11TH EDITION

KOVELS'
BOTTLES
PRICE LIST

ILLUSTRATED

RALPH & TERRY KOVEL

THREE RIVERS PRESS
NEW YORK

BOOKS BY RALPH AND TERRY KOVEL

American Country Furniture 1780–1875

A Directory of American Silver, Pewter, and Silver Plate

Kovels' Advertising Collectibles Price List

Kovels' American Art Pottery: The Collector's Guide to Makers, Marks, and Factory Histories

Kovels' American Silver Marks: 1650 to the Present

Kovels' Antiques & Collectibles Fix-It Source Book

Kovels' Book of Antique Labels

Kovels' Bottles Price List

Kovels' Collector's Guide to American Art Pottery

Kovels' Collectors' Source Book

Kovels' Depression Glass & Dinnerware Price List

Kovels' Dictionary of Marks—Pottery & Porcelain

Kovels' Guide to Selling, Buying, and Fixing Your Antiques and Collectibles

Kovels' Guide to Selling Your Antiques & Collectibles

Kovels' Illustrated Price Guide to Royal Doulton

Kovels' Know Your Antiques

Kovels' Know Your Collectibles

Kovels' New Dictionary of Marks—Pottery & Porcelain

Kovels' Organizer for Collectors

Kovels' Price Guide for Collector Plates, Figurines, Paperweights, and Other Limited Editions

Kovels' Quick Tips—799 Helpful Hints on How to Care for Your Collectibles

The Label Made Me Buy It: From Aunt Jemima to Zonkers— The Best-Dressed Boxes, Bottles, and Cans from the Past

Published by Three Rivers Press, a division of Crown Publishers, Inc., 201 East 50th Street, New York, New York 10022. Member of the Crown Publishing Group.

Random House, Inc. New York, Toronto, London, Sydney, Auckland
www.randomhouse.com

Three Rivers Press is a registered trademark of Random House, Inc.

Printed in the United States of America

Library of Congress Cataloging-in-Publication Data

ISBN 0-609-80312-3

10 9 8 7 6 5 4 3 2 1

Keep Up On Prices All Year Long

Have you kept up with prices? They change! Prices change with discoveries, auction records, even historic events. Every entry and every picture in this book is new and current, thanks to modern computer technology. It even includes prices from the now popular Internet bottle auctions. This book is a handy overall price guide, but you also need news and the very latest stories of bottle sales and discoveries.

Books on your shelf get older each month, and prices do change. Important sales produce new record prices. Rarities are discovered. Fakes appear. You will want to keep up with developments from month to month rather than from year to year. *Kovels on Antiques and Collectibles,* a nationally distributed, illustrated newsletter, includes up-to-date information on bottles and other collectibles. This monthly newsletter reports current prices, collecting trends, and landmark auction results for all types of antiques and collectibles, including bottles, and also contains tax, estate, security, and other pertinent news for collectors.

Additional information and a free sample newsletter are available from the authors at P.O. Box 22200-B, Beachwood, Ohio 44122. Read excerpts or order from our Web site: www.kovel.com.

Clues To The Contents Of This Book

Some product slogans brag, "We did it right the first time." But we know that anything can be improved; and, once again with a new book, we have put in a few extra features. This is the all-new, better-than-ever, eleventh edition of *Kovels' Bottles Price List.* We wrote the first bottle price guide twenty-eight years ago. This year, the book's format has been updated to reflect the changing interests of the 1990s. Paragraphs have been expanded. The histories of companies and their products have been researched, and we have tried to note any important changes in ownership of modern brands. A new color-picture section shows some of the interesting bottles sold in the past year.

All of the prices in the book are new. They are compiled from sales and offerings of the past two years. You will find that many modern bottles are no longer listed by brand, because collector interest has waned. We still have extensive listings of the more popular modern bottles like Jim Beam and Ezra Brooks. The pictures of old bottles are all new and were taken with special equipment so that they will be clearer and more informative.

"Go-withs," the bottle-related items that are bought and sold at all the bottle shows, are listed in their own section at the end of the book. Jar openers, advertisements, corkscrews, bottle caps, and other items that picture or are used with bottles have been classified as bottle go-withs. There is a bibliography and a listing of publications included in this book to aid you in further research. This list was checked and is accurate as of January 1999. The national and state club lists are also accurate as of January 1999. Unfortunately, addresses do change; if you cannot find one of the listed clubs, write to us at P.O. Box 22200-B, Beachwood, Ohio 44122.

Note: Bottles which contained alcoholic beverages must be sold empty to conform with the law in most states. To sell a filled liquor bottle, you must have a liquor license from the state where you live or where you sell the bottle. It is illegal to ship full bottles across state lines. The value is the same for full or empty liquor bottles.

DEFINITIONS

Novice collectors may need a few definitions to understand the terms used in this book. A *pontil mark* is a scar on the bottom of a bottle. It was made by the punty rod that held the glass for the glassblower. If the scar is rough, it is called a *pontil*. If it is smoothed out, it is called a *ground pontil*. *Free-blown* or *blown* means that the glass was blown by the glassmaker, using a blowpipe; it was not poured into a mold. *Mold-blown* means it was blown into a mold as part of the forming process. A *kick-up* is the deep indentation on the bottom of a bottle. Kick-ups are very often found on wine bottles. Describing glass as *whittled* or having *whittle marks* means there are irregular marks that look like the rough surface of a piece of whittled wood. Such marks are found on bottles that were made before 1900 and were caused by hot glass being blown into a cold mold. *Embossed* lettering is raised lettering. *Etched* lettering was cut into the bottle with acid or a sharp instrument. *Bubbles, teardrops,* or *seeds* describe types of bubbles that form in glass. A *seam* is the line left on the bottle by the mold. A seam may go up the neck of the bottle. If it goes over the lip, the bottle was machine made. An *applied lip* is handmade and applied to the bottle after the glassmaker has formed the bottle. A *sheared lip* is found on bottles made before 1840. The top of the bottle was cut from the blowpipe with shears and the result is the sheared lip. The *2-piece,* or *BIMAL,* mold was used from about 1860 to 1900. The *3-piece mold* was used from 1820 to 1880. The automatic bottle machine was invented in 1903 and *machine-made* bottles were the norm after that date. *Black glass* is not really black. It is very dark olive green or olive amber and appears black unless seen in a bright light. *Milk glass* is an opaque glass made by using tin or zinc in the mixture. Although most milk glass is white, it is correct to call colored glass of this type "blue" or "green" milk glass. If glass that was made from 1880 to 1914 is left in strong sunlight, it often turns colors. This is because of the chemical content of the old glass. Bottles can turn purple, pale lavender, or shades of green or brown. These bottles are called *sun-colored.* Bottles can also be *iridized* and colored by a radiation process similar to that used for preserving vegetables. There are a few other terms that relate to only one type of bottle, and these terms have been identified in the proper paragraphs.

Bottle clubs and bottle shows have set the rules for this edition of *Kovels' Bottles Price List.* We have used the terms preferred by the collectors and have tried to organize the thousands of listings in an easy-to-use format. Many abbreviations have been included that are part of the bottle collectors' language. The abbreviations are listed below and appear throughout the book.

ABM means automatic bottle machine.

ACL means applied color label, a pyroglaze or enamel lettering.

BIMAL means blown in mold, applied lip.

DUG means literally dug from the ground.

FB means free blown.

IP means iron pontil.

ISP means inserted slug plate. Special names were sometimes embossed on a bottle, especially a milk bottle, with a special plate inserted in the mold.

OP means open pontil.

Pyro means pyroglaze or enamel lettering often found on milk bottles and soda bottles.

SC means sun-colored.

SCA means sun-colored amethyst.

To make the descriptions of the bottles as complete as possible, an identification number has been added to the description in some categories. The serious collector knows the important books about a specialty, and these books have numbered lists of styles of bottles. Included in this book are identification numbers for flasks from McKearin, bitters from Ring, and fruit jars from *Red Book of Fruit Jars,* now by Leybourne. The full titles of the books used are included in the Bibliography and listed in the introductory paragraph for each category.

Medicine bottles include all medicine bottles except those under the more specific headings such as "Bitters" or "Sarsaparilla." Modern bottles of major interest are listed under the brand name.

If you are not a regular at bottle shows, it may take a few tries to become accustomed to the method of listing used in this book. If you cannot find a bottle, try several related headings. For instance, hair products are found under "Cosmetic" and "Cure."

Many named bottles are found under "Medicine," "Food," "Fruit Jar," etc. If your fruit jar has several names, such as "Ball Mason," look under "Fruit Jar, Ball" or "Fruit Jar, Mason." If no color is listed, the bottle is clear. We edit color descriptions to make the comparisons of bottles easier. It is impossible to explain the difference between "olive yellow," "light olive yellow," "yellow olive," "light greenish yellow," all terms used in the sales. Where possible we used the description selected by the seller.

PICTURE DICTIONARY OF BOTTLE SHAPES

Collectors and bottle makers have often given shape-inspired nicknames to their bottles.

FLASKS

The **calabash** flask is shaped like the calabash gourd, a vegetable that was often hollowed out to hold water.

The **punkinseed,** or **pumpkinseed** flask, is relatively flat and is shaped like the seed of a pumpkin. In the early 1900s the bottle manufacturers called them picnic flasks.

The **coffin** flask has a hexagonal-shaped base that tapers slightly at the bottom. It resembles a coffin.

The **shoofly** flask was popular in the South. The name was used by early bottle manufacturers.

The **chestnut** flask is almost round, and is named for the well-known nut. The nut comes from the chestnut trees that grow in Europe and the northern parts of the United States.

The **Pitkin-type** flask is named for the Pitkin Glassworks of East Hartford, Connecticut. The name is used to describe similarly shaped bottles made by other factories, too. The blowers used the "German" method of putting a second gather of glass halfway up the post, making the glass walls of the flask thicker. The bottle was then blown into a rib mold to impress ribs. The finished bottle could have vertical or swirled ribs.

INKS

Perhaps because so many ink bottles are unmarked, ink bottle collectors have given them descriptive nicknames.

igloo

teakettle

turtle

umbrella

OTHERS

The **demijohn** is a large, narrow-necked bottle that is often encased in wicker.

The **gemel** is really two bottles joined together. It was made to hold two different liquids, like oil and vinegar. Many gemel bottles don't have flat bases and must be kept lying flat on a table.

A **jar** is a wide-mouthed cylindrical bottle made of glass or earthenware. The fruit jar or canning jar is the most common jar found today.

A **lady's leg** is a long-necked bottle that only slightly resembles the leg of a woman. The trademarked bottle shape was first used by Boker's Stomach Bitters.

The **case gin** bottle is shaped to fit into a wooden case for shipping. The bottles were rectangular so they could sit flat against each other in a case. The shape was especially favored by the Dutch, who used these bottles for exporting gin.

The black glass bottles used by the English in the 17th century were made in several shapes. One, the **mallet**, was thought to resemble a short-handled hammer.

The **onion** was named for the vegetable.

A **seal** bottle, used about 1630 to 1750, was named for the extra glob of glass or the seal attached to the outside of the bottle. The seal was impressed with initials and sometimes a date.

Zanesville-type bottles are named for the shape of the bottles made by the Zanesville Manufacturing company in Zanesville, Ohio, from 1815 to 1838 and from 1842 to 1851. Like the Pitkin-type flask, the name is used for other companies' bottles of the same shape.

The prices shown for bottles are the *actual* prices asked for or bid for bottles during the past two years. We know collectors try to get discounts, so some of these bottles may have sold for a little less than the average price. Prices vary in different parts of the country. The condition of the bottle is a major factor in determining price. We do not list broken or chipped bottles, but sometimes flaws or scratches are noticed after a sale. If more than one price for a bottle has been recorded, a range is given. When selling your bottles, remember that the prices here are retail, not the wholesale price paid by a dealer. You can sell your collection to a dealer at about half the prices listed here. At auction you may get the same prices found in the book, but auctions are unpredictable. Prices may be high or low because of a snowstorm or a very determined pair of bidders. Internet auctions have the added risk of an unknown seller, so the condition may not be accurately reported. Low-priced bottles sell best at flea markets and garage sales. Because of the idiosyncrasies of the computer, it is impossible to place a range on prices of bottles that are illustrated. The price listed for each bottle pictured in the book is the actual sale price for that bottle.

Particular spellings are meant to help the collector. If the original bottle spelled "Catsup" as "Ketchup," that is the spelling that appears. The abbreviation "Dr." for doctor may appear on bottles as "Dr" (no period) or "Dr." (period). However, we have included a period each time to keep the computer alphabetizing more consistent, except in the case of bottles of Dr Pepper. The period was omitted in Dr Pepper by the company in 1950, and we use whatever appeared on the bottle. Also, if a word is written, for example, "Kennedy's," "Kennedys'," or "Kennedys," we have placed the apostrophe or omitted it as it appeared on the bottle. A few bottles are included that had errors in the original spelling in the bottle mold. In these cases the error is explained. Medicine, bitters, and other bottle types sometimes use the term "Dr." and sometimes use just the last name of the doctor. We have used the wording as it appears on the bottle, except for "Whiskey" which is used even if the bottle held scotch or Canadian or was spelled "Whisky."

Every bottle or go-with illustrated in black and white is indicated by the abbreviation "Illus" in the text. Bottles shown in color pictures are priced in the center section where they appear.

We have tried to be accurate, but cannot be responsible for any errors in pricing or information that may appear. Any information about clubs, prices, or content for future books will be considered for the next book. Please send it to Kovels, P.O. Box 22200, Dept. BPL, Beachwood, Ohio 44122.

Ralph M. Kovel, Life Member,
Federation of Historical Bottle Clubs

Terry H. Kovel, Life Member,
Federation of Historical Bottle Clubs

ACKNOWLEDGMENTS

Those who sell bottles are the most informed experts in the field. Special thanks to Jim Hagenbuch of Glass Works Auctions, Norm Heckler Jr. and Norm Heckler Sr. of Norman C. Heckler & Co., Jeff Wichmann of Pacific Glass Auctions, and Christie Mayer Lefkowith of Phillips International Auctioneers. Thanks also to Gary Metz's Muddy River Trading Co., Charles G. Moore, Pettigrew Auction Company, and Bruce and Vicki Waasdorp for their special help with information and photographs.

Pictured items and information were furnished by AB!C Absentee Auctions; Americana Resources Antiques & Collectibles; Antique Bottle & Glass Collector; Gary Bagnall; Roger Behrens; Carol Bloom; Larry Caddell; Tom & Deena Caniff; Christie's; Dan Clark; Collectors Auction Service; Howard Crowe; Diane De Volder; J.C. Devine Inc.; Ralph Finch; Fink's Off the Wall Auctions; Gary Fitz; Michael A. Florer; Brad Fortier; Susan Fox; Dale Diana Frazier; Albert E. French; Jen Galletta; George W. Gideon Sr.; Bob & Sue Gilbert; Rob & Kath Goodacre; Steve Guion; Stacey Halliday; James E. Herring; Buddy Hinton; Roger Huff; Paul Irby; James D. Julia, Inc.; Billy Johnsen; Engvard Johnson; Robert Karle; Tony Knipp; Dan Kreeger; Dan Leonard; Leslie's Antiques & Auctions; Katharine Mattmiller; Jerry McCann; Pete McCue; McMurray Antiques & Auctions; Edward E. Miller; Joe R. Myhand; Ruben Negron; Nostrums & Quackery; NSA Auctions; Ross Oehling; Phillips New York; Glenn Poch's; Margaret Protze; Dick Roller; Jeff Scharnowske; Sally Schulze; Tom Shaughnessy; Shot Glass Exchange; Skinner, Inc.; Phillip Smith; Sotheby's; Ann Stokes; J. Carl Sturm; Robert Swartz; Jan Thalberg; Ralph Van Brocklin; Dianne Vetraomile; George Waddy; Wallingford Internet Antique Bottle Web; Les Whitman; John & Mary Wolf; Mark Yates; and members and dealers at the Ohio Bottle Club's 20th Annual Show. Thanks.

And to Gay and staff, who double-checked everything; PJ, our editor; Pam, production editorial–wonder; and Steve, the ultimate problem solver—hurrah!

RESOURCES
MUSEUMS & ARCHIVES

COCA-COLA COMPANY ARCHIVES, Industry & Consumer Affairs, P.O. Drawer 1734, Atlanta, GA 30301, 800-438-2653, Web site: cocacola.com.

CORNING MUSEUM OF GLASS, Rakow Library, One Museum Way, Corning, NY 14830-2253, 607-937-5371.

DR PEPPER MUSEUM, 300 S. 5th St., Waco, TX 76701, 254-757-2433.

NATIONAL BOTTLE MUSEUM, 76 Milton Ave., Ballston Spa, NY 12020, 518-885-7589, Web site: www.crisny.org/not-for-profit/nbm.

PEPSI-COLA COMPANY ARCHIVES, One Pepsi Way, Somers, NY 10589, 914-767-6000, Web site: www.pepsi.com.

SEAGRAM MUSEUM, 57 Erb St. W., Waterloo, ON, Canada N2L 6C2, 519-885-1857, fax: 519-746-1673, Web site: www.seagram-museum.ca.

PUBLICATIONS OF INTEREST TO BOTTLE COLLECTORS

See the club list for other publications

NEWSPAPERS

These are general newspapers with some articles and ads for bottles.

Antique Trader Weekly
P.O. Box 1050
Dubuque, IA 52004-1050
e-mail: traderpubs@aol.com
Web site: www.collect.com/antique-
   trader

Collector's News
P.O. Box 156
Grundy Center, IA 50638
e-mail: collectors@collectors-news.com
Web site: collectors-news.com

NEWSLETTERS

Advertising Collectors Express
P.O. Box 221
Mayview, MO 64071

Avon Times
P.O. Box 9868
Kansas City, MO 64134

Creamers
P.O. Box 11
Lake Villa, IL 60046-0011

Foss Collectibles
1224 Washington Ave.
Golden, CO 80401

Fruit Jar Newsletter
364 Gregory Ave.
West Orange, NJ 07052-3743

Just For Openers
P.O. Box 64
Chapel Hill, NC 27514

**Kovels on Antiques
   and Collectibles**
P.O. Box 22200
Beachwood, OH 44122

Mini-Scents
28227 Paseo El Siena
Laguna Niguel, CA 92677
e-mail: perfumemel@aol.com
(miniature perfume bottles)

Root Beer Float
609 Devils Ln.
Walworth, WI 53184
e-mail: nader@elknet.net

MAGAZINES

Antique Bottle & Glass Collector
P.O. Box 180
East Greenville, PA 18041
e-mail: glswrk@enter.net
Web site: glswrk-auction.com

Bottles & Bygones
30 Brabant Rd.
Cheadle Hulme
Cheadle, Cheshire, UK SK8 7AU
e-mail: Mike@tithebar.co.demon.uk
Web site: members.tripod.com/
   ~MikeSheriden/index.htm

British Bottle Review
Elsecar Heritage Centre
Barnsley, S. Yorkshire, UK S74 8HJ

The Miniature Bottle Collector
P.O. Box 2161
Palos Verdes Peninsula, CA 90274

BOTTLE CLUBS

There are hundreds of bottle clubs that welcome new members. The list of local clubs is arranged by state and city so you can find the club nearest your home. If no club is listed nearby, we suggest you contact the national organizations, which follow. Any active bottle club that is not listed and wishes to be included in future editions of *Kovels' Bottles Price List* should send the necessary information to the authors, P.O. Box 22200, Beachwood, Ohio 44122. The information in this list has been compiled with the help of the Federation of Historical Bottle Collectors, *The Miniature Bottle Collector,* and the National Bottle Museum.

NATIONAL CLUBS

Many of these clubs have local chapters and shows.
Write to them for more information.

American Breweriana Association, Inc.
American Breweriana Journal (magazine)
P.O. Box 11157
Pueblo, CO 81001
e-mail: Breweriana
@amigo.net
Web site: www.a-b-a.com

American Collectors of Infant Feeders
Keeping Abreast (newsletter)
1849 Ebony Dr.
York, PA 17402-4706

Anheuser-Busch Collectors Club
First Draft (magazine)
2700 S. Broadway
St. Louis, MO 63118
Web site: www.
budweiser.com

Antique Advertising Association of America
Past Times (newsletter)
P.O. Box 1121
Morton Grove, IL 60053

Canadian Corkscrew Collectors Club
The Quarterly Wormer (newsletter)
P.O. Box 5295
Englewood, NJ 07631
e-mail: clarethous
@aol.com

Candy Container Collectors of America
Candy Gram (newsletter)
P.O. Box 352
Chelmsford, MA 01824-0352

Classic Wheaton Club
Classic Wheaton Club Newsletter (newsletter)
P.O. Box 59
Downington, PA 19335-0059
e-mail: cwc@cwcusa.com
Web site; www.
cwcusa.com

Coca-Cola Collectors Club International
Coca-Cola Collectors News (newsletter)
P.O. Box 49166
Atlanta, GA 30359-1166

Cream Separator Collectors Association
Cream Separator & Dairy Newsletter (newsletter)
W20772 State Rd. 95
Arcadia, WI 54612

Crown Collectors Society International
Crown Cappers' Exchange (newsletter)
4300 San Juan Dr.
Fairfax, VA 22030
e-mail: crownking
@theonramp.net
(crown caps from beer and soda bottles)

Dr Pepper Collectors Club
Lion's Roar (newsletter)
3100 Monticello, Suite 890
Dallas, TX 75205

Eastern Coast Breweriana Association
The Keg (magazine)
P.O. Box 349
West Point, PA 19846
e-mail: brhntr@aol.com

Federation of Historical Bottle Collectors
Bottles and Extras (magazine)
c/o Kevin Sives
1485 Buck Hill Dr.
Southampton, PA 18966
e-mail: sives@erols.com
Web site: www.fohbc.com

Figural Bottle Opener Collectors
The Opener (newsletter)
1953 Sugar Stick Rd.
Harrington, DE 19952

International Association of Jim Beam Bottle and Specialties Clubs
Beam Around the World (newsletter)
2015 Burlington Ave.
Kewanee, IL 61443
Web site:
www2.tcc.com.net/
~eagle.beam-wade
collectables.htm

International Chinese Snuff Bottle Society
Journal (magazine)
2601 N. Charles St.
Baltimore, MD 21218
Web site: www.
snuffbottle.org

International Perfume Bottle Association
Perfume Bottle Quarterly (newsletter)
3314 Shamrock Rd.
Tampa, FL 33629

International Swizzle Stick Collectors Association
Swizzle Stick News (newsletter)
P.O. Box 1117
Bellingham, WA 98227-1117

Jelly Jammers
Jelly Jammers Journal (newsletter)
6086 West Boggstown Rd.
Boggstown, IN 46110
e-mail: emshaw@in.net
(jelly jars)

Lilliputian Miniature Bottle Club
Gulliver's Gazette (newsletter)
54 Village Circle
Manhattan Beach, CA 90266-7222

The Mini Bottle Club
The Mini Bottle Club (newsletter)
47 Burradon Rd.
Burradon, Carmlington,
Northumberland, UK
NE23 7NF

National Association of Avon Collectors Club
P.O. Box 7006
Kansas City, MO 64113

National Association Breweriana Advertising
The Breweriana Collector (magazine)
2343 Met-To-Wee Ln.
Wauwatosa, WI 53226

National Association of Milk Bottle Collectors, Inc.
The Milk Route (newsletter)
4 Ox Bow Rd.
Westport, CT 06880-2602

National Association of Paper and Advertising Collectors
P.A.C. (newspaper)
P.O. Box 500
Mount Joy, PA 17552-9984

National Ski Country Bottle Club
Ski Country Collector (newsletter)
1224 Washington Ave.
Golden, CO 80401

New England Moxie Congress
Nerve Food News (newsletter)
2783 No. Triphammer Rd.
Ithaca, NY 14850-9756

Painted Soda Bottle Collector's Association
Soda Net (newsletter)
9418 Hilmer Dr.
LaMesa, CA 91942
e-mail: aclsrus@msn.com

Pepsi-Cola Collectors Club
Pepsi-Cola Collectors Club Newsletter (newsletter)
P.O. Box 817
Claremont, CA 91711

Saratoga-Type Bottle Collectors Society
The Spouter (newsletter)
1198 Main St., Box 685
Warren, MA 01083

Society of Inkwell Collectors
The Stained Finger (newsletter)
5136 Thomas Ave. S.
Minneapolis, MN 55410
e-mail: soic@
concentric.net
Web site: woic.org

**Southeastern Antique
Bottle Club**
The Whittle Mark
(newsletter)
143 Scatterfoot Dr.
Peachtree City, GA 30269
e-mail: fred-taylor@
worldnet.att.net
Web site: home.att.
net/~fred-taylor

**Violin Bottle Collectors
Association of
America**
Fine Tuning (newsletter)
24 Sylvan St.
Danvers, MA 01923

**Whisky Pitcher
Collectors Association
of America**
Black & White (newsletter)
19341 W. Tahoe Dr.
Mundelein, IL
60060-4061

STATE CLUBS

ALABAMA
**Mobile Bottle
Collectors Club**
8844 Lee Circle
IRVINGTON, AL 36544

ARIZONA
**Phoenix Antique Bottle
& Collectors Club**
4708 W. Solano Dr. S.
GLENDALE, AZ 85301

ARKANSAS
**Indian Country Antique
Bottle & Relic Society**
3818 Hilltop Dr.
JONESBORO, AR 72401

**Little Rock Antique
Bottle Collectors Club**
16201 Highway 300
ROLAND, AR 72135

CALIFORNIA
**California
Miniature Bottle Club**
1911 Willow St.
ALAMEDA, CA 94501

**Los Angeles
Historical Bottle Club**
5569 Hallowell Ave.
ARCADIA, CA 91007

**Bakersfield Bottle &
Insulator Collectors**
1023 Baldwin Rd.
BAKERSFIELD, CA
93304

**Fresno Antique Bottle
& Collectors Club**
281 N. Magill Ave.
CLOVIS, CA 93612

**Mother Lode
Antique Bottle Club**
P.O. Box 165
DOWNIEVILLE, CA
95936

**San Diego
Antique Bottle Club**
2265 Needham Rd., #20
EL CAJON, CA 92020

**San Luis Obispo
Bottle Society**
124-21st St.
PASO ROBLES, CA
93446

**'49er Historical
Bottle Association**
P.O. Box 561
PENRYN, CA 95663

**Superior California
Bottle Club**
3220 Stratford Ave.
REDDING, CA 96001

**Golden Gate Historical
Bottle Society**
6019 Arlington Blvd.
RICHMOND, CA 94805

**Mission Trail
Historical Bottle Club**
1475 Teton Ave.
SALINAS, CA 93906

**Northwestern Bottle
Collectors Association**
P.O. Box 1121
SANTA ROSA, CA
95402

**San Bernardino County
Historical Bottle &
Collectors Club**
1458 W. Winn Dr.
UPLAND, CA 91786

**Sequoia Antique Bottle
& Collectable Society**
P.O. Box 3695
VISALIA, CA 93278

COLORADO
**Southern Colorado
Antique Bottle Collectors**
843 Ussie Ave.
CANON CITY, CO 81212

**Peaks & Plains
Antique Bottle &
Collectors Club, Inc.**
308 Maplewood Dr.
COLORADO SPRINGS,
CO 80907-4326

Antique Bottles & Collectables of Colorado
P.O. Box 245
LITTLETON, CO 80160

Western Slope Bottle Club
P.O. Box 354
PALISADE, CO 81526

CONNECTICUT
Somers Antique Bottle Club
27 Plank Ln.
GLASTONBURY, CT 06033-2523

Southern Connecticut Antique Bottle Collectors Association, Inc.
34 Dartmouth Dr.
HUNTINGTON, CT 06484

DELAWARE
Delmarva Antique Bottle Collectors
57 Lakewood Dr.
LEWES, DE 19958

Tri-State Bottle Collectors & Diggers Club
2225 Naamans Rd.
WILMINGTON, DE 19810

FLORIDA
M-T Bottle Collectors Association Inc.
P.O. Box 1581
DELAND, FL 32720

Treasure Coast Bottle Collectors
6301 Lilyan Parkway
FT. PIERCE, FL 34951

Antique Bottle Collectors of North Florida
P.O. Box 380022
JACKSONVILLE, FL 32205

Mid-State Antique Bottle Collectors, Inc.
717 Clemwood Dr.
ORLANDO, FL 32803

Association of Florida Antique Bottle Clubs
P.O. Box 3105
SARASOTA, FL 34230

Sun Coast Antique Bottle Collectors Association, Inc.
12451 94th Ave. N.
SEMINOLE, FL 33707

Central Florida Insulator Collectors Club
3557 Nicklaus Dr.
TITUSVILLE, FL 32780

GEORGIA
Rome Bottle Club
105 Central High Rd.
CARROLTON, GA 30116

HAWAII
Hawaii Historical Bottle Collectors Club
P.O. Box 90456
HONOLULU, HI 96835

ILLINOIS
Metro-East Bottle & Jar Association
309 Bellevue Dr.
BELLEVILLE, IL 62223

First Chicago Bottle Club
P.O. Box A3382
CHICAGO, IL 60690

Antique Bottle Collectors of Northern Illinois
215 Coventry
MT. PROSPECT, IL 60056

Pekin Bottle Collectors Association
P.O. Box 372
PEKIN, IL 61555

INDIANA
Fort Wayne Historical Bottle Club
2015 Trinity St.
HUNTERTOWN, IN 46748

Midwest Antique Fruit Jar & Bottle Club
1201 Cowing Dr.
MUNCIE, IN 47304

Wabash Valley AB & P Club
3283 N. Co. Rd., 700 E.
POLANDIN, IN 47868

IOWA
Iowa Antique Bottleers
2815 Druid Hill Dr.
DES MOINES, IA 50315

KANSAS
Southeast Kansas Bottle & Relic Club
302 S. Western
CHANUTE, KS 66720

KENTUCKY
Kentuckiana Antique Bottle & Outhouse Society
5801 River Knolls Dr.
LOUISVILLE, KY 40222

MARYLAND
Baltimore Antique Bottle Collectors, Inc.
P.O. Box 36061
TOWSON, MD 21286

MASSACHUSETTS
Little Rhody Bottle Club
27 Irving Ave.
SOUTH ATTLEBORO, MA 02703

MICHIGAN

**Huron Valley Bottle
& Insulators Club**
11843 Knob Hill
BRIGHTON, MI
48116-9220

**Metropolitan Detroit
Antique Bottle Club**
410 Lothrop Rd.
GROSSE POINT
FARMS, MI 48236

**Great Lakes
Miniature Bottle Club**
19745 Woodmont
HARPER WOODS, MI
48225

**Kalamazoo
Antique Bottle Club**
1121 Maywood
KALAMAZOO, MI
49001

**Flint Antique Bottle
& Collectable Club**
6349 Silver Lake Rd.
LINDEN, MI 48451

MINNESOTA

**Midwest Miniature
Bottle Club**
P.O. Box 240388
APPLE VALLEY, MN
55124-0388

**Minnesota First
Antique Bottle Club**
5001 Queen Ave. N.
MINNEAPOLIS, MN
55430

**North Star Historical
Bottle Association**
3308 32nd Ave. S.
MINNEAPOLIS, MN
55406

MISSOURI

**St. Louis Antique Bottle
Collectors Association**
2236 S. Highway N.
PACIFIC, MO 63069

NEBRASKA

**Nebraska Antique Bot-
tle & Collectors Club**
2902 Kendel Dr.
ASHLAND, NB 68003

NEVADA

Las Vegas Bottle Club
3901 E. Stewart, #16
LAS VEGAS, NV 89110

**Antique Bottle Club
of Reno & Sparks**
P.O. Box 1061
VERDI, NV 89439

NEW HAMPSHIRE

Yankee Bottle Club
382 Court St.
KEENE, NH 03431-2534

**Merrimack Valley
Antique Bottle
Collectors**
776 Harvey Rd., Rt. 10
MANCHESTER, NH
03103

**New England
Antique Bottle Club**
4 Francoeur Dr.
SOMERSWORTH, NH
03878

**Central New Hampshire
Antique Bottle Club**
RFD 2, Box 1A
Winter St.
TILTON, NH 03276

NEW JERSEY

**South Jersey's
Heritage Bottle
& Glass Collectors**
P.O. Box 122
GLASSBORO, NJ 08028

**North Jersey
Antique Bottle
Collectors Association**
36 William St.
LINCOLN PARK, NJ
07035

**Central Jersey
Bottle Club**
92 N. Main St.
NEW EGYPT, NJ 08533

**New Jersey
Antique Bottle Club**
24 Charles St.
SOUTH RIVER, NJ
08882

Jersey Shore Bottle Club
P.O. Box 995
TOMS RIVER, NJ 08754

NEW YORK

**Western New York
Miniature Liquor Club**
P.O. Box 182
CHEEKTOWAGA, NY
14225

**Hudson Valley
Bottle Club**
6 Columbus Ave.
CORNWALL ON
HUSDON, NY 12520

**Mohawk Valley
Antique Bottle Club**
275 Brockway Rd.
FRANKFORT, NY 13340

**Finger Lakes Bottle
Collectors Association**
3250 Dubois Rd.
ITHACA, NY 14850

**Genesee Valley Bottle
Collectors Association**
Box 15528
West Ridge Station
ROCHESTER, NY
14615

**Long Island Antique
Bottle Association**
10 Holmes Ct.
SAYVILLE, NY 11782

**Empire State Bottle
Collectors Association**
P.O. Box 3421
SYRACUSE, NY 13220

Berkshire Antique
Bottle Association
1 Dudley Heights
TROY, NY 12180

NORTH CAROLINA
Western North Carolina
Antique Bottle Club
P.O. Box 18481
ASHEVILLE, NC 28814

OHIO
Ohio Bottle Club, Inc.
3937 Lake Shore Dr.
CORTLAND, OH 44410

Findlay Antique
Bottle Club
407 Cimarron Ct.
FINDLAY, OH 45840

Southwestern Ohio
Antique Bottle
& Jar Club
273 Hilltop Dr.
DAYTON, OH 45415

Superior Eleven
Bottle Club
22000 Shaker Blvd.
SHAKER HEIGHTS,
OH 44122

OKLAHOMA
Tulsa Antique Bottle
and Relic Club
4 Gawf Place
MUSKOGEE, OK 74403

Oklahoma Territory
Bottle & Relic Club
1300 S. Blue Haven Dr.
MUSTANG, OK 73064

OREGON
Northwest Miniature
Bottle Club
P.O. Box 566
BORING, OR 97228

Siskiyou Antique
Bottle Collectors
2668 Montara Dr.
MEDFORD, OR 97504

Oregon Bottle Collectors
1762 Sunset Ave.
WEST LINN, OR 97068

PENNSYLVANIA
Washington County
Antique Bottle Club
P.O. Box 488
CLAYSVILLE, PA
15323

Laurel Valley
Bottle Club
P.O. Box 131
HOSTETTER, PA 15658

Ligonier Historical
Bottle Collectors
P.O. Box 188
LIGONIER, PA 15658

Forks of the
Delaware Bottle
Collectors Association
164 Farmview Rd.
NAZARETH, PA
18064-2500

Pittsburgh Antique
Bottle Club
235 Main Entrance Dr.
PITTSBURGH, PA
15228

Bedford County
Bottle Club
497 Plum Creek Blvd.
ROARING SPRING, PA
16673

Jefferson County
Antique Bottle Club
6 Valley View Dr.
WASHINGTON, PA
15301

Pennsylvania Bottle
Collectors Association
251 Eastland Ave.
YORK, PA 17402

TENNESSEE
Memphis Bottle
Collectors Club
3706 Deerfield Cove
BARTLETT, TN 38135

Middle Tennessee
Bottle Collectors Club
1750 Keyes Rd.
GREENBRIER, TN
37073

East Tennessee
Bottle Society
314 Patty Rd.
KNOXVILLE, TN 37924

TEXAS
Gulf Coast Bottle
& Jar Club
P.O. Box 1754
PASADENA, TX 77501

UTAH
Utah Antique Bottle
& Relic Club
517 S. Hayes
MIDVALE, UT 84047

VIRGINIA
Potomac
Bottle Collectors
8411 Porter Ln.
ALEXANDRIA, VA
22308

Historical Bottle
Diggers of Virginia
145 Third St.
BROADWAY, VA 22815

Richmond Area
Bottle Collectors
Association Inc.
3511 Clydewood Ave.
RICHMOND, VA 23234

**Apple Valley Bottle
Collectors Club**
3015 N. Western Pike
WINCHESTER, VA
22603

WASHINGTON
**Washington Bottle
Collectors Association**
5492 Hannegan Rd.
BELLINGHAM, WA
98226

WISCONSIN
**Antique Bottle Club of
Northern Illinois**
P.O. Box 571
LAKE GENEVA, WI
53147

**Milwaukee Antique
Bottle Club**
514 Lafayette St.
WATERTOWN, WI
53094

CANADA
**Bytown Bottle
Seekers' Club**
7 Queenston Dr.
RICHMOND, ON,
CANADA K0A 2ZO
e-mail: af262@
freenet.carleton.ca

**Four Seasons Bottle
Collectors Club**
129 Main St. N.
MARKHAM, ON,
CANADA L3P 1Y2

AUCTION GALLERIES

Some of the prices and pictures in this book were furnished by these auction houses and dealers, and we thank them. If you are interested in buying or selling bottles or related collectibles, you may want to contact these firms.

**AB!C Absentee
Auctions**
139 Pleasant Ave.
Dundas, ON, Canada
L9H 3T9
905-628-3433
e-mail: draaks@
netaccess.on.ca
Web site: www.nas.
net/~draaks

**Antique Bottle
Connection**
147 Reserve Rd.
Libby, MT 59923
406-293-8442
fax: 406-293-8442
e-mail: letsgo@libby.org

**Bothroyd & Detwiler
On-line Auctions**
1290 1/2 S. 8th Ave.
Yuma, AZ 85364-4509
e-mail:detwiler
@primenet.com
Web site: www.primenet.
com/~detwiler/index.htm

BBR Auctions
Elsecar Heritage Centre
Barnsley, S. Yorkshire,
UK S74 8HJ
01226-745156
fax: 01226-351561
e-mail: sales@
bbrauctions.co.uk
Web site: www.
bbrauctions.co.uk

**Bruce and Vicki
Waasdorp Stoneware
Auctions**
P.O. Box 434
Clarence, NY 14031
716-759-2361
fax: 716-759-2397
e-mail: waasdorp@
antiques-stoneware.com
Web site: www.
antiques-stoneware.com

**Collectors Auction
Services**
R.R. 2, Box 431
Oil City, PA 16301
814-677-6070
fax: 814-677-6166
e-mail: manderton@
mailchoice.net

**DuMouchelle's
Art Galleries, Inc.**[1]
409 East Jefferson Ave.
Detroit, MI 48226
313-963-0248
fax: 313-963-8199
Web site: www.
demouchelles.com
(Royal Doulton)

Early Auction Co.
123 Main St.
Milford, OH 45150
513-831-4833
fax: 513-831-1441

**Fink's Off The Wall
Auctions**
108 E. Seventh St.
Lansdale, PA 19446-2622
215-855-9732
fax: 215-855-6325
e-mail: lansbeer
@finksauction.com
Web site: www.
finksauctions.com

Garth's Auctions, Inc.
P.O. Box 369
Delaware, OH 43015
740-362-4771
fax: 740-363-0164
e-mail: info@garths.com
Web site:
  www.garths.com

**Gary Metz's Muddy
  River Trading Co.**
P.O. Box 1430
251 Wildwood Rd.
Salem, VA 24153
540-387-5070
fax: 540-387-3233

Glass-Works Auctions
P.O. Box 180
East Greenville, PA
  18041
215-679-5849
fax: 215-679-3068
e-mail:glaswrk@enter.net
Web site: www.
  glswrk-auction.com

Howard B. Parzow
P.O. Box 3464
Gaithersburg, MD
  20885-3464
301-977-6741
fax: 301-208-8947

John R. Pastor Auctions
7288 Thorncrest Dr. SE
Ada, MI 49301
616-285-7604

Monsen and Baer
P.O. Box 529
Vienna, Virginia 22183
703-938-2129
fax: 708-242-1357
(perfume bottles)

**Norman C. Heckler
  & Company**
79 Bradford Corner Rd.
Woodstock Valley, CT
  06282
860-974-1634
fax: 860-974-2003
e-mail: heckler
  @neca.com
Web site:
  hecklerauction.com

**Nostalgia
  Publications, Inc.**
21 S. Lake Dr.
Hackensack, NJ 07601
201-488-4536
fax: 201-883-0938
e-mail: nostpub@
  Webtv.net
Web site: www.
  nostalgiapubs.com

NSA Auctions
Newton-Smith Antiques
88 Cedar St.
Cambridge, ON, Canada
  N1S 1V8
519-623-6302
e-mail:nsa@mgl.ca/nsa
Web site: mgl.ca/~nsa

Pacific Glass Auctions
1507 21st St., Suite 203
Sacramento, CA 95814
800-806-7722
fax: 916-443-3199
e-mail: info@pacglass
Web site: pacglass.com

**Pettigrew Antique &
  Collector Auctions**
Division of R.G. Canning
  Attractions
P.O. Box 38159
Colorado Springs, CO
  80973
719-633-7963
fax: 719-633-5035

**Phillips International
  Auctioneers & Valuers**
406 E. 79th St.
New York, NY 10021
212-570-4830
fax: 212-570-2207
Web site: www.
  phillips-auctions.com

Pop Shoppe Auctions
10566 Combie Rd.,
  #106521
Auburn, CA 95602
530-268-6333
e-mail: popshoppe
  @aol.com
(specializing in
  ACL soda bottles)

**Richard Opfer
  Auctioneering, Inc.**
1919 Greenspring Dr.
Timonium, MD 21093
410-252-5035
fax: 410-252-5863

Shot Glass Exchange
Box 219
Western Springs, IL
  60558
708-246-1559
fax: 708-246-1559

Skinner, Inc.
357 Main St.
Bolton, MA 01740
978-779-6241
fax: 978-779-5144
Web site: www.
  skinnerinc.com

**Richard W. Withington,
  Inc.**
590 Center Rd.
Hillsboro, NH 03244
603-464-3232

BIBLIOGRAPHY

We've found these books to be useful. Some of them may be out of print, but your local library should be able to get them for you through interlibrary loan.

GENERAL

Blakeman, Alan. *Antique Bottles Collectors Encyclopedia with Price Guide,* 2 vols. Elsecar, England: BBR Publishing, 1986, 1995.

Brown, William E. *The Auction Price Report,* 1998 edition. Privately printed (8251 NW 49th Ct., Coral Springs, FL 33067).

Feldhaus, Ron. *The Bottles, Breweriana and Advertising Jugs of Minnesota: 1850-1920,* 2 vols. Privately printed, 1986, 1987 (6724 Xerxes Ave. S., Edina, MN 55423).

Fletcher, Johnnie W. *Kansas Bottles: 1854 to 1915.* Privately printed, 1994 (1300 S. Blue Haven Dr., Mustang, OK 73064).

Ketchum, William C., Jr. *A Treasury of American Bottles.* Indianapolis: Bobbs-Merrill, 1975.

Kovel, Ralph and Terry. *Kovels' Antiques & Collectibles Price List 1999,* 31st edition. New York: Three Rivers Press/Crown, 1999.

———. *Kovels' Know Your Antiques.* New York: Crown, 1990.

———. *Kovels' Bottles Price List,* 11th edition. New York: Three Rivers Press/Crown, 1999.

McKearin, George L. and Helen. *Two Hundred Years of American Blown Glass.* New York: Crown, 1950.

Mario's Price Guide to Modern Bottles. Privately printed, issued quarterly (146 Sheldon Ave., Depew, NY 14043).

Megura, Jim. *Official Price Guide: Bottles.* New York: House of Collectibles, 1996.

Montague, H.F. *Montague's Modern Bottle Identification & Price Guide,* 3rd edition. Privately printed, 1984 (P.O. Box 4059, Overland Park, KS 66204).

Munsey, Cecil. *The Illustrated Guide to Collecting Bottles.* New York: Hawthorn Books, 1970.

Odell, John. *Indian Bottles and Brands.* Privately printed, 1997 (467B Yale Dr., Lebanon, OH 45036).

———. *Digger Odell's Official Antique Bottle & Glass Collector Magazine Price Guide:* 10 vols.: Barber Bottles (1), Bitters (2), Flasks (3), Inks (4), Medicines (5), Colognes, Pattern Mold, Label under Glass, Fire Extinguishers and Target Balls (6), Sodas and Mineral Waters (7), Whiskeys (8), Black Glass (9), Poisons, Drugstore & Apothecary Bottles (10). Privately printed, 1995–1998 (1910 Shawhan Rd., Morrow, OH 45152).

Ohio Bottles, 20th Anniversary Edition. Barberton, OH: Ohio Bottle Club, 1989.

Polak, Michael. *Bottles Identification and Price Guide,* 2nd edition. New York: Avon Books, 1997.

Toulouse, Julian Harrison. *Bottle Makers and Their Marks.* Camden, NJ: Thomas Nelson, 1971.

AVON

Avon 8 and *Avon 8: Supplement 1.* Pleasant Hill, CA: Western World Publishing, 1985, 1987.

Hastin, Bud. *Bud Hastin's Avon Products & California Perfume Co. Collector's Encyclopedia,* 15th edition. Privately printed, 1998 (P.O. Box 9868, Kansas City, MO 64134).

BARBER

Holiner, Richard. *Collecting Barber Bottles.* Paducah, KY: Collector Books, 1987.

BEAM

Cembura, Al, and Constance Avery. *A Guide to Jim Beam Bottles,* 12th edition. Privately printed, 1984 (139 Arlington Ave., Berkeley, CA 94707).

Honeyman, Betty, ed. *Jim Beam Bottles: A Pictorial Guide.* Privately printed, 1982 (International Association of Jim Beam Bottle & Specialties Clubs, 2015 Burlington Ave., Kewanee, IL 61443). Price guide update, 1998.

Jim Beam Bottles 1993 Price Guide. Privately printed, 1993 (International Association of Jim Beam Bottle & Specialties Clubs). Price guide update, 1998.

BEER

Bull, Donald, et al. American Breweries. Privately printed, 1984 (P.O. Box 106, Trumbull, CT 06611).

Friedrich, Manfred, and Donald Bull. *The Register of United States Breweries 1876–1976,* 2 vols. Privately printed, 1976 (P.O. Box 106, Trumbull, CT 06611).

Van Wieren, Dale P. *American Breweries II.* Privately printed, 1995 (Eastern Coast Breweriana Association, P.O. Box 1354, North Wales, PA 19454).

Yenne, Bill. *The Field Guide to North America's Breweries and Microbreweries.* New York: Crescent Books, 1994.

BITTERS

Brown, William E. *The Auction Price Report, 1995 Edition: Bitters, Historical Flasks, Medicines, Whiskeys, Sodas & Mineral Waters.* Privately printed, 1995 (8251 NW 49th Ct., Coral Springs, FL 33067).

Ring, Carlyn, and W.C. Ham. *Bitters Bottles.* Privately printed, 1998 (P.O. Box 427, Downieville, CA 95936).

Watson, Richard. *Bitters Bottles.* Fort Davis, TX: Thomas Nelson & Sons, 1965.

————. *Supplement to Bitters Bottles.* Camden, NJ: Thomas Nelson & Sons, 1968.

Wichman, Jeff. *Antique Western Bitters Bottles.* Sacramento, CA: Pacific Glass Books, 1999.

BLACK GLASS

Morgan, Roy, and Gordon Litherland. *Sealed Bottles: Their History and Evolution (1630–1930).* Burton-on-Trent, England: Midland Antique Bottle Publishing, 1976.

————. *A Bottle Collector's Guide: European Seals, Case Gins and Bitters.* London: Latimer New Dimensions Ltd., 1976.

CANDY CONTAINERS

Candy Containers: A Price Guide. Gas City, IN: L-W Book Sales, 1996.

Dezso, Douglas M., J. Leon Poirier, and Rose D. Poirier. *Collector's Guide to Candy Containers,* Paducah, KY: Collector Books, 1998.

Eikelberner, George, Serge Agadjanian, and Adele L. Bowden. *The Compleat American Glass Candy Containers Handbook.* Privately printed, 1986 (6252 Cedarwood Rd., Mentor, OH 44060).

Long, Jennie D. *An Album of Candy Containers.* 2 vols. Privately printed, 1978, 1983 (P.O. Box 552, Kingsburg, CA 93631).

COCA-COLA

The Coca-Cola Company: An Illustrated Profile. Atlanta, GA: The Coca-Cola Co., 1974.

Goldstein, Shelley and Helen. *Coca-Cola Collectibles with Current Prices and Photographs in Full Color,* 4 vols. and index. Privately printed, 1971–1980 (P.O. Box 301, Woodland Hills, CA 91364).

Hill, Deborah Goldstein. *Price Guide to Coca-Cola Collectibles.* Radnor, PA: Wallace-Homestead, 1991.

Hoy, Anne. *Coca-Cola: The First Hundred Years.* Atlanta, GA: The Coca-Cola Company, 1986.

Mix, Richard. *The Mix Guide to Commemorative Coca-Cola Bottles.* Privately printed, 1990 (P.O. Box 558, Marietta, GA 30061-0558).

Munsey, Cecil. *The Illustrated Guide to the Collectibles of Coca-Cola.* New York: Hawthorn Books, 1972.

Petretti, Allan. *Petretti's Coca-Cola Collectibles Price Guide,* 10th edition. Dubuque, IA: Antique Trader Books, 1997.

Schaeffer, Randy, and Bill Bateman. *Coca-Cola: A Collector's Guide to New and Vintage Coca-Cola Memorabilia.* London: Courage Books, 1995.

Schmidt, Bill and Jan. *The Schmidt Museum Collection of Coca-Cola Memorabilia.* Privately printed, 1986 (P.O. Box 647, Elizabethtown, KY 42701).

Spontak, Joyce. *Commemorative Coca-Cola Bottles: An Unauthorized Guide.* Atglen, PA: Schiffer, 1998.

Wilson, Al. *Collectors Guide to Coca-Cola Items.* Gas City, IN: L-W Book Sales, 1985.

COLOGNE, SEE PERFUME

COSMETIC

Fadely, Don. *Hair Raising Stories: A Comprehensive Look at 19th & Early 20th Century Hair Preparations and the Bottles They Came In.* Privately printed, 1992 (P.O. Box 273, U.S. Air Force Academy, Colorado Springs, CO 80840).

CURES, SEE MEDICINE; SARSAPARILLA

DECANTER

Davis, Derek C. *English Bottles & Decanters: 1650–1900.* New York: World Publishing, 1972.

DRUG, SEE MEDICINE

FIGURAL, SEE ALSO BITTERS

Christensen, Don and Doris. *Violin Bottles: Banjos, Guitars & Other Novelty Glass.* Privately printed, 1995 (21815 106th St. E., Buckley, WA 98321).

Revi, Albert Christian. *American Pressed Glass and Figure Bottles.* New York: Thomas Nelson & Sons, 1964.

Umberger, Jewel and Arthur L. *Collectible Character Bottles.* Privately printed, 1969 (Corker Book Co., 819 W. Wilson, Tyler, TX 75701).

Wearin, Otha D. *Statues that Pour: The Story of Character Bottles.* Privately printed, 1965 (Sage Books, 2679 S. York St., Denver, CO 80205).

FLASKS

Blakeman, Alan. *A Collectors Guide: Reform Flasks.* Elsecar, England: BBR Publishing, 1997.

Brown, William E. *The Auction Price Report, 1995 Edition: Bitters, Historical Flasks, Medicines, Whiskeys, Sodas & Mineral Waters.* Privately printed, 1995 (8251 NW 49th Ct., Coral Springs, FL 33067).

Clark, Lois. *Wheaton's: My Favorite Collectibles.* Privately printed, 1998 (Classic Wheaton Club, P.O. Box 59, Downington, PA 19335).

McKearin, Helen, and Kenneth M. Wilson. *American Bottles & Flasks and Their Ancestry.* New York: Crown, 1978.

Roberts, Mike. *Price Guide to All the Flasks.* Privately printed, 1980 (840 Elm Ct., Newark, OH 43055).

Thomas, John L. *Picnics, Coffins, Shoo-Flies.* Privately printed, 1974 (P.O. Box 446, Weaverville, CA 96093).

Van Rensselaer, Stephen. *Early American Bottles & Flasks,* revised edition. Privately printed, 1969 (J. Edmund Edwards, 61 Winton Place, Stratford, CT 06497).

FOOD, SEE ALSO FRUIT JARS; VINEGAR

Caniff, Tom. *The Label Space: The Book.* Privately printed, 1997 (5003 W. Berwyn Ave., Chicago, IL 60630-1501).

FRUIT JARS

Arnold, Ken. *Australian Preserving & Storage Jars: Pre-1920.* Privately printed, 1983 (16 Montgomery Crescent, Bendigo, Victoria 3550, Australia).

Bond, Ralph. *Fruit Jar Patents.* Privately printed, 1970.

Bowditch, Barbara. *American Jelly Glasses: A Collector's Notebook.* Privately printed, 1986 (400 Dorchester Rd., Rochester, NY 14610).

Caniff, Tom, ed. *The Guide to Collecting Fruit Jars: Fruit Jar Annual,* 3 vols. Privately printed, 1996–1998 (5003 W. Berwyn Ave., Chicago, IL 60630).

Creswick, Alice. *The Fruit Jar Works,* 2 vols. Privately printed, 1987 (Douglas Leybourne, P.O. Box 5417, North Muskegon, MI 49445).

Leybourne, Douglas M., Jr. *The Collector's Guide to Old Fruit Jars: Red Book 8.* Privately printed, 1997 (P.O. Box 5417, North Muskegon, MI 49445).

Roller, Dick. *Fruit Jar Patents,* Vol. II (1870–1884; 1885–1899), Vol. III

(1900–1942). Privately printed, 1996 (Jerry McCann, 5003 W. Berwyn Ave., Chicago, IL 60630-0443).

―――. *The Standard Fruit Jar Reference.* Privately printed, 1983 (607 Driskell, Paris, IL 61944).

Schroeder, Bill. *1000 Fruit Jars Priced and Illustrated,* 5th edition, 1996. Paducah, KY: Collector Books, 1996).

Toulouse, Julian Harrison. *Fruit Jars: A Collector's Manual.* Jointly published by Camden, NJ: Thomas Nelson & Sons and Hanover, PA: Everybody's Press, 1969.

INK

Blakeman, Alan. *A Collectors Guide: Inks.* Elsecar, England: BBR Publishing, 1996.

Covill, William E., Jr. *Ink Bottles and Inkwells.* Taunton, MA: William S. Sullwold, 1971.

Rivera, Betty and Ted. *Inkstands and Inkwells.* New York: Crown, 1973.

JAR, SEE FRUIT JAR

MEDICINE

Baldwin, Joseph K. *A Collector's Guide to Patent and Proprietary Medicine Bottles of the Nineteenth Century.* New York: Thomas Nelson, 1973.

Blasi, Betty. *A Bit about Balsams: A Chapter in the History of Nineteenth Century Medicine.* Privately printed, 1974 (5801 River Knolls Dr., Louisville, KY 40222).

Brown, William E. *The Auction Price Report, 1995 Edition: Bitters, Historical Flasks, Medicines, Whiskeys, Sodas & Mineral Waters.* Privately printed, 1995 (8251 NW 49th Ct., Coral Springs, FL 33067).

Wilson, Bill and Betty. *19th Century Medicine in Glass.* Privately printed, 1971 (Box 245, Amador City, CA 95601).

MILK

Edmondson, Bill. *The Milk Bottle Book of Michigan.* Privately printed, 1995 (317 Harvest Ln., Lansing, MI 48917).

Giarde, Jeffrey L. *Glass Milk Bottles: Their Makers and Marks.* Bryn Mawr, CA: The Time Travelers Press, 1980.

MILK GLASS, SEE ALSO FIGURAL

Belknap, E.M. *Milk Glass.* New York: Crown, 1959.

Ferson, Regis F. and Mary F. *Yesterday's Milk Glass Today.* Privately printed, 1981 (122 Arden Rd., Pittsburgh, PA 15216).

MINERAL WATER, SEE SODA

MINIATURES

Cembura, Al, and Constance Avery. *A Guide to Miniature Bottles.* Privately printed, 1973 (139 Arlington Ave., Berkeley, CA 94708).

Kay, Robert E. *Miniature Beer Bottles & Go-Withs.* Privately printed, 1980 (216 N. Batavia Ave., Batavia, IL 60510).

Keegan, Alan. *Scotch in Miniature: A Collector's Guide.* Privately printed, 1982 (Chiisai Bin, P.O. Box 1900, Garden Grove, CA 92642).

NURSING

Ostrander, Diane Rouse. *A Guide to American Nursing Bottles.* Privately printed, 1984, revised 1992 (Will-O-Graf, P.O. Box 24, Willoughby, OH 44094).

Pastor, John R. *Nursing Bottle Absentee Auction* (from the Estate of Laure Kimpton, Madison, Wisconsin), 1998 (7288 Thorncrest Dr. SE, Ada, MI 49301).

PEPSI-COLA

Ayers, James C. *Pepsi-Cola Bottles Collectors Guide.* Privately printed, 1995 (RJM Enterprises, P.O. Box 1377, Mount Airy, NC 27030).

Lloyd, Everette and Mary. *Pepsi-Cola Collectibles with Price Guide.* Atglen, PA: Schiffer, 1993.

Rawlingson, Fred. *Brad's Drink: A Primer for Pepsi-Cola Collectors.* Privately printed, 1976 (FAR Publications, Box 5456, Newport News, VA 23605).

Stoddard, Bob. *Introduction to Pepsi Collecting.* Privately printed, 1991 (Double Dot Enterprises, P.O. Box 1548, Pomona, CA 91769).

Vehling, Bill, and Michael Hunt. *Pepsi-Cola Collectibles (with Prices),* 3 vols. Gas City, IN: L-W Book Sales, 1988–1993.

PERFUME, COLOGNE, AND SCENT

Avon & California Perfume Co.: Collector's Encyclopedia, 15th edition. Privately printed, 1998 (P.O. Box 9868, Kansas City, MO 64134).

Baccarat: Bud Hastin's The Perfume Bottles. Privately printed, 1986 (Addor Associates, P.O. Box 2128, Westport, CT 06880).

Ball, Joanne Dubbs, and Dorothy Hehl Torem. *Fragrance Bottle Masterpieces.* Atglen, PA: Schiffer, 1996.

Bowman, Glinda. *More Miniature Perfume Bottles.* Atglen, PA: Schiffer, 1996.

Forsythe, Ruth A. *Made in Czechoslovakia.* Privately printed, 1982 (Box 327, Galena, OH 43021).

Gaborit, Jean-Yves. *Perfumes: The Essences and Their Bottles.* New York: Rizzoli, 1985.

Latimer, Tirza True. *The Perfume Atomizer: An Object with Atmosphere.* Atglen, PA: Schiffer, 1991.

Lefkowith, Christie Mayer. *The Art of Perfume: Discovering and Collecting Perfume Bottles.* New York: Thames and Hudson, 1994.

Martin, Hazel. *A Collection of Figural Perfume & Scent Bottles.* Privately printed, 1982 (P.O. Box 110, Lancaster, CA 93535).

North, Jacquelyn Y. Jones. *Commercial Perfume Bottles.* Atglen, PA: Schiffer, 1986.

———. *Perfume, Cologne and Scent Bottles.* Atglen, PA: Schiffer, 1986.

Ringblum, Jeri Lyn. *A Collector's Handbook of Miniature Perfume Bottles.* Atglen, PA: Schiffer, 1996.

Sloan, Jean. *Perfume and Scent Bottle Collecting with Prices.* Radnor, PA: Wallace-Homestead, 1989.

Utt, Mary Lou and Glen, and Patricia Bayer. *Lalique Perfume Bottles.* New York: Crown, 1985.

PICKLE

Zumwalt, Betty. *Ketchup Pickles Sauces.* Privately printed, 1980 (P.O. Box 413, Fulton, CA 95439).

POISON

Durflinger, Roger L. *Poison Bottles Collectors Guide.* Privately printed, 1972 (132 W. Oak St., Washington Court House, OH 43160).

Kuhn, Rudy. *Poison Bottle Workbook.* Privately printed, 1988 (3954 Perie Ln., San Jose, CA 95132).

ROYAL DOULTON

Dale, Jean. *The Charlton Standard Catalog of Royal Doulton Jugs.* Privately printed, 1991 (Charlton Press, 2010 Yonge St., Toronto, Ontario M4S 1Z9, Canada).

Lukins, Jocelyn. *Doulton Kingsware Whisky.* Yelverton, Devon, England: M.P.E., 1981.

SARSAPARILLA

DeGrafft, Joan. *American Sarsaparilla Bottles.* Privately printed, 1980 (47 Ash St., North Attleboro, MA 92760).

Shimko, Phyllis. *Sarsaparilla Bottle Encyclopedia.* Privately printed, 1969 (Box 117, Aurora, OR 97002).

SKI COUNTRY

Ski Country Collector's Guide and Catalog of Decanters. Privately printed, 1983 (1224 Washington Ave., Golden, CO 80401).

SCENT, SEE PERFUME

SODA, SEE ALSO COCA-COLA; PEPSI-COLA

Bowers, Q. David. *The Moxie Encyclopedia.* Vestal, NY: The Vestal Press, 1984.

Brown, William E. *The Auction Price Report, 1995 Edition: Bitters, Historical Flasks, Medicines, Whiskeys, Sodas & Mineral Waters.* Privately printed, 1995 (8251 NW 49th Ct., Coral Springs, FL 33067).

Dietz, Lawrence. *Soda Pop.* New York: Simon & Schuster, 1973.

Ellis, Harry E. *Dr Pepper, King of Beverages.* Dallas, TX: Dr Pepper Company, 1979.

Ferguson, Joel. *New Orleans Soda Water Manufacturers History.* Privately printed, 1995 (106 Dixie Circle, Slidell, LA 70458).

Fowler, Ron. *Washington Sodas: The Illustrated History of Washington's Soft Drink Industry.* Privately printed, 1986 (Dolphin Point Writing Works, P.O. Box 45251, Seattle, WA 98145).

Marsh, Thomas E. *The Official Guide to Collecting Applied Color Label Soda Bottles,* Vol. II. Privately printed, 1995 (914 Franklin Ave., Youngstown, OH 44502).

Petretti, Allan. *Petretti's Soda Pop Collectibles Price Guide.* Dubuque, IA: Antique Trader Books, 1996.

Sweeney, Rick. *Collecting Applied Color Label Soda Bottles,* 2nd edition. Privately printed, 1995 (9418 Hilmer Dr., La Mesa, CA 91942).

Tucker, Donald. *Collector's Guide to the Saratoga Type Mineral Water Bottles.* Privately printed, 1986 (North Berwick, ME 03906).

TONIC, SEE MEDICINE

Smith, Levin J. *White House Vinegar Book.* Privately printed, 1971 (P.O. Box 102, Independence, VA 24348).

WHISKEY

Barnett, R. E. *Western Whiskey Bottles,* Privately printed, 1997 (P.O. Box 109, Lakeview, OR 97630).

Brown, William E. *The Auction Price Report, 1995 Edition: Bitters, Historical Flasks, Medicines, Whiskeys, Sodas & Mineral Waters.* Privately printed, 1995 (8251 NW 49th Ct., Coral Springs, FL 33067).

Spaid, David, and Henry Ford. *The One Hundred and One Rare Whiskeys.* Privately printed, 1989 (P.O. Box 2161, Palos Verdes, CA 90274).

Thomas, John, L. *Whiskey Bottles & Liquor Containers from the State of Washington,* Privately printed, 1998 (4805 Grace St., Apt. C, Capitola, CA 95010-2655).

————.*Whiskey Bottles & Liquor Containers from the State of Oregon,* Privately printed, 1998, (4805 Grace St., Apt. C, Capitola, CA 95010-2655).

WINE

Dumbrell, Roger. *Understanding Antique Wine Bottles.* Suffolk, England: Antique Collectors' Club, 1983.

GO-WITHS

Byrne, Thomas. *The U.S. Beer Coaster Guide.* Privately printed, 1980 (P.O. Box 173, E. Hanover, NJ 07936).

Congdon-Martin, Douglas. *America for Sale.* Atglen, PA: Schiffer, 1991.

Edmonson, Barbara. *Historic Shot Glasses.* Bend, OR: Maverick Publications, 1985.

————. *Old Advertising: Spirits Glasses.* Bend, OR: Maverick Publications, 1988.

Hake, Ted, and Russ King. *Price Guide to Collectible Pin-Back Buttons: 1896–1986.* Privately printed, 1986 (Hake's Americana & Collectible Press, P.O. Box 1444, York, PA 17405).

Huxford, Sharon and Bob. *Huxford's Collectible Advertising: An Illustrated Value Guide,* 2nd Edition. Paducah, KY: Collector Books, 1995.

Klug, Ray. *Antique Advertising Encyclopedia,* 2 vols. Gas City, IN: L-W Book Sales, 1978, 1985.

Morrison, Tom. *Root Beer Advertising: A Collector's Guide.* Privately printed, 1990 (2930 Squaw Valley Dr., Colorado Springs, CO 80918).

Summers, B.J. *Value Guide to Advertising Memorabilia.* Paducah, KY: Collector Books, 1994.

─────────────────────── **AESTHETIC SPECIALTIES** ───────────────────────

In 1979 the first bottle was released by ASI, or Aesthetic Specialties, Inc., of San Mateo, California. It was a ceramic vodka bottle that was made to honor the 1979 Crosby 38th National Pro-Am Golf Tournament. According to the company president, Charles Wittwer, 400 cases of the bottle were made. The company continued making bottles: the 1979 Kentucky Derby bottle (600 cases); 1909 Stanley Steamer (5,000 cases in three different colors made in 1979); 1903 Cadillac (2 colors made in 1979, gold version, with and without trim, made in 1980); World's Greatest Golfer (400 cases in 1979); World's Greatest Hunter (1979); 38th and 39th Crosby Golf Tournaments (1979 and 1980); 1981 Crosby 40th Golf Tournament (reworked version of World's Greatest Golfer, 100 cases); Crosby Golf Tournaments (1982, 1983, and 1984); Telephone Service Truck (1980); Ice Cream Truck (1980); 1910 Oldsmobile (1980, made in three colors); Packard (1980); 1911 Stanley Steamer (1981, 1,200 cases); 1937 Packard (1981, produced with McCormick); 1914 Chevrolet (1981); and Fire engine (1981).

AESTHETIC SPECIALTIES, Bing Crosby, 38th, 1979	14.00
Bing Crosby, 39th, 1980	25.00 to 28.00
Bing Crosby, 40th, 1981	36.00
Bing Crosby, 41st, Otter, 1982	65.00
Bing Crosby, 42nd, Seal, 1983	40.00
Bing Crosby, 43rd, Clam, 1984	45.00 to 50.00
Bing Crosby, 44th, 1985	50.00
Cadillac, 1903 Model, Blue, White, 1979	70.00
Cadillac, 1980 Model, Gold	124.00
Chevrolet, 1914 Model, 1979	60.00
Chevrolet, 1980 Model, Gold	170.00
Kentucky Derby, 1979	26.00
Model T Ice Cream Truck, Ford, 1980	75.00 to 85.00
Oldsmobile, 1910 Model, Black, 1980	75.00 to 80.00
Oldsmobile, Gold, 1980	165.00
Oldsmobile, Platinum, 1980	307.00
Stanley Steamer, 1909 Model, Black, 1981	50.00 to 65.00
Stanley Steamer, 1911 Model, Black, 1981	75.00
Stanley Steamer, Gold, 1981	113.00
Stanley Steamer, Green, 1981	42.00
World's Greatest Golfer, 1979	35.00 to 40.00
World's Greatest Hunter, 1979	29.00 to 35.00
ALPHA, see Lewis & Clark	
AUSTIN NICHOLS, see Wild Turkey	

─────────────────────────────── **AVON** ───────────────────────────────

David H. McConnell started a door-to-door selling company in 1886. He recruited women as independent sales representatives to sell his perfume. The company was named the California Perfume Company even though it was located in New York City. The first product was a set of five perfumes called Little Dot. In 1928 it was decided that CPC was too limiting a name so a new line called Avon was introduced. By 1936, the Avon name was on all of the company's products, including perfumes, toothbrushes, and baking items. Avon became a public company in 1946. Collectors want the bottles, jewelry, figurines, sales awards, early advertising, pamphlets, and other go-withs. For information on national and local clubs, books, and other publications, contact the National Association of Avon Collector Clubs, P.O. Box 7006, Kansas City, MO 64113.

AVON, Albee, 1981, Box	65.00
Albee, 1982	20.00
Albee, 1983	20.00
Albee, 1985	20.00 to 25.00
Albee, 1988	20.00 to 25.00
Albee, 1989	20.00
Auto Lantern, 1973	12.00
Avon Calling, 1905, Phone, 1973	10.00
Bell, Hearts Delight, 1993	10.00
Bell, Paul Revere, 1979	8.00
Bo Peep, Soap, Box, 1953	75.00
California Perfume Co., Furniture Polish, 1915, 4 Oz.	50.00
California Perfume Co., Jardin D'Amour Powder Sachet, 1929	75.00

California Perfume Co., Red Food Coloring, 1915, 2 Oz.	75.00
California Perfume Co., Trailing Arbutus Powder Sachet, 1925	75.00
Car, Chevy '55, Box, 1975, 7 In. ....*Illus*	9.00
Car, Stanley Steamer, Silver, 1978	10.00
Car, Station Wagon, 1971	8.00
Car, Straight Eight, 1973	10.00
Car, Volkswagen, Black, 1970	12.00
Chess Set, Box, 32 Piece	100.00
Clock, see Avon, Leisure Hours	
Cologne, Little Girl Blue, 1972-1973	25.00
Come Rain Or Shine, Box, 1989	10.00
Covered Wagon, 1970	10.00
Decanter, Crystalique, 1975	40.00
Decanter, Homestead, 1973-1974	7.00
Decanter, Indian Head Penny, 1970-1972	3.00
Decanter, Owl Fancy, 1974-1976	6.00
Decanter, Period Piece, 1972-1973	8.00
Decanter, Short Pony, 1968-1969	10.00
Decanter, Snoopy Surprise, 1969-1971	11.00
Decanter, Stylish Lady, 1982-1983	10.00
Decanter, Wild Turkey, 1974-1976	9.00
Decanter, Wise Choice Owl, 1969-1970	9.00
Dinosaur, Bubble Bath, Triceratops, Brontosaurus, Tyrannosaurus, Box, 1975-1978, 3 Piece	20.00
Football Helmet, see Avon, Opening Play	
Four Seasons Calendar Plate, 1987	10.00
Garden Girl, Pink	4.00
Helmet, see Avon, Opening Play	
La Belle Telephone, 1974-1976	3.00
Lamp, see Avon, Tiffany Lamp	
Leisure Hours, 1970, 5 1/4 In. ....*Illus*	6.00
Linus, Bubble Bath, Box, 1968	20.00 to 35.00
Little Girl Blue, 1972	25.00
Lucy, Bubble Bath, Painted, 1970-1972	25.00 to 30.00
Merry Mouse	88.00
Mother's Love, 1981	10.00
My First Call, 1980	40.00
NAAC, McConnell Club, 1978	25.00
Opening Play, 1968-1969, 4 1/4 In. ....*Illus*	14.00
Pipe, Dutch, 1973	5.00
Pipe Dream, 1967	12.00
Pipe Full, 1971-1976	2.00
Pistol, 1850 Pepper Box, Box, 1979	35.00
Right Connection, Fuse, 1977	1.50
Roaring Twenties, 1972-1974	4.00
Scottish Lass, 1975	3.00
Spanish Senorita, 1975-1976	4.00
Spice Jar, House, Yellow	5.00

Avon, Car, Chevy '55, Box, 1975, 7 In.

Avon, Leisure Hours, 1970, 5 1/4 In.

Avon, Opening Play, 1968-1969, 4 1/4 In.

Avon, Super Cycle, 1971, 7 1/4 In.

Spice Jar, Townhouse, Blue	5.00
Steer Horns, see Avon, Western Choice	
Stein, American Armed Forces, 1990	35.00
Stein, Blacksmith, 1985	6.00
Stein, Car Classic, 1979	25.00
Stein, Christopher Columbus, Box, 1992	12.00
Stein, Collector, 1976, Large	25.00
Stein, Ducks Of American Wilderness, Box, 1988	26.00
Stein, Endangered Species, 1990	9.00
Stein, Flying, 1981	10.00 to 25.00
Stein, Great American Football, Box, 1983	16.00
Stein, Great American Baseball, 1984	25.00
Stein, Sailing Ships, 1977	25.00
Stein, Shipbuilder, 1986	19.00
Stein, Sporting, 1983	9.00
Stein, Western Round-Up, 1980	25.00
Super Cycle, 1971, 7 1/4 In. *Illus*	9.00
Telephone, see Avon, Avon Calling; Avon, La Belle Telephone	
Tiffany Lamp, 1973	7.00
Viking Horn, 1966	5.00
Western Choice, Steer Horns, 1967	15.00
Wishful Thoughts, 1982, Box	10.00

―――――――――――――――― **BALLANTINE** ――――――――――――――――

Ballantine's Scotch was sold in figural bottles in 1969. The five bottles were shaped like a golf bag, knight, mallard, zebra, or fisherman. Ballantine also made some flasks and jugs with special designs.

BALLANTINE, Fisherman, 1969	15.00 to 17.00
Golf Bag, 1969 *Illus*	25.00
Jug, Miniature	5.00 to 10.00
Mallard Duck, 1969	10.00
Zebra, 1969 *Illus*	15.00

Ballantine, Golf Bag, 1969

Ballantine, Zebra, 1969

BARBER

The nineteenth-century barber either made his own hair tonic or purchased it in large containers. Barber bottles were used at the barbershop or in the home. The barber filled the bottles each day with hair oil, bay rum, tonic, shampoo, witch hazel, rosewater, or some other cosmetic. He knew what was inside each bottle because of its distinctive shape and color. Most of the important types of art glass were used for barber bottles. Spatter glass, milk glass, cranberry, cobalt, cut, hobnail, vaseline, and opalescent glass were used alone or in attractive combinations. Some were made with enamel-painted decorations. Most of the bottles were blown. A pontil mark can be found on the bottom of many bottles. These special fancy bottles were popular during the last half of the nineteenth-century. In 1906 the Pure Food and Drug Act made it illegal to use refillable, nonlabeled bottles in a barbershop and the bottles were no longer used.

BARBER, Amber, Lady's Leg Neck, Bulbous, 7 3/4 In.	60.00
Amber, Ribs, Orange, White, Yellow Enamel, Rolled Lip, 1925, 8 In.	105.00
Amber, White Enamel Flowers, 8 1/4 In.	190.00
Amethyst, Allover Pink Iridescent, Light Yellow Amber, Cylindrical, 1920, 7 1/4 In.	360.00
Amethyst, Bell Shape, Ribs, Orange, White Enamel, Sheared Lip, 8 In.	110.00
Amethyst, Bell Shape, White, Gold Gilt Flowers, Sheared Lip, 8 In.	550.00
Amethyst, Corset Waist, Ribs, White, Red, Gold Enamel, 7 1/2 In.	80.00
Amethyst, Corset Waist, White & Gold Enamel Design, Pontil, 7 7/8 In.	95.00
Amethyst, Enamel Flowers, Gold Gilt, Sheared Lip, IP, 7 1/2 In.	75.00
Amethyst, Enamel Flowers, Painted Red Orange Band, Sheared Lip, OP, 7 3/4 In.	45.00
Amethyst, Enamel Flowers, Tooled Mouth, Corset, Long Neck, Pontil, 7 3/4 In.	90.00
Amethyst, Enamel Flowers, White & Orange, Pontil, 1885-1925, 7 1/2 In.	165.00
Amethyst, Gilt Enamel, Pontil, c.1900, 7 7/8 In.	105.00
Amethyst, Gold Art Nouveau Flowers, OP, 7 3/4 In.	475.00
Amethyst, Gold Enamel Flowers, Gold Rim, Bulbous, OP, c.1860	220.00
Amethyst, Green & White Enamel, Pontil, c.1900, 7 1/4 In.	130.00
Amethyst, Ground Lip, Polished, 7 5/8 In.	200.00
Amethyst, Hobnail, Rolled Lip, 7 1/4 In.	255.00
Amethyst, Hobnail, Rolled Lip, Metal Stopper, 7 1/2 In.	145.00
Amethyst, Hobnail, Rolled Lip, Porcelain Stopper, 7 In.	145.00
Amethyst, Hobnail, Rolled Lip, Smooth Base, 7 1/8 In.	470.00
Amethyst, Mary Gregory Type, 7 3/4 In.	525.00
Amethyst, Mary Gregory Type, White Enamel Victorian Woman, Bulbous, 7 1/2 In.	210.00
Amethyst, Melon Sides, Butterfly & Flowers, Pontil, Rolled Lip, 8 1/4 In.	95.00
Amethyst, Melon Sides, White, Orange Butterfly, Flowers, 8 1/4 In.	175.00
Amethyst, Orange, White Enamel, Bulbous, OP	60.00
Amethyst, Orange, White Enamel, Pontil Base, 8 In.	100.00
Amethyst, Orange, White Flowers, Sheared Mouth, Pontil, Cylindrical, 1920, 8 In.	80.00
Amethyst, Ribs, Art Nouveau Flowers, Sheared Lip, Porcelain Stopper, 8 In.	110.00
Amethyst, Ribs, Bell Shape, White Enamel, Sheared Lip, 7 7/8 In.	100.00
Amethyst, Ribs, Corset Waist, Blue, Orange, Green Enamel Flowers, 1925, 8 In.	770.00
Amethyst, Ribs, Corset Waist, Flowers, Sheared Lip, 7 3/4 In.	6325.00
Amethyst, Ribs, Corset Waist, White, Red, Gold Enamel, Sheared Lip, 7 In.	130.00
Amethyst, Ribs, Flowers, Rolled Lip, Metal Stopper, Pontil, 7 3/4 In.	165.00
Amethyst, Ribs, Flowers, Rolled Lip, Porcelain Stopper, Pontil, 7 5/8 In.	95.00
Amethyst, Ribs, Flowers, Sheared Lip, Pontil, 6 3/4 In.	55.00
Amethyst, Ribs, Girl, Holding Flowers, 7 7/8 In.	245.00
Amethyst, Ribs, Green, Pink, Red Enamel Flowers, 6 7/8 In.	255.00
Amethyst, Ribs, Mary Gregory Type, Porcelain Stopper, 8 In., 2 Piece	250.00
Amethyst, Ribs, Mary Gregory Type, White Enamel Boy With Butterfly Net, 8 1/8 In.	330.00
Amethyst, Ribs, Mary Gregory Type, White Enamel Girl With Basket, 7 7/8 In.	305.00
Amethyst, Ribs, Mary Gregory Type, White Enamel Girl, Rolled Lip, 7 3/4 In.	330.00
Amethyst, Ribs, Red, Pink, Green Enamel Thistle, Sheared Lip, 1925, 8 In.	305.00
Amethyst, Ribs, Red, White Enamel, 6 5/8 In.	60.00
Amethyst, Ribs, Red, White Enamel, Sheared Lip, 6 In.	30.00
Amethyst, Ribs, Red, White Enamel, Sheared Lip, 7 7/8 In.	95.00
Amethyst, Ribs, Red, White, Yellow Enamel Flowers, Sheared Lip, 6 3/4 In.	145.00
Amethyst, Ribs, Red, Yellow Enamel Flowers, 7 3/4 In.	105.00
Amethyst, Ribs, Red, Yellow, White Enamel, Sheared Lip, 1925, 6 3/4 In.	100.00
Amethyst, Ribs, Silver Overlay Flowers, Pontil Base, 7 1/2 In.	1265.00
Amethyst, Ribs, White Enamel, 8 1/8 In.	165.00

Amethyst, Ribs, White Enamel, Rolled Lip, 7 1/8 In. 120.00
Amethyst, Ribs, White Enamel, Sailing Vessel, 6 5/8 In. 305.00
Amethyst, Ribs, White, Blue Enamel, Sheared Lip, 7 1/2 In. . . . . .60.00 to 100.00
Amethyst, Ribs, White, Blue Enamel, Sheared Lip, 7 In. 145.00
Amethyst, Ribs, White, Gilt, Sheared Lip, 6 5/8 In. 210.00
Amethyst, Ribs, White, Gold Gilt Flowers, Rolled Lip, 7 7/8 In. . . . . .265.00 to 330.00
Amethyst, Ribs, White, Orange, Gilt Flowers, Rolled Lip, Pontil, 6 5/8 In. 70.00
Amethyst, Ribs, White, Orange, Gilt Flowers, Sheared Lip, Pontil, 6 5/8 In. 55.00
Amethyst, Ribs, White, Orange, Gold Enamel, Pontil Base, 8 In. 95.00
Amethyst, Ribs, White, Yellow & Orange Flowers, Sheared Lip, Pontil, 7 7/8 In. 165.00
Amethyst, Ribs, White, Young Boy, Standing With Outstretched Arm, 8 1/8 In. 210.00
Amethyst, Ribs, Yellow, Gold Art Nouveau Flowers, 7 1/2 In. 495.00
Amethyst, Ribs, Yellow, Gold Flowers, 7 7/8 In. 500.00
Amethyst, Ribs, Yellow, Gold Gilt Flowers, Rolled Lip, 7 3/4 In. 60.00
Amethyst, Ribs, Yellow, Green Enamel Flowers, 7 In. 145.00
Amethyst, Ribs, Yellow, Green, White, Rolled Lip, Stopper, 8 In. 190.00
Amethyst, Sheared Lip, Metal Stopper, OP, 7 1/2 In. 90.00
Amethyst, Vertical Ribs, Flowers, Rolled Lip, Pontil, 7 3/4 In. 360.00
Amethyst, White & Orange Flowers, Tooled Mouth, Pontil, Bulbous, 6 1/2 In. 120.00
Amethyst, White Enamel Flowers, Pontil, c.1900, 7 7/8 In. . . . . .40.00 to 105.00
Amethyst, White Women, Holding Glass High In Air, Rolled Lip, 1925, 8 In. 2585.00
Amethyst, White, Gilt Art Nouveau Flowers, 7 1/2 In. 690.00
Amethyst, White, Gilt Flowers, Rolled Lip, 7 3/4 In. 630.00
Amethyst, White, Yellow, Orange Enamel, Rolled Lip, 8 3/8 In. 90.00
Amethyst, Yellow, Gold, Art Nouveau Floral, Rolled Lip, 7 3/4 In. . . . . *Illus* 605.00
Amethyst, Yellow, White Enamel Flowers, Tooled Mouth, 1920, 8 3/4 In. 275.00
Apple Green, Enamel, Rolled Lip, OP, 8 1/2 In. 85.00
Apple Green, Ribs, Gold Art Nouveau Flowers, Metal Stopper, OP, 8 1/2 In. 225.00
Apple Green, Ribs, Orange & White Flowers, Sheared Lip, OP, 7 1/4 In. 55.00
Apple Green, Thumbprint, Yellow, White, Orange Enamel, 1925, 8 3/8 In. 185.00
Apricot, Orange & White Enamel Flowers, Tooled Mouth, Pontil, Bulbous, 8 In. 145.00
Aqua Milk Glass, Lavender Flowers, Painted, Screw Stopper, Chas. J. Firth, 9 In. 715.00
Art Glass, Applied Ruby Crackle, Ground & Polished Lip, 1920s, 7 3/4 In. 500.00
Barbasol Shaving Cream, Embossed, 2 7/8 In. . . . . *Illus* 10.00
Bay Rum, Amber, Monogram, Applied Mouth, Reddington & Co., San Francisco, 10 In. . 110.00
Bay Rum, Amethyst, Ribs, White Enamel Grist Mill, 8 In. 260.00
Bay Rum, Amethyst, White Enamel Grist Mill, 7 5/8 In. 230.00
Bay Rum, Amethyst, White Enamel Grist Mill, Pontil, Rolled, Lip, 8 1/2 In. 235.00
Bay Rum, Black Glass, H. Michelson, St. Thomas, Cylindrical 40.00
Bay Rum, Blue Milk Glass, Winter Cabin, Painted, Screw Stopper, J. Gaghan, 10 1/2 In. . 470.00
Bay Rum, Light Amber, Weeks & Potter, Boston, Mass. 50.00
Bay Rum, Milk Glass, Bird, Snowy Roof, Pewter Screw Cap, A. Winkel Sr., 9 1/2 In. . . . 550.00
Bay Rum, Milk Glass, Blue & Red Flowers & Beads, Joe Sheetz, W.T. & Co., 9 1/2 In. . . 150.00
Bay Rum, Milk Glass, Bride With Flowers, Ground Lip, 9 1/2 In. 495.00
Bay Rum, Milk Glass, Clover, Green & Red Enamel, Rolled Lip, Pontil, 8 3/4 In. 90.00
Bay Rum, Milk Glass, Enamel Flowers, Sheared Lip, OP, Stopper 330.00
Bay Rum, Milk Glass, Enamel Flowers, Tooled Lip, 8 1/2 In. 120.00
Bay Rum, Milk Glass, Flowers, Joe Sheetz, W.T. & Co., 9 1/2 In. 250.00
Bay Rum, Milk Glass, Flowers, Multicolor, Ground Lip, J.N. Hogarth, 1885, 9 In. 470.00
Bay Rum, Milk Glass, Girl, Label Under Glass, Metal Stopper, Fred Gordon, 10 In. 415.00
Bay Rum, Milk Glass, Label Under Glass, W.J. Reynar, Metal Neck Band, 10 3/4 In. . . . 200.00
Bay Rum, Milk Glass, Multicolor Clover, 9 3/8 In. 160.00
Bay Rum, Milk Glass, Multicolor Enamel Flowers, Tooled Mouth, 9 1/8 In. 175.00
Bay Rum, Milk Glass, Multicolor, 5 Birds In Flight, Marked, 9 In. 415.00
Bay Rum, Milk Glass, Opalescent, Flowers, Multicolor, Enamel, Marked, 7 1/4 In. 155.00
Bay Rum, Milk Glass, Opalescent, Grist Mill, Rolled Lip, Pontil, 9 In. 275.00
Bay Rum, Milk Glass, Pretty Girl, Reverse Painted Label, Metal Screw Top, 11 In. 150.00
Bay Rum, Milk Glass, Winter Scene, Cottage, Pewter Screw Cap, C.F. Hawman, 9 1/2 In. 470.00
Bay Rum, Milk Glass, Woman Label Under Glass, Chas. L. Auger, 11 In. 880.00
Bay Rum, Milk Glass, Woman, Label Under Glass, Rolled Lip, R.H. Wilson, 9 7/8 In. . . 715.00
Bay Rum, Opalescent, Milk Glass, Multicolor Clover, 8 5/8 In. 90.00
Bay Rum, Opalescent, Milk Glass, Swirl Ribs, Red Enamel Lettering, 9 In. 60.00
Bay Rum, Opaque Blue, Woman Label Under Glass, Gilt, 10 7/8 In. 990.00

Bay Rum, Pretty Woman On Label, Screw Top, J. Frank Morse, 9 3/4 In. 75.00
Bay Rum, Puerto Rico & Baileys On Label, LaTraen, 1890s, Some Contents 35.00
Bay Rum, Yellow, Ribs, Red, White, Green, Gold Enamel Flowers, Marked, 8 3/4 In. ... 415.00
Before & After, Figural, Face, Sad & Happy, Rolled Lip, Cork Stopper, 12 In. 935.00
Belt Buckle, Ribs, Yellow Topaz, Pontil, 8 1/8 In. 230.00
Black Amethyst, Ribs, White, Orange Enamel Flowers, 7 In. 105.00
Blown, Diamond Mold, Cranberry & White Vertical Stripes, Bulbous, 7 In. 2530.00
Blown, Grass Green, White, Gold Art Nouveau, Sheared Lip, 8 In. 360.00
Blue, Corset Waist, Opalescent Wandering Vine, 7 In. 230.00
Blue, Enamel Daisies, Sheared Lip, Metal Stopper, OP, 8 In. 130.00
Blue & White, Splotch, Polished Lip, Polished Pontil, 7 3/4 In. 330.00
Blue Milk Glass, Cherub, Yellow, 7 1/2 In. ....415.00 to 550.00
Blue Opalescent, Daisy & Fern, Rolled Lip, Metal Stopper, 7 3/4 In. 105.00
Blue Opalescent, Fern Pattern, Rolled Lip, 7 In. 110.00
Blue Opalescent, Spanish Lace, Pontil, 7 1/4 In. 170.00
Brilliantine, Cobalt Blue, Pontil, 3 1/2 In. ....65.00 to 110.00
Brilliantine, Ruby Red, Tooled Lip, Crown Type Stopper, 4 In. 330.00
Canary Yellow Opalescent, Daisy & Fern, Melon Sides, Rolled Lip, 7 1/8 In. 130.00
Canary Yellow Opalescent, Vertical Stripe, Melon Sides, 7 1/4 In. 120.00
Carnival-Type, Swirled Ribs, Smooth Base, Polished Lip, 7 7/8 In. ....*Illus* 303.00
Chas. L. Auger, Bay Rum, Label Under Milk Glass, Victorian Lady, Pink Ground, 11 In. . 885.00
Checkerberry, Copper Wheel Cut Lettering, Rolled Lip, 6 5/8 In. 80.00
Citron, Enamel Flowers, OP, 7 7/8 In. 160.00
Clambroth Opalescent, Hobnail, Pink, Tooled Mouth, 6 5/8 In. 415.00
Clear, Pale Blue Satin, Ribs, Enamel Flowers, Sheared Lip, OP, 8 In. 105.00
Clear, Raised Ribs, Cobalt Blue Base, 7 1/2 In. 330.00
Cobalt Blue, 22 Vertical Ribs, Flowers, Rolled Lip, Metal Stopper, 8 3/4 In. 145.00
Cobalt Blue, 552 On Base, Screw-On Pewter Stopper, 9 1/2 In. 200.00
Cobalt Blue, Bell Shape, Red, White, Gold Enamel, 7 7/8 In. 210.00
Cobalt Blue, Bird On A Branch, Sheared Lip, 8 3/8 In. 495.00
Cobalt Blue, Enamel Flowers, Rolled Lip, Pontil, 8 In. 220.00
Cobalt Blue, Fluted Neck, Base, Embossed, N. Wapler, N.Y. 40.00
Cobalt Blue, Iridescent Mother-Of-Pearl, Vine, Applied Mouth, 7 3/4 In. 1815.00
Cobalt Blue, Mallet Shape, Orange, Yellow, White Enamel, 7 3/4 In. 190.00
Cobalt Blue, Mary Gregory Type, White Enamel Boy Playing Tennis, 8 In. .....265.00 to 385.00
Cobalt Blue, Mary Gregory Type, White Enamel Girl Playing Tennis, 8 1/4 In. . .305.00 to 360.00
Cobalt Blue, Orange, White Enamel, Rolled Lip, Pontil, 6 5/8 In. 90.00
Cobalt Blue, Ribs, Bell Shape, Flowers, Sheared Lip, Pontil, 7 1/2 In. 145.00
Cobalt Blue, Ribs, Bell Shape, Pink, White Enamel, Sheared Lip, 1925, 8 In. 80.00
Cobalt Blue, Ribs, Bell Shape, White, Gold Gilt, 7 3/4 In. 550.00
Cobalt Blue, Ribs, Corset Waist, Red, White Enamel Flowers, 7 In. 175.00
Cobalt Blue, Ribs, Corset Waist, White, Orange Enamel, Sheared Lip, 7 7/8 In. 465.00
Cobalt Blue, Ribs, Corset Waist, White, Orange, Gold Enamel, Rolled Lip, 7 3/4 In. 155.00
Cobalt Blue, Ribs, Enamel Flowers, Rolled Lip, Pontil, 7 5/8 In. 255.00
Cobalt Blue, Ribs, Flowers, Rolled Lip, Porcelain Stopper, 7 1/4 In. 90.00
Cobalt Blue, Ribs, Gold, Silver Persian Style Enamel, 6 3/4 In. 95.00
Cobalt Blue, Ribs, Green, White, Pink, Gold Gilt Flowers, 6 3/4 In. 95.00
Cobalt Blue, Ribs, Mary Gregory Type, White Enamel Boy Holding A Bird, 7 In. 415.00
Cobalt Blue, Ribs, Mary Gregory Type, White Enamel Girl With A Flower, 8 In. 550.00

If you discover a cache of very dirty bottles and you are not dressed in work clothes, make a temporary cover up from a plastic garbage bag.

Barber, Barbasol Shaving
Cream, Embossed, 2 7/8 In.

Cobalt Blue, Ribs, Multicolor, Enamel Flowers, Rolled Lip, 7 5/8 In. 200.00
Cobalt Blue, Ribs, Orange, Silver Persian Design, Sheared Lip, 6 In. 110.00
Cobalt Blue, Ribs, Pink, Green, White Enamel Flowers, Sheared Lip, 1925, 7 In. 145.00
Cobalt Blue, Ribs, Red, White Enamel, Corset Waist Form, 7 In. 145.00
Cobalt Blue, Ribs, White & Green Enamel, Sheared Lip, 7 1/2 In. 155.00
Cobalt Blue, Ribs, White & Yellow Flowers, Rolled Lip, Pontil, 8 1/4 In. 80.00
Cobalt Blue, Ribs, White Enamel, Rolled Lip, Pontil, 7 In. ....70.00 to 95.00
Cobalt Blue, Ribs, White Enamel, Sheared Lip, 6 7/8 In. ....80.00 to 110.00
Cobalt Blue, Ribs, White Enamel, Sheared Lip, Pontil, 7 5/8 In. 145.00
Cobalt Blue, Ribs, White, Gold Enamel, Sheared Lip, 6 3/4 In. 90.00
Cobalt Blue, Ribs, White, Green, Pink Enamel Flowers, 7 In. 145.00
Cobalt Blue, Ribs, White, Orange Enamel Flowers, 6 7/8 In. ....105.00 to 140.00
Cobalt Blue, Ribs, White, Pink, Yellow Enamel Flowers, Sheared Lip, 1925, 8 In. 90.00
Cobalt Blue, Ribs, White, Pink, Yellow Flowers, Sheared Lip, 7 In. 95.00
Cobalt Blue, Ribs, White, Yellow, Gold Flowers, Sheared Lip, 7 3/4 In. 220.00
Cobalt Blue, Ribs, White, Yellow, Orange Enamel, Rolled Lip, 8 In. 230.00
Cobalt Blue, Ribs, Yellow & Gold, Rolled Lip, Pontil, 7 5/8 In. ....*Illus* 440.00
Cobalt Blue, Thumbprint, Yellow, Orange, White Enamel, 8 1/4 In. 110.00
Cobalt Blue, Thumbprint, Yellow, White, Orange Enamel, Rolled Lip, 1925, 8 In. 55.00
Cobalt Blue, White & Gold Enamel, 7 1/4 In. 110.00
Cobalt Blue Cut To Clear, Tooled Lip, 7 3/4 In. 740.00
Cobalt Blue Cut To Clear, Tooled Lip, Spring-Loaded Closure, 9 5/8 In. ....*Illus* 578.00
Coin Spot, Amber, Yellow, Orange, White Enamel, 8 In. ....85.00 to 110.00
Coin Spot, Apple Green, Melon Sides, White, Orange Butterfly, 8 In. 90.00
Coin Spot, Clear, Cranberry Flashed, Melon Sides, Tooled Lip, 8 5/8 In. 95.00
Coin Spot, Cobalt Blue, Mary Gregory Type, White Enamel Cameo, 8 1/4 In. 770.00
Coin Spot, Cranberry Opalescent, Flattened Bulbous Body, 7 In. 200.00
Coin Spot, Cranberry Opalescent, Melon Sides, 7 1/8 In. 145.00
Coin Spot, Cranberry Opalescent, Melon Sides, Rolled Lip, 8 1/2 In. ....130.00 to 230.00
Coin Spot, Cranberry Opalescent, Melon Sides, Rolled Lip, Metal Stopper, 7 In. 75.00
Coin Spot, Cranberry Opalescent, Melon Sides, Smooth Base, 6 5/8 In. 135.00
Coin Spot, Cranberry Opalescent, Smooth Base, Rolled Lip, 6 5/8 In. ....*Illus* 633.00
Coin Spot, Cranberry Opalescent, White, Rolled Lip, 7 In. 495.00
Coin Spot, Light Yellow Green, White, Yellow, Orange Enamel, 8 In. 115.00
Coin Spot, Melon Sides, Opalescent Turquoise, Rolled Lip, 7 1/8 In. 155.00
Coin Spot, Melon Sides, Sapphire Blue, Original Metal Stopper, 8 1/2 In. 110.00
Coin Spot, Milk Glass Opalescent, Melon Sides, Rolled Lip, 6 7/8 In. 120.00
Coin Spot, Milk Glass, Opalescent, Melon Sides, Rolled Lip, Stopper, 7 In. 60.00
Coin Spot, Teal Blue, Melon Sides, Rolled Lip, 8 1/2 In. 120.00
Coin Spot, Teal Blue, Melon Sides, Rolled Lip, Porcelain Stopper, 8 3/8 In. 180.00
Coin Spot, Turquoise Opalescent, Melon Sides, Smooth Base, 6 3/4 In. 135.00
Coin Spot, Yellow Straw, White Enamel, Rolled Lip, 8 In. 275.00
Cologne, Bark Encased, Clear, Girl, Label Under Glass, 7 3/4 In. 770.00
Cologne, Bark Encased, Multicolor Label Under Glass, 7 3/4 In. 220.00
Copper Wheel Cut, Clear, 7 1/8 In. 55.00
Copper Wheel Cut, Floral, Tooled Lip, Sterling Silver Stopper, 7 In. 135.00
Crackle, Indented On All 4 Sides, Original Metal Stopper, 7 3/4 In. 140.00
Cranberry, Broken Ribs, Swirled Right, Sheared Lip, 6 3/4 In. 715.00
Cranberry, Diamond Pattern, White Stripes, Sheared Mouth, Square, 1920, 8 In. 305.00
Cranberry, Hobnail, Rolled Lip, Polished Pontil, 7 1/8 In. 175.00
Cranberry, Hobnail, Rolled Lip, Pontil, 7 In. 120.00
Cranberry, Ribs, Enamel, Pontil, 7 3/8 In. 715.00
Cranberry, Ribs, Flowers, Globular, 8 1/8 In. 275.00
Cranberry, Ribs, Multicolor Flowers, Rolled Lip, 7 1/4 In. 385.00
Cranberry, Ribs, White, Yellow, Blue Enamel, Sheared Lip, 7 3/4 In. 575.00
Cranberry, Rolled Lip, 8 1/2 In. 140.00
Cranberry, White Stars & Stripes, Rolled Lip, 7 1/4 In. 360.00
Cranberry, White Stripes, Rolled Lip, Metal Stopper, 7 3/4 In. 180.00
Cranberry, White, Swirled Left, Ground Pontil, Porcelain Stopper, 8 In. 225.00
Cranberry Opalescent, Daisy & Fern, Melon Sides, Rolled Lip, 7 In. ....230.00 to 305.00
Cranberry Opalescent, Daisy & Fern, Melon Sides, Rolled Lip, 8 In. 135.00
Cranberry Opalescent, Daisy & Fern, Rolled Lip, Metal Stopper, 7 1/4 In. 185.00
Cranberry Opalescent, Fern, Swirl Lines Throughout, Rolled Lip, 8 In. 240.00

Barber, Carnival-Type, Swirled Ribs, Smooth Base, Polished Lip, 7 7/8 In.
Barber, Yellow Green, Bell Shape, Ribs, Enamel Flowers, 7 7/8 In.
Barber, Cobalt Blue, Ribs, Yellow & Gold, Rolled Lip, Pontil, 7 5/8 In.
Barber, Cobalt Blue Cut To Clear, Tooled Lip, Spring-Loaded Closure, 9 5/8 In.
Barber, Amethyst, Yellow, Gold, Art Nouveau Floral, Rolled Lip, 7 3/4 In.
Barber, Turquoise, Frosted Ribs, Art Nouveau, Rolled Lip, Pontil, 8 3/4 In.
Barber, Coin Spot, Cranberry Opalescent, Smooth Base, Rolled Lip, 6 5/8 In.

Cranberry Opalescent, Hobnail, Ground Pontil, Sheared Lip, 8 1/4 In. 305.00
Cranberry Opalescent, Hobnail, Rolled Lip, 7 5/8 In. 145.00
Cranberry Opalescent, Hobnail, Rolled Lip, Metal Stopper, Pontil, 7 In. 185.00
Cranberry Opalescent, Hobnail, Rolled Lip, Polished Pontil, 7 5/8 In. 60.00
Cranberry Opalescent, Hobnail, Rolled Lip, Porcelain Stopper, Polished Pontil, 6 5/8 In.   60.00
Cranberry Opalescent, Hobnail, White, Rolled Lip, Polished Pontil, 7 In. 210.00
Cranberry Opalescent, Melon Shape, Milk Glass Stripes, Cylindrical, 7 In. 200.00
Cranberry Opalescent, Melon Sides, White Vertical Stripes, 6 7/8 In. 190.00
Cranberry Opalescent, Milk Glass, Fern, Tooled Mouth, 8 1/4 In. 360.00
Cranberry Opalescent, Milk Glass, Tooled Mouth, 8 1/2 In. 175.00
Cranberry Opalescent, Opalescent Milk Glass, Daisy, Fern, 8 In. 130.00
Cranberry Opalescent, Stripes Swirled Right, Rolled Lip, 6 7/8 In. . . . . .175.00 to 185.00
Cranberry Opalescent, White Hobnail, Metal Stopper, Ground Pontil, 8 1/2 In. 220.00
Cranberry Opalescent, White Rib Swirl, Pewter Crown Stopper, 9 3/8 In. 605.00
Cranberry Opalescent, White Spanish Lace, Rolled Lip, 8 1/8 In. 440.00
Cranberry Opalescent, White Stars & Stripes, Rolled Lip, 6 7/8 In. 495.00
Cranberry Opalescent, White Stripes, Melon Sides, Rolled Lip, 7 3/8 In. . . . . . .130.00 to 145.00
Cranberry Opalescent, White Stripes, Rolled Lip, Porcelain Stopper, 7 1/4 In. . .120.00 to 130.00
Cranberry Opalescent, White Swirl, Polished Pontil, 6 7/8 In.   305.00
Cranberry Opalescent, White Swirl, Rolled Lip, 6 7/8 In. 210.00
Cranberry Opalescent, White Swirled Stripes, Rolled Lip, 8 1/8 In. 690.00
Cranberry Opalescent, White Vertical Stripes, Rolled Lip, 7 1/4 In. 415.00
Cranberry Top, Lower-Half Splotch, Tooled Mouth, 9 In. 65.00
Cremex, Shampooing Vase, Cobalt Blue, Finger Grooves, 7 3/4 In. 110.00
Custard Milk Glass, Tooled Mouth, 9 1/2 In. 140.00
Dark Green, Mary Gregory Type, White Enamel Boy With Butterfly Net, 8 In. 275.00
Demon Brand Hair Oil, Label, Metal Screw Top, 11 In. 305.00
Eiffel Tower Shape, Tooled Lip, 7 1/2 In. 130.00
Emerald, Teal Green, White, Gold Gilt, Rolled Lip, Pontil, 8 3/8 In. 660.00
Emerald Green, Bell Shape, Pink, Red Thistle, Sheared Lip, 7 5/8 In. 525.00
Emerald Green, Bell Shape, White Enamel Flowers, Pontil, 8 1/2 In. 230.00
Emerald Green, Corset Waist, White Enamel, Gilt, Sheared Mouth, 7 In. 440.00
Emerald Green, Enamel Flowers, Tooled Mouth, Bulbous, Pontil, 6 1/4 In. 110.00
Emerald Green, Mary Gregory Type, Rolled Lip, Pontil, 7 3/4 In. 385.00

Emerald Green, Modified Corset Waist, Light Green Enamel, 7 In. 300.00
Emerald Green, Multicolor Acanthus, Flowers, 8 1/2 In. 8800.00
Emerald Green, Ribs, Bell Shape, White, Orange Floral, Sheared Lip, 8 In. 200.00
Emerald Green, Ribs, Flowers, Rolled Lip, Porcelain Stopper, Pontil, 7 3/4 In. 275.00
Emerald Green, Ribs, Orange, Blue, White, Gold Enamel, 7 In. 230.00
Emerald Green, Ribs, White Enamel, Sheared Lip, Smooth Base, 6 5/8 In. 50.00
Emerald Green, Ribs, White, Orange Enamel Flowers, 6 3/8 In. 200.00
Emerald Green, Silver Overlay Flowers, Rolled Lip, 7 7/8 In. 100.00
Emerald Green, White, Gilt, Flared Lip, 7 1/4 In. 185.00
Emerald Green, White, Gilt, Rolled Lip, 7 7/8 In. 240.00
Emerald Green, White, Orange Enamel, 8 1/8 In. 85.00
Florida Water, Milk Glass, Winter Scene, Cottage, I. Wolstencroft, Ground Lip, 9 3/8 In. 275.00
Florida Water, Murray & Lanman, New York, Paper, Neck Label, 9 1/2 In. 50.00
Fore After Shaving, Golfer, Label, 9 1/2 x 4 1/2 In. 265.00
Fred W. Suttle, Bay Rum, Label Under Glass, Milk Glass, Pewter Collar, 1860, 11 In. .. 510.00
Gold Carnival Overlay, Thumbprint, Mary Gregory Type, White Enamel Cameo, 8 In. . 230.00
Golfer's, Multicolor Enamel, Cut Shoulder, Stopper, 7 In. 1210.00
Grass Green, Corset Waist, White, Black, Gold Enamel, Sheared Lip, 7 3/4 In. 110.00
Grass Green, Ribs, Blue, White, Orange Enamel, Sheared Lip, 7 7/8 In. 165.00
Grass Green, Ribs, White Enamel, Sheared Lip, 6 3/4 In. 100.00
Grass Green, Ribs, White, Gold Enamel, Tooled Lip, 7 3/8 In. 440.00
Grass Green, Ribs, White, Yellow, Blue, Orange Enamel Flowers, Sheared Lip, 7 In. ... 100.00
Green, Hobnail, Rolled Lip, 7 1/4 In. ....65.00 to 85.00
Green, Mary Gregory Type, White, Wide Rolled Lip, 7 In. 440.00
Green, Ribs, Gold Gilt Flowers, Rolled Lip, 7 5/8 In. 990.00
Green, Ribs, Red, White, Gold, Brown Enamel, 7 7/8 In. 90.00
Green, Ruby Over Clear, Fluted Base, Rolled Lip, 7 In. 260.00
Green, Silver Berry, Leaf Overlay, Pontil, 7 3/4 In. 1540.00
Green, Swirled Agate, White & Brown, OP, 6 1/2 In. 195.00
Green, Thumbprint, Rolled Lip, 7 7/8 In. 330.00
Green, White & Orange Enamel Flowers, Tooled Mouth, Cylindrical, Pontil, 8 In. 220.00
Green, White Enamel, 8 1/4 In. 50.00
Green, White, Gilt Art Nouveau Flowers, 7 5/8 In. 635.00
Green, White, Landscape, Tooled Mouth, Metal Stopper, 8 In. 745.00
Green & White Splotches, Clear Ground, Striped Neck, Tooled Mouth, Square, 7 In. ... 385.00
Hair Tonic, Blue Milk Glass, Sailboats, Enamel, Screw Stopper, J. Gaghan, 10 1/2 In. 470.00
Hair Tonic, Label Under Glass, Milk Glass, Victorian Woman In Pink, 10 1/2 In. 990.00
Hair Tonic, Milk Glass, Painted Cranes, Metal Screw Top, A.H. Matlack, 10 1/2 In. 360.00
Hair Tonic, Milk Glass, Victorian Woman Label Under Glass, Cylindrical, 10 In. 990.00
Hair Tonic, Milk Glass, Winter Scene, Cottage, Pink Ground, Pewter Screw Cap, 9 1/2 In. 580.00
Hair Tonic, West Point Laboratories, New York, Label, Screw Lid, West Point, 1935, 8 In. 195.00
Herpicide, For The Hair & Scalp, Shaker, Label, Sprinkler Cap, Newbro's, 10 3/4 In. ... 15.00
Imperial Red, Blue & Yellow Enamel, Gilt, 8 1/2 In. 2310.00
Klondike Head Rub, Robin's Egg Blue, Tooled Lip, OP, Metal Stopper, 9 3/4 In. 220.00
Latticinio, White, Red, Pale Green Vertical Stripes, Cylindrical, Pontil, 8 1/4 In. 210.00
Lemon Yellow, Frosted, Flowers, Tooled Lip, 7 In. 85.00
Lime Green Opalescent, White Stripe, Smooth Base, Rolled Lip, 7 In. 440.00
Medium Green, White, Gilt Art Nouveau Flowers, Transfer Cherub, 7 5/8 In. 415.00
Milk Glass, 2 Cranes Among Reeds, Multicolor, W.T. & Co., 9 1/2 In. 360.00
Milk Glass, 2 Swans On A Pond, Multicolor, Pewter Screw Cap Stopper, 1925, 9 In. 200.00
Milk Glass, 4 Cranberry Stripes, Melon Sides, Tooled Mouth, 8 In. 780.00
Milk Glass, Allover Brown Splatter, Tooled Mouth, 6 1/2 In. 605.00
Milk Glass, Bell Shape, Cherubs, Sheared Lip, Porcelain Stopper, Pontil, 7 5/8 In. 360.00
Milk Glass, Black Enamel Bands, Sheared Lip, Pewter Stopper, Marked, 8 In. 145.00
Milk Glass, Black, Brown Design, Bird, On A Roof, Tan Ground, W.T. & Co., 9 1/2 In. .. 145.00
Milk Glass, Blue Flowers, Tooled Mouth, 9 In. 240.00
Milk Glass, Blue, Pink, Brown, Gold Enamel, 7 3/4 In. 305.00
Milk Glass, Bohemian Design, Multicolor, Polished Lip, 1925, 8 1/2 In. 110.00
Milk Glass, Canary Yellow, Hobnail, Rolled Lip, Pontil, 7 1/4 In. 185.00
Milk Glass, Canary Yellow, Opalescent Daisy & Fern, Melon Shape, 7 1/4 In. 145.00
Milk Glass, Cottage In A Forest, Multicolor, Pewter Screw Cap, 1925, 9 In. 690.00
Milk Glass, Cottage, Enamel, Multicolor, Jas. Wolfinger Hair Tonic, 1920, 9 In. 470.00
Milk Glass, Dark Powder Blue, Tooled Lip, 10 1/4 In. 105.00

Milk Glass, Enamel Bird, Multicolor, Pewter Screw Cap, 9 In. 360.00
Milk Glass, Enamel Flowers, Multicolor, Rolled Lip, 1925, 8 7/8 In. 155.00
Milk Glass, Enamel Flowers, Multicolor, Sheared Lip, 8 7/8 In. 390.00
Milk Glass, Flowers, Bird, Multicolor, Pewter Screw Stopper, 1925, 9 In. 550.00
Milk Glass, Flowers, Lake Shore Scene, Multicolor, Pewter Screw Cap, 9 In. 215.00
Milk Glass, Flowers, Multicolor, 8 In. 255.00
Milk Glass, Flowers, Multicolor, Ground Lip, Pewter Screw Cap, 1925, 9 1/2 In. 230.00
Milk Glass, Honey Yellow Overlay, Enamel Flowers, M. Loveall, Stopper, 7 3/4 In. 495.00
Milk Glass, Multicolor Floral, Gray Blue Ground, W.T. & Co., 9 In. 550.00
Milk Glass, Opalescent Powder Blue, 9 3/8 In. 130.00
Milk Glass, Opalescent, Green, Black Clover, Original Metal Stopper, 1925, 9 1/8 In. ... 120.00
Milk Glass, Opalescent, Hobnail, 7 3/4 In. 100.00
Milk Glass, Opalescent, Reliable Trademark Brand Twin Action Shampoo, ABM, 6 7/8 In. 35.00
Milk Glass, Pink Satin Glass, Smooth Base, Flared Lip, 8 1/2 In. 145.00
Milk Glass, Robin's Egg Blue, Thumbprint, Tooled Mouth, 8 1/2 In. 165.00
Milk Glass, Robin's Egg Blue, Tooled Mouth, Ground Pontil, 8 1/4 In. 165.00
Milk Glass, Robin's Egg Blue, Tooled Mouth, Pontil, Conical, 6 3/4 In. 110.00
Milk Glass, Satin Glass, Yellow, Green, Red, White Enamel Flowers, Rolled Lip, 7 3/8 In. 80.00
Milk Glass, Sparrow, Multicolor, Rolled Lip, 1925, 8 3/4 In. 230.00
Milk Glass, Yellow, Melon Sides, Overlay Heart, Rolled Lip, 20th Century, 8 In. 185.00
Morning After Rub, Reverse Glass Label, T. Noonan & Co., Boston, Mass., 2 Piece, 7 In. 635.00
Multicolor Butterfly, Enamel, Flared Lip, Ground Pontil, 6 In. 105.00
Multicolor Roses, Thumbprint, Rolled Lip, 8 3/8 In. 550.00
Opalescent, Bell Shape, Allover Enamel, Cherubs, OP, Pt. 370.00
Opalescent, Hobnail, Tooled Lip, Polished Pontil, 6 1/2 In. 50.00
Opalescent, Melon Sides, Fern Pattern, Rolled Lip, Polished Pontil, 6 3/4 In. 100.00
Opalescent, Spanish Lace, Rolled Lip, 7 1/8 In. 100.00
Opalescent, Stars & Stripes, Tooled Mouth, 7 1/8 In. 180.00
Opalescent, White Spanish Lace, Rolled Lip, 7 In. 185.00
Opalescent, White Spanish Lace, Rolled Lip, Polished Pontil, 8 1/4 In. 255.00
Opalescent, White Stars & Stripes, Rolled Lip, Pontil, 7 In. 230.00
Opalescent, White Stripes, Swirled Right, Rolled Lip, Porcelain Stopper, 7 1/2 In. 110.00
Opalescent, White Swirl, Rolled Lip, Pontil, 7 In. 145.00
Orange, Pink, Light Blue Highlights, 7 7/8 In. 205.00
Pink Amethyst, Red, White Enamel, 8 In. 55.00
Pink Amethyst, Ribs, Lavender, White, Orange, Blue Enamel, 7 In. 305.00
Pink Amethyst, Ribs, White Enamel, Rolled Lip, Pontil Base, 7 In. 95.00
Pink Cranberry Opalescent, Splotch, Fountain Shape, Flared Lip, 8 1/4 In. 855.00
Pink Swirl, White Alternating, Rolled Lip, 5 3/4 In. 360.00
Pompeian Hair Massage Does Remove Dandruff, Label Under Glass, Stopper, 8 In. 230.00
Pressed Glass, Fluted, Peppermint, Rolled Lip, Metal Stopper, 7 In. 55.00
Puce, Overall White Enamel, Polished Lip, 7 7/8 In. 415.00
Purple, Gold, Loetz Glass, Ground & Polished Lip, 8 1/8 In. 415.00
Red, Grape & Vine, Applied Mouth, Neck Ring, Squat, 1925, 6 3/8 In. 125.00
Red, Splotch, White, Polished Lip, Pontil, 7 3/4 In. 360.00
Red, Stag, Running, Ground Lip, 8 1/2 In. 800.00
Red, White Alternating Bands, Ground Lip, Porcelain Stopper, 8 1/2 In. 245.00
Red, White, Gilt Enamel, Rolled Lip, Pontil, 8 3/8 In. 470.00
Red, White, Yellow, Allover Splotch, Tooled Lip, 9 1/4 In. 605.00
Red & Blue Enamel, Bell Shape, 9 In. 335.00
Red Cut To Clear, Bohemian Style Deer, 8 1/2 In. ....495.00 to 550.00
Red Cut To Clear, Mary Gregory Type, Boy & Butterfly, Tooled Lip, Pontil, 8 1/4 In. ... 470.00
Red Flashed, Cut To Clear, Bohemian Style Design, Ground Lip, 7 3/4 In. 90.00
Red Flashed, Cut To Clear, Bohemian Style Design, Porcelain Stopper, 8 1/2 In. 275.00
Ribs, Barrel, White, Orange, Gold Enamel Flowers, 7 5/8 In. 415.00
Ris Tol Antiseptic Toilet Lotion, Reverse Painted Glass, Metal Stopper, 7 In. 150.00
Robin's Egg Blue, Enamel Flowers, Long Neck, Bulbous, Pontil, 7 5/8 In. 100.00
Robin's Egg Blue Opalescent, Daisy & Fern, Melon Sides, 7 1/8 In. 230.00
Ruby Red, Web, Polished Lip, 7 3/4 In. 690.00
Ruby Red Cut To Clear, Bohemian Style Copper Wheel Cut, 8 In. 150.00
Ruby Red Cut To Clear, Frosted Bohemian Style Design, 7 7/8 In. 360.00
Sapphire Blue, Butterfly, Melon Sides, Rolled Lip, Metal Stopper, Pontil, 8 1/4 In. 95.00
Sapphire Blue, Diamond, Multicolor Enamel Flowers, 8 5/8 In. 415.00

Sapphire Blue, Iridescent Mother-Of-Pearl, Vine, Polished Lip, 7 3/4 In. 850.00
Sapphire Blue, Mary Gregory Type, White Enamel, Bulbous, 8 In. 165.00
Sapphire Blue, Ribs, White & Orange Enamel, Sheared Lip, Porcelain Stopper, 6 5/8 In. 120.00
Sapphire Blue, White Enamel Flowers, Gilt, Pontil, 7 1/2 In. 260.00
SEN, Reverse Painted Label, Metal Screw Top, 10 In. 2090.00
Shampoo, Milk Glass, Flowers, Rolled Lip, E.W. Inc., 9 1/8 In. 330.00
Silver, Blue Tiffany Design, Multicolor, Smooth Base, 7 1/2 In. 495.00
Silver Overlay, Tooled Lip, Rabbit Stopper, Polished Pontil, 6 In. 440.00
Silver Plate, Raised Acanthus Leaf, Stopper, Adelphi Silver Plate Co., 7 In. 175.00
Smoky Olive, Hobnail, Rolled Lip, Pontil, 6 7/8 In. 100.00
Smoky Pink, Hobnail, Rolled Lip, 6 7/8 In. 95.00
Swirled Rib, Metallic Design, 1925, 8 In. 305.00
T. Noonan & Co., Barber's Supplies, Boston, Mass., Tooled Mouth, 1885-1915, 8 3/8 In. 70.00
Toilet Water, 3-Piece Mold, Cobalt Blue, Pontil, Flared Lip, 1820-1830, 5 5/8 In. 145.00
Toilet Water, 3-Piece Mold, Deep Sapphire Blue, Tooled Mouth, 1830-1850, 6 3/4 In. .. 200.00
Toilet Water, 3-Piece Mold, Light Sapphire Blue, Flared Lip, Pontil, 1830, 5 1/4 In. 130.00
Toilet Water, 3-Piece Mold, Light Violet Blue, Tooled Mouth, Incorrect Stopper, 5 In. .. 260.00
Toilet Water, 3-Piece Mold, Tam-O'-Shanter Stopper, 6 3/4 In. 200.00
Toilet Water, 3-Piece Mold, Violet Cobalt Blue, Pontil, 1830, 5 1/4 In. 715.00
Toilet Water, Amethyst, White Enamel, Windmill, Rolled Lip, Pontil, 7 3/4 In. 265.00
Toilet Water, Deep Cobalt Blue, 12-Sided, Flared Lip, 1850-1860, 6 In. 385.00
Toilet Water, Milk Glass, Multicolor Flowers, Rolled Lip, 7 3/4 In. 100.00
Toilet Water, Milk Glass, Red, Green, Black Flowers, Marked, 9 In. 200.00
Toilet Water, Milk Glass, Tulip, Rolled Lip, Pontil, 8 5/8 In. 230.00
Toilet Water, Red, Rolled Lip, Polished Pontil, 7 In. 175.00
Toilet Water, Sapphire Blue, Stopper, 5 1/2 In. 302.00
Topaz, Flowers, Smooth Base, ABM Lip, 8 In. 305.00
Topaz, Ribs, Enamel, Corset Waist, Pontil, 7 7/8 In. 525.00
Topaz, Ribs, Frosted, Multicolor Roses, Sheared Lip, 8 In. 800.00
Topaz, Ribs, Multicolor Roses, Enamel, Sheared Lip, 8 1/8 In. 580.00
Topaz, White Enamel Flowers, Polished Lip, 8 1/8 In. 240.00
Turquoise, Bell Shape, Mary Gregory Type, White Enamel, 7 1/2 In. 575.00
Turquoise, Corset Waist, Ribs, White, Gold Enamel, 7 5/8 In. 85.00
Turquoise, Cut & Polished Flutes On Neck, Tooled Lip, 6 1/2 In. 25.00
Turquoise, Frosted Ribs, Art Nouveau, Rolled Lip, Pontil, 8 3/4 In. ....*Illus* 550.00
Turquoise, Frosted, Ribs, Multicolor Art Nouveau, 8 3/8 In. 415.00
Turquoise, Hobnail, Rolled Lip, Polished Pontil, 7 In. ....90.00 to 105.00
Turquoise, Hobnail, Rolled Lip, Pontil, 7 1/4 In. 145.00
Turquoise, Opalescent Lime Green, White Stripe, 7 In. 440.00
Turquoise, Red, White, Yellow Enamel Flowers, Rolled Lip, 7 In. 110.00
Turquoise, Ribs, Bell Shape, Multicolor Panel, Enamel, Sheared Lip, 1925, 8 In. 65.00
Turquoise, Ribs, Enamel Flowers, Rolled Lip, Pontil, 7 5/8 In. 90.00
Turquoise, Ribs, Frosted, Multicolor Flowers, Rolled Lip, 1925, 8 3/4 In. 550.00
Turquoise, Ribs, Gilt Flowers, 7 5/8 In. 330.00
Turquoise, Ribs, Mary Gregory Type, White Enamel, Rolled Lip, 7 3/4 In. 330.00
Turquoise, Ribs, Red, White Enamel, Sheared Lip, 7 1/2 In. 120.00
Turquoise, Ribs, Red, White, Gilt, Corset Waist, 7 5/8 In. 130.00
Turquoise, Ribs, Red, White, Yellow Enamel, Sheared Lip, 8 In. 145.00
Turquoise, Ribs, Red, Yellow, White Enamel Flowers, 7 3/4 In. 175.00
Turquoise, Ribs, White, Gold Enamel, Sheared Lip, 7 3/4 In. 145.00
Turquoise, Ribs, White, Orange Enamel, Rolled Lip, 8 3/8 In. 135.00
Turquoise, Ribs, White, Red Enamel, Sheared Lip, 7 3/4 In. 105.00
Turquoise, Ribs, White, Red, Gold Enamel, 1925, 8 In. 190.00
Turquoise, Ribs, Yellow, White, Red Enamel Flowers, 6 3/4 In. 100.00
Turquoise, Spanish Lace, Rolled Lip, 8 1/8 In. 525.00
Turquoise, Thumbprint, Yellow, White, Orange Enamel, Rolled Lip, 8 In. 210.00
Turquoise, White, Gold Gilt, Polished Lip, Stopper, 12 1/4 In. 110.00
Turquoise, Yellow, White Flowers, Flared Lip, 8 1/4 In. 155.00
Turquoise Opalescent, Blue, Vertical White Stripe, Sheared Lip, 6 In. 165.00
Turquoise Opalescent, Daisy & Fern, Rolled Lip, 8 1/2 In. 165.00
Turquoise Opalescent, Hobnail, Blue, White, Rolled Lip, 7 1/4 In. 205.00
Turquoise Opalescent, Hobnail, Rolled Lip, Metal Stopper, Polished Pontil, 6 7/8 In. .. 165.00
Turquoise Opalescent, Hobnail, Rolled Lip, Polished Pontil, 7 In. 100.00

Turquoise Opalescent, Hobnail, Rolled Lip, Pontil, 8 1/8 In. 55.00
Turquoise Opalescent, Stars & Stripes, Rolled Lip, 7 1/4 In. ....440.00 to 550.00
Turquoise Opalescent, Stars & Stripes, Rolled Lip, Porcelain Stopper, 7 In. 155.00
Turquoise Opalescent, Swirl, Rolled Lip, 7 In. ....265.00 to 525.00
Turquoise Opalescent, Thumbprint, White Splotches, 8 In. 550.00
Turquoise Opalescent, White Fern, Smooth Base, 8 1/2 In. 210.00
Turquoise Opalescent, White Spanish Lace, Rolled Lip, 7 In. 275.00
Turquoise Opalescent, White Spanish Lace, Rolled Lip, Pontil, 8 In. 415.00
Turquoise Opalescent, White Stars & Stripes, Smooth Base, 7 3/8 In. 660.00
Turquoise Opalescent, White Swirl, Rolled Lip, Pontil, 6 7/8 In. 415.00
Turquoise Opalescent, White Vertical Stripe, Melon Sides, 7 1/4 In. 110.00
Vegederma, Amethyst, White Enamel, Tooled Mouth, Bulbous, 8 In. 140.00
Vegederma, Amethyst, Woman, Flowing Hair, Faded Wording, Pontil, 1870-1880 ...... 290.00
Vegederma, Apple Green, Mary Gregory Type, Porcelain Stopper, 7 7/8 In. .....415.00 to 690.00
Venetian, Blue & White Stripes, Swirled Right, Pontil, Porcelain Stopper, 9 1/2 In. 275.00
Venetian, White & Cobalt Stripes, Ground Lip, Porcelain Stopper, Pontil, 8 5/8 In. 185.00
White Porcelain, Multicolor Flowers, Gold Trim, 7 1/8 In. 1045.00
White Shaded To Cranberry Opalescent, Hobnail, Rolled Lip, Pontil, 7 In. 100.00
Witch Hazel, Amber, Label Under Glass, Pewter Stopper, 7 In. 187.00
Witch Hazel, Milk Glass, Barber Supply Co., Octagonal, 1895-1905 .... 45.00
Witch Hazel, Milk Glass, Enamel Flowers, Rolled Lip, Stopper 175.00
Witch Hazel, Milk Glass, Enamel Flowers, Sheared Lip, OP, Stopper 330.00
Witch Hazel, Milk Glass, Flowers, Rolled Lip, 8 7/8 In. 140.00
Witch Hazel, Milk Glass, Multicolor Flowers, Tooled Lip, 9 In. 90.00
Witch Hazel, Milk Glass, Opalescent, Multicolor Flowers, Stopper, 1925, 9 1/2 In. 55.00
Witch Hazel, Milk Glass, Red & Green Clover, Rolled Lip, 9 1/4 In. 155.00
Witch Hazel, Roses, Amber, Multicolor Label Under Glass, 7 1/8 In. 330.00
Yellow, Bell Shape, Ribs, Flowers, Enamel, Pink, White, 7 5/8 In. 120.00
Yellow, Bell Shape, Ribs, White, Green, Orange Flowers, Sheared Lip, 7 In. 330.00
Yellow, Green, Vertical Rib, White, Red Enamel, 7 3/4 In. 70.00
Yellow, Hobnail, Rolled Lip, 7 1/8 In. 120.00
Yellow, Thumbprint, Rolled Lip, 8 1/8 In. 140.00
Yellow Amber, Bell Shape, Ribs, Enamel Flowers, Sheared Lip, Pontil, 7 1/2 In. 75.00
Yellow Amber, Hobnail, Rolled Lip, 7 1/2 In. ....80.00 to 175.00
Yellow Amber, Ribs, White, Yellow, Gilt Flowers, Sheared Lip, Porcelain Stopper, 7 In. . 305.00
Yellow Amber, Thumbprint, Yellow, Orange, White Enamel, 8 1/4 In. 175.00
Yellow Green, Bell Shape, Ribs, Enamel Flowers, 7 7/8 In. ....*Illus* 523.00
Yellow Green, Bell Shape, Ribs, White, Green, Orange, Sheared Lip, 7 3/4 In. 145.00
Yellow Green, Floral & Flag, Wide Mouth, Bulbous, 6 1/2 In. 385.00
Yellow Green, Flowers, Ground Mouth, Globular, Pontil, 8 In. 220.00
Yellow Green, Hobnail, Rolled Lip, Porcelain Stopper, 7 5/8 In. 100.00
Yellow Green, Mallet Shape, White, Orange Enamel, Rolled Lip, 8 In. 180.00
Yellow Green, Mary Gregory Type, Girl Playing Tennis, Inverted Conical, Pontil, 8 In. ... 200.00
Yellow Green, Mary Gregory Type, Rolled Lip, Porcelain Stopper, Pontil, 8 In. ..140.00 to 255.00
Yellow Green, Ribs, Bell Shape, Multicolor Enamel Flowers, Sheared Lip, 8 In. 525.00
Yellow Green, Ribs, Corset Waist, Red, Yellow, White Flowers, 8 In. 100.00
Yellow Green, Ribs, Enamel Flowers, Rolled Lip, Pontil, 7 7/8 In. ....65.00 to 75.00
Yellow Green, Ribs, Fleur-De-Lis & Flowers, Sheared Lip, Pontil, 7 3/4 In. 85.00
Yellow Green, Ribs, Flowers, Sheared Lip, Pewter Stopper, 6 5/8 In. 85.00
Yellow Green, Ribs, Mary Gregory Type, White Enamel Girl Playing Tennis, 8 1/8 In. .. 275.00
Yellow Green, Ribs, Multicolor Enamel Flowers, 6 1/8 In. 190.00
Yellow Green, Ribs, Multicolor Enamel Flowers, Polished Pontil, 1925, 8 In. 220.00
Yellow Green, Ribs, Red, White Enamel Flowers, 6 3/4 In. 135.00
Yellow Green, Ribs, Red, White Enamel, Corset Waist, 7 5/8 In. 90.00
Yellow Green, Ribs, Red, White Enamel, Sheared Lip, Pontil, 7 3/4 In. ....90.00 to 120.00
Yellow Green, Ribs, Red, White, Gold Enamel, Sheared Lip, 8 In. 60.00
Yellow Green, Ribs, Red, Yellow, White Enamel Flowers, 7 5/8 In. 105.00
Yellow Green, Ribs, White Enamel Boy Standing With Outstretched Arm, Stopper, 9 In. . 440.00
Yellow Green, Ribs, White Enamel, Gilt, Sheared Lip, 6 7/8 In. 100.00
Yellow Green, Ribs, White Enamel, Rolled Lip, 8 1/8 In. 440.00
Yellow Green, Ribs, White Enamel, Sheared Lip, Pontil, 7 In. 95.00
Yellow Green, Ribs, White, Blue Enamel, Sheared Lip, 7 3/8 In. 110.00
Yellow Green, Ribs, White, Gold Gilt Flowers, Sheared Lip, 1925, 7 5/8 In. 220.00

Yellow Green, Ribs, White, Orange Enamel Flowers, Stopper, Pontil, 1925, 8 In. 230.00
Yellow Green, Ribs, White, Yellow & Orange Flowers, Rolled Lip, Pontil, 7 7/8 In. 95.00
Yellow Green, Ribs, White, Yellow Enamel Daisy, 6 1/8 In. 175.00
Yellow Green, Ribs, White, Yellow, Green Flowers, 7 5/8 In. 120.00
Yellow Green, Ribs, Yellow, Orange, White Enamel Daisy, 1925, 6 In. 55.00
Yellow Green, Thumbprint, Yellow, Orange, White Enamel, 8 In. 130.00
Yellow Olive, Ribs Green, White, Orange, Gold Enamel Flowers, Rolled Lip, 7 In. 210.00
Yellow Olive, Ribs, Red, Yellow, White Enamel Flowers, Rolled Lip, 7 7/8 In. 120.00
Yellow Olive, Ribs, White Enamel, Marked, Cybeline, 7 5/8 In. 825.00
Yellow Olive, Ribs, White, Red Enamel, Sheared Lip, 7 7/8 In. 65.00
BATTERY JAR, see Oil

--------------------------------- **BEAM** ---------------------------------

The history of the Jim Beam company is confusing because the progeny of the founder, Jacob Beam, favored the names David and James. Jacob Beam had been a whiskey distiller in Virginia and Maryland before moving to Kentucky in 1788. He was selling Kentucky Straight Bourbon in bottles labeled *Beam* by 1795. His son David continued to market Beam bourbon. His grandson, David M. Beam, was the next to inherit the business. One of David M.'s brands was Old Tub, started in 1882 at Beam's Clear Springs Distillery No. 230. The company was called David M. Beam. The next Beam family member in the business was Col. James B. Beam, son of David M., who started working at the distillery in 1880 at the age of 16. By 1914 he owned the Early Times Distillery No. 7 in Louisville, Kentucky. J.B. Beam and B.H. Hurt were partners in the distillery from 1892 to 1899. In 1915, when the colonel died, the distillery was acquired by S.L. Guthrie and some partners. Then T. Jeremiah Beam, son of James B. Beam, inherited the James Beam Company, and with his cousin, Carl Beam, continued to make the famous bourbon. Booker Noe, Baker Beam, and David Beam, sixth-generation descendants of Jacob Beam, continued in the business. Today, Jim Beam Brands is a wholly-owned subsidiary of Fortune Brands.

Beam bottles favored by today's collectors were made as containers for Kentucky Straight Bourbon. In 1953, the company began selling some Christmas season whiskey in special decanters shaped like cocktail shakers instead of the usual whiskey bottles. The decanters were so popular that by 1955 the company was making Regal China bottles in special shapes. Executive series bottles started in 1955 and political figures in 1956. Customer specialties were first made in 1956, decanters (called *trophy series* by collectors) in 1957, and the state series in 1958. Other bottles are classed by collectors as Regal China or Glass Specialty bottles. A small number of special bottles were made by The Royal Doulton Company in England from 1983 to 1985. The rarest Beam bottle is the First National Bank of Chicago bottle; 117 were issued in 1964. The Salute to Spiro Agnew bottle made in 1970 was limited to 196. Six men making counterfeits of the very rare Beam bottles were arrested in 1970. Jim Beam stopped making decanters for the commercial trade in 1992.

The Foss Company made a limited number of decanters exclusively for the International Association of Jim Beam Bottle and Specialties Club (IJBBSC). Cinnamon Teal was issued in 1994 and Harlequin Duck in 1995 with the Ducks Unlimited label.

The Jim Beam company has also made many other advertising items or *go-withs* such as ashtrays and openers. The International Association of Jim Beam Bottle & Specialties Clubs (2015 Burlington Avenue, Kewanee, IL 61433) has regional and sectional meetings. They sell a book, *Jim Beam Bottles, A Pictorial Guide,* and a price list is also available.

Bottles are listed here alphabetically by name or as Convention, Executive, Political, or other general headings. This is because beginning collectors find it difficult to locate bottles by type. Miniature bottles are listed here also. Go-withs are in the special section at the end of the book.

BEAM, 101st Airborne Division, Armed Forces, 1977 .... 10.00
A-C Spark Plug, 1977 ....*Illus* 36.00
A.H. Steve Stephenson, Past Presidents, 1982 .... 5000.00
ABC Florida, 1973 ....10.00 to 12.00
AHEPA, 1972 ....6.00 to 7.00
Aida, Opera, 1978 ....75.00 to 85.00

Beam, A-C Spark
Plug, 1977

Beam, Bartender's
Guild, Crystal, 1973

Beam, Boy's Town,
Italy, 1973

Alaska Purchase, Centennial, 1966 .... 5.00
Alaska Star, State, 1958 ....35.00 to 45.00
Ambulance, Emergency, White, 1985 .... 40.00
American Brands, 1989 .... 275.00
American Cowboy, 1981 ....15.00 to 25.00
AMVETS, 25th Anniversary Of American Wars, 1970, 11 3/4 In. 5.00
Angelo's Delivery Truck, 1984 .... 85.00
Antioch, 1967 .... 5.00
Antique Trader, 1968 ....5.00 to 10.00
Arizona, State, 1968 ....5.00 to 6.00
Armadillo, 1981 ....15.00 to 18.00
Armanetti, Award Winner, 1969 ....7.00 to 9.00
Armanetti, Bacchus, 1970 .... 10.00
Armanetti, Fun Shopper, 1971 .... 9.00
Armanetti, Vase, 1968 .... 9.00
Army Jeep, Regal China, 1987 ....35.00 to 45.00
Barney's Slot Machine, 1978 ....25.00 to 30.00
Barry Berish, Presidential, Bowl On Pedestal Decanter, 1986 .... 65.00
Barry Berish, Presidential, Carolers, 1988 .... 65.00
Barry Berish, Presidential, Musical Bell, 1984 .... 90.00
Barry Berish, Presidential, Twin Doves, 1987 .... 70.00
Barry Berish, Presidential, Urn On Base Decanter, 1984 .... 97.00
Barry Berish, Presidential, Urn On Pedestal Decanter, 1985 .... 75.00
Bartender's Guild, Crystal, 1973 ....*Illus* 9.00
Baseball, 1969 ....25.00 to 35.00
Bass Boat, 1988 ....32.00 to 37.00
Beam Pot, 1980 .... 12.00
Beatty Burro, Glass, 1970 .... 18.00
Beaver Valley Club, 1977 .... 15.00
Bell Ringer, A Fore Ye Go, 1970 .... 7.00
Bell Ringer, Plaid Apron, 1970 ....7.00 to 8.00
Bell Scotch, Miniature, 1969 .... 17.00
Bell Scotch, Qt., 1969 .... 23.00
Big Apple, New York, Regal, 1979 ....10.00 to 20.00
Bing Crosby, 29th National Pro-AM, 1970, 12 In. ....5.00 to 10.00
Bing Crosby, 30th, 1971, 13 In. ....5.00 to 8.00
Bing Crosby, 31st, 1972, 11 In. ....20.00 to 22.00
Bing Crosby, 32nd, 1973, 11 In. ....25.00 to 35.00
Bing Crosby, 33rd, 1974, 12 In. ....25.00 to 35.00
Bing Crosby, 34th, 1975, 13 In. 65.00
Bing Crosby, 35th, 1976, 12 In. ....25.00 to 40.00
Bing Crosby, 36th, 1977, 11 1/2 In. 35.00
Binion's Horseshoe Casino, Las Vegas, 1970 .... 10.00
Blue Daisy, 1967 .... 5.00
Blue Jay, 1969 .... 10.00
Blue Slot Machine, 1967 .... 10.00
Bluegill, 1974, 9 3/4 In. 20.00
Bob Hope Desert Classic, 14th, 1973 ....10.00 to 14.00

Bob Hope Desert Classic, 15th, 1974 . . . . .14.00 to 19.00
Bohemian Girl, 1974 . . . . .15.00 to 19.00
Bonded Gold, 1975 . . . .   5.00
Bonded Mystic, 1979 . . . . .6.00 to 8.00
Bonded Silver, Regal, 1975 . . . .   5.00
Boothill, 1972 . . . .   8.00
Boris Godunov, Opera, 1982 . . . . .200.00 to 300.00
Boy's Town, Italy, 1973 . . . .*Illus*   10.00
BPAA, Bowling Proprietors, 1974 . . . .   5.00
BPO Does, 1971 . . . .   6.00
Broadmoor Hotel, 1968 . . . .   5.00
Buccaneer, Multicolor, 1982 . . . .   50.00
Buccaneer, Solid Gold, 1982 . . . .   50.00
Buffalo Bill, 1971 . . . . .15.00 to 20.00
Bull Dog, Armed Forces, 1979 . . . .   25.00
Cable Car, 1968 . . . .   5.00
Cable Car, 1983 . . . . .48.00 to 50.00
Cal Neva, 1969 . . . .   9.00
California Derby, With Glasses, 1971 . . . .   35.00
California Mission, 1970 . . . .*Illus*   15.00
Camellia City Club, 1979 . . . . .18.00 to 20.00
Cameo, Blue, Glass, 1965 . . . . .3.00 to 5.00
Cannon With Chain, Glass, 1970 . . . .   3.00
Canteen, 1979 . . . . .15.00 to 18.00
Captain & Mate, 1980 . . . .   10.00
Cardinal, Female, 1973 . . . .   10.00
Cardinal, Male, 1968 . . . .*Illus*   25.00
Carmen, Opera, 1978 . . . .   70.00
Carolers, Holiday, 1988 . . . .   55.00
Cat, Burmese, 1967 . . . .   10.00
Cat, Katz, Black, 1968 . . . . .12.00 to 15.00
Cat, Katz, Yellow, 1967 . . . . .15.00 to 20.00
Cat, Siamese, 1967 . . . . .25.00 to 26.00
Cat, Tabby, 1967 . . . .   10.00
Catfish, 1981 . . . . .35.00 to 47.00
Cathedral, Radio, 1979 . . . .   10.00
Cedars Of Lebanon, 1971 . . . .   6.00
Charisma, Decanter, 1970 . . . . .10.00 to 11.00
Charlie McCarthy, 1976 . . . . .35.00 to 45.00
Chateaux, Martini, Glass, 1953 . . . . .20.00 to 28.00
Chateaux Classic Cherry, 1976 . . . .   2.00
Cherry Hills Country Club, 1973 . . . .   10.00
Chevrolet, Bel Air, 1957 Model, Black, 1988 . . . .   90.00
Chevrolet, Bel Air, 1957 Model, Dark Blue, 1987 . . . .   75.00
Chevrolet, Bel Air, 1957 Model, Gold, 1988 . . . . .100.00 to 125.00
Chevrolet, Bel Air, 1957 Model, Red, 1987 . . . . .75.00 to 90.00

Beam, California   Beam, Cardinal,
Mission, 1970   Male, 1968

Chevrolet, Bel Air, 1957 Model, Turquoise, 1987 . . . . .65.00 to 70.00
Chevrolet, Bel Air, 1957 Model, Turquoise, 1992 . . . . 55.00
Chevrolet, Bel Air, 1957 Model, White, 1992 . . . . 500.00
Chevrolet, Camaro, 1969 Model, Blue, 1989 . . . . 65.00
Chevrolet, Camaro, 1969 Model, Green, 1989 . . . . .125.00 to 165.00
Chevrolet, Camaro, 1969 Model, Pace Car, 1989 . . . . .70.00 to 90.00
Chevrolet, Camaro, 1969 Model, Silver, 1989 . . . . .95.00 to 110.00
Chevrolet, Convertible, 1957 Model, Black 75.00
Chevrolet, Convertible, 1957 Model, Cream . . . . .95.00 to 100.00
Chevrolet, Convertible, 1957 Model, Red . . . . .79.00 to 95.00
Chevrolet, Corvette Stingray, 1963 Model, Black, 1987 . . . . 90.00
Chevrolet, Corvette, 1953 Model, White, 1989 . . . . .150.00 to 160.00
Chevrolet, Corvette, 1954 Model, Blue, 1989 . . . . .85.00 to 120.00
Chevrolet, Corvette, 1955 Model, Black, 1990 . . . . .120.00 to 125.00
Chevrolet, Corvette, 1955 Model, Copper, 1989 . . . . .80.00 to 95.00
Chevrolet, Corvette, 1955 Model, Red, 1990 . . . . 125.00
Chevrolet, Corvette, 1957 Model, Black, 1990 . . . . 75.00
Chevrolet, Corvette, 1957 Model, Blue, 1990 . . . . 75.00
Chevrolet, Corvette, 1957 Model, Blue, 1991 . . . . 500.00
Chevrolet, Corvette, 1957 Model, Copper, 1991 . . . . 125.00
Chevrolet, Corvette, 1957 Model, Green, 1991 . . . . 180.00
Chevrolet, Corvette, 1957 Model, Red, 1991 . . . . 195.00
Chevrolet, Corvette, 1957 Model, White, 1990 . . . . .125.00 to 150.00
Chevrolet, Corvette, 1963 Model, Blue, 1987 . . . . 100.00
Chevrolet, Corvette, 1963 Model, Red, 1988 . . . . 65.00
Chevrolet, Corvette, 1963 Model, Silver, 1988 . . . . 65.00
Chevrolet, Corvette, 1978 Model, Black, 1984 . . . . .110.00 to 150.00
Chevrolet, Corvette, 1978 Model, Pace Car, 1987 . . . . 195.00
Chevrolet, Corvette, 1978 Model, Red, 1988 . . . . 55.00
Chevrolet, Corvette, 1978 Model, White, 1985 . . . . 70.00
Chevrolet, Corvette, 1978 Model, Yellow, 1985 . . . . 60.00
Chevrolet, Corvette, 1984 Model, Bronze, 1989 . . . . .95.00 to 110.00
Chevrolet, Corvette, 1984 Model, Gold, 1989 . . . . 95.00
Chevrolet, Corvette, 1984 Model, Red, 1988 . . . . .80.00 to 90.00
Chevrolet, Corvette, 1985 Model, White 55.00
Chevrolet, Corvette, 1985 Model, Yellow 45.00
Chevrolet, Corvette, 1986 Model, Bronze 89.00
Chevrolet, Corvette, 1986 Model, Pace Car, Yellow 150.00
Chevrolet, Corvette, 1986 Model, Red . . . . .89.00 to 95.00
Chevrolet, Hot Rod, 1957 Model, Yellow, 1988 . . . . .95.00 to 100.00
Cheyenne, 1967 . . . . .5.00 to 7.00
Chicago Art Museum, 1972 . . . . .10.00 to 12.00
Chicago Club Loving Cup, 1978 . . . . .14.00 to 15.00
Chicago Cub, 1985 . . . . 35.00
Chicago Fire, 1971 . . . . .15.00 to 20.00
Chicago Show, 1977 . . . . 10.00
Chocolomi, 1976 . . . . 2.00
Christmas Tree, 1986 . . . . .100.00 to 135.00
Circus Wagon, 1979 . . . . .23.00 to 25.00
Civil War, North, 1961 . . . . 20.00
Civil War, South, 1961 . . . . 30.00
Cleopatra, Rust, Glass, 1962 . . . . .3.00 to 5.00
Cleopatra, Yellow, Glass, 1962 . . . . .10.00 to 15.00
Clint Eastwood, Tennis, 1973 . . . . 12.00
Clock, Antique, 1985 . . . . .35.00 to 40.00
Coach Devaney, Nebraska, 1972 . . . . 10.00
Cocktail Shaker, Glass, 1953 . . . . 6.00
Coffee Grinder, Antique, 1979 . . . . .12.00 to 14.00
Coffee Warmer, Pyrex, Black, 1954 . . . . 10.00
Coffee Warmer, Pyrex, Gold Metal Band, 1956 . . . . 10.00
Coffee Warmer, Pyrex, Gold, 1954 . . . . 10.00
Coho Salmon, 1976 . . . . .15.00 to 19.00
Colin Mead, 1984 . . . . 150.00

Collectors Edition, Vol. 1, Aristide Braunt, 1966 .... 4.00
Collectors Edition, Vol. 1, Artist, 1966 .... 4.00
Collectors Edition, Vol. 1, Blue Boy, 1966 .... 6.00
Collectors Edition, Vol. 1, Laughing Cavalier, 1966 .... 2.00 to 4.00
Collectors Edition, Vol. 1, Mardi Gras, 1966 .... 2.00 to 3.00
Collectors Edition, Vol. 1, On The Terrace, 1966 .... 6.00 to 7.00
Collectors Edition, Vol. 2, George Gisze, 1967 .... 5.00
Collectors Edition, Vol. 2, Man On A Horse, 1967 .... 5.00
Collectors Edition, Vol. 2, Night Watch, 1967 .... 5.00
Collectors Edition, Vol. 2, Nurse & Child, 1967 .... 5.00
Collectors Edition, Vol. 2, Soldier & Girl, 1967 .... 5.00
Collectors Edition, Vol. 2, The Jester, 1967 .... 5.00
Collectors Edition, Vol. 3, American Gothic, 1968 .... 2.00 to 4.00
Collectors Edition, Vol. 3, Buffalo, 1968 .... 2.00 to 4.00
Collectors Edition, Vol. 3, Indian Maiden, 1968 .... 2.00 to 5.00
Collectors Edition, Vol. 3, The Kentuckian, 1968 .... 2.00
Collectors Edition, Vol. 3, The Scout, 1968 .... 4.00
Collectors Edition, Vol. 3, Whistler's Mother, 1968 .... 2.00
Collectors Edition, Vol. 4, Paintings, Balcony, 1969 .... 2.00
Collectors Edition, Vol. 4, Paintings, Boy With Cherries, 1969 .... 4.00
Collectors Edition, Vol. 4, Paintings, Emile Zola, 1969 .... 4.00
Collectors Edition, Vol. 4, Paintings, Fruit Basket, 1969 .... 4.00
Collectors Edition, Vol. 4, Paintings, Sunflowers, 1969 .... 4.00
Collectors Edition, Vol. 4, Paintings, The Judge, 1969 .... 4.00
Collectors Edition, Vol. 4, Paintings, Zouave, 1969 .... 4.00
Collectors Edition, Vol. 5, Paintings, Au Cafe, 1970 .... 2.00
Collectors Edition, Vol. 5, Paintings, Gare Saint Lazare, 1970 .... 2.00
Collectors Edition, Vol. 5, Paintings, Old Peasant, 1970 .... 2.00
Collectors Edition, Vol. 5, Paintings, The Jewish Bride, 1970 .... 2.00
Collectors Edition, Vol. 5, Paintings, Titus At Writing Desk, 1970 .... 5.00
Collectors Edition, Vol. 6, Paintings, Boy Holding Flute, 1971 .... 3.00
Collectors Edition, Vol. 6, Paintings, Charles I, 1971 .... 3.00
Collectors Edition, Vol. 6, Paintings, The Merry Lute Player, 1971 .... 3.00
Collectors Edition, Vol. 7, Paintings, Maidservant, 1972 .... 3.00
Collectors Edition, Vol. 7, Paintings, Prince Baltasor, 1972 .... 3.00
Collectors Edition, Vol. 7, Paintings, The Bag Piper, 1972 .... 3.00
Collectors Edition, Vol. 8, Musicians, Frederic F. Chopin, 1973 .... 3.00
Collectors Edition, Vol. 8, Musicians, Ludwig Van Beethoven, 1973 .... 3.00
Collectors Edition, Vol. 8, Musicians, Wolfgang Mozart, 1973 .... 3.00
Collectors Edition, Vol. 9, Birds, Cardinal, 1974 .... 4.00
Collectors Edition, Vol. 9, Birds, Woodcock, 1974 .... 4.00
Collectors Edition, Vol. 10, Fish, Largemouth Bass, 1975 .... 4.00
Collectors Edition, Vol. 10, Fish, Rainbow Trout, 1975 ....*Illus* 28.00
Collectors Edition, Vol. 10, Fish, Sailfish, 1975 .... 4.00
Collectors Edition, Vol. 11, Wildlife, Bighorn Sheep, 1976 .... 5.00
Collectors Edition, Vol. 11, Wildlife, Chipmunk, 1976 .... 3.00
Collectors Edition, Vol. 12, Dogs, Irish Setter, 1977 .... 3.00
Collectors Edition, Vol. 12, Dogs, Labrador Retriever, 1977 .... 4.00
Collectors Edition, Vol. 12, Dogs, Springer Spaniel, 1977 .... 4.00
Collectors Edition, Vol. 14, Wildlife, Cottontail Rabbit, 1978 .... 5.00
Collectors Edition, Vol. 14, Wildlife, Mule Deer, 1978 .... 5.00
Collectors Edition, Vol. 14, Wildlife, Red Fox, 1978 ....*Illus* 5.00
Collectors Edition, Vol. 15, Remington, Cowboy 1902, 1979 .... 5.00
Collectors Edition, Vol. 15, Remington, Indian Trapper 1908, 1979 .... 5.00
Collectors Edition, Vol. 15, Remington, Lt. S.C. Robertson 1890, 1979 .... 5.00
Collectors Edition, Vol. 16, Waterfowl, Canvas Back, 1980 .... 5.00
Collectors Edition, Vol. 16, Waterfowl, Mallard, 1980 .... 5.00
Collectors Edition, Vol. 17, Waterfowl, Pintail Duck, 1981 .... 3.00
Collectors Edition, Vol. 17, Wildlife, Great Elk, 1981 .... 3.00
Collectors Edition, Vol. 18, Birds, Cardinal, 1982 .... 4.00
Collectors Edition, Vol. 18, Wildlife, Whitetail Deer, 1982 .... 4.00
Collectors Edition, Vol. 19, Birds, Scarlet Tanager, 1983 .... 4.00
Collectors Edition, Vol. 20, Duck Stamps, 1984 .... 7.00

Beam, Collectors
Edition, Vol. 10, Fish,
Rainbow Trout, 1975

Beam, Collectors
Edition, Vol. 14,
Wildlife, Red Fox, 1978

Collectors Edition, Vol. 21, Duck Stamps, 1985 .... 8.00
Collectors Edition, Vol. 22, Duck Stamps, 1986 .... 6.00
Colorado, State, 1959 .... 20.00
Colorado Centennial, 1976 .... 10.00
Colorado Springs, 1972 .... 9.00
Convention, No. 1, Denver, U.S. Map On Bottle, 1971 .... 10.00
Convention, No. 2, Anaheim, Fox On Top, June 19-25, 1972 .... 37.00
Convention, No. 2, Anaheim, June 19-25, 1972 .... 35.00
Convention, No. 3, Detroit, Fox On Top, 1973 ....16.00 to 19.00
Convention, No. 4, Lancaster, 1974 ....17.00 to 70.00
Convention, No. 5, Sacramento, 1975 ....11.00 to 12.00
Convention, No. 6, Hartford, 1976 .... 5.00 to 9.00
Convention, No. 7, Louisville, Square, Bird On Top, 1977 .... 5.00 to 9.00
Convention, No. 8, Chicago, 1978 .... 5.00 to 10.00
Convention, No. 9, Houston, Cowboy, 1979 .... 58.00
Convention, No. 9, Houston, Tiffany On Rocket, 1979 .... 49.00
Convention, No. 10, Norfolk, Ship & Wheel, 1980 .... 25.00
Convention, No. 11, Las Vegas, 1981 ....20.00 to 25.00
Convention, No. 12, New Orleans, King Rex On Throne, Atop Float, 1982 .... 7.00 to 29.00
Convention, No. 13, St. Louis, 1983 ....50.00 to 151.00
Convention, No. 14, Hollywood, Florida, 1984 ....20.00 to 24.00
Convention, No. 15, Las Vegas, 1985 .... 45.00
Convention, No. 15, Las Vegas, Showgirl On Dice, 1985 .... 40.00
Convention, No. 16, Boston, Black & White Dress, 1986 .... 37.00
Convention, No. 16, Boston, Pilgrim Woman, 1986 .... 55.00
Convention, No. 17, Louisville, Ship Picture, 1987 ....65.00 to 66.00
Convention, No. 18, Portland, Bucky Beaver, 1988 ....29.00 to 35.00
Convention, No. 19, Kansas City, Picture Of Horse & Wagon, 1989 .... 45.00
Convention, No. 20, Kissimmee, Beach Hut, Barrels, 1990 .... 37.00
Convention, No. 21, Reno, Sheriff With Guns, Dice & Money, 1991 .... 64.00
Convention, No. 22, St. Louis, 1992 .... 50.00
CPO, 1974 .... 9.00
Crappie, 1979 .... 9.00 to 15.00
Crispus Attucks, 1976 .... 5.00
CRLDA, 1973 .... 7.00 to 10.00
Crystal, Amaretto, 1975 .... 3.00
Crystal, Amber, 1973 .... 5.00
Crystal, Azur-Glo, 1975 .... 2.00 to 4.00
Crystal, Black, 1974 .... 6.00
Crystal, Blue, 1971 .... 5.00 to 6.00
Crystal, Clear, Bourbon, 1966 .... 10.00
Crystal, Clear, Vodka, 1967 .... 10.00
Crystal, Emerald, Bourbon, 1968 .... 7.00 to 10.00
Crystal, Opaline, 1969 .... 7.00
Crystal, Smoked Geni, 1964 ....40.00 to 45.00
Crystal, Sunburst, Black, 1974 .... 4.00

Beam, Duesenberg, 1935, Convertible,
Coupe, Gray, 1983

Beam, Emmett Kelly, Native
Son Of Kansas, 1973

Beam, Executive, 1968,
Presidential

Crystal, Sunburst, Red, 1974	4.00
Dancing Scot, Glass, Short, 1963	60.00 to 75.00
Dancing Scot, Glass, Tall, 1964	20.00 to 25.00
Dancing Scot, Glass, Tall, Couple, 1964	300.00 to 375.00
Dark Eyes Vodka, Jug, 1978	6.00
Delaware, State, 1972	6.00 to 7.00
Delco Battery, 1978	25.00
Delft Blue, Glass, 1963	3.00 to 5.00
Delft Rose, Glass, 1963	5.00 to 6.00
Denver Rush To Rockies, 1970	10.00
District Executive Urn, 1986	36.00
Doe, 1963	15.00 to 20.00
Don Giovanni, Opera, 1980	120.00
Duck, 1957	18.00
Duck Decoy, 1988, 375 Ml.	19.00
Ducks & Geese, Glass, 1955	4.00 to 6.00
Ducks Unlimited, No. 1, Mallard, 1974	40.00
Ducks Unlimited, No. 2, Wood Duck, 1975	40.00 to 45.00
Ducks Unlimited, No. 3, 40th Anniversary, 1977	40.00 to 50.00
Ducks Unlimited, No. 4, Mallard, 1978	45.00
Ducks Unlimited, No. 5, Canvasback, Drake, 1979	40.00 to 50.00
Ducks Unlimited, No. 6, Blue-Winged Teal, 1980	50.00
Ducks Unlimited, No. 7, Green-Winged Teal, 1981	40.00 to 45.00
Ducks Unlimited, No. 8, Woody & His Brood, 1982	65.00
Ducks Unlimited, No. 9, American Widgeons, 1983	65.00
Ducks Unlimited, No. 10, Mallard, 1984	65.00 to 90.00
Ducks Unlimited, No. 11, Pintail, Pair, 1985	60.00
Ducks Unlimited, No. 12, Redhead, 1986	30.00 to 50.00
Ducks Unlimited, No. 13, Bluebill, 1987	30.00 to 50.00
Ducks Unlimited, No. 14, Gadwall Family, 1988	40.00 to 45.00
Ducks Unlimited, No. 15, Black Duck, 1989	85.00 to 95.00
Ducks Unlimited, No. 16, Canada Goose, 1989	75.00
Ducks Unlimited, No. 17, Tundra Swan, 1991	40.00
Ducks Unlimited, No. 18, Ringneck, 1992	80.00
Ducks Unlimited, No. 19, Loon, 1992	300.00
Ducks Unlimited, No. 20, Cinnamon Teal, 1993	100.00
Ducks Unlimited, No. 21, Harlequin Duck, 1995	125.00
Duesenberg, 1934 Model J, Dark Blue, 1981	125.00
Duesenberg, 1935, Convertible, Coupe, Gray, 1983	*Illus* 245.00
Duesenberg, Light Blue, 1982	110.00
Eagle, 1966	10.00 to 12.00
Elks, 1968	5.00 to 6.00
Emmett Kelly, Native Son Of Kansas, 1973	*Illus* 65.00
Emmett Kelly, Willie The Clown, 1973	25.00 to 35.00
Ernie's Flower Cart, 1976	25.00
Evergreen State Club, 1974	11.00 to 12.00

Executive, 1955, Royal Porcelain, Black ....235.00 to 300.00
Executive, 1956, Royal Gold Round ....60.00 to 65.00
Executive, 1957, Royal Di Monte ....35.00 to 45.00
Executive, 1958, Gray Cherub ....135.00 to 175.00
Executive, 1959, Tavern Scene ....35.00 to 54.00
Executive, 1960, Blue Cherub ....60.00 to 70.00
Executive, 1961, Golden Chalice 25.00
Executive, 1962, Flower Basket ....28.00 to 30.00
Executive, 1963, Royal Rose ....20.00 to 25.00
Executive, 1964, Royal Gold Diamond ....25.00 to 30.00
Executive, 1965, Marbled Fantasy ....25.00 to 30.00
Executive, 1966, Majestic ....22.00 to 25.00
Executive, 1967, Prestige ....10.00 to 15.00
Executive, 1968, Presidential ....*Illus*   13.00
Executive, 1969, Sovereign ....8.00 to 10.00
Executive, 1970, Charisma ....10.00 to 14.00
Executive, 1971, Fantasia ....10.00 to 14.00
Executive, 1972, Regency 12.00
Executive, 1973, Phoenician ....10.00 to 12.00
Executive, 1974, Twin Cherubs ....12.00 to 15.00
Executive, 1975, Reflection In Gold 25.00
Executive, 1976, Floro De Oro 25.00
Executive, 1977, Golden Jubilee 12.00
Executive, 1978, Yellow Rose Of Texas 15.00
Executive, 1979, Mother Of Pearl Vase 15.00
Executive, 1980, Titian 15.00
Executive, 1981, Royal Filigree, Cobalt Deluxe ....16.00 to 18.00
Executive, 1982, Americana Pitcher...............................18.00 to 20.00
Executive, 1983, Musical Bell ....20.00 to 35.00
Executive, 1984, Musical Bell, Noel 25.00
Executive, 1985, Vase, Italian Marble 16.00
Executive, 1986, Bowl, Italian Marble 25.00
Executive, 1987, Twin Doves 15.00
Expo 74, 1974 ....9.00 to 25.00
Falstaff, Opera, 1979 ....   125.00
Father's Day, 1988 ....   19.00
Fiesta Bowl, 1973 ....   17.00
Figaro, Opera, 1977 ....   120.00
Fighting Bull, 1981 ....15.00 to 20.00
Fiji Islands, 1971 ....   8.00
Fire Engine, Ford, 1930 Model A, 1983 ....   165.00
Fire Engine, Mississippi, 1978 ....   115.00
Fire Pumper Truck, Ford, 1934 Model, 1988 ....   90.00
Fire Truck, Mack, 1917 Model, 1982 ....   125.00
First National Bank Of Chicago, 1964 ....1585.00 to 2000.00
Five Seasons Club, 1980 ....   10.00
Fleet Reserve, 1974 ....4.00 to 6.00
Florida Shell, 1968 ....   5.00
Football, 1989 ....   55.00
Football Hall Of Fame, 1972 ....15.00 to 19.00
Ford, Delivery Truck, Angelo's, Black, 1900 Model, 1984 ....   695.00
Ford, Fire Chief, 1928 Model A, 1988 ....70.00 to 125.00
Ford, Fire Chief, 1934 Model A, 1988 ....50.00 to 95.00
Ford, International Delivery Wagon, Black, 1984 ....   95.00
Ford, Model A, 1903 Model, Black, 1978 ....   50.00
Ford, Model A, 1903 Model, Red, 1978 ....   35.00
Ford, Model A, 1928 Model, 1980 ....65.00 to 70.00
Ford, Model A, 1928 Model, Black, 1978 ....   55.00
Ford, Model T, 1913 Model, Black, 1974 ....50.00 to 58.00
Ford, Mustang, 1964 Model, Black, 1986 ....   110.00
Ford, Mustang, 1964 Model, Red, 1986 ....60.00 to 90.00
Ford, Mustang, 1964 Model, White, 1986 ....60.00 to 70.00
Ford, Phaeton, 1929 Model, 1982 ....55.00 to 60.00

Ford, Pickup Truck, 1935 Model, 1988 . . . . 59.00
Ford, Pickup Truck, Angelo's, 1935 Model, 1990 . . . . .70.00 to 80.00
Ford, Police Car, 1929 Model, Blue, 1982 . . . . .80.00 to 90.00
Ford, Police Car, 1929 Model, Yellow, 1983 . . . . .395.00 to 440.00
Ford, Police Tow Truck, 1935 Model, 1988 . . . . 60.00
Ford, Roadster, 1934 Model, Cream, 1990 . . . . .80.00 to 90.00
Ford, Salesman's, 1928 Model, Black, 1981 . . . . .900.00 to 1200.00
Ford, Salesman's, 1928 Model, Yellow, 1981 . . . . .650.00 to 800.00
Ford, Thunderbird, 1956 Model, Black, 1986 . . . . .75.00 to 90.00
Ford, Thunderbird, 1956 Model, Blue, 1986 . . . . 85.00
Ford, Thunderbird, 1956 Model, Gray, 1986 . . . . .65.00 to 95.00
Ford, Thunderbird, 1956 Model, Green, 1986 . . . . .75.00 to 100.00
Ford, Thunderbird, 1956 Model, Yellow, 1986 . . . . 100.00
Ford, Woodie Wagon, 1929 Model, 1983 . . . . .70.00 to 90.00
Foremost, Black & Gold, 1956 . . . . 175.00
Foremost, Gray & Gold, 1956 . . . . 200.00
Foremost, Pink Speckled Beauty, 1956 . . . . .200.00 to 230.00
Fox, Blue, 1967 . . . . 60.00
Fox, Gold, 1969 . . . . .25.00 to 30.00
Fox, Green Coat, 1965 . . . . 14.00
Fox, Green Coat, 1967 . . . . 14.00
Fox, On Dolphin, 1980 . . . . 30.00
Fox, Rennie The Runner, 1974 . . . . 14.00
Fox, Rennie The Surfer, 1975 . . . . .10.00 to 12.00
Fox, Rennie, Red Coat, Distillery, 1973 . . . . 800.00
Fox, Uncle Sam, 1971 . . . . 15.00
Fox, White, 1969 . . . . .22.00 to 25.00
Franklin Mint, 1970 . . . . .6.00 to 8.00
Gem City Club, 1983 . . . . 30.00
General Stark, 1972 . . . . .12.00 to 15.00
George Washington, 1976 . . . . .15.00 to 19.00
Germany, Armed Forces, 1970 . . . . 5.00
Germany, Hansel & Gretel, 1971 . . . . 9.00
Germany, Pied Piper, 1974 . . . . 9.00
Germany, Wiesbaden, 1973 . . . . 9.00
Giant Panda, 1980 . . . . 20.00
Gibson Girl, Yellow, Blue, 1983 . . . . .50.00 to 60.00
Gladiolas Festival, 1974 . . . . .7.00 to 25.00
Glen Campbell, 1976 . . . . .15.00 to 25.00
Globe, Antique, 1980 . . . . 10.00
Golden Gate Casino, 1969 . . . . .75.00 to 79.00
Golden Nugget Casino, 1969 . . . . .48.00 to 50.00
Golf Cart, Regal China, 1986 . . . . .30.00 to 60.00
Goose, Blue, 1971 . . . . 5.00
Goose, Blue, 1979 . . . . .10.00 to 12.00
Grand Canyon, 1969 . . . . .5.00 to 10.00
Great Dane, 1976 . . . . .10.00 to 15.00
Grecian, Glass, 1961 . . . . .3.00 to 5.00
Green China Jug, Pussy Willow, 1965 . . . . .6.00 to 7.00
Hannah Duston, 1973 . . . .*Illus*   30.00
Harley-Davidson, 1988 . . . . 170.00
Harolds Club, Covered Wagon, 1969 . . . . .5.00 to 8.00
Harolds Club, Covered Wagon, Reno Or Bust, 1974 . . . . .25.00 to 35.00
Harolds Club, Man In Barrel, No. 1, 1957 . . . . 400.00
Harolds Club, Man In Barrel, No. 2, 1958 . . . . 150.00
Harolds Club, Nevada, Gray, 1963 . . . . 100.00
Harolds Club, Nevada, Silver, 1964 . . . . 150.00
Harolds Club, Pinwheel, 1965 . . . . .35.00 to 40.00
Harolds Club, Silver Opal, 1957 . . . . 20.00
Harolds Club, Slot Machine, Blue, 1967 . . . . 12.00
Harolds Club, Slot Machine, Gray, 1968 . . . .*Illus*   9.00
Harolds Club, VIP, 1967 . . . . .40.00 to 55.00
Harolds Club, VIP, 1968 . . . . 57.00

| Beam, Hannah Duston, 1973 | Beam, Harolds Club, Slot Machine, Gray, 1968 | Beam, Hawaiian Open, 9th, Tiki God, 1974 | Beam, Hemisfair, San Antonio, 1968 |

Harolds Club, VIP, 1969 . . . . .250.00 to 275.00
Harolds Club, VIP, 1970 . . . .   50.00
Harolds Club, VIP, 1971 . . . . .50.00 to 60.00
Harolds Club, VIP, 1972 . . . .   20.00
Harolds Club, VIP, 1973 . . . . .15.00 to 25.00
Harolds Club, VIP, 1974 . . . . .15.00 to 20.00
Harolds Club, VIP, 1975 . . . . .15.00 to 20.00
Harolds Club, VIP, 1976 . . . .   20.00
Harolds Club, VIP, 1977 . . . . .20.00 to 25.00
Harolds Club, VIP, 1978 . . . .   25.00
Harolds Club, VIP, 1979 . . . . .25.00 to 30.00
Harolds Club, VIP, 1980 . . . .   20.00
Harolds Club, VIP, 1981 . . . .   95.00
Harolds Club, VIP, 1982 . . . .   50.00
Harrah's Club, Nevada, Gray, 1963 . . . . .500.00 to 650.00
Harrah's Club, Nevada, Silver, 1963 . . . . .500.00 to 600.00
Harvey's, 1969 . . . .   12.00
Hatfield, 1973 . . . .   20.00
Hawaii, State, 1959 . . . .   35.00
Hawaii, State, 1967 . . . . .35.00 to 40.00
Hawaii Aloha Club, 1971 . . . . .9.00 to 15.00
Hawaii Paradise, 1978 . . . .   15.00
Hawaiian Open, 7th, Pineapple, 1972 . . . .   15.00
Hawaiian Open, 8th, Golf Ball, 1973 . . . .   17.00
Hawaiian Open, 9th, Tiki God, 1974 . . . . .Illus   15.00
Hawaiian Open, 10th, Menehune, 1975 . . . .   20.00
Hawaiian Open, 11th Outrigger, 1976 . . . . .15.00 to 20.00
Hawaiian Open, 11th, US Emblem, 1976 . . . .   14.00
Helmet & Boots, Short Timer, 1984 . . . .   29.00
Hemisfair, San Antonio, 1968 . . . . .Illus   10.00
Hen, Blue, 1982 . . . . .18.00 to 20.00
Herre Bros., 1972 . . . . .30.00 to 40.00
Hoffman, 1969 . . . . .6.00 to 7.00
Home Builders, 1978 . . . .   25.00
Hone Heke, 1981 . . . . .155.00 to 195.00
Hongi Hika, 1980 . . . .   140.00
Horse, 1961 . . . . .20.00 to 22.00
Horse, 1966 . . . .   20.00
Horse, 1967 . . . .   15.00
Horse, 1968 . . . .   15.00
Horse, Appaloosa, 1974 . . . . .10.00 to 12.00
Horse, Black, 1962 . . . . .20.00 to 25.00
Horse, Brown, 1962 . . . .   15.00

Horseshoe Club, Reno, 1969	8.00
Hyatt House, Chicago, 1971	10.00
Hyatt Regency, New Orleans, 1976	10.00 to 12.00
Idaho, State, 1963	35.00
Illinois, State, 1968	6.00 to 8.00
Indian Chief, 1979	15.00 to 20.00
Indianapolis Sesquicentennial, 1971	8.00 to 10.00
Indianapolis Speed Race, 1970	19.00
International Chili Society, 1976	10.00
International Petroleum, 1971	5.00 to 7.00
Jackelope, 1971	10.00 to 15.00
Jaguar, 1981, Trophy	30.00
Jewel Tea, 50th Anniversary, 1982	50.00 to 70.00
Jewel Tea Wagon, 1974	65.00 to 75.00
Jim Beam Jug, Black, 1982	35.00
Jim Beam Jug, Dark Blue, 1982	25.00 to 35.00
Jim Beam Jug, Dark Green, 1982	35.00
Jim Beam Jug, Light Blue, 1982	35.00
John Arthur, Past Presidents, 1977	5000.00
John Henry, 1972	35.00
Kaiser International, Open, 1971	15.00
Kangaroo, 1977	15.00
Kansas, State, 1960	35.00 to 40.00
Kentucky, 1982	75.00
Kentucky, Black Horse Head Stopper, State, 1967	12.00 to 18.00
Kentucky, Brown Horse Head Stopper, State, 1967	25.00
Kentucky, White Horse Head Stopper, State, 1967	24.00 to 30.00
Kentucky Colonel, 1970	5.00 to 10.00
Kentucky Derby, 95th, Pink Roses, 1969	20.00
Kentucky Derby, 95th, Red Roses, 1969	20.00
Kentucky Derby, 96th, Double Roses, Stopper, 1970	30.00
Kentucky Derby, 97th, Horse & Rider, 1971	18.00
Kentucky Derby, 98th, Horse & Rider In Wreath, 1972	24.00 to 25.00
Kentucky Derby, 100th, 1974	19.00
Key West, Florida, 1972	6.00 to 8.00
King Kamehameha, 1972	10.00 to 15.00
King Kong, 1976	20.00
Kiwi Bird, 1974	5.00 to 7.00
Koala Bear, Gray, 1973	35.00
Laramie, Centennial Jubilee, 1968	5.00 to 6.00
Largemouth Bass, 1973	15.00 to 28.00
Las Vegas, 1969	6.00 to 9.00
Las Vegas Show Girl, Blond, 1981	50.00
Las Vegas Show Girl, Brunette, 1981	50.00
Legion Music, Joliet Legion Band, 1978	10.00
Light Bulb, 1979	14.00
Lombard, Lilac, 1969	5.00 to 6.00
London Bridge, 1971	5.00 to 8.00
London Bridge With Medallion, 1969	165.00 to 175.00
Louisville Downs, 1978	16.00
Madame Butterfly, Opera, 1977	225.00 to 250.00
Magpies, 1977	18.00 to 20.00
Maine, State, 1970	6.00 to 8.00
Marbled Fantasy, 1965	37.00
Mare & Foal, Horse, For The Love Of A Foal, 1982	50.00
Marina City, 1962	10.00 to 20.00
Marine Corps, 1975	35.00 to 40.00
Mark Anthony, Glass, 1962	20.00
Martha Washington, 1975	10.00 to 14.00
McCoy, 1973	20.00
Mephistopheles, Opera, 1979	150.00 to 170.00
Mercedes Benz, 1974 Model, Blue, 1987	35.00 to 45.00

Mercedes Benz, 1974 Model, Gold, 1988 ....50.00 to 75.00
Mercedes Benz, 1974 Model, Green, 1987 ....   45.00
Mercedes Benz, 1974 Model, Mocha, 1987 ....   45.00
Mercedes Benz, 1974 Model, Sand Beige, Pa., 1987 ....35.00 to 50.00
Mercedes Benz, 1974 Model, Silver, Australia, 1987 ....100.00 to 130.00
Mercedes Benz, 1974 Model, White, 1986 ....45.00 to 60.00
Michigan, State, 1972 ....   6.00
Milwaukee, Stein, 1972 ....   28.00
Mint, Cycle, Stopper, 1971 ....   12.00
Mint 400, 3rd, China Stopper, 1970 ....   90.00
Mint 400, 3rd, Metal Stopper, 1971 ....   8.00
Mint 400, 5th, 1972 ....8.00 to 12.00
Mint 400, 6th, 1973 ....8.00 to 12.00
Mint 400, 7th, 1975 ....9.00 to 12.00
Mint 400, 8th, 1976 ....10.00 to 15.00
Montana, State, 1963 ....50.00 to 60.00
Monterey Bay Club, 1977 ....9.00 to 10.00
Mortimer Snerd, 1976 ....40.00 to 45.00
Mr. Goodwrench, 1978 ....30.00 to 45.00
Mt. St. Helens, 1980 ....   22.00
Multi-Glo, Glass, 1975 ....   6.00
Musicians On Wine Cask, 1964 ....5.00 to 7.00
Muskie, 1971 ....15.00 to 16.00
Muskie, Gold, 1971 ....   16.00
Muskie, National Freshwater Fishing Hall Of Fame, 1983 ....27.00 to 34.00
National Licensed Beverage Assoc., 1975 ....   5.00
Nebraska, State, 1967 ....   19.00
Nevada, State, Gold Letters, 1964 ....   100.00
Nevada, State, Silver Letters, 1963 ....   27.00
New Hampshire, State, 1967 ....5.00 to 6.00
New Hampshire Eagle, 1971 ....   20.00
New Jersey, Blue Gray, State, 1963 ....   35.00
New Jersey, Yellow, State, 1963 ....   35.00
New Mexico, Bicentennial, 1976 ....   10.00
New Mexico, State, 1972 ....   5.00
New Mexico, Wedding Vase, 1972 ....10.00 to 14.00
New York, The Big Apple, 1979 ....   12.00
New York World's Fair, 1964 ....10.00 to 14.00
Noel, Executive Bell, 29th, 1983 ....   30.00
Noel, Executive Bell, 30th, 1984 ....   25.00
North Dakota, State, 1964 ....   35.00
Northern Pike, 1978 ....15.00 to 20.00
Nutcracker, 1978 ....100.00 to 120.00
Nutcracker, Barry Berish, Presidential, 1989 ....   100.00
Nutcracker, Barry Berish, Presidential, Silver, 1990 ....   100.00
Nutcracker, Holiday, 1989 ....   50.00
Nutcracker, Holiday, Drummer, 1990 ....*Illus*   15.00
Nutcracker, Holiday, Presidential, 1991 ....15.00 to 35.00
Nutcracker, Presidential, Gold, 1991 ....   100.00
Oatmeal Jug, 1966 ....   45.00
Ohio, State, 1966 ....5.00 to 6.00
Ohio State Fair, 1973 ....   9.00
Oldsmobile, 1904 Model, 1972 ....   28.00
Olsonite Eagle Race Car, No. 48, 1975 ....60.00 to 65.00
Oregon, State, 1959 ....   22.00
Oregon Liquor Control, 1984 ....   32.00
Osco Drug, 1987 ....   20.00
Owl, L.V.N.H., English, 1982 ....   45.00
Paddy Wagon, 1983 ....   140.00
Passenger Car, 1981 ....   45.00
Paul Bunyan, 1970 ....   9.00
Paul Saroff, Past Presidents, 1976 .... 5000.00
Pearl Harbor, 1972 ....   16.00

Beam, Nutcracker,
Holiday, Drummer, 1990

Beam, Political, Elephant,
1980, Superman

Beam, Saturday Evening Post, Game
Called Because Of Rain, 1975

Pearl Harbor, Blue & White, 1972 .... 65.00
Pearl Harbor Survivors, 1976 ....10.00 to 65.00
Pennsylvania, State, 1967 .... 12.00
Pennsylvania Dutch Club, 1974 .... 11.00
Perch Pretty, 1980 .... 15.00
Permian Basin Oil Show, 1972 .... 9.00
PGA 53rd Golf Tournament, 1971 .... 15.00
Pheasant, 1960 .... 10.00
Phi Sigma Kappa, 1973 .... 15.00
Phoenician, 1973 .... 10.00
Police Car, 1929 Model, 1982 .... 100.00
Police Car, 1929 Model, Yellow, 1983 .... 450.00
Police Patrol Car, 1934 Model, Black & White, 1989 .... 72.00
Police Patrol Car, 1934 Model, Yellow, 1989 .... 130.00
Political, Donkey, 1960, Campaigner ....16.00 to 18.00
Political, Donkey, 1964, Boxer 16.00
Political, Donkey, 1968, Clown 10.00
Political, Donkey, 1972, Football 15.00
Political, Donkey, 1976, Drum, New York 20.00
Political, Donkey, 1980, Superman 20.00
Political, Donkey, 1984, Computer 30.00
Political, Donkey, 1988, Drummer ....30.00 to 35.00
Political, Elephant, 1960, Campaigner 16.00
Political, Elephant, 1964, Boxer ....15.00 to 20.00
Political, Elephant, 1968, Clown 10.00
Political, Elephant, 1970, Spiro Agnew, Dinner 1000.00
Political, Elephant, 1972, Football 15.00
Political, Elephant, 1972, Miami Beach, Dinner ....400.00 to 550.00
Political, Elephant, 1972, Washington, D.C., Feb. 10 Dinner ....350.00 to 400.00
Political, Elephant, 1976, Drum 8.00
Political, Elephant, 1976, Drum, Kansas City ....15.00 to 25.00
Political, Elephant, 1980, Superman ...._Illus_ 20.00
Political, Elephant, 1984, Computer 30.00
Political, Elephant, 1988, Drummer 35.00
Ponderosa, 1969 ....10.00 to 15.00
Pony Express, 1968 ....8.00 to 10.00
Poodle, Gray, 1970 .... 10.00
Poodle, White, 1970 .... 10.00
Portland Bottle & Rose, Convention, Red, 1988 .... 35.00
Portland Bottle & Rose, Convention, Yellow, 1988 .... 35.00
Portland Rose Festival, 1972 .... 10.00
Poulan Chain Saw, 1979 ....25.00 to 27.00
Powell Expedition, 1969 .... 6.00
Preakness, 100th, Pimlico, 1975 ....20.00 to 25.00

Pretty Perch, 1980 .... 15.00
Prima Donna, 1969 .... 8.00
Queensland, 1978 .... 20.00
Rabbit, 1971 .... 45.00
Rabbit, Texas, 1971 .... 14.00
Ralph's Market, 1973 .... 14.00
Ram, 1958, Trophy 40.00
Ramada Inn, 1976 .... 4.00 to 8.00
Red Mile, Race Track, 1975 .... 16.00 to 18.00
Redwood Empire, 1967 .... 5.00 to 6.00
Reflection In Gold, 1975 .... 15.00
Reidsville, 1973 .... 9.00
Republic Of Texas Club, 1980 .... 12.00 to 15.00
Richard's, New Mexico, 1967 .... 6.00 to 7.00
Robin, 1969 .... 8.00 to 10.00
Rocky Marciano, 1973 .... 25.00 to 40.00
Rubber Capitol Club, 1973 .... 15.00
Ruidoso Downs, Pointed Ears, 1968 .... 25.00 to 35.00
Sahara Invitational, Golf, 1971 .... 15.00
Sailfish, 1957 .... 17.00 to 20.00
Salesman Glass Bottle, Award, 1980 .... 250.00
Samoa, 1973 .... 5.00 to 7.00
San Diego, 1968 .... 5.00
San Francisco Cable Car, 1983 .... 35.00 to 45.00
Santa Claus, 1983 .... 130.00 to 150.00
Santa Fe, 1960 .... 70.00 to 80.00
Saturday Evening Post, Benjamin Franklin, 1975 .... 4.00
Saturday Evening Post, Game Called Because Of Rain, 1975 .... *Illus* 4.00
Saturday Evening Post, Ye Pipe & Bowl, 1975 .... 4.00
Screech Owl, Gray, 1979 .... 22.00
Screech Owl, Red, 1979 .... 22.00
Seafair, 1972 .... 13.00 to 15.00
Seattle World's Fair, 1962 .... 16.00
Seoul, Korea, 1988 .... 20.00
Setter, 1958 .... 20.00
Sheraton Hotel, 1975 .... 8.00
Short Timer, Armed Forces, 1975 .... 20.00 to 23.00
Shriners, El Kahir Pyramid, 1975 .... 15.00
Shriners, Moila, Purple Camel, 1975 .... 15.00 to 30.00
Shriners, Moila, Purple Sword, 1972 .... 19.00
Shriners, Order Of Shriners, 1970 .... 5.00 to 6.00
Shriners, Rajah Temple, 1977 .... 25.00
Shriners, Western Association, 1980 .... 20.00
Sigma Nu Fraternity, Kentucky, 1977 .... 10.00
Sigma Nu Fraternity, Michigan, 1977 .... 10.00 to 15.00
Slot Machine, Gray, Regal China, 1968 .... 8.00
Smith's North Shore Club, 1972 .... 12.00 to 15.00
Smoke Glo, Glass 4.00
Snow Goose, 1979 .... 15.00 to 30.00
South Carolina, State, 1970 .... 10.00 to 26.00
South Dakota, Mt. Rushmore, 1969 .... 9.00
South Dakota, State, 1969 .... 5.00
Space Shuttle, 1986 .... 30.00 to 50.00
Spenger's Fish Grotto, 1977 .... 19.00 to 20.00
Sports Car Club Of America, 1976 .... 15.00
St. Bernard, 1979 .... 30.00
St. Louis Arch, 1964 .... 10.00 to 20.00
St. Louis Club, 1972 .... 10.00 to 12.00
Statue Of Liberty, 1975 .... 10.00 to 20.00
Stein, German, 1983 .... 18.00 to 20.00
Stone Mountain, 1974 .... 10.00 to 20.00
Sturgeon, 1980 .... 15.00 to 18.00
Stutz Bearcat, 1914, Blue, 1977 .... 250.00

Beam, Telephone,
100 Digit, 1983

Beam, Thomas Flyer, White, 1976

Stutz Bearcat, 1914, Bronze, 1977 .... 450.00
Stutz Bearcat, 1914, Gray, 1977 ....45.00 to 55.00
Stutz Bearcat, 1914, Yellow, 1977 ....45.00 to 58.00
Submarine Redfin, 1970 ....5.00 to 8.00
Superdome, New Orleans, 1975 .... 5.00
Swagman, 2nd National Convention, Australia, 1979 ....15.00 to 38.00
Sydney Opera House, 1977 ....20.00 to 23.00
Te Rauparaha, 1982 .... 155.00
Telephone, 100 Digit, 1983 ....*Illus* 50.00
Telephone, 1897 Model, 1978 ....25.00 to 35.00
Telephone, 1919 Dial, 1980 ....45.00 to 50.00
Telephone, 1919 Dial, 1981 .... 50.00
Telephone, Battery, 1982 ....35.00 to 45.00
Telephone, French Cradle, 1979 ....15.00 to 25.00
Telephone, Pay Phone, 1981 .... 45.00
Telephone, Wall Set, 1975 ....18.00 to 25.00
Thailand, 1969 ....5.00 to 6.00
Thomas Flyer, Blue, 1976 ....60.00 to 65.00
Thomas Flyer, White, 1976 ....*Illus* 65.00
Tiffany Poodle, 1973 .... 15.00
Tigers, 1977 .... 15.00
Tobacco Festival, 1973 ....15.00 to 17.00
Tombstone, 1970 ....*Illus* 20.00
Train, Box Car, 1983 .... 55.00
Train, Caboose, Gray, 1988 ....50.00 to 60.00
Train, Caboose, Orange, 1980 .... 75.00
Train, Caboose, Yellow, 1985 ....65.00 to 80.00
Train, Casey Jones Accessory Set 60.00
Train, Casey Jones Bumpers 12.00
Train, Casey Jones Caboose, 1989 ....22.00 to 32.00
Train, Casey Jones Tank Car, 1990 .... 40.00
Train, Casey Jones Track ....6.00 to 7.00
Train, Casey Jones With Tender, 1989 .... 39.00
Train, General Locomotive, 1986 ....70.00 to 100.00
Train, General, Flat Car, 1987 .... 65.00
Train, Grant Baggage Car, 1981 ....40.00 to 45.00
Train, Grant Combination Car, 1988 .... 40.00
Train, Grant Dining Car, 1982 ....80.00 to 85.00
Train, Grant Locomotive, 1979 .... 80.00
Train, Grant Passenger Car, 1981 .... 40.00
Train, Log Car, 1984 ....65.00 to 75.00
Train, Lumber Car, 1985 .... 45.00
Train, Tank Car, 1983 ....40.00 to 50.00
Train, Track ....10.00 to 20.00
Train, Water Tower, 1985 ....40.00 to 45.00
Train, Wood Tender, 1988 ....50.00 to 75.00

Beam, Volkswagen, Red, 1973

Beam, Tombstone, 1970

TraveLodge, Sleepy Bear, 1972 . . . . .15.00 to 20.00
Treasure Chest, 1979 . . . . 10.00
Trout Unlimited, 1977 . . . . 15.00
Truth Or Consequences, 1974 . . . . .8.00 to 20.00
Turquoise China Jug, 1966 . . . . 6.00
Turtle, Short Neck, 1975 . . . . 10.00
Twin Bridges Club, 1971 . . . . .22.00 to 25.00
Twin Cherubs, 1974 . . . . 10.00
U.S. Open, 1972 . . . . 25.00
Uncle Sam With Eagle, Royal Doulton, 1984, 5 In. . . . . .45.00 to 50.00
Veterans Of Foreign Wars, 1971 . . . . .5.00 to 10.00
Viking, 1973 . . . . .12.00 to 25.00
Volkswagen, Blue, 1973 . . . . 65.00
Volkswagen, Red, 1973 . . . .*Illus* 70.00
Von's 75th Anniversary, 1981 . . . . .25.00 to 35.00
Walleye Pike, 1977 . . . . 15.00
Walleye Pike, Hall Of Fame, 1987 . . . . 21.00
Washington Bicentennial, 1976 . . . . .12.00 to 17.00
Washington State, State, 1975 . . . . .10.00 to 15.00
Waterman, Glazed, 1980 . . . . 50.00
Waterman, Norfolk Convention Gift, Pewter, 1980, Pair 6.00
West Virginia, State, 1963 . . . . .100.00 to 115.00
WGA, Western Open, 1971 . . . . 15.00
Wolverine Club, 1975 . . . . 10.00
Woodpecker, 1969 . . . . 8.00
Wyoming, State, 1965 . . . . .45.00 to 50.00
Yellowstone, 1972 . . . . .5.00 to 7.00
Yosemite, Decal Map, 1967 . . . . 5.00
Yuma Rifle Club, 1968 . . . . .17.00 to 19.00
Zimmerman Liquors, 2-Handled Jug, 1965 . . . . .50.00 to 55.00
Zimmerman Liquors, 50th Anniversary, 1983 . . . . .30.00 to 40.00
Zimmerman Liquors, Bell, Dark Blue, 1976 . . . . .6.00 to 10.00
Zimmerman Liquors, Blue Beauty, 1969, 10 In. . . . . .10.00 to 12.00
Zimmerman Liquors, Blue Daisy, 1967 . . . . 6.00
Zimmerman Liquors, Cherubs, Lavender, 1968 . . . . .5.00 to 9.00
Zimmerman Liquors, Cherubs, Salmon, 1968 . . . . .5.00 to 7.00
Zimmerman Liquors, Chicago, Z, 1970 . . . . .5.00 to 10.00
Zimmerman Liquors, Eldorado, Gray Blue, 1978 . . . . 5.00
Zimmerman Liquors, Peddler, 1971 . . . . .5.00 to 10.00
Zimmerman Liquors, Vase, Green, 1972 . . . . .5.00 to 10.00

---------------------------------- BEER ----------------------------------

History says that beer was first made in America in the Roanoke Colony of Virginia in 1587. It is also claimed that the Pilgrims brought some over on the already crowded Mayflower. William Penn started a brewery in 1683. By the time of the Civil War, beer was made and bottled in all parts of the United States. In the early years the beer was poured from kegs or sold in ordinary unmarked black glass bottles. English stoneware bottles were in common use in this country from about 1860 to 1890. Excavations in many inner cities still unearth these sturdy containers. A more or less standard bottle was used by about 1870. It held a quart of liquid and measured about 10 inches high. The early ones were plain and had a cork stopper. Later bottles had embossed lettering on the sides. The lightning stopper was invented in 1875 and many bottles had various types of wire and lever-type seals that were replacements for the corks. In the 1900s Crown corks were used. It wasn't long before plain bottles with paper labels appeared, but cans were soon the containers preferred by many. The standard thick-topped glass beer bottle shape of the 1870s, as well as modern beer bottles, are included in this category. The bottles can be found in clear, brown, aqua, or amber glass. A few cobalt blue, milk glass, or red examples are known. Some bottles have turned slightly amethyst in color from the sun. Collectors are often interested in local breweries and books listing the names and addresses of companies have been written. (See Bibliography.) Beer bottle collectors often search for advertising trays, signs, and other *go-withs* collected as *breweriana*. These are listed under Go-Withs at the end of this book.

BEER, A. Gettelman Brewing Co., Milwaukee, Hand Holding Glass, Reverse Label, Qt. .   25.00
A. Scheidt's Brewing Co., Norristown, Pa., Blob Top, Squat 15.00
A. Templeton Cream Ale, Louisville, Blob Top, Squat, Qt. 65.00
A.M. Heinly, Hamburg, Pa., Lady's Leg, Amber 30.00
A.W. Kennison, Auburn, Calif., Qt. 7.00
Aberdeen Brewg. Co., Aberdeen, Wash., Amber, Girl Picture, Tooled Top, Qt. 65.00
ABG Co., On Base, Cobalt Blue, 9 1/2 In. 30.00
Adam Scheidt Br'g., Norristown, Pa., Aqua, Crown Top 3.00
Adam Scheidt Brewing Co., Norristown, Pa., 9 In. 20.00
Adam Scheidt Brewing Co., Norristown, Pa., Aqua, Monogram, Blob Top 16.00
Adam's Ale House, Milwaukee Lager, Concord, N.H., Emerald Green, Stopper, Pt. 525.00
Adam's Ale House, Milwaukee Lager, Concord, N.H., Yellow, Stopper, Pt. 345.00
Adolph Haser, Chester, Pa., Blob Top, Stopper 15.00
Ahrens Bottling Co., Oakland, 1/2 Pt. 30.00
Ainslie Leeds Street Brewery, Liverpool, Black Glass, Amber, 1790-1810, 8 3/4 In. . .   580.00
Albert Aherns, N.Y., Medium Green, Blob Top, Ceramic Stopper 80.00
Angel's Brewery & Bottling Works, Ernst F. Hubler, 4-Piece Mold, Yellow Amber, Qt.   100.00
Anheuser-Busch, New Jersey Bottling Association, New Brunswick, N.J., BIMAL 50.00
Anheuser-Busch, Washington, D.C., Aqua, Blob Top 35.00
Anheuser-Busch Brew. Assn., St. Louis & New York, O. Meyer & Co., Amber 20.00
Anheuser-Busch Brew. Assn., St. Louis, Mo., Washington, D.C., Eagle, Logo, Aqua . . .   70.00
Anheuser-Busch Brewing Co., Pre-Prohibition, 12 Oz. 39.00
Anheuser-Busch Brewing Co., Watertown Branch, Eagle, Monogram, Amber 15.00
Anheuser-Busch Malt Nutrine, St. Louis, Label, 1920s, 7 Oz. 71.00
Anthracite Brewing Co., Mt. Carmel, Pa., Crown Bail, 1890s, 8 1/4 In. 18.00
Arnholt & Schaefer, Philada., Aqua, Crown Top 3.00
Atlantic City Brewing Co., Atlantic City, N.J., Lighthouse, BIMAL, Crown Top 25.00
Augusta Brewing Co., Augusta, Ga., Amber, Pt. 50.00
B.J. King, York, Pa., Aqua, Blob Top 8.00
Bath Bottling Works, Bath, Me., Blob Top, Stopper, Pt. 15.00
Bay View Brewing Co., Seattle, Wa., Medium Olive Green, 1890, 11 3/4 In. 3005.00
Becker's Cereal, Oldon, Label, 1920s, 6 Oz. 26.00
Belleville, Ill., Cobalt Blue, 9 1/2 In. 60.00
Belmont Brewing Co., Martins Ferry, O., Bell, Amber, Blob Top, Pt. 15.00
Belmont Brewing Co., Martins Ferry, O., Bell, Aqua, Blob Top, Qt. 20.00
Belmont Brewing Co., Martins Ferry, Ohio, Bell, Amber, Blob Top, Qt. . . . . .15.00 to 20.00
Berghoff Brewing Co., Fort Wayne, Ind., Amber, Blob Top, Qt. 15.00
Berghoff Brewing Co., Fort Wayne, Ind., Amber, Round Slug, Blob Top, Pt. 10.00
Birdsboro Bottling Works, Birdsboro, Pa., Aqua, Blob Top, Stopper 12.00
Blatz, Vertical Ribs, Star On Back 5.00
Boule & Rosy, Stoneware 25.00
Brown Stout, Blue Green, Single Collar, Squat, IP, 6 1/2 In. 60.00
Bruske Bros. Bottling Works, Manistee, Mich., Amber, Blob Top, 1882-1884, Qt. 200.00
Buckeye Bottling Works, Toledo, Ohio, Aqua, Round Slug, Blob Top 15.00
Buffalo Brewing, Sacramento, Cal., Amber, Tooled Top, Qt. 45.00
Buffalo Brewing Co., S.F. Agency, Monogram In Shield, Yellow, Blob Top 50.00
Buffalo Brewing Co., Sacramento, Ca., Red Amber, Applied Mouth, 12 1/8 In. 140.00

Burgermeister, Hamm Brewing, Los Angeles, Pottery, 1960s, 9 Oz. 6.00
C. Conrad & Co., Original Budweiser, Aqua, Pat. No. 6376, 1880-1890, 12 In. 145.00
C. Conrad & Co., Original Budweiser, Aqua, Pat. No. 6376, Applied Mouth, 1890, 9 In. . 100.00
C. Pfund, Philada., Crown Top 3.00
C. Thomas Truckee, 4-Piece Mold, Olive, Tooled Top, Bent Neck, Stopper, 1/2 Pt. Split . 880.00
C.B. & Co., Chattanooga, Tenn., Aqua, Marble, Burst Bubble, 11 In. 10.00
C.C. Haley & Co., California Pop Beer, Pat. Oct. 29th, 1872, Black Glass, 11 1/2 In. 80.00
C.D. Kaier, Mahanoy City, Pa., Yellow Green, Applied Mouth, 1875-1885, 11 1/4 In. 190.00
C.H. Daniels Brewery, Manistee, Mich., Amber, Blob Top, Qt. 45.00
C.L. Centlivre Brewing Co., Ft. Wayne, Ind., Amber, Blob Top, Qt. 15.00
C.W. Queen, Norristown, Pa., Weiss Beer 25.00
Calumet Brewing Co., Calumet, Mich., Amber, Blob Top, Qt. 15.00
Camden Bottling Co., Camden, N.J., Script, Amethyst, Blob Top 6.00
Canadian Ace, Cone Top, Simulated Wood Lithograph, 12 Oz. 25.00
Carlisle Bottling Works, Geo. N. Bacon, Lime Yellow, Blob Top 100.00
Charles E. Porter, Pittsburgh, Pa., Blob Top 15.00
Charles Hobleman, Cincinnati, Teal Blue, Backward S, IP, 9 1/8 In. 2585.00
Chas. B. Hepler, Avenue, Pa., Yellow Amber, Blob Top 15.00
Chas. Ihne, 66 Crown St., New Haven, Ct., Green Aqua, Blob Top, 9 In. 15.00
Chas. Joly, No. 9 So. Seventh St., Phila., Yellow Green, Blob Top 20.00
Chas. Joly, No. 9, Philadelphia, Pa., Deep Olive Green 70.00
Chas. Knorr, West Philada, Amethyst, Blob Top 8.00
Chas. R. Puckhaber Beers, Fresno, Cal., Amber, 1/2 Pt. 48.00
Chattanooga Brewing Co., Chattanooga, Tenn., Aqua, 9 1/2 In. 25.00
Chicago Bottling Works, D. Meineke, San Francisco, Stopper, Bail, 1/2 Pt. 15.00
Chicago Consolidated Bottling Co., 14 To 18 Charles Place, Aqua, 11 1/2 In. 12.00
Chris Nacrelli, Marcus Hook, Pa., Script, Blob Top 15.00
Cincinnati Brewing Co., Star In Round Slug, Aqua, Blob Top 15.00
City Bottling Works, Toledo, Ohio, Aqua, Blob Top, Qt. 15.00
City Brewery, John Buehler, Steubenville, Ohio, Amber, Blob Top, Pt. 15.00
City Brewery, Titusville, Pa., Amber, Monogram With Hops, Blob Top 18.00
City Brewing Co., Steubenville, O., Amber, Blob Top, Qt. 20.00
Clinton Brewing Co., Clinton, Iowa, Stopper, Picnic 40.00
Cobalt Blue, Applied Top, Bubbles, 9 1/4 In. 75.00
Colaluga Bros., Providence, R.I., Blob Top, Bubbles, Cork 10.00
Columbia Brewing Co., Logansport, Ind., Amber, Blob Top, Qt. 15.00
Columbia Preferred Beer, Shenandoah, Pa., Amber, 8 In. 15.00
Conrad's Budweiser, Aqua, Blob Top, Pt. 40.00
Consumer's Bottling Co., Redwood, Ca., Amber, Qt. 375.00
Consumer's Park Brewing Co., Brooklyn, N.Y., Aqua, Blob Top, Stopper 4.00
Consumers Brewing Co., Phila., Aqua, Crown Top, ABM 3.00
Continental Brew. Co., Philadelphia, Pa., Aqua, Blob Top 50.00
Continental Brewing Company, Philada., Blob Top, Stopper 8.00
Cosgrave & Sons Lager Beer, Toronto, Ont., Aqua, 1878-1882, 9 1/8 In. 60.00
Cream Ale, Templeton, Louisville, Ky., Red Amber, 5-Pointed Star On Base, 1875, Qt. ... 85.00
Crescent Brewing Co., Aurora, Ind., Amber, Blob Top, Qt. 25.00
Crystal Rock, Amber, Blob Top, Pt. ....10.00 to 15.00
Cunningham & Co., Philada., Aqua, Blob Top 4.00
D. & R., Dover, N.H., Deep Aqua, Mug Base, Qt. 25.00
D. Alampi, Philada., Aqua, Blob Top 10.00
D. Lutz & Son, Allegheny, Pa., Amber, Blob Top 15.00
D.W. DeFrest, R, Stoneware, Cream, Cobalt Blue Letters, Blob Top, Qt. 95.00
Daniel Toohey, Chester, Pa., Blob Top 6.00
Daniel Toohey, Chester, Pa., Crown Top 3.00
Davenport Brewing Company, Davenport, Iowa, Amber, Blob Top, Stopper, 14 1/2 In. 20.00
David Mayer Brewery, N.Y., Blob Top, Stopper, Pt. ....15.00 to 25.00
Dawson & Son Brewers, 1893, New Bedford, Mass., Porcelain Stopper, Blob Top, Pt. . 20.00
Des Moines Brewing Co., Des Moines, Iowa, Amber, Round Slug, Picnic 40.00
Des Moines Brewing Co., Picnic, Porcelain Stopper 45.00
Diehl & Lord Bottlers, Nashville, Qt. 85.00
Dr. Cronk's, Gibbons & Co., Superior Ale, Buffalo, N.Y., Green, Blob Top, IP, 6 3/4 In. . 470.00
Dr. Cronk's, Yellow Green, 12-Sided, Pontil, 1850-1865 .... 1155.00
Dr. Smith's Pat. White Root, Hathaway, Stoneware, Brown, Tan, Blob Top, Qt. 80.00

E. Wagner, Manchester, N.H., Emerald Green, Stopper, Pt. 445.00
E. Wagner, Manchester, N.H., Maltese Cross, Lemon Yellow, Blob Top, Pt. 55.00
E. Wagner, Manchester, N.H., Maltese Cross, Lemon Yellow, Olive, Stopper, Pt. 35.00
E.G. Rosche ABC Sparkling Lager, Albany, N.Y., Blob Top, Amber, Pt. 45.00
E.L. Kerns, Trenton, N.J., Elk's Head, Aqua, Blob Top 12.00
Edmott's Porter & Ale, Blue Green, Blob Top, Squat 60.00
Ekhardt & Becker, Detroit, Embossed, 1910s 6.00
El Dorado Brewing Co., Stockton, Cal., Amber, Blob Top 25.00
Elk Brewing Co., Kittaning, Pa., Elk Head, Aqua, Blob Top, Pt. ....5.00 to 12.00
Elk Brewing Co., Kittaning, Pa., Embossed Elk, Blob Top, Qt. 15.00
Emmerling Brewing Co., Embossed, Pre-Prohibition, 12 Oz. 4.50
Empire Bottling Works, Lancaster, Pa., Blob Top 7.00
Empire Bottling Works, Lancaster, Pa., Crown Top 3.00
Erie Brg. Co., Erie, Pa., Amber, Blob Top 5.00
Escanaba Brewing Co., Amber, Blob Top, 12 In. 15.00
Excelsior Lager Beer, C On Base, Aqua, Blob Top, Lopsided, Pt. 35.00
Excelsior Lager Beer, Plattsburg, N.Y., Deep Aqua, Stopper, Pt. 40.00
F. & M. Schaefer Brewing Co., N.Y., Aqua, Stopper, 1842, Pt. 100.00
F. Engle, Lancaster, Pa., Aqua, Blob Top 7.00
F. Herman, New Haven, Ct., Aqua, Blob Top, 9 In. 15.00
F.J. McCarthy, Havre Street, East Boston, Mass., Amber, Blob Top, Pt. 10.00
Falstaff Lemp, St. Louis, Embossed, Pre-Prohibition, 12 Oz. 11.00
Ferro-Phos Brewing, Embossed, Pre-Prohibition, 14 Oz. 4.50
Finnegan & Fitzsimmons, Fall River, Mass., Blob Top 15.00
Fitzgerald Bros., Troy, N.Y., Amber, Blob Top 4.00
Foss-Schneider Brewing Co., Cincinnati, O., Aqua, Blob Top 10.00
Frank Fehr Brewing Co., Louisville, Ky., Amber, Blob Top, Qt. ....15.00 to 20.00
Frank Goeltz, Essington, Pa., Crown Top 3.00
Frank McKeone, Phoenixville, Pa., Aqua, Crown Top 3.00
Frank McKeone, Phoenixville, Pa., Lady's Leg, Amber, Blob Top 60.00
Frank McKeone, Phoenixville, Pa., Light Green, Blob Top 6.00
Fred Kobolt Jr., N. 6th St., Amethyst, Blob Top, Stopper 12.00
Fredericksburg Bottling Co., S.F., Olive Green, Applied Top, Qt. 45.00
Fredericksburg Brewery, Red Amber, Qt. 50.00
Fresno Brewing Co., Fresno, Amber, Qt. 8.00
G. Snyder, Cold Spring N.Y., Honey Amber, Citron, Pt. 25.00
G.F. Hewitt, Theater Building, Stoneware, Salt Glaze, Gray, 1855-1875, 10 In. 120.00
G.F. Washurn, Stoneware, Blue Letters 60.00
G.F.T.T., Stoneware, Debossed Blue Letters, Qt. 25.00
G.W. Hoxie's Premium, Green, Applied Collar Mouth, 1855-1865, 6 1/2 In. ....165.00 to 180.00
G.W. Hoxie's Premium, Green, Squat, Pt. 40.00
Gambrinus Brewing Co., Portland, Or., Amber, Tooled Mouth, 1880-1900, 11 1/4 In. .. 35.00
Gambrinus Stock Co., Cincinnati, O., Amber, Round Slug, Blob Top, Pt. ....10.00 to 15.00
Geo. Goganzer, Philada., Amethyst, Blob Top 8.00
Geo. Goganzer, Philada., Blob Top, Stopper 12.00
George Bechtel Brewing Co., Stapleton, Staten Island, Soldier, Aqua, Blob Top 15.00
George Bechtel Brewing Co., Excelsior, Stapleton, Staten Island, Knight, Blob Top ... 60.00
George Ch. Gemuenden Brown Stout, Blue Emerald Green, IP, 1845-1855, 6 7/8 In. .. 90.00
George Ringele, Phila., Blob Top 6.00
Gerhard Lang's Bottling Works, Buffalo, N.Y., Blob Top 15.00
Glennon's Beer, Pittston, Pa., Embossed 3.50
Gold Crest, Storz Brewing, Label, 1940s, 12 Oz. 7.00
Golden Gate Bottling Works, San Francisco, Bear, Amber, Stopper, Split ......50.00 to 75.00
Golden Gate Bottling Works, San Francisco, Ca., Yellow Amber, 1910, 7 3/4 In. 55.00
Gruber & Sons, Philadelphia, Aqua, Blob Top 6.00
H. Bohn, Branford, Ct., Blob Top, 9 1/4 In. ....5.00 to 7.00
H. Denhalter, Salt Lake City, Utah, Aqua, Applied Mouth, 1880s, 7 1/4 In. 220.00
H. Floto's Lager Beer, Reading, Pa. 25.00
H. Ingermanns XXX Ale, Cambridge City, Ind.,Yellow Amber, Blob Top, Squat, Qt. .. 130.00
H. Ingermanns XXX Ale, Cambridge City, Ind., Amber, Stopper, Blob Top, Squat, Qt. ... 100.00
H. Ricketts & Co., Liverpool, Bristol, 3-Piece Mold, Olive Green, Pontil, Qt. 45.00
H.F. Krieger, Bottler, Louisville, Ky., Light Amber, Blob Top, Closure, 11 1/2 In. 40.00
Hartmann & Fehrenbach Brewing Co., Wilmington, Del., Winged Horse, Crown Top 6.00

Harvard Brewing, Lowell, U.S.A., Amber, Blob Top, 1902, Pt. 12.00
Heiss, Philadelphia, Star, Cobalt Blue, IP 185.00
Henry Bohn, Branford, Conn., Dean Foster & Co., Aqua, Blob Top, 9 1/2 In. 15.00
Henry Bohn, Registered, Branford, Conn., 8-Sided, Light Aqua, Blob Top, 9 In. 15.00
Henry Braun Beer Bottling, Oakland, Calif., Amber, Tooled Mouth, 7 3/4 In. 55.00
Henry Elias Brewing Co., New York, Aqua, Blob Top 5.00
Henry K. Wampole & Co., Philada, Orange Amber, Bulbous Neck, Inside Haze, 8 In. . . .   6.00
Herman Goring, Green, Lightning Stopper 85.00
Home Brewing Co., Braddock, Pa., Amber, Qt. 30.00
Home Brewing Co., Indianapolis, Ind., Amber, Blob Top, Qt. . . . . .15.00 to 20.00
Home Brewing Co., Indianapolis, Ind., Monogram, Amber, Blob Top, Pt. 10.00
Home Brewing Co., Indianapolis, Ind., Monogram, Aqua, Blob Top, Pt. 10.00
Home Brewing Co., Indianapolis, Ind., Round Slug, Blob Top 15.00
Homestead Brewing Co., Homestead, Pa., Amber, Blob Top, Pt. 15.00
Homestead Brewing Co., Homestead, Pa., Golden Amber, Blob Top, Qt. 30.00
Honolulu Brewing & Malting Co., Ltd., Honolulu, T.H., Aqua, Crown Top, 12 Oz. . . .   15.00
Honolulu Brewing & Malting Co., Ltd., Honolulu, T.H., Aqua, Crown Top, 16 Oz. 20.00
Hoosick Bottling Works 1892, Hoosick Falls, N.Y., Amber, Blob Top, Pt. 20.00
Howe & Streeter, Schlitz Milwaukee Lager, Manchester, N.H., Original Bail, Stopper . .   100.00
Huntington Brewing Co., Amber, Crown Top, 9 1/4 In. 9.00
I. Sutton & Co., Covington, Ky., Blue Aqua, 12-Sided, IP, 8 3/8 In. 935.00
I.C. Clark Bottlers, Atlanta, Ga., Aqua, Marble, Slug, 9 1/4 In.   15.00
Indiana Brewing Association, Marion, Embossed, 1920s, 20 Oz. 5.00
Indianapolis Brewing Co., Indianapolis, Ind., Amber, Blob Top, Qt. 15.00
Indianapolis Brewing Co., Indianapolis, Ind., Aqua, Blob Top, Qt. 15.00
Indianapolis Brewing Co., Indianapolis, Ind., Qt. 22.00
Indianapolis Brewing Co., Indianapolis, U.S.A., Aqua, Winged Lady, Marble, 9 1/2 In.   15.00
Iroquois, Brewing Co., Buffalo, N.Y., Indian In Headdress 6.00
Iroquois, Buffalo, Indian In Headdress, Amber, Blob Top 50.00
Iroquois Beverage, Indian Head, Pre-Prohibition, 12 Oz. 11.00
Iroquois Brewing Co., Buffalo, Amber, Indian Chief, Crown Top, 9 1/2 In. 25.00
J. Gahm & Son, Boston, Mass., Amethyst, Blob Top, Bail & Porcelain Stopper, 9 1/4 In.   12.00
J. Gahm Beer, Charlestown, Mass., Straw Yellow, Olive 90.00
J. Straubmuller, Philada, Aqua, Crown Top 3.00
J.F. Koenig, Phila., Pa., Blob Top, Stopper 12.00
J.H. Brickel, Waterbury, Conn., Aqua, Blob Top, 9 1/4 In. 15.00
J.H. Myers, Bainbridge, Pa., Aqua, Crown Top 3.00
J.J. Steinhilber, Flushing, Pa., Aqua, Blob Top, Stopper 12.00
J.M. Ingermanns XXX Ale, Cambridge City, Ind., Dark Amber, Stopper, Blob Top, Qt. .   100.00
J.W. Thomas, Stoneware, Blue Letters, 7 1/2 In. 60.00
Jackson Brewing, Green, Man On Horse, Crown Top, 9 In. 10.00
Jacob Hornung, Philada, Aqua, Blob Top, Stopper 10.00
Jacob Jocker's, Philadelphia, Pa., Aqua, Stopper, 9 1/2 In. 50.00
Jacob Ruppert Brewers, New York, Green Aqua, Crown Top, Embossed 3.00
Jacob Ruppert's New York Lager, Trademark, Bottle Not To Be Sold, Aqua, Blob Top   15.00
James Hyman, Chester, Pa., Blob Top 7.00
James Hyman, Chester, Pa., Blob Top, Stopper 12.00
Jas. Watson, Philada., Brown Stout, Flower, Aqua, Squat 50.00
Johann Hoff, Dark Olive, Embossed Shoulder, Cork, 5 3/8 In.   8.00
John Campbell, Philadelphia, Camel, Aqua, Blob Top, Pt. 25.00
John F. Betz & Son, Philada, Script, Aqua, Crown Top 3.00
John Gephardt, Boston, Mass, Forest Green, Stopper, Pt. 80.00
John Getz & Son, York, Penna., Crown Top 5.00
John H. Young, Philada., Aqua, Blob Top 10.00
John Hohenadel, Falls Brewery, Phila., Aqua, Crown Top, ABM 4.00
John Kauffman Brewing Co., Cincinnati, O., Round Slug, Aqua, Blob Top 15.00
John Maher, Fernwood, Pa., Aqua, Crown Top 3.00
John Pforr, Chicago, Green 50.00
John Rapp & Son, San Francisco, Calif., Bail, Stopper, Qt. 7.00
John Stanton Brewing Co., Troy, N.Y., Yellow Green, Blob Top 60.00
John Tons, Stockton, Cal., Amber, Blob Top, Qt. 27.00
John Wagner Brewing Co., Sidney, Ohio, Amber, Blob Top, Qt. 15.00
Jos. Serwazi, Manayunk, Pa., Aqua, Blob Top 10.00

Jos. Straubmuller, Philadelphia, Aqua, Blob Top 4.00
Joseph Hess, Philada., Aqua, Blob Top 7.00
Joseph Hess, Philada., Aqua, Blob Top, Stopper 10.00
Joseph Schlitz, Milwaukee, Embossed, Label, 1910s 5.00
JSP, Monogram, Teal Blue, Sloping Collar Mouth, Cork, 9 In. 25.00
Kahny & Burbacher, Bottlers, Redding, Cal., 3-Piece Mold, Amber, Tooled Top, 1/2 Pt . 45.00
Keystone Bottling Company, Reading, Pa., Lady's Leg, Amber, Blob Top 60.00
Kiehl & Keefer, Lancaster, Pa., Aqua, Mug Base, Blob Top ....5.00 to 7.00
Kiehl & Keefer, Lancaster, Pa., Blob Top 7.00
Koppitz-Melchers Brewing Co., Registered Detroit, Mich., Star, Aqua, Blob Top 20.00
L. Hillemann, Phila., Aqua, Crown Top, ABM 3.00
L. Hillemann, Philada., Script, Blob Top, Stopper 10.00
L. Hillemann, Philadelphia, Pa., Porcelain Stopper, 9 1/4 In. 45.00
L. Meegan, Sand Bank, N.Y., Amber, Blob Top, Qt. ....30.00 to 40.00
L. Mueller, Phila., Blob Top 6.00
Leisy Brewing Co., Green, Mug, Pt. 55.00
Leo Braun, New Haven, Conn., Aqua, Blob Top, 9 In. 15.00
Lewistown Brew, Label, 1910, 12 Oz. 40.00
M. Conway, Philada., Crown Top 3.00
M. Dippold Oriental, Stopper, Pt. 15.00
M.B.C.V., Perth & Fremantle Bottle Exchange Co., Ltd., Aqua, Australia, 12 In. 10.00
Mathie Brewing Co., Los Angeles, Amber, Blob Top, Qt. ....20.00 to 40.00
Max Blumberg, Chester, Pa., Star, Aqua, Blob Top 13.00
McAvoy Brew Co., Malt Marrow, Chicago, Ill., Embossed Base, Amber, Blob Top 10.00
McCarty & Co., East Boston, Mass., Honey Amber, Pt. 20.00
Meadville Brewing Co., Meadville, Pa., Eagle, Yellow Amber, Crown Top 6.00
Men Around A Table Playing Cards, Long Neck, Yellow Olive, Germany, 1910, 14 In. 100.00
Metzler Bros. Brewery, N.Y., Aqua, Blob Top, Pt. 20.00
Moerlein Old Jug Lager Krug Bier, Stoneware, Black Transfer, Cherubs, 8 1/2 In. 40.00
Mokelumne Hill Brewery, Amber, Tooled Lip, 1890-1900, 11 In. ....35.00 to 90.00
Monumental Brewing Co., Baltimore, Md., Monument, Aqua, ABM, Crown Top 3.00
Murphy's Bottling Works, Port Jervis, N.Y., Blue Aqua, Porcelain Stopper, Pt. 20.00
N.G. Gurnsey & Co., Keene, N.H., Aqua, Blob Top, Stopper, Pt. 20.00
Narragansett Brewing Co., Providence, R.I., Famous Lager & Ale, Crown Top, 9 1/4 In. 2.00
National Bottling Co., San Francisco, Ca., A.D.B. Lang, Eagle, Amber, Blob Top 75.00
National Bottling Co., San Francisco, Eagle, Qt. 35.00
New Freeland Brewing Co., Freeland, Pa., Grass Green, ABM, 9 1/2 In. 10.00
Northampton Brewing & Bottling Co., Northampton, Pa., Blob Top 5.00
Norton Bros., Amesbury, Mass., Pink SCA, Blob Top, Stopper, Pt. 35.00
Nyman's Pure Malt Leader For Temperance Drink, Chicago, Flag Logo 40.00
OBC, Mauch Chunk, Pa., On Base, Lady's Leg, Amber, 7 In. 40.00
Obermeyer & Liebmanns Bottling Dept., New York City, Amber, Bail, Stopper, Pt. . 35.00
Old Jug Bier, Stoneware, Logo, Label, Pre-Prohibition 5.50
Oriental Bottling Department, Philada., Aqua, Blob Top 7.00
Oriental Bottling Department, Philada., Blob Top, Stopper 12.00
Oscar Altpeter, Baraboo, Wis., Aqua, Round Slug, Blob Top 20.00
P. Ebner, Wil., Del., Aqua, Blob Top 3.00
P. Harrington, Milwaukee Lager, Manchester, N.H., Honey Amber, Blob Top, Pt. ..10.00 to 25.00
P. Mansfield, Stoneware, Gray, Cobalt Blue, Blob Top, 1/2 Pt. 120.00
P. McGuinness, Utica, N.Y., Eagle, Aqua, Round Slug, Blob Top 40.00
P.F. Cullin, Chester, Pa., Aqua, Blob Top 12.00
Pabst, Milwaukee, A.M. Finkbeiner, Philada., Pa. 20.00
Pabst Blue Ribbon, Milwaukee, Wis., Orange Amber, Porcelain Stopper, Pt. 50.00
Paul Pohl, Chicago, Medium Olive Green, Pt. 85.00
Paul Weil, New Haven, Ct., Light Aqua, Blob Top, 9 In. 10.00
Peaslee's Ale, Dubuque, Ia., Black Glass, Qt. 150.00
People's Brewing Company, Embossed, Pre-Prohibition, 12 Oz. 8.00
Perkiomen Valley Brewery, Green Lane, Pa., Aqua, Wire Stopper, Squat, 7 In. 75.00
Peter Hand's, Label, 1950s, 12 Oz. 3.50
Peter Hauck & Co., Harrison, N.J., Aqua, Crown Top, ABM 3.00
Peter Mugler, Brewer, Sisson, Cal., 4-Piece Mold, Amber, 1/2 Pt. 45.00
Pfeiffer's Jumbo Beer, 1950s, 32 Oz. 11.00
Phil Scheuermann Brewery, Hancock, Mich., Amber, Blob Top, Qt. 15.00

Phil Scheuermann Brewery, Hancock, Mich., Amber, Round, 1900-1915, 12 In. 10.00
Philadelphia XXX Porter & Ale, M. Flanagan, Petersburg, Va., Green, Olive Tone, IP . 250.00
Philadelphia XXX Porter & Ale, Yellow Olive Green, Blob Top, 1865, 6 3/4 In. 95.00
Philip Walker, Chester, Pa., Script, Amethyst, Blob Top 8.00
Phillipp Zum Weiss Beer Brewery Philadelphia, Stoneware, Orange Brown, 7 3/8 In. 90.00
Phoenix Bottling Works, Buffalo, N.Y., Embossed Phoenix Bird, Blob Top 15.00
Quandt Brewing Co., Mercury, Swirled Base, Blob Top, Stopper, Pt. 30.00
Quandt Brewing Co., Troy, N.Y., Embossed Figure, Blob Top 20.00
Quandt Brewing Co., Troy, N.Y., Running Indian, Aqua, Pt. 35.00
R. Robinson, 376 Bowery, N.Y., XX, Blue Green, Blob Top, Squat 30.00
R.C. & T., New York Brown Stout, Blue Green, IP, Polished 70.00
Raffaele Dabruzzo, Philada., Pa., Blob Top, Stopper 15.00
Rainier, Fresno Bottling, Amber, Pt. 60.00
Rainier, Seattle, Wa., Amber, Tooled Lip, 1890-1910, 5 1/2 In. 65.00
Raspiller Brewing Co., West Berkeley, Eagle, 1/2 Pt. 50.00
Raspiller Brewing Co., West Berkley, Amber, Blob Top, Qt. 130.00
Reading Brewing Co., Reading, Pa., Crown Top, ABM 3.00
Reichard & Weaver Pilsener, Wilkes-Barre, Yellow Green, ABM, 9 1/2 In. 10.00
Reno Brewing Co., Reno, Nev., Amber, Blob Top 65.00
Richmond Bottling Works, California, Qt. 20.00
Richmond Brewing Co., Richmond, Va., Star With Hops & Grain, Aqua 50.00
Robert Portner Brewing Co., Alexandria, Va., Olive Green, Blob Top, 1880-1895, 10 In. 165.00
Robertson & Co., Phila., California Pop Beer, Yellow Olive Amber, Blob Top, Squat . . . 160.00
Robinson & Moore, Wil., Del., Aqua, Blob Top 9.00
Rock Island Brewing Co., Rock Island, Ill., Stopper, Picnic 35.00
Roessle Brewery, Boston, Premium Lager, Blob Top, Pt. 15.00
Roxborough Bottling, Roxborough, Pa., ABM, Crown, Qt. 7.00
Royal Ruby Anchor Glass, On Base, Ruby Red, ABM, Qt., 9 5/8 In. 12.00
Rudolph's, Philada., Blob Top, Stopper 10.00
S. Erven & Co., Bottlers, Philada., Brown Stout, Light Blue Green, IP, 1845-55, 6 7/8 In. 120.00
S. Shapiro, Chester, Pa., Aqua, Crown Top, ABM 3.00
S.S.B., Property Of Silver Springs Brewery, Victoria, B.C., Amber, c.1920, 9 1/8 In. 20.00
Samuel Trout, Philadelphia, Pa., Aqua, Stopper, Pt. 20.00
Schafer-Meyer Brg. Co., Louisville, Ky., Amber, Blob Top, Qt. 20.00
Schick & Fett, Reading, Pa., Aqua, Blob Top 5.00
Schlitz, Aqua, Blob Top, Qt. 20.00
Schlitz, Gold Amber, Blob Top, Qt. 40.00
Schlitz, Royal Ruby, Label, 1950s, 7 Oz. 12.00
Schmidt's Bottling Works, Hanover, Pa., Aqua, Mug Base, Crown Top 3.00
Schmulbach Brewing Co., Wheeling, West Va., Eagle, Blob Top, 11 In. 30.00
Schroeder's B.W.B. Co., St. Louis, Mo., Deep Green, Blob Top, Pt. 65.00
Seneca Club Export Brew, Utica, N.Y., Clyde Glassworks, Applied Top, Pt. 35.00
Smethport Bottling Works, A.J. Warshafsky, Smethport, Pa., Blob Top 10.00
Snyder, Lebanon, Pa., On Base, Lady's Leg, Amber, Pony, 6 3/4 In. 40.00
Sprenger Brew. Co., Registered, Amber, Crown Top 4.00
Sprenger Brew. Co., Script, Aqua, Crown Top 7.00
Springfield Breweries, Registered, Springfield, O., Round Slug, Amber 10.00

Beer, Tam O' Shanter Ale,
Dry Hopped, Rochester
N.Y., Green, Plaid Label,
11 1/2 In.

Beer, Utica Club Pilsener
Beer, Utica, N.Y., Amber, Red,
Blue & White Label, 9 1/4 In.

Springfield Breweries, Springfield, O., Amber, Blob Top, Qt. 10.00
Springfield Breweries, Springfield, Ohio, Qt. 7.00
St. Marys Brewing Co., St. Marys, Pa., Yellow, Blob Top 20.00
Stoddard, Dot On Base, Olive Amber, Blob Top, Squat 40.00
Stoddard Ale, X On Base, Yellow To Red Amber, Elongated Bulged Neck 75.00
Stoll Brewing Co., Troy, N.Y., Embossed Eagle, Aqua Stopper, 9 In. 18.00
Stroudsburg Brewing Co., Hutchinson 7.50
T.J. Murphy, Bridgeport, Ct., Blob Top, Wire Bail & Stopper, 9 In. 10.00
Tacoma Bottling Co., San Francisco, 1/2 Pt. 15.00
Tam O' Shanter Ale, Dry Hopped, Rochester, N.Y., Green, Plaid Label, 11 1/2 In. .*Illus* 5.00
Tennant's Sheffield, W In Shield, Light Strawberry Pink Puce, England, Pt. 35.00
Terre Haute Bottling Co., Aqua, Blob Top, Pony 15.00
Terre Haute Brewing, Aqua, Crown Top 8.00
Terre Haute Brewing Co., Terre Haute, Ind., Aqua, Blob Top, Qt. 15.00
Thompson Bottler Of Stout For Invalids, Blyth, Stoneware, White, Black Stencil, 8 In. 58.00
Thos. L. Reilly, Grays Ferry Rd., Phila., Crown Top 3.00
Trenton Brewing Co., Trenton, N.J., Red Amber, Stopper, Pt. 100.00
Trenton Brewing Co., Trenton, N.J., Tiger Head, Amber, Blob Top 60.00
Turtle Bay Brewery, Oceanic, N.J., Man, Riding Turtle, Blue, Aqua, Pt. 50.00
Tweedie Red Hand, San Francisco, Green, Hand Picture, Qt. 715.00
U.S. Bottling Co., John Fausner, San Francisco, Cal., Blob Top 40.00
Union, Shoofly, Pt. 180.00
Utica Club Pilsener Beer, Utica, N.Y., Amber, Red, Blue & White Label, 9 1/4 In. *Illus* 7.00
Val Blatz, Milwaukee, Aqua, Embossed Star, Blob Top 15.00
Vallance, Widemouth, Stoneware, Brown & Tan 35.00
W. Kuebler's Sons, Easton, Pa., Orange Amber, Crown Top 3.00
W. Massey New Orleans, Stoneware, Salt Glaze, Gray, 1870-1885, 6 1/2 In. 145.00
W.H. Cawley Co., Somerville Dover Flemington, N.J., Lime Citron, Blob Top 45.00
W.H. Cawley Co., Somerville, N.J., Light Yellow Green, Blob Top, Stopper 40.00
Wacker & Birk, Aqua, Crown Top 6.00
Wacker Brewery, Lancaster, Pa. 4.00
Wall & Heverin, Auburn, N.Y., Orange Amber, Crown Top 6.00
Walter-Raupfer Brewing Co., Columbia City, Ind., Eagle, Aqua, Blob Top, Qt. 20.00
Weber's Weiss Beer, John Worf, Rondout, N.Y., Orange Amber, Blob Top, Squat . .30.00 to 40.00
Weisbrod & Hess, Oriental Bottling Department, Philadelphia, Blob Top 7.00
Weiss Beer, John Worf, Rondout, N.Y., Amber, Blob Top, Squat, Pt. 25.00
Weiss Beer, St. Louis, Mo., Stopper 60.00
Weiss Beer, Thomas Uleckie, Shenandoah, Pa., BIMAL, Squat, 7 In. 15.00
Weiss Bier, M.J. Ryan, Mahanoy City, Pa., Amber, Blob Top, Squat 45.00
Westford, Dark Amber, Blob Top 35.00
Wheaton & Sons, New Bedford, Mass., Whale, Seltzer Bottle, Aqua, Blob Top, Pt. 15.00
William Gebhardt, Morris, Ill., Amber, Round Slug, Blob Top 20.00
William Krebs, Congers, N.Y., Blob Top 20.00
William Pond & Co., N.Y. 80.00
Willow Springs Beer, Aqua 8.00
Wm Pfeifer, Chicago, Trademark, Amber, Porcelain Closure, Some Contents, 1895-1910 8.00
Wm. Pfeifer, Chicago, Green, Pt. 75.00
Wm. Robinson, 102 Sudbury St., Boston, Not To Be Sold, Aqua, Lightning Stopper 15.00
Wunder Bottling Co., San Francisco, Cal., Blob Top, 1/2 Pt. ....15.00 to 20.00
Yellow, Screw Top, Stopper, Qt. 30.00
York Brewing Co., York, Pa., Aqua, 1896, Blob Top 22.00
BENNINGTON, see Pottery

———————————————————————— BININGER ————————————————————————

Bininger and Company of New York City was a family-owned grocery and dry goods
store. It was founded by the 1820s and remained in business into the 1880s. The store
sold whiskey, wine, and other liquors. After a while they began bottling their products
in their own specially designed bottles. The first bottles were ordered from England but
it wasn't long before the local glass factories made the Bininger's special figural containers. Barrels, clocks, cannons, jugs, and flasks were made. Colors were usually
shades of amber, green, or puce.

BININGER, A.M. & Co., 19 Broad St., N.Y., Hammer & Star, Cannon, Amber, 12 1/2 In. .. 330.00
A.M. & Co., Bininger's Travelers Guide, Teardrop, Gold Amber, 7 In. ....220.00 to 250.00

Tired of scrubbing and scrubbing glass to remove marks from masking tape and labels? Get some commercial hand cleaner, pat some on the stain, let it stay for 30 minutes. Then rub it off with a cloth and wash the glass.

Bininger, Old Kentucky Bourbon, N.Y., 1849, Medium Amber, 9 1/2 In.

A.M. & Co., Cannon, Whiskey, Golden Amber, 1860-1880, 12 In.	525.00
A.M. & Co., Jug, Gold Amber, Applied Mouth, 1860-1880, 7 7/8 In.	275.00
A.M. & Co., Jug, New York, Medium Amber, 8 In.	230.00
A.M. & Co., Jug, No. 19 Broad St., New-York, Medium Amber, Applied Top	305.00
A.M. & Co., Jug, Yellow Olive Green, Applied Handle, 1860-1870, 8 In.	1540.00
A.M. & Co., London Dock Gin, Honey Amber, Small	200.00
A.M. & Co., N.Y., Old London Dock Gin, Root Beer, 1865, 8 In., Bin-33	150.00
A.M. & Co., New York, Square, Deep Yellow Green, Sloping Collar, 9 5/8 In.	175.00
A.M. & Co., No. 19 Broad St., N.Y., Cannon, Gold Amber, 12 1/2 In.	690.00
A.M. & Co., No. 19 Broad St., N.Y., Jug, Gold Amber, 7 In.	110.00
A.M. & Co., No. 19 Broad St., N.Y., Jug, Medium Amber, 7 3/4 In.	130.00
A.M. & Co., No. 19 Broad St., New York, Jug, Yellow Amber, 7 3/4 In.	385.00
A.M. & Co., No. 19 Broad St., New York, Medium Amber, Applied Handle	325.00
A.M. & Co., Old Kentucky 1849 Reserve Bourbon, Barrel, Golden Amber, OP, 8 In.	180.00
A.M. & Co., Old Kentucky Bourbon, Barrel, Amber, 7 3/4 In.	175.00
A.M. & Co., Old Kentucky Bourbon, Double Collar, 9 1/4 In.	255.00
A.M. & Co., Old Kentucky Reserve Bourbon, Barrel, Amber, Pontil, 8 In.	200.00
A.M. & Co., Old London Dock Gin, Deep Amber, 8 In.	165.00
A.M. & Co., Old London Dock Gin, Forest Green	160.00
A.M. & Co., Old London Dock, Yellow, Olive Tone, Applied Sloping Collar, 9 7/8 In.	195.00
A.M. & Co., Old London Dock, Yellow, Olive, Part Label, Square, 9 5/8 In.	110.00
Barrel, Light Amber, OP	210.00
Clock, Knickerbocker, N.Y., Gold Amber, Double Pontil, 6 In.	380.00
Clock, Regulator, Amber, Pontil, 5 7/8 In.	210.00
Clock, Regulator, Gold Amber, Pontil, 1840-1860, 5 7/8 In.	330.00
Clock, Regulator, Medium Amber, 1855-1870, 6 In.	2365.00
Old Kentucky Bourbon, N.Y., 1849, Medium Amber, 9 1/2 In. ....*Illus*	125.00
Old Kentucky Reserve Bourbon, A.M. Bininger & Co., Barrel, 8 In. ....220.00 to 385.00	
Peep-O-Day, Medium Amber, Double Collar, 7 5/8 In.	465.00
Traveler's Guide, N.Y., Teardrop, Amber, Applied Double Collar, 6 3/4 In.	305.00

BISCHOFF

Bischoff Company, founded in 1777 in Trieste, Italy, made fancy decanters. The modern collectible Bischoff bottles were imported into the United States from about 1950. Glass, porcelain, and stoneware decanters and figurals were made.

African Head, 1962	14.00
Alpine Pitcher, 1969	27.00
Amber Flower, 1952	32.00 to 35.00
Amber Leaf, 1952	32.00 to 35.00
Amphora, 2 Handles, 1950	25.00
Ashtray, Green Striped, 1958	12.00 to 14.00
Bell House, 1960	17.00 to 39.00
Bell Tower, 1959	20.00
Blue Gold, 1956	45.00 to 50.00
Candlestick, 1958	25.00
Candlestick, Clown, 1963	8.00
Cat, Black, 1969	20.00 to 23.00
Chariot Urn, 1966, 2 Sections	25.00

Chinese Boy Or Girl, 1962 . . . .   35.00
Christmas Tree, 1957 . . . .   55.00
Clown, Black Hair, Low, 1963 . . . .   35.00
Deer, 1969 . . . . .15.00 to 20.00
Egyptian Musician, 1963 . . . .   15.00
Floral, Canteen, 1969 . . . .   18.00
Fruit, Canteen, 1969 . . . .   20.00
Mask, Gray, 1963 . . . .   25.00
Porcelain Cameo, 1962 . . . .   20.00
Spanish Boy Or Girl, 1961 . . . .   30.00

───────────────────────── **BITTERS** ─────────────────────────

Bitters seems to have been an idea that started in Germany during the seventeenth century. A tax was levied against gin in the mid-1700s and the clever salesmen simply added some herbs to the gin and sold the mixture as medicine. Later, the medicine was made in Italy and England. Bitters is the name of this mixture. By the nineteenth century, bitters became a popular local product in America. It was usually of such a high alcoholic content that the claim that one using the product felt healthier with each sip was almost true. One brand had over 59% alcohol (about 118 proof). Although alcoholism had become a problem and social drinking was frowned upon by most proper Victorians, the soothing bitters medicine found wide acceptance. At that time there was no tax on the medicine and no laws concerning ingredients or advertising claims.

The word *bitters* must be embossed on the glass or a paper label must be affixed to the bottle for the collector to call the bottle a bitters bottle. Most date from 1862, the year of the Revenue Act tax on liquor, until 1906, the year the Food and Drug Act placed restrictions on the sale of bitters as a medicinal cure. Over 1,000 types are known. Bitters were sometimes packaged in figural bottles shaped like cabins, human figures, fish, pigs, barrels, ears of corn, drums, clocks, horses, or cannons. The bottles came in a variety of colors. They ranged from clear to milk glass, pale to deep amethyst, light aqua to cobalt blue, pale yellow to amber, and pale to dark green. A bottle found in an unusual color commands a much higher price than a clear bottle of the same shape. The numbers used in the entries in the form R-00 refer to the book *Bitters Bottles* by Carlyn Ring and W.C. Ham. Each bottle is pictured and described in detail in the book.

A. Lambert's, Philada., Olive Amber, Applied Mouth, 11 In., R-L 5.5 . . . .   800.00
A.S. Hopkins Union Stomach, Apricot Puce, Collared Mouth, 9 3/4 In., R-H178 . . . . .   525.00
African Stomach, Amber, Applied Mouth, 1880-1890, 9 5/8 In., R-A15 . . . . .85.00 to 130.00
African Stomach, Orange Amber, Applied Top, 9 5/8 In., R-A16 . . . .   55.00
African Stomach, Spruance Stanley & Co., Red Amber, 1875-1880, 9 1/2 In., R-A17 . . .   130.00
Alpenkraeuter Magenbitter, Interlaken Dennler, Torpedo, Yellow Green, 11 In., R-A33   110.00
Alpine Herb, Amber, Square, 10 In., R-A37 . . . .   175.00
Amer Picon, Philippeville, Olive Green, Lady's Leg Neck, ABM, 11 3/4 In., R-A 44.5 . .   50.00
American Life, P.E. Iler, Tiffin, Oh., Cabin, Amber, 8 7/8 In., A-49 . . . .   4730.00
Angelica Bitters Or Poor Mans Tonic, Aqua, 7 3/4 In., R-A58 . . . . .110.00 to 240.00
Angostura, Green, Shoulder & Base Embossed, BIMAL, Tooled Lip, 4 1/4 In., R-A60 . .   35.00
Angostura Bark, Eagle Liqueur Distille, Amber, 7 In., R-A68 . . . .   260.00
Appetine, Geo. Benz & Sons, St. Paul, Minn., Amber, Pat. Nov. 23 1897, 8 1/4 In., A-78   385.00
Appetine, Geo. Benz & Sons, St. Paul, Minn., Gold Amber, Labels, 3 1/2 In., R-A79 . . .   990.00
Arabian, Lawrence & Weichselbaum, Savannah, Ga., Amber, 9 3/4 In., R-A80 . . .195.00 to 360.00
Argyle, E.B. Wheelock, Amber, Applied Mouth, 1875-1885, 9 3/4 In., R-A83 . . . .135.00 to 185.00
Aromatic Orange Stomach, Berry, Demoville & Co., Amber, 10 In., R-A90 . . .550.00 to 580.00
Atwood's Jaundice, Free Sample, Aqua, 12-Sided, ABM, 4 In., R-A113 . . . .   40.00
Atwood's Jaundice, M. Carter, Aqua, 12-Sided, 6 In., R-A123 . . . .   120.00
Atwood's Quinine Tonic, Aqua, Rectangular, 8 7/16 In., R-A129 . . . . .85.00 to 90.00
Atwood's Vegetable Dyspeptic, Aqua, Tooled Mouth, Label, 6 3/4 In., R-A130 . . . . . .   90.00
Augauer, Chicago, Yellow Green, Tooled Lip, 1900-1910, 7 7/8 In., A-134 . . . .   90.00
Ayala Mexican, M. Rothenberg & Co., Red, Amber, Tooled Lip, 9 3/8 In., A-142 . . . . . .   255.00
Ayala Mexican, M. Rothenberg & Co., Yellow Amber, Tooled Lip, 9 In., A-142 . . . .   105.00
Baker's Orange Grove, Amber, Applied Collar Mouth, 9 1/2 In., R-B9 . . . . .120.00 to 415.00
Baker's Orange Grove, Emerald Green, Amber Neck & Shoulders, 9 1/2 In., R-B9 . . . .   8800.00
Baker's Orange Grove, Pink Apricot Puce, Sloping Collar, 9 1/2 In., R-B9 . . . .   660.00
Baker's Orange Grove, Red Puce, Applied Sloping Collar, 9 1/2 In., R-B9 . . . .   145.00
Baker's Orange Grove, Root Beer Amber, Sloping Collar, 9 1/2 In., R-B9 . . . .   240.00

Baker's Orange Grove, Yellow Amber, Applied Collar Mouth, 9 1/2 In., R-B9 ..330.00 to 495.00
Balsdons Golden, 1856, N.Y., Gold Amber, Applied Double Collar, 9 3/4 In., R-B15 ... 1020.00
Barrel, Black Olive Amber, Applied Blob Top, 1865-1875, 10 1/8 In. 105.00
Barrel, Cobalt Blue, 10-Rings Above, Below Center Panel, 1870-1875, 9 3/4 In. 2200.00
Barrel, Medium To Deep Sapphire Blue, Applied Mouth, 1880, 9 3/4 In. 2200.00
Barrel, Strawberry Puce, IP, 1845-1860, 9 3/4 In. 880.00
Beck's Herb, York, Pa., Amber, Applied Top, Square, 9 1/2 In., R-B46 .... 350.00
Begg's Dandelion, Amber, Square, 9 1/4 In., R-B52 .... 65.00
Beggs Dandelion, Olive Yellow, Sloping Mouth, Square, 9 1/4 In., R-B53 .... 385.00
Ben Franklin, Barrel, Blue Green, Applied Mouth, 1860, 10 In., R-F80 .... 3575.00
Ben-Hur, Amber, Square, 9 1/2 In., R-B69 ....100.00 to 128.00
Bennet's Celebrated Stomach, Gold Amber, Applied Top, 9 In., R-B73 .... 470.00
Bennet's Celebrated Stomach, Orange Amber, Applied Mouth, Square, 9 In., R-B74 . 305.00
Bennet's Wild Cherry Stomach, San Francisco, Smoky Amber, 1879, 9 In., R-B7474 . 825.00
Bennett Pieters & Co., Red Jacket, Medium Amber, Square, 9 1/2 In., R-R19 .... 85.00
Berkshire, Amann & Co., Cincinnati, O., Pig, Variant, Amber, 9 1/2 In., R-B81 .... 1375.00
Berlin Magen, S.B. Rothenberg, Sole Agent, U.S., Gray Blue Milk Glass, 9 In., R-B82 .. 100.00
Big Bill Best, Amber, Tooled Mouth, Labels, 1900-1910, 12 1/8 In., R-B95 .....100.00 to 195.00
Big Bill Best, Fat Man, Figural, Amber, Tooled Lip, 11 1/2 In. 200.00
Bismarck, W.H. Muller, Gold Amber, Square, 7 1/4 In., R-B106 ....60.00 to 65.00
Bodeker's Constitution, Flask, Strapside, Amber, Tooled Mouth, 6 3/4 In., R-B132 ... 305.00
Boneco Stomach, Paper Labels, Cork, Contents, 9 3/8 In. 255.00
Bourbon Whiskey, Barrel, Cherry Puce, Applied Mouth, 9 1/4 In., R-B171 .....165.00 to 200.00
Bourbon Whiskey, Barrel, Pink Topaz, 9 1/4 In., R-B171 .... 4510.00
Bourbon Whiskey, Barrel, Smoky Apricot Puce, Applied Mouth, 9 1/4 In., R-B171 .... 880.00
Bourbon Whiskey, Barrel, Strawberry Puce, 9 1/4 In., R-B171 ....240.00 to 545.00
Bouvier Buchu, Bouvier Specialty, Louisville, Ky., Amber, ABM, 10 1/2 In., R-B172 .. 605.00
Boyer's Stomach, Cincinnati, Picture Of Lady's Leg, 11 In., R-B184 .... 100.00
Brady's Family, Gold Amber, Applied Sloping Collar, Square, 9 1/2 In., R-B193 .... 85.00
Brobst & Rentschler, Reading, Pa., Barrel, Yellow Amber, Tooled Mouth, 10 In. 470.00
Brophy's Bitters, Nokomis, Illinois, Moon & Star, Aqua, 7 1/2 In., R-B217 ......75.00 to 100.00
Brown & Drake Catawba, Binghamton, N.Y., Root Beer, Lady's Leg, 11 3/8 In., R-C81 . 12100.00
Brown's Aromatic, Hannibal, Mo., Aqua, Applied Top, 8 3/4 In., R-B219 .... 300.00
Brown's Castilian, Amber, Applied Mouth, 11 1/4 In., R-B221 .... 120.00
Brown's Celebrated Indian Herb, H. Pharazyn, Phila., Gold Amber, 12 In. ...880.00 to 1430.00
Brown's Celebrated Indian Herb, Patented 1867, Chocolate Amber, 12 In., R-B223 .. 5280.00
Brown's Celebrated Indian Herb, Patented 1867, Amber, 12 1/4 In., R-B223 .550.00 to 700.00
Brown's Celebrated Indian Herb, Patented 1868, Amber, 12 In., R-B225 .....465.00 to 660.00
Brown's Celebrated Indian Herb, Patented 1868, Yellow Olive, 12 In., R-B225 ..... 5060.00
Brown's Celebrated Indian Herb, Patented Feb. 11, 1868, Yellow Amber, R-B226 *Illus* 2530.00
Brown's Iron, Yellow Olive, Applied Double, 8 5/8 In., R-B231 .... 230.00
Bryant's Stomach, Lady's Leg, Forest Green, 8-Sided, 12 5/8 In., R-B243 .... 8000.00
Bryant's Stomach, Lady's Leg, Olive Green, 8-Sided, 12 5/8 In., R-B243 .... 7425.00
Buhrer's Gentian, S. Buhrer Proprietor, Yellow Amber, Square, 9 In., R-B252 ...115.00 to 130.00
Buhrer's Gentian, Yellow Amber, Applied Sloping Collar, 8 1/4 In., R-B251 .... 200.00
Burdock Blood, Buffalo, NY, Aqua, Partial Label, 8 1/2 In., R-B262 .... 28.00
Burdock Blood, T. Milburn & Co., Toronto, Ont., Aqua, Rectangular, 4 1/4 In., R-B265 . 75.00
Burdock Blood, T. Milburn & Co., Toronto, Ont., Aqua, Rectangular, 8 1/4 In., R-B264 . 85.00
Burkhart's Homestead, Fond Du Lac, Wis., Amber, Tooled Mouth, 9 In., B-269 ..... 265.00
Burton's Ginger Wine, Aqua, Tooled Mouth, 4 1/8 In., R-B274 .... 550.00
Burton's Stomach, Amber, Applied Sloping Collar Mouth, 8 7/8 In., R-B275 .... 120.00
Byrne, see Bitters, Professor Geo. J. Byrne
C.G. Gates & Co., Life Of Man, Smoky Sapphire Blue, Label, 8 1/4 In., R-G7 .... 210.00
C.H. Swain's Bourbon, Amber, Applied Topsquare, 9 In., R-S227 .... 110.00
C.W. Roback's, see Bitters, Dr. C.W. Roback's
Cabin, see Bitters, Drake's Plantation; Bitters, Golden; Bitters, Kelly's Old Cabin;
Bitters, Old Homestead Wild Cherry
Caldwell's Herb, Great Tonic, Amber, IP, Applied Collar Mouth, 12 3/8 In., R-C8 220.00 to 305.00
Caldwell's Herb, Great Tonic, Medium Amber, IP, Sloping Collar, 12 3/4 In., R-C7 .... 160.00
California Cocktail, Acme Wine Co., Lady's Leg, Amber, Partial Label, 13 In. 65.00
California Sherry Wine, Amber, Label, BIMAL, Contents, 12 1/4 In. 55.00
California Wine, Amber, Square, 9 In., R-M69L 90.00
California Wine, Lady's Leg, Medium Amber, 1870, 12 1/4 In., R-C24 .... 230.00

Bitters, Brown's
Celebrated
Indian Herb,
Patented Feb. 11,
1868, Yellow
Amber, R-B226

To ship small pieces of glass, try this trick. Put the glass in a Styrofoam cup, then wrap in bubble wrap or several layers of paper. Stuff sides and bottom of a large box with Styrofoam trays. Then put the antiques on the trays. Pack more Styrofoam around them. Maybe you can get extra trays at your grocery store.

Calisaya, Burlington, Vt., Amber, 10 In., R-C27 .... 125.00
Cannon's Dyspeptic, Cannon Ball Corners, Gold Amber, 10 In., R-C33 .... 3575.00
Canteen, John Hart & Co., Lancaster, Pa., Medium Blue Green, 9 7/8 In., R-C34 ...... 1595.00
Canton, Star, Lady's Leg, Amber, Embossed, 12 1/4 In., R-C35 .... 375.00
Capuziner Stomach, Amber, Label, Square, 8 1/4 In., R-C41 .... 465.00
Caracas, E. Eising & Co., New York, Red Amber, 8 3/4 In., R-C44 .... 75.00
Carlsbader, Crown, SCA, 10 In., R-C50 .... 110.00
Carmeliter Stomach, New York, Yellow Olive Green, 9 1/8 In., R-C54 .... 165.00 to 330.00
Caroni, Amber, Sample, 5 In., R-C61 .... 135.00
Caroni, Green, Tooled Top, 5 1/16 In., R-C60 .... 75.00
Catawba Wine Grapes, Green, Square, 9 3/8 In., R-C85 .... 3300.00
Celebrated Crown, Amber, Applied Mouth, 8 7/8 In., R-C93 .... 165.00
Celebrated Nectar Stomach Bitters & Nerve Tonic, Green, Square, 9 3/4 In., R-C99 1540.00
Celery, S. Cty. W. Co., Round, 5 1/2 In., R-C104 .... 35.00
Chalmer's Catawba Wine Trademark, Aqua, Applied Mouth, 11 3/4 In., R-C119 ... 550.00
Cherry Cordial, Yellow Amber, Tooled Mouth, 9 In., R-C137 .... 150.00
Clarke's, Vegetable Sherry Wine, 75 Cents, Aqua, 11 3/4 In., R-C159 .... 425.00
Clarke's Compound Mandrake, Aqua, 7 3/4 In., R-C151 .... 75.00
Clarke's Sherry Wine, Aqua, Applied Mouth, 8 In., R-C165 .... 185.00
Clarke's Sherry Wine, Rockland, Me., Aqua, 9 5/8 In., R-C162 .... 125.00
Clarke's Sherry Wine, Sharon, Mass., Deep Aqua, Applied Mouth, 9 1/2 In., R-C163 .. 165.00
Clarke's Vegetable Sherry Wine, Only 70 Cts, Blue Aqua, OP, 11 3/5 In., R-C157 .... 165.00
Clarke's Vegetable Sherry Wine, Sharon, Mass., Aqua, 12 1/4 In., R-C156 .... 90.00
Clarke's Vegetable Sherry Wine, Sharon, Mass., Aqua, 14 In., R-C155 .... 425.00
Cliffs Aromatic, Joseph Clifford, Proprietor, Amber, Tooled Mouth, 10 In., R-C173.9 ... 55.00
Coca, Indian Carrying Man, Emerald Green, Cylindrical, 10 5/8 In., R-C179 .... 385.00
Cognac, S. Steinfeld, Olive Green, Applied Double Collar Mouth, 11 In., R-C187 ...... 440.00
Colombo Peptic, Amber, Square, 9 In., R-C200 .... 30.00
Commander's Aromatic, New Orleans, Amber, Tooled Mouth, 11 In., R-C205 .... 190.00
Comus Stomach, Cierc Bros. & Co. Limited, Amber, Square, 9 In., R-C212 .... 165.00
Congress, Gold Amber, Tooled Sloping Mouth, Rectangular, 9 1/4 In., R-C216 ...130.00 to 185.00
Constitution, 1964, Seward & Bentley, Buffalo, N.Y., Gold Amber, 9 1/4 In., R-C223 .. 1000.00
Constitution, Seaward & Bentley, Buffalo, N.Y., Amber, Rectangular, 9 1/4 In., R-C223 525.00
Cumberland, Nashville, Tenn., Amber, Applied Mouth, 9 7/8 In., R-C256 .... 635.00
Curtis & Perkins Wild Cherry, Aqua, Label, Applied Collar, 6 7/8 In., R-C262 .100.00 to 145.00
Curtis Cordial Calisaya, Great Stomach Bitters, Amber, 11 3/4 In., R-C261 ...855.00 to 1350.00
David Andrews Vegetable Jaundice, Providence, R.I., Aqua, Tombstone, 8 In., R-A57 . 385.00
De Witt's Stomach, Chicago, Amber, BIMAL, Square, 9 1/4 In., R-D64 .... 40.00
De Witts Stomach, Amber, Strapside, 7 1/2 In., R-D66 .... 65.00
De Witts Stomach, Chicago, Amber, Peened Out Variant, Strapside, 9 1/2 In., R-D64 .. 85.00
DeKuyper, Orange, Olive Green, Label, 7 3/4 In., R-D40L 25.00
Devil Cert Stomach, 4 In., R-D59 .... 40.00
Didier's, Gold Amber, Tooled Mouth, Rectangular, 7 7/8 In., R-D72 .... 95.00
Digestine, Medium Amber, Tooled Mouth, 3 3/8 In., R-D74 .... 855.00
Dingens Napoleon Cocktail, Banjo Shape, SCA, IP, 10 1/2 In., R-N3 .... 5775.00

Dingens' Napoleon Cocktail, Lady's Leg, Banjo Yellow Olive Amber, 9 1/2 In., R-N4 .   5500.00
Doyles Hop, Yellow Amber, 9 5/8 In., R-D93 . . . . .45.00 to 75.00
Doyles Hop, 1872, Yellow Olive, Applied Double Collar, 9 3/4 In., R-D93 . . . .   660.00
Doyles Hop, Yellow Green, Applied Mouth, 9 5/8 In., R-D93 . . . .   275.00
Dr. A.S. Hopkins Union Stomach, Amber, Sample, 4 3/4 In., R-H183 . . . .   300.00
Dr. A.S. Hopkins Union Stomach, Hartford, Conn., Yellow Olive, 9 3/4 In., R-H180 . .   305.00
Dr. A.S. Hopkins Union Stomach, Gold Yellow Amber, 9 1/2 In., R-H179 . . . . . .85.00 to 135.00
Dr. A.W. Coleman's Anti Dyspeptic & Tonic, Blue Aqua, Ring Mouth, 9 In., R-C194 .   1375.00
Dr. A.W. Coleman's Anti Dyspeptic & Tonic, Emerald Green, IP, 9 In, R-C194 . . . . . .   4730.00
Dr. A.W. Coleman's Anti Dyspeptic & Tonic, Olive Amber, 1865, 9 1/4 In., R-C194 . .   2970.00
Dr. A.W. Coleman's Anti Dyspeptic & Tonic, Green, IP, 9 1/4 In., R-C194 . . . .   3630.00
Dr. Allen's Stomach, Pittsburgh, Pa., Aqua, Applied Mouth, 12 In., R-A31 . . . .   330.00
Dr. B. Olen's Life, N.Y., Aqua, Flared Lip, Pontil, 5 In., R-O57 . . . .   415.00
Dr. B.L. Kauffman Stomach Lancaster, Green, IP, 9 1/4 In., R-K13.5 . . . .   4290.00
Dr. Banker's Home Bitters, N.Y., Aqua, Applied Mouth, 9 In., R-B18 . . . . .110.00 to 120.00
Dr. Baxter's Mandrake, Aqua, 12-Sided, 6 1/2 In., R-B36 . . . .   25.00
Dr. Bell's Blood Purifying, Great English Remedy, Amber, 9 3/4 In., R-B56 . . . . .85.00 to 120.00
Dr. Bell's Liver & Kidney, Green Aqua, Applied Mouth, Square, 9 In., R-B61 . . . .   1040.00
Dr. Blake's Aromatic, New York, Aqua, Rectangular, OP, 7 In., R-B120 . . . .   225.00
Dr. Brown's Berry, Houts Mfg. Co., St. Louis, May 27, 1890, 8 1/4 In., R-B221 . . . . . .   85.00
Dr. Bull's Superior Stomach, W.H. Bull & Co., St. Louis, Amber, 9 In., R-B258 . . . . .   180.00
Dr. C.G. Garrison's Bitters For Dyspepsia, Phila., Pa., Aqua, 8 In., R-G6.5 . . . .   325.00
Dr. C.H. Smith's American Stomach, Tooled Lip, 8 In., R-S121 . . . .   165.00
Dr. C.W. Roback's Stomach, Barrel, Amber, IP, 10 In., R-R73 . . . . .410.00 to 440.00
Dr. C.W. Roback's Stomach, Barrel, Gold Amber, 9 3/8 In., R-R74 . . . . .130.00 to 255.00
Dr. C.W. Roback's Stomach, Cincinnati, O., Barrel, Yellow Amber, 9 3/8 In., R-74 . . . .   1705.00
Dr. C.W. Roback's Stomach, Cincinnati, O., Barrel, Amber, 9 3/8 In., R-R75 . .210.00 to 360.00
Dr. C.W. Roback's Stomach, Cincinnati, O., Barrel, Yellow Amber, IP, 10 In., R-R74 . .   745.00
Dr. C.W. Roback's Stomach, Cincinnati, O., Barrel, Yellow Olive, 9 3/8 In., R-R75 . . .   1155.00
Dr. C.W. Roback's Stomach, Cincinnati, O., Barrel, Yellow Olive, Cork, 10 In., R-R73 .   6600.00
Dr. Campbell's Scotch, Gold Yellow Amber, Tooled Mouth, 6 1/8 In., R-C31 . .275.00 to 470.00
Dr. Chandler's Jamaica Ginger, Lowell, Mass., Barrel, Yellow Green, 10 In., R-C127 . 13750.00
Dr. DeAndries Sarsaparilla, E.M. Rusha, New Orleans, Yellow Amber, 10 In., R-D35 .   1400.00
Dr. F. Fleschut's Celebrated Stomach, LaPorte, Pa., Aqua, 8 3/4 In., R-F54 . . . .   415.00
Dr. F. Woodbridge, Headache, Root Beer Amber, Sloping Collar, 9 1/4 In., R-H74 . . . . .   5280.00
Dr. Fenner's Liditol, Aqua, Rectangular, 10 1/2 In. 65.00
Dr. Fisch's, Fish, Gold Amber, Applied Mouth, 11 3/4 In., R-F44 . . . . .175.00 to 200.00
Dr. Fisch's, Fish, Patented 1866, Amber, Applied Mouth, 11 3/4 In., R-F44 . . . .   330.00
Dr. Fisch's, Patented 1866, Amber, Applied Mouth, 11 3/4 In., R-F44 . . . .   110.00
Dr. Fisch's, W.H. Ware, Pat. 1866, Fish, Yellow Amber, 11 3/4 In., R-F44 . . . . . . .260.00 to 690.00
Dr. Flint's Quaker, Providence, R.I., Aqua, 9 1/2 In., R-F58 . . . .   85.00
Dr. Flint's Stomach, Aqua, 9 In., R-F60 . . . .   35.00
Dr. Forest's Tonic, Harrisburg, Pa., Yellow Amber, Applied Mouth, 9 1/2 In., R-F69 . . . .   195.00
Dr. Frank's Laxative Tonic, Gold Yellow Amber, Tooled Mouth, 6 1/2 In., R-F78 . . . . .   230.00
Dr. Geo. Pierce's Indian Restorative, Lowell, Mass., Aqua, 7 7/8 In., R-P96 . . . .   60.00
Dr. Gillmore's Laxative Kidney & Liver, SCA, 10 1/8 In., R-G43 . . . . .95.00 to 115.00
Dr. H.A. Jackson's, Aqua, OP, 7 1/2 In., R-J5 . . . .   275.00
Dr. H.C. Stewart's Tonic, Col., O., Amber, Rectangular, 7 3/4 In., R-S194 . . . .   80.00
Dr. H.C. Stewart's Tonic, Col., O., Gold Yellow Amber, Tooled Lip, 7 3/4 In., R-S194 .   45.00
Dr. Harters Cherry, St. Louis, Blue Aqua, 9 1/2 In., R-H42 . . . .   165.00
Dr. Harter's Wild Cherry, Amber, 7 7/8 In., R-H45 . . . . .40.00 to 45.00
Dr. Harter's Wild Cherry, Dayton, Oh., Amber, 7 7/8 In., R-H46 . . . .   30.00
Dr. Harter's Wild Cherry, St. Louis, Amber, Label, Sample, 2 3/4 In., R-H54 . . . .   95.00
Dr. Harter's Wild Cherry, St. Louis, Gold Amber To Red Amber, 7 1/3 In., R-H51 . . . .   70.00
Dr. Harter's Wild Cherry, St. Louis, Amber, Tooled Mouth, 7 7/8 In., R-H50 . . . . .50.00 to 90.00
Dr. Harters Wild Cherry, St. Louis, Amber, Sample, 4 1/2 In., R-H52 . . . .   15.00
Dr. Henley's Wild Grape Root IXL, Aqua, Pontil, 12 1/2 In., R-H85 . . . . .165.00 to 185.00
Dr. Henley's Wild Grape Root IXL, Aqua, Tooled Lip, 12 1/2 In., R-H85 . . . .   110.00
Dr. Henley's Wild Grape Root IXL, Aqua, Applied Mouth, 12 1/2 In., R-H85 . . .90.00 to 120.00
Dr. Henley's Wild Grape Root IXL, Blue Aqua, Applied Mouth, 12 In., R-H84 . . . . . .   100.00
Dr. Henley's Wild Grape Root IXL, Light Aqua, Bent Neck, 9 3/8 In., R-H86 . . . .   1100.00
Dr. Henley's Wild Grape Root IXL, Olive Green, 12 1/2 In., R-H85 . . . .   1760.00
Dr. Henry Weis, Guard On The Rhine Stomach, Dayton, Ohio, Amber, 9 In., R-W69 . . .   260.00

Dr. Hentz's Curative, Aqua, Sample, Aquare, 4 1/4 In., R-H89 . . . .   175.00
Dr. Herbert John's Indian, Amber, Tooled Mouth, 8 5/8 In., R-J43 . . . .   105.00
Dr. Hoofland's German, Liver Complaint, C.M. Jackson, Aqua, 8 1/2 In., R-H168 .30.00 to 32.00
Dr. Hoofland's German, Liver Complaint, C.M. Jackson, Aqua, 9 1/2 In., R-H168 . . . .   40.00
Dr. J. Hostetter's Stomach, 18 Fluid Oz., Amber, ABM, 8 3/4 In., R-H197 . . . .   5.00
Dr. J. Hostetter's Stomach, Amber, 9 1/2 In., R-H194 . . . .   90.00
Dr. J. Hostetter's Stomach, L. & W., Yellow Olive, 8 7/8 In., R-H195 . . . .   95.00
Dr. J. Hostetter's Stomach, Medium Honey Amber, 8 3/4 In., R-H196 . . . .   40.00
Dr. J. Hostetter's Stomach, Medium Olive Green, 9 1/2 In., R-H194 . . . .   230.00
Dr. J. Hostetter's Stomach, Olive Green, 9 1/2 In., R-H194 . . . . .155.00 to 330.00
Dr. J. Hostetter's Stomach, Olive Green, Sloping Collar, 9 1/2 In., R-H194 . . . .   605.00
Dr. J. Hostetter's Stomach, W. MCG & Co., Black Amber, 9 1/2 In., R-H194 . . .60.00 to 175.00
Dr. J. Hostetter's Stomach, Yellow Olive Amber, 9 1/2 In., R-H194 . . . .   225.00
Dr. J. Sweet's Strengthening, Aqua, Square, 8 1/4 In., R-S234 . . . . .50.00 to 60.00
Dr. J.G.B. Siegert & Sons Angustura, Green, 8 1/4 In., R-A65 . . . .   25.00
Dr. J.R.B. McClintock's Dandelion, Philadelphia, Aqua, 7 1/4 In., R-M52 . . . .   155.00
Dr. Jacob's, New Haven, Ct., Blue Aqua, Applied Mouth, 10 1/4 In., R-J110 . . . .   230.00
Dr. Jacob's, New Haven, Ct., S.A. Spencer, Aqua, Rectangular, 10 1/4 In., R-J10 . . . .   120.00
Dr. Jacob's, New Haven, Ct., S.A. Spencer, Aqua, Rectangular, 8 1/2 In., R-J11 . . . .   185.00
Dr. John Bull's Cedron, Yellow Amber, Allover Swirl Ground Lines, 10 In., R-B255 . . .   185.00
Dr. John Bull's Cedron, Yellow Olive Green, 10 In., R-B254 . . . .   880.00
Dr. John Bull's Cedron, Cabin, Gold Amber, 10 3/8 In., R-B253.3 . . . .   690.00
Dr. Lamot's Botanic, Gold Yellow Amber, Applied Mouth, 8 1/2 In., R-L9 . . . .   120.00
Dr. Lamot's Botanic, Medium Amber, Tooled Mouth, 8 1/2 In., R-L9 . . . . .130.00 to 145.00
Dr. Langley's Root & Herb, 99 Reversed, Union St., Aqua, Tapered Top, 6 3/4 In., R-L24   175.00
Dr. Langley's Root & Herb, Amber, Applied Mouth, 6 In., R-L20 . . . . .90.00 to 120.00
Dr. Lawrence's Wild Cherry, Amber, Sample, 5 1/2 In., R-L51 . . . .   350.00
Dr. Loew's Celebrated Stomach Bitters & Nerve Tonic, Amber, 3 1/2 In., R-L113 .   350.00
Dr. Loew's Celebrated Stomach Bitters & Nerve Tonic, Amber, 4 3/4 In., R-L112 .   75.00
Dr. Loew's Celebrated Stomach, Olive Green, Tooled Mouth, 1910, 9 In., R-L111 . . .   330.00
Dr. Lovegood's Family, XX, Cabin, Root Beer Amber, 9 1/8 In., R-L125 . . . .   2475.00
Dr. M. Smith's Stomach, Cabin, Root Beer Amber, 9 5/8 In., R-S128 . . . .   550.00
Dr. Manly Hardy's Genuine Jaundice, Blue Aqua, OP, 6 1/4 In., R-H34 . . . . . .175.00 to 230.00
Dr. Med Koch's Universal Magen, Green, Applied Mouth, 1880, 7 7/8 In., R-K65.5 . . .   715.00
Dr. Petzold's Genuine German, Incpt. 1862, Amber, 10 1/8 In., R-P75 . . . . . . .140.00 to 170.00
Dr. Petzold's Genuine German, Incpt. 1862, Amber, 10 5/8 In., R-P74 . . . .   95.00
Dr. Petzold's Genuine German, Incpt. 1862, Amber, Ring Mouth, 10 5/8 In., R-P78 . .   220.00
Dr. Petzold's Genuine German, Incpt. 1862, Medium Amber, 10 3/4 In., R-P79 . . . . . .   130.00
Dr. Petzold's Genuine German, Pat'd 1884, Medium Amber, 7 In., R-P77 . . . .   175.00
Dr. Place's Cundurango, Blue Green Aqua, Indented Panel, Square, 9 3/8 In., R-P106 . .   415.00
Dr. Planett's, Aqua, Applied Sloping Collar, IP, 9 3/4 In., R-P107 . . . .   240.00
Dr. Renz's Herb, Olive Amber, Applied Top, 9 7/8 In., R-R38 . . . . .385.00 to 415.00
Dr. Renz's Herb, Yellow Olive Green, 9 7/8 In., R-R36 . . . .   660.00
Dr. Roback's Stomach, Barrel, Amber, 10 In., R-R73 . . . .   200.00
Dr. Saylor's German Rheuma Stomachic Herb, Amber, 8 5/8 In., R-S45 . . . .   605.00
Dr. Skinner's Celebrated, 25 Cent, So. Reading, Mass., Aqua, 8 1/2 In., R-S115 .90.00 to 155.00
Dr. Soule Hop, Hop Flowers & Leaf, Cabin, Red Amber, 9 1/4 In., R-S145 . . . .   90.00
Dr. Soule's Hop, Hop Flowers & Leaf, Cabin, Black, 7 3/4 In., R-S147 . . . .   185.00
Dr. Soule's Hop, Hop Flowers & Leaf, Cabin, Topaz, 7 3/4 In., R-S147 . . . .   130.00
Dr. Soule Hop, Hop Flowers & Leaf, Cabin, Yellow Puce, 1872, 9 1/4 In., R-S145 . . . . .   300.00
Dr. Sperry's Female Strengthening, Waterbury, Ct., Tooled Mouth, 9 In., R-S161 . . . .   165.00
Dr. Sperry's Rheumatic, Hartford, Ct., Aqua, Applied Top, 10 1/8 In., R-S162 . . . .   200.00
Dr. Stanley's South American Indian, Yellow Amber, Square, 9 In., R-S174 . . . .   175.00
Dr. Stewart's Tonic, Columbus, O., Amber, 7 3/4 In., R-S194 . . . .   80.00
Dr. Stoever's, Kryder & Co., Philadelphia, Yellow Amber Olive, 9 1/2 In., R-S199 . . . . .   110.00
Dr. Stoughten's National, Hamburg, Pa., Amber, 9 7/8 In., R-S208 . . . .   1815.00
Dr. Thos. Hall's California Pepsin Wine, Amber, Square, 9 In., R-H11 . . . .   140.00
Dr. Tompkin's Vegetable, Medium Teal Blue, Tooled Mouth, 9 In., R-T36 . . . .   1485.00
Dr. Von Hopf's Curaco, Chamberlain & Co., Des Moines, Iowa, Amber, 9 1/4 In., R-V27   210.00
Dr. Von Hopf's Curaco, Des Moines, Iowa, Amber, Tooled Mouth, 9 1/4 In., R-V25 . . .   75.00
Dr. Von Hopf's Curaco, Marion, Iowa, Amber, 7 1/2 In., R-V28 . . . .   75.00
Dr. W. Simon's Indian, Yellow Green, Tooled Mouth, 5 1/4 In., R-S111 . . . .   580.00
Dr. Washington's American Life, Amber, Tooled Mouth, 9 In., R-W53 . . . .   230.00

Dr. Wheeler's Sherry Wine, Green, Applied Sloping Collar, 7 3/4 In., R-W86 . . . . . .   525.00
Dr. Wilson's Herbin, Aqua, 6 In., R-W125 . . . .   40.00
Dr. Wonser's U.S.A. Indian Root, Light To Medium Gold Amber, 11 In., R-W146 . . . .   6600.00
Dr. Wood's Sarsaparilla & Wild Cherry, Aqua, OP, 9 In., R-W151 . . . .   303.00
Dr. Zabriskie's, Jersey City, N.J., Pontil, Square, 6 3/4 In., R-Z1 . . . .   595.00
Drake's Plantation, 4 Log, Amber, Applied Mouth, 10 1/4 In., R-D110 . . . . .90.00 to 110.00
Drake's Plantation, 4 Log, Yellow Amber, Applied Mouth, 1870, 10 3/8 In., R-D110 . .   95.00
Drake's Plantation, 4 Log, Lemon Yellow, 10 1/4 In., R-D110 . . . .   385.00
Drake's Plantation, 4 Log, Olive Yellow, 10 1/4 In., R-D110 . . . .   650.00
Drake's Plantation, 4 Log, Yellow Amber, 10 1/4 In., R-D110 . . . . .90.00 to 120.00
Drake's Plantation, 4 Log, Yellow Amber, 10 In., R-D110 . . . .   330.00
Drake's Plantation, 4 Log, Yellow Amber, Olive Tone, 10 In., R-D110 . . . .   1495.00
Drake's Plantation, 4 Log, Yellow Topaz, 10 1/8 In., R-D110 . . . .   355.00
Drake's Plantation, 5 Log, Apricot Puce, Applied Mouth, 10 In., R-D109 . . . . .300.00 to 415.00
Drake's Plantation, 5 Log, Chocolate Amber, 10 In., R-D109 . . . .   220.00
Drake's Plantation, 5 Log, Gold Amber, Sloping Collar, 10 In., R-D109 . . . .   200.00
Drake's Plantation, 5 Log, Strawberry Puce, Applied Mouth, 10 In., R-D109 . . . .   240.00
Drake's Plantation, 5 Log, Yellow Amber, 10 1/4 In., R-D110 . . . .   605.00
Drake's Plantation, 5 Log, Yellow Green, 10 In., R-D109 . . . .   550.00
Drake's Plantation, 6 Log, Amber, 9 3/4 In., R-D108 . . . .   100.00
Drake's Plantation, 6 Log, Amber, Applied Mouth, 10 In., R-D105 . . . .   105.00
Drake's Plantation, 6 Log, Amber, Expanded Mouth, Folded Lip, 10 In., R-D108 . . . . .   2255.00
Drake's Plantation, 6 Log, Apricot Puce, Applied Sloping Collar, 10 In., R-D105 . . . . .   660.00
Drake's Plantation, 6 Log, Cherry Puce, 9 7/8 In., R-D106 . . . .   360.00
Drake's Plantation, 6 Log, Copper Puce, Applied Mouth, 10 In., D-105 . . . .   230.00
Drake's Plantation, 6 Log, Copper Topaz, 10 In., R-D108 . . . .   175.00
Drake's Plantation, 6 Log, Dark Burgundy Puce, 10 In., R-D105 . . . .   305.00
Drake's Plantation, 6 Log, Dark Strawberry Puce, 10 In., R-D105 . . . .   145.00
Drake's Plantation, 6 Log, Deep Burgundy Puce, 10 In., R-D108 . . . . .165.00 to 200.00
Drake's Plantation, 6 Log, Deep Burgundy Puce, Sloping Collar, 10 In., R-D105 . . . . .   120.00
Drake's Plantation, 6 Log, Deep Root Beer Amber, 10 In., R-D105 . . . . .90.00 to 120.00
Drake's Plantation, 6 Log, Deep Ruby Amber, 10 In., R-D106 . . . .   400.00
Drake's Plantation, 6 Log, Gasoline Topaz, Sloping Collar, 10 1/8 In., R-D105 . . . .   305.00
Drake's Plantation, 6 Log, Gold Amber, Applied Collar Mouth, 10 In., R-D108 . . . . . .   415.00
Drake's Plantation, 6 Log, Gold Yellow Amber, Applied Mouth, 10 In., R-D103 . . . . . .   175.00
Drake's Plantation, 6 Log, Green Amber, Crooked Neck & Top, 10 In., R-D107 . . . . . .   880.00
Drake's Plantation, 6 Log, Light To Medium Yellow Olive, 10 In., R-D108 . . . .   3080.00
Drake's Plantation, 6 Log, Medium Amber, 10 In., R-D105 . . . .   110.00
Drake's Plantation, 6 Log, Medium Amber, 10 In., R-D108 . . . .   220.00
Drake's Plantation, 6 Log, Medium Amber, Variant, 10 In., R-D104 . . . .   220.00
Drake's Plantation, 6 Log, Medium Copper Puce, 10 In., R-D105 . . . .   230.00
Drake's Plantation, 6 Log, Medium Peach Puce, 10 In., R-D105 . . . .   360.00
Drake's Plantation, 6 Log, Medium Puce, 10 In., R-D106 . . . .   250.00
Drake's Plantation, 6 Log, Medium Strawberry Puce, 9 3/4 In., R-D105 . . . .   330.00
Drake's Plantation, 6 Log, Medium Yellow Amber, Olive Tone, 10 In., R-D105 . . . . . .   230.00
Drake's Plantation, 6 Log, Red Amethyst, 10 In., R-D105 . . . .   175.00
Drake's Plantation, 6 Log, Root Beer Amber, Applied Collar Mouth, 10 In., R-D108 . .   120.00
Drake's Plantation, 6 Log, Smoky Yellow Olive, 10 In., R-D105 . . . .   855.00
Drake's Plantation, 6 Log, Strawberry Puce, Applied Mouth, 10 In., R-D105 . . .195.00 to 305.00
Drake's Plantation, 6 Log, Strawberry Puce, Sloping Collar, 10 In., R-D105 . . . .   155.00
Drake's Plantation, 6 Log, Tobacco Amber, Applied Mouth, 10 In., R-D105 . . . .   100.00
Drake's Plantation, 6 Log, Yellow Amber, Olive Tone, 10 In., R-D106 . . . .   385.00
Drake's Plantation, 6 Log, Yellow Green, 10 1/8 In., R-D108 . . . .   550.00
Drake's Plantation, 6 Log, Yellow Green, Olive Tone, Sloping Collar, 10 In., R-D109 .   6050.00
Dyspepsia, D.W. Dowen, A.B. Jenner, Druggist, Saratoga Springs, Blue Aqua, 7 1/4 In. .   255.00
E. Baker's Premium, Richmond, Va., Aqua, Applied Mouth, 6 3/4 In., R-B10.2 . . . .   305.00
E. Bull's Luxury, Louisville, Ky., Lady's Leg, Amber, 9 1/8 In., R-D256 . . . . .220.00 to 395.00
E. Dexter Loveridge Wahoo, DWD Patd 1863, Cabin, Amber, 10 In., R-L126 . . . .   500.00
E. Long's Indian Herb, Indian Queen, Amber, Yellow Amber Arm, 12 In., R-L119 . . . .   12650.00
E.F. Kunkel's Bitter Wine Of Iron, Philadelphia, Pa., Sunken Panel, Aqua, 7 3/4 In. . .   8.00
E.J. Rose's Magador For Stomach, Kidney & Liver, Amber, 8 5/8 In., R-R98 . . . .35.00 to 80.00
E.S. Royer's Excelsior, Root Beer Amber, Sloping Double Collar, 9 3/8 In., R-R121 . . . .   175.00
E.S. Royer's Excelsior, Yellow Amber, Ring Mouth, Rectangular, 9 1/4 In., R-R121 . . . .   120.00

Bitters, Electric,
Chicago, Amber,
9 7/8 In., R-E29

Bitters, Emerson's
Excelsior Botanic,
8 In., R-E41

Eagle Angostura Bark, Eagle Liqueur Distilleries, Amber, 7 In., R-E2 . . . .   75.00
Ear Of Corn, see Bitters, National, Ear of Corn
Edw. Wilder's, Wholesale Druggists, Louisville, K.Y., Cabin, 10 1/2 In., R-W116 . . . . . .   220.00
Edw. Wilder's Bourbon, Louisville, Ky., Cabin, Applied Mouth, 10 1/4 In., R-W115.5 .   745.00
Edw. Wilder's Stomach, Cabin, 10 1/2 In., R-W116 . . . . .155.00 to 325.00
Electric, Chicago, Amber, 9 7/8 In., R-E29 . . . .*Illus*   45.00
Electric Brand, Gold Amber, Labels, 8 5/8 In., R-E33 . . . .   45.00
Electric Brand, H.E. Bucklen & Co., Chicago, Ill., Amber, 10 In., R-E32 . . . . .10.00 to 30.00
Electric Brand, Medium Amber To Red Amber, 8 5/8 In., R-E33 . . . .   25.00
Emerson's Excelsior Botanic, 8 In., R-E41 . . . .*Illus*   85.00
Empire Tonic, Donnell Tilden & Co., St. Louis, Mo., Yellow Amber, 9 In., R-E44 . . . . .   30.00
English Female, Louisville, Ky., Droomgoole, Aqua, Tooled Mouth, 8 1/2 In., R-E45 . . .   120.00
Excelsior, Applied Top 9, Amber, Square, 9 In., R-E62 . . . .   200.00
F. Brown Sarsaparilla & Tomato, Aqua, 9 1/2 In., R-S36 . . . .   140.00
Faith Whitcomb's, Boston, Mass., Aqua, Applied Mouth, 9 1/2 In., R-W90 . . . .   95.00
Ferro Quina, D.P Rossi Dogliani Italia, S.F., Red Amber, 3 3/4 In., R-F34 . . . .   65.00
Ferro Quina, San Francisco, Amber, 3 3/4 In., R-F33 . . . .   235.00
Ferro Quina Stomach, Red Amber, Tooled Mouth, 9 In., R-F40 . . . .   70.00
Ferro-China-Bisleri, Milano, New York, Bisleri's Iron Chinchona, Green, 10 In., R-F31 .   25.00
Fish, W.H. Ware, Pat. 1866, Clear, Tooled Lip, 11 1/2 In., R-F46 . . . .   855.00
Fish, W.H. Ware, Pat. 1866, Gold Amber, Applied Mouth, 11 1/2 In., R-F45 . . . . .175.00 to 255.00
Fish, W.H. Ware, Pat. 1866, Gold Amber, Round Collared Mouth, 11 3/8 In., R-F46 . . . . .   175.00
Fish, W.H. Ware, Pat. 1866, Root Beer Amber, Applied Mouth, 11 1/2 In., R-F45 .215.00 to 230.00
Fish, W.H. Ware, Pat. 1866, Root Beer Amber, Applied Mouth, 11 5/8 In., R-F46 . . . .   215.00
Fish, W.H. Ware, Pat. 1866, Yellow Amber, 11 1/2 In., R-F45 . . . .   240.00
Fish, W.H. Ware, Pat. 1866, Yellow Olive, Aqua Corners, 11 3/8 In., R-F46 . . . .   3300.00
Frank Miller & Co.'s Stomach, Amber, Sloping Mouth, Square, 8 1/2 In., R-M87 . . . .   55.00
Fredericksburg Bottling Co., San Francisco, Olive Green, 1885-1900, 11 3/8 In. 45.00
French Tonic Bitters, McDonald & Lake, Pigton, Ont., Aqua, 12 3/8 In., R-F86.5 . . . . .   3080.00
G.C. Blake's, Anti Deseptic, Aqua, IP, Applied Mouth, 7 1/4 In., R-B119 . . . .   550.00
G.C. Segur's Golden Seal, Aqua, OP, Applied Sloping Collar, 8 In., R-S84 . . . .   110.00
Gary Owen Strengthening, Ball & Lyons, New Orleans, La., Amber, 9 1/8 In., R-O96 .   165.00
Genl Scott's New York Artillery, Cannon, Yellow Amber, 12 3/8 In., R-S78 . . . .   6325.00
Gentiana Root & Herb, Boston, Mass., Aqua, Applied Mouth, 9 1/2 In., R-G12 . . . . . .   135.00
Gentiana Root & Herb, Seth E. Clapp & Co., Aqua, Tapered Square, 9 7/8 In., R-G11 .   145.00
Genuine Angostura, Yellow Amber, Shoulder Embossed, Cylindrical, 8 1/4 In., R-G13 .   80.00
German Balsam, W.M. Watson & Co., Blue Milk Glass, Square, 9 In., R-G18 . . . .   825.00
German Balsam, W.M. Watson & Co., Milk Glass, 9 In., R-G18 . . . . .385.00 to 690.00
Germania, Seated Lady, Milk Glass, Case Gin Form, Tooled Mouth, 9 1/2 In., R-G33 . . .   825.00
Germania Magen, Lady's Leg, Amber, Square Ring Collar, Cylindrical, 12 In., R-G36 . .   90.00
Gilbert's Sarsaparilla, Yellow Amber, Square Collar, 8-Sided, 8 3/4 In., R-G42 . . . .   605.00
Globe Tonic, Gold Amber, Applied Sloping Collar Mouth, Square, 9 5/8 In., R-G49 . . . .   130.00
Globe Tonic, Medium Amber, Applied Sloping Collar, 9 5/8 In., R-G49 . . . .   105.00
Golden, Geo. C. Hubbel & Co., Cabin, Aqua, 10 3/8 In., R-G63 . . . .   600.00

Golden, Geo. C. Hubbel & Co., Cabin, Aqua, Label, Double Collar, 10 3/8 In., R-G63 .. 155.00
Good Samaritan Stomach, Gold Yellow Amber, Square, 1885, 9 1/4 In., R-G66.5 .... 470.00
Gordon's Kidney & Liver, Yellow Amber, Sloping Collar, 9 1/4 In., R-G77 .... 75.00
Grand Prize, Light To Medium Amber, Applied Mouth, 9 1/4 In., R-G89 .... 355.00
Greeley's Bourbon, Barrel, Apricot Puce, 9 3/8 In., R-G101 .... 200.00
Greeley's Bourbon, Barrel, Copper Puce, 9 3/8 In., R-G101 ....255.00 to 305.00
Greeley's Bourbon, Barrel, Deep Strawberry Puce, 9 3/8 In., R-G101 .... 135.00
Greeley's Bourbon, Barrel, Gray Apricot Puce, Square Collar, 9 3/8 In., R-G101 ...... 265.00
Greeley's Bourbon, Barrel, Gray Puce, Square Collar, 9 3/8 In., R-G101 .... 220.00
Greeley's Bourbon, Barrel, Root Beer, Puce Tone, 9 3/8 In., R-G101 .... 250.00
Greeley's Bourbon, Barrel, Smoky Olive Topaz, 9 3/8 In., R-G101 ....*Illus* 1210.00
Greeley's Bourbon, Barrel, Smoky Puce, 9 3/8 In., R-G101 ....305.00 to 415.00
Greeley's Bourbon, Barrel, Smoky Topaz Olive, Applied Mouth, 9 3/8 In., R-G101 ... 770.00
Greeley's Bourbon Whiskey, Barrel, Blue Aqua, Applied Mouth, 9 1/2 In., R-G102 ... 3135.00
Greeley's Bourbon Whiskey, Barrel, Copper Puce, 9 1/2 In, R-G102 .... 130.00
Greeley's Bourbon Whiskey, Barrel, Moss Green, Square Mouth, 9 1/2 In., R-G102 .. 1600.00
Greeley's Bourbon Whiskey, Barrel, Pink Amethyst, 9 1/2 In., R-G102 .... 470.00
Greeley's Bourbon Whiskey, Barrel, Pink Puce, Square Collar, 9 1/2 In., R-G102 ..... 715.00
Greeley's Bourbon Whiskey, Barrel, Strawberry Puce, 9 1/2 In., R-G102 .... 550.00
Greeley's Bourbon Whiskey, Barrel, Topaz Puce, Label, 9 3/8 In., R-G102 .... 1375.00
Green Mountain Cider, Aqua, Double Collar, Partial Label, 10 1/4 In., R-G103 ...... 210.00
Green Mountain Cider, Blue Aqua, Applied Mouth, 10 1/4 In., R-G103 .... 145.00
Greenhut's, Prepared By S. Greenhut, Cleveland, O., Medium Amber, 11 In., R-G109 .. 180.00
Greer's Eclipse, Amber, Applied Collar Mouth, 8 3/8 In., R-G111 .... 185.00
Greer's Eclipse, Amber, Applied Sloping Collar Mouth, Square, 8 5/8 In., R-G112 ..... 80.00
Greer's Eclipse, Gold Amber, Sloping Mouth, Square, 9 1/2 In., R-G110 .... 110.00
Griel's Herb, Griel & Young, Pale Aqua, Tooled Mouth, 9 3/8 In., R-G115 .... 110.00
Griel's Herb, Griel's & Young, Lancaster, Pa., Aqua, Tooled Mouth, 9 3/8 In., R-G115 .. 525.00
H. Bowman Druggist, Sacramento, Calif., Aqua, Applied Mouth, 7 1/4 In. 50.00
H.M. Crookes's Stomach, Lady's Leg, Olive Green, Sloping Collar, 10 1/8 In., R-C253 195.00
H.N. Winfree's Aromatic Stomach, Chester, Va., Aqua, 6 1/2 In., R-W135 .... 305.00
H.P. Herb Wild Cherry, Cabin, Gold Yellow, Roped Corners, Ring Collar, 10 In., R-H93 330.00
H.P. Herb Wild Cherry, Cabin, Medium Amber, 10 In., R-H93 .... 325.00
H.P. Herb Wild Cherry, Cabin, Green, Tooled Mouth, 8 7/8 In., R-H94 .....4400.00 to 5060.00
H.P. Herb Wild Cherry, Reading, Pa., Cabin, Amber, 8 7/8 In., R-H94 .... 260.00
Hagan's, Amber, Applied Mouth, 9 7/8 In., R-H5 ....525.00 to 550.00
Hall's, Barrel, Gold Amber, Applied Mouth, 9 1/8 In., R-H10 .... 175.00
Hall's, Barrel, Orange Amber, Square Collar, 9 1/8 In., R-H10 ....220.00 to 440.00
Hall's, Barrel, Yellow Amber, Olive Tone, Wrapper, Cork, 9 1/8 In., R-H10 .... 375.00
Hall's, Barrel, Yellow Amber, Square Collar, 9 1/8 In., R-H10 ....110.00 to 200.00
Hall's, E.E. Hall, New Haven, Conn., Barrel, Amber, Applied Mouth, 9 1/8 In., R-H10 .. 220.00
Hansard's Genuine Hop, Swansea & Llanelly, 7 3/4 In., R-H25 ....*Illus* 75.00
Hart's Star, O.B.L.P.C., 1868, Philadelphia, Pa., Tooled Mouth, 9 1/4 In., R-H58 ..... 305.00
Hart's Star, Philadelphia, Pa., 1868, Aqua, Tooled Mouth, 9 1/4 In., R-H58 .... 275.00
Hartwig Kantorowicz, Posen, Germany, Milk Glass, 9 1/2 In., R-C179 .... 150.00
Hellman's Congress, St. Louis, Mo., Amber, Square, 8 3/4 In., R-H79 ....210.00 to 225.00
Hellman's Congress, St. Louis, Mo., Root Beer Amber, Olive, 8 3/4 In., R-H79 .... 305.00
Hentz's Curative, Aqua, Square, 9 5/8 In., R-H88 .... 80.00
Herkules, AC Monogram, Yellow Green, Tooled Lip, 7 1/2 In., R-H98 .... 1100.00
Herkules, Green, Tooled Mouth, 2 Label Panels, Globular, 7 In., R-H98 .... 990.00
Hertrich's Gesundheits, Deep Olive Green, Globular, 9 3/8 In., R-H104 .... 385.00
Hertrich's Gesundheits, Olive Green, 12 In., R-H104 .... 715.00
Hertrich's Gesundheits, Olive Green, Bulbous, 8 1/4 In., R-H104 .... 1155.00
Hi-Hi, Rock Island, Ill., Amber, Triangular, 9 3/8 In., R-H118 .... 80.00
Hibernia, Braunschweiger & Bumsted, San Francisco, Amber, 10 In., R-H113 .... 800.00
Hibernia, Medium Yellow Amber, Square, 9 3/4 In., R-H112 .... 80.00
Highland Bitters & Scotch Tonic, Barrel, Gold Yellow Amber, 9 3/4 In., R-H117 .... 3300.00
Highland Bitters & Scotch Tonic, Barrel, Medium Amber, 9 3/4 In., R-H117 .... 1210.00
Hirsch's Malt Whiskey Reliable Stimulant, Amber, 10 3/4 In. 65.00
Hochstadter Co., Burgunder Wein Bitter Leipziger, Lime Green, 3-Piece Mold, 11 3/4 In. 100.00
Holtzermann's Patent Stomach, Cabin, 2-Sided, Amber, 9 1/4 In., R-H155 .... 2200.00
Holtzermann's Patent Stomach, Cabin, 4-Sided, Amber, 9 5/8 In., R-H154 ...200.00 to 690.00
Holtzermann's Patent Stomach, Cabin, 4-Sided, Red Amber, 9 5/8 In., R-H154 ..... 180.00

Holtzermann's Patent Stomach, Cabin, Red Amber, Tooled Mouth, 9 5/8 In., R-H154   230.00
Holtzermann's Stomach, Cabin, 4-Sided, Gold Amber, Label, 4 In., R-H153 . . . .   330.00
Home Bitters, Jas. A. Jackson Proprietors, St. Louis, Mo., Amber, 9 In., R-H158 . . . . . .   60.00
Honolulu Brewing Co., Honolulu, Aqua, 1880-1900, 12 In. 40.00
Hops & Malt Trade, Cabin, Amber, 9 1/4 In., R-H186 . . . .   300.00
Hops & Malt Trade, Cabin, Amber, Solidified Contents, 9 1/4 In., R-H186 . . . .   240.00
Hops & Malt Trade, Cabin, Red Amber, Applied Mouth, 9 1/4 In., R-H186 . . . .   275.00
Hostetter's, see Bitters, Dr. J. Hostetter's
Houck's Patent Panacea, Baltimore, Md., Aqua 50.00
Hubbell Co., see Bitters, Golden
Hurley Bros. Pepsinized, Hurley Bros., St. Paul, Minn., Red Amber, 7 7/8 In., R-H213.8   120.00
Hutchings Curative, Aqua, OP, 8 1/2 In. 230.00
Hutchings Dyspepsia, New York, Blue Aqua, IP, 8 1/2 In., R-H218 . . . .   165.00
Hutchings Dyspepsia, New York, Blue Aqua, Sloping Collar, IP, 8 1/2 In., R-H218 . . . .   90.00
I. Newton's Jaundice, Norwich, Vt., Aqua, Rolled Lip, OP, 6 3/4 In., R-N25 . . . .   275.00
I. Newton's Jaundice, Norwich, Vt., Aqua, Tooled Mouth, 6 3/4 In., R-N25 . . . .   770.00
Indian Queen, see Bitters, Brown's Celebrated Indian Herb
Indian Vegetable & Sarsaparilla, Geo. C. Goodwin, Boston, Aqua, 8 3/8 In., R-I25 . . .   440.00
J. Walker's Vinegar, Aqua, Applied Top, 8 3/8 In., R-W11 . . . .   55.00
J. Walker's Vinegar, Light Green, Bubbles, 8 3/8 In., R-W11 . . . .   100.00
J.F.L. Capitol, Pineapple, Gold Amber, Applied Mouth, IP, 9 In., R-C40 . . . .   715.00
J.W. Hutchinson's Tonic, Blue Aqua, Applied Double Collar, 9 In., R-H220 . . . .   910.00
Jackson's Stonewall, Quinlin Bros. & Co., Cabin, Gold Amber, 9 1/2 In., R-J8 . . . .   5500.00
Jenkins' Stomach, Gold Amber, Applied Mouth, 9 1/2 In., R-J28 . . . .   400.00
Jno Moffat, Phoenix, Price $1, Yellow Amber, Olive Tone, Pontil, 5 1/2 In., R-M110 . . .   910.00
Joel Whary's Herb, Medium Amber, Tooled Mouth, 9 1/8 In., R-W79.9 . . . .   100.00
John Moffat, Price $1.00, Phoenix, Medium Olive Green, Pontil, 5 1/2 In., R-M112 . . . .   525.00
John Moffat, Price $1.00, Phoenix, Olive Amber, Applied Mouth, 5 3/8 In., R-M113 . . .   910.00
John Moffat, Price $1.00, Phoenix, Yellow Olive Green, Pontil, 5 1/2 In., R-M112 . . . . .   500.00
John Root's, Buffalo, N.Y., Cabin, Blue Green, 10 1/4 In., R-R90.4 . . . . .210.00 to 910.00
John Root's, Buffalo, N.Y., Cabin, Emerald Green, 10 1/4 In., R-R90.4 . . . .   1540.00
John W. Steele's Niagara Star, Cabin, Deep Amber, 10 In., R-S182 . . . .   690.00
John W. Steele's Niagara Star, Cabin, Medium Amber, 10 1/4 In., R-S183 . . . .   415.00
Johnson's Calisaya, Burlington, Vt., Apricot Puce, Applied Mouth, Square, 10 In., R-J45   330.00
Johnson's Calisaya, Burlington, Vt., Gold Amber, Ring Mouth, Square, 10 In., R-J45 . . .   90.00
Johnson's Calisaya, Burlington, Vt., Yellow Amber, Square, 10 In., R-J45 . . . .   230.00
Johnson's Indian Dyspeptic, Burlington, Vt., Aqua, OP, 6 5/8 In., R-J46 . . . . .400.00 to 415.00
Jones Universal Stomach, Williamsport, Pa., Amber, Collar Mouth, 9 In., R-J53 . . . . . .   220.00
Jones Universal Stomach, Williamsport, Pa., Orange Amber, 9 1/8 In., R-J53 . . . .   120.00
Jug, A.L. Heintz Co., Stoneware, Cream, Black Transfer, 9 1/4 In., R-H76 . . . .   105.00
Julien's Imperial Aromatic, Wear Upham & Ostrom, Lady's Leg, 12 1/2 In., R-J57 . . .   2695.00
Jung & Wulff, Cocktail & Flavoring, ABM Lip, Original Label, 5 1/2 In., R-J58.5 . . . . .   50.00
Kagy's Superior Stomach, Amber, Applied Sloping Collar, 9 1/2 In., R-K3 . . . .   150.00

Bitters, Greeley's Bourbon,
Barrel, Smoky Olive Topaz,
9 3/8 In., R-G101

Bitters, Hansard's Genuine
Hop, Swansea & Llanelly,
7 3/4 In., R-H25

Bitters, Lash's, Natural
Laxative, Amber,
Label, 9 3/8 In.

Kaiser Wilhem Bitters Co., Sandusky, O., 10 1/8 In., R-K5 .... 28.00
Kelly's Old Cabin, Cabin Shape, Medium Chocolate, 9 1/4 In., R-K22 .... 1850.00
Kelly's Old Cabin, Patented 1863, Cabin Shape, Chocolate Amber, 9 5/8 In., R-K21 .... 2585.00
Kelly's Old Cabin, Patented 1863, Cabin Shape, Deep Amber, 9 5/8 In., R-K21 ...... 1540.00
Keystone, Barrel, Amber, 9 3/4 In., R-K36 .... .575.00 to 645.00
Keystone, Barrel, Red Amber, Applied Mouth, 9 3/4 In., R-K36 .... 580.00
Kimball's Jaundice, Troy, N.H., Yellow Olive Amber, IP, Label, 7 In., R-K42 ...230.00 to 630.00
Knapp's Health Restorative, Aqua, 8 1/8 In., R-K62 .... 580.00
Koehler & Hinrichs, Red Star Stomach, Amber, Fluted Top & Base, 11 1/4 In., R-R25 .. 400.00
L. Goldheim Celebrated Swiss Wine Stomach, Amber, 9 3/4 In., R-C101 .... 303.00
L.F. Atwood's Improved Vegetable Physical Jaundice, Label, 6 3/4 In., R-A126 .... 22.00
Lacour's Sarsapariphere, Medium Amber, Applied Top, 9 In., R-L3 .... 935.00
Lady's Leg, Red Amber, Embossed, 12 1/8 In. 48.00
Lash's, Amber, Sample, 4 1/4 x 1 5/16 In., R-L31 .... 125.00
Lash's, Natural Laxative, Amber, Label, 9 3/8 In. .... .Illus 65.00
Lash's, Natural Tonic Laxative, Amber, Square, 9 1/2 In., R-L32 .... 25.00
Lash's Kidney & Liver, Best Cathartic & Blood Purifier, Amber, 8 7/8 In., R-L34 ..... 20.00
Lash's Kidney & Liver, Best Cathartic & Blood Purifier, Red Amber, 1910, 9 In., R-L37 185.00
Lediard's Celebrated Stomach, Green, Applied Mouth, 9 1/2 In., R-L60 ..... .660.00 to 745.00
Lediard's O.K. Plantation, 1840, Cabin, Yellow Amber, 10 In., R-L62 .... 3960.00
Leopold Sahl's, Aromatic Stomach, Pittsburgh, Pa., Root Beer Amber, 10 In., R-S7 .... 3960.00
Lippman's Great German, New York & Savannah, Georgia, Amber, 9 In., R-L99 ..... 230.00
Lippman's Great German, Savannah, Ga., Copper Puce, 10 In., R-L98 .... 880.00
Lippman's Great German, Savannah, Geo., Yellow Amber, 10 In., R-L98 .... 360.00
Lippman's Great German, Yellow Amber, Double Collar Mouth, 10 In., R-L98 ...... 265.00
Litthauer Stomach, see also Bitters, Hartwig Kantorowicz
Litthauer Stomach, Hartwig Kantorowicz, Hamburg, Milk Glass, 10 3/4 In., R-L105 .. 45.00
Litthauer Stomach, Hartwig Kantorowicz, Berlin, Amber, 9 1/2 In., R-L105 .... 175.00
Litthauer Stomach, Hartwig Kantorowicz, Berlin, Amber, 9 1/2 In., R-L106 .... 90.00
Litthauer Stomach, Hartwig Kantorowicz, Berlin, Yellow Green, 3 3/4 In., R-L107 ... 50.00
Litthauer Stomach, Hartwig Kantorowicz, Milk Glass, 3 3/4 In., R-L107 ..... .120.00 to 205.00
Litthauer Stomach, Hartwig Kantorowicz, Yellow Olive Green, 9 1/2 In., R-L106 .... 85.00
Litthauer Stomach, Josef Loewenthal Berlin, Milk Glass, 9 1/2 In., R-L102 ..... .85.00 to 205.00
Litthauer Stomach, Milk Glass, Applied Mouth, Case Gin, 9 1/2 In., R-L102 .... 65.00
Lohengrin, Adolf Marcus Von Buton, Germany, Milk Glass, Gin Case, 9 1/2 In., R-L117 175.00
London Style Orange, E.G. Lions & Raas Co., San Francisco, Cal., Label, Fifth 55.00
Lorimer's Juniper Tar, Elmira, N.Y., Teal Blue, 9 1/2 In., R-L121 .... 1540.00
Lyons Bitter Co., New Haven, Conn., Gold Amber, Square, 8 3/4 In., R-L141 .... 30.00
Malabac, M. Cziner, Chemist, Lady's Leg, Gold Amber, 11 1/2 In., R-M13 .... 145.00
Malort, 20 Vertical Ribs, Fluted Shoulders, Neck, Copper Letters, 11 3/4 In., R-M19.7 .. 140.00
Mandrake, see Bitters, Dr. Baxter's
McConnon's Stomach, McConnon & Company, Winona, Minn., Amber, 8 3/4 In., R-M53 105.00
McCullough Druggist, Reno, Nevada, Tooled Lip, 1891-1910, 8 In. 110.00
McDowall's Eclectic, Aqua, Allover Iridescent, Tooled Mouth, 7 3/4 In., R-M54 ...... 55.00
McKeever's Army, Drum, Amber, Applied Mouth, 10 1/2 In., R-M58 ....1595.00 to 2310.00
McKelvy's Stomach, Pittsburgh, Pa., Aqua, Square, 8 1/2 In., R-M57 .... 260.00
Mishler's Herb, Dr. S.B. Hartman & Co., Yellow Amber, Square, 9 In., R-M99 ..135.00 to 525.00
Mishler's Herb, Dr. S.B. Hartman & Co., Yellow, Square, 9 In., R-M100 .... 175.00
Mishler's Herb, Tablespoon Graduation, Gold Yellow Amber, 9 In., R-M101 .... 85.00
Mishler's Herb, Tablespoon Graduation, Yellow Amber, 9 In., R-M100 .... 70.00
Morning Inceptum, Star, Gold Amber, IP, 12 7/8 In., R-M135 ....160.00 to 245.00
Morning Inceptum, Star, Root Beer Amber, IP, 12 7/8 In., R-M135 .... 330.00
Morning Inceptum, Star, Root Beer Amber, Red IP, 12 7/8 In., R-M135 .... 1210.00
Morning Inceptum, Star, Yellow Olive To Yellow Green, 12 7/8 In., R-M135 .... 2090.00
Moulton's Oloroso, Pineapple Trade Mark, Aqua, 11 3/8 In., R-M146 .... 210.00
Napoleon, Dingen Brothers, 1866, Cabin, Root Beer Amber, Square, 10 In., R-N2 ..... 2750.00
National, Ear Of Corn, 1867, Amber, Applied Mouth, 12 5/8 In., R-N8 .... .Illus 330.00
National, Ear Of Corn, 1867, Gold Olive, Ring Mouth, 12 5/8 In., R-N8 ......1100.00 to 1650.00
National, Ear Of Corn, 1867, Medium Amber, Applied Mouth, 12 1/2 In., R-N8 ..275.00 to 420.00
National, Ear Of Corn, Aqua, Pat. 1867, Applied Mouth, 12 5/8 In., R-N8 .... 2475.00
National, Ear Of Corn, Amber, Applied Collar, 12 5/8 In., R-N8 ....255.00 to 495.00
National Tonic, Blue Aqua, Applied Collar, Square, 9 1/2 In., R-N13 .... 1020.00
New York Hop Bitters Co., Semi-Cabin, Deep Aqua, 9 1/2 In., R-N28 .... 230.00

Newman's Golden Fruit, Gold Amber, Sloping Collar, 10 3/4 In., R-N22.5 . . . .   880.00
Nibol Kidney & Liver, Amber, Tooled Mouth, 9 1/2 In., R-N31 . . . . .175.00 to 330.00
Nightcap, Schmidlapp & Co., A Good Beverage, Cincinnati, O., 9 In., R-N32 . . . .   75.00
Normandy Herb & Root Stomach, Olive Yellow, Rectangular, 7 3/4 In., R-N38 . . . . .   110.00
O'Hare Bitters Co., Pittsburgh, Pa., Amber, Square, 9 1/4 In., R-O10 . . . .   100.00
O'Leary's 20th Century, Amber, 8 1/2 In., R-O55 . . . .   150.00
Old Cabin, Cabin, Red Amber, Sloping Collar, 9 1/4 In., R-019 . . . .   1870.00
Old Carolina, Goodrich Wineman & Co., Deep Red Puce, 10 In., R-O20 . . . .   2700.00
Old Dr. Townsend's Celebrated Stomach, Yellow Amber, 8 3/4 In., R-T51 . . . .   11550.00
Old Dr. Townsend's Stomach, New York, Blue Green, 10 In., R-T51 . . . .   965.00
Old Homestead Wild Cherry, Cabin, Amber, 9 7/8 In., R-O37 . . . . .155.00 to 415.00
Old Homestead Wild Cherry, Cabin, Yellow Amber, 9 7/8 In., R-O37 . . . . .165.00 to 230.00
Old Homestead Wild Cherry, Cabin, Yellow Olive, 9 3/4 In., R-37 . . . .*Illus*   2255.00
Old Homestead Wild Cherry, Cabin, Yellow, Amber Tone, 9 7/8 In., R-O37 . . . .   1320.00
Old Homestead Wild Cherry, Dark Chocolate, 9 7/8 In., R-O37 . . . .   350.00
Old Sachem & Wigwam Tonic, Barrel, Amber, 9 1/2 In., R-O46 . . . . .200.00 to 660.00
Old Sachem & Wigwam Tonic, Barrel, Aqua, Yellow, 10 1/8 In., R-O45 . . . .   5225.00
Old Sachem & Wigwam Tonic, Barrel, Cherry Puce, 9 1/2 In., R-O46 . . . . . .525.00 to 660.00
Old Sachem & Wigwam Tonic, Barrel, Gold Amber, 9 1/2 In., R-O46 . . . . . . .305.00 to 415.00
Old Sachem & Wigwam Tonic, Barrel, Gold Amber, Pontil, 9 3/8 In., R-O46 . . . .   1045.00
Old Sachem & Wigwam Tonic, Barrel, Gold Yellow, Square Collar, 9 1/2 In., R-O46 . .   440.00
Old Sachem & Wigwam Tonic, Barrel, Light Pink Topaz, 9 1/2 In., R-O46 . . . .   3410.00
Old Sachem & Wigwam Tonic, Barrel, Light To Medium Pink Puce, 9 1/2 In., R-O46 .   855.00
Old Sachem & Wigwam Tonic, Barrel, Olive Yellow, 9 1/2 In., R-O46 . . . .   1870.00
Old Sachem & Wigwam Tonic, Barrel, Pink Amethyst, 9 1/2 In., R-O46 . . . .   635.00
Old Sachem & Wigwam Tonic, Barrel, Plum Puce, Square Collar, 9 1/2 In., R-O46 . . .   275.00
Old Sachem & Wigwam Tonic, Barrel, Red Puce, Applied Mouth, 9 1/2 In., R-O46 . . .   440.00
Old Sachem Bitters & Wigwam Tonic, Barrel, Red Copper Puce, 9 1/2 In., R-O46 . . .   635.00
Owl Drug Iron, Apothecary, Clear, Acid Etched, Tooled Mouth, Stopper, 10 In., R-O98.5   470.00
Oxygenated For Dyspensia Asthma, Aqua, Rectangular, 7 5/8 In., R-O99 . . . . .68.00 to 140.00
Palmer's Tonic, Andrus & Palmer, Cabin, Green, 10 1/4 In., R-P12 . . . .   17050.00
Panknin's Hepatic, New York, Amber, Applied Mouth, Square, 8 5/8 In., R-P18 . . . . . .   70.00
Pepsin, Golden Gate Medicine Co., Light To Medium Yellow Amber, 9 1/8 In., R-P46 .   55.00
Pepsin, R.W. Davis Drug Co., Green, 8 1/4 In., R-P44 . . . .   95.00
Pepsin, R.W. Davis Drug, Green, 4 1/8 x 2 1/4 In., R-P45 . . . .   145.00
Pepsin Calisaya, Dr. Russell Med. Co., Green, 4 1/8 In., R-P51 . . . .   85.00
Pepsin Calisaya, Dr. Russell Med. Co., Green, 7 7/8 In., R-P50 . . . . .35.00 to 60.00
Peruvian, Chas. Noelle & Co., Amber, Applied Double Collar, 9 1/4 In., R-P63.5 . . . . . .   150.00
Peruvian, P. Shaw, M.D., Portland, Pa., Amber, Picnic, Applied Mouth, 5 In., R-P66 . . .   145.00
Peruvian, W. & K., Monogram In Shield, Amber, Applied Mouth, 9 1/8 In., R-P67 . . . . .   95.00
Petzold's Genuine German, Amber 160.00
Pig, see Bitters, Berkshire; Bitters, Suffolk
Pineapple, W. & Co., N.Y., Amber, Double Collar, OP, 8 7/8 In., R-P100 . . . .   360.00
Pineapple, W. & Co., N.Y., Amber, IP, 8 1/8 In., R-P100 . . . .   410.00
Pineapple, W. & Co., N.Y., Yellow Green, 8 7/8 In., R-P100 . . . .   470.00
Plantation, 1862, Pan't. Secured 1863, Amber, Applied Top, Crude, 9 1/2 In., R-P108 . .   65.00
Plow's Sherry, Bunch Of Grapes, Medium Amber, Applied Mouth, 8 In., R-P111 . . . . .   9350.00
Polo Club Trade Mark Stomach, Amber, 9 1/8 In., R-P117 . . . . .110.00 to 120.00
Poor Man's Family, Aqua, Tooled Lip, 6 3/8 In., R-P123 . . . .   105.00
Prickley Ash Bitters Co., Honey Amber, Applied Top, Square, 9 1/4 In., R-P140 . . . . .   75.00
Professor B.E. Mann's Oriental Stomach, Cabin, Amber, 10 In., R-M29 . . . .   745.00
Professor B.E. Mann's Oriental Stomach, Gold Yellow, Square, 9 1/4 In., R-M29 . . . .   330.00
Professor Geo. J. Byrne, Great Universal Compound, Olive, 10 1/4 In., R-B280 . . . . . .   3520.00
Professor Geo. J. Byrne, N.Y., Great Universal Compound, Amber, 10 1/4 In., R-B280 .   1485.00
Prune Bitters Gives Strength Quickly, Amber, Tooled Mouth, 9 1/4 In., R-P150 . . . .   175.00
Prune Stomach & Liver, Amber, Square, 9 1/4 In., R-P151 . . . .   85.00
Prussian, Yellow Amber, Tooled Mouth, 8 1/2 In., R-P152 . . . .   90.00
Quinine Tonic Manf. By G.T.B. Chemical Co., Lexington, Ky, 8 In., R-Q6 . . . .   100.00
R.H. Becker's Russian, Tooled Mouth, 10 1/2 In., R-B45 . . . .   330.00
R.L. Egerton's Stomach, Louisville, Ky., Honey Amber, 10 1/2 In., R-E25 . . . .   305.00
Red Jacket, Monheimer & Co., Medium Amber, Tooled Mouth, 9 1/2 In., R-R20 . . . . . .   105.00
Reed's, Lady's Leg, Amber, Applied Mouth, 12 1/2 In., R-R28 . . . . .130.00 to 495.00
Reed's, Lady's Leg, Gold Amber, Ring Mouth, Cylindrical, 12 1/2 In., R-R28 . . . .   185.00

Rex Kidney & Liver, Gold Yellow Amber, Tooled Mouth, 6 3/4 In., R-R45 . . . .   145.00
Rising Sun, John C. Hurst, Philada., Amber, Square, 9 3/8 In., R-R66 . . . . .65.00 to 110.00
Rose Hill Stomach, H.M. Mosher & Co., New York, Amber, Square, 9 3/8 In., R-R92 . .   355.00
Rosswinkle's Crown, Gold Yellow Amber, Applied Sloping Collar, 8 7/8 In., R-R102 . .   415.00
Rothery's, Chicago, Amber, Tooled Mouth, 8 In., R-R105 . . . .   85.00
Royal Italian Bitters Registered Trade Mark, Amethyst, 13 1/2 In., R-R111 . .745.00 to 815.00
Royal Pepsin Stomach, L & A Scharff, Sole Agents, Amber, 6 3/8 In., R-R115 . . . .   70.00
Royal Pepsin Stomach, L & A Scharff, St Louis & Canada, Amber, 7 3/8 In., R-R114 . .   80.00
Royal Pepsin Stomach, L & A Scharff, St. Louis, Canada, 8 3/4 In., R-R113 . . .120.00 to 185.00
Royal Pepsin Stomach, L & A Scharff, St. Louis, Tooled Mouth, 8 3/4 In., R-R113 . . . .   145.00
Royce's Sherry Wine, Aqua, Applied Sloping Collar, Label, 8 In., R-R119 . . . .   55.00
Royce's Sherry Wine, Blue Aqua, Smooth Base, 8 In., R-119 . . . .   90.00
Rush's, A.H. Flanders M.D., New York, Amber, Applied Top, 8 7/8 In., R-R124 . . . .   45.00
Russ' St. Domingo, New York, Amber, Square, 9 7/8 In., R-R125 . . . .   175.00
Russ' St. Domingo, New York, Yellow Topaz, Applied Mouth, 9 7/8 In., R-R125 . . . . . .   415.00
Russian Imperial Tonic, Blue Aqua, Applied Mouth, 9 1/2 In., R-N133 . . . .   2035.00
Russian Lithuanian Litovsky Liquor Co., Australia, Amber, Label, 9 1/2 In. 175.00
S & S, Der Doktor, Tooled Mouth, Square, 9 1/2 In., R-S4 . . . . .85.00 to 120.00
S. Kaufman's Celebrated Anti Cholera, Pat. 1865, Amber, Square, 9 7/8 In., R-K16 . .   1760.00
S. Kaufman's Celebrated Anti Cholera, Patd 1865, Cabin, Amber, 10 In., R-K16 . . . .   2200.00
S.C. Smiths Druid, B.T. 1865 S.C., Barrel, Yellow, Applied Mouth, 9 In., R-S124 . . . . .   2970.00
S.O. Richardson's, South Reading, Mass., Aqua, Rectangular, 6 7/8 In., R-R57 . . . .95.00 to 330.00
S.O. Richardson's, South Reading, Mass., Blue Aqua, IP, 6 7/8 In., R-R57 . . . . . .155.00 to 180.00
S.T. Drake's, see Bitters, Drake's Plantation
Saint Jacob's, KYGW Co, Honey Amber, 8 3/4 In., R-S13 . . . . .90.00 to 220.00
San Joaquin Wine, Amber, Applied Sloping Double Collar, 9 3/4 In., R-S26 . . . .   230.00
Sanborn's Kidney & Liver Vegetable Laxative, Amber, Ring Mouth, 10 In., R-S28 . .   55.00
Sanitarium, Hi-Hi Bitters Co., Rock Island, Ill., Yellow Green, 9 11/16 In., R-S31 . . . . .   130.00
Sarracenia Life, Mobile, Ala., Amber, Square, 9 1/4 In., R-S34 . . . .   175.00
Saxlehner's Hunyadi Janos, Bitterquelle, Olive Green, Cork, 9 1/4 In., R-S42B 10.00
Sazerac Aromatic, PHD & Co., Lady's Leg, Gold Amber, 10 1/8 In., R-S48 . . . .   165.00
Sazerac Aromatic, PHD & Co., Lady's Leg, Milk Glass, 12 In., R-S 47 . . . . . . .200.00 to 230.00
Sazerac Aromatic, PHD & Co., Lady's Leg, Yellow Olive, 10 1/8 In., R-S48 . . . .155.00 to 170.00
Schroeder's, Established 1845, Lady's Leg, Amber, 8 1/2 In., R-S67 . . . .   225.00
Schroeder's, Louisville, Ky., Lady's Leg, Amber, 9 In., R-S63 . . . .   220.00
Schroeder's, Louisville, Ky., Rooster, Lady's Leg, Amber, 4 In., R-S66 . . . .   990.00
Schroeder's, Louisville, Ky., S.B. & G. Co., Lady's Leg, Amber, 9 In., R-S65 . . . .   195.00
Schroeder's, Louisville, Ky., S.B. & G. Co., Lady's Leg, Amber, 11 5/8 In., R-S68 . . . . .   265.00
Schroeder's, Louisville, Ky., S.B. & G. Co., Lady's Leg, Red Amber, 9 In., R-S65 . . . . .   385.00
Schroeder's, Louisville, Ky., S.B. & G. Co., Lady's Leg, Yellow Amber, 9 In., R-S65 . . .   330.00
Schroeder's Stomach, Gold Yellow Amber, Applied Mouth, 9 15/16 In., R-S75 . . . .   210.00
Sealed, Deep Red Amber, Applied Ribbon Seal, Elichtwitz & Co., 1890, 7 1/2 In. 55.00
Seaworth Bitters Co., Cape May, N.J., Lighthouse Amber, 6 1/2 In., R-S82 . . . .   3190.00
Seaworth Bitters Co., Lighthouse, Medium To Yellow Amber, 11 1/2 In., R-S81 . . . . .   5775.00
Sharp's Mountain Herb, Chocolate Amber, Sloping Collar, 9 5/8 In., R-S95 . . . .   200.00

Bitters, Old
Homestead Wild
Cherry, Cabin,
Yellow Olive,
9 3/4 In., R-37

Bitters, National,
Ear Of Corn,
1867, Amber,
Applied Mouth,
12 5/8 In., R-N8

Bitters, Triner's
American Elixer
Of Bitter Wine,
Amber, 9 In.,
R-T55

Shedd's Spring, Medium Amber, Tooled Mouth, Square, 9 3/4 In., R-S97 . . . .   155.00
Sheetz's Celebrated Bitter Cordial, Philadelphia., Pa., Aqua, 10 In. 45.00
Simon's Centennial Trade Mark, Geo. Washington Bust, Amber, 9 3/4 In., R-S110 . . .   1800.00
Simon's Centennial Trade Mark, Geo. Washington Bust, Aqua, 9 3/4 In., R-S110 . . . . .   715.00
Simon's Prussian Vegetable, Amber, Square, 10 5/8 In., R-S113 . . . . .165.00 to 175.00
Sir Robert Edgar's English Life, Ruland, Vt., Amber, Square, 8 3/4 In., R-E18 . . . . . .   825.00
Sir Robert Edgar's English Life, Rutland, Vt., Yellow Amber, 8 3/4 In., R-E18 . . . . . .   190.00
Smiths Druid, Barrel, Deep Cherry Puce, Applied Disc Mouth, 9 In., R-S124 . . . .   1020.00
Smiths Druid, Barrel, Yellow Amber, Square Mouth, 9 In., R-S124 . . . .   660.00
Smyrna Stomach, Dayton, Ohio, Tooled Ring Sloping Mouth, Square, 9 In., R-S134 . . .   145.00
Snyder's Celebrated Cordial, Phila., Pa., Amber, Applied Mouth, 9 5/8 In., R-S136 . . .   165.00
Sol Frank's Panacea, Lighthouse, Amber, Applied Mouth, 10 1/4 In., R-F79 . . . .   210.00
Solomons' Strengthening & Invigorating, Cobalt Blue, 9 5/8 In., R-S139 . . . .   715.00
Solomons' Strengthening & Invigorating, Cobalt Blue, 9 5/8 In., R-S140 . . . .   1020.00
St. Gotthard Herb, St. Louis, Mo., Light Amber, Square, 8 7/8 In., R-S12 . . . .   95.00
Stanwood's Dandelion, Yellow Dock & Wild Cherry, Amber, IP, 8 5/8 In., R-S175 . . . .   165.00
Star Kidney & Liver, Amber, Square, 8 7/8 In., R-S178 . . . .   85.00
Steinfeld's French Cognac, Amber, Applied Double Collar, 11 1/4 In., R-S185 . . . .   330.00
Suffolk, Philbrook & Tucker, Pig, Amber, Double Collar, 10 1/8 In., R-S217 . . . . .305.00 to 855.00
Sunny Castle Stomach, Jos. Dudenhoefer, Milwaukee, Deep Amber, 9 In., R-S223 . . . .   155.00
Texas Blood Purifier & Tonic, San Antonio, Texas, Gold Amber, 10 In., R-T14 . . . . . .   1375.00
Thomas A. Hurley's Stomach, Louisville, Ky., Amber, 10 1/2 In., R-H214 . . . .   305.00
Tippecanoe, H.H. Warner & Co., Light Yellow Amber, Flared Lip, 9 In., R-T30 . . .80.00 to 190.00
Tippecanoe, Misspelled Rochester, Light Amber 145.00
Toneco Stomach, Labels, Metal Seal, Stopper, Contents, Square, 9 In., R-T38 . . . .   100.00
Triner's American Elixer Of Bitter Wine, Amber, 9 In., R-T55 . . . .*Illus*   20.00
Turner Brothers, New York, Buffalo, N.Y., Olive Green, Square, 9 3/4 In., R-T70L 355.00
Turner Brothers, New York, Buffalo, N.Y., Red Amber, Square, 9 1/2 In., R-T70L 1500.00
Tyler's Standard American, Gold Amber, Sloping Mouth, Square, 9 1/4 In., R-T72 . . .   145.00
Tyler's Standard American, Root Beer Amber, Applied Sloping Collar, 9 1/4 In., R-T72   185.00
Uhler's Purifying & Strengthening, Philada, Pa., Blue Aqua, Pontil, 7 7/8 In., R-U1 . .   145.00
Ulmer's Mountain Ash Bitters, Remedy, New German, Aqua, 7 1/8 In., R-U2 . . . .   990.00
Underberg, Lady's Leg, Amber, Partial Label, ABM, 4 1/4 In., R-U8 . . . .   40.00
Von Koster Stomach, Fairfield, Conn., Amber, Tooled Sloping Mouth, 9 In., R-V32 . . .   175.00
W.C., Brobst & Rentschler, Barrel, Yellow Amber, 10 5/8 In., R-W57 . . . .   415.00
W.F. Severa Stomach, Gold Amber, Square, 9 5/8 In., R-S87 . . . .   65.00
W.L. Richardson's, South Reading, Mass., Aqua, Flared Lip, OP, 7 In., R-R58 . . . .   170.00
Wahoo & Calisaya, Jacob Pinkerton, Cabin, Gold Amber, 9 5/8 In., R-W3 . . . .   440.00
Wahoo & Calisaya, Jacob Pinkerton, Cabin, Medium Amber, Label, 9 5/8 In., R-W3 . . .   1100.00
Wait's Kidney & Liver Bitters, PCGW, Amber, Square, 9 In., R-W6 . . . . .60.00 to 70.00
Wallace's Tonic Stomach, Chicago, Ill., Amber, 9 In., R-W17 . . . .   120.00
Wampoo, Siegel & Bro., New York, Amber, Square, 9 3/4 In., R-W25 . . . .   170.00
Warner's Safe, Rochester, N.Y., Amber, Applied Mouth, 7 1/2 In., R-W35 . . . .   605.00
Warner's Safe Tonic, Gold Yellow, Tooled Mouth, Oval, 7 1/2 In., R-W39 . . . .   715.00
Warsaw Stomach, Amber, Applied Collar Mouth, 8-Sided, 10 In. 4200.00
We Never Sleep, Mugge's, Vibrant Yellow Green, Tooled Lip, 1900, 8 1/4 In. 145.00
Webb's Improved Stomach, Gold Amber, Sloping Mouth, Square, 9 In., R-W60 . . . . .   75.00
Webbs Old Rye, Jackson, Mich., Root Beer Amber, Applied Mouth, 9 In., R-W61 . . . . .   1100.00
West India Stomach, St. Louis, Mo., Amber, Square, 8 1/2 In. . . . . .85.00 to 90.00
Wheeler's Berlin, Baltimore, Yellow Green, Graphite IP, 8-Sided, 9 1/2 In., R-W83 . . . .   5500.00
Wheeler's Berlin, Baltimore, Yellow Olive, Double Collar, IP, 6-Sided, 9 1/2 In., R-W83   5500.00
Wheeler's Genuine, Aqua, 9 1/2 In., R-W85 . . . .   100.00
White's Stomach, Amber, Square, 9 1/2 In., R-W101 . . . .   125.00
White's Stomach, Gold Amber, Applied Sloping Collar, 9 1/2 In., R-W101 . . . .   100.00
Whitwell's Temperance, Boston, Aqua, OP, 7 3/4 In., R-W105 . . . . .80.00 to 95.00
Wild Cherry, C.C. Richards & Co., Pale Green Aqua, 6 1/4 In., R-W112 . . . .   75.00
William Allen's Congress, Aqua, Indented Panels, 10 In., R-A29 . . . .   80.00
William Allen's Congress, Yellow Amber, Olive Tone, 10 In., R-A29 . . . .   1870.00
Wilmerding & Co., Sole Agent For Peruvian Bitters, Flask, Amber, 6 In., R-P68 . . . . . .   6930.00
Wm. Ritmeier's California Wine, T.W. & Co., Amber, Square, 9 1/2 In., R-R67 . . . . . .   90.00
Woodcock Pepsin, John H. Schroeder, Amber, Rectangular, 8 In., R-W158 . . . .   80.00
Woodcock Pepsin, St. Louis, Mo., Tooled Mouth, 8 In., R-W159.5 . . . .   185.00

Wryghte's, London, Olive Green, Concave Panels, Pontil, 6 In., R-W165 . . . . 745.00
Yerba Buena, Flask, Amber, Ghost Y, 9 1/2 In., R-Y3 . . . . 85.00
Yerba Buena, Flask, Red Amber, Strap Side, 9 1/2 In., R-Y3 . . . . 55.00
Yerba Buena, San Francisco, Cal., Yellow Olive, R-Y3 . . . . 225.00
Young America Stomach, P. Rindskopf & Bro., Amber, 9 1/4 In., R-Y7 . . . . 440.00
Zingari, F. Rahter, Lady's Leg, Amber, Applied Mouth, 12 In., R-Z4 . . . . .185.00 to 280.00
Zingari, F. Rahter, Lady's Leg, Orange Amber, Applied Mouth, 12 In., R-Z4 . . . . .145.00 to 175.00
Zingari, F. Rahter, Lady's Leg, Red Amber, Applied Mouth, 12 In., R-Z4 . . . . 110.00
Zoeller's Stomach, Amber, Tooled Mouth, Rectangular, 9 1/2 In., R-Z7 . . . . .130.00 to 275.00
Zuzu, Amber, Square, 8 3/4 In., R-Z9 . . . . 110.00

--------------------------------- **BLACK GLASS** ---------------------------------

Black glass is not really black. It is dark green or brown. In the seventeenth century, blown black glass demijohns were used to carry liquor overseas from Europe. They were usually heavy glass bottles that were made to withstand shipping. The kick-up bottom also helped deter breakage. Many types of bottles were made of very dark glass that appeared black. This was one of the most common colors for glass wine bottles of the eighteenth and early-nineteenth centuries.

BLACK GLASS, 3-Piece Mold, Deep Kick-Up Base, Qt. 30.00
Apothecary, Olive Amber, England, 1870, 12 1/2 In. 175.00
Apothecary, Olive Amber, Pontil, Rolled Mouth, 1830, 12 1/2 In. 360.00
Bladder, Seal, Ino Hawkins, 1741, Olive Amber, Applied String Lip, England, 7 In. 2700.00
Champagne, Olive Amber, Deep Kick-Up, Pontil, 1780-1810, 10 1/4 In. 70.00
Cylindrical, Yellow Olive, Sheared Mouth, Pontil, 1750-1780, 11 1/4 In. 210.00
Dutch Kidney, Olive Amber, Applied Mouth, Pontil, 1750-1770, 7 1/8 In. 495.00
Dutch Mallet, Amber, Applied Top, OP, 1740-1760 . . . . 130.00
Dutch Onion, Blown, Applied Ring, Bubbles, OP, 7 3/4 In. 185.00
Dutch Onion, Dark Green, Applied Top, OP, c.1720 . . . . 75.00
Dutch Onion, Emerald Green, Sheared Lip, Laid On Ring, OP, c.1720s 130.00
Dutch Onion, Green Aqua, Applied Seal, 1810-1830, 3 1/2 In. 155.00
Dutch Onion, Horsehoof, Applied String Lip, OP, 1725-1735, 8 In. 100.00
Dutch Onion, Horsehoof, Wide Mouth, Crude Neck 625.00
Dutch Onion, Olive Amber, Applied Ring, OP, 1720s 90.00
Dutch Onion, Olive Amber, Expanded Mouth, String Lip, 1830, 8 3/8 In. 525.00
Dutch Onion, Olive Amber, Horsehoof, Painted Portrait, Coat Of Arms, 8 3/4 In. 415.00
Dutch Onion, Olive Amber, Horsehoof, Wide Mouth, String Lip, 1725-40, 8 1/2 In. 525.00
Dutch Onion, Olive Amber, Laid On Ring, OP, 1720s 65.00
Dutch Onion, Olive Green, Applied Ring, OP, 1740 . . . . 120.00
Dutch Onion, Olive Green, Applied String Lip, OP, 1725-1835, 5 7/8 In. 110.00
Egg Shape, Blown, Sheared Top, String Rim, 1770-1800, 19 1/2 In. 240.00
English Mallet, Olive Amber, Applied String Lip, 1740-1750, 8 1/8 In. 120.00
English Mallet, Olive Green, String Lip, 1730-1740, 7 In. 190.00
English Mallet, Olive Green, Wide Mouth, String Lip, Pontil, 1770-1790, 5 7/8 In. 550.00
English Mallet, Yellow Olive, Crude String Rim, 1750, Continental, Small 125.00
English Onion, Olive Amber, Straight Sides, Pontil, 1710-1725, 6 1/4 In. 200.00
English Onion, Squat, 1725-1730 . . . . 550.00
Globular, Medium Yellow Olive Green, Applied Mouth, Pontil, 1810, 9 5/8 In. 275.00
Globular, Yellow Olive Amber, Rolled Lip, Pontil, 1790-1820, 10 3/4 In. 855.00
Isco California Sherry, Hudson's Bay Co., Winnipeg, 3-Piece Mold, Label, 12 In. 15.00
Kidney Shape, Medium Yellow Olive Green, Dutch, 1760-1780, 7 3/8 In. 605.00
Kidney Shape, Olive Amber, Sheared Lip, Pontil, Holland, 1750-1770, 3 3/4 In. 2310.00
Ludlow, Pontil, 1810-1825, 9 3/8 In. 65.00
Mallet, Olive Green, Amber Tone, Long Neck, Deep Kick-Up, OP, Belgium, 9 1/2 In. . . . 385.00
Onion, Yellow Olive Green, Applied String Lip, Pontil, 1715-1730, 7 In. 145.00
Pancake Onion, Olive Amber, Upside-Down String Lip, 1700, 5 x 5 3/4 In. 305.00
Porter, Yellow Olive To Olive Amber, Thin String Rim, Long Neck 45.00
Red Amber, Rolled Lip, New England, 1855-1865, 8 1/4 In. 465.00
Shaft & Glob, Light Blue Green, Kick-Up, Continental, 1660-1680, 4 3/4 In. 3080.00
Spirits, Blown, Long Neck, Yellow Olive, Ring Mouth, Netherlands, 1740, 6 In. 85.00
Storage, Aqua, Wide Mouth, Flared Lip, Blown, Pontil, 1810-1830, 10 7/8 In. 330.00
Storage, Emerald Green, Flared Rim, Belled Base, Pontil, 10 3/8 In. 220.00
Storage, Medium Olive Green, Wide Mouth, Cylindrical, Pontil, Holland, 11 In. 120.00
Storage, Olive Amber, Applied String Lip, 1780-1820, 9 1/2 In. 165.00

Storage, Olive Amber, Sheared & Flared Mouth, Applied String Lip, 14 7/8 In. 240.00
Storage, Olive Amber, Sheared Lip, Applied Neck Ring, Pontil, 1880, 8 1/2 In. 215.00
Storage, Olive Amber, Sheared Mouth, Pontil, 1810, 15 In. 360.00
Storage, Olive Amber, Wide Mouth, Flared Rim, Pontil, 10 1/8 In. 150.00
Storage, Olive Green, Turn Mold, Applied Mouth, Pontil, 12 In. 100.00
Storage, Yellow Amber, Olive Tone, 3-Piece Mold, Rolled Lip, 13 7/8 In. 230.00
Storage, Yellow Olive Green, Tooled & Flared Lip, Pontil, 1780-1830, 12 3/4 In. 195.00
Storage, Yellow Olive Green, Tooled & Flared Lip, Pontil, 9 3/4 In. 165.00
Wine, Yellow Olive Green, 8-Sided, Pontil, England, 1780-1800, 9 3/4 In. 550.00
BLACKING, see Household, Blacking

---------------------------------- **BLOWN** ----------------------------------

The American glass industry did not flourish until after the Revolution. Glass for windows and blown-glass bottles were the most rewarding products. The bottles were blown in large or small sizes to hold liquor. Many glassworks made blown and pattern-molded bottles. Midwestern factories favored twisted swirl designs. The colors ranged from green and aquamarine to dark olive green or amber. Sometimes blue or dark purple bottles were blown. Some were made of such dark glass they are known as *black glass* bottles.

BLOWN, Aqua, Applied Handle, Foot, Bulbous, 6 1/4 In. 1540.00
Blue, Rope Of Blue Glass Coiled At Neck, 16 x 6 In. 35.00
Carboy, Golden Amber, Applied Top, 7 3/4 In. 65.00
Clear, Floral Enameled, 6 1/4 In. 192.00
Clear, Floral Enameled, Pewter Top, 5 3/4 In. 247.00
Decanter, 3-Piece Mold, Flared Lip, Pontil, Ground Glass Stopper, 1825, 9 In. 80.00
Decanter, Blue, Pinch, Vertical Ribs, Pontil, Pewter Cap, Trailings, Europe, 1770-1790 . . 875.00
Decanter, Leaded Glass, Dark Purple, Vertical Ribs, Pontil, Square, 1780-1810 . . . . 125.00
Engraved Floral & Brandy, 3 Applied Rings, 9 1/2 In. 60.00
Fly Trap, Pat. Appd. For, Clear, Ground Mouth, Applied String Lip, 1880-1910, 6 7/8 In. . 360.00
Globular, Bright Yellow Amber, Applied Mouth, Pontil, 1783-1830, 11 1/4 In. 410.00
Globular, Gold Amber, Heavy Applied Mouth, Pontil, 1800-1830, 9 1/4 In. 255.00
Globular, Light Olive Green, Pontil, 1780-1810, 4 1/8 In. 465.00
Globular, Pale Aqua, Flared Lip, Pontil, 1770-1810, 3 In. 100.00
Globular, Yellow Amber, Olive Tone, Rolled Mouth, Pontil, 1783-1830, 3 1/4 In. 990.00
Globular, Yellow Olive, Painted, Admiral, Ships, Coat Of Arms, Netherlands, 11 x 10 In. 1760.00
Globular, Yellow Olive, Rolled Lip, Pontil, 1780-1810, 6 5/8 In. 120.00
Gold Amber, Puce Striations Throughout, Pontil, Cylindrical, 1840-1860, 18 In. 340.00
Ludlow, Green, Applied Lip, 8 1/2 In. 200.00
Olive Green, Tooled Mouth, Pontil, 1783-1830, 7 1/4 In. 175.00
Olive Green, White Splotches, Pontil, Congressville Glass Works, 1840, 7 1/2 In. 75.00
Onion, Blue Green, Pontil, Deep Pointed Kick-Up, 1770-1810, 4 7/8 In. 355.00
Storage, Dark Olive Amber, Applied Mouth, Chamfered Corners, Pontil, 1800-1830, 8 In. 305.00
Storage, Dip Molded, Deep Olive Amber, Applied Mouth, Pontil, 1780-1810, 15 1/4 In. . 495.00
Storage, Gold Amber, Crude, 1760-1790 . . . . 140.00
Storage, Olive Green, Sheared Lip, Pontil, Holland, c.1760s 175.00
Storage, Yellow Olive, Applied Mouth, Cylindrical, 1840-1860, 13 1/2 In. 110.00
Storage, Yellow Olive, Rolled Mouth, Pontil, 1800-1830, 4 1/2 In. 210.00
Storage, Yellow Olive, Rolled Mouth, Pontil, New England, 1830-1860, 4 1/2 In. 230.00
Vial, Sapphire Blue, White Combed Swirls, Pewter Cap, 2 1/2 In. 2365.00
BROOKS, see Ezra Brooks
C.P.C., CALIFORNIA PERFUME COMPANY, see Avon
CABIN STILL, see Old Fitzgerald
CALABASH, see Flask

---------------------------------- **CANDY CONTAINER** ----------------------------------

The first figural glass candy containers date from the nineteenth century. They were made to hold candy and to be used later as toys for children. These containers were very popular after World War I. Small glass figural bottles held dime-store candy. Cars, trains, airplanes, animals, comic figures, telephones, and many other imaginative containers were made. The fad faded in the Depression years but returned in the 1940s. Today many of the same shapes hold modern candy in plastic bottles. The paper labels on the containers help a little with the dating. In the 1940s the words *Contents* or *Ingredients* were included on the labels. Earlier, this information was not necessary. Screw tops and corks were used. Some of the most popular early shapes have been reproduced in Taiwan and Hong Kong in recent years. A club with a newsletter is Candy Container Collectors of America, PO Box 352, Chelmsford, MA 01824-0352.

Airplane, Spirit Of Goodwill, Replacement Closure		100.00
Airplane, Spirit Of St. Louis, Closure, Metal		650.00
Airplane, Spirit Of St. Louis, Pink		350.00
Barney Google Riding Spark Plug, Sheared Lip, 1925, 4 1/8 In.		605.00
Baseball Player, With Bat, Closure		695.00
Battleship, On Waves, Closure		200.00
Boat, Battleship On Waves, Closure		150.00
Boat, Colorado, Closure, 1914		300.00
Bulldog, On Round Base, Closure		75.00
Cannon, 2 Wheels, No. 1, Closure		350.00
Car, Gum, Fresh Pak Co., Moline, Ill., Contents, Cap, 4 1/2 In.	*Illus*	15.00
Charlie Chaplin, Closure		150.00
Chick, In Shell Auto, Closure		375.00
Chicken, On Sagging Basket, Closure		150.00
Chicken On Nest, Closure		150.00
Clock, Alarm, Closure		335.00
Dog, Brown, U.S.A., 4 In.	*Illus*	40.00
Don't Park Here, Closure		325.00
Duck, Large Bill, No Closure	125.00 to	175.00
Duck, On Basket, Closure		150.00
Duck, On Round Base, Closure		450.00
Fire Engine, Ladder Truck, Closure		295.00
Gun, Stough, 1939		25.00
Horn, Horn O'Candy, Plastic Mouth Piece & Rim, Contents, 7 In.	*Illus*	10.00
Horn, With Candy & Sticker, Millstein, 1948		25.00
Independence Hall, Closure		125.00
Jackie Coogan, Frosted, Closure		1000.00
Kiddies Breakfast Bell, Closure		65.00
Lamp, Closure		230.00

Candy Container, Car,
Gum, Fresh Pak Co.,
Moline, Ill., Contents, Cap,
4 1/2 In.

Candy Container,
Dog, Brown,
U.S.A., 4 In.

Candy Container,
Horn, Horn O'Candy,
Plastic Mouth Piece &
Rim, Contents, 7 In.

Candy Container,
McKinley, Full Dinner Pail,
Glass Top

Candy Container, Pistol, Original Cap,
Contents, 7 1/2 In.

Candy Container, Rabbit,
Contents, 6 in.

Candy Container,
Spark Plug, 3 In.

Candy Container,
Suitcase, 3 1/2 In.

Lantern, Barn, Gray, No Closure	60.00
Lantern, Beaded Trim, No. 1, Closure	50.00
Lantern, Bond Electric Corp., Closure	25.00
Lantern, Tiny Plain, Closure	25.00
Liberty Bell, With Label, Closure	225.00
Liberty Motor Plane, Wing Span 6 1/4-In.	2200.00
Locomotive, Lithographed Tin Closure, Purple Tint Glass	110.00
McKinley, Full Dinner Pail, Glass Top ....*Illus*	45.00
Milk Carrier	125.00
Mule, Pulling Water Barrel, Closure	100.00
Petunia Pig	25.00
Piano, Ruby Flashed, Closure	400.00
Picolo, Closure	150.00
Pipe, With Candy, Closure, Germany	65.00
Pistol, Original Cap, Contents, 7 1/2 In. ....*Illus*	35.00
Rabbit, Contents, 6 In. ....*Illus*	20.00
Rabbit, On Log, Glass	265.00
Racer, Metal Closure	250.00
Rocking Horse, Clown Rider, Replacement Closure	200.00
Rolling Pin, Closure	250.00
Rooster, Crowing, Closure	325.00
Spark Plug, 3 In. ....*Illus*	125.00
Suitcase, 3 1/2 In. ....*Illus*	50.00
Tank	30.00
Telephone, Flat Top, Closure	50.00
Telephone, Victory Glass, Closure ....50.00 to	120.00
Telephone, West Co., 1907	95.00
Tune In Radio, Closure	200.00
U.S. Postal Mail Box, Glass	115.00
Uncle Sam, Closure	495.00
Watch, Complete	750.00
Watermelon	195.00
Windmill, 5 Windows, Ruby Flashed, Closure	500.00
Windmill, Blade, Dutch	100.00
World Globe On Stand, Closure	550.00
Ye Olde Oaken Bucket, Closure	100.00

CANNING JAR, see Fruit Jar
CASE, see Gin

--------------------- **COCA-COLA** ---------------------

Coca-Cola was first served in 1886 in Atlanta, Georgia. John S. Pemberton, a pharmacist, originated the syrup and sold it to others. He was trying to make a patent medicine to aid those who suffered from nervousness, headaches, or stomach problems. At first the syrup was mixed with water; but in 1887, Willis E. Venable mixed it with carbonated water, and Coca-Cola was made. Pemberton sold his interest in the company to Venable and a local businessman, George S. Lowndes, in 1888. Later that year, Asa

Griggs Candler, an owner of a pharmaceutical company, and some business friends became partners in Coca-Cola. A short time later they purchased the rest of the company. After some other transactions, Asa Candler became the sole owner of Coca-Cola for a grand total of $2,300. The first ad for Coca-Cola appeared in the *Atlanta Journal* on May 29, 1886. Since that time the drink has been sold in all parts of the world and in a variety of bottles and cans. The *waisted* bottle was first used in 1916. Over 1,000 commemorative Coca-Cola bottles have been issued since 1949. The company advertised heavily, and bottles, trays, calendars, signs, toys, and lamps, as well as thousands of other items, can be found. See listings under Go-Withs at the back of the book.

Coca-Cola written in script was trademarked in 1893. Coke was registered in 1945. The first 16-ounce bottle was introduced in 1960. The brand name Diet Coke was first used in 1982. In 1985 the company introduced a new formula but didn't change the name. Six months later they were forced by popular opinion to bring back the old formula under the name Classic Coke. Cherry Coke was also introduced in 1985. There is a national club with a newsletter, The Coca-Cola Collectors Club, P.O. Box 49166, Atlanta, GA 30359-1166. You can learn from the national about local meetings. Price guides and books about the history of Coca-Cola are listed in the Bibliography. The Schmidt Coca-Cola Museum in Elizabethtown, Kentucky, is associated with Coca-Cola bottlers. The Coca-Cola Company Archives (PO Drawer 1734, Atlanta, GA 30313) can answer questions about Coca-Cola memorabilia. The World of Coca-Cola museum at 55 Martin Luther King Dr. in Atlanta has exhibits of interest to collectors.

COCA-COLA, Albermarle, N.C., Aqua, Script, Crown Top 35.00
  Alua, Ok., Hobbleskirt 5.00
  Amarillo, Tex., Hobbleskirt 5.00
  Baton Rouge, La., Hobbleskirt 5.00
  Beidenharn, Vicksburg, Miss., Script 70.00
  Berkshire Bottling Co., Pittsfield, Ma., Nov. 6, 1923 .... 10.00
  Big Chief C.C. Bottling, Pittsburg, Kan., Aqua, Straight Sides ... 20.00
  Binghampton Bottling Co., Yellow Olive Citron, Contents, 6 1/2 Oz. ... 150.00
  Binghamton Bottling Co. Inc., Lime Citron ....100.00 to 130.00
  Birmingham, Ala., Aqua, Script 35.00
  Birmingham, Ala., Straight Sides, Script 15.00
  Buddy Holly, Music Festival, Limited Edition, Box 30.00
  Canada, H On Base, Straight Sides, ABM, 1915, 7 3/4 In. 45.00
  Canada, Olive To Emerald Green, Straight Sides, ABM, 1915, 7 3/4 In. ... 125.00
  Chattanooga, 75th Anniversary, 1974 ....*Illus* 5.00
  Christmas, Bradford, Pa., 1923, 6 Oz. 12.00
  Christmas, Norfolk, Va., 1923 .... 10.00
  Cleveland, Ohio, Amber, Arrow, Straight Sides ....*Illus* 75.00
  Denver Bottling Co., Colo., Dark Blue 600.00
  Display Bottle, Christmas, Gal. 300.00
  First Throwaway, 9 In. ....*Illus* 4.00
  Gilley's, Pasadena, Texas, 1984, 10 Oz. ....*Illus* 30.00

Coca-Cola, Chattanooga,   Coca-Cola, Cleveland, Ohio,   Coca-Cola, First
75th Anniversary, 1974   Amber, Arrow, Straight Sides   Throwaway, 9 In.

Coca-Cola, Unforgettable
Forties, 1984, 10 Oz.
Coca-Cola, Jimmy Carter,
39th President, 10 Oz.
Coca-Cola, Gilley's, Pasadena,
Texas, 1984, 10 Oz.;

Coca-Cola, Hebrew
Script, 6 In.
Coca-Cola, Trademark
Registered, Pat. D105529,
Light Green

Gold Seal, Property Of The Coca-Cola Co. Of Canada Limited, ABM, 1920s, 7 1/4 In. . .	10.00
Hebrew Script, 6 In. . . . . *Illus*	2.00
Hygeia Bottling Works, Pensacola, Fla., Aqua	55.00
Jackson, Tenn., Amber, Script, Crown Top	85.00
Jimmy Carter, 39th President, 10 Oz. . . . . *Illus*	195.00
Knoxville, Tenn., Amber, Crown Top, 7 1/2 In. . . . . .60.00 to 80.00
Lake Charles, La., Hobbleskirt	5.00
Memphis, Tenn., Amber, Arrow, Script	30.00
Morgantown, W. Va., Amber, Crown Top, ABM	60.00
Philadelphia, Amber	30.00
Pittsburgh, Pa., Amber	35.00
Prorerty (Error) Of The Coca-Cola Company, Canada, Teal, Straight Sides, 7 3/4 In.	75.00
Royal Palm Soda, Property Of Coca-Cola, Palm Tree, Pat. Nov. 6, 1923, 6 Oz.	20.00
Seltzer, 10-Sided, Sapphire Blue, Metal Dispenser, 1880-1920, 12 1/8 In.	185.00
Smile Bottling Works, Hagerstown, Me., 1910, 7 3/8 In.	15.00
Trademark Registered, Pat. D105529, Light Green . . . . *Illus*	2.00
Unforgettable Forties, 1984, 10 Oz. . . . . *Illus*	40.00
W. Palm Beach, Fla., Hobbleskirt	15.00
Williamsburg Bottling Works, Williamsburg, Pa., Amethyst	15.00

-------------------------------- **COLLECTORS ART** --------------------------------

Collectors Art bottles are made of hand-painted porcelain. The bird series was made in the 1970s. The first issued was the bluebird, then the meadowlark, canary, hummingbird, parakeet, and cardinal. Only 12 birds were issued each year and each was limited to 1,200 pieces. The later editions included bulls (1975), dogs, other animals, and a 1971 Corvette Stingray.

COLLECTORS ART, Afghan Hound, 1975, Miniature	15.00
Angus Bull, 1975, Miniature . . . . .20.00 to 25.00
Basset Hound, 1977, Miniature	20.00
Blue Bird, 1971, Miniature	24.00
Blue Jay, 1972, Miniature	25.00
Brahma Bull, 1975, Miniature	32.00
Bunting, 1973, Miniature	18.00
Canary, 1971, Miniature	22.00
Cardinal, 1971, Miniature	20.00
Charolais Bull, 1975, Miniature	26.00
Chipmunks, 1972, Miniature	18.00
Collie, 1976, Miniature	22.00
Corvette, Goodyear Tires, 1971	30.00
Corvette Stingray, Blue, 1971	60.00
Corvette Stingray, Red, 1971	30.00
Dachshund, 1977, Miniature	21.00
Dalmatian, 1976, Miniature	25.00
Doberman, Black, 1976, Miniature	20.00
Doberman, Red, 1976, Miniature	25.00
Goldfinch, 1972, Miniature	22.00

Hereford, 1972	36.00
Hummingbird, 1971, Miniature	20.00
Irish Setter, 1976, Miniature	18.00
Koala, 1972, Miniature	30.00
Longhorn Bull	30.00
Meadowlark, 1971, Miniature	20.00
Mexican Fighting Bull, 1975, Miniature	30.00
Oriole, 1972, Miniature	24.00
Parakeet, 1971, Miniature	20.00
Pointer, Brown, White, 1976, Miniature	15.00
Poodle, Black, 1976, Miniature	15.00 to 20.00
Poodle, Brown, 1976, Miniature	15.00 to 20.00
Rabbits, 1972, Miniature	40.00
Raccoons, 1973, Miniature	28.00
Robin, 1972, Miniature	18.00
Schnauzer, 1976, Miniature	20.00
Shepherd, Black, 1976, Miniature	25.00 to 30.00
Shepherd, German, Brown, 1976, Miniature	18.00
Skunks, 1972, Miniature	20.00
St. Bernard, 1977, Miniature	20.00

COLOGNE

Our ancestors did not bathe very often and probably did not smell very good. It is no wonder that the perfume and cologne business thrived in earlier centuries. Perfume is a liquid mixture with alcohol. Cologne is a similar mixture but with more alcohol, so the odor is not as strong or as lasting. Scent was also popular. It was a perfume with some ammonia in the mixture so it could be used to revive someone who felt faint. The mixture dictated the type and size of bottle. Scent bottles usually had screw tops to keep the ammonia smell from escaping. Because its odor did not last as long as that of perfume, cologne was used more often and was sold in larger bottles. Cologne became popular in the United States about 1830; the Boston and Sandwich Glass Company of Sandwich, Massachusetts, was making cologne bottles at that time. Since cologne bottles were usually put on display, they were made with fancy shapes, brightly colored glass, or elaborate labels. Blown figural and scroll bottles were favored. The best-known cologne bottle is the 1880 Charlie Ross bottle. It has the embossed face of Charlie, a famous kidnap victim—a strange shape to choose for a cologne bottle! Today the name *perfume* is sometimes used incorrectly as a generic term meaning both cologne and perfume. Old and new bottles for cologne, perfume, and scents are collected. Related bottles may be found in the Perfume and Scent categories.

COLOGNE, 6-Sided, Amethyst, Sheared Lip, OP, J.M. Farina, 4 3/4 In.	35.00
6-Sided, Corset Waist, Teal Blue, Rolled Lip, Sandwich, 1865-1875, 4 3/4 In.	495.00
6-Sided, Sapphire Blue, Tooled Mouth, Pontil, C. & B., 1840-1860, 3 5/8 In.	155.00
8-Sided, Corset Waist, Purple Amethyst, 1865-1875, 7 In.	1070.00
8-Sided, Corset Waist, Purple Amethyst, Rolled Lip, Sandwich, 1860-1874, 7 In.	110.00
8-Sided, Corset Waist, Purple Amethyst, Sandwich, 4 In.	200.00
8-Sided, Pink Amethyst, 1865-1875, 4 3/4 In.	330.00
10-Sided, Engraved Cologne, Pressed Glass, Stopper, 8 1/4 In. ....*Illus*	175.00
11-Sided, Powder Blue, Milk Glass, Tooled Lip, Pontil, 1865-1880, 2 5/8 In.	190.00
12-Sided, Amethyst, Boston & Sandwich Glass Works, 6 3/8 In.	300.00
12-Sided, Blue, Flared Lip, Tubular Pontil, 6 In.	355.00
12-Sided, Cobalt Blue, Sloped Shoulders, Sandwich, 7 1/4 In.	165.00
12-Sided, Emerald Green, Sloped Shoulders, Rolled Lip, Pontil, 1865-1875, 10 In.	855.00
12-Sided, Paneled, Bunch Of Grapes With Leaves, Aqua, 1840-1860, 6 1/4 In.	415.00
12-Sided, Paneled, Inward Rolled Mouth, Smooth Base, 1860-1880, 7 1/8 In.	175.00
12-Sided, Paneled, Teal Blue, Blue Opalescent Neck, 1860-1880, 5 1/2 In.	385.00
12-Sided, Sapphire Blue, Pontil, Sandwich, 1840-1860, 7 1/4 In.	275.00
12-Sided, Sapphire To Electric Blue, 2-Piece Mold, Boston & Sandwich, 5 7/8 In.	130.00
12-Sided, Teal Blue, Rolled Lip, Sandwich, 1860-1875, 4 7/8 In.	165.00
16 Vertical Ribs, Cobalt Blue, Rolled & Flared Lip, Pontil, Toilet Water, 5 1/8 In.	175.00
16 Vertical Ribs, Sapphire Blue, Flared Lip, Pontil, Toilet Water, 1825-1835, 6 1/4 In.	275.00
16 Vertical Ribs, Sapphire Blue, Inward Rolled Mouth, Pontil, 1820-1860, 5 1/2 In.	265.00
Amethyst, 3-Piece Mold, Flared Mouth, 1820-1840, 6 In.	330.00
Amethyst, Corset Waist, Paneled, 4 1/2 In.	450.00

Cologne, 10-Sided,
Engraved Cologne,
Pressed Glass,
Stopper, 8 1/4 In.

Cologne, Boy On
Chair, 4 1/2 In.

Cologne, Monument,
6 1/2 In.

Amethyst, Gothic Corner Columns, Cork Stopper, 5 1/2 In. 40.00
Aqua, Indian, Arches & Columns, OP, 3 3/4 In. 115.00
Aqua, Urn & Floral Design, Outward Rolled Mouth, Pontil, 6 1/2 In. 105.00
B.P.O.E., Canteen Shape, Indian, Elk & Arrows, Cream, Brown Transfer, 1870, 3 1/4 In. .   55.00
Birds & Florals, Etched, Pontil, Toilet Water, 1760-1800 . . . .   355.00
Blue Opalescent, Thumbprint, Herringbone Corners, Sandwich, 1880, 6 In. 880.00
Blue Opalescent, Tooled Mouth, Pontil, Boston & Sandwich, 12 In. 165.00
Boy On Chair, 4 1/2 In. . . . .*Illus*   75.00
Buddha, Sitting Under Arch, Twisted Columns, Rectangular, Flared Mouth, Pontil, 6 In. .   110.00
Cake Walk, Blue, Yellow, Fuschia, Purple, Green, Brown, Black Man Dancing, 11 In. . . .   1100.00
Citron, 3-Piece Mold, Pontil, Boston & Sandwich, Toilet Water, 6 In. 1430.00
Cobalt Blue, 3-Piece Mold, Flared Lip, Blown Stopper, 1835, 5 In. 240.00
Cobalt Blue, 3-Piece Mold, Flared Lip, Pontil, Toilet Water, 1815-1825, 5 1/2 In. 130.00
Cobalt Blue, 3-Piece Mold, Ribbed, Flared & Rolled Lip, Pontil, Toilet Water, 5 3/4 In. .   110.00
Cobalt Blue, Alternating Diamond Pattern & Plain Panels, Rolled Lip, 5 5/8 In. 90.00
Cobalt Blue, Cut Glass Neck Panels, Square Base, Flared Lip, Stopper, 3 1/2 In. 360.00
Cobalt Blue, Flared Lip, Pontil, Blown Stopper, Toilet Water, 1820-1830, 5 1/2 In. 55.00
Cobalt Blue, Knight Between 2 Columns, Flared Lip, 1845-1860, 4 1/8 In. 770.00
Cobalt Blue, Rolled Lip, Sandwich, 1865-1880, 4 3/4 In. 465.00
Cobalt Blue, Vertical Ribs, Flanged Lip, Pontil, Toilet Water, 5 In. 210.00
Cone, Amethyst, Inward Rolled Mouth, Pontil, 1860, 8 1/8 In. 360.00
Corset Waist, Canary Yellow, Tooled Lip, Sandwich, 1860-1870, 4 7/8 In. 1595.00
Corset Waist, Paneled, Amethyst, Tooled Mouth, Sandwich Type, 1840-1860, 6 In. 770.00
Cut Glass, Clear, Cobalt Blue Overlay, Pedestal Base, Stopper, Sandwich, 6 1/2 In. 195.00
Cylindrical, Beaded Rib Pattern, Milk Glass, Sandwich, 10 1/4 In. 145.00
Cylindrical, Blue Opalescent, Tapered, Floral Label, Pontil, 10 7/8 In. 275.00
Cylindrical, Milk Glass, Fluted Ribs, Sandwich, 10 1/4 In. 95.00
Dancing Indians, Aqua, Rolled Lip, OP, 1845-1855, 4 7/8 In. 155.00
Eau De Ybry, Old Fashioned Garden, Hourglass, Yellow, BIMAL, 7 In. 60.00
Elephant Shape, Tooled Flared Mouth, Pontil, 1840-1860, 4 3/4 In. 550.00
Emerald Green, Rolled Lip, Bubbles, OP, 5 1/2 In. 175.00
General Sherman, Coin Shape, Brown Transfer, Cream, 1880, 3 3/8 In. 105.00
Green, Flared Top, Sandwich, 5 In. 130.00
Guerlain, Eau De Cologne Hegemonienne, Beehive Shape, Ball Stopper, 9 1/2 In. 1270.00
House Of Men, Inc., His, Man's Torso Shape, Enamel, Ivory Head Stopper, 6 1/2 In. 200.00
Inverted Pear, Pressed & Cut Floral, Acorn Stopper, Toilet Water, 9 1/2 In. 75.00
L. Kossuth, Bust, Aqua, Pontil, Rolled Lip, 1860, 5 3/4 In. 85.00
Lavender Blue, 3-Piece Mold, Toilet Water, 5 1/2 In. 180.00
Light Yellow Olive, Applied Lip, Pointed Kick-Up, Pontil, 1790-1820, 4 1/8 In. 385.00
Milk Glass, Beaded Flute, Tooled Lip, 8 In. 55.00
Milk Glass, Gold, Black, Blue Label Under Glass, Glass Stopper, Toilet Water, 6 In. 605.00
Milk Glass, Gold, Black, Pink Label Under Glass, Glass Stopper, Toilet Water, 6 In. 800.00
Milk Glass, Large Logo, Stopper, E.N. Lightner & Co., Detroit, Mich, 7 1/2 In. 80.00
Milk Glass, Opalescent, Thumbprint, Herringbone Corners, Sandwich, 1880, 9 In. 245.00

Cologne, Monument
With Lion, 5 In.

Cologne, Nina Violet, Triple
Extract, C.B. Goodworth
Sons Co, 2 1/8 In.

Milk Glass, Star & Stripe, Partial Flared Lip, 1870-1880, 7 1/2 In. 110.00
Monument, 6 1/2 In. ....*Illus* 75.00
Monument, Cobalt Blue, Building Shape, Tooled Mouth, 1860-1880, 6 3/8 In. 130.00
Monument, Milk Glass, Tapered, 8 In. ....85.00 to 95.00
Monument, Milk Glass, Tapered, Stopper, Sandwich, 1880, 15 In. 305.00
Monument, Opaque Blue Gray, On Pedestal, France, 1845-1865, 8 1/2 In. 440.00
Monument, Teal Green, Flared Lip, 1865-1875, 12 In. 1700.00
Monument With Lion, 5 In. ....*Illus* 125.00
Multicolor Butterfly & Reeds, Cut Glass, Enamel, Screw Cap, 1893, 4 In. 70.00
Nina Violet, Triple Extract, C.B. Goodworth Sons Co, 2 1/8 In. ....*Illus* 18.00
Pillar Mold, Canary Yellow, Pontil, 1860-1870, 5 In. 140.00
Pocahontas, Indian, Aqua, Sheared Mouth, 5 In. 100.00
Pocahontas, Indian, Diamond Shape, Aqua, Inward Rolled Mouth, Pontil, 4 3/4 In. 175.00
Pomegranate, Open Flower, Vaseline, Pressed Glass Stopper, Sandwich, 8 In. 770.00
Purple Cobalt Blue, 3-Piece Mold, Ribbed, Flared Lip, Stopper, Toilet Water, 6 In. 150.00
Purple Cobalt Blue, 3-Piece Mold, Toilet Water, 5 1/2 In. 170.00
Sapphire Blue, 2-Piece Mold, Flared Mouth, Period Stopper, 1860-1880, 7 In. 275.00
Sapphire Blue, 3-Piece Mold, Flared Mouth, Sandwich, Toilet Water, 5 1/4 In. 185.00
Sapphire Blue, Flared Mouth, Pontil, Sandwich, Toilet Water, 6 1/4 In. 155.00
Sapphire Blue, Flat Corset Form, Palmette, Scrolled Acanthus, 1840-1860, 5 1/2 In. ... 1980.00
Sapphire Blue, Polished Lip, Ground Glass Stopper, Sandwich, 1850, 5 In. 440.00
Slender Cone Shape, Yellow Olive, Pointed Ground Stopper, OP, 11 In. 55.00
Thumbprint, Purple Amethyst, Rolled Lip, 1860-1870, 5 3/4 In. 305.00
Turquoise, Flared Top, Sandwich, 5 1/3 In. 110.00
Vantines Oriental Toilet Water, Japanese Flags & Characters 22.00
Vertical Ribs, Swirled Left At Neck, Flared Lip, Toilet Water, 6 In. 60.00

─────────────────────── **CORDIAL** ───────────────────────

Cordials are liqueurs that are usually drunk at the end of the meal. They consist of pure
alcohol or cognac, plus flavors from fruits, herbs, flowers, or roots. A cordial may also
be a medicinal drink. Curacao is a cordial containing orange peel, Creme de Menthe
contains mint, Triple Sec has orange and cognac, and Kummel has coriander and car-
away seeds.

CORDIAL, Balm Of Gilead, Prepared Only By Dr. Solomon, Amber, 1790-1820, 6 7/8 In. . . 4400.00
  Booth & Sedgwick's, Deep Blue Green, Beveled Corners, IP, 1845-1860, 9 3/4 In. 415.00
  Booth & Sedgwick's, London, Amber, Applied Mouth, 9 1/2 In. 220.00
  Booth & Sedgwick's, London, Forest Green, Sloping Mouth, Square, Pontil, 7 In. 210.00
  Brandy, S.M. & Co., N.Y., Gold Yellow Amber, Applied Medallion, Necklace, 10 In. ... 1485.00
  Charles', Medium Olive Amber, Applied Mouth, London, 1865-1875, 9 3/4 In. 130.00
  Constitution Beverage, W. Olmsted & Co., New York, Gold Amber, 10 In. 210.00
  Dr. Bigger's Huckleberry, Atlanta, Ga., Clear, Label, Tooled Mouth, 5 1/8 In. 40.00
  Dr. McBride, World's Relief, Aqua, Applied Top, 6 1/2 In. 65.00
  Dr. Morse's Invigorating, Aqua, Sloping Collar, OP, 7 3/8 In. 85.00
  Ewbank's Topaz Cinchona, Amber, Applied Sloping Collar Mouth, 9 3/8 In. 140.00
  Flora Delle Alpi, Gold Star-Shaped Paper Labels, Cork, 10 In. ....*Illus* 5.00
  Lediard's Morning Call, Olive Green, 1865-1875, 9 3/4 In. ....35.00 to 195.00

McLean's Strengthening Cordial Blood Purifier, Aqua, 9 In. 20.00
Morley's Liver & Kidney, Deep Amber, Tooled Mouth, 1880-1890, 9 In. 330.00
Mrs. E. Kidder Dysentery, Boston, Aqua, Cylindrical, Pontil, 7 1/4 In. . . . . .105.00 to 110.00
Olivers Lemon Pineapple, Orange Horehound, Rye Rock, New York, ABM, Qt. 20.00
Peychaud's American Aromatic Bitter Cordial, L.E. Jung, Amber 38.00
R.E. Messenger & Co., London, Olive Green, Rectangular, 1840-1860, 7 3/4 In. 75.00
Roboline R & C., N.Y., Amber, Ring Top, 1880s, 9 In. 375.00
Shaker Digestive, 8 In. 75.00
Spain's Golden Cream Sherry, Foil Wrapped Amber Bottle, Label, 12 In. . . . .*Illus*   10.00
Strasdowsky, Green, Produce Of France, Paper Label, Cork, 12 In. . . . .*Illus*   15.00
W.H. Jones & Co. Importers Wines, Spirits, Boston, Mass., Green, Strapside, 10 In. . .   26.00
Wishart's Pine Tree Tar, Medium Blue Green, 1870, 9 3/4 In. . . . . .130.00 to 190.00
Wishart's Pine Tree Tar, Phila., Light Copper Amber, 7 1/2 In. 80.00
Wishart's Pine Tree Tar, Phila., Patent 1859, Emerald Green, 9 1/2 In. . . . . .90.00 to 230.00
Wishart's Pine Tree Tar Cordial, Phila., Pine Tree, Teal Green, 1870, 8 In. 175.00

────────────────────────────── **COSMETIC** ──────────────────────────────

Cosmetics of all kinds have been packaged in bottles. Hair restorer, hair dye, creams, rosewater, and many other product bottles can be found. Paper labels on early bottles add to their value.

COSMETIC, Ainaxab Celebrated Eygyptian Elixer For The Skin, Hieroglyphics 85.00
Ayer's Hair Vigor, Peacock Blue, Tooled Top, 6 1/2 In. . . . . .55.00 to 75.00
Baldplate Hair Tonic Co., New York, 8 Oz., Light Amethyst, 6 1/2 In. 25.00
Barrow Evans Hair Restorer, Medium Blue, Bevelled Edge, 6 In. . . . . .26.00 to 35.00
Barry's Safe Hair Dye, N.Y., Cobalt Blue, Tooled Lip, 1880-1890, 4 1/8 In. 35.00
Barry's Tricopherous For The Skin & Hair, New York, Aqua, BIMAL 15.00
Batchelor's Liquid Hair Dye, Aqua 12.00
Binder Dandruff Eradicator, Pottstown, Pa., Aqua, 8 In. 30.00
Bogle's Hair, Aqua, OP 55.00
Boswell & Warner's Colorific, Cobalt Blue, Tooled Top, 5 1/2 In. 35.00
Bowen's Genuine Crude Oil Products, Hair Grower, 1910-1915, 6 3/4 In. 145.00
Burma Shave, Jar, Lid, 1 Lb. 12.00
C.S. Emerson American Hair Restorative, Cleveland, Oh., Aqua, Oval, 6 1/2 In. 215.00
Canadian Booster Hair Tonic & Dandruff Cure, Windsor, Ont., 6 1/2 In. 50.00
Cara Nome Talcum, Langlois, New York, Shaker Top, 5 1/4 In. . . . .*Illus*   10.00
Chamberlain's Lotion, Yellow Label, Instructions Around Bottle, 1940, Sample 1.00
Chevalier's Life For The Hair, Aqua, 7 In. 20.00
Circassian Hair Rejuvenator, Pearson & Co., Brooklyn N.Y., Amber, 1865, 7 In. 195.00
Circassian Hair Restorative, Cincinnati, Amber, Fancy Panels, 7 In. 200.00
Coke Dandruff Cure, Embossed Base, Light Amethyst Tint, 5 In. 15.00
Concreta Molinard, Rouge, Toute Le Provence, Paris, 1 1/8 In. . . . .*Illus*   2.00
D. Damschinsky Liquid Hair Dye, New York 8.00
De Meridor's Liquid Beauty Powder, Amethyst, 5 In. 20.00
Dodge Brothers Melanine Hair Tonic, Purple Amethyst, 7 1/4 In. 500.00
Dr. D. Jayne's Hair Tonic, Philada., Aqua, Oval, Pontil, 4 1/2 In. 70.00

Cordial, Flora Delle Alpi, Gold Star-Shaped Paper Labels, Cork, 10 In.

Cordial, Spain's Golden Cream Sherry, Foil Wrapped Amber Bottle, Label, 12 In.

Cordial, Strasdowsky, Green, Produce Of France, Paper Label, Cork, 12 In.

Dr. D. Jayne's Hair Tonic, Aqua, Oval, Pontil, 6 3/4 In. . . . . .40.00 to 60.00
Dr. Leon's Electric Hair Renewer, Ziegler & Smith, Phila., Pink Amethyst, 7 In. 250.00
Dr. Mathews' Gray Hair Restorer, San Francisco, Applied Mouth, Paper Label, 7 In. .   85.00
Dr. Tebbett's Physiological Hair Regenerator, Amber, Rectangular, 6 1/4 In. 60.00
Dr. Tebbett's Physiological Hair Regenerator, Burgundy Amethyst, 7 1/2 In. 160.00
Dr. Tebbett's Physiological Hair Regenerator, Medium To Deep Amethyst, 8 In. . . .   330.00
Dr. Wilson's Hair Restorer, Amber, Rectangular, 6 5/8 In. 12.00
Dresser, Red, Onion Shape, Long Neck, Wheel Cut Flutes, 7 In. 95.00
E.S. Russell's Castanaine For The Hair, Nashua, N.H., Amber 50.00
Edward Harlene Astol Hair Colour Restorer, Honey Amber, Rectangular, 6 3/4 In. . .   12.00
Electric Blue Florida Water, Aqua, Applied Top, 7 In. 22.00
Elysian Mfg. Co. Chemists & Perfumers, Bloom Of Youth Face Powder, Cobalt Blue .   80.00
Empress Instantaneous Hair Color Restorer, Amber, 4 1/4 In. 10.00
Espy's Fragrant Cream, Light Amethyst, 6 In. 10.00
Fagret's Hair Tonic, Balto, Md. 10.00
Fish's Hair Restorative, San Francisco, Aqua, Applied Top, 7 1/4 In. 770.00
Florentine Hair Promoter, Label, Contents 15.00
Florida Water, Cherub In Ship Label, Tax Stamp, 6 3/4 In. 12.00
Fountain Of Youth Hair Restorer, Trenton, N.J., Amber, Rectangular, 7 1/4 In. .80.00 to 130.00
G.A.P. Mason Alpine Hair Balm, Providence, R.I., Yellow Olive, Pontil, 1840, 7 In. . . .   415.00
Gallagher's Magical Hair Oil, Philada., Amethyst, BIMAL, 6 In. 15.00
Guerlain Cream, Jar, Porcelain, Rose Design Lid, Mid-19th Century, Sample, 1 1/4 In. .   1585.00
Hall's Hair Renewer, R.P.H. & Co., C.G., Peacock Blue, Glass Stopper, 7 3/4 In. 495.00
Harrison's Columbian Hair Dye, Backwards S, 3 1/4 In. 25.00
Harrison's Columbian Hair Dye, Beveled Edges, Sheared Lip, Pontil, 1850, 3 1/2 In. .   145.00
Harrison's Hair Colour Restorer, Amber, Sunken Panel, 6 1/2 In. 18.00
Hays's Hair Health, Pale Amber, Label, Rectangular, Box, 6 1/2 In. 25.00
Heinrick's Rose Cream Lotion, Minneapolis, Label, Stopper, Rectangular, 6 3/4 In. . . .   15.00
Humphrey's New York Witch Hazel Oil, SCA, 3 In. 20.00
Ingrams Milk Weed Cream, Milk Glass 25.00
J. Cristadoro Liquid Hair Dye, Aqua, Pontil, 2 7/8 In. 20.00
J. Cristadoro's Hair Restorative & Beautifier, N.Y., Light Aqua, Applied Top 35.00
John Hart & Co., Heart, Amber, 7 1/4 In. 465.00
John Hart & Co., Heart, Amber, Double Collar, 1875-1885, 7 In. 360.00
Kickapoo Sage Hair Tonic, Cobalt Blue, Tooled Lip, 4 1/2 In.   185.00
Lady Esther Face Cream, 4-Purpose, U.S. Tax $.15, Chicago, Ill., 10 Oz. . . . .*Illus*   20.00
Larkin Rose Talcum, Larkin Co. Perfumers, Buffalo, Contents, 4 1/4 In. . . . .*Illus*   28.00
Larkin Soap Co., Green, Stopper, 3 In. 20.00
Liquid Green Soap, Willow Of Boston, Bath, Crown Stopper, 7 3/8 In. . . . .*Illus*   18.00
Lockyer's Sulpher Hair Restorer, Aqua, Oval, 7 1/2 In. 15.00
Lorrimers Excelsior Hair Tonic, Amber, 8 1/4 In. 45.00
Lyon's For The Hair, Kathairon, N.Y., Blue Aqua, Cork, 6 1/4 In. . . . . .15.00 to 35.00
M.A. Reaves Great Electric Hair Tonic . . . . .90.00 to 110.00
Mack's Florida Water, Blue Aqua, Green Streak, Applied Top, 8 3/4 In. 45.00
Maltin M'f'g Co. Chemists, New York, Amber, Label, Rectangular, 8 1/2 In. 15.00
Mascaro Tonique For The Hair, Rochester, N.Y., BIMAL, SCA . . . . .22.00 to 25.00

Cosmetic, Cara Nome
Talcum, Langlois, New
York, Shaker Top, 5 1/4 In.

Cosmetic, Concreta Molinard, Rouge, Toute
Le Provence, Paris, 1 1/8 In.

Cosmetic, Lady Esther Face
Cream, 4-Purpose, U.S. Tax
$.15, Chicago, Ill., 10 Oz.

Cosmetic, Liquid
Green Soap, Willow
Of Boston, Bath,
Crown Stopper,
7 3/8 In.

Cosmetic, Larkin Rose
Talcum, Larkin Co.
Perfumers, Buffalo,
Contents, 4 1/4 In.

Cosmetic, Merrell's
Dousan, For Personal
Hygiene, Cincinnati,
5 3/8 In.

Cosmetic, Modjeska
Talcum, Larkin Co.,
1-Cent Revenue Stamp,
4 1/2 In.

Masta's Indian Pulmonic Balsam, Aqua, 5 5/8 In.	60.00
Merrell's Dousan, For Personal Hygiene, Cincinnati, 5 3/8 In. *Illus*	10.00
Mexican Hair Renewer, Cobalt Blue, Rectangular, 7 In.	25.00 to 34.00
Modjeska Talcum, Larkin Co., 1-Cent Revenue Stamp, 4 1/2 In. *Illus*	20.00
Montgomery's Hair Restorer, Philada., Amber, 7 1/2 In.	40.00
Mrs. S.A. Allen's Hair Color Restorer, New York, Amber, Label, Contents, 7 1/4 In.	120.00
Mrs. S.A. Allen's World's Hair Balsam, Aqua, Tooled Lip, OP, 6 1/2 In.	360.00
Mrs. S.A. Allen's World's Hair Restorer, New York, Amber, Applied Top, 7 1/4 In.	75.00
Mrs. S.A. Allen's World's Hair Restorer, New York, Yellow Amber, BIMAL, 7 1/4 In.	45.00
Mrs. S.A. Allen's World's Hair Restorer, New York, Yellow Olive, 1860, 7 1/4 In.	355.00
Mrs. S.A. Allen's World's Hair Restorer, New York, Yellow, 7 1/4 In.	120.00
Nattan's Crystal Discovery For The Hair, Star, Cobalt Blue, Tooled Lip, 7 1/2 In.	75.00
Nature's Hair Restorative, Aqua, Labels, BIMAL, 6 1/2 In.	15.00
Noxzema For Shaving, Cobalt Blue, Label, Lid, 4 Lb.	50.00
Noxzema Skin Care, Cobalt Blue, Label, Lid, 1/4 Lb.	30.00
Oldridge's Balm Of Columbia For Restoring Hair, Philadelphia, Aqua, 6 3/4 In.	330.00
Owl Drug Co. Hair Tonic, 1 Wing, SCA, 8 3/4 In.	25.00
Parisian Sage, Ciroux Mfg. Co., Buffalo, A Hair Dye, Rectangular, 7 In.	20.00
Parker's Hair Balsam, Amber, 7 1/2 In.	8.00 to 10.00
Parker's Hair Balsam, Orange Amber, Tooled Lip, 6 1/2 In.	20.00
Perry's Hungarian Balm For The Hair, Aqua, Pontil, 5 3/4 In.	75.00 to 125.00
Phalon's Chemical Hair Invigorator, N.Y., Aqua, Oval, OP, 5 1/2 In.	60.00
Phalon's Chemical Hair Invigorator, N.Y., Green Aqua, Oval, OP, 6 3/4 In.	150.00
Phalon's Magic Hair Dye No. 2, Aqua, 2 3/4 In.	12.00
Pond's Extract, Light Aqua, Double Collar, Strap Side, 1846, Cork, 5 1/2 In.	6.00
Prof. I. Hubers Malvina Lotion, Toledo, Ohio, Amber, Haze, 5 In.	7.00
Prof. J.R. Tilton, San Francisco, Great Hair Producer, Medium Cobalt Blue, 7 In.	305.00
Professor Mott's Magic Hair Invigorator, A.J. Green, Highgate, Vt., Aqua, 8 In.	275.00
Professor Mott's Magic Hair Invigorator, Highgate, Vt., Aqua, 1860, 6 3/8 In.	210.00
Professor Wood's Hair Restorative Depot, St. Louis & New York, Aqua, OP, 7 In.	75.00
Queen Florida Water, French Richards & Co., Aqua, 6 1/2 In.	20.00
Rauchfuss Hair Invigorator, N.Y., Dark Aqua, Rectangular, Pontil, 7 In.	225.00
Reeves Ambrosia, Aqua, Rectangular, 7 1/4 In.	42.00
Renovo For Hair, D.Skidmore & Co., Seneca Falls, N.Y., Purple Amethyst, 7 3/4 In.	1815.00
Riker's American Hair Restorer, Amber, Oval, 6 3/4 In.	70.00
S. Cristadoro Liquid Hair Dye	20.00
S.A. Chevalier's Life For The Hair, Applied Top	40.00
Saniktol For The Teeth, Milk Glass	20.00
Scalp Food Cranitonic Hair Food, 1890s, Square, 11 In.	35.00
Shookum Root Hair Grower, Cobalt Blue, Haze	75.00
Sportsman Talc, Sportsman Div. N.Y., White, Mallard Duck, Contents, c.1953, 4 1/2 In.	35.00
St. Clair's Hair Lotion, Cobalt Blue, Tooled Lip, 1890-1900, 7 1/4 In.	65.00
Stearns Hair Remover, Price $1.00, Milk Glass, Fancy Stopper, 3 In.	36.00
Sterling's Ambrosia For The Hair, Aqua, Rectangular, 6 In.	6.00

Cosmetic, Wav-Ola
Hair Lotion, Figural
Stopper, 8 In.

Cosmetic, Varifluer
Talcum, Martha
Matilda Harper,
Rochester, N.Y., 5 In.

Cosmetic, Zanol Peroxide
Cream, American Beauty
Products Co., Cinti, Oh., 3 In.

Storr's Chemical Hair Invigorator, Aqua, Applied Sloping Collar Mouth, 1855, 6 In. .	60.00
Tooth Powder, Milk Glass	8.00
U Ar Das For The Complexion, Woodward Clarke & Co., Ore., Cobalt, 5 In. . . . . .45.00 to 65.00
Van Buskirb's Fragrant Sozodont For The Teeth & Breath, Aqua, BIMAL, 5 In. . .	10.00
Varifluer Talcum, Martha Matilda Harper, Rochester, N.Y., 5 In. . . . .*Illus*	10.00
W.C. Montgomery's Hair Restorer, Philadelphia, Amber, Rectangular, 7 1/2 In. . .10.00 to 30.00
W.C. Montgomery's Hair Restorer, Philadelphia, Purple Amethyst, 1870, 7 1/2 In. . . .	275.00
Wagner's Sapajo For The Hair, W.T. & Co., U.S.A., Cobalt Blue, Tooled Lip, 6 1/8 In.	75.00
Wards Tooth Powder, Jar, 16-Sided, Clambroth, Opalescent, Pewter Lid, 1880, 1 3/8 In.	190.00
Wav-Ola Hair Lotion, Figural Stopper, 8 In. . . . .*Illus*	32.00
White Hair Regenevator, W. White Chemist, Phila., Amber, Label, 5 1/2 In.	80.00
Yucca For The Hair, Yucca Co., Burlington, Vt., Aqua, Tooled Mouth, 1900, 7 5/8 In. . .	305.00
Zanol Peroxide Cream, American Beauty Products Co., Cinti, Oh., 3 In. . . . .*Illus*	37.00

CURE

Collectors have their own interests and a large group of bottle collectors seek medicine bottles with the word *cure* embossed on the glass or printed on the label. A cure bottle is not a *remedy bottle*. The word *cure* was originally used for a medicine that treated many diseases. A *specific* was made for only one disease. The Pure Food and Drug Act of 1906 made label changes mandatory and the use of the word *cure* was no longer permitted. Related bottles may be found in the Medicine and Bitters categories.

CURE, A.C. Barrows Cor. Mortar & Pestle, Honey Amber, 4 1/8 In.	55.00
Alaska Drug Co., Douglas, Alaska, Tooled Lip, Flat Sides, 1890-1910, 5 3/8 In.	175.00
Ambrose Morse Compound Dockroot, OP	180.00
Arctic Frost Bite, Aqua, 2 1/2 In.	14.00
Ayer's Ague, Lowell, Mass., Aqua, OP, 7 1/4 In.	250.00
B.W. Hair & Son Asthma, London, Amber, Rectangular, 6 1/2 In. . . . . .20.00 to 30.00
Baker's Vegetable Blood & Liver, Greeneville, Tenn., 9 1/2 In.	250.00
Barry's Tricopherous, OP	40.00
Bennett's Hyssop, Stockport, Aqua, Sunken Panel, Rectangular, 5 1/2 In.	26.00
Bettison's English Horse Liniment, Louisville, Ky., Aqua, OP, Rolled Lip, 1855, 4 In.	415.00
Bro. Benjamin's Cough Cure	75.00
Brown's Blood Cure, Phila., Pa., Green, Tooled Mouth, 1890-1900, 6 1/4 In.	120.00
Burkhardt's Fever & Ague Remedy, Louisville, Ky., Aqua, Pontil, 1840-1855, 6 3/4 In.	415.00
Calqueur, Quehen & Smith, Cobalt Blue, Pillar Shape, 4 Sunken Panels, Rectangular . . .	30.00
Coke Dandruff Cure, A.R. Bremer Co., New York, Chicago, ACL, Stopper, 7 1/2 In. . . .	240.00
Conn's Kidney Cure, Philadelphia, Pa., Aqua, 1890, 6 In.	10.00
Craig Kidney Cure Company, Amber, Double Collar, 1890, 9 1/2 In. . . . . .110.00 to 305.00
Criswell's Bromo-Pepsin Cures Headache & Indigestion, Amber	12.00
Curtis Cough Cure, J.J. Mack & Co., San Francisco, Cal., Tooled Top, 7 In.	110.00
Cuticura System Of Curing Constitutional Humors, Aqua, Square, 9 In.	15.00
Da Costa's Radical Cure, Aqua, Small	20.00
Dana's Sarsaparilla, Martin's Catarrh Cure, Belfast, Label	22.00
Doct. Curtis Inhaling/Hygean Vapor, N.Y., Smoky, Applied Mouth, OP, 7 In.	150.00

Dr. B.W. Hair's Asthma Cure, Cincinnati, Aqua, Square, 5 7/8 In. 15.00
Dr. B.W. Hair's Asthma Cure, Square, Aqua, 7 3/4 In. 10.00
Dr. C. Crooke's Never Fail, Louisville, Ky., Aqua, Rolled Lip, 1840-1855, 4 1/4 In. 330.00
Dr. Elliot's Speedy Cure, Aqua, 7 1/2 In. 25.00
Dr. Fenner's Kidney & Backache Cure, Amber, 10 1/2 In. 90.00
Dr. Hutchinson's Paralysis Cure, Aqua 80.00
Dr. J. Kauffmann's Angeline Internal Rheumatism Cure, Hamilton, Ohio, 7 1/2 In. .   25.00
Dr. Kilmer's Catarrh Cough Consumption Oil Specific, Aqua, 1895, 8 1/2 In. 715.00
Dr. Kilmer's Swamp Root Kidney Liver & Bladder Cure, Aqua, 7 In. 10.00
Dr. Kilmer's Swamp Root Kidney Cure, Binghamton, N.Y., Aqua, Round, 3 In. . . .5.00 to 10.00
Dr. L.E. Keeley's Cure For Drunkenness, Inside Stain 50.00
Dr. L.E. Keeley's Double Chloride Of Gold Cure For Neurasthenia, 6 In. 415.00
Dr. L.E. Keeley's Gold Cure For Drunkenness, Dwight, Ill., Spout, 5 1/2 In. . . . .75.00 to 95.00
Dr. M.M. Fenner's People's Remedies, Kidney & Backache Cure, Amber, 10 In. . .45.00 to 75.00
Dr. Mile's New Heart Cure, Amber 45.00
Dr. Vanderpool's S.B. Cough & Consumption Cure, Aqua, 6 1/8 In. 115.00
Dr. W.W. Brown, Louisville, Ky., Blue Aqua, Pontil, Rolled Lip, 1845-1855, 4 1/2 In. . . .   40.00
Dr. Whittlesey's Dyspepsia Cure, Deep Aqua 75.00
Elepizone, A Certain Cure For Fits & Epilepsy, Dr. H.C. Root, London, Aqua, 6 1/2 In. .   55.00
F.W. Fitch's Ideal Dandruff Cure 10.00
Floraplexion, Cures Dyspepsia Liver Complaint & Consumption, Aqua, 6 In. . . . . . .20.00 to 30.00
Foley's Kidney & Bladder Cure, Amber, 9 1/2 In. 15.00
Foley's Kidney Cure, Cylindrical, Aqua, Sample 25.00
Frankfort Safe Cure, Emerald Green, Blob Top, Contents, Pt. 500.00
Fulton's Radical Remedy, Sure Kidney Liver & Dyspepsia Cure, Amber, 9 In. . .140.00 to 470.00
Gauss Elixir, Amber, 8 In. 15.00
Ginseng-Panacea, Deep Aqua, Rolled, OP, 1845-1855, 4 1/2 In. 175.00
Great Blood & Rheumatism Cure, Matt Johnson Co., St. Paul, Minn., Aqua, 9 In. . . .   35.00
Grover Graham's Dyspepsia Cure, Newburgh, N.Y., 6 In. . . . .*Illus*   5.00
H.G. Hotchkiss, Lyons, N.Y., Cobalt Blue, Applied Mouth, 1880-1900, 8 3/4 In. 120.00
H.H. Purdy, Downieville, Calif., Popular Kidney & Liver Cure, Tooled Mouth, 1890, 9 In.   330.00
Hall's Catarrh Cure, Aqua, 4 1/2 In. 4.00
Hermanu's Germany's Infallible Dyspepsia Cure, Amber, 2 7/8 In. 20.00
Hernia Cure Co., Westbrook, Maine, Rupturine Cures Ruptures, SCA . . . . .25.00 to 90.00
Holland Cough & Consumption Cure, Aqua, 6 In. 45.00
Hydrolithia, Cures Headache, Amber 15.00
J.A. Melvin's Rheumatic & Dyspepsia Cure, Aqua 20.00
J.B. Gotthelf Headache Cure, 2 1/2 In. 15.00
Johnson's Chill & Fever Tonic, Guaranteed To Cure, Ga. 20.00
K.K. Cures, Bright's Disease & Systitis, Rectangular, 7 1/2 In. . . . . .30.00 to 45.00
Kendall's Spaven Cure, Enosburgh Falls, Vt., Amber, 12 Vertical Panels, 5 5/8 In. 3.00
Kendall's Spavin Cure For Human Flesh, Aqua . . . . .20.00 to 45.00
Kodol Dyspepsia Cure For Indigestion, Aqua, Labels, Rectangular, 8 3/4 In. 15.00
L.F. Ganter Magic Chicken Cholera Cure, Light Amber, 6 In. . . . . .50.00 to 100.00
Langenbach's Dysentery, San Francisco, Amber, Label, Tooled Top, Contents, 5 1/2 In.   55.00
Liquifruta Cough Cure, Aqua, 5 In. 10.00
Martha J. Allen's Female Restorative, Aqua, Tooled Lip, 1890-1910, 10 5/8 In. 88.00
McBurney's Kidney & Bladder Cure, Los Angeles, Cal., Tooled Top, 5 In. . . . . . .22.00 to 70.00
Mexican Mustang Liniment, Aqua, Crude Top, OP, 7 1/2 In. 30.00
Minard's Liniment, Amethyst, 5 In. 15.00
Mrs. S.A. Allen's World's Hair Restorer, Amethyst, 7 1/4 In. 200.00
Munyon's Inhaler Cures Colds Catarrh & All Throat & Lung Diseases, 4 1/2 In. . .   35.00
Negative Electric Fluid, N.W. Seet, Md., N.Y., Aqua, Rolled Lip, 1845-1855, 3 3/8 In. .   105.00
One Night Cough Cure, Kohler Mf'g. Co., Baltimore, Md., Aqua, 5 1/4 In. . . . . . .*Illus*   12.00
Original Copper Cure, Amber, Tooled Lip, 1885-1795, 7 3/4 In. 55.00
Otto's Cure, B.H. Bacon, Rochester, N.Y., Aqua, 2 3/4 In. 12.00
Otto's Cure For The Throat & Lungs, Aqua, 6 In. . . . . .15.00 to 30.00
P. Hoppe, Amsterdam, Olive Green, Applied Top, Squat, 11 1/2 In. 40.00
Pettit's American Cough Cure, Howard Bros., Aqua, 7 In. 40.00
Piso's Cure For Consumption, Hazelton & Co., Aqua, 5 1/2 In. 10.00
Piso's Cure For Consumption, Hazelton & Co., Yellow Olive, 5 In. 20.00
Polar Star Cough, Aqua, 4 In. . . . . .5.00 to 20.00
Porter's Cure Of Pain, Cleveland, Aqua, 6 3/4 In. 20.00

Cure, Grover Graham's
Dyspepsia Cure,
Newburgh, N.Y., 6 In.

Cure, One Night
Cough Cure, Kohler
Mf'g. Co., Baltimore,
Md., Aqua, 5 1/4 In.

Cure, Sayman's Veget.
Liniment, Cures
Catarrh & Colds,
Amethyst, 6 1/2 In.

Pratt's Distemper & Pink Eye Cure, Amber, Tooled Top, 6 3/4 In. 120.00
Prescriptions Get It At Bell's Cut Rate Drug Store, Reading, Pa., Green, 8 In. 385.00
River Swamp Chill & Fever Cure, Embossed Alligator, Amber, 1880s, 6 In. . . .660.00 to 1020.00
Rock's Cough Cold Cure, Cha'sa Darby, N.Y., Aqua, Rectangular, 5 3/4 In. . . . . . . .5.00 to 20.00
Rohrer's Expectoral Wild Cherry Tonic, Lancaster, Pa., 1860-1870, 10 1/2 In. .330.00 to 385.00
S. Grover Graham's Dyspepsia Cure, 8 In. . . . . .12.00 to 15.00
S. Grover Graham's Dyspepsia Cure, Newburgh, N.Y., 6 3/4 In. . . . . .10.00 to 20.00
S.B. Vanderpool's Headache And Liver Cure 100.00
S.B.N. Catarrh, Smith Bros., Fresno, Cal., Aqua, Round, 8 In. . . . . .16.00 to 25.00
S.C. Wells, Shilos Consumption Cure, Aqua, BIMAL, 7 1/2 In.   10.00
S.E. Bowen & Co., Bridgeton, N.J., Cobalt Blue, Cylindrical, 4 7/8 In. 90.00
Safe Cure, London, Amber, 1/2 Pt. . . . . .45.00 to 48.00
Sanford's Radical, Cobalt Blue, Tooled Mouth, Labels, 1880-1890, 7 3/8 In. . . . . . .30.00 to 95.00
Sayman's Veget. Liniment, Cures Catarrh & Colds, Amethyst, 6 1/2 In. . . . .*Illus*   6.00
Shiloh's Consumption, Aqua, Sample, 3 3/8 In. 12.00
Such's California Cure For Asthma & Lung Disease, Aqua, 1865-1875, 8 1/8 In. . . .   470.00
Veno's Lightning Cough Cure, Aqua, 5 In. . . . . .25.00 to 45.00
Warner's Safe Cure, Embossed Around Neck, No Safe 165.00
Warner's Safe Cure, Frankfort, Olive Green, Applied Mouth, 9 1/8 In. 415.00
Warner's Safe Cure, Green, Sample, 4 1/2 In. 395.00
Warner's Safe Cure, Left Hand, Amber 145.00
Warner's Safe Cure, London, Gold Amber, 9 3/8 In. .75.00 to 120.00
Warner's Safe Cure, London, Honey Yellow, Sample, 4 1/2 In. 500.00
Warner's Safe Cure, London, Olive Green, 7 1/2 In. 90.00
Warner's Safe Cure, London, Olive Green, 9 1/2 In. . . . . .105.00 to 110.00
Warner's Safe Cure, London, Yellow Green, 4 1/2 In. 595.00
Warner's Safe Cure, London, Yellow Orange, Bubbles, Slugplate Variant, 7 In. 130.00
Warner's Safe Cure, Melbourne, Red Amber, 5 1/2 In. 65.00
Warner's Safe Cure, Melbourne, Red Amber, 9 1/2 In. 58.00
Warner's Safe Cure, Red Amber, Applied Mouth, 9 1/8 In. 265.00
Warner's Safe Cure, Rochester, Amber, 7 1/4 In. 25.00
Warner's Safe Cure, Rochester, N.Y., Amber, Label, Oval, 9 1/2 In. 85.00
Warner's Safe Cure, Rochester, N.Y., Honey Amber, 7 In. 35.00
Warner's Safe Cure, Rochester, N.Y., London, Eng., & Toronto, Canada, 11 In. 110.00
Warner's Safe Cure, Safe, Blood Red, Smooth Base, Germany, 1880-1895, 9 1/2 In. . . .   660.00
Warner's Safe Cure, Trademark, Melbourne, Safe, Red Amber, 9 1/2 In. . . . . .70.00 to 125.00
Warner's Safe Cure, Yellow Olive Green, Safe, Germany, 1885-1900, 9 In. 260.00
Warner's Safe Diabetes Cure, Rochester, N.Y., Amber, Tooled Top, 9 1/4 In. 75.00
Warner's Safe Kidney & Liver Cure, Amber, Slug Plate, Variant . . . . .65.00 to 75.00
Warner's Safe Kidney & Liver Cure, Rochester, N.Y., Amber, Blob Top, 9 1/4 In. 20.00
Warner's Safe Kidney & Liver Cure, Rochester, N.Y., Yellow Amber, 1890, 9 1/2 In. . .   665.00
Warner's Safe Rheumatic Cure, Amber, Safe, England, 1885-1900, 9 1/4 In. 190.00
Warner's Safe Rheumatic Cure, Red Amber, Tooled Lip, 1885-1900, 9 1/2 In. . .65.00 to 175.00
Warner's Safe Rheumatic Cure, Rochester, N.Y., Amber, 9 1/2 In. . . . . .50.00 to 155.00
Wm. Radam's No. I Cure, Jug, Gal. 85.00
Wood's Great Peppermint Cure For Cough & Colds, Aqua, 1895, 5 1/2 In. 495.00

─────────────────────── **CYRUS NOBLE** ───────────────────────

This complicated story requires a cast of characters and names: Cyrus Noble, a master distiller; Ernest R. Lilienthal, owner of Bernheim Distillery; Crown Distillers, trade name of Lilienthal & Company; Haas Brothers, successor to Lilienthal & Co.; and another Ernest R. Lilienthal and grandson of the original Ernest Lilienthal, president of Haas Brothers Distributing. Cyrus Noble was in charge of the quality of the whiskey made at the Bernheim Distillery in Kentucky. He was said to be a large man, over 300 pounds, and liked to taste his own product. According to the stories, he tasted to excess one day, fell into a whiskey vat, and drowned. The company, as a tribute, named the brand for him in 1871 and so Cyrus Noble Bourbon came into being.

Ernest R. Lilienthal, the original owner of Bernheim Distillery, moved to San Francisco and opened Lilienthal & Company with the trade name of Crown Distillers. Their best-selling brand was Cyrus Noble. It was made in three grades and sold by the barrel. The company later became Haas Brothers Distributing Company.

In 1901 John Coleman, a miner in Searchlight, Nevada, was so discouraged with the results of his digging that he offered to trade his mine to Tobe Weaver, a bartender, for a quart of Cyrus Noble whiskey. The mine was named Cyrus Noble and eventually produced over $250,000 worth of gold.

One of the early bottles used for Cyrus Noble whiskey was amber with an inside screw top; it was made from the 1860s to 1921. Haas Brothers of San Francisco marketed special Cyrus Noble bottles from 1971 to 1980. The first, made to commemorate the company's 100th anniversary, pictured the miner, the unfortunate John Coleman. Six thousand bottles were made and sold, filled, for $16.95 each. Tobe Weaver, the fortunate bartender, was pictured in the next bottle. A mine series was made from 1971 to 1978, the full size about 14 inches high and the miniatures about 6 inches; a wild animal series from 1977 to 1978; and a carousel series in 1979 and 1980. Other series are birds of the forest, olympic bottles, horned animals, and sea animals. W.A. Lacey, a brand of 86 proof blended whiskey distributed by Haas Brothers, was also packed in a variety of figural bottles. They are listed separately under Lacey. Production of decanters for both brands ended in 1981.

CYRUS NOBLE, Assayer, 1972	115.00
Bartender, 1971	115.00
Bear & Cubs, 1978, 1st Edition	110.00
Bear & Cubs, 1978, 2nd Edition	75.00
Beaver & Kit, 1978, 1st Edition	65.00
Blacksmith, 1976	40.00
Buffalo Cow & Calf, 1977, 1st Edition ....*Illus*	108.00
Buffalo Cow & Calf, 1977, 2nd Edition	74.00
Burro, 1973	60.00
Carousel, Horse, Black Flyer, 1979	50.00
Carousel, Horse, White Charger, 1979	50.00
Carousel, Lion, 1979	40.00
Carousel, Pipe Organ, 1980	50.00
Carousel, Tiger, 1979	100.00
Deer, Mule, 1980	52.00
Deer, White Tall Buck, 1979	50.00
Delta Saloon, 1971, Miniature	270.00
Dolphin, 1979	46.00
Elk, Bull, 1980	45.00
Gambler, 1974 ....40.00 to 50.00
Gambler's Lady, 1977, Miniature	44.00
Gold Miner, 1970	170.00
Harp Seal, 1979 ....50.00 to 75.00
Landlady, 1977	30.00
Middle Of Piano, Trumpeter, 1979 ....25.00 to 40.00
Mine Shaft, 1978	40.00
Miner's Daughter, 1975	40.00
Moose, 1976, 1st Edition	90.00
Mountain Lion & Cubs, 1977, 1st Edition	65.00
Mountain Sheep, 1978, 1st Edition	85.00

Cyrus Noble,
Tonopah, 8-Sided,
White, 1972

Cyrus Noble, Buffalo Cow & Calf, 1977,
1st Edition

Cyrus Noble, Whiskey
Drummer, 1975

Music Man, 1978, Miniature	30.00
Oklahoma Dancers, 1978	32.00
Olympic Skater, 1980	40.00
Owl In Tree, 1980 . . . . .35.00 to 37.00
Penguins, 1978	50.00
Sea Turtle, 1979	42.00
Seal Family, 1978	45.00
Snowshoe Thompson, 1972	130.00
South Of The Border, Dancers, 1978	35.00
Tonopah, 8-Sided, White, 1972 . . . .*Illus*	100.00
USC Trojan, 1980	75.00
Violinist, 1978, Miniature	35.00
Walrus Family, 1978 . . . . .40.00 to 50.00
Walrus Family, 1980, Miniature	42.00
Whiskey Drummer, 1975 . . . .*Illus*	32.00
Whiskey Drummer, 1977, Miniature	32.00
Wood Duck	40.00

--------------------------------- **DANT** ---------------------------------

Dant figural bottles were first released in 1968 to hold J.W. Dant alcoholic products.
The figurals were discontinued after a few years. The company made an Americana
series, field birds, special bottlings, and ceramic bottles. Several bottles were made with
errors. Collectors seem to have discounted this in determining value.

DANT, Alamo, 1969 . . . .*Illus*	4.00
American Legion, 1969 . . . .*Illus*	10.00
Atlantic City, 1969	6.00
Boeing 747, 1970 . . . .*Illus*	8.00

Dant, Alamo, 1969

Dant, American Legion, 1969

Dant, Boeing 747, 1970

Boston Tea Party, Eagle Right, 1968 .... 5.00
Boston Tea Party, Reverse Eagle, 1968 ....5.00 to 10.00
Burr-Hamilton Duel, 1969 .... 6.00
Constitution & Guerriere, 1969 .... 6.00
Field Bird Series, No. 1, Ring-Necked Pheasant, 1969 .... 7.00
Field Bird Series, No. 2, Chukar Partridge, 1969 .... 7.00
Field Bird Series, No. 3, Prairie Chicken, 1969 .... 7.00
Field Bird Series, No. 4, Mountain Quail, 1969 .... 7.00
Field Bird Series, No. 5, Ruffled Grouse, 1969 .... 7.00
Field Bird Series, No. 6, California Quail, 1969 .... 7.00
Field Bird Series, No. 7, Bob White, 1969 .... 8.00
Field Bird Series, No. 8, Woodcock, 1969 ....7.00 to 9.00
Ft. Sill, 1969 .... 8.00
Indy 500, 1969 ....7.00 to 10.00
Mt. Rushmore, 1969 ....6.00 to 8.00
Patrick Henry, 1969 ....6.00 to 8.00
Paul Bunyan, 1969 ....5.00 to 8.00
San Diego Harbor, 1969 ....5.00 to 7.00
Washington At Delaware, 1969 ....5.00 to 8.00

———————————————— DECANTER ————————————————

Decanters were first used to hold the alcoholic beverages that had been stored in kegs. The undesirable sediment that formed at the bottom of old wine kegs was removed by carefully pouring off the top liquid, or decanting it. At first a necessity, the decanter later became merely an attractive serving vessel. A decanter usually has a bulbous bottom, a long neck, and a small mouth for easy pouring. Most have a cork or glass stopper. They were popular in England from the beginning of the eighteenth century. By about 1775 the decanter was elaborate, with cut, applied, or enameled decorations. Various early American glassworks made decanters. Mold-blown decanters were the most popular style and many were made in the East and the Midwest from 1820 to the 1860s. Pressed glass was a less expensive process introduced in about 1850, and many decanters were made by this method. Colored Bohemian glass consisting of two or three cased layers became popular in the late-nineteenth century. Many decanters are now made for home or restaurant use or with special logos to promote products. Bar bottles, decanter-like bottles with brand names in the glass, were used from about 1890 to 1920 in saloons. The law no longer permits the use of bar bottles because no bottle may be refilled from another container. Other decanters may be found in the Beam, Bischoff, and other modern bottle categories.

DECANTER, 8-Pillar Mold, Tooled & Flared Lip, Stopper, Polished Pontil, 9 3/8 In. 110.00
16 Diamonds, 3 Applied Neck Rings, Flared Mouth, Pontil, No Stopper, Qt. 350.00
Always Pure Old Elk Whiskey, Ear Of Corn Shape, Green, Gold Paint, Handle, 9 In. ... 450.00
Blown, 6 Cathedral Arched Panels, Cobalt Blue, Tooled Mouth, 9 1/2 In. 130.00
Blown, 8-Pillar Mold, Amethyst Highlights On Each Rib, Pittsburgh, Pa., Pontil, 11 In. ... 1100.00
Blown, Flared Lip, Ground Glass Stopper, Pontil, 7 In. 120.00
Blown, Light Olive Green, Rigaree, Sheared Lip, Graphite IP, Iran, 8 In. 75.00
Blown, Olive Green, Applied Double Collar, Pontil, 8 1/4 In. 2250.00
Blown, Ribs, Swirled Right, Sunburst In Diamond Band, Stopper, 7 In. 165.00
Blown, Sapphire Blue, Flared Mouth, Pontil, Sandwich, 1/2 Pt. 550.00
Blown, Yellow Green, Sloping Collar, Ring, Pontil, Pt. 1760.00
Blown, Yellow Olive, Tooled Mouth, Pontil, 1820-1840, Qt. 715.00
Bluebell Design, 1930s, 10 In. 155.00
Brandy, Amber, Painted Gold, Tubular Pontil, 14 In. 65.00
Brandy, Blown, Amethyst, Painted Label, Cylindrical, Pontil, 1840-1860, 11 In. 275.00
Brandy, Blown, Light Emerald Green, Tooled Flared Mouth, Pontil, England, 9 1/4 In. ... 385.00
Cable Pattern, Sandwich Type, Backbar, Polished Pontil, 10 1/2 In. 85.00
Canary, Corset Paneled Bell Shape, Applied Mouth, Pontil, Sandwich Type, Qt., Pair ... 1100.00
Claret, Chestnut Glass, Barley Corn Handle, Sky Blue, 1860, 9 1/2 In. 135.00
Cobalt Blue, Pillar Mold, Applied Shoulder, Neck Rings, 1855-1870, 11 In. 60.00
Cobalt Blue, Ring Of Rings Pattern, Stopper, 10 In. 36.00
Coin Spot, Sandwich Type, Cut & Polished Panels, Backbar, Pontil, 10 3/4 In. 95.00
Commemorative, Jim Thorpe, Tooled Mouth, 1925-1930, 8 3/8 In. 95.00
Cornflower Blue, 8 Panels, Applied Bulbous Lip, Stopper, 10 3/4 In. 825.00
Cut Glass, Diamond Pattern, Apricot Amber, Fluted Neck, Shoulders, Qt., 9 1/4 In. 150.00

Decanter,
Kentucky Tavern,
Paper Label, 10
In.

Decanter, James
E. Pepper, Paper
Label

Decanter, Old
Tom Moore
Whiskey, 10

Cut Glass, Flared Mouth, Pontil, 19th Century, Qt.	255.00
Emerald Green, Sandwich Type, Backbar, Metal Stopper, Polished Pontil, 10 1/4 In.	1320.00
Etched Glass, Silver Mounted, Cherubs, Figural Finial Stopper, 8 1/2 In.	65.00
Gin, Dark Amber, Gold Lettering, Applied Top, Tubular Pontil, 1850, 13 In.	65.00
Gold, Vertical Rib, Yellow Enamel, Green Shoulder, Neck, Glass Stopper, 1910, 8 In.	85.00
James E. Pepper, Paper Label ....*Illus*	5.00
John Lennon, Beatles	170.00
Keene, Blown, Olive Green, 1810-1830, 10 In.	2090.00
Keene, Forest Green, Marlboro Street, Pontil, Pt.	630.00
Keene, Olive Green, OP, 7 1/2 In.	305.00
Kentucky Tavern, Paper Label, 10 In. ....*Illus*	7.00
Old Tom Moore Whiskey, 10 In. ....*Illus*	35.00
Old Tucker Whiskey, White Enamel, Fluted	95.00
Pillar Mold, Clear, Cranberry Cased Interior, Panels & Notches, 11 1/4 In.	1045.00
Pillar Mold, Cobalt Blue, Applied Mouth, Neck Ring, Polished Pontil, 10 3/8 In.	1210.00
Pillar Mold, Cut Panels Neck & Ribs, Star Cut Base, Stopper, 11 In.	495.00
Pillar Mold, Milk Glass, Opalescent, Tooled & Flared Mouth, Pontil, 7 In.	330.00
Pillar Mold, Red Encased In Clear, Notches, Polished Pontil, 9 1/8 In.	935.00
Pittsburgh Type, Deep Purple Amethyst, Pontil, Original Silver Stopper, 1870, 11 In.	770.00
Rum, Blown, Clear, Mismatched Stopper, 8 1/2 In.	220.00
Rye, Peacock Blue, Gold Letters, White Scrolls, Stopper, 10 In.	150.00
Thomas Caines Type, Chain Design, Bulbous, Pontil, Stopper, 1820-1840, Qt.	160.00
Whiskey, Blown, Rolled Lip, England, 1770-1800, 8 In.	135.00

DEMIJOHN

A demijohn is a very large bottle that is usually blown. Many held alcoholic beverages, molasses, or other liquids. It was usually bulbous with a long neck and a high kick-up. Early examples have open pontils. Many were covered with wicker to avoid breakage when the bottles were shipped. A demijohn could hold from one to ten gallons. Most early demijohns were made of dark green, amber or black glass. By the 1850s the glass colors were often aqua, light green, or clear.

DEMIJOHN, 2-Piece Mold, Light Blue, Applied Sloping Mouth, 12 1/2 In.	55.00
3-Piece Mold, Yellow Olive Green, Medallion On Shoulder, 2 Gal., 21 In.	165.00
4-Piece Mold, Light Sapphire Blue, Applied Mouth, 1860-1880, 17 3/8 In.	245.00
Apple Green, Applied Sloping Collared Mouth, Cylindrical, 1860-1890, 14 1/4 In.	130.00
Apple Shape, Yellow Green, 5 Gal.	190.00
Aqua, Wicker Design, Pontil, 3 In.	35.00
Black Olive Amber, Applied String Lip, OP, 1770-1790, 12 3/8 In.	180.00
Bladder Shape, Olive Green, Applied Mouth, 1840-1870, 16 1/2 In.	360.00
Blown, 3-Piece Mold, Light Olive Green, Pontil, 1830-1860, 16 1/4 In.	215.00
Blown, Yellow Amber, Applied Mouth, Cylindrical, 1840-1870, 11 In.	35.00
Blue Green, Crude, OP, 2 Gal.	40.00
Blue Green, IP, 1/2 Gal.	50.00
Blue Green, OP, 3 Gal.	65.00
Bread Loaf Shape, Yellow Amber Flowers, Pontil, 1860-1880, 9 5/8 In.	690.00
Cobalt Blue, Tooled Lip, 1880-1900, 13 1/2 In.	200.00

Cobalt Blue, Turn Mold, Flared Lip, Pontil, 1860-1880, 11 7/8 In. 550.00
Consolidated Ice Co., Pittsburgh, Pa., Aqua, Applied Mouth, 1880, 17 In. 55.00
Dark Olive Green, IP, 20 In. 85.00
Deep Root Beer Amber, Allover Etching, Pontil, 1840-1870, 16 1/2 In. 135.00
Dip Mold, Olive Green, Pontil, 10 x 4 In. 90.00
Emerald Green, Applied Top, OP, 15 In. 90.00
Flattened Shape, Yellow Olive Green, Tri-Pontil Base, 1840-1870, 19 1/2 In. 220.00
Fred C. White, N.Y., Light Amber, Tooled Mouth, 1860-1890, 20 1/2 In. 185.00
Heart Shape, Chocolate Puce Amber, Pontil, 3 Gal. 165.00
Kidney Shape, 3-Piece Mold, Olive Green, OP, Long Crooked Neck, 19 In. 85.00
Kidney Shape, Blown, Yellow Olive Green, Sloping Mouth, Pontil, 17 In. 255.00
Kidney Shape, Emerald Green, Applied Mouth, Pontil, 1840-1860, 18 In. 285.00
Kidney Shape, Gold Amber, Sheared Mouth, 1830-1860, 18 1/2 In. 220.00
Kidney Shape, Olive Green, String Lip, 1780-1810, 16 7/8 In.   330.00
Kidney Shape, Olive Yellow, Sheared Mouth, 1830-1860, 17 In. . . . . .110.00 to 165.00
Kidney Shape, Yellow, Applied Mouth, 1860-1880, 17 In. 285.00
Light Blue Green, Applied String Rim, Sheared Mouth, Pontil, 1780-1830, 3 3/4 In. . . .   440.00
Lockport, Low Dome, Center Dot Blue Green, 2 Gal., 14 In. 165.00
Medium Cobalt Blue, Applied Sloping Collar, 1870-1885, 12 In. 240.00
Olive Green, Applied Sloping Collar Mouth, 1830, 20 In. . . . . .110.00 to 165.00
Olive Green, Yellow Tone, Applied Collar Mouth, Pontil, 1800-1830, 18 3/8 In. 80.00
Olive Yellow, Crude, IP, New England, 3 Gal. 125.00
Onion Shape, Yellow Olive, Kick-Up Base, Embossed 2, Sheared & Applied Top, 2 Qt. .   70.00
Stoddard, Gold Amber, Cylindrical, 18 In. 110.00
Stoddard, Red Olive Amber, Cylindrical, OP, 20 In. 110.00
Straw Yellow, Applied Sloping Collar Mouth, 1865-1880, 17 7/8 In. 130.00
Yellow Olive Green, Applied Mouth, Cylindrical, Pontil, 1870, 20 In. 120.00

─────────────────────────── **EZRA BROOKS** ───────────────────────────

Ezra Brooks fancy bottles were first made in 1964. The Ezra Brooks brand was purchased by Glenmore Distilleries Company of Louisville, Kentucky, in 1988, three years
after Ezra Brooks had discontinued making decanters. About 300 different ceramic figurals were made between 1964 and 1985. The dates listed here are within a year of the
time they appeared on the market. Bottles were often announced and then not produced
for many months. Glenmore sold the Ezra Brooks label to Heaven Hill Distillery in
Bardstown, Kentucky, who sold it to David Sherman Corporation of St. Louis, Missouri, in 1994.

EZRA BROOKS, 100th Award, 1972 . . . .   25.00
   American Legion, Champaign, Urbana, 1983 . . . .   25.00
   American Legion, Chicago, Salute, 1972 . . . .   50.00
   American Legion, Denver, 1977 . . . . .15.00 to 20.00
   American Legion, Hawaii, 1973 . . . . .12.00 to 15.00
   American Legion, Houston, 1971 . . . . .30.00 to 35.00
   American Legion, Miami Beach, 1974 . . . . .9.00 to 12.00
   American Legion, New Orleans, 1978 . . . .   25.00
   American Legion, Salt Lake City, 1984 . . . . .45.00 to 50.00
   American Legion, Seattle, 1983 . . . . .30.00 to 35.00
   American Legion, Water Tower, 1982 . . . . .15.00 to 20.00
   AMVET, 1974 . . . .   10.00
   AMVET, Polish Legion, 1978 . . . . .10.00 to 12.00
   Antique Cannon, Gold, 1969 . . . . .8.00 to 10.00
   Arizona, Desert Scene, 1969 . . . .   10.00
   Auburn, Boat Tail, 1932 Model, 1978 . . . . .25.00 to 30.00
   Auburn, U-War Eagle, 1982 . . . . .19.00 to 22.00
   Badger, Boxer, No. 1, 1973 . . . . *Illus*   18.00
   Badger, Football, No. 2, 1975 . . . .   17.00
   Badger, Hockey, No. 3, 1975 . . . .   15.00
   Baltimore Oriole, 1979 . . . .   29.00
   Bareknuckle Fighter, 1972 . . . . .25.00 to 30.00
   Basketball Player, 1974 . . . .   16.00
   Beaver, 1973 . . . . *Illus*   12.00
   Betsy Ross, 1975 . . . .   10.00
   Bicycle, Penny-Farthington, 1973 . . . .   10.00

Ezra Brooks, Badger, Boxer, No. 1, 1973

Ezra Brooks, Beaver, 1973

Ezra Brooks, Bowler, 1973

Big Daddy Lounge, 1969 .... 5.00 to 11.00
Bird Dog, 1971 .... 12.00 to 15.00
Bird Dog, Gold, 1971 .... 25.00
Bordertown Nevada, 1970 .... 10.00
Bowler, 1973 .... *Illus* 12.00
Brahma Bull, 1972 .... *Illus* 18.00
Bronco Buster, 1974 .... *Illus* 15.00
Bucket Of Blood, 1970 .... 9.00
Buffalo Hunt, 1971 .... 10.00 to 12.00
C.B. Convoy Radio, 1976 .... 8.00 to 10.00
Canadian Honker, 1975 .... 13.00 to 15.00
Card, Jack Of Diamonds, 1969 .... 12.00 to 14.00
Card, King Of Clubs, 1969 .... 14.00
Card, Queen Of Hearts, 1969 .... 14.00
Casey At Bat, 1973 .... 60.00
Charlois Bull, 1973 .... *Illus* 15.00
Cheyenne Shootout, 1970 .... 10.00 to 12.00
Chicago Fire Team, 1974 .... 25.00 to 27.00
Chicago Water Tower, 1969 .... 8.00 to 12.00
Christmas Tree, 1980 .... *Illus* 22.00
Cigar Store Indian, 1968 .... 8.00 to 10.00
Clown, No. 1, Smiley, 1979 .... *Illus* 27.00
Clown, No. 2, Cowboy, 1979 .... 26.00 to 30.00
Clown, No. 3, Pagliacci, 1979 .... 19.00 to 22.00
Clown, No. 4, Keystone Cop, 1980 .... 30.00
Clown, No. 5, Cuddles, 1981 .... 26.00 to 27.00
Clown, No. 6, Tramp, 1981 .... 26.00 to 28.00
Clown With Accordion, 1972 .... 25.00 to 27.00
Clown With Balloons, 1974 .... 25.00

Ezra Brooks, Brahma Bull, 1972

Ezra Brooks, Bronco Buster, 1974

Ezra Brooks, Charlois Bull, 1973

Ezra Brooks,
Christmas Tree, 1980

Club, No. 1, Distillery, 1970	7.00
Club, No. 2, Birthday Cake, 1972	7.00
Club, No. 3, Map, 1973	7.00
Clydesdale, 1974 ....*Illus*	22.00
Conquistadors, Drum & Bugle, 1972	10.00
Corvette, 1957 Model, Blue, 1976	125.00
Corvette, 1957 Model, Yellow, 1976	125.00
Corvette, 1962 Model, Mako Shark, 1979	30.00
Creighton, Blue Jay, 1976	25.00
Dakota Cowboy, 1975	30.00
Dakota Cowgirl, 1976	30.00
Dakota Grain Elevator, 1978	25.00
Dakota Shotgun Express, 1977 ....15.00 to 18.00	
Deadwagon, Nevada, 1970	10.00
Decanter, Glass, 1964 ....10.00 to 12.00	
Decanter, Glass, 1965	15.00
Decanter, Glass, 1966	7.00
Decanter, Glass, 1967	6.00
Decanter, Glass, 1968	7.00
Decanter, Glass, 1969	7.00
Deer, Whitetail, 1974	15.00
Delta Belle, Riverboat, 1969	10.00
Dirt Bike, 1973	16.00
Dog, Setter, 1974	10.00
Duesenberg, Model SJ, 1971	35.00
Eagle, Gold, 1971	15.00
Elephant, Asian, 1973	20.00
Elephant, Big Bertha, 1970	20.00
Elk, 1972	25.00
Equestrian, 1974 ....10.00 to 12.00	
F.O.E. Eagle, 1978	15.00
F.O.E. Eagle, 1979	20.00
F.O.E. Eagle, 1980	35.00
F.O.E. Eagle, 1981	35.00
Fire Engine, 1971	25.00
Fireman, 1975	28.00
Fisherman, 1975	12.00
Football Player, 1974	12.00
Ford Thunderbird, 1956 Model, Blue, 1977	80.00
Ford Thunderbird, 1956 Model, Yellow, 1977	60.00
Foremost Astronaut, 1970	20.00
Fox, Redtail, 1979	35.00
Fresno Grape, 1970	10.00
Fresno Grape, With No Gold, 1970	60.00
Gamecock, 1970	15.00
Gator, Florida, No. 1, Passing, 1972	15.00
Gator, Florida, No. 2, Running, 1973	15.00

Ezra Brooks, Clown,
No. 1, Smiley, 1979

Ezra Brooks, Clydesdale, 1974

Ezra Brooks, Jester, 1972

Gator, Florida, No. 3, Blocker, 1975 .... 22.00
Gavel, President, 1982 ....50.00 to 55.00
Gavel & Block, V.I.P., 1982 .... 15.00
Georgia Bulldog, 1972 .... 20.00
Go Big Red, No. 1, Football, 1970 ....28.00 to 30.00
Go Big Red, No. 2, With Hat, 1971 .... 21.00
Go Big Red, No. 3, Football, 1972 ....22.00 to 23.00
Golden Grizzly Bear, 1968 .... 8.00
Goldpanner, 1970 .... 8.00
Goose, Happy, 1975 .... 15.00
Gopher, Minnesota Hockey Player, 1975 .... 18.00
Grandfather Clock, 1970 ....7.00 to 10.00
Greater Greensboro Open, No. 1, 1972 .... 25.00
Greater Greensboro Open, No. 1, Gold, 1972 .... 40.00
Greater Greensboro Open, No. 2, 1973 .... 25.00
Greater Greensboro Open, No. 3, 1974 .... 40.00
Greater Greensboro Open, No. 4, 1975 .... 25.00
Greater Greensboro Open, No. 5, 1976 .... 25.00
Greater Greensboro Open, No. 6, 1977 .... 23.00
Groucho Marx, 1977 .... 40.00
Hambletonian, Gold, 1971 .... 25.00
Hambletonian, Race Track, 1971 .... 15.00
Hardy, Oliver, 1976 .... 35.00
Harold's Club Dice, 1968 .... 14.00
Hereford, 1972 ....17.00 to 19.00
Historical Flask, 1970 ....4.00 to 6.00
Horseshoe Casino, 1970 .... 14.00
Hunter & Dog, 1973 .... 20.00
Idaho, Skier, 1972 .... 10.00
Indian, Ceremonial, 1970 .... 20.00
Indy Pace Car, Corvette, 1978 .... 45.00
Indy Pace Car, Ford Mustang, 1979 .... 40.00
Indy Pace Car, Penske Pacemaker, No. 1, Gold, 1982 .... 125.00
Indy Pace Car, Pontiac, 1980 .... 50.00
Indy Pace Car, Pontiac, Black Special, 1980 .... 40.00
Indy Race Car, No. 3, Norton Spirit, 1982 .... 90.00
Indy Race Car, No. 21, 1970 ....45.00 to 60.00
Indy Race Car, Penske Pacemaker, No. 1, 1982 .... 95.00
Indy STP, No. 40, Gold, 1983 .... 125.00
Indy STP, No. 40, Silver, 1983 .... 125.00
Iowa Farmer, 1977 .... 30.00
Iowa Farmer's Elevator, 1978 .... 30.00
Jayhawk, Kansas, 1969 .... 14.00
Jester, 1972 ....*Illus* 10.00

Jug, Old Time, 1977	20.00
Jug, Owl, 1.75 Liter, 1980	10.00
Kachina, No. 1, Morning Singer, 1971	80.00
Kachina, No. 2, Hummingbird, 1973	80.00
Kachina, No. 3, Antelope, 1975	80.00
Kachina, No. 4, Maiden, 1975	35.00
Kachina, No. 5, Longhair, 1976	45.00 to 48.00
Kachina, No. 6, Buffalo Dancer, 1977	47.00
Kachina, No. 7, Mudhead, 1978	50.00 to 55.00
Kachina, No. 8, Drummer, 1979	80.00
Kachina, No. 9, Watermelon, 1980	25.00
Kansas Wheat Shocker, 1971	14.00
Katz Cat, Gray, 1969	11.00
Katz Philharmonic, Cat, 1970	10.00 to 12.00
Keystone Cops In Car, 1972	60.00 to 75.00
Kitten On Pillow, 1975	10.00 to 12.00
Laurel, Stan, 1976	35.00
Leopard, Snow, 1980	35.00
Liberty Bell, 1970	6.00
Lighthouse, Maine, 1971	25.00
Lincoln Continental, 1979	30.00
Lion, African, 1980	20.00
Lion On Rock, 1971	10.00
Liquor Square, 1972	8.00 to 10.00
Lobster, 1970	22.00
Loon, 1979	25.00 to 27.00
M & M, Brown Jug, 1974	18.00
Macaw, 1980	48.00
Maine Potato, 1973	10.00
Man O'War, Horse, 1969	25.00
Max The Hat Zimmerman, 1976	28.00
Minuteman, 1975	15.00
Moose, 1972	25.00
Motorcycle, 1972	15.00
Mr. Foremost Dancing Man, 1969	22.00
Mr. Merchant, 1970	8.00
Mule, Missouri, Gold, 1972	45.00
New Hampshire, State House, 1969	8.00
North Carolina Bicentennial, 1975	12.00
Nugget Classic, 1970	15.00
Nugget Rooster, No. 1, 1969	30.00
Oil Gusher, 1969	10.00
Old Capital, Iowa, 1971	35.00 to 40.00
Old Ez Owl, No. 1, Barn Owl, 1977	25.00
Old Ez Owl, No. 2, Eagle, 1978	55.00
Old Ez Owl, No. 3, Snowy, 1979	30.00
Old Ez Owl, No. 4, Scops, 1980	22.00
Old Ez Owl, No. 5, Great Gray, 1982	30.00
Old Man Of The Mountain, New Hampshire, 1970	12.00
Panda, 1972	15.00 to 17.00
Penguin, 1973	12.00
Phoenix Bird, 1971	24.00
Phonograph, 1970	25.00
Pirate, 1971	8.00 to 10.00
Pistol, Dueling, Flintlock, 1968	11.00
Pistol, Dueling, Flintlock, Made In Japan, 1968	40.00
Political, Democratic & Republican Conventions, 1976, Pair	28.00 to 30.00
Quail, California, 1970	10.00
Raccoon, 1978	35.00
Ram, 1973	18.00
Razorback Hog, Arizona, 1970	20.00 to 40.00
Razorback Hog, Arizona, No. 2, 1979	35.00
Reno Arch, 1969	10.00

Ezra Brooks, San Francisco Cable Car,
Gray, Green, Brown, 1968

Ezra Brooks, Tank, Military, 1972

Saddle, Silver, 1973	.25.00 to 50.00
Sailfish, 1971	.8.00 to 12.00
Salmon, Washington, 1971	25.00
San Francisco Cable Car, Gray, Green, Brown, 1968	*Illus* 9.00
Sea Captain, 1971	12.00
Seal, Gold, 1972	.10.00 to 12.00
Senator, 1972	.8.00 to 10.00
Senator, Gold, 1972	25.00
Shark, White, 1977	10.00
Shriner, Clown, 1978	.15.00 to 18.00
Shriner, Fez, 1976	7.00
Shriner, Golden Pharaoh, 1981	35.00
Shriner, King Tut Tomb Guard, 1979	20.00
Shriner, Sphinx, 1980	12.00
Silver Dollar 1804, 1970	.8.00 to 10.00
Silver Spur, 1971	16.00
Ski Boot, 1972	10.00
Slot Machine, Liberty Bell, 1971	.18.00 to 20.00
Snow Egret, 1981	20.00
Snowmobile, 1972	15.00
South Dakota Air National Guard, 1976	20.00
Spirit Of '76, Drummer, 1974	10.00
Spirit Of St. Louis, 1977	.10.00 to 12.00
Stagecoach, 1969	13.00
Stonewall Jackson, 1974	25.00
Stove, Potbelly, 1968	.8.00 to 10.00
Strongman, 1974	20.00
Sturgeon, 1975	25.00
Tank, Military, 1972	*Illus* 35.00
Tecumseh, 1969	10.00
Telephone, 1971	15.00
Tennis Player, 1973	12.00
Terrapin, Maryland, 1974	14.00
Texas Longhorn, 1971	25.00
Ticker Tape, 1970	8.00
Tiger, Bengal, 1979	27.00
Tiger, On Stadium, 1973	16.00
Tonapah, 1972	15.00
Totem Pole, No. 1, 1972	16.00
Totem Pole, No. 2, 1973	17.00
Tractor, Fordson, 1971	20.00
Train, Casey Jones Locomotive, 1980	20.00
Train, Iron Horse Engine, 1970	9.00
Trojan, Horse, 1974	20.00
Trojan, USC, 1973	22.00
Trout & Fly, 1970	10.00

Truckin' An' Vannin', 1977 .... 11.00
Turkey, White, 1971 .... 26.00
Vermont Skier, 1973 .... 12.00
VFW, Blue, 75th Anniversary, 1973 .... 12.00
VFW, Cobalt Blue, Red, White & Gold, No. 185, 1973 .... 75.00
VFW, Illinois, 1982 .... 25.00
VFW, No. 2, White, 1975 .... 6.00
Virginia, Cardinal, 1973 .... 14.00
Virginia Mountain Lady, 1972 .... 20.00
Walgreen Drugs, 1974 .... 34.00
Weirton Steel, 1974 .... 18.00
West Virginia Mountain Man, 1971 .... 60.00
Whale, 1973 .... 20.00
Whooping Crane, 1982 .... 22.00
Wichita Centennial, 1970 .... 5.00
William Penn, 1981 .... 65.00
Winston Churchill, 1969 .... 6.00 to 9.00
Zimmerman Top Hat, 1968 .... 5.00

---------------------------------- FAMOUS FIRSTS ----------------------------------

Famous Firsts Ltd. of Port Chester, New York, was owned by Richard E. Magid. The first figural bottles, issued in 1968, were a series of race cars. The last figurals were made in 1985.

FAMOUS FIRSTS, Animals, Mother & Baby, 1981, Miniature 220.00
Balloon, 1971 .... 34.00
Bell, Alpine, 1970 .... 18.00
Bell, Liberty, 1976 .... 8.00
Bell, St. Pol, 1970 .... 22.00
Bennie Bow Wow, 1973 .... 16.00
Bersaglieri, 1969 .... 34.00
Bucky Badger Mascot 12.00
Bugatti Royale, 1930-1973 .... 310.00
Butterfly, 1971 .... 12.00
Cable Car, 1973 .... 50.00
Centurian, 1969 .... 40.00
China Clipper, 1979 .... 130.00
Circus Lion, 1979 .... 25.00
Circus Tiger, 1979 .... 25.00
Coffee Mill, 1979 .... 35.00
Corvette Stingray, 1953 Model, 1975 .... 90.00
Corvette Stingray, 1963 Model, 1977 .... 95.00
Dino Ferarri, Green, 1975 .... 65.00
Dino Ferarri, Red, 1983 .... 65.00
Dino Ferarri, White, 1975 .... 35.00
Don Sympatico, 1973 .... 18.00
Duesenberg, 1980 .... 85.00
Duesenberg, 50th Anniversary, Red, 1982 .... 250.00
Egg House, 1975 .... 16.00
Fireman, 1980 .... 60.00
Fireman, 1981 .... 60.00

For a pollution-free glass cleaner use a mixture of white vinegar and water.

Famous Firsts, Honda
Motorcycle, 1975

Famous Firsts, Roulette Wheel, 1972

Famous Firsts, Scale,
Lombardy, 1970

Garibaldi, 1969	37.00
Golfer, He, 1973	32.00
Golfer, She, 1973	32.00
Hen, Filamena, 1973	22.00
Hippo, Baby, 1980	60.00
Honda Motorcycle, 1975 ....*Illus*	71.00
Hurdy Gurdy, 1971	18.00
Indy Racer, No. 11, 1971	18.00
Lockheed Transport, Jungle, 1982	63.00
Lockheed Transport, Marine Gray, 1982	81.00
Lockheed Transport, USAF Rescue, 1982	80.00
Locomotive, Clinton, 1969	30.00
Lotus, Racer, No. 2, 1971	112.00
Macaw	60.00
Marmon Wasp, No. 32, 1968	75.00
Marmon Wasp, No. 32, Gold, 1/2 Pt., 1971	30.00
Minnie Meow, 1973	18.00
Mustang, P-51-D, Fighter Plane, 1974	110.00
Napoleon, 1969	22.00
Natchez Riverboat, 1975	45.00
National Racer, No. 8, 1972	55.00
Panda, Baby, 1981	86.00
Pepper Mill, 1978	20.00
Phonograph, 1969	48.00
Phonograph, 1969, Miniature	18.00
Porsche Targa, 1979	75.00
Renault Racer, No. 3, 1969	65.00
Riverboat, Robert E. Lee, 1971	60.00
Rooster, Ricardo, 1973	18.00
Roulette Wheel, 1972 ....*Illus*	30.00
Scale, Lombardy, 1970 ....*Illus*	30.00
Sewing Machine, 1979, 200 Milliliter	45.00
Ship, Sea Witch, 1976	70.00
Ship, Sea Witch, 1980, 200 Milliliter	25.00
Skier, He, 1973	18.00
Skier, Jack & Jill, 1975	20.00
Skier, She, 1973	18.00
Spirit Of St. Louis, 1969	95.00
Spirit Of St. Louis, 1972, Miniature	62.00
Spirit Of St. Louis, Golden, 1977	65.00
Stamps, 1847, 1980	26.00
Swiss Chalet, 1974	32.00
Telephone, Floral, 1973	25.00
Telephone, French, 1969	40.00
Telephone, French, 1973	63.00
Telephone, French, White, 1973, Miniature	18.00
Telephone, Johnny Reb, 1973	30.00
Telephone, Yankee Doodle, 1973	30.00

Tennis, He, 1973	27.00
Tennis, She, 1973	27.00
Warriors, 1979, Miniature	23.00
Winnie Mae, Airplane, 1972	95.00
Winnie Mae, Airplane, 1972, Miniature	70.00
Yacht America, 1970, 24 In.	70.00
Yacht America, 1978	70.00

---------------------- **FIGURAL** ----------------------

Figural bottles are specially named by the collectors of bottles. Any bottle that is of a
recognizable shape, such as a human head, a pretzel, or a clock, is considered to be a
figural. There are no restrictions as to date or material. A *Soaky* is a special plastic bottle that holds shampoo, bubble bath, or another type of bath product. They were first
made by Colgate-Palmolive in the late 1950s. Figurals are also listed by brand name or
type in other sections of this book, such as the Bitters, Cologne, Perfume, Pottery, and
Whiskey categories.

FIGURAL, Acrobat, Lady, Frosted, 13 1/4 In.	35.00 to 40.00
Atterbury Duck, Patd. April 11th 1871, Milk Glass, Ground Lip, 12 In.	145.00 to 305.00
Auto, With Driver, 8 In.	150.00 to 165.00
Ballet Dancer, Milk Glass, Painted, Sheared Mouth, Pontil, 12 In.	580.00
Banjo, Amethyst, Metal Holder, 9 1/2 In.	40.00 to 85.00
Barrel, Amber, ABM Lip, 1915-1925, 6 1/8 In.	40.00
Barrel, Globe Tobacco Company, Detroit, Pat. Oct. 10th, 1882, Yellow Amber, No Lid	80.00
Barrel, Scroll, Feet, Mouth, 1790-1840, 5 1/8 In.	110.00
Bartender Joe, Red Clay, Cork In Head, With 4 Whiskeys, 1930s, 9 In., 5 Piece	85.00
Baseball, Embossed Stitch Pattern, Ground Lip, 2 3/4 In.	165.00
Bather-On-A-Rock, Stained, Clear, 10 In.	45.00
Bear, Amber, Applied Snout, Sheared Lip, 1875-1886, 10 3/4 In.	330.00
Bear, Embossed Container Made By Cia, Leaning On Shield, Pontil, 10 3/4 In.	80.00
Bear, Kummel, Black Amethyst, 11 In.	55.00 to 60.00
Bear, Kummel, Olive Green, 11 In.	50.00 to 85.00
Bear, Olive Amber, Tooled Mouth, Applied Face, 1890-1910, 9 5/8 In.	550.00
Bear, Polar, Hugging Lamp Post, Milk Glass, Ground Lip, 1880-1900, 11 1/4 In.	185.00
Bear, Seated, Blue Aqua, Applied Face, Sheared Lip, 1880-1900, 10 3/8 In.	990.00
Bear, Seated, Distre Mercator Sa Anvers Belgiour, Olive Green, Applied Face, 9 3/4 In.	440.00
Bear, Snow Crest Beverage Bank, Salem, Mass., 6 7/8 In. ....*Illus*	23.00
Bear, Vinho Do Urso Wine, Portugal, Ceramic, Cork, 1950s	12.00
Book, Bennington Type, Brown, Tan, Green Glaze, 1840-1880, 5 3/4 In.	230.00 to 385.00
Book, Coming Thro' The Rye, Pottery, Allover Blue Glaze, 1870-1890, 5 In.	175.00
Book, Departed Spirits, Bennington Type, Dark Brown, Yellow Mustard, 5 1/2 In.	470.00
Book, History Of Bourbon Co., Pottery, Allover Blue Glaze, 1890, 7 1/4 In.	200.00
Book, History Of Holland, Pottery, Blue Glaze, 1890, 5 3/4 In.	120.00
Book, Life Of Kossuth, Bennington Type, Brown, Cream, Green Glaze, 1840-1880, 6 In.	275.00

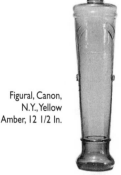

Figural, Canon,
N.Y., Yellow
Amber, 12 1/2 In.

Figural, Bear, Snow
Crest Beverage Bank,
Salem, Mass., 6 7/8 In.

Figural, Boot, Clear, Embossed
Fort, Church & Ruins, Laced
Up Front, 11 In.

Boot, Clear, Embossed Fort, Church & Ruins, Laced Up Front, 11 In. . . . .*Illus*   9.00
Brewmaster, Louis Buehler, Philadelphia, Pa., Pouring Beer, Blob Top 50.00
Bunker Hill, Blue Green, 12 In. 695.00
Bust, Czarine, Kick-Up, BIMAL, 13 In. 95.00
Bust, George Washington, Amber, 4 In. 45.00
Bust, George Washington, Cobalt Blue, 4 In. 65.00
Bust, Granger, Pat. June 2, 1874 . . . .   35.00
Bust, Grover Cleveland, Frosted, 10 In. 185.00
Bust, La Tsarine, Milk Glass, Original Tin Lid, 1895-1910, 13 1/8 In. 415.00
Bust, President Harrison, Frosted, Black Column 525.00
Bust, President James Garfield, Ground Mouth, 1880-1900, 7 In. 90.00
Bust, Wiseman, Clear, Original Tin Lid, 1890-1915, 11 1/8 In.   605.00
Cabin, Bank, Cobalt Blue Paint, Save With Pittsburgh Paints, 1900s, 3 In. 150.00
Cabin, Clear, Rope Sides, Wide Mouth, France 125.00
Candle, Frosted, Flame Stopper, 5 1/2 In. 40.00
Canon, N.Y., Yellow Amber, 12 1/2 In. . . . .*Illus*   633.00
Cherub Holding Medallion, Frosted, Ground Pontil, 13 In. 130.00
Child, Kneeling, Ground Lip, Original White Rose Label, 1890-1910, 3 1/2 In. 45.00
Clam, Clear, 4 In. 40.00
Clam, Cobalt Blue, Ground Lip, Metal Screw Cap, 1885-1910, 5 1/8 In. 350.00
Claw & Egg, Clear, 16 In. 25.00
Clock, Lewis 66 Rye, The Strauss, Pritz Co., Reverse Painted, White, Silver, Black, 12 In.   175.00
Clown, Sun Clear Glass, Pontil, Glass Head Stopper, 1890-1910, 13 In. 55.00
Clown, Turquoise Blue, Frosted, Ground Lip, Depose, 1890-1925, 13 5/8 In. . . . . .210.00 to 330.00
Clown On Ball, Deponiert, Clear Frosted, Ground Lip, Germany, 1885-1910, 13 3/8 In. .   155.00
Clown's Head, 7 In. 55.00
Coachman, Van Dunck's Genever, Ware & Schmitz, Amber, 1895, 8 3/4 In. . . . . . .90.00 to 130.00
Columbus Monument, Milk Glass, 1892, 20 In. . . . . .550.00 to 990.00
Cottage, Cottage Brand, Green Aqua, Tooled Lip, 1890-1900, 6 3/8 In. 155.00
Crying Baby, Clear, Patd. 1874, 6 1/2 In. 50.00
Cucumber, Light Blue Green, 1885-1900, 4 1/2 In. 145.00
Czar Nicholas II, Satin Milk Glass, Head Stopper, 1890-1910, 10 In. 1017.50
Dice, Milk Glass, Black Dots, Tooled Mouth, 1891, 3 5/8 In. 220.00
Dirigible, Bon-Bon Jar, MU-MU, Clear Frosted, Gold Paint, ABM Lip, France, 9 3/8 In. .   120.00
Dog, Amber, 10 In. 30.00
Domino 40.00
Donald Duck's Head, 4 1/4 In. 25.00
Duck, Atterbury, Milk Glass, 1865-1875, 11 5/8 In. .185.00 to 305.00
Duck, Rynbende Liquor, Red, Black, Clear, Milk Glass, Appied, Feet & Wings, 4 5/8 In. .   55.00
Ear Of Corn, Amber, Applied Mouth, 1870-1880, 9 3/4 In. . . . . .100.00 to 110.00
Eiffel Tower, Gray Ceramic, 14 3/4 In. . . . . .50.00 to 55.00
Elephant, Amber, ABM, 10 1/2 In. 30.00
Elephant, Deponiert, Clear Frosted, Sheared Lip, Germany, 1890-1910, 9 1/2 In. 255.00
Elephant, Seated, Castle Products, Newark, NJ, Tin Screw-On Lid, Bank, 7 In. 25.00
Elephant Head, Clear Frosted, Tooled Lip, 1880-1910, 12 1/8 In. 145.00
Fantasia, Frosted, 13 3/4 In. . . . . .40.00 to 45.00
Fat Man, Medium Amber, 10 In. 270.00
Fish, Amber, 9 7/8 In. 30.00
Fish, Antinori Soave Wine, Green, Julius Wile Sons & Co. Inc., Italy, 13 In. 15.00
Fish, Aqua, Sheared Lip, 1890-1910, 11 In. 65.00
Fish, Clear, 13 In. . . . .*Illus*   7.00
Fish, Sitting On Tail & 2 Fins, Mouth Open, 14 In. 20.00
Fish, Turquoise Blue, Sheared Lip, c.1895-1915, 10 7/8 In. 85.00
Flamingo, Hand Blown, Clear, Applied Legs, Rynbende Glass, Holland, 6 In. 55.00
Fox, Screw Top, 8 1/2 In. . . . .*Illus*   20.00
General Boulanger, Painted, Depose, 1890-1915, 14 3/4 In. 75.00
Golfer, Frosted, With 4 Head Cups, Lid, 1920, 11 1/2 In., 5 Piece 440.00
Grant's Tomb, Milk Glass, 1893, 11 3/4 In. 75.00
Ham, Clear, Screw Cap, 6 In. 50.00
Hand Holding Dagger, Clear, Pontil, 1890-1910, 14 In. 525.00
Hand Holding Leaves, Space For Label, 1890s, 5 1/4 In. 15.00
Hand Raised, Fingers & Thumb Together, Plastic Screw Top, 5 In. 15.00
Hand With Ring, Glad Hand, Whiskey Nip, Pottery, Flesh Tone Glass, Cork, 6 1/4 In. . .   50.00

Figural, Parrot,
Curacao, Clear,
Gold Beak, Red
Eyes, Destilerias
El Lorito, 10 In.

Figural, Fish,
Clear, 13 In.

To remove a dried cork that has fallen inside a bottle, try this. Pour some household ammonia in the bottle. Let it sit for a few days. Most of the cork should dissolve and can easily be removed.

Hat, Embossed B P & R, Stovepipe Form, Forest Green, 3 7/8 In. 230.00
Hatchet, Washington & World Fair 1893, Amethyst, 8 1/4 In. 160.00
Heart, Amber, Wood Covered Cork Top, Paul Masson, 8 1/2 In. 10.00
Hessian Soldier, Clear, Cannon Ball Base, 7 1/4 In. 30.00
Horn, Pressed Glass, Clear, 8 1/2 In. 45.00
Human Skull, Cobalt Blue, Tooled Mouth, 4 1/4 In. 935.00
Indian Queen, see Bitters, Brown's Celebrated
Joan Of Arc, At Stake, Frosted, Square Mouth, 14 3/8 In. . . . . .55.00 to 80.00
Joan Of Arc, Crusader Uniform, Milk Glass, Gold Paint Traces, France, 17 In. 605.00
Joan Of Arc, Frosted, Hands Folded, 13 1/2 In. 325.00
Joan Of Arc, John Tavernier, Milk Glass, Stopper, France, 16 1/2 In. 305.00
John Bull, Tree Stump, Amber, Tooled Mouth, 11 3/4 In. . . . . .155.00 to 230.00
Jules Grevy Bust, Jo Janvier, D & D Depose, France, 11 1/2 In. . . . . .75.00 to 135.00
King Humbert, Queen Margarita, Victor Emmanuell III, Busts, Milk Glass, 13 5/8 In. . . 65.00
Klondike, Gold Nugget, Milk Glass, Ground Lip, Metal Screw Cap, 1880-1895, 6 In. . . . 95.00
Liberty Bell, Proclaim Liberty, Yellow, Amber Tone, Tooled Lip, 20th Century, 8 5/8 In. 30.00
Life Preserver, Frosted, Pontil, Ground & Polished Lip, 6 5/8 In. . . . . .50.00 to 100.00
Lighthouse, Sapphire Blue, Copper Balcony Top, 1920, 12 3/4 In. 580.00
Lincoln, Bank, Clear, 8 1/2 In. 15.00
Lion, Display Statue, Lion Crouching, Blue Sponge Glaze, 7 1/2 In. 175.00
Lobster, Flared Lip, Marked Depose, Pontil, 1880-1900, 11 5/8 In. 90.00
Log Cabin, Alfred Andersen & Co., Minneapolis, Minn., Red Amber, 1890-1900, 7 In. . . 255.00
Log Cabin, Bank, Embossed Log Cabin Both Sides, Screw Opening, 4 3/4 In. 40.00
Madam, Cobalt Blue, Depose At Foot, Pontil, Stopper, France, 1915, 12 3/8 In. 1155.00
Man, Standing, Amber, Primicerio & Co., Baltimore, 1900, 7 In. 1485.00
Man & Woman Dancing Tango, Gilt Edge Saloon, Stockton, Cal., Cork, 1900, 5 1/4 In. 185.00
Monk, Ceramic, Cork In Head, West Germany, 8 In. 40.00
Moses, Amber, Hiram Ricker & Sons Inc., Water Bottle, 12 In. . . . .*Illus* 22.00
Moses, In The Bullrushes, Clear, 4 3/4 In. 45.00
Moses, Poland Springs Water, Aqua, 1880-1890, 10 1/2 In. . . . . .55.00 to 110.00
Negro Waiter, Frosted, Black Painted Head, 14 In. 230.00
Nicholas II & La Tsarine, Bust, Milk Glass, Europe, 12 1/4 In., Pair 175.00
Nightstick, Yellow Olive, Ground Lip, Metal Screw Cap, c.1885-1910, 10 1/2 In. 145.00
Nude, Draped Cloth, Monterrey Cocktail, Art Deco, 1940-1950, 1/2 Gal. 25.00
Nude, In Clamshell, Cobalt Blue, Plastic Base, ABM, Plastic Screw Lid, 10 1/8 In. 40.00
Nude, In Foliage, Frosted, 13 1/2 In. 40.00
Octopus, Draped Over American Silver Dollar, Milk Glass, 1901, 4 1/2 In. 415.00
Owl, 5 1/2 In. . . . . .40.00 to 70.00
Owl, Hand Blown, Clear, Applied Wings, Feet, Rynbende Glass, Holland, 4 In. 45.00
Oyster, Light Green, 6 In. 45.00
Oyster, Whiskey, Amber, Ground Screw Top, 6 In. 110.00
Parrot, Curacao, Clear, Gold Beak, Red Eyes, Destilerias El Lorito, 10 In. . . . .*Illus* 48.00
Pear, Blown, Peach Blow, World's Fair, Etched, 1893 . . . . 175.00
Pelican, Green, 14 3/4 In. 25.00
Piece Of Coal, Black Amethyst, Metal Screw Cap, 1890-1910, 3 1/2 In. 90.00

Pig, Drink While It Lasts From The Hogs, 7 In. 150.00
Pig, Duffy Crescent, Louisville, Ky., Inside Crescent Moon, Aqua, 1880, 8 In. ...745.00 to 1815.00
Pig, From The World's Fair, With A Little Good Old Rye In, 7 1/4 In. 1760.00
Pig, Good Old Bourbon In A Hog's..., Yellow Amber, Dark Amber Head, 6 5/8 In. ..235.00 to 260.00
Pig, Good Ole Bourbon In A Hogs..., 6 3/4 In. ....50.00 to 70.00
Pig, Kirkpatrick Brothers, Ill., World's Fair, 1893, Anna Pottery, 6 In. 1760.00
Pig, Pure Old Bourbon In A Hog's..., E.R.R., Pottery, Tan, 1875-1885, 6 7/8 In. 460.00
Pig, Railroad & River Guide, Stoneware, Cobalt Blue, Anna Pottery, 6 In. 5500.00
Pig, Something Good In A Hog's..., He Won't Squeal, On Belly, Tooled Mouth, 1910, 4 In. 120.00
Pig, Standing, Clear, Tooled Lip, 1880-1890, 7 In. 255.00
Pineapple, Applied Double Collar Mouth, 1865-1870, 8 7/8 In. 155.00
Pineapple, Amber, Ring Mouth, 11 3/4 In. 145.00
Policeman, Cobalt Blue, Painted Features, France, 1880-1920, 18 3/4 In. ....120.00 to 155.00
Policeman, French, Cobalt Blue, 8 In. 175.00
Policeman, Liqueur, Raspail, Paris, Cobalt Blue, Painted, 14 1/2 In. 85.00
Poodle, Amber, 1933, 8 In. 18.00
Potato, Idaho, 1893, World's Fair, 4 3/4 In. 40.00
Potbelly Stove, 10 1/4 In. ....*Illus* 15.00
Pretzel, Ceramic, Beige, 3 1/2 In. 75.00
Rebecca At Well, Frosted & Clear, 7 3/4 In. 40.00
Revolver, Amethyst, Solid Glass Rim, 5 In. 60.00
Revolver, Aqua, Ground Top, Threads, USA, Avor., 8 In. 40.00
Revolver, Flintlock, Honey Amber, Ground Top, Metal Cap, 9 1/2 In. 60.00
Revolver, Ground Top, Tin Cap, Octagon Barrel, 4 1/2 In. 30.00
Revolver, Mercury Silver, Black Butt Plates, 5 In. 40.00
Revolver, Yellow, Ground Top, Metal Cap, 8 In. 80.00
Roast Fowl, Amber, Screw Cap, 6 1/2 In. ....75.00 to 150.00
Rooster, Amber, Taiwan, 1973, 11 1/2 In. 15.00
Russian Peasant, M.G. Husted, 1915, 12 1/8 In. 90.00
Sailors On Ship, Clear, Amethystine Tint, Tooled Mouth, Depose, France, 11 3/4 In. ... 90.00
Saint Joseph, Frosted, Halo Stopper, 6 In. 135.00
Saint Joseph, John Tavernier, Bonbon, Painted, France, 16 In. 110.00
Saint Nicholas, Sheared Lip, Germany, 3 In. 85.00
Santa Claus, 12 In. ....75.00 to 90.00
Santa Claus, M.C. Husted, Clear, Tooled Mouth, 1910, 12 1/4 In. 85.00
Scallop, Stained, 4 3/4 In. 30.00
Scottish Sailor, Clear Frosted, Hat Lid, Ground Lip, 1890-1910, 12 1/4 In. 110.00
Senorita, With Fan, Clear, By Dalmau Hermanos, Spain, 12 In. ....*Illus* 9.00
Shell Tree, Blue, 13 In. 15.00
Shoe, Black Amethyst, Painted Toe, Metal Screw Cap, c.1910, 3 5/8 In. 120.00
Shoe, Dark Amethyst, Protruding Big Toe, Screw Threads, Cap, 1860-1890, 6 In. ...75.00 to 90.00
Skate, Dress Shoe, Electric Blue, Metal Tassel Band, Cork, 6 5/8 In. 440.00
Soaky, Baloo, Colgate 75.00
Soaky, Batman 65.00
Soaky, Bullwinkle Moose, Plastic, Red, Yellow Antlers, 1966, 10 In. 50.00
Soaky, Creature From The Black Lagoon, Plastic, Green, 10 In. 60.00

Figural, Moses, Amber, Hiram Ricker & Sons Inc., Water Bottle, 12 In.

Figural, Fox, Screw Top, 8 1/2 In.

Figural, Potbelly Stove, 10 1/4 In.

Figural, Senorita,
With Fan, Clear,
By Dalmau
Hermanos, Spain,
12 In.

Figural, Trunk,
Embossed,
Modern, Light
Olive, 10 In.

Figural,
Violin, Aqua,
9 1/2 In.

Soaky, Dick Tracy, 1960 .... 40.00
Soaky, Felix The Cat, Box 25.00
Soaky, King Louie, Colgate 75.00
Soaky, Mister Magoo, 1960s, 9 In. 35.00
Soaky, Tennessee Tuxedo 35.00
Soaky, Top Cat, Yellow, Hanna-Barbera, Contents, 10 In. 45.00
Soaky, Tweety 68.00
Space Scout, Galaxy Grape & Orange Syrup, Bank, 1950s, 8 1/2 In. 40.00
Spirit Of St. Louis, Cobalt Blue, Original Brass Propeller, 1927, 12 In. 855.00
Statue Of Liberty, Milk Glass Base, Bronze, 1893-1895, 15 1/8 In. .....440.00 to 550.00
Statue Of Liberty, Milk Glass, Ground Mouth, 15 1/2 In. 210.00
Tree Trunk, Pres. Franklin D. Roosevelt, Souvenir Of Chicago, c.1934, 12 In. 470.00
Trunk, Embossed, Modern, Light Olive, 10 In. ....*Illus* 12.00
Turtle, Amber, 5 In. 150.00
U.S. Mailbox, Rye, Embossed Eagle, 7 In. ....60.00 to 80.00
Uncle Sam, Clear, 1898, Flaccus Bros., 9 1/2 In. ....85.00 to 130.00
Uncle Sam, Pat. Apl'd For, Clear, Metal Screw High Cap, 1910, 9 1/2 In. 60.00
Violin, Amber, Tooled Lip, 7 In. ....30.00 to 40.00
Violin, Amber, Wooden Neck, Tooled Mouth, 1890-1910, 14 1/4 In. 175.00
Violin, Amethyst, Hanging Chain, Pontil, 10 In. ....60.00 to 125.00
Violin, Amethyst, Metal Holder, 7 1/2 In. ....40.00 to 45.00
Violin, Apple Green, Metal Hanger, OP, 9 1/2 In. 45.00
Violin, Aqua, 9 1/2 In. ....*Illus* 20.00
Violin, Blue, 10 In. ....30.00 to 40.00
Violin, Cobalt Blue, 3 3/4 In. ....25.00 to 100.00
Violin, Light Apple Green, Pontil, 9 3/4 In. 60.00
Violin, Light Blue, Musical Notes On Back, 10 In. 40.00
Violin, Ruby Red Glass Overlay, 6 In. 80.00
Violin, Sailing Ship Design, Tooled Flared Mouth, Pontil, 1860, 4 3/4 In. 255.00
Violin, Sapphire Blue, Tooled Lip, 7 1/2 In. 65.00
Violin, Yellow Green, Metal Hanger, OP, 9 1/2 In. ....45.00 to 50.00
Washington, Cork, ABM, 9 1/2 In. 10.00
Whisk Broom, Bisque, 6 In. 30.00
Whisk Broom, Brown, Blue, Red, Porcelain, Germany, 1885-1920, 7 1/4 In. 185.00
Woman, Holding Fan & Flowers, Pottery, B.F. & Co., Tan & Green Glaze, 10 1/4 In. ... 155.00
Woman, Standing, D.D. Alsace, Depose, Blue Milk Glass, 1895-1910, 13 3/8 In. 635.00
Woman, Wearing Flowing Dress, Marked, Fox Land, France, 1890-1915, 13 3/4 In. 45.00
Woman With Basket, Clear Frosted, Painted, Tooled Mouth, Europe, 10 1/4 In. 100.00
Young Boy, C.F. Knapp, Patent Applied For, Tooled Mouth, 1890-1910, 6 3/4 In. 165.00

―――――――――――――――――――――― **FIRE GRENADE** ――――――――――――――――――――――

Fire grenades were popular from about 1870 to 1910. They were glass containers filled
with a fire extinguisher such as carbon tetrachloride. The bottle of liquid was thrown at
the base of a fire to shatter and extinguish the flames. A particularly ingenious *automatic* type was hung in a wire rack; theoretically, the heat of the fire would melt the sol-
der of the rack and the glass grenade would drop into the fire. Because they were
designed to be broken, not too many have survived for the collector. Some are found

today that still have the original contents sealed by cork and wax closures. Handle these with care. Fumes from the contents are dangerous to your health.

FIRE GRENADE, Acanthus Leaf & Lion Head, Aqua, Ground Lip, 1875-1895, 6 3/8 In. . 165.00
American Fire Extinguisher Co., Clear, Quilted, Footed Base, Pt., 6 1/4 In. 330.00
Barnum's, Handfire, June 26, 1869, Amber, 6 In. . . . .*Illus* 1100.00
Fire Plug, Fire Dep't., Throw Into Fire, Fred Adams Advertising, 4 3/8 In. 275.00
Firex, Cobalt Blue, Box, 3 1/4 In. 75.00
Flagg's Hand, Aug. 4, 1868, Amber, 6 1/2 In. . . . .*Illus* 800.00
H.N.S., Yellow Amber, Ground Lip, Qt., 7 1/8 In. 115.00
H.N.S., Yellow, Amber, Ground Lip, Smooth Base, 1880-1895, 7 1/4 In. 110.00
Harden's Hand, Cobalt Blue, Diamond Pattern, Contents, 6 1/4 In. 120.00
Harden's Hand, Fire Extinguisher, Pat. No. 1, Aug. 8, 1877, Turquoise, 6 1/4 In. 55.00
Harden's Hand, Fire Extinguisher, Turquoise Blue, Sheared, Ground Lip, 7 In. 385.00
Harden's Hand, Pat. No. 1, Aug. 8 1871, Deep Turquoise, Ground Lip, 6 In. 105.00
Harden's Hand, Star In Circle, Ribbed, Sapphire Blue, c.1890, 7 In. 270.00
Harden's Hand, Star, Cobalt Blue, Contents, Wire Bail, 6 1/2 In. 130.00
Harden's Hand, Star, Fire Extinguisher, Band Around Middle, 1880-1890, 7 In. 440.00
Harden's Improved, Pat. Oct. 7th 1884, Cobalt Blue & Clear, 2 3/8 In. 770.00
Harkness Fire Destroyer, Cobalt Blue, Tooled Lip, Bubbles, Contents, 6 1/4 In. 470.00
Hayward's Hand, Apple Green, Pat. Aug. 8, 1871, Contents, Pt., 6 1/4 In. 225.00
Hayward's Hand, Aqua, Pat. Aug. 8, 1871, Partial Label, Contents, Pt., 5 7/8 In. 175.00
Hayward's Hand, Clear, Applied Mouth, Smooth Base, 1871-1885, 6 1/8 In. 140.00
Hayward's Hand, Cobalt Blue, Design Patd., Tooled Mouth, Contents, Qt. 250.00
Hayward's Hand, Cobalt Blue, Pat. Aug. 8, 1871, Tooled Mouth, Contents, 6 In. .180.00 to 220.00
Hayward's Hand, Green, Pat. Aug. 8, 1871, 6 1/8 In. 415.00
Hayward's Hand, Lavender, 4 Bulbous Panels, 1860-1890, 6 1/4 In. 1210.00
Hayward's Hand, Yellow Olive, Tooled Mouth, 1871-1885, 6 1/8 In. 275.00
Hayward's Hand, Yellow, Pat. Aug. 8, 1871, Tooled Lip, Contents, 6 In. 165.00
Hazelton's High Pressure Chemical Fire Keg, Brown, 11 1/2 In. . . . .*Illus* 200.00
Healy's Hand, U Upside Down, Amber, 11 In. . . . .*Illus* 900.00
Healy's Hand, Yellow Amber, Applied Mouth, Qt., 11 1/2 In. 910.00
Horizontal Rib, Light Aqua Glass, Tooled Mouth, 1880-1895, 7 In. . . . . .825.00 to 855.00
HSN, Large Diamond, Yellow Topaz, Ground, Globular, 1870-1900, 7 In. 110.00
HSN, Light To Medium Straw Yellow, Ground Lip, 1880s, Qt., 7 1/8 In. 340.00
L'Urbaine, Medium Straw Yellow, Ground Lip, 1880-1890, 6 1/2 In. 550.00
L.B., Cobalt Blue, Vertical Rib Pattern, Ground Lip, France, 1885-95, Pt., 5 3/8 In. 550.00
Louisville & Nashville Railroad, Orange Amber, Tooled Mouth, 1880-1890, Qt. 1100.00
Magic Fire Extinguisher Co., Yellow Amber, Ground Lip, 1880-1890, 6 1/4 In. 105.00
O.J. Childs Co. Sulphuric Acid, Utical, No. 1, Amber 40.00
Oval Label Panel, Cobalt Blue, Horizontal Ribs, BIMAL, 1885-1895, 6 1/2 In. 240.00
Prevoyante Extinteur Grenade, Orange Amber, Ground Lip, France, Pt., 5 5/8 In. . . . 415.00
Recessed Band, Deep Opening For Peg In Base, Ground Lip, 1890-1910, Pt., 6 In. 825.00
Red Paint, Clear, Metal Framework, Contents, 9 1/2 In. 150.00
Systeme Labbe, Paris, Medium Orange Amber, 1880-1900, 5 3/4 In., Pt. . . . . . . .305.00 to 330.00
Unic Extingtrice, Yellow Amber, Orange Amber Neck, 4-Panels, Round, 5 In. 303.00

Fire Grenade,
Barnum's,
Handfire,
June 26, 1869,
Amber, 6 In.

Fire Grenade,
Flagg's Hand,
Aug. 4, 1868,
Amber, 6 1/2 In.

Fire Grenade,
Hazelton's High
Pressure Chemical Fire
Keg, Brown, 11 1/2 In.

Fire Grenade, Healy's
Hand, U Upside Down,
Amber, 11 In.

Vertical Rib, Ground Lip, Smooth Base, 1880-1895, 5 1/2 In. 415.00
Vertical Rib, Yellow Orange Amber, Ground Lip, France, 1880-1895, 5 5/8 In. 305.00
FITZGERALD, see Old Fitzgerald

────────────────── **FLASK** ──────────────────

Flasks have been made in America since the eighteenth century. Hundreds of styles and variations were made. Free-blown, mold-blown, and decorated flasks are all popular with collectors. Prices are determined by rarity, condition, and color. In general, bright colors bring higher prices. The numbers used in the entries in the form McK G I-000 refer to the book *American Bottles and Flasks* by Helen McKearin and Kenneth M. Wilson. Each flask listed in that book is sketched and described and it is important to compare your flask with the book picture to determine value, since many similar flasks were made.

Many reproductions of flasks have been made, most in the last 25 years, but some as early as the nineteenth century. The reproduction flasks that seem to cause the most confusion for the beginner are the Lestoil flasks made in the 1960s. These bottles, sold in grocery stores, were filled with Lestoil, a liquid cleaner, and sold for about 65 cents. Three designs were made: a Washington Eagle, a Columbia Eagle, and a ship Franklin Eagle. Four colors were used—purple, dark blue, dark green, and amber—and mixes were also produced. Over one million of the flasks were made and they now are seen at the collectible shows. The only mark on the bottles was the name Lestoil on the stopper. Other reproductions that are often found are marked *Nuline* or *Taiwan*.

FLASK, 3-Piece Mold, Blown, Smoky Clear, Pontil, 5 1/2 In. 1100.00
8 Ribs, Swirled To Right, Teardrop Shape, Amethyst, 1860, 7 In. 120.00
10 Diamond, Medium Amber, Pontil, 5 In. 770.00
11 Ribs, Swirled To Right, Teardrop Shape, Emerald Green, 1800-1860, 6 7/8 In. 120.00
12 Diamond, Amethyst, Pontil, 1930, 6 In. 120.00
12 Diamond, Amethyst, Pontil, Emil Larson, 1930, 4 7/8 In. 100.00
12 Ribs, Fold Down Lip, Midwest, Globular, Pontil, 1830, 8 3/8 In. 330.00
14 Ribs, Swirled To Right, Gold Amber Red, Pontil, 4 3/4 In. 605.00
15 Diamond, Blue Aqua, Pontil, 1820-1830, 9 1/2 In. 605.00
16 Diamond, Teardrop Shape, Blue Aqua, Pontil, 6 1/4 In. 200.00
16 Ribs, Swirled To Left, Aqua, Pontil, 6 In. 220.00
16 Ribs, Swirled To Left, Blue Green, Club, Midwest, Pontil, 8 1/2 In. 1595.00
16 Ribs, Swirled To Right, Cobalt Blue, Flared Mouth, Pontil, 1800-1830, 3 3/4 In. 210.00
16 Ribs, Swirled To Right, Globular, Applied Mouth, Green Aqua, 1820-1835, 8 3/8 In. .. 80.00
16 Ribs, Teardrop, Gold Amber, White Enamel Lines, Pontil, Europe, 1840, 4 1/2 In. ... 305.00
16 Ribs, Vertical, Amber, Midwest, Globular, Pontil, 3 5/8 In. 175.00
18 Ribs, Swirled To Right, Amethyst, Emil Larson, Vineland, N.J., 1920, 5 3/4 In. 130.00
18 Ribs, Swirled To Right, Amethyst, Emil Larson, Vineland, N.J., 1930, Pontil, 4 5/8 In. 230.00
20 Ribs, Swirled To Right, Sapphire Blue, Flared Mouth, 1830, 3 7/8 In. 525.00
20 Ribs, Vertical, Green Aqua, Rolled Mouth, Midwest, Globular, Pontil, 9 1/4 In. 230.00
22 Ribs, Swirled To Right, Cobalt Blue, Amethyst Tone, Midwest, Pontil, 4 5/8 In. 495.00
24 Broken Ribs, Swirled To Right, Blue Aqua, Midwest, Pontil, 1830, 8 5/8 In. 155.00

24 Broken Ribs, Swirled To Right, Cornflower Blue, Midwest, 7 7/8 In. 305.00
24 Ribs, Swirled To Left, Amber, Handle, Midwest, Globular, Pontil, 6 1/2 In. 4620.00
24 Ribs, Swirled To Left, Amber, Rolled Mouth, Midwest, Globular, 8 1/4 In. .....415.00 to 440.00
24 Ribs, Swirled To Left, Aqua, Midwest, Globular, Pontil, 8 1/8 In. 240.00
24 Ribs, Swirled To Left, Globular Melon Shape, Gold Amber, Pontil, 7 7/8 In. 1100.00
24 Ribs, Swirled To Left, Gold Amber, Midwest, Globular, Pontil, 8 In. 385.00
24 Ribs, Swirled To Left, Green Aqua, Midwest, Globular, Pontil, 7 1/4 In. 110.00
24 Ribs, Swirled To Left, Green, Pontil, 1830, 5 7/8 In. 240.00
24 Ribs, Swirled To Left, Medium Amber, Rolled Mouth, 1820-1835, Globular, 8 1/4 In. 635.00
24 Ribs, Swirled To Left, Red Amber, Rolled Mouth, Midwest, Globular, 8 1/4 In. 550.00
24 Ribs, Swirled To Left, Yellow Amber, Midwest, Globular, Pontil, 7 5/8 In. 715.00
24 Ribs, Swirled To Left, Yellow, Wide Neck, Midwest, Globular, Pontil, 7 3/8 In. 1015.00
24 Ribs, Swirled To Right, Amber, Midwest, Globular, Pontil, 7 7/8 In. ....360.00 to 385.00
24 Ribs, Swirled To Right, Amber, Rolled Mouth, Midwest, Globular, Pontil, 8 5/8 In. .. 440.00
24 Ribs, Swirled To Right, Aqua, Rolled Mouth, Pontil, Club, 7 7/8 In. 110.00
24 Ribs, Swirled To Right, Blue Aqua, Rolled Mouth, Midwest, Globular, 7 5/8 In. 415.00
24 Ribs, Swirled To Right, Gold Amber, Midwest, Globular, Pontil, 8 1/8 In. 355.00
24 Ribs, Swirled To Right, Medium Amber, Midwest, Globular, Pontil, 8 1/4 In. 305.00
24 Ribs, Swirled To Right, Red Amber, Midwest, Globular, Pontil, 8 3/8 In. 495.00
24 Ribs, Swirled To Right, Rolled Mouth, Globular, 1820-1830, 7 1/2 In. ....500.00 to 935.00
24 Ribs, Vertical, Blue Aqua, Midwest, Globular, Pontil, 7 3/4 In. 495.00
24 Ribs, Vertical, Gold Amber,1800-1830, 7 7/8 In. 715.00
24 Ribs, Yellow Amber, Rolled Mouth, Midwest, Globular, Pontil, 7 1/2 In. 1100.00
36 Ribs, Swirled, Light Yellow Olive, Pontil, 5 1/2 In. 300.00
A. Williams & Son, Family Wine Store, Estab. 1870, Boston, Strap Side, Pt. 30.00
Acanthus Leaf, Flared Mouth, Pontil, 5 3/8 In. 65.00
Admiral Dewey, Remember The Maine, Blue Ground, 1885-1900, 4 7/8 In. 230.00
Admiral Dewey, Remember The Maine, Label Under Glass, Canteen Shape 350.00
Ahrens-Bullwinkle Co., San Francisco, Light To Medium Orange Amber, 11 5/8 In. ... 745.00
Ain't What It Used To Be, Horse On Mound, Light Apricot Amber, Pontil, 6 1/2 In. .. 200.00
Amber, Embossed Anchor, Glob Top, Qt. 25.00
Amber, Rolled Mouth, Midwest, Globular, Pontil, 3 3/8 In. 740.00
Amber, Rolled Mouth, Midwest, Globular, Pontil, 8 In. 465.00
Amethyst, Boy With Dog, Carrying Bird, Girl With Bundle, Continental, Pontil, 1/2 Pt. . 255.00
Andy Balich, Pumpkinseed, Tooled Mouth, 1909-1915, 5 3/8 In. 70.00
Andy Balich, Pumpkinseed, Tooled Mouth, 1909-1915, 6 7/8 In. 55.00
B.F. Jellison, San Francisco, Pumpkinseed, Sun Colored Amethyst, 1900-1906, 7 In. 1210.00
B.P.O.E., Portland, 1912, Elk & Tulips, Lotus Bar, 1912, 4 3/4 In. 185.00
Basketweave, Amethyst, 1/2 Pt. 30.00
Bellows, Cranberry & White Loops, OP, c.1834 .... 700.00
Bergleen & Little, Doctor Bar, Raymond, Wash., Tooled Mouth, 1890-1910, 8 1/2 In. .. 55.00
Billiken, Hip, 1921 .... 195.00
Boar's Head, Deer, Purple Amethyst, Flattened Coin Shape, Pontil, 1850-1860, 1/2 Pt. .. 385.00
Brandes Brothers, New York, Amber, Strap Side, 1/2 Pt. 25.00
Braunschweiger & Co., Pumpkinseed, Tooled Mouth, 1890-1912, 5 3/8 In. 100.00
Brown, Thompson & Co., Louisville, Ky., Beech Fork Whiskey, Coffin, 1/2 Pt. 20.00
Byron & Scott, Portrait, Amber, OP, 1/2 Pt. 120.00
C.P. Mormon, Only Manuf'r Of J.H. Cutter Old Bourbon, Brown Amber, 7 3/4 In. 120.00
C.R. Gibson, Salamango, N.Y. 40.00
Cahn, Belt & Co., Baltimore, Maryland, 8 1/2 In. 25.00
Cap & Bead, Flared Mouth, Europe, Pontil, 6 3/8 In. 140.00
Capitol, W.A. Gaines & Co's, Old Crow Whiskey, Screw Threaded, 1/2 Pt. 265.00
Cascade Lincoln Co. Whiskey, Springfield, Tenn., Ribbed, Tooled Mouth, 7 1/4 In. ... 170.00
Chestnut, 10 Diamond, Blue Aqua, Midwest, Pontil, 4 5/8 In. ....635.00 to 1155.00
Chestnut, 10 Diamond, Gold Amber, Pontil, 1820-1830, 4 1/2 In. ....990.00 to 2090.00
Chestnut, 10 Diamond, Green, Pontil, 4 3/4 In. 4510.00
Chestnut, 10 Diamond, Olive Yellow, Pontil, 1820-1830, 5 1/2 In. ....2190.00 to 3190.00
Chestnut, 10 Diamond, Tobacco Amber, Pontil, 5 3/4 In. ....1020.00 to 2200.00
Chestnut, 10 Diamond, Yellow Olive Amber, Pontil, 4 7/8 In. ....*Illus* 855.00
Chestnut, 14 Ribs, Cobalt Blue, Pontil, 1832, 4 3/4 In. 220.00
Chestnut, 16 Ribs, Amber, 5 1/8 In. ....220.00 to 330.00
Chestnut, 16 Ribs, Aqua, Midwest, Pontil, 4 1/2 In. 175.00
Chestnut, 16 Ribs, Medium Pink Amethyst, 1820-1830, 6 In. 580.00

Chestnut, 16 Ribs, Olive Yellow, Midwest, Pontil, 6 In. .440.00 to 770.00
Chestnut, 18 Broken Ribs, Swirled To Right, Amber, Midwest, Pontil, 1830, 6 1/8 In. . . 1045.00
Chestnut, 18 Diamond, Citron To Amber, Flattened, Pontil, 6 1/4 In. 1210.00
Chestnut, 18 Diamond, Yellow Green, Applied Mouth, Midwest, 6 1/8 In. 330.00
Chestnut, 18 Ribs, Apple Green, Midwest, Pontil, 4 7/8 In. 85.00
Chestnut, 18 Ribs, Sapphire Blue, Teardrop Shape, Pontil, 6 1/2 In. 990.00
Chestnut, 18 Ribs, Straw Color, Teardrop Shape, Pontil, 6 7/8 In. 825.00
Chestnut, 20 Broken Ribs, Swirled To Left, Yellow Olive, Midwest, Pontil, 7 3/8 In. . . . 3850.00
Chestnut, 20 Ribs, Citron, Teardrop Shape, Pontil, 6 3/8 In. 770.00
Chestnut, 20 Ribs, Cobalt Blue, Europe, Pontil, 4 7/8 In. 230.00
Chestnut, 20 Ribs, Golden Yellow, Midwest, Pontil, 5 1/8 In. 245.00
Chestnut, 24 Broken Ribs, Swirled To Left, Amber, Midwest, 7 1/8 In. 2200.00
Chestnut, 24 Broken Ribs, Swirled To Left, Blue Aqua, Midwest, 7 5/8 In. 935.00
Chestnut, 24 Broken Ribs, Swirled To Right, Aqua, Midwest, Pontil, 1830, 6 3/4 In. . . . 635.00
Chestnut, 24 Broken Ribs, Swirled To Right, Red Amber, Midwest, Pontil, 8 1/4 In. . . . 990.00
Chestnut, 24 Ribs, Gold Amber, Red Tone, Flattened, Pontil, 8 5/8 In. 1430.00
Chestnut, 24 Ribs, Light Green, Pontil, 5 1/2 In. 120.00
Chestnut, 24 Ribs, Olive Yellow, Midwest, 1830, 5 In. 525.00
Chestnut, 24 Ribs, Swirled To Left, Gold Amber, Midwest, 1830, 5 In. . . . . .305.00 to 465.00
Chestnut, 24 Ribs, Swirled To Left, Gold Amber, Midwest, Pontil, 8 3/8 In. 3850.00
Chestnut, 24 Ribs, Swirled To Right, Blue Green, Flattened, Pontil, 6 1/8 In. 220.00
Chestnut, 24 Ribs, Yellow Amber, Midwest, Pontil, 5 1/4 In. . . . . .240.00 to 495.00
Chestnut, 24 Ribs, Yellow Olive, Midwest, 1830, 6 1/4 In. . . . . .385.00 to 1210.00
Chestnut, 30 Ribs, Gold Amber, Daisy, Midwest, Pontil, 5 1/8 In. 3960.00
Chestnut, 32 Ribs, Puce Amethyst, Pontil, 4 7/8 In. 825.00
Chestnut, 38 Ribs, Swirled To Right, Sapphire Blue, Pontil, 4 3/4 In. 1540.00
Chestnut, Amber, Multicolored Painted Soldier & European Words, 1890, 7 7/8 In. 110.00
Chestnut, Blue Green, Applied Mouth, Pontil, 5 3/8 In. 185.00
Chestnut, Dark Green, Laid On Ring, OP, 9 3/4 In. 255.00
Chestnut, Dark Strawberry Puce, Handle, IP, 1860-1870, 8 5/8 In. 305.00
Chestnut, Forest Green, Tooled Mouth, Seed Bubbles, Pontil, 12 1/2 In. 495.00
Chestnut, Light Olive Amber, Applied Mouth, 1830, 5 5/8 In. . . . . .100.00 to 165.00
Chestnut, Medium Olive Green Amber, Applied Mouth, Pontil, 1790-1820, 6 3/8 In. . . . 175.00
Chestnut, Moss Green, Applied Mouth, Pontil, 1770-1810, 7 3/4 In. . . . . .230.00 to 440.00
Chestnut, Olive Green, Rolled Mouth, Flattened, Pontil, 1780-1810, 6 5/8 In. . . . .155.00 to 200.00
Chestnut, Olive Yellow, Applied Mouth, Pontil, 9 3/4 In. . . . . .165.00 to 200.00
Chestnut, Olive Yellow, Applied Rim, New England, Pontil, 1783-1830, 5 1/2 In. 154.00
Chestnut, Olive Yellow, Flattened, 1820-1835, 5 3/8 In. . . . . .185.00 to 230.00
Chestnut, Olive Yellow, Sheared Mouth, Applied Rim, Pontil, 5 3/4 In. 200.00
Chestnut, Olive Yellow, Tooled Mouth, Flattened, 5 3/8 In. . . . . .175.00 to 340.00
Chestnut, Red Amber, Flared Lip, Midwest, Pontil, 6 1/2 In. 330.00
Chestnut, Yellow Amber, Sloping Collar, Flattened, 8 1/4 In. 185.00
Chestnut, Yellow Green, Olive Tone, Sheared Mouth, Applied Rim, 1780-1830, 10 In. . . 360.00
Chestnut, Yellow Green, Olive Tone, Sheared Mouth, New England, 6 In. 165.00
Chestnut, Yellow Olive, Sheared Mouth, Applied Rim, Pontil, 5 1/4 In. 200.00
Chestnut, Yellow Olive, Sheared Mouth, New England, 1780-1830, 8 1/4 In. 65.00
Chestnut, Yellow Olive, Sheared Mouth, Pontil, 1780-1830, 7 In. 175.00
Christmas Greetings, M. Lurey, Richmond, Calif., Label Under Glass, 7 In. 150.00
Cleveland & Stephenson, Barrel, Amber, Polished Pontil, 1/2 Pt. 305.00
Clevenger Brothers, Clayton, N.J., Gold Amber, Eagle, 1960s, Qt. 5.00
Clinch & Co. Liquor Dealers, Grass Valley, Coffin, 1/2 Pt. 305.00
Clock Face, Grandfather's Clock & Star Back, Pumpkinseed, 1/2 Pt. 60.00
Clock Face, Spiderweb Pattern, Pumpkinseed, 1/2 Pt. 30.00
Coffin, A. Livingston Wholesale & Retail, Carson City, Nev., Amethyst, 1885-1905, 6 In. . 1815.00
Columbian Jubilee, Santa Maria Picture, 1492-1892, Amber, Coffin, Pt. 500.00
Com. W.S. Schley U.S.N., Flag, Label Under Glass, Metal Screw Cap, 1895-1900, 6 In. . 470.00
Crest, Lion With Battleaxe, Cobalt Blue, Swirled, OP, 6 1/2 In. 150.00
Cunningham & Ihmsen Glassmakers, Pittsburgh, Pa., Aqua, Strap Side, Pt. 40.00
D.B. Lester, Grocer, Savannah, Ga., Gold Amber, Strap Side, 1890, 9 3/4 In. 110.00
Deer, Oak Tree & Boar, Cobalt Blue, Tooled Mouth, Pontil, 1840-1860, 7 3/8 In. 330.00
Deer's Head Brand Rye Whiskey, Meagher Bros. & Co., Montreal, Aqua, Cork, 8 In. . . 15.00
Devil's Island Endurance Gin, Oval, Fluted, Pt. 15.00
Dillon Mont, Louis W. Potter, PIX, 1900, Pt. 355.00

Double Eagle, Stoneware, Light Brown Sewer Tile, 1890, 1/2 Pt., 5 3/8 In. 95.00
Duffy's Crescent Saloon, Pig Shape, Aqua, 7 1/2 In. 1050.00
Edward Canlan & Co., Cincinnati, Ohio, Amber, Double Mouth, Wooden Cork, 5 3/4 In. 440.00
Edwd. Jno. Rose & Compy., Wine & Brandy Dealers, Aqua, BIMAL, 5 1/4 In. 15.00
Firecracker, Aqua, OP, Pt. 185.00
Flowers Mfg. Co., Greenville, Tenn, SCA, Shoofly, 1/2 Pt. 15.00
Geekie, 123 Baltimore, Md., Blue Aqua, Strap Side, Applied Mouth, 1880, Pt. 145.00
Geo. A. Berry & Co., Aqua, Eagle, Qt. 75.00
Grove Whiskey, Chestnut, Applied Seal & Handle, Flattened, Pontil, 8 1/2 In. 170.00
H. Brickwedel & Co., Orange Yellow Amber, Tooled Mouth, 1880s, 7 1/4 In. 220.00
Henderson N.C. Dispensary, Strap Side, 1/2 Pt. 95.00
Henry Chapman & Co., Montreal, Amber, 1860-1990, Glass Screw Cap, 6 In. 120.00
Hildebrandt Posner, San Francisco, Pumpkinseed, Purple, Pt. 70.00
Hirschfeld & Beck, New York, Rectangular, 7 In. 10.00
Honest Measure, Double Collar, Strap Side, 9 1/2 In. 3.00
Honest-One, Double Collar, Rectangular, Cork, 8 1/4 In. 3.00
Hotel Statler, Cleveland, Ohio, Pumpkinseed, 3 1/4 In. 10.00
Hunter's, Cobalt Blue, Europe, OP, 7 In. 75.00
I Got My Fill At Jakes, Pumpkinseed, Applied Double Collar Mouth, 6 3/8 In. . .260.00 to 525.00
I. Hayes & Co., Manchester, N.Y., Amber, 1/2 Pt. 35.00
I. Trager Co., Cincinnati, Ohio, Amber, ABM, Pt. . . . . .10.00 to 20.00
J. Fox & Co., Cincinnati, Saloon, Birmingham, Ala., Strap Side, Light Stain, 1/2 Pt. 275.00
J.J. Cannon Palmer House, Label Under Glass, Clock Face, Screw Cap, 5 1/8 In. 330.00
James Noel, Los Angeles, Ca., Pumpkinseed, Clear, Tooled Mouth, 1890, 6 3/8 In. 355.00
Jas. S. Fox, Hudson, N.Y., Coffin, 1/2 Pt. 25.00
Jas. Tharp Wines & Liquors, Washington, D.C., Amber, Slug Plate, Strap Side, 1/2 Pt. . 40.00
Jim McCarty's Place, Chattanooga, Tenn., Coffin, Pt. 175.00
Jno. F. Horne, Knoxville, Tenn., Gold Amber, Strap Side, Tooled Mouth, Qt. 85.00
John Mitchell, 35 Bridge St., Portsmouth, Aqua, Strap Side, 7 1/2 In. 35.00
Jos. Melczer & Co., San Francisco, Cal., 1/2 Pt. 100.00
L. Gerstle, Bluff City, Tenn., Pumpkinseed, Tooled Mouth, 1885-1900, 4 3/4 In. . .155.00 to 330.00
L.K. & Co., Syracuse, N.Y., Amber, Strap Side, 1/2 Pt. 30.00
Label Under Glass, Kaiser Wilhelm Photo, Metal Screw Cap, Germany, 1915, 5 1/4 In. . . 220.00
Lilienthal & Co., San Francisco, Amber, Double Mouth, 1872-1880, 8 1/2 In. 550.00
Louis J. Vessel, Washington, D.C., K, Amber, Slug Plate, Strap Side, Pt. 45.00
Louis XVI, Pinch, Pewter Cap, 6 1/8 In. 125.00
Louisville Liquor House, Cripple Creek, Col., 1/2 Pt. 1210.00
Lynn & Parker, Hollister, Cal., Monogram, 1889-1894, Pt. 176.00
M. Geary Liquor Dealer, Woodstock, Va., Amber, Applied Mouth, 1885, 8 In. 580.00
M.D. Lucy, 189 Merrimack St., Newburyport, Aqua, Strap Side, 6 In. 35.00
McCormick & Co., Beer Brand, Baltimore, Md., SCA, 1/2 Pt. 20.00
McK G I-1, Washington & Eagle, Green Aqua, OP, Pt. 325.00
McK G I-1, Washington & Eagle, Light Blue Green, Pontil, Pt. 605.00
McK G I-2, Washington & Eagle, Green Aqua, Pontil, Pt. . . . . .110.00 to 290.00
McK G I-7, Washington & Eagle, Green Aqua, Pontil, Pt. . . . . .550.00 to 605.00

Flask, Chestnut,
10 Diamond, Yellow
Olive Amber,
Pontil, 4 7/8 In.

Flask, McK G I-11,
Washington &
Eagle, Blue Aqua,
Pontil, Pt.

McK G 1-10, Washington & Eagle, Green Aqua, Pontil, Pt. 100.00
McK G 1-11, Washington & Eagle, Blue Aqua, Pontil, Pt. ....*Illus* 635.00
McK G 1-14, Washington & Eagle, Aqua, Pontil, Pt. ....200.00 to 385.00
McK G 1-16, Washington & Taylor, Green Aqua, Pontil, Pt. 120.00
McK G 1-17, Washington & Taylor, Green, Pontil, Pt. 1100.00
McK G 1-17, Washington & Taylor, Wine, Pontil, Pt. 2750.00
McK G 1-17, Washington & Taylor, Yellow Amber, Pontil, Pt. ....*Illus* 3025.00
McK G 1-19, Washington & Monument, Copper Puce, Pontil 4070.00
McK G 1-20, Washington & Monument, Cobalt Blue, Pontil, Pt. 30250.00
McK G 1-20, Washington & Monument, Light Amethyst, Pontil, Pt. ....495.00 to 605.00
McK G 1-20, Washington & Monument, Pink Amethyst, Pontil, Pt. ....1430.00 to 1650.00
McK G 1-21, Washington & Monument, Olive Amber, Pontil, Qt. 3575.00
McK G 1-21, Washington & Monument, Pink Amethyst, Pontil, Qt. 850.00
McK G 1-21, Washington & Monument, Sapphire Blue, Pontil, Qt. 12100.00
McK G 1-22, Washington & Clay, Taylor, Green, Pontil, Qt. 2750.00
McK G 1-24, Washington & Taylor, Blue Green, Seed Bubbles, Pt. 470.00
McK G 1-25, Washington, Classical Bust, Aqua, Pontil, Qt. 90.00
McK G 1-26, Washington & Eagle, Blue Aqua, Pontil, Qt. 105.00
McK G 1-27, Washington & Eagle, Aqua, Qt. 1760.00
McK G 1-28, Washington & Sailing Ship, Aqua, Double Collar, Pontil, Pt. 305.00
McK G 1-28, Washington & Sailing Ship, Aqua, Sloping Collar, Pontil, Pt. ....155.00 to 305.00
McK G 1-28, Washington & Sailing Ship, Blue Aqua, Double Collar, Pontil, Pt. 275.00
McK G 1-28, Washington & Sailing Ship, Gray Puce, Pt. 3025.00
McK G 1-31, Washington & Jackson, Olive Amber, Pontil, Pt. 200.00
McK G 1-31, Washington & Jackson, Yellow Amber, Pontil, Pt. 175.00
McK G 1-32, Washington & Jackson, Medium Olive Amber, Pontil, Pt. 210.00
McK G 1-34, Washington & Jackson, Amber, Pontil, 1/2 Pt. 265.00
McK G 1-34, Washington & Jackson, Aqua, Pontil, 1/2 Pt. 210.00
McK G 1-34, Washington & Jackson, Forest Green, Pontil, 1/2 Pt. 1045.00
McK G 1-34, Washington & Jackson, Olive Amber, Pontil, 1/2 Pt. ....120.00 to 305.00
McK G 1-34, Washington & Jackson, Yellow Amber, Pontil, 1/2 Pt. ....155.00 to 385.00
McK G 1-35, Washington & Tree, Calabash, Aqua, Applied Mouth, OP, Qt. 210.00
McK G 1-35, Washington & Tree, Calabash, Cobalt Blue, Tooled Mouth, OP, Qt. 11000.00
McK G 1-36, Washington & Tree, Calabash, Aqua, Sloping Collar, Pontil, Qt. .....165.00 to 190.00
McK G 1-37, Washington & Taylor Never Surrenders, Aqua, OP, Qt. 70.00
McK G 1-37, Washington & Taylor Never Surrenders, Cobalt Blue, OP, Qt. 3740.00
McK G 1-37, Washington & Taylor Never Surrenders, Olive Green, OP, Qt. 295.00
McK G 1-37, Washington & Taylor Never Surrenders, Pink Puce, Pontil, Qt. 2310.00
McK G 1-37, Washington & Taylor Never Surrenders, Sapphire Blue, Pontil, Qt. .770.00 to 2200.00
McK G 1-38, Washington & Taylor Never Sirremders, Olive Green, Pontil, Pt. 440.00
McK G 1-38, Washington & Taylor Never Surrenders, Sapphire Blue, Pt. 715.00
McK G 1-38, Washington & Taylor Never Surrenders, Amethyst, Pt. ....880.00 to 1015.00
McK G 1-38, Washington & Taylor Never Surrenders, Green, Applied Mouth, Pt. 415.00
McK G 1-38, Washington & Taylor Never Surrenders, Red Puce, Pt. ....605.00 to 935.00
McK G 1-38, Washington & Taylor Never Surrenders, Yellow Olive, Pontil, Pt. ..440.00 to 1265.00
McK G 1-39, Washington & Taylor, Blue Green, OP, Qt. ....525.00 to 1075.00
McK G 1-39, Washington & Taylor, Cobalt Blue, OP, Qt. 3190.00
McK G 1-39, Washington & Taylor, Medium Olive Amber, OP, Qt. 1018.00
McK G 1-40, Washington & Taylor, Olive Amber, Pontil, Pt. 880.00
McK G 1-40a, Washington & Taylor, Cobalt Blue, Pontil, Pt. ....2365.00 to 2530.00
McK G 1-40a, Washington & Taylor, Yellow Amber, Pontil, Pt. ....935.00 to 1210.00
McK G 1-40c, Washington & Taylor, Blue Green, Bubbles, Pontil, Pt. 550.00
McK G 1-41, Washington & Taylor, Cobalt Blue, OP, 1/2 Pt. 3740.00
McK G 1-41, Washington & Taylor, Colorless, Smoky Gray Cast, Pontil, 1/2 Pt. 385.00
McK G 1-41, Washington & Taylor, Olive Green, Pontil, 1/2 Pt. 1870.00
McK G 1-42, Washington & Taylor, Cobalt Blue, Pontil, Qt. 4400.00
McK G 1-42, Washington & Taylor, Milky Aqua, Pontil, Qt. ....220.00 to 245.00
McK G 1-44, Washington & Taylor, Cobalt Blue, Mouth Flake, Pontil, Pt. 1925.00
McK G 1-44, Washington & Taylor, Deep Amber, Pontil, Pt. 825.00
McK G 1-47, Washington & Taylor, Blue Green, OP, Qt. 375.00
McK G 1-47, Washington & Taylor, Teal Blue, Graphite Pontil, Qt. 350.00
McK G 1-48, Washington, Father Of His Country, Blue Green, Pontil, Pt. 660.00
McK G 1-48, Washington, Father Of His Country, Olive Green, Pontil, Pt. 990.00

Flask, McK G I-99,
Jenny Lind, Calabash,
Light Blue Green,
Pontil, Qt.

Flask, McK G I-17, Washington &
Taylor, Yellow Amber, Pontil, Pt.

McK G I-48, Washington, Father Of His Country, Yellow Olive, Pontil, Pt. 3025.00
McK G I-49, Washington & Taylor, Aqua, OP, Pt. 70.00
McK G I-50, Washington & Taylor, Emerald Green, Pontil, Pt. 880.00
McK G I-50, Washington & Taylor, Smoky, OP, Pt. 330.00
McK G I-51, Washington & Taylor, Aqua, OP, Qt. 125.00
McK G I-51, Washington & Taylor, Dark Amber, Pontil, Pt. 660.00
McK G I-52, Washington & Taylor, Dark Amber, Double Collar, IP, Pt. 715.00
McK G I-52, Washington & Taylor, Yellow Amber, Pontil, Pt. 770.00
McK G I-53, Washington & Taylor, Blue Green, 1/2 Pt. 1155.00
McK G I-53, Washington & Taylor, Medium Blue Green, Pontil, 1/2 Pt. 1210.00
McK G I-54, Washington & Taylor, Emerald Green, Applied Mouth, Qt. 525.00
McK G I-54, Washington & Taylor, Pink Amethyst, OP, Qt. 2700.00
McK G I-54, Washington & Taylor, Sapphire Blue, Sloping Collar, Qt. 2420.00
McK G I-54, Washington & Taylor, Yellow Green, Blob Top, Seed Bubbles, OP, Qt. 470.00
McK G I-55, Washington & Taylor, Blue Green, Pontil, Pt. 440.00
McK G I-55, Washington & Taylor, Yellow Olive, Pontil, Pt. 690.00
McK G I-58, Washington, Aqua, Open Pontil, Pt. 95.00
McK G I-59, Washington & Sheaf, Cobalt Blue, Pontil, 1/2 Pt. 23100.00
McK G I-67, Jackson & Eagle, Aqua, Pontil, Pt. 525.00
McK G I-71, Taylor & Ringgold, Rough & Ready, Aqua, Pontil, Pt. 255.00
McK G I-71, Taylor & Ringgold, Rough & Ready, Blue Aqua, Pontil, Pt. 165.00
McK G I-71, Taylor & Ringgold, Rough & Ready, Jade Green, Pontil, Pt. 2200.00
McK G I-71, Taylor & Ringgold, Rough & Ready, Medium Blue Green, Pt. 1045.00
McK G I-72, Taylor & Ringgold, Rough & Ready, Aqua, Pontil, Pt. 185.00
McK G I-73, Taylor & Monument, Amethyst, Pontil, Pt. 10450.00
McK G I-73, Taylor & Monument, Pale Aqua, Pontil, Pt. 200.00
McK G I-73, Taylor & Monument, Pink, Seared Mouth, Pontil, Pt. 2090.00
McK G I-73, Taylor & Monument, Puce, Inward Rolled Mouth, Pontil, Pt. 5500.00
McK G I-73, Taylor & Monument, Yellow Green, Inward Rolled Mouth, Pontil, Pt. 1265.00
McK G I-74, Taylor & Corn, Sapphire Blue, Pontil, Pt. 41250.00
McK G I-75, Taylor & Corn, Yellow Olive Green, Pontil, Pt. 9350.00
McK G I-79, Grant & Eagle, Aqua, Ring Mouth, Pt. 275.00
McK G I-80, Lafayette & Clinton, Light Yellow Olive, Pontil, Pt. 1045.00
McK G I-80, Lafayette & Clinton, Olive Amber, Pontil, Pt. . . . . .220.00 to 605.00
McK G I-81, Lafayette & Clinton, Yellow Olive, Pontil, 1/2 Pt. . . . . .580.00 to 1100.00
McK G I-85, Double Eagle, Yellow Olive, Pontil, Pt. 145.00
McK G I-86, Lafayette & Liberty, Medium Amber, OP, 1/2 Pt. 500.00
McK G I-86, Lafayette & Liberty, Olive Amber, Pontil, 1/2 Pt. . . . . .210.00 to 605.00
McK G I-86, Lafayette & Liberty, Olive Green, Pontil, 1/2 Pt. 385.00
McK G I-88, Lafayette & Masonic, Yellow Olive, Pontil, Pt. 1090.00
McK G I-89, Lafayette & Masonic, Yellow Green, Pontil, 1/2 Pt. 3300.00
McK G I-90, Lafayette & Eagle, Aqua, OP, Pt. 275.00
McK G I-94, Franklin & Dyott, Aqua, Pontil, Pt. . . . . .90.00 to 385.00

McK G I-96, Franklin & Dyott, Pale Aqua, Pontil, Qt. 265.00
McK G I-97, Franklin & Franklin, Green Aqua, Pontil, Qt. 160.00
McK G I-99, Jenny Lind, Calabash, Aqua, Broad Sloping Collar, IP 100.00
McK G I-99, Jenny Lind, Calabash, Blue Aqua, IP, Qt. 90.00
McK G I-99, Jenny Lind, Calabash, Light Blue Green, Pontil, Qt. ....*Illus* 30500.00
McK G I-99, Jenny Lind, Calabash, Yellow Olive, Double Collar, Pontil, Qt. . . .2585.00 to 3190.00
McK G I-100, Jenny Lind, Kossuth, Calabash, Aqua, OP, Qt. 200.00
McK G I-101, Jenny Lind, Calabash, Aqua, OP, Qt. 130.00
McK G I-101, Jenny Lind, Calabash, Aqua, Sloping Collar, Pontil, Qt. 190.00
McK G I-102, Jenny Lind & Glasshouse, Calabash, Aqua, OP, Qt. ....110.00 to 175.00
McK G I-103, Jenny Lind & Glasshouse, Calabash, Lavender Blue, Pontil, Qt. 1485.00
McK G I-104, Jenny Lind & Glasshouse, Calabash, Cornflower Blue, Applied Mouth, IP   605.00
McK G I-104, Jenny Lind & Glasshouse, Calabash, Sapphire Blue, IP, Qt. 1105.00
McK G I-109, Jenny Lind & Lyre, Aqua, Pontil, Pt. 550.00
McK G I-109, Jenny Lind & Lyre, Aqua, Pontil, Qt. ....825.00 to 1485.00
McK G I-109, Jenny Lind & Lyre, Blue Aqua, Pontil, Qt. ....800.00 to 935.00
McK G I-111, Kossuth & Frigate, Blue Green, Pontil, Pt. 365.00
McK G I-112, Kossuth & Frigate, Calabash, Blue Aqua, IP, Qt. ....255.00 to 330.00
McK G I-112, Kossuth & Frigate, Calabash, Blue Green, Sloping Collar, IP, Qt. 1430.00
McK G I-113, Kossuth & Tree, Calabash, Blue Green, IP, Qt. 100.00
McK G I-113, Kossuth & Tree, Calabash, Light Apple Green, IP, Qt. 355.00
McK G I-113, Kossuth & Tree, Calabash, Light Blue Green, Ring Collar, IP, Qt. 165.00
McK G I-113, Kossuth & Tree, Calabash, Olive Green, Applied Top, OP, Qt. 230.00
McK G I-114, Bryon & Scott, Olive Green, Pontil, 1/2 Pt. 255.00
McK G I-114, Byron & Scott, Amber, OP, 1/2 Pt. 175.00
McK G I-114, Byron & Scott, Yellow Olive Amber, OP, 1/2 Pt. 210.00
McK G I-115, Wheat Price, Short Haired Bust, Pale Blue Green, Pontil, Pt. 5500.00
McK G I-116, Wheat Price, Bushy Haired Bust, Fairview Works, Blue Green, Pontil, Pt. . 210.00
McK G I-117, Columbia & Eagle, Blue Aqua, Pontil, Pt. ....220.00 to 745.00
McK G I-121, Columbia & Eagle, Aqua, Pontil, Pt. ....165.00 to 305.00
McK G I-121, Columbia & Eagle, Blue Aqua, Pontil, Pt. 255.00
McK G I-127, Columbus & Globe, Ground Mouth, Metal Screw Cap, 1/2 Pt. 245.00
McK G II-1, Double Eagle, Blue Aqua, Pontil, Pt. ....220.00 to 325.00
McK G II-1, Double Eagle, Light Blue Green, Pontil, Pt. 245.00
McK G II-4, Cornucopia & Urn, Deep Green, OP, Pt. 175.00
McK G II-6, Eagle & Cornucopia, Green Aqua, Pontil, Pt. ....295.00 to 325.00
McK G II-11, Eagle & Cornucopia, Aqua, Pontil, 1/2 Pt. ....*Illus* 130.00
McK G II-11, Eagle & Cornucopia, Pale Citron, Pontil, 1/2 Pt. 415.00
McK G II-11a, Eagle & Cornucopia, Light Citron, Pontil, 1/2 Pt. 3200.00
McK G II-17, Eagle & Cornucopia, Aqua, Pontil, 1/2 Pt. 230.00
McK G II-19, Eagle & Morning Glory, Blue Aqua, Double Collar, OP, Pt. 580.00
McK G II-19, Eagle & Morning Glory, Light Blue Green, Double Collar, Pontil, Pt. 660.00
McK G II-21, Eagle & Prospector, Blue Aqua, Applied Mouth, Pt. 165.00
McK G II-22, Eagle & Lyre, Aqua, Pontil, Pt. 715.00
McK G II-22, Eagle & Lyre, Medium Amber, Pontil, Pt. 7975.00
McK G II-24, Double Eagle, Aqua, Pontil, Pt. ....105.00 to 210.00
McK G II-24, Double Eagle, Citron, Pontil, Pt. 230.00
McK G II-24, Double Eagle, Gold Amber, Pontil, Pt. 605.00
McK G II-24, Double Eagle, Light Emerald Green, Pontil, Pt. 495.00
McK G II-24, Double Eagle, Light Yellow Green, Pontil, Pt. ....440.00 to 660.00
McK G II-24, Double Eagle, Sapphire Blue, Pontil, Pt. ....1540.00 to 2860.00
McK G II-26, Double Eagle, Aqua Clambroth, Pontil, Qt. 305.00
McK G II-26, Double Eagle, Aqua, Pontil, Qt. ....105.00 to 120.00
McK G II-26, Double Eagle, Blue Aqua, Applied Mouth, IP, Qt. 110.00
McK G II-26, Double Eagle, Blue Green, IP, Qt. 825.00
McK G II-26, Double Eagle, Gray Blue, IP, Qt. 2310.00
McK G II-26, Double Eagle, Yellow Green, Pontil, Qt. 990.00
McK G II-30, Double Eagle, Aqua, Pontil, 1/2 Pt. 230.00
McK G II-31, Double Eagle, Vertical Ribs, Aqua, OP, Qt. 190.00
McK G II-35, Eagle, Louisville, Ky., Vertical Ribs, Blue Aqua, Qt. ....180.00 to 185.00
McK G II-36, Eagle & Louisville, Vertical Ribs, Aqua, Pt. ....120.00 to 185.00
McK G II-36, Eagle & Louisville, Vertical Ribs, Blue Aqua, Olive Streak, Pt. 90.00
McK G II-36, Eagle & Louisville, Vertical Ribs, Blue Aqua, Pt. 100.00

Flask, McK G II-11,
Eagle & Cornucopia,
Aqua, Pontil, 1/2 Pt.

Flask, McK G II-55,
Eagle & Grapes,
Blue Aqua,
Pontil, Qt.

McK G II-37, Eagle & Ravenna, Blue Green, Ring Mouth, IP, Pt. 550.00
McK G II-37, Eagle & Ravenna, Light Blue Green, Pt. 285.00
McK G II-37, Eagle & Ravenna, Medium Green, IP, Pt. 990.00
McK G II-38, Eagle & Dyottville, Aqua, Pt. 330.00
McK G II-39, Eagle & Shield, Yellow Green, Applied Mouth, Pt. 2035.00
McK G II-40, Double Eagle, Aqua, Pontil, Pt. 130.00
McK G II-40, Double Eagle, Teal Blue, Pontil, Pt. 1020.00
McK G II-42, Masonic, Clasped Hands & Eagle, Calabash, Yellow Green, Tubular, Qt. ... 360.00
McK G II-45, Eagle & Cornucopia, Blue Green, Pontil, 1/2 Pt. 330.00
McK G II-46, Eagle & Cornucopia, Aqua, Pontil, 1/2 Pt. 210.00
McK G II-48, Eagle & Coffin, Blue Green, Pontil, Qt. 1930.00
McK G II-48, Eagle & Coffin, Smoky Green, Pontil, Qt. 285.00
McK G II-51, Eagle & Coffin, Aqua, Pontil, Pt. 1210.00
McK G II-52, Eagle & Flag, Aqua, OP, Pt. 230.00
McK G II-53, Eagle & Flag, Aqua, OP, Pt. ....145.00 to 170.00
McK G II-53, Eagle & Flag, Root Beer Amber, Pontil, Pt. 3410.00
McK G II-54, Eagle & Flag, Aqua, Pontil, Pt. ....105.00 to 240.00
McK G II-55, Eagle & Grapes, Blue Aqua, Pontil, Qt. ....*Illus* 155.00
McK G II-55, Eagle & Grapes, Gold Amber, Pontil, Qt. 2255.00
McK G II-55, Eagle & Grapes, Root Beer Amber, OP, Qt. 1705.00
McK G II-56, Eagle & Grapes, Aqua, Pontil, 1/2 Pt. 315.00
McK G II-60, Eagle & Oak Tree, Aqua, Pontil, 1/2 Pt. ....260.00 to 375.00
McK G II-60, Eagle & Oak Tree, Gold Amber, Pontil, 1/2 Pt. 6050.00
McK G II-60, Eagle & Oak Tree, Root Beer Amber, Pontil, 1/2 Pt. 405.00
McK G II-61, Eagle & Willington, Medium Golden Amber, Qt. 210.00
McK G II-61, Eagle & Willington, Olive Green, Applied Mouth, Qt. 145.00
McK G II-61, Eagle & Willington, Olive, Applied Double Collared Mouth, Qt. ...185.00 to 200.00
McK G II-61, Eagle & Willington, Yellow Olive, Sloping Collar, Qt. 200.00
McK G II-62, Eagle & Willington, Blue Green, Sloping Collar, Pt. 605.00
McK G II-62, Eagle & Willington, Medium Olive, OP, Pt. 225.00
McK G II-62, Eagle & Willington, Yellow Olive, Pt. ....120.00 to 175.00
McK G II-63, Eagle & Willington, Amber, Double Collar, 1/2 Pt. 230.00
McK G II-63, Eagle & Willington, Blue Green, Double Collar, 1/2 Pt. 1540.00
McK G II-63, Eagle & Willington, Forest Green, Double Collar, 1/2 Pt. ....190.00 to 255.00
McK G II-63, Eagle & Willington, Medium Olive Green, Double Collar, 1/2 Pt. 175.00
McK G II-63, Eagle & Willington, Olive Green, Double Collar, 1/2 Pt. 130.00
McK G II-63, Eagle & Willington, Yellow Amber, Double Collar, 1/2 Pt. 155.00
McK G II-63, Eagle & Willington, Yellow Olive, 1/2 Pt. 120.00
McK G II-63, Eagle & Willington, Yellow Olive, Double Collar, 1/2 Pt. ....155.00 to 165.00
McK G II-63a, Eagle & Willington, Forest Green, Double Collar, 1/2 Pt. 145.00
McK G II-64, Eagle & Willington, Medium Yellow Olive, Pontil, Pt. 300.00
McK G II-64, Eagle & Willington, Olive Amber, Double Collar, Pt. ....95.00 to 120.00
McK G II-64, Eagle & Willington, Olive Green, Sloping Collar, Pt. 120.00
McK G II-64, Eagle & Willington, Orange Amber, Double Collar, Pt. 255.00
McK G II-64, Eagle & Willington, Yellow Olive, Pontil, Pt. ....165.00 to 245.00

McK G II-67, Eagle & Anchor, Gold Amber, Red Tone, Double Collar, 1/2 Pt. 495.00
McK G II-67, Eagle & Anchor, Honey Amber, Double Collar, 1/2 Pt. 1155.00
McK G II-68, Eagle & Anchor, Emerald Green, Pontil, Pt. 770.00
McK G II-68, Eagle & Anchor, Yellow, Olive, Double Collar, Pt. 605.00
McK G II-69, Eagle & Cornucopia, Aqua, Pontil, 1/2 Pt. . . . . .165.00 to 475.00
McK G II-70, Double Eagle, Dark Yellow Olive, Pontil, Pt. 175.00
McK G II-70, Double Eagle, Olive Amber, Pontil, Pt. 130.00
McK G II-71, Double Eagle, Olive Amber, Bubbles, Pontil, 1/2 Pt. 230.00
McK G II-72, Eagle & Cornucopia, Forest Green, Pontil, Pt. 255.00
McK G II-72, Eagle & Cornucopia, Green Amber, OP, Pt. . . . . .135.00 to 150.00
McK G II-72, Eagle & Cornucopia, Olive Amber, Pontil, Pt. 100.00
McK G II-72, Eagle & Cornucopia, Olive Green, Pontil, Pt. . . . . .75.00 to 145.00
McK G II-72b, Eagle & Cornucopia, Green Amber, OP, Pt. 175.00
McK G II-73, Eagle & Cornucopia, Dark Olive Green, OP, Pt. 70.00
McK G II-73, Eagle & Cornucopia, Olive Amber, Pontil, Pt. 120.00
McK G II-73, Eagle & Cornucopia, Yellow Green, OP, Pt. 125.00
McK G II-73, Eagle & Cornucopia, Yellow Olive, Pontil, Pt. . . . . .100.00 to 145.00
McK G II-74, Eagle & Cornucopia, Aqua, Pontil, Pt. . . . . .155.00 to 220.00
McK G II-74, Eagle & Cornucopia, Clear Green, Pontil, Pt. 355.00
McK G II-78, Double Eagle, Yellow Olive Amber, Pontil, Pt. 145.00
McK G II-79, Double Eagle, Deep Olive Amber, Pontil, Qt. 275.00
McK G II-80, Double Eagle, Yellow Olive Amber, Pontil, Qt. 1100.00
McK G II-81, Double Eagle, Bright Yellow Amber, Pontil, Pt. 90.00
McK G II-81, Double Eagle, Olive Amber, Pontil, Pt. .165.00 to 210.00
McK G II-81, Double Eagle, Yellow Olive Amber, Pontil, Pt. . . . . .185.00 to 242.00
McK G II-81, Double Eagle, Yellow Olive, Pontil, Pt. 210.00
McK G II-82, Double Eagle, Gold Amber, Pontil, Pt. 145.00
McK G II-82, Double Eagle, Olive Amber, Pontil, Pt. 165.00
McK G II-82, Double Eagle, Yellow Amber, Pontil, Pt. 165.00
McK G II-83, Double Eagle, Yellow Amber, Pontil, Pt. 120.00
McK G II-85, Double Eagle, Olive Amber, Pontil, Pt. 130.00
McK G II-86, Double Eagle, Green Amber, OP, 1/2 Pt. 125.00
McK G II-86, Double Eagle, Olive Amber, Pontil, 1/2 Pt. . . . . .105.00 to 145.00
McK G II-86, Double Eagle, Yellow Olive Amber, Pontil, 1/2 Pt. . . . . .120.00 to 220.00
McK G II-88, Double Eagle, Yellow Olive, Pontil, 1/2 Pt. 200.00
McK G II-89, Double Eagle, Citron, Round Collar, Pt. 385.00
McK G II-91, Double Eagle, Blue Aqua, Applied Mouth, IP, Qt. 265.00
McK G II-91, Double Eagle, Cobalt Blue, Ring Mouth, Qt. 1870.00
McK G II-92, Double Eagle, Teal Blue, Ring Mouth, Pt. 1320.00
McK G II-92, Double Eagle, Yellow Olive Amber, OP, Pt. 80.00
McK G II-93, Double Eagle, Gold Amber, Applied Round Mouth, IP, Pt. 240.00
McK G II-93, Double Eagle, Red Amber, Applied Mouth, Pt. 175.00
McK G II-101, Double Eagle, Green, Applied Mouth, Qt. 305.00
McK G II-103, Double Eagle, Medium Amber, Applied Mouth, Pt. 230.00
McK G II-103, Double Eagle, Yellow Olive, Double Collar, Qt. 495.00
McK G II-104, Double Eagle, Dark Olive Green, Ring Mouth, Qt. 305.00
McK G II-105, Double Eagle, Medium Olive Amber, Applied Mouth, Pt. 275.00
McK G II-105, Double Eagle, Yellow Amber, Applied Mouth, Pt. 210.00
McK G II-106, Double Eagle, Forest Green, Ring Mouth, Pontil, Pt. 230.00
McK G II-106, Double Eagle, Yellow Olive Green, Pontil, Pt. 440.00
McK G II-107, Double Eagle, Citron, Double Collar, Pt. 360.00
McK G II-107, Double Eagle, Medium Amber, Applied Mouth, Pt. 305.00
McK G II-109, Double Eagle, Pale Yellow Green, Applied Aqua Ring Mouth, 1/2 Pt. . . . 210.00
McK G II-118, Double Eagle, Gold Amber, Ring Mouth, Pt. . . . . .155.00 to 275.00
McK G II-118, Double Eagle, Sapphire Blue, Ring Mouth, Pt. . . . . .880.00 to 1100.00
McK G II-122, Double Eagle, Blue Aqua, Pontil, Pt. 855.00
McK G II-126, Double Eagle, Gold Yellow, 1/2 Pt. 415.00
McK G II-126, Double Eagle, Pink Amethyst, Tooled Mouth, 1/2 Pt. 715.00
McK G II-126, Double Eagle, Yellow Amber, Applied Mouth, 1/2 Pt. 305.00
McK G II-127, Double Eagle, Aqua, 1/2 Pt. 95.00
McK G II-129, Double Eagle, Blue Aqua, Pt. 605.00
McK G II-130, Double Eagle, Aqua, Pt. 80.00
McK G II-139, Eagle, Gold Amber, Pt. 240.00

McK G II-142, Eagle & Indian Shooting Bird, Blue Aqua, Applied Mouth, Qt. 210.00
McK G II-142, Eagle & Indian Shooting Bird, Cornflower Blue, Ring Mouth, Qt. 1320.00
McK G II-142, Eagle & Indian Shooting Bird, Yellow, Ring Mouth, Qt. 550.00
McK G II-143, Eagle, Calabash, Emerald Green, Sloping Collar, IP 495.00
McK G II-143, Eagle, Calabash, Grass Green, IP, Qt. ....120.00 to 165.00
McK G II-143, Eagle, Calabash, Yellow Green, IP ....185.00 to 220.00
McK G III-2, Cornucopia & Medallion, Aqua, Pontil, 1/2 Pt. ....90.00 to 155.00
McK G III-3, Double Cornucopia, Aqua, OP 120.00
McK G III-4, Cornucopia & Urn, Olive Amber, Pontil, Pt. 90.00
McK G III-4, Cornucopia & Urn, Olive Green, Pt. 1210.00
McK G III-4, Cornucopia & Urn, Yellow Olive, Pontil, Pt. 330.00
McK G III-7, Cornucopia & Urn, Light To Medium Blue Green, OP, 1/2 Pt. 275.00
McK G III-7, Cornucopia & Urn, Olive Amber, 5 1/4 In. 120.00
McK G III-7, Cornucopia & Urn, Olive Green, OP, 1/2 Pt. ....75.00 to 130.00
McK G III-7, Cornucopia & Urn, Root Beer Amber, Pontil, 1/2 Pt. 100.00
McK G III-7, Cornucopia & Urn, Yellow Green, Pontil, 1/2 Pt. 155.00
McK G III-7, Cornucopia & Urn, Medium To Deep Olive Amber, OP, 1/2 Pt. 120.00
McK G III-10, Cornucopia & Urn, Amber, 1/2 Pt. 90.00
McK G III-11, Cornucopia & Urn, Medium Olive Green, Pontil, 1/2 Pt. 65.00
McK G III-11, Cornucopia & Urn, Yellow Olive, Pontil, 1/2 Pt. 70.00
McK G III-12, Cornucopia & Urn, Yellow Olive, Pontil, 1/2 Pt. ....130.00 to 230.00
McK G III-13, Cornucopia & Urn, Teal Green, OP, 1/2 Pt. 635.00
McK G III-14, Cornucopia & Urn, Blue Green, Pontil, 1/2 Pt. ....355.00 to 385.00
McK G III-14, Cornucopia & Urn, Emerald Green, OP, 1/2 Pt. 465.00
McK G III-14a, Cornucopia & Urn, Blue Green, Pontil, 1/2 Pt. 305.00
McK G III-15, Cornucopia & Urn, Aqua, Pontil, 1/2 Pt. 220.00
McK G III-15, Cornucopia & Urn, Blue Green, OP, 1/2 Pt. 525.00
McK G III-16, Cornucopia & Urn, Blue Aqua, IP, Pt. 250.00
McK G III-16, Cornucopia & Urn, Blue Green, IP, Pt. 415.00
McK G III-16, Cornucopia & Urn, Olive, Amber, Pt. 100.00
McK G III-17, Cornucopia & Urn, Blue Aqua, Double Collar, OP, Pt. 185.00
McK G III-17, Cornucopia & Urn, Blue Green, Applied Mouth, OP, Pt. ....325.00 to 605.00
McK G III-17, Cornucopia & Urn, Emerald Green, Pontil, Pt. 330.00
McK G III-34, Cornucopia & Urn, Olive Green, OP, Pt. 130.00
McK G IV-1, Masonic & Eagle, Blue Green, Pontil, Pt. 255.00
McK G IV-1a, Masonic & Eagle, Light Blue Green, Pontil, Pt. ....210.00 to 265.00
McK G IV-2, Masonic & Eagle, Blue Green, Tooled Mouth, Pontil, Pt. 605.00
McK G IV-2, Masonic & Eagle, Light Green, Pt. 825.00
McK G IV-2, Masonic & Eagle, Olive Green, Pontil, Pt. 2530.00
McK G IV-3, Masonic & Eagle, Aqua Tint, Pontil, Pt. 525.00
McK G IV-3, Masonic & Eagle, Ice Blue, Rolled Collar, Pontil, Pt. ....*Illus* 770.00
McK G IV-4, Masonic, J.K.B., Yellow Green Amber, Tooled Mouth, Pontil, Pt. 1870.00
McK G IV-5, Masonic & Eagle, Medium Green, Pt. 825.00
McK G IV-11, Masonic & Eagle, Blue Green, Tooled Mouth, Pontil, Pt. 1015.00
McK G IV-14, Masonic & Eagle, Light To Medium Green, Pontil, 1/2 Pt. 880.00
McK G IV-14, Masonic & Eagle, Pale Yellow Green, Tooled Mouth, Pontil, 1/2 Pt. 465.00
McK G IV-17, Masonic & Eagle, Forest Green, Tubular Pontil, Pt. 200.00
McK G IV-17, Masonic & Eagle, Olive Amber, Pontil, Pt. 155.00
McK G IV-17, Masonic & Eagle, Olive Green, Pontil, Pt. 355.00
McK G IV-18, Masonic & Eagle, Yellow Amber, Pontil, Pt. ....160.00 to 220.00
McK G IV-18, Masonic & Eagle, Yellow Olive Amber, Pontil, Pt. 210.00
McK G IV-19, Masonic & Eagle, Light Amber Olive, Pontil, Pt. 165.00
McK G IV-19, Masonic & Eagle, Yellow Olive Green, Pontil, Pt. 205.00
McK G IV-20, Masonic & Eagle, Olive Amber, Pontil, Pt. 130.00
McK G IV-20, Masonic & Eagle, Yellow Amber, Pontil, Pt 175.00
McK G IV-21, Masonic & Eagle, Light Yellow Olive, Pontil, Pt. 230.00
McK G IV-24, Masonic & Eagle, Forest Green, Pontil, 1/2 Pt. 210.00
McK G IV-24, Masonic & Eagle, Light Yellow Olive, Pontil, Pt. 220.00
McK G IV-24, Masonic & Eagle, Olive Green, Pontil, 1/2 Pt. 195.00
McK G IV-24, Masonic & Eagle, Yellow Olive, Pontil, 1/2 Pt. ....175.00 to 465.00
McK G IV-27, Masonic & Eagle, Yellow Green, Wide Rolled Mouth, Pontil, Pt. 220.00
McK G IV-28, Double Masonic, Blue Green, Inward Rolled Mouth, Pontil, 1/2 Pt. 360.00
McK G IV-28, Double Masonic, Light Green, Pontil, 1/2 Pt. 175.00

Flask, McK G IV-3,
Masonic & Eagle,
Ice Blue, Rolled
Collar, Pontil, Pt.

Flask, McK G VI-4,
Corn For The World,
Prussian Blue, Sloping
Collar, Qt.

McK G IV-29, Double Masonic, Yellow Olive, Pontil, 1/2 Pt. 4675.00
McK G IV-32, Masonic & Eagle, Aqua, Pontil, Pt. 175.00
McK G IV-32, Masonic & Eagle, Blue Aqua, Pontil, Pt. 355.00
McK G IV-32, Masonic & Eagle, Gold To Red Amber, Pontil, Pt. 440.00
McK G IV-32, Masonic & Eagle, Light Green Blue, Inward Rolled Mouth, Pontil, Pt. ... 385.00
McK G IV-32, Masonic & Eagle, Red Amber, Pontil, Pt. 440.00
McK G IV-32, Masonic & Eagle, Yellow Amber, Pontil, Pt. 1020.00
McK G IV-32, Masonic & Eagle, Yellow Olive, Pontil, Pt. 2860.00
McK G IV-34, Masonic Arch & Frigate, Aqua, Pontil, 1816-1838, Pt. 110.00
McK G IV-34, Masonic Arch & Frigate, Aqua, Pontil, Pt. 200.00
McK G IV-36, Masonic Arch & Frigate, Green Aqua, Pontil, Pt. 715.00
McK G IV-36, Masonic Arch & Frigate, Pale Green, Pontil, Pt. 550.00
McK G IV-37, Masonic & Eagle, Aqua, Pontil, Pt. ....110.00 to 200.00
McK G IV-42, Masonic Clasped Hands & Eagle, Aqua, Pontil, Qt. 60.00
McK G IV-42, Masonic Clasped Hands & Eagle, Calabash, Citron, Pontil, Qt. 330.00
McK G IV-43, Masonic & Seeing Eye, Aqua, Pontil, Pt. 415.00
McK G IV-43, Masonic & Seeing Eye, Gold Amber, OP, Pt. 195.00
McK G IV-43, Masonic & Seeing Eye, Olive Amber, OP, Pt. ....145.00 to 200.00
McK G IV-43, Masonic & Seeing Eye, Yellow Olive Amber, Pt. ....125.00 to 255.00
McK G V-1, Success To The Railroad, Aqua, OP, Pt. ....265.00 to 275.00
McK G V-1, Success To The Railroad, Gold Yellow Amber, OP, Pt. 4550.00
McK G V-1a, Success To The Railroad, Sapphire Blue, OP, Pt. 4290.00
McK G V-1b, Success To The Railroad, Apricot, Pontil, Pt. 3520.00
McK G V-3, Success To The Railroad, Aqua, Pontil, Pt. 495.00
McK G V-3, Success To The Railroad, Yellow Olive Green, OP, Pt. ....170.00 to 385.00
McK G V-4, Success To The Railroad, Yellow Olive, Pontil, Pt. ....330.00 to 495.00
McK G V-5, Success To The Railroad, Emerald Green, Pt. 320.00
McK G V-5, Success To The Railroad, Moss Green, Pontil, Pt. 440.00
McK G V-5, Success To The Railroad, Olive Green, Pontil, Pt. 415.00
McK G V-5, Success To The Railroad, Yellow Olive, Sloping Collar, Pt. 330.00
McK G V-6, Success To The Railroad, Gold Olive Amber, Pontil, Pt. 230.00
McK G V-6, Success To The Railroad, Olive Amber, Tubular Pontil, Pt. 160.00
McK G V-6, Success To The Railroad, Olive Green, Striations, OP, Pt. 240.00
McK G V-9, Horse Pulling Cart & Eagle, Gold Amber, Pontil, Pt. 145.00
McK G V-9, Horse Pulling Cart & Eagle, Yellow Olive Amber, Pontil, Pt. 175.00
McK G V-10, Lowell Railroad & Eagle, Golden Amber, Pontil, 1/2 Pt. 285.00
McK G V-10, Lowell Railroad & Eagle, Moss Green, OP, 1/2 Pt. 990.00
McK G V-10, Lowell Railroad & Eagle, Olive Green, OP, 1/2 Pt. ....185.00 to 200.00
McK G V-10, Lowell Railroad & Eagle, Yellow Olive Green, Pontil, 1/2 Pt. 155.00
McK G V-12, Success To The Railroad, Clambroth, Small Crack, Pontil, Pt. 30250.00
McK G VI-1, Monument, A Little More Grape, Apricot Puce, Pontil, 1/2 Pt. 2850.00
McK G VI-2, Monument & Fells Point, Claret, Pontil, 1/2 Pt. 3960.00
McK G VI-2, Monument & Fells Point, Green Aqua, Pontil, 1/2 Pt. 305.00
McK G VI-2, Monument & Fells Point, Pale Aqua, Pontil, 1/2 Pt. 220.00
McK G VI-2, Monument & Fells Point, Puce, Base Slag, Pontil, 1/2 Pt. 4125.00
McK G VI-2, Monument & Fells Point, Topaz, Pontil, 1/2 Pt. 4125.00

Flask,
McK G VIII-2,
Sunburst, Medium

Flask, McK G IX-10,
Scroll, Amber,
Pontil, Pt.

McK G VI-2, Monument & Fells Point, Yellow Green, Pontil, 1/2 Pt. 4400.00
McK G VI-2, Monument & Fells Point, Yellow Olive, Pontil, 1/2 Pt. 2750.00
McK G VI-4, Corn For The World, Aqua, Square Collar Mouth, Qt. . . . . .100.00 to 265.00
McK G VI-4, Corn For The World, Bright Green, Sloping Collar, Qt. 2420.00
McK G VI-4, Corn For The World, Copper Puce, Pontil, Qt. . . . . .770.00 to 935.00
McK G VI-4, Corn For The World, Cornflower Blue, Sloping Collar, Qt. 2200.00
McK G VI-4, Corn For The World, Gold Yellow, Apricot Tone, Double Collar, Qt. 1210.00
McK G VI-4, Corn For The World, Orange Amber, Double Collar, Qt. 1320.00
McK G VI-4, Corn For The World, Prussian Blue, Sloping Collar, Qt. . . . .*Illus* 8250.00
McK G VI-4, Corn For The World, Purple, Sloping Collar, Qt. 38500.00
McK G VI-4, Corn For The World, Teal Green, Double Collar, Qt. 4125.00
McK G VI-4, Corn For The World, Yellow Amber, IP, Qt. 1760.00
McK G VI-4, Corn For The World, Yellow Olive Green, IP, Qt. 3575.00
McK G VI-4, Corn For The World, Yellow Olive, Short Sloping Collar, Qt. 2090.00
McK G VI-4a, Corn For The World, Aqua, Pontil, Qt. 385.00
McK G VI-5, Corn For The World, Aqua, Pontil, Qt. . . . . .250.00 to 605.00
McK G VI-5, Corn For The World, Citron, Amber Striations, Pontil, Qt. 8800.00
McK G VI-5, Corn For The World, Yellow Amber, Bubbles, IP, Qt. 1595.00
McK G VI-6, Corn For The World, Aqua, Pontil, Pt. 240.00
McK G VI-6, Corn For The World, Gold Amber, Pontil, Pt. 5225.00
McK G VI-7, Corn For The World, Claret, Pontil, 1/2 Pt. 7700.00
McK G VI-7, Corn For The World, Yellow Olive Green, Pontil, 1/2 Pt. 5225.00
McK G VII-4, E.G. Booz Old Cabin Whiskey, Amber, Sloping Collar, Qt. 2310.00
McK G VIII-1, Sunburst, Clear Green, Pontil, Pt. 525.00
McK G VIII-1, Sunburst, Pale Yellow Green, Pontil, Pt. .605.00 to 770.00
McK G VIII-2, Sunburst, Clear Green, Pontil, Pt. 440.00
McK G VIII-2, Sunburst, Light Green, Pontil, Pt. . . . . .440.00 to 660.00
McK G VIII-2, Sunburst, Medium Green, Pt. . . . .*Illus* 715.00
McK G VIII-3, Sunburst, Yellow Olive Amber, Pontil, Pt. . . . . .415.00 to 525.00
McK G VIII-3, Sunburst, Yellow Olive, Pontil, Pt. . . . . .525.00 to 605.00
McK G VIII-7, Sunburst, Yellow Olive Amber, Pontil, Pt. . . . . .465.00 to 1375.00
McK G VIII-8, Sunburst, Medium Olive Green, Pontil, Pt. 415.00
McK G VIII-8, Sunburst, Yellow Olive Amber, Pontil, Pt. . . . . .385.00 to 495.00
McK G VIII-9, Sunburst, Yellow Amber, Bubbles, Pontil, 1/2 Pt. 255.00
McK G VIII-9, Sunburst, Yellow Amber, OP, 1/2 Pt. 635.00
McK G VIII-9, Sunburst, Yellow Olive, Pontil, 1/2 Pt. 275.00
McK G VIII-10, Sunburst, Keen, Yellow Olive, Tooled Mouth, Pontil, 1/2 Pt. 290.00
McK G VIII-10, Sunburst, Yellow Olive Green, Pontil, 1/2 Pt. 230.00
McK G VIII-14, Sunburst, Blue Green, Pontil, 1/2 Pt. .900.00 to 1045.00
McK G VIII-14, Sunburst, Yellow Green, Pontil, 1/2 Pt. 415.00
McK G VIII-15, Sunburst, Pale Green, Pontil, 1/2 Pt. 1100.00
McK G VIII-16, Sunburst, Forest Green, Pontil, 1/2 Pt. 440.00
McK G VIII-16, Sunburst, Moss Green, Pontil, 1/2 Pt. 425.00
McK G VIII-16, Sunburst, Olive Green, Shared Mouth, Pontil, 1/2 Pt. 605.00
McK G VIII-16, Sunburst, Yellow Olive Green, Pontil, 1/2 Pt. . . . . .305.00 to 385.00
McK G VIII-18, Sunburst, Light To Medium Gold Tan, OP 425.00

McK G VIII-18, Sunburst, Olive, OP, 1/2 Pt. 440.00
McK G VIII-20, Sunburst, Blue Aqua, Pt. 325.00
McK G VIII-20, Sunburst, Pale Green Aqua, Pt. 190.00
McK G VIII-22, Sunburst, Pale Green, Pontil, Pt. 305.00
McK G VIII-24, Sunburst, Aqua, OP, 1/2 Pt. 325.00
McK G VIII-24, Sunburst, Chocolate Amber, Pontil, 1/2 Pt. 2035.00
McK G VIII-24, Sunburst, Gold Amber, Pontil, 1/2 Pt. 1430.00
McK G VIII-25, Sunburst, Aqua, Pontil, 1/2 Pt. ....175.00 to 325.00
McK G VIII-25, Sunburst, Copper Puce, 1/2 Pt. 6050.00
McK G VIII-25, Sunburst, Medium Pink Amethyst, OP, 1/2 Pt. 3190.00
McK G VIII-26, Sunburst, Green Aqua, Pt. 325.00
McK G VIII-26, Sunburst, Yellow Olive, Pontil, Pt. 2640.00
McK G VIII-27, Sunburst, Pale Clambroth, Inward Rolled Mouth, Pontil, 1/2 Pt. 220.00
McK G VIII-27, Sunburst, Pale Yellow Green, Pontil, 1/2 Pt. 265.00
McK G VIII-28, Sunburst, Yellow Green, Ball OP, 1/2 Pt. 385.00
McK G VIII-29, Sunburst, Blue Aqua, Pontil, Pt. 275.00
McK G VIII-29, Sunburst, Blue Green, Tooled Mouth, Pontil, Pt. 260.00
McK G VIII-29, Sunburst, Light Green, Tooled Mouth, Pontil, 1/2 Pt. 120.00
McK G IX-1, Scroll, Blue Aqua, OP, Qt. .... 85.00 to 90.00
McK G IX-1, Scroll, Medium Green, OP, Qt. 165.00
McK G IX-1, Scroll, Yellow Green, Graphite Pontil, Qt. 825.00
McK G IX-2, Scroll, Aqua, IP, Qt. .... 95.00 to 120.00
McK G IX-2, Scroll, Gold Amber, Ring Mouth, IP, Qt. 330.00
McK G IX-3, Scroll, Sapphire Blue, Ring Mouth, IP, Qt. 1320.00
McK G IX-3b, Scroll, Gold Amber, Ring Mouth, IP, Qt. 495.00
McK G IX-6, Scroll & Louisville, Blue Aqua, IP, Qt. 120.00
McK G IX-9, Scroll & Louisville, Citron, Irregular, IP, Pt. 190.00
McK G IX-10, Scroll, Amber, Pontil, Pt. .... *Illus* 440.00
McK G IX-10a, Scroll, Blue Green, Pontil, Pt. 385.00
McK G IX-10b, Scroll, Amber, Pontil, Pt. 825.00
McK G IX-10b, Scroll, Olive Amber, Pt. .... 440.00 to 660.00
McK G IX-10c, Scroll, Teal Blue, Mouth Flake, OP, Pt. 1650.00
McK G IX-11, Scroll, Aqua, Tubular Pontil, Pt. 90.00
McK G IX-11, Scroll, Gold Amber, High Base, Variant, OP 500.00
McK G IX-11, Scroll, Gold Amber, Round Collar, IP, Pt. 355.00
McK G IX-11, Scroll, Moonstone, Pink Tint, Pontil, Pt. 1540.00
McK G IX-11, Scroll, Root Beer Amber, Applied Mouth, IP, Pt. 385.00
McK G IX-11, Scroll, Sapphire Blue, IP, Pt. 2145.00
McK G IX-11a, Scroll, Citron, Pontil, Pt. 470.00
McK G IX-11a, Scroll, Cornflower, Pontil, Pt. 385.00
McK G IX-11a, Scroll, Sapphire Blue, Milky Interior, IP, Pt. 1985.00
McK G IX-11a, Scroll, Yellow, Olive, Pontil, Pt. 690.00
McK G IX-12, Scroll, Olive Moss Green, Pontil, Pt. 770.00
McK G IX-12, Scroll, Yellow Olive, Pontil, Pt. 605.00
McK G IX-13, Scroll, Amber, IP, Pt. 385.00
McK G IX-13, Scroll, Olive Amber, IP, Pt. 440.00
McK G IX-16, Scroll, Yellow Olive Amber, OP, Pt. 495.00
McK G IX-20, Scroll, Blue Aqua, Open Bubble, Pontil, Pt. 130.00
McK G IX-20, Scroll, Medium Yellow Green, Pontil, Pt. 1430.00
McK G IX-24, Scroll, Blue Aqua, OP, Pt. ....240.00 to 305.00
McK G IX-25, Scroll, Light Yellow Green, Pontil, Pt. 50.00
McK G IX-29, Scroll, Aqua, Pontil, 1/2 Gal. 305.00
McK G IX-29, Scroll, Blue Aqua, OP, 1/2 Gal. ....360.00 to 410.00
McK G IX-30a, Scroll, Green Aqua, Polished Pontil, 12 In. 955.00
McK G IX-31, Scroll, Blue Aqua, OP, 1/2 Pt. 90.00
McK G IX-31, Scroll, Citron, IP, 1/2 Pt. 580.00
McK G IX-31, Scroll, Lime Green, Pontil, 1/2 Pt. 990.00
McK G IX-32, Scroll, Yellow Olive Green, Disc Mouth, IP, 1/2 Pt. 1540.00
McK G IX-32, Scroll, Yellow Olive Green, Square Collar, IP, 1/2 Pt. 1320.00
McK G IX-34, Scroll, Apple Green, 1/2 Pt. 90.00
McK G IX-34, Scroll, Cornflower Blue, OP, 1/2 Pt. 220.00
McK G IX-34, Scroll, Gold Amber, Pontil, 1/2 Pt. 495.00
McK G IX-34, Scroll, Yellow Green, Pontil, 1/2 Pt. 770.00

McK G IX-34a, Scroll, Light Green, Pontil, 1/2 Pt. 100.00
McK G IX-34a, Scroll, Olive Green, IP, 1/2 Pt. 2530.00
McK G IX-43, Scroll, Aqua, IP, Pt. 440.00
McK G IX-44, Scroll, Aqua, Pontil, Pt. . . . . .465.00 to 575.00
McK G IX-44, Scroll, Blue Aqua, Pontil, Pt. . . . . .470.00 to 525.00
McK G IX-45, Scroll, Aqua, Pontil, Pt. . . . . .440.00 to 465.00
McK G IX-46, Scroll, Blue Aqua, Pontil, Qt. 715.00
McK G IX-46, Scroll, Emerald Green, OP, Qt. 3520.00
McK G IX-50, Scroll, McCarty & Torreyson, Light Blue Green, IP, Qt. 2310.00
McK G X-1, Stag & Willow Tree, Aqua, Pontil, Pt. . . . . .155.00 to 275.00
McK G X-1, Stag & Willow Tree, Blue Aqua, OP, Pt. 275.00
McK G X-3, Sheaf Of Rye & Grapes, Apple Green, Pontil, 1/2 Pt. 385.00
McK G X-3, Sheaf Of Rye & Grapes, Aqua, OP, 1/2 Pt. . . . . .165.00 to 275.00
McK G X-4, Cannon, A Little More Grape, Apricot, Pontil, Pt. 3025.00
McK G X-4, Cannon, A Little More Grape, Copper Puce, Pontil, Pt. 4950.00
McK G X-4, Cannon, A Little More Grape, Light Yellow Green, Pontil, Pt. 3300.00
McK G X-4, Cannon, A Little More Grape, Olive Green, OP, Pt. 5390.00
McK G X-5, Cannon, A Little More Grape, Olive Green, Pontil, Pt. 3575.00
McK G X-6, Cannon, A Little More Grape, Honey Amber, Pontil, 1/2 Pt. 1870.00
McK G X-6, Cannon, A Little More Grape, Strawberry Puce, Pontil, 1/2 Pt. 5500.00
McK G X-6, Cannon, A Little More Grape, Yellow Green, Pontil, 1/2 Pt. 2750.00
McK G X-7, Sloop & Bridgeton, Aqua, OP, 1/2 Pt. 600.00
McK G X-8, Sloop & Star, Aqua, Pontil, 1/2 Pt. 120.00
McK G X-9, Sloop & Star, Aqua, OP, 1/2 Pt. 120.00
McK G X-9, Sloop & Star, Light Blue Green, Sheared Base, Pontil, 1/2 Pt. 440.00
McK G X-10, Sheaf Of Rye & Star, Aqua, Inward Rolled Mouth, Pontil, Pt. 660.00
McK G X-11, Sheaf Of Rye & Star, Aqua, Pontil, 1/2 Pt. 935.00
McK G X-14, Murdock & Cassel, Green Aqua, Pontil, Pt. 1775.00
McK G X-15, Summer & Winter, Aqua, Double Collar, Pt. 65.00
McK G X-15, Summer & Winter, Dark Cherry Puce, Pt. 1100.00
McK G X-16, Summer & Winter, Aqua, Double Collar, 1/2 Pt. 200.00
McK G X-17, Summer & Winter, Aqua, Double Collar, Pt. 100.00
McK G X-18, Summer & Winter, Blue Green, Double Collar, OP, Qt. 1705.00
McK G X-18, Summer & Winter, Citron, Double Collar, OP, Qt. 1100.00
McK G X-18, Summer & Winter, Pale Blue Green, Pontil, Qt. 165.00
McK G X-18, Summer & Winter, Smoky Ice Blue, Pontil, Qt. 415.00
McK G X-19, Summer & Winter, Blue Aqua, Applied Mouth, OP, Qt. . . . . .100.00 to 110.00
McK G X-19, Summer & Winter, Ice Blue, Qt. . . . . .150.00 to 185.00
McK G X-19, Summer & Winter, Yellow Olive, Double Collar, Pontil, Qt. 1540.00
McK G X-27, Flag & Stoddard, Yellow Olive Amber, Pontil, Pt. 7150.00
McK G X-30, Hunter & Stag, Aqua, Ring Mouth, Pt. 385.00
McK G XI-8, For Pike's Peak, Prospector, Blue Aqua, Applied Mouth, Qt. 95.00
McK G XI-8, For Pike's Peak, Prospector, Teal Blue, Qt. 225.00
McK G XI-11, Prospector & Eagle, Aqua, Large OP, Pt. 190.00
McK G XI-26, For Pike's Peak, Prospector, Aqua, 1/2 Pt. 120.00
McK G XI-30, For Pike's Peak, Prospector, Eagle, Aqua, Qt. 75.00
McK G XI-30, For Pike's Peak, Prospector, Eagle, Yellow Olive Amber, Qt. 965.00
McK G XI-34, For Pike's Peak, Prospector, Eagle, Yellow Olive, Applied Mouth, Qt. . . . 855.00
McK G XI-34, For Pike's Peak, Prospector, Olive Amber, Applied Mouth, Qt. 690.00
McK G XI-41, For Pike's Peak, Prospector, Eagle, Aqua, Pt. 70.00
McK G XI-41, For Pike's Peak, Prospector, Eagle, Blue Aqua, Applied Mouth, Pt. . .50.00 to 90.00
McK G XI-44, Prospector & Eagle, Blue Aqua, Applied Mouth, Pt. 965.00
McK G XI-46, For Pike's Peak, Prospector, Hunter, Aqua, 7 1/2 In. . . . . .95.00 to 165.00
McK G XI-46, For Pike's Peak, Prospector, Hunter, Aqua, Ring Mouth, Qt. 330.00
McK G XI-47a, For Pikes Peak, Prospector, Green Aqua, Qt. 750.00
McK G XI-50, For Pike's Peak, Prospector, Hunter, Yellow Green, Ring Mouth, Pt. 440.00
McK G XI-50, For Pike's Peak, Prospector, Hunter, Root Beer Amber, Pt. 990.00
McK G XI-51, For Pike's Peak, Prospector, Hunter, Olive Green, Applied Mouth, Pt. 1100.00
McK G XI-52, For Pike's Peak, Prospector, Blue Aqua, Applied Mouth, 1/2 Pt. 145.00
McK G XI-54, For Pike's Peak, Prospector, Aqua, Applied Mouth, Qt. 580.00
McK G XII-2, Clasped Hands & Eagle, Waterford, Aqua, Double Collar, IP, Qt. 250.00
McK G XII-2, Clasped Hands & Eagle, Waterford, Yellow Olive, Qt. 1210.00
McK G XII-6, Clasped Hands & Eagle, Golden Yellow, Ring Collar, Qt. 825.00

McK G XII-7a, Clasped Hands & Eagle, Aqua, Pt. 45.00
McK G XII-8, Union, Clasped Hands & Eagle, Yellow Olive, Ring Mouth, Qt. 550.00
McK G XII-9, Union, Clasped Hands & Eagle, Yellow Olive, Applied Mouth, Qt. 550.00
McK G XII-15, Union, Clasped Hands & Eagle, Blue Aqua, Applied Mouth, Qt. 140.00
McK G XII-18, Union, Clasped Hands & Eagle, Lime Green, Ring Mouth, Pt. 220.00
McK G XII-19, Union, Clasped Hands & Eagle, Amber, Applied Mouth, Pt. 205.00
McK G XII-23, Union, Clasped Hands & Eagle, Citron, Ring Mouth, Pt. 245.00
McK G XII-24, Union, Clasped Hands & Eagle, Citron, Ring Mouth, Qt. 245.00
McK G XII-25, Union, Clasped Hands & Eagle, Citron, Round Collar, Qt. 8250.00
McK G XII-29, Union, Clasped Hands & Eagle, Amber, Applied Mouth, 1/2 Pt. 120.00
McK G XII-29, Union, Clasped Hands & Eagle, Aqua, 1/2 Pt. 55.00
McK G XII-29, Union, Clasped Hands & Eagle, Red Amber, Ring Mouth, 1/2 Pt. 220.00
McK G XII-30, Union, Clasped Hands & Eagle, Gold Amber, Ring Mouth, 1/2 Pt. 275.00
McK G XII-31, Union, Clasped Hands & Eagle, Gold Amber, Applied Mouth, 1/2 Pt. 210.00
McK G XII-31, Union, Clasped Hands & Eagle, Orange Amber, Ring Collar, 1/2 Pt. 200.00
McK G XII-31, Union, Clasped Hands & Eagle, Yellow Olive, Applied Mouth, 1/2 Pt. .. 330.00
McK G XII-37, Union, Clasped Hands, Aqua, Applied Mouth, IP, Qt. 110.00
McK G XII-37, Union, Clasped Hands, Cornflower Blue, Ring Mouth, Qt. .....605.00 to 1430.00
McK G XII-38, Union, Clasped Hands & Cannon, Blue Aqua, Applied Mouth, Pt. 145.00
McK G XII-39, Union, Clasped Hands & Cannon, Gold Amber, Pt. 355.00
McK G XII-39, Union, Clasped Hands & Cannon, Red Amber, Ring Mouth, Pt. 195.00
McK G XII-41, Union, Clasped Hands & Cannon, Aqua, Round Collar, Pt. 100.00
McK G XII-41, Union, Clasped Hands & Cannon, Gold Yellow, Ring Collar, Pt. 550.00
McK G XII-42, Union, Clasped Hands & Cannon, Aqua, Ring Mouth, 1/2 Pt. 145.00
McK G XII-42, Union, Clasped Hands & Cannon, Aqua, Applied Mouth, 1/2 Pt. ..100.00 to 440.00
McK G XII-43, Union, Clasped Hands & Eagle, Calabash, Amber, IP, Qt. ....275.00 to 415.00
McK G XII-43, Union, Clasped Hands & Eagle, Calabash, Aqua, Qt. 100.00
McK G XII-43, Union, Clasped Hands & Eagle, Orange Amber, IP, Qt. 240.00
McK G XII-53, Eagle & Anchor, Gold Amber, Pt. 325.00
McK G XIII-3, Girl Riding Bicycle & Eagle, Aqua, Applied Mouth, Pt. ....165.00 to 200.00
McK G XIII-4, Hunter & Fisherman, Calabash, Apricot, IP, Qt. 355.00
McK G XIII-4, Hunter & Fisherman, Calabash, Aqua, Pontil, Qt. 90.00
McK G XIII-4, Hunter & Fisherman, Calabash, Blue Green, Pontil, Qt. 230.00
McK G XIII-4, Hunter & Fisherman, Calabash, Copper Puce, Sloping Collar, IP 360.00
McK G XIII-4, Hunter & Fisherman, Calabash, Gold Amber, Sloping Collar, IP 265.00
McK G XIII-5, Hunter & Fisherman, Calabash, Aqua, OP, Qt. ....80.00 to 90.00
McK G XIII-6, Hunter & Fisherman, Calabash, Blue, OP, Qt. 120.00
McK G XIII-7, Hunter & Hounds, Aqua, Double Collar, Pontil, Pt. 200.00
McK G XIII-8, Sailor & Banjo Player, Copper Amber, Tubular Pontil, 1/2 Pt. 1650.00
McK G XIII-8, Sailor & Banjo Player, Orange Amber, Double Collar, 1/2 Pt. 990.00
McK G XIII-8, Sailor & Banjo Player, Yellow Olive Green, Tubular Pontil, 1/2 Pt. 1540.00
McK G XIII-10a, Sailor & Banjo Player, Yellow Olive Green, Pontil, 1/2 Pt. 3025.00
McK G XIII-11, Soldier & Dancer, Aqua, Pontil, Pt. 110.00
McK G XIII-11, Soldier & Dancer, Blue Green, Ring Collar, Pt. 660.00
McK G XIII-11, Soldier & Dancer, Gold Amber, Ring Collar, Pt. 660.00
McK G XIII-11, Soldier & Dancer, Ice Blue, IP, Pt. 605.00
McK G XIII-11, Soldier & Dancer, Lemon Yellow Green, Pontil, Pt. 2090.00
McK G XIII-11, Soldier & Dancer, Pink, Pontil, Pt. 6050.00
McK G XIII-12, Soldier & Dancer, Aqua, Pt. 145.00
McK G XIII-12, Soldier & Dancer, Blue Aqua, Applied Mouth, Pt. 175.00
McK G XIII-12, Soldier & Dancer, Yellow Green, Ring Mouth, Pt. 770.00
McK G XIII-13, Soldier & Dancer, Medium Olive Green, Pt. 1100.00
McK G XIII-13, Soldier & Dancer, Yellow Olive Green, Ring Collar, Pt. 1760.00
McK G XIII-14, Soldier & Dancer, Yellow Olive, Applied Mouth, Pt. 935.00
McK G XIII-15, Soldier & Daisy, Calabash, Aqua, Sloping Collar, IP, Qt. 330.00
McK G XIII-15, Soldier & Daisy, Calabash, Light Blue Green, Qt. 330.00
McK G XIII-15, Soldier & Daisy, Calabash, Light Green, Oil Treated Interior, IP, Qt. ... 200.00
McK G XIII-16, Soldier & Hound, Citron, Ring Mouth, Qt. 385.00
McK G XIII-16, Soldier & Hound, Gold Yellow, Ring Mouth, Pontil, Qt. 355.00
McK G XIII-16, Soldier & Hound, Red Amber, Pontil, Qt. 470.00
McK G XIII-16, Soldier & Hound, Yellow Olive, Pontil, Qt. 440.00
McK G XIII-16, Soldier & Hound, Yellow Olive, Ring Collar, Pontil, Qt. 660.00
McK G XIII-17, Horseman & Hound, Citron, Double Collar, Pt. 605.00

McK G XIII-17, Horseman & Hound, Claret, Tubular Pontil, Pt. 4675.00
McK G XIII-17, Horseman & Hound, Yellow Amber, Double Collar, Pt. 495.00
McK G XIII-17, Horseman & Hound, Yellow Olive, Double Collar, Pt. 495.00
McK G XIII-18, Horseman & Hound, Puce Amber, Double Collar, 1/2 Pt. 1100.00
McK G XIII-18, Horseman & Hound, Sapphire Blue, Pontil, 1/2 Pt. 9350.00
McK G XIII-18, Horseman & Hound, Yellow, Double Collar, 1/2 Pt. 1540.00
McK G XIII-19, Flora Temple, Burgundy Puce, Applied Mouth, Handle, Qt. 255.00
McK G XIII-19, Flora Temple, Yellow Amber, Puce Tone, Handle, Qt. 415.00
McK G XIII-20, Flora Temple, Copper Puce, Applied Mouth, Pt. 385.00
McK G XIII-21, Flora Temple, Blue Aqua, Pt. 355.00
McK G XIII-21, Flora Temple, Smoky Copper Color, Applied Handle & Mouth, Pt. 1925.00
McK G XIII-22, Flora Temple, Apricot Amber, Ring Mouth, Pt. 335.00
McK G XIII-22, Flora Temple, Red Puce To Copper, Applied Handle & Mouth, Pt. 190.00
McK G XIII-23, Flora Temple, Copper Olive Tone, Pt. 495.00
McK G XIII-23, Flora Temple, Medium Blue Green, Applied Mouth, Pt. 715.00
McK G XIII-23, Flora Temple, Puce, Applied Mouth, Pt. 230.00
McK G XIII-24, Flora Temple, Aqua, Ring Collar, Pt. 465.00
McK G XIII-24, Flora Temple, Cherry Puce, Applied Mouth & Handle, Pt. 495.00
McK G XIII-24, Flora Temple, Light Blue Green, Applied Collar, Pt. 330.00
McK G XIII-34, Sheaf Of Grain, Aqua, Pontil, Qt. 110.00
McK G XIII-35, Sheaf Of Grain, Westford Glass Co., Amber, 1/2 Pt. ....90.00 to 165.00
McK G XIII-35, Sheaf Of Grain, Westford Glass Co., Gold Red Amber, Pt. 60.00
McK G XIII-35, Sheaf Of Grain, Westford Glass Co., Olive Amber, Double Collar, Pt. ... 145.00
McK G XIII-35, Sheaf Of Grain, Westford Glass Co., Olive Green, Double Collar, Pt. ... 135.00
McK G XIII-35, Sheaf Of Grain, Westford Glass Co., Yellow Amber, Pt. 210.00
McK G XIII-36, Sheaf Of Grain, Westford Glass Co., Gold Amber, Double Collar, Pt. ... 130.00
McK G XIII-36, Sheaf Of Grain, Westford Glass Co., Olive Amber, Pt. 120.00
McK G XIII-37, Sheaf Of Grain, Westford Glass Co., Amber, Double Collar, 1/2 Pt. 155.00
McK G XIII-37, Sheaf Of Grain, Westford Glass Co., Golden Amber, 1/2 Pt. 100.00
McK G XIII-37, Sheaf Of Grain, Westford Glass Co., Olive Amber, 1/2 Pt. 155.00
McK G XIII-37, Sheaf Of Grain, Westford Glass Co., Yellow Olive, Double Collar, 1/2 Pt. 165.00
McK G XIII-38, Sheaf Of Grain & Star, Yellow Olive, IP, Qt. 685.00
McK G XIII-39, Sheaf Of Grain & Star, Aqua, Yellow Green Tint, Pontil, Pt. 100.00
McK G XIII-39, Sheaf Of Grain & Star, Green, Double Mouth, OP, Pt. 1210.00
McK G XIII-39, Sheaf Of Grain & Star, Yellow Green, Double Collar, Pontil, Pt. .330.00 to 935.00
McK G XIII-40, Sheaf Of Grain & Star, Yellow, Double Collar, IP, 1/2 Pt. 550.00
McK G XIII-40, Sheaf Of Grain & Star, Yellow Grass Green, Pontil, 1/2 Pt. 2090.00
McK G XIII-44, Sheaf Of Grain & Star, Calabash, Amber, IP, Qt. 230.00
McK G XIII-45, Sheaf Of Grain, Star, Calabash, Gold Amber, Ring Mouth, IP, Qt. 275.00
McK G XIII-46, Sheaf Of Grain & Tree, Calabash, Bright Green, Pontil, Qt. 440.00
McK G XIII-48, Anchor & Sheaf Of Grain, Amber, Applied Mouth, Qt. 635.00
McK G XIII-48, Anchor & Sheaf Of Grain, Prussian Blue, Short Collar, Qt. 16500.00
McK G XIII-48, Anchor & Sheaf Of Grain, Teal Blue, Qt. 2475.00
McK G XIII-48, Anchor & Sheaf Of Grain, Yellow Amber, Double Collar, Qt. ....935.00 to 990.00
McK G XIII-48, Anchor & Sheaf Of Grain, Yellow Olive, Pontil, Qt. 3850.00
McK G XIII-49, Anchor & Sheaf Of Grain, Aqua, 1/2 Pt. 145.00
McK G XIII-49, Anchor & Sheaf Of Grain, Emerald Green, Ring Mouth, 1/2 Pt. 2200.00
McK G XIII-49, Anchor & Sheaf Of Grain, Strawberry Amethyst, 1/2 Pt. 1650.00
McK G XIII-49, Anchor & Sheaf Of Grain, Yellow, Ring Mouth, 1/2 Pt. 8250.00
McK G XIII-51, Anchor & Sheaf Of Wheat, Topaz, Pontil, 1/2 Pt. 2200.00
McK G XIII-52, Anchor & Sheaf Of Grain, Calabash, Sapphire Blue, Pontil, Qt. 6600.00
McK G XIII-53, Eagle & Anchor, Resurgam, Aqua, Applied Collared Mouth, Pt. 130.00
McK G XIII-53, Eagle & Anchor, Resurgam, Claret, Double Collar, Pt. 2750.00
McK G XIII-53, Eagle & Anchor, Resurgam, Prussian Blue, Short Sloping Collar, Pt. ... 9350.00
McK G XIII-53, Eagle & Anchor, Resurgam, Yellow Green, Sloping Collar, Pt. 1870.00
McK G XIII-53, Eagle & Anchor, Resurgam, Yellow Olive, Sloping Collar, Pt. 1100.00
McK G XIII-54, Anchor & Eagle, Resurgam, Yellow Apricot, Double Collar, Pt. 1540.00
McK G XIII-55, Isabella & Anchor, Aqua, OP, Qt. 250.00
McK G XIII-58, Spring Garden & Anchor, Prussian Blue, Sloping Collar, Pt. 11000.00
McK G XIII-58, Spring Garden & Anchor, Sapphire Blue, Double Collar, Pt. 13200.00
McK G XIII-58, Spring Garden & Anchor, Smoky Pink Puce, Double Collar, Pt. 1705.00
McK G XIII-58, Spring Garden & Anchor, Yellow, Double Collar, Base Flake, Pt. 910.00
McK G XIII-60, Spring Garden & Anchor, Aqua, Tooled Mouth, 1/2 Pt. 145.00

Be very careful when handling old bottles or medical equipment. The remains of old drugs, even toxic materials, may still cling to the surface. A broken bit of glass or a sliver could let these toxic materials reach your bloodstream.

Flask, Merry Christmas, Happy New Year, Label Under Glass, Screw Cap, 4 7/8 In.

McK G XIII-60, Spring Garden & Anchor, Puce Amber, Pontil, 1/2 Pt. 605.00
McK G XIII-60, Spring Garden & Anchor, Root Beer Amber, Pontil, 1/2 Pt. 350.00
McK G XIII-60, Spring Garden & Anchor, Yellow Green, Tooled Mouth, 1/2 Pt. 550.00
McK G XIII-61, Spring Garden & Anchor, Claret, Double Collar, 1/2 Pt. 4675.00
McK G XIII-61, Spring Garden & Anchor, Forest Green, Double Collar, 1/2 Pt. 2530.00
McK G XIII-83, Star & Ravenna, Yellow Olive, Applied Mouth, Pt. 1595.00
McK G XIV-1, Traveler's Companion & Star, Medium Amber, Qt. 155.00
McK G XIV-1, Traveler's Companion & Star, Olive Amber, Qt. 150.00
McK G XIV-1, Traveler's Companion & Star, Red Amber, Qt. 200.00
McK G XIV-1, Traveler's Companion & Star, Root Beer Amber, Bubbles, Qt. 150.00
McK G XIV-1, Traveler's Companion & Star, Yellow Olive, Qt. 230.00
McK G XIV-2, Traveler's Companion, Ravenna, Gold Amber, Ring Mouth, Qt. 330.00
McK G XIV-2, Traveler's Companion, Ravenna, Medium Amber, Qt. 470.00
McK G XIV-3, Traveler's Companion, Ravenna, Blue Aqua, Applied Mouth, Qt. 130.00
McK G XIV-3, Traveler's Companion, Ravenna, Gold Amber, Ring Mouth, IP, Pt. 495.00
McK G XIV-3, Traveler's Companion, Ravenna, Yellow Olive, Double Collar, IP, Pt. 1210.00
McK G XIV-6, Traveler's Companion, Lockport, Blue Green, Round Collar, Pt. 3630.00
McK G XIV-6, Traveler's Companion, Lockport, Red Amber, Double Collar, Pt. 225.00
McK G XIV-7, Traveler's Companion & Star, Aqua, IP, 1/2 Pt.   210.00
McK G XIV-7, Traveler's Companion & Star, Golden Amber, Round Collar, Pt. 210.00
McK G XIV-7, Traveler's Companion, Amber, IP, 1/2 Pt. 575.00
McK G XIV-7, Traveler's Companion, Yellow Amber, IP, 1/2 Pt. 355.00
McK G XV-6, Granite Glass Co., Stoddard, N.H., Gold Amber, Red Tone, Qt. 880.00
McK G XV-6, Granite Glass Co., Stoddard, N.H., Olive Amber, Pontil, Qt. 1100.00
McK G XV-7, Granite Glass Co., Stoddard, N.H., Gold Amber, Pt. 155.00
McK G XV-7, Granite Glass Co., Stoddard, N.H., Gold Yellow, Olive, Bubbles, Pontil, Pt.   385.00
McK G XV-7, Granite Glass Co., Stoddard, N.H., Orange Amber, Applied Mouth, Pt. . . .   250.00
McK G XV-15, Newburgh Glass Co., Black Olive Amber, Double Collar, 1/2 Pt. 1760.00
McK G XV-15, Newburgh Glass Co., Yellow Olive, Striations, Pt. 1870.00
McK G XV-28, Zanesville City Glass Works, Aqua, Strap Side, Applied Mouth, Pt. 100.00
McK G XV-28, Zanesville Cut Glass Works, Yellow Amber, Strap Side, Pt. 605.00
Merry Christmas, Happy New Century, Clock Face, Screw Threads, 1900, 4 1/2 In. 230.00
Merry Christmas, Happy New Year, Label Under Glass, Screw Cap, 4 7/8 In. . . . . .*Illus*   204.00
Merry Christmas & Happy New Year, Embossed Wreath, Pumpkinseed, 1/2 Pt. 30.00
Milk Glass, Morning Nip, Grandmother's Face On Front, Metal Screw, 1905, 5 In. 175.00
Milk Glass, Splotch, Red, Yellow, Green, Purple, Sheared, Tooled Lip, 1860, 5 In. 230.00
Molded Ribs, Swirled To Right, Amethyst, Pontil, Emil Larson, 1930, 8 In. 385.00
Naber Alfs & Brune, San Francisco, Tooled Mouth, Phoenix, 1891-1906, 5 1/4 In. 330.00
Nailsea Type, Cranberry, Criss-Cross Looped Design, Pontil, Egg Shape, 1840-1870, 7 In.   745.00
O.G.W., Whiskey, Amber, Double Rolled Mouth, Pt. 55.00
Old Oscar Pepper Whiskey, Frankfort Distillery, For Medicinal Purposes Only, Label, Pt.   15.00
Olive Green, Inward Rolled Lip, Applied Rigaree, 1780-1830, 6 3/8 In. 330.00
Olive Green, Strap Side, Qt. 25.00
Ortion & Gerhardt, Pumpkinseed, Tooled Mouth, 1895-1898, 5 3/8 In. 110.00
Owl Weber, Owl On Branch, Nevada City, SCA, 6 3/8 In. 205.00
Park Square Hotel, Westfield, Mass., Aqua, Strap Side, 1/2 Pt. 20.00
Picnic, Amber, Twisted Neck, Tooled Top, 1/2 Pt. 100.00

Pinch, Blue Aqua, Applied Mouth, Pontil, 1820-1830, 3 1/2 In. 355.00
Pinch, Gold Amber, Pontil, 4 3/4 In. 385.00
Pink Amethyst, Dark Striations Swirls, Pontil, Qt. 465.00
Pitkin Type, 10 Broken Ribs, Swirled To Right, Pontil, Midwest, 1825, 4 3/4 In. 495.00
Pitkin Type, 14 Ribs, Swirled To Right, Apple Green, Midwest, 4 1/2 In. 605.00
Pitkin Type, 16 Broken Ribs, Swirled To Right, Emerald Green, Midwest, Pontil, 6 1/4 In. 1250.00
Pitkin Type, 16 Broken Swirled Ribs, Green, Half Post Neck, 6 In. 550.00
Pitkin Type, 16 Ribs, Swirled To Right, Emerald Green, Midwest, Pontil, 4 3/4 In. 355.00
Pitkin Type, 16 Ribs, Swirled To Right, Midwest, Pontil, 4 7/8 In. 355.00
Pitkin Type, 16 Ribs, Swirled To Right, Yellow Olive Green, 6 In. 385.00
Pitkin Type, 16 Ribs, Vertical, Emerald Green, Pontil, 5 1/4 In. 605.00
Pitkin Type, 18 Ribs, Swirled To Right, Cobalt Blue, Pontil, 5 5/8 In. 3300.00
Pitkin Type, 19 Ribs, Swirled To Right, Green, Pontil, 6 In. 440.00
Pitkin Type, 19 Ribs, Swirled To Right, Yellow Green, Pontil, 6 3/8 In. 295.00
Pitkin Type, 22 Broken Ribs, Swirled To Right, Smoky Clear, Pontil, 5 5/8 In. 240.00
Pitkin Type, 24 Broken Swirled Ribs, Light Green, Half Post Neck, 4 5/8 In. 495.00
Pitkin Type, 24 Ribs, Swirled To Left, Emerald Green, Pontil, 7 In. 330.00
Pitkin Type, 24 Ribs, Swirled To Right, Emerald Green, Pontil, 5 7/8 In. 305.00
Pitkin Type, 26 Ribs, Swirled To Right, Gold Amber, Midwest, Pontil, 4 3/4 In. 1045.00
Pitkin Type, 30 Broken Ribs, Swirled To Left, Light Green, Pontil, 5 7/8 In. 275.00
Pitkin Type, 30 Ribs, Swirled To Left, Sea Green, Pontil, 5 1/2 In. 305.00
Pitkin Type, 31 Ribs, Swirled To Right, Aqua, 1840, Pontil, 6 1/2 In. . . . . .130.00 to 265.00
Pitkin Type, 32 Broken Ribs, Swirled To Right, Yellow Tobacco Amber, 1830, 5 7/8 In. . 825.00
Pitkin Type, 32 Broken Swirled Ribs, Peacock Green, Half Post Neck, 6 In. 495.00
Pitkin Type, 32 Ribs, Sea Green, Pontil, 6 7/8 In. 275.00
Pitkin Type, 32 Ribs, Swirled To Right, Aqua, Pontil, 6 In. 175.00
Pitkin Type, 32 Ribs, Swirled To Right, Olive Green, 7 1/4 In. 850.00
Pitkin Type, 32 Ribs, Swirled To Right, Yellow Olive Amber, Midwest, Pontil, 5 3/8 In. . 605.00
Pitkin Type, 32 Ribs, Swirled To Right, Yellow Olive, Pontil, 7 1/8 In. 1210.00
Pitkin Type, 36 Broken Ribs, Swirled To Left, Root Beer Amber, 1800-1820, 6 In. 495.00
Pitkin Type, 36 Broken Ribs, Swirled To Left, Yellow Olive, Pontil, 5 1/8 In. 580.00
Pitkin Type, 36 Broken Ribs, Swirled To Right, Olive Green, 6 In. 275.00
Pitkin Type, 36 Ribs, Swirled To Left, Gold Amber, Pontil, 6 1/8 In. 605.00
Pitkin Type, 36 Ribs, Swirled To Left, Light Green, Pontil, 1810, 6 3/8 In. 690.00
Pitkin Type, 36 Ribs, Swirled To Left, Light Yellow Olive, Pontil, 5 3/4 In. . . . . .310.00 to 910.00
Pitkin Type, 36 Ribs, Swirled To Left, Light Yellow Olive, Pontil, 6 3/8 In. 440.00
Pitkin Type, 36 Ribs, Swirled To Left, Root Beer Amber, Pontil, 5 3/4 In. 495.00
Pitkin Type, 36 Ribs, Swirled To Left, Root Beer Amber, Pontil, 6 1/4 In. 410.00
Pitkin Type, 36 Ribs, Swirled To Left, Yellow Olive, Pontil, 5 In. 440.00
Pitkin Type, 36 Ribs, Swirled To Left, Yellow Olive, Pontil, 6 3/4 In. 415.00
Pitkin Type, 36 Ribs, Swirled To Right, Light Olive Yellow, Pontil, 4 7/8 In. 440.00
Pitkin Type, 36 Ribs, Swirled To Right, Sea Green, Pontil, 5 3/4 In. 415.00
Pitkin Type, 36 Ribs, Swirled To Right, Yellow Olive, Pontil, 5 In. . . . . .335.00 to 465.00
Pitkin Type, 36 Ribs, Swirled To Right, Yellow Olive, Pontil, 6 In. 4400.00
Pumpkinseed, Applied Mouth, SCA, 1890-1900, 6 3/8 In. 145.00
Pumpkinseed, Diamonds, Cross Embossing, 5 3/4 In. 15.00
Pumpkinseed, Tooled Mouth, SCA, 1890-1910, 5 1/2 In. 145.00
Pure Whisky Put Up At Geo. A. Riggins Wonderful Drugstore, Label, Amber, Pt. . 165.00
Rabbit, Working A Butter Churn, Multicolored Enamel Design, 1817, 5 1/2 In. 990.00
Rang's Syrup Of Tar, Blue Aqua, Teardrop Shape, Applied Mouth, 1855, 5 1/2 In. 415.00
Ratto & Foppiano, Oakland, Cal., Coffin, 1/2 Pt. 90.00
Reclining Deer, Tree Stump, Purple Amethyst, Coin Shape, Germany, Pontil, 1/2 Pt. . . . 355.00
Red, White, Blue, Gold Label Under Glass, Metal Screw Cap, 1880-1900, 6 In. 1100.00
Sailor's Snug Harbor, Staten Island, N.Y., Winter Scene, Pumpkinseed, 1905, 6 7/8 In. . 45.00
Scroll, Aqua, IP, Applied Ring Collar, Qt. 60.00
Senate Saloon, Grand Junction, Colo., Screw Threaded, 1905, Pt. 355.00
Sheaf Of Grain, Westford Glass Co., Olive Amber, Pt. . . . . .65.00 to 150.00
Sheaf Of Wheat & Star, Bright Golden Amber, Applied Mouth, 1860, Pt. 132.00
Silver Deposit, Scrolled Foliate, Cap Foot, Alvin, 1900, 5 1/2 In. 290.00
Spruance, Stanley & Co., San Francisco, Amber, Strap Side, Applied Top, Pt. . . . .660.00 to 700.00
Standing Lion, Axe, Grapes, Cobalt Blue, Pontil, Europe, 1860, 1/2 Pt. 230.00
Stiegel Type, Floral, Engraved KRN, Teardrop, Pontil, 6 3/8 In. 330.00
Sunburst & Medallion, Gray Cornflower Blue, Herringbone Sides, Pontil, 1860, 1/2 Pt. 550.00

Teardrop, Cranberry Red Tight Looping, Pontil, 1840-1870, 5 3/4 In. 100.00
Teardrop, Cranberry, Pontil, 7 1/2 In. 330.00
Teardrop, Flattened, Orange Amber, Double Collar, Pontil, Blown, 8 7/8 In. 100.00
Teardrop, TMW, Floral Design, Engraved Bird, Ferns, Tooled Mouth, 1780-1820, 9 1/2 In. 220.00
Tombstone, Amber, Ground Top, Keystone, Cap, Pt. 145.00
Tree On Seal, Black Glass 160.00
Try It, Red Amber, Pumpkinseed, Twisted Neck, Gouged Shoulder, Tooled Top, 1/2 Pt. ... 90.00
Victoria Duchess Of Kent, Bourne, Denby, Stoneware 65.00
W.A. Reist, Colonial, York, Pa., Fluted, Hotel View, Mold Blown, Pewter Cap, Pt. 55.00
W.K.Yc. Co., Shoofly, Amber, Pt. 30.00
Winchell & Davis, Albany, N.Y., Strap Side, 1/2 Pt. 25.00
Woman's Torso In Corset, Silver Screw Top, Ground Lip, 6 In. 85.00
Wormser Bros., San Francisco, Orange Amber, Double Roll Mouth, 1867-1872, 8 1/2 In. 330.00
Yellow Amber, Tooled Mouth, Midwest, Pontil, 11 5/8 In. 305.00
Yellow Olive Base, Black Top, Pocket, Pontil, 1830, 5 1/2 In. 155.00

FOOD

Food bottles include all of the many grocery store containers, such as those for catsup, horseradish, jelly, and other foodstuffs. Vinegar bottles and a few other special bottles are listed under their own headings.

FOOD, A.C. Benner & Co., New Haven, Ct., Aqua, Tapered Rectangular, Cork, 5 In. 3.00
A.L. Murdock Liquid Food, Amber, Embossed 15.00
Acker's Select Tea, Finley Acker & Co., Man On Elephant, Green, Crown Lid, 11 In. .. 305.00
Acker's Select Tea, Finley Acker & Co., Yellow Green, Smooth Lip, Crown Lid, 8 3/8 In. . 415.00
Acker's Select Tea, Yellow Green, Original Glass Lid, Crown Shape, 1910-1920, 11 In. . 330.00
Akron Pure Milk Co., Creamed Cottage Cheese, Embossed, 12 Oz., 5 1/4 In. .....*Illus* 14.00
Alpha Salad Cream, Threaded Ground Top, Tapered, 7 In. 2.00
Armour Creameries, Louisville, Ky., Jar, Sour Cream, Embossed, ISP, Round, Pt. 10.00
Arrow Root, Jar, White, Black Letters, Stoneware, Lid, 5 1/4 In. 75.00
Bacorn Co., Pure Fruit Flavors, Elmira, N.Y., Tooled Lip, Rectangular, Cork, 4 1/2 In. .. 2.00
Baker's Standard Flavoring Extracts, Imitation Banana, Partial Label, 7 3/4 In. 15.00
Benton Meyers & Co. Fruit Juices, Cleveland, Jug, 1/2 Pt. 125.00
Berry, Blue Green, Wide Mouth, Applied Lip, c.1860-1880, 11 In. 90.00
Berry, Green, Wide Mouth, Applied Lip, 10 3/4 In. 40.00
Berry, Medium Blue Green, Applied Mouth, 1855-1865, 11 1/4 In. 110.00
Berry, Root Beer Amber, Fluted Neck, New England, 1855-1870, 11 3/8 In. 360.00
Berry, Yellow Green, Wide Mouth, c.1860-1880, 12 1/4 In. 100.00
Blue Aqua, Wide Mouth, Flared Lip, Pontil, Blown, Paddle Marks, Europe, 9 In. 255.00
Bob White Crystal White Syrup, Louisville, Ky., Orange Label, 7 1/2 In. ......*Illus* 8.00
Borden's Malted Milk, Raised & Painted Letters, Stopper, Square, 6 1/2 x 4 1/2 In. 225.00
Brandt's Pure Horse Raddish, Cleveland, O., Jar, Cream, Cobalt Transfer, 1910, 6 In. . 130.00
Bromo Caffeine, Cornflower Blue, Inside Haze, Cork, 3 In. 10.00
Brooke's Lemons, Embossed Lemon, 11 In. 35.00
Bruder's Orange Ade, Modern Milk Plant, Orange & Green, ACL, Gal. ....*Illus* 49.50

Food, Akron Pure Milk Co., Creamed Cottage Cheese, Embossed, 12 Oz., 5 1/4 In.

Food, Bob White Crystal White Syrup, Louisville, Ky., Orange Label, 7 1/2 In.

Food, Bruder's Orange Ade, Modern Milk Plant, Orange & Green, ACL, Gal.

Food, Distillata, Distilled Water, City Ice & Fuel Co., Cleveland, Ohio, 10 3/4 In.	Food, Figaro Wood Smoke, Jug Shape, Yellow, Red & Blue Label, Cork, 8 In.	Food, Jumbo Peanut Butter, Frank Tea & Spice Co., Cincinnati, Ohio, 5 In.	Food, Kim's Pure Horseradish, Pittsburgh, Pa., Orange Paper Label, 6 In.

Butterine, Penn Meat Co., Blue & White Bands, Stoneware, Pat. 6/2/1914, 1/2 Gal. 100.00
C.B. & Co., Ketchup, Miniature 15.00
California Perfume Co., see Avon, California Perfume Co.
Campbell's Beefsteak Tomato Ketchup, Label Only, Screw Cap Trademark, c.1900 . . 65.00
Campbell's Soup Company Ketchup, Ribbed, 1890 . . . . 25.00
Carnation Malted Milk, Milk Glass, Aluminum Lid, Jar, 1940s-1950s 175.00
Catsup, 8-Sided, Amethyst, Screw Top, ABM, 9 In. 2.00
Chas. Gulden Mustard, N.Y., Wide Mouth, Squat, 3 3/4 In. 5.00
Chas. Gulden Mustard, N.Y., Wide Mouth, Squat, 4 5/8 In. 10.00
Cider & Vinegar, Jug, Louisville, Ky., Stoneware, Cream, Cobalt, Handle, 1910, 3 In. . . 55.00
Cleveland Fruit Juice Co., Jug, Cleveland, O., Stoneware, Cream, Blue, 1915, 4 In. . . . 130.00
Cloverdale Cottage Cheese & Sour Cream, Bismarck, N.D., Jar, Red & Blue, 12 Oz. 35.00
Cocoa Nut Oil, C. Toppan, Aqua, Applied Disc Mouth, Pontil, 1845-1855, 6 In. 145.00
Columbia Catsup Extra Quality, Crown Top, 1890, 7 7/8 In. 10.00
Concentrated Extract Of Lemon Abrams & Carroll, San Francisco, Label, 5 In. . . . 45.00
Concentrated Extract Of Vanilla Abrams & Carroll, San Francisco, Label, 5 In. . . . 45.00
Cottage Cheese, Dannon Real Yogurt, Jar, Brown & Orange ACL, Round, 1/2 Pt. 20.00
Cottage Cheese, Honicker's Dairy, St. Clair, Pa., Jar, Red Pyro, Round, Pt. 4.50
Cover, Horlick's Malted Milk, Jar, Gal. 150.00
Curtice Brothers, CB, Rochester, Aqua, IP, Applied Sloping Collar, 1850s, 8 3/8 In. . . . 275.00
Curtice Brothers Blue Label Tomato Ketchup, Embossed, Label, 1920-1930, Small 15.00
Curtice Brothers Preservers, Rochester, N.Y., Ketchup Bottle Shape, SCA 12.00
D & H Co., Sauce Bottle, Aqua, IP, 1845-1860, 6 1/8 In. 60.00
Davidson's Clam Chowder, Camden, N.Y., Aqua, Embossed, Cylindrical, 8 In. 18.00
Deneen's Cottage Cheese, Sharon, Pa., Large Mouth, Embossed, 1 Pt. 1600.00
Diamond Packing Co., Bridgeton, N.J., Pat. Feb. 1, 1870, Aqua, Squat, 8 In. 28.00
Distillata, Distilled Water, City Ice & Fuel Co., Cleveland, Ohio, 10 3/4 In. . . . .*Illus* 22.00
Down On The Farm Preserves, C.W. Rodefer Co., Shadyside, Ohio, Stoneware, Ears, Qt. 160.00
E. Frese, San Francisco, Flavoring, Light Green, Applied Top, 6 1/2 In. 130.00
E.R. Durkee & Co., Salad Dressing, New York, Threaded Ground Lip, Pat. 1877, 6 3/4 In. 5.00
Eat Tom's Toasted Peanuts, 5 Cents, Jar, Glass Lid, Red Knob, 8 In. 65.00
Edwardsburg Corn Syrup, Crown, Perfect Seal Jar, ABM, Lightning, Qt., 8 In. 20.00
Falcon Brand Olives 15.00
Figaro Wood Smoke, Jug Shape, Yellow, Red & Blue Label, Cork, 8 In. . . . .*Illus* 22.50
Foss's Liquid Fruit Flavors, Portland, Me., Cork, 4 3/4 In. 1.00
Foss's Liquid Fruit Flavors, Portland, Me., Rectangular, Cork, 3 1/4 In. 1.00
French's Medford Brand Prepared Mustard, Embossed, Pt., 5 In. 10.00
Ginger, W In Oval, Light Green, Applied Top, 6 In. 55.00
Golden Tree Brand Syrup, Qt. 27.00
Grand Union Tea Company, Screw Top, Embossed, 4 3/4 In. 2.00
Grand Union Tea Company, Sunken Panels Sides, Rectangular, Cork, 5 1/4 In. 2.00
Green & Clark Missouri Cider, Aug. 27, 1878, Amber, Blob Top, Qt. 48.00

BOTTLES
OF THE YEAR

BOTTLE COLLECTING has been a popular hobby since the days of the ancient Greeks and Romans. But collectors today are not concerned with ancient glass; they want to buy pieces made in America or Europe from the eighteenth century to the present. In the 1920s a few wealthy collectors began to look at early American glass. They were interested in goblets, decanters, bowls, and lamps, but also in a few types of bottles. Historic flasks were the commercial whiskey bottles of the day. Most were made by glassworks east of the Mississippi, from New England to Ohio. The earliest book we have seen for bottle collectors was written in 1921 by Stephen Van Rensselaer. It was about bottles and flasks and had a checklist that was the best available for many years. When the Ohio home of the Van Sweringen brothers, founders of the New York Central Railroad, was sold in the 1930s, the library had two copies of the book and several old flasks. The brothers, who were among the richest men in the nation, chose to collect bottles.

Collecting antiques became a hobby of the middle class in the 1950s. National newspaper columns were published, price books appeared, antiques shows were started in many states, and the first national bottle collectors club was founded. The Antique Bottle Collectors Association of California formed in 1959. We first became aware of bottle collecting around 1960, when we started collecting labeled food-product bottles. *Western Collector* magazine began a series of well-researched articles in a special section in 1965. Our 1967 book, *Know Your Antiques*, included a chapter on dating bottles. By then, bottle collecting was one of the three most popular collecting hobbies in America, topped only by coins and stamps. In 1971, in our first price book about bottles, we listed old and new bottles. Collectors today would like to be able to buy at those prices. An 1897 cone-shaped Carter's ink bottle was $7; a Brown's Celebrated Indian Herb Bitters, $250; a hunter and fisherman calabash flask, $25 to $90; an olive amber Eagle and Cornucopia flask, $55. The most expensive fruit jar was a Canton cobalt blue jar for $100 to $450. Most sold for under $10.

Bottle collecting has changed through the years. Historic flasks are still desirable, but very expensive. Modern bottles are wanted by some collectors, but cost less than they did a few years ago. Milk and soda bottles made since the 1940s are saved by many. And bottles with the product labels still intact bring a premium. Perfume bottles are bringing high prices, especially when sold with the box. The biggest change is that many bottles are now sold on the Internet.

Here are some highlights from the thousands of bottles sold at auctions and shows in the past two years. Some set records, some are unusual, some are just fun.

The biggest news last year was the famous "San Francisco dig," which turned up two cone-shaped Bryant's Stomach Bitters bottles. The "rarer than rare" dark green bottles were found ten feet underground. One, in remarkably good condition, sold on the West Coast for the **record price of $68,750**—making it the most expensive bottle ever sold at auction. There are only two or three uncracked versions of the Bryant's bottle, and this was the first one to be offered in a public auction. Its companion, with several cracks and a hole, sold at a Pennsylvania auction for $11,825. The 14-inch Bryant's bottle was produced for less than a year in 1857. But even its replacement, called the "eight-sided lady's leg" because of the shapely neck of the bottle, is hard to find.

A perfect example of the Brown's Celebrated Indian Herb Bitters, dated 1867, sold for $5,280 in 1997. The 12 1/4-inch bottle is made of dark chocolate amber glass and has 90 percent of its original paint.

The Simon's Centennial Bitters Trademark bottle is a bust of General George Washington. The 10-inch bottle, made around 1875, is plentiful in aqua, more scarce in the amber color shown here. This one sold for $1,650 in 1997. Beware of reproductions in amethyst.

Prices ranged from $17 to $25,300 at a sale of a famous ink bottle collection belonging to Jan and Watt White. Many rare bottles were sold.

Many ink bottles are classified by shape, like turtle, umbrella, teakettle, or cone. This embossed David's turtle bottle is golden amber—an extremely rare color. The 2-inch bottle, made around 1885, sold for $560.

A collector paid $1,100 for this exceptional labeled Harrison's Columbian Ink made between 1840 and 1850. The 4 1/8-inch sapphire blue bottle has an applied flanged collar.

There are few known examples of this 11 1/2-inch Harrison's Columbian Ink bottle made about 1850. The 12-sided, medium blue master ink auctioned for $25,300.

Ink collectors look for paper labels, like the colorful example on this 1850s deep green Howe's Unchangeable Blue master ink bottle, which sold for $672. It is 7 1/8 inches high and features an applied mouth.

Target balls bring high prices because they were made to be broken. Only fragments of the deep aqua Liddle & Keading Agents ball were found until 1977, when two whole deep aqua balls were unearthed during a downtown renovation in Marysville, California. One of them sold for $3,600 at the 1992 Toledo Bottle Exposition. The other (above right) sold for $7,700 at a 1997 Pennsylvania auction. The yellow amber target ball (right) is notable for its hobnail pattern. It sold for $1,430. Both balls are 2³/₄ inches in diameter.

This turn-of-the-century Mary Gregory–type barber bottle sold for a **record price of $2,585.** A collector paid almost five times the pre-sale estimate for the 8-inch amethyst bottle. It has white enamel decoration showing an unusual fountain shaped like a woman.

Bottles and other collectibles are all over the World Wide Web, and phone and mail auctions are posting catalogs on the Internet. A 1998 stoneware auction that took mail and phone bids also got bids from all fifty states when the catalog was posted on the auction's Web site. High bids were posted each day, and collectors could then phone in new bids. Prices were above expectations.

The 14-inch, 2-gallon jug decorated with a bantam rooster in a dotted geometric frame sold for $5,280. It was made by J.C. Waelde North Bay around 1860.

The 13-inch, 1¹/₂-gallon jug with a basket of flowers was made by the Fort Edward Pottery Company about the same time. It sold for $1,540.

A sale in Geneva, Switzerland, devoted almost entirely to "perfume presentations"—the bottles with all of their packaging—was the highest grossing auction of its kind. This blown, enameled flacon in the shape of a champagne flute sold for $7,535. It was made for Les Créations Guyla for their Caresse Parisienne perfume.

The 1927 black glass flacon with the words "Merry Christmas," made for Benoît, sold for $3,014.

This Femme Divine bottle made in 1923 for Parfums Loulette sold for $2,062 at the perfume bottle auction. It was designed by Julien Viard. Collectors might encounter the same bottle filled with Fidelwood perfume by the The House of Fragrance. The Bermuda company bought leftover bottles from Loulette.

S ome fruit jars sell for very fancy prices. The hand-blown jars, made before 1896, are the most desirable. These examples are unusual for their color, closure, size, or embossed wording.

The green jar marked Mason's Patent, Nov. 30th, 1858, E.H.E. (RB-1849)* sold for $3,410.

The amber Mason's Patent, Nov. 30th, 1858, C.F.J. Co. (unlisted) was $2,640.

The tall aqua Salem Jar (RB-2543) was $1,320.

Glass-Works Auctions

The amber Mason's Patent, Nov. 30th,1858, N.C.L. (RB-861) sold for $1,320.

Mason's 5 Patent, Nov 30th, 1858, an unusual blue jar (RB-2050-6), brought $2,420.

*The RB numbers refer to *The Red Book of Fruit Jars.*

George and Helen McKearin, the gurus of the bottle-collecting world, categorized historic flasks by subject in 1941. They sorted, listed, numbered, and sketched all of the known American historic flasks. More than fifty years later, bottle collectors still use the McKearin numbering system.

This 1850s medium amber Eagle and Lyre pint flask (McK GII-22) sold at auction last year for $7,975. The color is very rare.

(Eagle—front)   *(Lyre—back)*

Glass-Works Auctions

Other historic flasks from a 1998 auction (left to right): Corn for the World (McK GVI-5), made 1840–1860, quart, yellow olive amber, $1,595; Union, Clasped Hands and Eagle (McK GXII-13), 1860–1880, quart, yellow olive, $1,210; Washington and Taylor (McK GI-55), 1840–1860, pint, medium blue green, $440.

There are many bottle collectors who buy whatever tickles their fancy. The possibilities for collections are as varied as the products put in bottles.

Medicine bottles are interesting because the names and decorations are strange to us now. The 1870s olive-colored Connell's Brahminical Moonplant East Indian Remedies bottle (left) is embossed with a pair of feet surrounded by stars. The unusual bottle, made by the Pacific Glass Works, auctioned for $495. The rare cobalt H. Bowman Druggist bottle (right) is embossed with the words "Citrate of Magnesia." It is one of many bottles made for the Oakland, California, druggist around 1890. It brought $220.

Whiskey bottles come in a variety of shapes. The Non Pareil Trademark Kolb & Denhard bottle is said to be the only Western whiskey jug that is embossed. It was made for a San Francisco distillery from 1895 to 1902. It brought $8,800 at auction.

One of the earliest flasks used in the Western states is embossed "Wormser Bro's S.F. Fine Old Cognac." The 6³/₄-inch bottle was made around 1870 for a San Francisco firm.

It was found years ago in a California Gold Rush town. A boy walking in the rain saw the brown glass and dug out the bottle. It auctioned for $11,000.

Many collectors like bright colors, especially cobalt blue. This blue M R Sacrimento soda sold for $6,600. The bottle was made between 1851 and 1863 by the Union Glass Works of Philadelphia. The misspelled city name adds to the value.

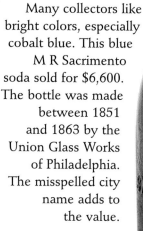

Only a handful of cobalt California Natural Seltzer Water H & G bottles are known. There is a bear embossed on the side. Some examples have grass near the bear; some do not. This grassless example sold for $1,320.

Some collectors search for bottles embossed with special words like "cure" or "hair." Fish's Infallible Hair Restorative is a rare cobalt blue example of a bottle made by Pacific Glass Works before 1863. Last year it sold for $4,620.

This E.H.V.B. NY pickle bottle in a rare color was made for Elias H. VanBenschoten, a New York City pickle packer, around 1850. It sold for $4,840 at a 1997 auction.

The only known fire grenade with a picture of an animal is the California Fire Extinguisher. This version with both California's state bear and the word "California" is not common. The 1870s bottle sold for $4,180. Another example of this bottle with its paper label intact sold for $8,500.

There are still collectors of the "modern" figural bottles made by Ezra Brooks, Jim Beam, Wild Turkey, and other liquor brands. Most of the companies stopped making new decanters by the 1990s. This Wild Turkey decanter was the first one in a series started in 1971 by Austin Nichols Distillery. It is known as Number 1, Standing Turkey. The company must have known that the decanter would seem odd to customers, because the tag that came with the bottle says, "Remove head stopper. Pour as indicated by directional arrow." The decanter originally retailed for about $20. In the early 1980s, when the company reissued a miniature series of the turkeys, the decanter was worth more than $300. Interest in modern bottles has decreased in the last few years, and so has the value of this bottle. It is now worth about $180.

Oddities like this gemel bottle are scarce and are sought by collectors of early American glass as well as bottle collectors. It is made of two bottles holding two different liquids, like oil and vinegar or two liqueurs, joined together. Gemels were usually made by glass workers in their spare time, not for commercial trade, thus making their origins hard to identify. This kind of gemel, made of aqua glass with white loopings and an irregular wafer base, is called a South Jersey type. The style originated at window glass factories in the New Jersey area in the mid- to late 1800s. It is worth about $200.

GO ~ WITHS

Many companies create advertising items that are used to promote their products. These include advertising signs, drink dispensers, giveaways like bottle openers or mirrors, and any other object that pictures or mentions the bottled product. Bottle collectors call all these items "go-withs."

This 19-inch-high Hires Root Beer urn dispenser was made in Mettlach, Germany, about 1910. It sold for a **record price of $106,700** at an auction of the largest privately owned Hires collection known. The famous Hires boy is pictured on one side. The bathrobe he wears helps to date the piece.

Everyone has seen lighted advertising clocks in gas stations or drugstores. Some of them are worth high prices now. This Art Deco–style Dr. Pepper clock is a countertop model made in the 1930s. It sold for $4,255 last year. The simple and less well-known Sun Crest root beer clock sold for $403.

Clever distillers long ago termed their products "medicinal" to increase their appeal. Advertising signs and trays tout the purifying and invigorating qualities of the mixtures. The 16½-inch lithographed tin Kalamazoo Celery Pepsin Bitters tray claimed, "Twill brace you up." It auctioned for $800.

Warner's made many different types of tonics and medicines. This sign pictured a grandmother and two grandchildren to advertise Warner's Log Cabin Sarsaparilla, The Best Blood Purifier. The 13¾-inch by 27½-inch lithographed paper sign sold for $1,895.

H. Graff & Co., Fresno, Cal., Aqua, Rectangular, Qt. 40.00
H.J. Heinz Co., Crock, Pittsburg, Gray, Cobalt Slip Decoration, Salt Glaze, 5 In. 440.00
H.J. Heinz Co., Mother Of All Catsups, Pat'd Jun 9th, 1891, 6-Sided, Store Display, 26 In. 675.00
H.J. Heinz Co., Patented 7, Bulbous Neck, Cork, 8 In. 4.00
Heinz Food, Jar, Figural Stopper, Logo, c.1900, 12 1/2 In. 295.00
Heinz Tomato Ketchup, Pittsburgh, USA, 1890s, 9 In. 18.00
Heinz Tomato Ketchup, Pittsburgh, USA, Bulbous, Rope Design 10.00
Holman's Baking Powder, Buffalo, N.Y., Light Blue Green, Tooled Mouth, 5 3/4 In. .. 110.00
Home Made Preserves, H.A. Johnson & Co., Boston, Mass., Stoneware, 1/2 Gal. 40.00
Horlick's Malted Milk, Jar, ABM, Screw Top Tin Lid, Sample 35.00
Horlick's Malted Milk, Racine, Wis., Embossed, Tin Screw-On Lid, 7 In. 45.00
Hub Punch, C.H. Graves & Sons, Boston, Mass., Amber, Label, Cylindrical, Pt. 70.00
Ingrams Milk Weed Cream, Milk Glass, 1 1/4 In. 25.00
Jar, Jelly, Aqua, Paneled, OP 55.00
Jeffry's Worcestershire, Light Aqua, Stopper, Applied Top, 7 1/2 In. 35.00
Jewel Tea Vanilla, 1917 .... 75.00
Jumbo Peanut Butter, 1/2 Pt. 20.00
Jumbo Peanut Butter, 3 1/2 Oz. 50.00
Jumbo Peanut Butter, 10 1/2 Oz. 15.00
Jumbo Peanut Butter, Frank Tea & Spice Co., Cincinnati, Ohio, 5 In. ....*Illus* 25.00
Jumbo Peanut Butter, Jumbo Good Enuf For Me, Ribbed, 1 Lb. 15.00
Jumbo Peanut Butter, Pantry Jar, Handle, Contents, 2 Lb. 75.00
Jumbo Peanut Butter, Tapered, 4 Oz. 45.00
Jumbo Peanut Butter, Tapered, 5 Oz. 45.00
Kim's Pure Horseradish, Pittsburgh, Pa., Orange Paper Label, 6 In. ....*Illus* 18.00
L. Rose & Co., Lime Juice, Tapered Cylindrical, 13 In. 34.00
Lakeshore Honey, Embossed, Pressed Lid, 5 1/2 In........................6.00 to 7.50
Lea & Perrins, Worcestershire Sauce, Aqua, Crown Top, Inside Stain, 7 In. 1.00
Liquid Yeast, Beer, Cobalt Blue, Pt. 60.00
Log Cabin Syrup, Bicentennial Flask, 1776, Red, White & Blue Label, 8 In. ......*Illus* 1.00
Lucky Horseshoe Jelly, Tin Cover 8.00
Maltine Mfg. Co., Red Amber, Tooled Lip, Bubbles, Cork, 7 1/2 In. 5.00
Mammoth Selected Olives, Smith-Perkins, Rochester, N.Y., Label, 10 1/2 In. ....*Illus* 30.00
Margaret O'Brien Candy Kitchen, Lemon Flavor, Label, 1 Oz. 40.00
McCormick & Co. Spice Grinders, Baltimore, Md., Bell Shape, Screw Cap, Metal, 5 In. 15.00
Mellins Food, Free Sample, 3 1/2 In. 12.00
Mocking Bird Food, Thos. Broom, Phila., Ground Lip, Threaded 10.00
Monarch Brand Tomato Catsup, Lion's Head On Label, Unopened 20.00
Mrs. Butterworth's Syrup, Green, 8 1/4 In. 1000.00
Nash's Brand Golden Cream Mustard, Chicago, Ill., Paper Label, 7 1/2 In. .....*Illus* 10.00
Necco Sweets Candy Jar, Marked On Lid, 10 In.............................. 85.00
Olive Oil, Frank Tea Spice, Cincinnati, Stippled, Olives, 1910s, 6 3/4 In. 15.00

Food, Log Cabin Syrup, Bicentennial Flask, 1776, Red, White & Blue Label, 8 In.

Food, Mammoth Selected Olives, Smith-Perkins, Rochester, N.Y., Label, 10 1/2 In.

Food, Nash's Brand Golden Cream Mustard, Chicago, Ill., Paper Label, 7 1/2 In.

Food, Scott Co. Tomato Catsup, Austin, Ind., White & Blue Paper Label, 9 1/2 In.

Olive Oil Type, Aqua, Bubbles, Crude Lip, Cork, 9 1/2 In. 2.00
One Pound Pure Honey, Embossed Beehive 5.00
Parke Davis Orange Extract, For Soda Fountain Use, Label, Contents 40.00
Pepper Sauce, see Pepper Sauce category
Pickle, see Pickle category
Polish Honey Drink, Jug, Amber, Labels, 4 1/2 In. 10.00
Prepared Mustard, Bank, Unpunctured Coin Slot, Milk Glass 22.00
Pure Honey, Jar, Beehive, Embossed, Aqua, 2 Lbs., 8 3/4 In. 40.00
R.D. Bisbee Pure Horse Radish, Chesterfield, Mass., Light Blue, Label, 7 1/8 In. 65.00
Relish, Square, Aqua, 6 1/2 In. 10.00
Robertson Candy Co., New York, USA, Aqua, Bubbles, 1/2 Gal. 115.00
Rose's Lime Juice, Embossed Vines & Flowers, BIMAL, Crown Top, England, 7 1/2 In.   25.00
Salad Dressing, Crock, Allover Blue Sponge, Cream, Stencil, Stoneware, Qt. 250.00
Sanitas Nut Food Co., Ltd., Battle Creek, Mich., Jar, Aqua, Ground Lip 3.00
Sauce, Wm. Underwood & Co., Boston, Blue Green, 18-Sided, Pontil, 1860, 7 3/8 In. . . .   770.00
Scott Co. Tomato Catsup, Austin, Ind., White & Blue Paper Label, 9 1/2 In. . . . . .*Illus*   10.00
Snider Tomato Juice, Rochester, N.Y., Paper Label With Tomato, 5 1/2 In. . . . .*Illus*   15.00
Snyders Sour Cream, 11Pa., Jar, Embossed, ISP, Round, Pt. 12.00
Spanish Queen Olives, Bordeaux, Label Only, Oval, 6 1/2 In.   10.00
Squirrel Salted Nuts, Jar, 14 1/2 In. 450.00
Stohrers Mustard & Pickle Works, Keystone Odd Shape, Est. 1870, 8 5/8 In. 12.00
Storage, Medium Olive Amber, Applied String Lip, OP, 1750-1770, 13 3/4 In. 195.00
Storage, Medium Olive Green, Amber Tone, Applied String Lip, 1780-1800, 14 3/8 In. . .   825.00
Storage, Medium Olive Green, Wide Mouth, Sheared & Tooled Mouth, 1780-1830, 11 In.   175.00
Storage, Medium Yellow Olive Green, Amber Tone, Applied Mouth, 1855-1865, 9 In. . .   80.00
Storage, Yellow Olive Amber, Wide Mouth, Sheared Lip, Pontil, 1800-1830, 9 5/8 In. . .   175.00
Storage, Yellow Olive Green, Wide Mouth, Sheared & Tooled Lip, 1780-1830, 13 3/4 In.   120.00
Strittmatter's Pure Honey, Edensburg, Pa., Embossed Bee, Blue 65.00
Swift & Co., Chicago, Jar, Screw Band, Insert, Ground Lip, 6 3/4 In. 45.00
T.A. Bryan & Co.'s Perfection Tomato Sauce, Baltimore, Md., Amber, 1895, 8 In. . . .   130.00
The Cudahy Packing Co., Jug, Omaha, U.S.A., Stoneware, Brown, Gray, 7 1/2 In. 55.00
Trade Mills Coffees & Spices, Montreal, Figural, Drum, Light Green Aqua, Lid, 6 5/8 In.   90.00
Trader Vic's Pomegranate Grenadine Syrup, 1946, Contents, 4/5 Pt. . . . .*Illus*   15.00
Truth Brand Lemon Extract, Blackstone Co., Newark, N.J., Box, 6 In. . . . .*Illus*   15.00
Utility, Yellow Olive Green, Wide Mouth, Sheared Lip, 1780-1830, 12 In. 230.00
Virginia Dare Genuine Brandy Sauce, Brooklyn, N.Y., 6 5/8 In. . . . .*Illus*   5.00
W.K. Lewis & Co., Boston, Blue Aqua, Iron Pontil, c.1850-1860, 10 1/2 In. 305.00
W.S. Kimball, N.Y., Jar, Lid, Yellow Amber, Ground Lip 100.00
Watkins Extract Of Orange 6.00
Watkins Lemon Extract, Large 9.00
Weidmanns' Since 1870, Have Some Peanut Butter, Crock, Stoneware, Brown, Pt. 180.00
Wells Miller & Provost, Aqua, IP, Applied Mouth, 1860, 11 5/8 In. 145.00

Food, Snider Tomato Juice, Rochester, N.Y., Paper Label With Tomato, 5 1/2 In.

Food, Trader Vic's Pomegranate Grenadine Syrup, 1946, Contents, 4/5 Pt.

Food, Truth Brand Lemon Extract, Blackstone Co., Newark, N.J., Box, 6 In.

Food, Virginia Dare Genuine Brandy Sauce, Brooklyn, N.Y., 6 5/8 In.

Wells Miller & Provost, Aqua, Open Pontil, 1860, 12 In. 580.00
White Vanilla Lemon Extract 5.00
William Underwood & Company, Boston, Blue Aqua, 1865, 64 Oz, 12 5/8 In. 210.00
Y & S, Licorice Lozenges, Ground Lip, 1880-1900, 9 1/4 In. 55.00

─────────────────── **FRUIT JAR** ───────────────────

Fruit jars made of glass have been used in the United States since the 1850s. More than 1,000 different jars have been found with varieties of closures, embossing, and colors. The date 1858 on many jars refers to a patent and not the age of the bottle. Be sure to look in this listing under any name or initial that appears on your jar. If not otherwise indicated, the jar listed is of clear glass and quart size. The numbers used in the entries in the form RB-0 refer to the book *Red Book of Fruit Jars Number 8* by Douglas M. Leybourne Jr. A publication for collectors is *Fruit Jar Newsletter,* 364 Gregory Avenue, West Orange, NJ 07052-3743.

FRUIT JAR, 2-Piece Mold, Gold Amber, Wax Sealer, Qt., RB-3047 . . . .   75.00
3-Piece Mold, Aqua, Amber Striations, Wax Seal Groove, Qt., RB-2267 . . . .   470.00
A. & D.H. Chambers, Pittsburgh, Pa., On Base, Wax Sealer, Qt., RB-582 . . . .   10.00
A. Dufour & Co. Bordeaux, Barrel, Green Aqua, Pewter Lid, 1860, 1/2 Gal., RB-860 . .   385.00
A. Stone & Co., Aqua, Groove Ring Wax Sealer, Tin Lid, IP, 1845, Pt., RB-2752 . . . . . .   1045.00
A. Stone & Co., Phila, Aqua, Internal Threaded Neck, 1880, Qt., RB-2749-1 . . . .   470.00
A. Stone & Co., Philada, Aqua, Applied Mouth, 1860-1880, 1/2 Gal., RB-2747 . . . .   190.00
A. Stone & Co., Philada, Aqua, Groove Ring Wax Sealer, 1860s, Qt. Plus, RB-2743-2 . .   770.00
A. Stone & Co., Philada, Aqua, Groove Ring Wax Sealer, Pt., RB-2743 . . . . . .1045.00 to 1210.00
A. Stone & Co., Philada, Aqua, Qt., RB-2750 . . . .   750.00
A. Stone & Co., Philada, Aqua, Threaded Stopper, Cylindrical, 1/2 Gal., RB-2746 . . . . .   550.00
Acme, On Shield With Stars & Stripes, Clear, Wire Bail, 1/2 Gal., RB-12 . . . .   15.00
Agee Special, Clear, Base Groove, Pt., RB-36 . . . .   45.00
Air-Tite, Barrel, Aqua, Wax Sealer, IP, Qt. RB-51 . . . . .275.00 to 330.00
All Right, Patd. Jan 28, 1868, Aqua, Ground Lip, 1/2 Gal., RB-61 . . . .   120.00
Amazon Swift Seal, Blue, Glass Lid, Wire Clamp, Pt., RB-69 . . . .   4.00
American, Eagle & Flag, Aqua, Glass Lid, Australia, Qt., 1880, RB-73 . . . .   100.00
American Porcelain Lined, NAGCO., Blue, Lid, Qt., RB-75 . . . .   55.00
Anchor, Clear, Green Tint, Slanted Anchor, Lid, Canada, 1894-1913, Midget Pt., RB-77 .   130.00
Aqua, Qt. . . . .*Illus*   10.00
Arthur Burnham & Gilroy, Patent, Jany 2, 1855, Aqua, Wax Groove, 7 1/4 In., RB-96 .   550.00
Arthur H. Bailey & Co., Boston, U.S.A., Oval, Aqua, Tooled Mouth, Qt., RB-184-1 . . .   145.00
Atlas E-Z Seal, Aqua, 1/2 Pt., RB-121 . . . .   28.00
Atlas E-Z Seal, Aqua, Glass Lid, Wire Clamp, 1/2 Pt., RB-120 . . . .   300.00
Atlas E-Z Seal, Aqua, Glass Lid, Wire Clamp, Qt., RB-108 . . . .   5.00
Atlas E-Z Seal, Aqua, Lid, 48 Oz., RB-124 . . . .   27.00
Atlas E-Z Seal, Aqua, Qt., RB-109 . . . .   4.00
Atlas E-Z Seal, Aqua, Squat, Qt., RB-116 . . . .*Illus*   20.00
Atlas E-Z Seal, Clear, 1/2 Pt., RB-121 . . . .   10.00
Atlas E-Z Seal, Clear, Glass Lid, Wire Clamp, Qt., RB-109 . . . . .2.00 to 3.00
Atlas E-Z Seal, Light Green, Pt., RB-109 . . . .   10.00
Atlas Good Luck, Clear, Qt., RB-129-1 . . . .   20.00

Fruit Jar, Aqua, Qt.

Fruit Jar, Atlas E-Z Seal, Aqua, Squat, Qt., RB-116

Atlas Good Luck, Embossed 4-Leaf Clover, Clear, Glass Lid, Wire Clamp, Qt., RB-128   5.00
Atlas HA Mason, Clear, Zinc Screw Lid, Qt., RB-134-2 ....   4.00
Atlas Mason, Erased Whitney, Aqua, Qt., RB-144-2 ....   20.00
Atlas Mason, Nov. 30th, 1858, Aqua, Strong Shoulder, Qt., RB-154-2 ....   34.00
Atlas Special Mason, Aqua, Wide Mouth, Glass Lid, Screw Band, 1/2 Gal., RB-158 ...   6.00
Atlas Strong Shoulder Mason, Aqua, Zinc Screw Lid, Pt., RB-164 ....3.00 to 4.00
Atlas Strong Shoulder Mason, Cornflower Blue, ABM Lip, 1925, Qt., RB-164 ......   100.00
Automatic Sealer, Aqua, Wire Clamp, Pt., RB-177 ....   435.00
B.B. Wilcox, Patd March 26th, 1867, Aqua, Ground Lip, Lid, Qt., RB-3003 ....   35.00
Ball 4 Half Pint, Clear, 1/2 Pt., RB-201-8 ....10.00 to 15.00
Ball A Century Of Quality Glass, Pt., RB-345-5 ....   25.00
Ball Deluxe, Clear, Erased Pine, Qt., RB-196 ....   8.00
Ball Eclipse, Pat. 7-14-08, Clear, Pt., RB-196-5 ....   6.00
Ball Freezer Jar, Clear, Wide Mouth, Zinc Screw Lid, Pt., RB-201-3 ....   2.00
Ball Ideal, Clear, Glass Lid, Wire Clamp, Pt., RB-209-5 ....   2.00
Ball Ideal, Clear, Glass Lid, Wire Clamp, Qt., RB-213 ....2.00 to 3.00
Ball Ideal, Clear, Inverted Bosses, Qt., RB-216-5 ....35.00 to 40.00
Ball Ideal, Clear, T Shape Boss, Pt., 203-5 ....   10.00
Ball Ideal, Pat'd July 14, 1908, Blue, Wire Bail, Qt., RB-212-5 ....4.00 to 5.00
Ball Improved, Blue, Glass Lid, Zinc Band, Square, Qt., RB-223 ....   15.00
Ball Improved, Clear, Glass Lip, Zinc Band, Pt., RB-223-5 ....   10.00
Ball Improved, Erased Mason, Aqua, Glass Insert, Zinc Band, Pt., RB-222-5 ....   15.00
Ball Improved Mason, Green Aqua, Pt., RB-226-5 ....   12.00
Ball Improved Masons Patent 1858, Aqua, 3-L Loop, Zinc Lid, Qt., RB-229-7 .....   10.00
Ball Jar Mason's Patent Nov 30th 1858, Aqua, 1/2 Gal., RB-232-5 ....   35.00
Ball Mason, Bull & Bear, 1978, Pt., RB-354-5 ....   25.00
Ball Mason, Clear, Old North Bridge, Bicentennial Design, Zinc Screw Lid, Qt., RB-351   5.00
Ball Mason, Yellow Olive, Zinc Screw Lid, 1920-1930, Qt., RB-339 ....   155.00
Ball Mason Improved, 3-L Loop, Aqua, Pt., RB-249-5 ....   10.00
Ball Mason's, Patent Nov. 30th, 1858, Aqua, Zinc Screw Lid, Qt., RB-264-5 ....   5.00
Ball Pat. Apl'd For, Clear, Repro Closure, Pt., RB-327 ....   480.00
Ball Perfect Mason, Amber, 1/2 Gal., RB-345 ....   35.00
Ball Perfect Mason, Amber, Vertical Ribs, Zinc Lid, 1/2 Gal., RB-345 ....   40.00
Ball Perfect Mason, Aqua, 1/2 Gal., RB-294 ....   20.00
Ball Perfect Mason, Blue, 1/2 Gal., RB-340-1 ....   10.00
Ball Perfect Mason, Emerald Green, Qt., RB-339 ....   70.00
Ball Perfect Mason, Erased Boyd, Blue, Qt., RB-271-5 ....   10.00
Ball Perfect Mason, Erased Boyd, Light Green, Qt., RB-271-6 ....   20.00
Ball Perfect Mason, Medium Green, Qt., RB-343 ....   40.00
Ball Perfect Mason, Olive Green, 1/2 Gal., RB-274 ....   225.00
Ball Perfect Mason, Olive Green, 2 On Base, Zinc Lid, Qt., RB-339 ....   40.00
Ball Perfect Mason, Olive Green, Zinc Lid, Qt., RB-274 ....   15.00
Ball Perfect Mason, Straw Yellow, Pt., RB-339 ....   25.00
Ball R Guest House, RBCMCO., Clear, 1983, Pt., RB-367-1 ....   30.00
Ball R Mason, Harvey Croman 1946, 38 Years, 1984, Clear, Threadless, Pt., RB-353 ...   40.00
Ball Special, Clear, Beaded Neck Seal, Pt., RB-307-5 ....   15.00
Ball Special, Shoulder Seal, Blue, 1/2 Gal., RB-302 ....   50.00
Ball Square Mason, Clear, Qt., RB-313-5 ....   25.00
Ball Sure Seal, Blue, 42 Oz., RB-317 ....   30.00
Ball Sure Seal, Blue, Dated Base, 1/2 Gal., RB-318-6 ....   15.00
Ball Sure Seal, Blue, Regular Mouth Size, Pt., RB-316-5 ....15.00 to 20.00
Ball Sure Seal, Erased Sanitary, Blue, Pt., RB-317-2 ....   20.00
Banner, Pat'd Feby 9th, 1864, Deep Aqua, Glass Lid, Cylindrical, 1880, Qt., RB-403 ...   145.00
Banner Wide Mouth, Blue, Glass Lid, Wire Clamp, Qt., RB-411-2 ....   13.00
BBGMCo., Monogram, Aqua, Ball Qt., RB-196 ....   85.00
Beaver, Facing Right, Aqua, Canada, c.1894, Midget Pt., RB-424 ....   205.00
Beaver, Facing Right, Clear, Green Tint, Canada, c.1894, Imperial Qt., RB-425 ....   40.00
Beaver, Facing Right, Clear, Lid, Canada, 1894-1903, Pt., RB-424 ....   140.00
Beaver, Facing Right, Dark Aqua, Lid, Canada, 1895-1903, Imperial Qt., RB-425 ......   60.00
Beaver, Facing Right, Double Dot, Green, Lid, 1/2 Gal., RB-424 ....   75.00
Beaver, Facing Right, Orange Amber, Lid, c.1894, Qt., RB-424 ....   745.00
Beck Phillips & Co., Pitts., Pa., Aqua, 3 Raised Portions, Tin Lid, Qt., RB-427-2 ......   95.00
Bee, Aqua, 1869-1875, 1/2 Gal., RB-429 ....*Illus*   770.00

Fruit Jar, Bellerjeaus Simplicity, Patd Mar. 31st 1868, Aqua, Qt., RB-440-1; Fruit Jar, Van Vliet
Improved, Patd May 3-81, Aqua, Repro Yoke, Qt., RB-2880; Fruit Jar, Bee, Aqua, 1869-1875,
1/2 Gal., RB-429; Fruit Jar, Van Vliet Jar Of 1881, Aqua, Repro Yoke, 1/2 Gal., RB-2878;
Fruit Jar, Newman's Patent Dec. 20th 1859, Deep Aqua, Qt., RB-2240

Bee, Aqua, Ground Lip, Reproduction Closure, c.1869-1875, 1/2 Gal., RB-429 .... 770.00
Bee Hive, Aqua, ABM, Lid, Canada, c.1910, 1/2 Gal., RB-433 ....140.00 to 170.00
Bee Hive, Aqua, Lid, Canada, c.1910, Qt., RB-433 ....125.00 to 140.00
Belle, Aqua, Glass Lid, Repro Metal Band & Wire Bail, Qt., RB-438-1 .... 360.00
Belle, Pat. Dec. 14th, 1869, Aqua, Metal Lid, Qt., RB-438 .... 975.00
Bellerjeaus Simplicity, Patd Mar. 31st 1868, Aqua, Qt., RB-440-1 ....*Illus* 798.00
Best, Amber, Glass Lid, Screw Band, Cylindrical, Canada, 1900, Qt., RB-453 ....220.00 to 325.00
Best, Green Aqua, Rayed Base, No Lid, Canada, 1/2 Gal., RB-454 .... 6.00
Best, Orange To Chocolate Amber, Ground Lip, Lid, Screw Band, Qt., RB-453 .... 315.00
Best Jar Pat. Pend., Light Green, Glass Lid, 1/2 Gal., RB-463 .... 470.00
Bloeser Jar, Aqua, Wire Clamp, Qt., RB-468 .... 275.00
Blown, Bell Shape, Aqua, Groove Ring, Wax Sealer, Qt., RB-3061-2 .... 3300.00
Boyd Perfect Mason, Light Green, Zinc Screw Lid, Qt., RB-500 .... 10.00
Boyds Perfect Mason, Blue, 1/2 Gal., RB-501 .... 15.00
Buckeye 1, Apple Green, Glass Lid, Iron Yoke Clamp, 1/2 Gal., RB-528 .... 825.00
Burlington, B.C.Go., R'd 1875, Clear, Error, Canada, Qt., RB-539 .... 95.00
C.F. Spencers Patd. 1868, Improvedaqua, Qt., RB-2685 .... 365.00
CFJ Co., see Fruit Jar, Mason's CFJ Co.
Champion, Pat. Aug. 31 1869, Aqua, Iron Yoke Clamp, Qt., RB-583 ....175.00 to 325.00
Clarke Fruit Jar Co., Cleveland, Ohio, Aqua, Striations, Glass Lid, Bail, 1/2 Gal., RB-603 155.00
Cleveland Fruit Juice Co., On Base, Clear, Glass Lid, 1/2 Gal., RB-608 .... 5.00
Clyde, In Script, Clear, Lightning Seal, Pt., RB-619 .... 40.00
Cohansey, Barrel, Aqua, Wax Sealer, Qt., RB-633-1 .... 100.00
Cohansey Echo Farm, Aqua, Glass Lid, Circular Wire Clamp, 1/2 Pt., RB-627 .... 825.00
Cohansey Glass Mfg. Co., Pat. Mch 20 '77, Barrel, Aqua, Ring Wax Sealer, RB-633 ... 100.00
Cohansey Glass Mfg. Co., Pat. Mch 20 '77, Barrel, Blue Aqua, 1890, Qt., RB-633 ..... 80.00
Columbia, Aqua, Wire Clamp, Pt., RB-638 .... 25.00
Compton Batchelder, Cleveland, O., Aqua, Tin Lid, 1875-1895, Qt., RB-651 .... 230.00
Cross Mason's Patent Nov. 30th 1858, Yellow Amber, Zinc Lid, 1895, Qt., RB-1938 230.00
Cunningham & Co., Pittsburgh, Pa., Aqua, Red IP, 1855-1865, Pt., RB-722 .... 1210.00
Daisy Jar, Clear, Metal Clamp, Qt., RB-745 ....265.00 to 275.00
Decker's Iowana, Mason City, Iowa, Pat.'d July 14, 1908, Clear, Clamp, Qt., RB-760 .. 50.00
Doolittle, Pat. Dec. 3, 1901, Swirls, ABM, Lid, Canada, Pt., RB-810 ....20.00 to 35.00
Double Safety, Clear, Glass Lid, Wire Clamp, Pt., RB-816 .... 2.00
Down On The Farm Preserves, C.W. Rodefer Co., Shadyside, Ohio, Stoneware, Qt. .. 160.00
E. Bennett's Patent Dec. 2 1856, Yellowware, Wax Sealer, Stamped Lid, Qt., RB-446 305.00
E.C. Flaccus Co., Clear, Deer & Flowers, Pt., RB-1016 .... 115.00
E.C. Flaccus Co., Milk Glass, Lid, Metal Band, Ground Lip, 1890, Pt., RB-1016 . .350.00 to 415.00
Eagle, Aqua, Applied Groove Ring, Glass Lid, Iron Yoke, Clamp, 1870, Qt., RB-872 ..... 120.00
Eagle, Aqua, Embossed, Iron Yoke, Clamp, 1/2 Gal., RB-872 ....165.00 to 175.00
Eagle, Reisd. June 16th, 1868, Aqua, Groove Ring, Lid, Iron, Yoke, Clamp, Qt., RB-873 . 155.00

Eclipse, Aqua, Tin Lid, 1875-1895, Qt., RB-884 .... 50.00
Electric Fruit Jar, Globe, Aqua, Ground Lip, Glass Lid, Metal Closure, Qt., RB-921 ... 120.00
Electric Fruit Jar, Globe, Aqua, Qt., RB-922 .... 100.00
Electric Fruit Jar, Globe, Aqua, Wire Clamp, Qt., RB-922-1 .... 170.00
Electric Trademark, Aqua, Lid, Pt., RB-916 .... 25.00
Empire, Aqua, Applied Mouth, Iron Stopple, 1860-1865, Qt., RB-924 .... 660.00
Empire, Deep Green Aqua, Glass Lid, Metal Yoke Lever Clamp, Qt., RB-927 .... 230.00
Erie Fruit Jar, E In Hexagon, Aqua, Ground Lip, Lid, 1/2 Gal., RB-941 .... 240.00
Eskay's Albumenized Food, Pat. July 11th, 1893, Label, Amber, Contents, Pt., RB-944 40.00
Eureka, Clear, Metal Clamp, Pt. Plus, RB-947 .... 20.00
Excelsior Improved, 1, Aqua, Light Swirls, Ground Lipcanada, 1/2 Gal., RB-959 ..... 45.00
F.A. & Co., Aqua, Square Collar, IP, 1/2 Gal., RB-968-2 .... 175.00
F.B. Co., Amber, Grove In Wax Sealer, 1870-1885, Qt., RB-987 .... 155.00
F.C.G.Co., Citron, Tin Lid, Wax Seal Groove, 1875-1895, 1/2 Gal., RB-988 .... 330.00
F.H. Co., Yellow Olive, Grove In Wax Sealer, 1870-1885, Qt., RB-987 .... 415.00
Federal Fruit Jar, Pale Yellow Green, Flag, Glass Lid, Wire Bail, Australia, Qt., RB-996 75.00
Flaccus Bros. Steers Head Fruit Jar, Amber, Ground Lip, 1910, Pt., RB-1014 ...... 355.00
Flaccus Bros. Steers Head Fruit Jar, Clear, Lid, RB-1014 .... 30.00
Flaccus Bros. Steers Head Fruit Jar, Yellow Amber, RB-1013 .... 350.00
Foster, see Fruit Jar, Sealfast
Fridley & Cornman's Patent Oct. 25th 1859, Ladies Choice, Aqua, 1/2 Gal., RB-1038 1500.00
Friedley & Cornman's Patent Oct. 25th 1859, Aqua, 1859-1870, 1/2 Gal., RB-1039 1320.00
Frisco A-1 Trade Mark, Aqua, Glass Lid, Wire Bail, Australia, 1/2 Gal., RB-1040 ..... 175.00
Galloway's Everlasting Jar, Patd. Feb. 8th. 1870, Stoneware, 1/2 Gal., RB-1045 ...... 90.00
Gem, Clear, Ground Lip Insert, Screw Band, Midget Pt., RB-1053 .... 35.00
Gilberds Improved Jar, Aqua, Ground Lip, 1890, Qt., RB-1108 .... 165.00
Glass Bros. & Co., London, Ont., Pat'd. July 1897, Stoneware, Brown, Lid, Qt., RB-1118 70.00
Globe, Aqua, Repro Lever, Pt., RB-1124 .... 35.00
Globe, Aqua, Wire & Iron Clamp, 1/2 Gal., RB-1124 .... 35.00
Globe, Aqua, Wire & Iron Clamp, Qt., RB-1124 .... 28.00
Globe, Orange Amber, Iron Clamp, Pt. 125.00
Globe, Yellow Amber, Glass Lid, Wire & Iron Clamp, Qt., RB-1123 ....100.00 to 130.00
Glocker Trademark Sanitary Pat. 1911 Others Pending, Aqua, Qt., RB-1126 .... 85.00
Griffen's Patent Oct. 7 1862, Aqua, Iron Cage-Like Clamp, Qt., RB-1154 ... 155.00
Griswold's, Fluid Or Dry Sealing, Adjustable By Atmospheric Pressure, Qt., RB-1156 ... 4400.00
Haine's Improved N E Plus Ultra, Aqua, 1/2 Gal., RB-1173 .... 450.00
Haines Combination, Aqua, Applied Mouth, Glass Lid, Cylindrical, Qt., RB-1190 .... 90.00
Hamilton Glass Works, Aqua, Clamp, 1/2 Gal., RB-1199 .... 325.00
Hamilton Glass Works, Aqua, Metal Lid, Canada, 1880s, Quart, RB-1190 .....215.00 to 360.00
Hamilton Glass Works, Cornflower Blue, Glass Lid, Iron Clamp, Qt., RB-1190 ...... 320.00
Hamilton No. 3 Glass Works, Aqua, Haze, Canada, 1/2 Gal., RB-1195 .... 395.00
Hamilton No. 4 Glass Works, Aqua, Clamp, Canada, 1/2 Gal., RB-1197 .... 875.00
Hartell's, Pat. Oct. 19 1858, Blue Green, Ground Lip, Glass Lid, Pt., RB-1211-1 .... 255.00
Helme's Railroad Mills, Amber, Lid, 1 1/2 Pt., RB-1235 .... 42.00
Hero Cross, see Fruit Jar, Mason's Cross
Honest Mason Jar, Pat. 1858, SCA, Lid, Pt., RB-1264 .... 33.00
Ideal, Aqua, Screw Band, Midget Pt., RB-1280 .... 45.00
Ideal Imperial Qt., Aqua, Swirls, Bubbles, Ground Lip, Canada, c.1893, RB-1282 .... 15.00
Imperial, Pat. April 20th, 1886, Aqua, Vertical Panels, Clear Lid, Qt., RB-1295 .... 65.00
Improved Standard, Pat. April 17th, 1888, Aqua, Wax Sealer, Tin Lid, Qt., RB-1307 .. 495.00
Indicator, Aqua, Ground Lip, 2-Piece Metal Closure, 1870-1880, Qt., RB-1313 .... 690.00
J. & B. Fruit Jar, Pat'd June 14th 1898, Aqua, Qt., RB-1321 .... 50.00
J.C. Baker's, Patent Aug. 14, 1860, Aqua, Ground Mouth, 1/2 Gal., RB-188 .... 495.00
J.E. Taylor & Co. Pure Food, Santa Ana, Cal., Aqua, Glass Lid, Qt., RB-2787 .... 25.00
J.T. Kinney, Trenton, N.J., Aqua, A. Kline Stopper, Applied Mouth, Qt., RB-1420 .90.00 to 210.00
Jeanette Mason Home Packer, J In Box Insignia, Glass Lid, Screw Band, Qt., RB-1324 8.00
Johnson & Johnson, New York, Amber, Ground Top, Qt., RB-1342 .... 30.00
K Stark Jar, Patented, Clear, K In Star, Qt., RB-2730 .... 100.00
K.Y.G.W., Aqua, Groove Ring, Wax Sealer, 1/2 Gal., RB-1446 .... 15.00
Kerr Self Sealing Mason, 65th Anniversary, 1903-1968, Blue Streaked, Qt., RB-1387 .. 45.00
Kerr Self Sealing Mason, Amber, 2 Piece Metal Lid, Qt., RB-1386 ....20.00 to 45.00
Kerr Self Sealing Mason, U.S. Bicentennial, Milk Glass, Set Of 3, RB-1389 .... 250.00
Kerr Self Sealing Trademark Reg. Patented Mason, Chicago, Qt., RB-1371 .60.00 to 100.00

King, On Banner, Clear, Oval, Qt., RB-1414 .... 15.00
King, Pat. Nov. 2 1860, Aqua, Glass Lid, Metal Clamp, 1870, Qt., RB-1418 .... 275.00
King, Pat. Nov. 2 1869, Aqua, Glass Lid, Iron Yoke Clamp, Qt., RB-1418 .... 110.00
Knowlton Vacuum Fruit Jar, Olive Green, Glass Lid, Zinc Cover, Qt., RB-1432 ..... 110.00
Knowlton Vacuum Fruit Jar, Star, Blue, Lid, Qt., RB-1432 ....35.00 to 45.00
Knox K Mason, Clear, Bail Handle, Square, 1/2 Gal., RB-1435-5 .... 30.00
Knox K Mason, Clear, Glass Lid, 1/2 Pt., RB-1436 .... 20.00
L & W, Manufactured For Rice & Burnett, Cleveland, Qt., RB-1529 ....195.00 to 305.00
L.G. Co., Amber, Wax Sealer, 1870-1885, 1/2 Gal., RB-1482 .... 75.00
L.G. Co., Aqua, Wax Sealer, Qt., RB-1482 .... 20.00
La Lorraine, Thistle, Green Aqua, Glass Lid, Metal Clamp Closure, Liter, RB-1453 .... 85.00
Lafayette, Aqua, Ground Lip, 3-Piece Glass, Metal Closure, 1880-1890, Qt., RB-1450 .. 1265.00
Lafayette, Aqua, Metal Stopper, Qt., RB-1452 .... 140.00
Lafayette, Aqua, Patented Sept. 2 1884, Applied Mouth, Qt., RB-1452 ....55.00 to 135.00
Le Parfait, Clear, Glass Lid, Locking Wire Clamp, France, 7 1/2 Liter, RB-1480-4 ..... 35.00
Leotric, Erased, Aqua, Qt., RB-1477-1 .... 10.00
Longlife Mason, Amber, Fruit Medallion, Qt., RB-1515 .... 10.00
Ludlow's Patent June 28, 1859, Aqua, Glass Lid, Metal Closure, 1/2 Gal., RB-1546 . 185.00
Lynchburg Standard Mason, Aqua, Qt., RB-1594............................... 20.00
M G M Co., Monogram, Clear, 1/2 Gal., RB-2171 .... 275.00
M.F.J. Co. 8, Aqua, Wax Sealer, Lid, Qt., RB-2168 .... 15.00
M.G. Co., Aqua, B On Base, Wax Sealer, Qt., RB-2170 .... 20.00
Macomb Pottery Co., Pat. Jan. 24, 1899, Stoneware, White, 1/2 Pt., RB-1601 .... 40.00
Macomb Pottery Co., Pat. Jan. 24, 1899, Stoneware, White, Qt., RB-1602 .... 30.00
Made In Canada, Crown, Clear, 12 Jewels, Pt., RB-695 .... 5.00
Made In Canada, Perfect Seal Adjustable, Yellow, Bubbles, Clear Lid, Qt., RB-2239 ... 100.00
Magic Fruit Jar, Star, Amber, Wire Clamp, 1/2 Gal., RB-1606 .... 975.00
Magic Fruit Jar, Wm.McCully & Co., Pittsburgh, Pa., June 6th, 1866, Aqua, Qt., RB-1607 975.00
Mankley & Cartwright, East Liverpool, Ohio, Pottery, Wax Sealer 250.00
Mansfield, Glass W'K's., Knowlton's, May '03, c.1903-1910, Qt., RB-1619 .... 330.00
Manufactured For N.O. Fansler, Cleveland, O., Aqua, Kline Stopper, 1880, Qt., RB-977 175.00
Mason, Clear, Liberty Bell, 1776 1976, Clear, Tin Lid, Screw Band, Qt., RB-1654 ...... 4.00
Mason, Light To Medium Yellow Green, Zinc Screw Lid, 1885-1900, RB-1642 .... 95.00
Mason, Shepherd's Crook, Clear, 1/2 Gal., RB-1633 ....10.00 to 12.00
Mason Jar Of 1858, Aqua, Qt., RB-1749 .... 50.00
Mason Keystone, Aqua, Lid, Qt., RB-1737 .... 32.00
Mason's, Amber, Ground Lip, Zinc Lid, 1875-1895, Pt., RB-1641 .... 190.00
Mason's, Amber, Smooth Lip, Zinc Screw Lid, 1910-1920, Pt., RB-1641 .... 65.00
Mason's 1 Patent Nov. 30th 1858, Aqua, Crowleytown, Zinc Lid, Pt., RB-1771 .... 1275.00
Mason's 2 Patent Nov. 30th 1858, Aqua, 1/2 Gal., RB-2030 .... 10.00
Mason's 3 Patent Nov. 30th 1858, Aqua, Qt., RB-2037 .... 5.00
Mason's 24 Patent Nov. 30th 1858, Aqua, Qt., RB-2030 .... 20.00
Mason's 31 Patent Nov. 30th 1858, Aqua, Qt., RB-2113 .... 40.00
Mason's CFJCo, Pat. Nov. 30th, 1858, 214 On Base, Light Olive Green, Pt., RB-1920 ... 30.00
Mason's CFJCo, Pat. Nov. 30th, 1858, Yellow Olive Green, Zinc Lid, Qt., RB-1920 ..... 715.00
Mason's CFJCo, Patent Nov. 30th 1858, Aqua, 1/2 Gal., RB-1920 .... 10.00
Mason's CFJCo, Patent Nov. 30th, 1858, Light Yellow Olive, Zinc Lid, Qt., RB-1920 ... 155.00
Mason's CFJCo. Improved, Amber, Hero Glass Works Lid, 1/2 Gal., RB-1723 .... 195.00
Mason's CFJCo. Improved, Aqua, Midget Pt., RB-1725 ....25.00 to 35.00
Mason's CFJCo. Improved, G-346 On Base, Aqua, Wire Clamp, Midget Pt., RB-1711 .. 20.00
Mason's CFJCo. Improved, Patent Nov. 30th 1858, Aqua, Midget Pt., RB-1818-1 .... 45.00
Mason's CFJCo. Improved, Red Amber, Ground Lip, 1875-1885, 1/2 Gal., RB-1711 .... 230.00
Mason's Cross Patent Nov. 30th 1858, Amber, Embossed, 1/2 Gal., RB-1939 ...... 165.00
Mason's Cross Patent Nov. 30th 1858, Amber, Qt., RB-1939 .... 150.00
Mason's Cross Patent Nov. 30th 1858, Amber, Zinc Lid, 1875-1895, Qt., RB-1939 .. 155.00
Mason's Cross Patent Nov. 30th 1858, Aqua, Embossed, Gal., RB-1942 .... 1500.00
Mason's Cross Patent Nov. 30th 1858, Aqua, Lid, Seed Bubbles, 1/2 Gal., RB-1939 . 27.00
Mason's Cross Patent Nov. 30th 1858, Aqua, Pt., RB-1939 ....8.00 to 15.00
Mason's Cross Patent Nov. 30th 1858, Aqua, Seed Bubbles, Zinc Lid, Qt., RB-1940 12.00
Mason's Cross Patent Nov. 30th 1858, Aqua, Zinc Lid, 1875-1890, Pt., RB-1939 ... 90.00
Mason's Cross Patent Nov. 30th 1858, Clear, Lid, 1/2 Gal., RB-1939 .... 26.00
Mason's Cross Patent Nov. 30th 1858, Yellow Green, Zinc Lid, RB-1934 .... 880.00
Mason's Crystal, Clear, Ground Lip, Zinc Screw Lid, 1875-1890, Pt., RB-1846 .... 145.00

Mason's Improved, Aqua, Screw Band, Midget Pt., RB-1724 .... 25.00
Mason's Improved, Cross, Apple Green, Lid, Qt., RB-1723 .... 100.00
Mason's Improved, Cross, Aqua, Lid, 1/2 Gal., RB-1723 .... 24.00
Mason's Improved, Erased Mascot, Amber, 1/2 Gal., RB-1695 .... 150.00
Mason's Improved, Fluting Shoulder & Base, Zinc Screw Band, 1900, Qt., RB-1695-1 . 330.00
Mason's Improved, Light Yellow Amber, Glass Lid, Zinc Band, 1/2 Gal., RB-1695 .... 120.00
Mason's Improved, Reverse CFGCo., Aqua, Lid, Qt., RB-1709 .... 28.00
Mason's Improved, Sky Blue, Glass Lid, Zinc Band, Qt., RB-1701 .... 935.00
Mason's Keystone, Pale Blue Green, Zinc Lid & Band, Qt., RB-1737 .... 880.00
Mason's KGBCo Patent Nov. 30th 1858, Clear, 1/2 Gal., RB-1958 .... 30.00
Mason's MFJ Patent Nov. 30th 1858, Green Aqua, Zinc Lid, Australia, Qt., RB-1971 . 65.00
Mason's N Patent Nov. 30th 1858, Aqua, Qt., RB-2009-1 .... 35.00
Mason's Patent 1858, Light Green, 1/2 Gal., RB-1766-1 .... 50.00
Mason's Patent 1858, Port On Reverse, Aqua, Qt., RB-1767..................... 10.00
Mason's Patent 1858, Port On Reverse, Aqua, Zinc Screw Lid, 1/2 Gal., RB-1767 .... 8.00
Mason's Patent Nov. 30th 1858, Amber, Qt., RB-1787 .... 125.00
Mason's Patent Nov. 30th 1858, Aqua, Lid, 1/2 Gal., RB-1787 .... 26.00
Mason's Patent Nov. 30th 1858, Aqua, Zinc Screw Lid, Qt., RB-1911-3 .... 5.00
Mason's Patent Nov. 30th 1858, Ball Mason Reverse, Aqua, 1/2 Gal., RB-1845-1 ... 30.00
Mason's Patent Nov. 30th 1858, Ball Underlined On Reverse, Aqua, Qt., RB-1815 .. 20.00
Mason's Patent Nov. 30th 1858, Christmas, Aqua, Pt., RB-1782-2 .... 100.00
Mason's Patent Nov. 30th 1858, Citron, Ground Lip, Zinc Screw Lid, Pt., RB-1836 .. 415.00
Mason's Patent Nov. 30th 1858, Clear, 1/2 Gal., RB-1787 .... 10.00
Mason's Patent Nov. 30th 1858, DuPont Reverse, Aqua, Zinc Lid, 1/2 Gal., RB-1848 415.00
Mason's Patent Nov. 30th 1858, Gold Yellow, Zinc Depressor Lid, 1/2 Gal., RB-1875 2530.00
Mason's Patent Nov. 30th 1858, Green, Amber Striations, 1920, 1/2 Gal, RB-1787 .. 360.00
Mason's Patent Nov. 30th 1858, Green Aqua, Ground Lip, 1/2 Gal., RB-1773 ...... 100.00
Mason's Patent Nov. 30th 1858, Green Aqua, Ground Mouth, 1/2 Gal., RB-1773 .... 100.00
Mason's Patent Nov. 30th 1858, Keystone In Circle, Amber, Lid, 1/2 Gal., RB-1964 . 360.00
Mason's Patent Nov. 30th 1858, Keystone In Circle, Aqua, Lid, 1/2 Gal., RB-1964 .. 36.00
Mason's Patent Nov. 30th 1858, Keystone In Circle, Aqua, Midget Pt., RB-1964 .... 45.00
Mason's Patent Nov. 30th 1858, Light Yellow Amber, Zinc Band, 1/2 Gal., RB-1784 . 415.00
Mason's Patent Nov. 30th 1858, Light Yellow Citron, Zinc Lid, Pt., RB-1787 ...... 185.00
Mason's Patent Nov. 30th 1858, Light Yellow Citron, Zinc Lid, Pt., RB-1941 ...... 1075.00
Mason's Patent Nov. 30th 1858, Medium Yellow Green, Pt., RB-1875 .... 80.00
Mason's Patent Nov. 30th 1858, P.B. On Base, Clear, Qt., RB-1892 .... 15.00
Mason's Patent Nov. 30th 1858, Pat. Nov. 26 67, Aqua, Zinc Lid, Midget Pt., RB-1890 20.00
Mason's Patent Nov. 30th 1858, Teal Blue, Flattened Emblem, Qt., RB-1787 .... 250.00
Mason's Patent Nov. 30th 1858, Tudor Rose, Aqua, Immerser Lid, RB-1875 .... 230.00
Mason's SGCo Patent Nov. 30th 1858, Apple Green, Qt., RB-1974 .... 45.00
Mason's SGCo Patent Nov. 30th 1858, Iridescent Aqua, 1/2 Gal., RB-1974 .... 15.00
Mastodon, T.A. Evans & Co., Aqua, Groove Ring Wax Sealer, Tin Lid, Qt., RB-2135 ... 80.00
McDonald New Perfect, Aqua, Glass Lid, Wire Clamp, Pt., RB-2147-1 .... 6.00
Medford Preserved Fruit, Buffalo, N.Y., Aqua, 1/2 Gal., RB-2163 ....120.00 to 195.00
Millville Atmospheric, Blue Aqua, Wax Grove, Glass Lid, Metal Yoke, Qt., RB-2181 .. 55.00
Millville Atmospheric, Whitall's Patent June 18th, 1861, Aqua, Pt., RB-2181 .....75.00 to 85.00
Millville Atmospheric, Whitall's Patent June 18th, 1861, Aqua, Pt., RB-2182 .... 45.00
Mom's Mason Jar, Home Products, Columbus, Ohio, Clear, Woman, Lid, Qt., RB-2198 . 5.00
Moore's, Patent Dec. 3 1861, Aqua, Applied Mouth, 1860-1870, Qt., RB-2204 .... 130.00
Myers Test Jar, Aqua, Glass Lid, Brass Strap Type Clamp, 1870-1890, Qt., RB-2218 ... 255.00
NE Plus Ultra Air Tight, Bodine & Bros., Wms' Town, N.J., Aqua, 1/2 Gal., RB-475 .. 1000.00
New Paragon, Aqua, Metal Band, 1/2 Gal., RB-2289 .... 225.00
New Paragon 3, Aqua, Ground Lip, Glass Insert, 1870, 1/2 Gal., RB-2290 .... 210.00
Newman's Patent Dec. 20th 1859, Deep Aqua, Qt., RB-2240 ....*Illus* 358.00
Ohio No. 11 Jelly, Ohio Fruit Jar Co. Of Upper Sandusky, Ohio, 1/2 Pt., RB-2261-1 ... 100.00
Ohio Quality Mason, Clear, 1/2 Gal., RB-2263 .... 15.00
P.J. Smyth & Co., Holly Springs, Miss., Stoneware, Cream, 1880-1900, 8 3/4 In. 40.00
Pansy, Erased Best, Aqua, Screw Band, Canada, 1890s, 1/2 Gal., 6 In., RB-2287 .... 195.00
Patent Sept. 18, 1860, Aqua, Qt., RB-2295 .... 120.00
Patented May 12 1863, Blue Aqua, Tin Lid, 1875-1895, 1/2 Gal., RB-2857 .... 303.00
Peoria Pottery, Brown Bennington Type Glaze, Wax Sealer, 7 1/4 In., RB-2329 ...... 35.00
Peoria Pottery, Brown, Groove Ring Wax Sealer, 1/2 Gal., RB-2329 .... 25.00
Petal, Aqua, Applied Mouth, IP, Qt., RB-3067 .... 210.00

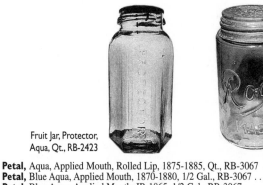

Fruit Jar, Protector,
Aqua, Qt., RB-2423

Fruit Jar, Root
Mason, Aqua, Pt.,
RB-2510

Petal, Aqua, Applied Mouth, Rolled Lip, 1875-1885, Qt., RB-3067	55.00
Petal, Blue Aqua, Applied Mouth, 1870-1880, 1/2 Gal., RB-3067	120.00
Petal, Blue Aqua, Applied Mouth, IP, 1865, 1/2 Gal., RB-3067	360.00
Petal, Blue Aqua, Applied Mouth, IP, 1865, Qt., RB-3067	305.00
Petal, Cobalt Blue, Red IP, 1850-1860, Qt., RB-3067	1210.00
Petal, Emerald Green, Applied Mouth, IP, Qt., RB-3067	1320.00
Petal, Medium Olive Green, Applied Mouth, Red IP, Qt., RB-3067	1485.00
Petal, Olive Green, Applied Mouth, IP, 1865, 1/2 Gal., RB-3067	2860.00
Petal, Wheaton Glassworks, Millville, N.J., Glass Lid, 1966, 1/2 Pt.	40.00
Pint Standard, Aqua, Groove Ring Wax Sealer, Pt., RB-2368	50.00
Pomona Immerser Fruit Jar, Aqua, Immerser Lid, Australia, Qt., RB-2371-2	350.00
Potter & Bodine Philada, Aqua, Qt., RB-2386	275.00
Potter & Bodine's Air-Tight Fruit Jar Philada, Aqua, 1860-1880, 1/2 Gal., RB-2383 .	385.00
Potter & Bodine's Air-Tight Fruit Jar Philada, Aqua, Tin Lid, 1880, Pt., RB-2383 . .	440.00
Potter & Bodine's Air-Tight Fruit Jar Philada, Barrel, Aqua, 1/2 Gal., RB-2386	185.00
Potter & Bodine's Air-Tight Fruit Jar Philada, Barrel, Aqua, 1/2 Gal., RB-2388	1595.00
Potter & Bodine's Air-Tight Fruit Jar Philada, Barrel, Aqua, OP, Pt., RB-2386	1500.00
Potter & Bodine's Air-Tight Fruit Jar Philada, Barrel, Aqua, OP, Qt., RB-2287	575.00
Potter & Bodine's Air-Tight Fruit Jar Philada, Barrel, Aqua, 1865, Qt., RB-2388 . . .	330.00
Protector, Aqua, 6-Sided, Ground Lip, Metal Lid, c.1885-1895, Qt., RB-2421	165.00
Protector, Aqua, Ground Mouth, Metal Lid, 1860-1880, Qt., RB-2420	80.00
Protector, Aqua, Qt., RB-2423 . . . . *Illus*	45.00
Put On Rubber Before Filling, Mrs. S.T. Rorer's, Star & Moon, Aqua, Qt., RB-2728 . .	440.00
Putnam, Amber, Lid, 1/2 Gal., RB-1492	75.00
Queen, Aqua, 1/2 Gal., RB-2433	35.00
Queen, Patented Nov. 2, 1868, Error, Aqua, Qt., RB-2433	25.00
Queensland, Pineapple, Light Green, Wire Bail, 1/2 Gal.	175.00
Quick Seal In Circle, Clear, Lid, Wire Clamp, Pt., RB-2451	7.00
R.M. Dalbey Fruit Jar, Pat. Nov. 16, 1858, Blue Aqua, Qt., RB-747	350.00
Railroad, see Fruit Jar, Helme's	
Robert Arthur's Patent 2nd Jan. 1855, Burham & Gilroy, Pottery, Qt., RB-98 .70.00 to 100.00	
Root Mason, Aqua, Pt., RB-2510 . . . . *Illus*	8.00
Root Mason, Aqua, Zinc Lid, Qt., RB-2510 . . . . .5.00 to 8.00	
Royal Trademark Full Measure Quart, Clear, Crown, Glass Lid, Qt., RB-2516 . . . .7.00 to 8.00	
S Mason's Patent 1858, Clear, 1/2 Gal., RB-1770	9.00
Safety, Amber, Wire Clamp, Qt., RB-2534	235.00
Safety Valve Patd May 21, 1895, HC, Aqua, Glass Lid, Metal Clamp, 1/2 Gal, RB-2539	50.00
San Francisco Glass Works, Blue Aqua, Groove Ring Wax Sealer, Qt., RB-2553	220.00
Schaffer Jar Rochester, N.Y., JCS Monogram, Aqua, Fin Glass Lid, 1/2 Gal., RB-2562	305.00
Sealfast, Foster, Clear, Glass Lid, Wire Clamp, Qt., RB-2581	6.00
Sherwood Pat. Applied For, On Glass Lid, Stoneware, White, Qt., RB-2623	20.00
SKO Improved Queen, Clear, Twin Side Toggle, 1/2 Pt., RB-2437-1	25.00
Smalley's Nu-Seal Trademark, In Diamond, Clear, Pt., RB-2657	15.00
Solidex In Oval, Light Green, Embossed Hinged Glass Lid, France, 1 1/2 Liter, RB-2678	30.00
Standard, Aqua, Groove Ring Wax Sealer, Qt., RB-2700	75.00
Standard, Blue Aqua, Groove Ring Wax Sealer, Tin Lid, 1895, 1/2 Gal., RB-2700-1	40.00
Standard, W. McC & Co., Amber, Groove Ring Wax Sealer, Tin Lid, Qt., RB-2701	470.00
Standard, W. McC & Co., Light To Medium Cobalt Blue, Tin Lid, Qt., RB-2701	855.00

Standard, W. McC & Co., Sky Blue, Tin Lid, Qt., RB-2701 . . . . 90.00
Star, Circled By Fruits, Aqua, Zinc Lid, Canada, Qt., RB-2724 . . . . 325.00
Star, Curled R, 6, Clear, Green Tint, Lid, Canada, c.1890, Qt., RB-2719 . . . . .35.00 to 45.00
Star & Crescent Self-Sealing Jar, Aqua, Zinc Press-Down Lid, 1900, Qt., RB-2727 . . . 470.00
Star Glass Co., New Albany, Ind., Aqua, Groove Ring Wax Sealer, Qt., RB-2729 . . . . . . 35.00
Star Glass Co., New Albany, Ind., Green Aqua, Groove Wax Sealer, Qt., RB-2729 . . . . . 65.00
Steer's Head, see Fruit Jar, Flaccus Bros.
Sterling Mason, Clear, Beaded Neck Seal, Zinc Screw Lid, Pt., RB-2735 . . . . 3.00
Stevens Tin Top, Pat'd July 27 1875, Aqua, Tin Lid, 1875-1895, Qt., RB-2739 . . . . 55.00
Stevens Tin Top, Pat'd July 27 1875, Aqua, Tin Lid, 1880-1895, Qt., RB-2741 . . . . 70.00
Stone Mason, Union Stoneware Co., Red Wing, Min., Stoneware, Lid, 1/2 Gal., RB-2754 275.00
Stone Mason, Union Stoneware Co., Red Wing, Min., Stoneware, Lid, Qt., RB-2754 . . . 200.00
Sun, Aqua, Ground Mouth, Glass Lid, 1870-1890, Qt., RB-2761-1 . . . . 140.00
Sun Trademark, J.P. Barstow, Aqua, Glass Lid, Metal Yoke Clamp, Qt., RB-2761 . . . . . 100.00
Sure Seal Made For L. Bamberger & Co., Blue, Pt., RB-401-2 . . . . 12.00
Swayzee's Improved Mason, Aqua, Pt., RB-2780 . . . . 8.00
Swayzee's Improved Mason, Aqua, Zinc Screw Lid, Qt., RB-2780-1 . . . . 6.00
Swayzee's Improved Mason, Light Green, Pt., RB-2780 . . . . 35.00
T.W. Beach Fruit Grower, Aqua, Cork, 6 In., RB-421-2 . . . . 28.00
Trademark Advance, JW Monogram, Pat. Apld. For, Aqua, Glass Lid, Wire, Qt., RB-27 415.00
Trademark Climax Registered, Clear, 1/2 Pt., RB-612-1 . . . . 75.00
Trademark Lightning, Amber, Lid, Qt., RB-1489 . . . . 55.00
Trademark Lightning, Aqua, Embossed, 1/2 Gal., RB-1490 . . . . 250.00
Trademark Lightning, Aqua, Glass Lid, Wire Clamp, Pt., RB-1489 . . . . 10.00
Trademark Lightning, Citron, Ground Mouth, Glass Lid, 1880-1900, Pt., RB-1489 . . . . 495.00
Trademark Lightning, Cornflower Blue, ABM Lip, 1920, 1/2 Gal., RB-1501 . . . . 145.00
Trademark Lightning, H.W.P. Monogram, Clear, Embossed, Qt., RB-1500 . . . . 175.00
Trademark Lightning, H.W.P. On Reverse, Aqua, Qt., RB-1500 . . . . 325.00
Trademark Lightning, H.W.P., Aqua, 48 On Base, Qt., RB-1498 . . . . 50.00
Trademark Lightning, H.W.P., Yellow Amber, 1/2 Gal., RB-1500 . . . . 175.00
Trademark Lightning, Honey Amber, Qt., RB-1489 . . . . .95.00 to 140.00
Trademark Lightning, M On Base, Clear, Ground Top, Australia, 1/2 Gal., RB-1507 . . . 125.00
Trademark Lightning, Olive Yellow, Glass Lid, 1800-1900, Qt., RB-1489 . . . . .185.00 to 210.00
Trademark Lightning, Reg. U.S. Pat. Office, Cornflower Blue, Lid, Qt., RB-1501-1 . . . 240.00
Trademark Lightning, Reg. U.S. Patent Office, Cornflower Blue, 1/2 Gal., RB-1501 . . . 375.00
Trademark Lightning, Registered U.S. Patent Office, Blue Aqua, Qt., RB-1502 . . . . . . 4.00
Trademark Lightning, Straw Yellow, Olive Tone, Glass Lid, 1885-1895, Qt., RB-1498 . . 140.00
Trademark Lightning, Yellow, Olive Tone, Glass Lid, 1880-1900, 1/2 Gal., RB-1498 . . 185.00
Trademark Lightning Putnam, 339, Yellow Amber, Ground Lip, Qt., RB-1491 . . . . . . 25.00
Trademark Lightning Putnam, Aqua, Glass Lid, Wire Clamp, Qt., RB-1491 . . . . 15.00
Trademark The Dandy, Amber, Gilberds Lid, Qt., RB-751 . . . . 185.00
Trademark The Dandy, Clear, Gilberds Lid, 1 1/2 Qt., RB-751 . . . . 55.00
Trademark The Dandy, Light Aqua, Clear Lid, Qt., RB-751 . . . . 35.00
Union No. 2, Aqua, 1/2 Gal., RB-2840 . . . . 35.00
Union No. 4, Aqua, Groove Ring Wax Sealer, Tin Lid, Cylindrical, Qt., RB-2851 . . . . . . 120.00
Unmarked, Groove Ring Wax Sealer, Amber, Base Embossed, 1870-1885, Qt., RB-3062 . . 145.00
Unmarked, Groove Ring Wax Sealer, Amethyst, Base Embossed, 1870-1885, Qt., RB-3062 255.00
Unmarked, Groove Ring Wax Sealer, Apple Green, Base Embossed, 1885, Qt., RB-3062 . 230.00
Vacu-Top, Clear, Metal Spring Band Clamp, Qt., RB-2860 . . . . 20.00
Valve Jar Co. Philadelphia, Aqua, Glass Lid, Wire Coil Clamp, 1/2 Gal., RB-2873 . . . . 415.00
Van Vliet Improved, Pat. May 3 1881, Aqua, Glass Lid, Qt., RB-2881 . . . . 330.00
Van Vliet Improved, Patd May 3-81, Aqua, Repro Yoke, Qt., RB-2880 . . . .*Illus* 358.00
Van Vliet Jar Of 1881, Aqua, Glass Lid, Metal Yoke Clamp, 1/2 Gal., RB-2878 . . . . . . 375.00
Van Vliet Jar Of 1881, Aqua, Glass Lid, Metal Yoke Clamp, 1/2 Gal., RB-2880 . . . . . . 495.00
Van Vliet Jar Of 1881, Aqua, Repro Yoke, 1/2 Gal., RB-2878 . . . .*Illus* 468.00
Van Vliet Jar Of 1881, Blue Aqua, Glass Lid, Metal Yoke Clamp, Pt., RB-2878 . . . . . . 910.00
Van Vliet Jar Of 1881, Pat. May 3 1881, Aqua, Ground Lip, Qt., RB-2880-1 . . . . 605.00
Victory 1, Patd. Feby. 9th, 1864, Reisd. June 22d, 1867, Aqua, 1/2 Gal., RB-2893 . .55.00 to 60.00
W. Zuttle, J.H. Stallo, Aqua, Glass Lid, Metal Clamp, Qt., RB-3045 . . . . 220.00
W.W. Lyman, Patd Feb. 9th, 1864, Aqua, Ground Lip, No Closure, 1/2 Gal., RB-1588 . . . 40.00
Wan-Eta Coca Boston, Aqua, Qt., RB-2909 . . . . 15.00
Wax Sealer, Cylindrical, Sapphire Blue, Sheared Moutn, Qt., RB-3063 . . . . 605.00
Wears Jar, Clear, Glass Lid, Wire Clamp, Qt., RB-2917 . . . . 11.00

Weir, Pat'd Mar. 1st, 1892, Stoneware, Brown, Cream, Lid, Bail, Pt., RB-2933 . . . .   60.00
Weir Seal No. 4, Western Stoneware, 2-Tone Brown, 5 Gal., RB-2938 . . . .   50.00
Western Pride Patented June 22, 1875, Aqua, Metal Clamp, Qt., RB-2945 . . . .   100.00
Whitall Tatum & Co. Philadelphia New York, Clear, Museum Jar, 1/2 Pt., RB-2956 .   75.00
White King Washes Everything, Aqua, Pt., RB-2963 . . . . .20.00 to 25.00
Whitmore's Patent, Rochester, N.Y., Aqua, Glass Lid, Wire Bail, 1/2 Gal., RB-2964 . .   525.00
Whitney Mason, Patd. 1858, Aqua, Pt., RB-2970 . . . .   10.00
Winslow Improved Valve Jar, Aqua, Iron Yoke Clamp, Qt., RB-3021 . . . .   675.00
Winslow Jar, Aqua, Glass Lid, Brass Wire Closure, 1/2 Gal., RB-3023 . . . .   90.00
Woodbury Improved WGW, Monogram, Aqua, Qt., RB-3029 . . . .   30.00
Woodbury WGW, Monogram, Aqua, Qt., RB-3028 . . . .   30.00

GARNIER

The house of Garnier Liqueurs was founded in 1859 in Enghien, France. Figurals have
been made through the nineteenth and twentieth centuries, except for the years of Prohibition and World War II. Julius Wile and Brothers, a New York City firm established
in 1877, became the exclusive U.S. agents for Garnier in 1885. Many of the bottles
were not sold in the United States but were purchased in France or the Caribbean and
brought back home. Only miniature bottles were sold in the United States from 1970 to
1973. From 1974 to 1978, Garnier was distributed in the United States by Fleischmann
Distilling Company. In 1978 the Garnier trademark was acquired by Standard Brands,
Inc., the parent company of Julius Wile Sons and Company and Fleischmann Distilling
Co., and a few of the full-sized bottles were again sold in the United States. Standard
Brands later merged with Nabisco Brands, Inc. In 1987 Nabisco sold the Garnier
Liqueurs trademark to McGuiness Distillers, Ltd. of Canada, which was sold to Corby
Distillers. The liquor is no longer made.

GARNIER, Acorn, 1910 . . . .   43.00
  Aladdin's Lamp, 1963 . . . . .40.00 to 50.00
  Alfa Romeo, 1913 Model, 1969 . . . . .27.00 to 29.00
  Alfa Romeo, 1924 Model, 1969 . . . .   30.00
  Alfa Romeo, 1929 Model, 1969 . . . .   25.00
  Apollo, 1969 . . . .   20.00
  Aztec, 1965 . . . .   18.00
  Baby Foot, 1963 . . . . .14.00 to 16.00
  Bacchus, 1967 . . . .   25.00
  Baseball Player, 1970 . . . . .18.00 to 20.00
  Bellows, 1969 . . . . .17.00 to 19.00
  Blue Bird, 1970 . . . .   17.00
  Bouquet, 1966 . . . .   20.00
  Bulldog 20.00
  Bullfighter, 1963 . . . . .22.00 to 27.00
  Burmese Man, 1965 . . . . .18.00 to 20.00
  Butterfly, 1970, Miniature 10.00
  Candlestick, Bedroom, 1967 . . . .   24.00
  Candlestick, Glass, 1965 . . . .   20.00
  Cannon, 1964 . . . .   55.00
  Cardinal, 1969 . . . .   16.00
  Cards, Miniature, 1970 . . . .   14.00
  Carrossee Coach, 1970 . . . .   28.00
  Cat, 1930 . . . .   76.00
  Cat, Black, Gray, 1962 . . . .   20.00
  Chalet, 1955 . . . . .40.00 to 45.00
  Chimney, 1956 . . . . .55.00 to 58.00
  Chinese Man, 1970 . . . .   20.00
  Chinese Woman, 1970 . . . .   20.00
  Christmas Tree, 1956 . . . . .60.00 to 65.00
  Citroen, 1922 Model, 1970 . . . .   25.00
  Clock, 1958 . . . . .20.00 to 30.00
  Clown, No. 20, 1910 . . . .   42.00
  Clown, With Tuba, 1955 . . . .   15.00
  Clown's Head, 1931 . . . .   75.00
  Coffee Mill, 1966 . . . .   25.00
  Coffeepot, 1962 . . . .   35.00

Collie, 1970 . . . . 20.00
Country Jug, 1937 . . . . 30.00
Diamond Bottle, 1969 . . . . 13.00
Drunkard, Millord, 1956 . . . . 22.00
Duck, No. 21, 1910 . . . . 16.00
Duckling, 1956 . . . . 35.00
Egg House, 1956 . . . . 73.00
Eiffel Tower, 1950 . . . . 21.00
Elephant, No. 66, 1932 . . . . 7.00
Empire Vase, 1962 . . . . 15.00
Fiat, 1913 Model, Nuevo, 1969 . . . . 28.00
Fiat, 1924 Model, 1969 . . . . 25.00
Football Player, 1970 . . . . 16.00
Ford, 1913 Model, 1969 . . . . 25.00
German Shepherd, 1970 . . . . 18.00
Goldfinch, No. 11, 1970 . . . . 17.00
Goose, 1955 . . . . 17.00
Greyhound, 1930 . . . . 75.00
Guitar & Mandolin 18.00
Harlequin, No. 166, 1958 . . . . 35.00
Hockey Player, 1970 . . . . 20.00
Hula Hoop, 1959 . . . . 30.00
Humoristiques, 1934, Miniature 30.00
Hunting Vase, 1964 . . . . 28.00
Inca, 1969 . . . . 17.00
Indian, 1958 . . . . 17.00
Indian Princess 14.00
Indy 500, No. 1, 1970 . . . . .35.00 to 40.00
Jockey, 1961 . . . . 28.00
LaDona, 1963 . . . . 35.00
Lafayette, 1949 . . . . 20.00
Laurel Crown, 1963 . . . . 22.00
Locomotive, 1969 . . . . 20.00
Log, Quarter, 1958 . . . . 30.00
Log, Round, 1958 . . . . 25.00
Loon, 1970 . . . . 14.00
Maharajah, 1958 . . . . 74.00
Marquis, 1931 . . . . 74.00
Marseilles, 1970 . . . . 20.00
Meadowlark, 1969 . . . . .15.00 to 20.00
MG, 1913 Model, 1970 . . . . 27.00
Mocking Bird, 1970 . . . . .20.00 to 25.00
Montmartre, 1960 . . . . 15.00
Napoleon, 1969 . . . . 27.00
Oasis, 1959 . . . . 20.00
Oriole, 1970 . . . . 20.00
Packard, 1930 Model, 1970 . . . . 20.00
Painting, 1961 . . . . 28.00
Paris Monuments, 1966 . . . . 35.00
Parrot, 1910 . . . . 34.00
Pelican, 1935 . . . . 50.00
Penguin, 1930 . . . . 75.00
Pheasant, 1969 . . . . 25.00
Pistol, Horse, 1964 . . . . 20.00
Poodle, Black, 1954 . . . . 15.00
Poodle, White, 1954 . . . . 15.00
Rainbow, No. 142, 1955 . . . . 28.00
Renault, 1911 Model, 1969 . . . . 29.00
Roadrunner, 1969 . . . . .20.00 to 25.00
Robin, 1970 . . . . 20.00
Rooster, Black, 1952 . . . . .14.00 to 16.00
Rooster, Maroon, 1952 . . . . .20.00 to 22.00
Soccer Shoe, 1962 . . . . .35.00 to 37.00

Soldier, Faceless, 1949 .... 61.00
SS France, 1962 .... 100.00
SS Queen Mary, 1970 .... 28.00
Stanley, 1907 Model, 1970 .... 27.00
Tam Tam, 1961 ....50.00 to 52.00
Taxi, Paris, 1960 ....54.00 to 60.00
Trout, 1967 .... 20.00
Vase, Miniature, 1935 .... 10.00
Violin, 1966 ....35.00 to 37.00
Watch, Blue, 1966 .... 26.00
Watch, Tan, 1966 .... 25.00
Watering Can, 1958 ....15.00 to 17.00
Woman, With Jug, 1930 .... 50.00
Young Deer, 1964 .... 28.00

-- GEMEL --

Gemel bottles are made in pairs. Two bottles are blown separately then joined together, usually with the two necks pointing in different directions. Gemels are popular for serving oil and vinegar or two different types of liqueurs.

GEMEL, Allover White Loopings, Tooled Lips, Rigaree Rim, Pontil, 1830-1860, 9 1/2 In.   110.00
Blown, Clear, Applied Foot, Tear Drop Stem, 8 1/2 In. 190.00
Blown, Green, Pontil, Applied Rigaree On Sides, 1830-1860 .... 125.00
Blue Aqua, White Checkerboard Striping, Tooled Lips, Pontil, 1830-1860, 7 In. 110.00
Nailsea Type, White Loops On Clear, Cobalt Bead Around Lip, Rigaree, 8 1/2 In. 180.00
Rigaree, Green Aqua, Flared Lip, OP, 6 1/2 In. 90.00
Wading Bird, Fish In Beak, Ferns, Monogram, Feathered Rigaree, 1780-1820, 9 In. 220.00

-- GIN --

The word gin comes from the Dutch word *genever,* meaning juniper. It is said that gin was invented in the seventeenth century in Holland to be used as a medicine. One of the earliest types of gin was what today is called *Geneva* or *Hollands* gin. It is made from a barley malt grain mash and juniper berries. The alcohol content is low and it is usually not used for cocktails. In some countries it is considered medicine. In England and America, the preferred drink is dry gin, which is made with juniper berries, coriander seeds, angelica root, and other flavors. The best dry gin is distilled, not mixed by the process used during Prohibition to make bathtub gin. Another drink is Tom gin, much like dry gin but with sugar added. Gin bottles have been made since the 1600s. Most of them have straight sides. Gin has always been an inexpensive drink, which is why so many of these bottles were made. Many were of a type called *case bottles* today. The case bottle was made with straight sides so that 4 to 12 bottles would fit tightly into a wooden packing case.

GIN, A. Houtman, Case, Yellow Olive, Applied Top 60.00
A. Van Hoboken & Co., Case, Olive Amber, SCA 55.00
A. Van Hoboken & Co., Rotterdam, A.V.H. In Shoulder Seal, Deep Green, c.1870s, 11 In.   50.00
A.C.A. Nolet, Schiedam, Green, Applied Top, 7 1/2 In. 45.00
A.C.A. Nolet, Schiedam, Pig Mouth, Seal, 11 In. 110.00
A.V.H., Shoulder Seal, Black Glass, Emerald Green, 1860s, 11 In. 85.00
African T. Co., Serval Cat Picture, Nigeria, c.1890, 8 3/4 In. 75.00
Barclay Grape Leaf Gin, B.W. Conant & Co., Boston, Jug, Pottery, 1900, 9 1/4 In. 100.00
Bininger, see the Bininger category
Blankenheym & Nolet, Case, Olive Green, 10 In. 25.00
Blankenheym & Nolet, Green, 6 1/2 In. 35.00
Blankenheym & Nolet, Script, Key On Reverse 45.00
Blown, Forest Green, Mushroom Mouth, Tapered, Pontil, 1780-1830, 10 1/2 In. 100.00
Blown, Forest Green, Rolled Mushroom Mouth, Tapered, 1780-1830, 10 1/4 In. 330.00
Blown, Forest Green, Tapered Gin, Applied Mushroom Mouth, Pontil, Netherlands, 10 In.   110.00
Blown, Medium Yellow Olive, Tooled Mouth, IP, 1800-1840, 17 In. 855.00
Blown, Yellow Olive, Applied Mushroom Mouth, Pontil, Netherlands, 1830, 9 In. 45.00
Blown, Yellow Olive, Applied Mushroom Mouth, Tapered, Netherlands, 1830, 8 In. 45.00
Blown, Yellow Olive, Owl On Front Panel, Mushroom Mouth, Tapered, 12 In. 825.00
Blown, Yellow Olive, Widemouth, Pontil, 1770-1800, 9 7/8 In. 305.00
Boll & Dunlop, Case, Rotterdam, Forest Green, Case, Rolled Top, Sealed 135.00

Gin, Gordon & Co.,
N.Y., Paper Label,
8 In.

Gin, J.J. Vogt &
Co., 9 In.

Gin, Melcher's
Finest, Geneva,
Montreal, 10 1/2 In.

Boll & Dunlop, Case, Rotterdam, Holland, Olive, Applied Top, 8 1/2 In. 35.00
C.A. Richards, Boston, Case, Amber, Applied Top 40.00
C.W. Herwig, Case, Crown Over H, Yellow Olive Green, 9 1/2 In. 100.00
Case, 3 Dots On Base, Olive Amber, Qt. 20.00
Case, Amber, Applied Top, African, 9 In. 45.00
Case, Amber, Applied Top, Crude, 8 1/4 In. 55.00
Case, Applied Mouth, Smooth Base, 1875-1890, 9 1/2 In. 90.00
Case, Black, Square Face, 4 3/8 In. 79.00
Case, Blown, Dark Amber, Applied Top, IP 55.00
Case, Dip Mold, Medium Blue, Emerald Green, Applied Mouth, OP, 1770-1800, 9 5/8 In.   120.00
Case, Dip Mold, Medium Olive Amber, Pontil, Dutch, 1770-1810, 11 In. 105.00
Case, Dip Mold, Olive Green, Rolled Lip, OP, 1780-1810, 10 In. 105.00
Case, Emerald Green, Applied Mouth, Seal, Dutch, 1875-1890, 11 In. 85.00
Case, Gold Amber, Applied Top, 1880s 45.00
Case, Light To Medium Green, String Lip, Dip Mold, 1800-1830, 12 In. 230.00
Case, Light Yellow Olive, Swirls, OP, 11 In. 190.00
Case, Medium Olive Green, OP, 9 5/8 In. 85.00
Case, Medium Yellow Olive, Dip Molded, Applied Mouth, Holland, 1770-1800, 11 In. . .   175.00
Case, Olive Amber, Silver Overlay Case, Original Silver, Cork Stopper, 1880-1900, 9 In. .   140.00
Case, Olive Green, AH On Seal, Blown, Pig Mouth, 11 In. 110.00
Case, Sample, 6 3/4 In. 40.00
Cosmopoliet, J.J. Melchers WZN, Standing Man In Coat & Straight-Brimmed Hat, 10 In.   145.00
Cosmopoliet, Standing Man In Fedora, Small Pedestal 140.00
Daniel Visser, Partial Label 25.00
Daniel Visser & Zonen, Schiedam, Shoulder Seal, Pinched Waist, Yellow Olive 60.00
Daniel Visser & Zonen, Schiedam, Case, Cobalt Blue, Seal, Holland, 1900, 11 In. 120.00
Devil's Island Endurance, Fluted Shoulder, 12 In. 15.00
E. Kiderlen, Case, Green, Applied Top, 7 3/4 In. 45.00
Gordon & Co., N.Y., Paper Label, 8 In. . . . . *Illus*   10.00
Holland, Jug, Gold Label, Large 140.00
I.A.I. Nolet, Schiedam, Case, Olive Green, Applied Mouth, Holland, 1870-1885, 8 In. . . .   80.00
J. & K., Royal Champion, In Embossed Circle, Green, Long Neck, Rolled Lip, 9 In. 30.00
J. Vandervalk & Co., Rotterdam, Case, SB & C In Seal, Olive Green 60.00
J.A. Gilka, Berlin, Red Amber 30.00
J.D.K.Z., Case, Blue Green, Applied Mouth, Africa 130.00
J.H. Henkes, Seal, Stork, 1810, 11 1/2 In. 100.00
J.J. Melchers, Case, W.Z.N., Olive, Applied Top, 9 In. 35.00
J.J. Peters, Case, Olive Green, Dog With Bird In Moutnh, 8 1/2 In. 60.00
J.J. Vogt & Co., 9 In. . . . . *Illus*   6.00
J.J.W. Peters, Dog & Prey, Nigeria . . . . .40.00 to 48.00
J.T. Clubhouse, Case, Reverse S, Amber, Applied Top, Graphite Pontil 360.00
J.T. Daly Club House, Case, Olive Amber, Bubbles, 1865-1875, 8 7/8 In. 145.00
Kinderlen, Rotterdam, Celebrated Old Gin, Barrel, Light Olive Green, 1900, 8 1/2 In. . .   175.00
Knickerbocker, Case, New York, Teal Blue, Applied Mouth, 1875-1885, 5 7/8 In. 385.00
Levert & Co., De Wildeman, Opgericht AO 1690, Windmill, Man With Pipe, Jug, 8 1/2 In.   160.00
London Jockey Club House, Jockey On Horse, Olive Amber, 1865, 9 1/4 In. 690.00

London Jockey Club House, Olive Green, Horse & Rider, IP, 1860, 9 3/8 In. 355.00
London Jockey Club House, Red Amber, Horse & Rider, 9 1/4 In. 550.00
London Jockey Club House, Yellow Green, Applied Mouth, IP, 1855-1865, 9 1/8 In. . . 965.00
London Jockey Club House, Yellow Green, Horse & Rider, 1860-1880, 10 In. 770.00
Meijer & Co., Case, Schiedam, Rampant Lion, Applied Mouth, Holland, 1890, 9 1/4 In. . 75.00
Melcher's Finest, Geneva, Montreal, 10 1/2 In. . . . .*Illus* 18.00
Milk Glass, 4-Panels, Beveled Corners, Enamel Flower Design On Each Panel, 4 1/4 In. . 360.00
Milshire Dry Gin, Heublein Bro., Hartford, Miniature 15.00
Moses Poland Water, Poland Spring Gin, Label, Amber, 9 In. 25.00
Olive Green, Tapered, Ribbed, 10 1/2 In. 25.00
P. Hoppe Night Cap, Old Schiedam, Holland Gin, Estbd. 1780, Label Only, 11 3/4 In. . ' 30.00
Ruby N' Sloe, Lady's Leg, Amber . . . . .125.00 to 345.00
Sapphire Blue, Milk Glass Loopings, Beveled Corners, Pewter Collar, Pontil, 7 1/8 In. . 1210.00
Schade & Buysing, Schiedam, Blown, Pig Mouth, Seal, 11 In. 155.00
Seahorse Holland's Gin, Label 100.00
Superfine Schiedam Geneva Gin, Case, Label, Qt. 25.00
T.J. Dunbar & Co., Square, Yellow Olive, Beveled Corners, Sloping Collar, 9 5/8 In. . . . 1980.00
V. Marken & Co., Olive Green, Embossed Script, 9 In. 34.00
Van Den Burgh & Co., Blown, Seal, 9 In. 110.00
W.H. & Co., Case, Light Green, Seal, 1880s, 11 In. 110.00
W.S.C. Clubhouse, Yellow Olive Green, Applied Mouth, 9 1/4 In. 220.00
Waldorf Astoria Dry Gin, BIMAL, Labels, Sample 20.00
Yellow Olive, OP, Applied Mouth, Holland, 1770-1800, 10 1/8 In. 175.00
Yellow Olive, OP, Applied Mouth, Holland, 1770-1800, 11 In. 145.00

---------------------------------- **GINGER BEER** ----------------------------------

Ginger beer was originally made from fermented ginger root, cream of tartar, sugar, yeast, and water. It was a popular drink from the 1850s to the 1920s. Beer made from grains became more popular and very little alcoholic ginger beer was made. Today it is an alcohol-free carbonated drink like soda. Pottery bottles have been made since the 1650s. A few products are still bottled in stoneware containers today. Ginger beer, vinegar, and cider were usually put in stoneware holders until the 1930s. The ginger beer bottle usually held 10 ounces. Blob tops, tapered collars, and crown tops were used. Some used a cork, others a Lightning stopper or inside screw stopper. The bottles were of shades of brown and white. Some were salt glazed for a slightly rough, glassy finish. Bottles were stamped or printed with names and usually the words *ginger beer.*

GINGER BEER, Akron Pottery, Akron, O., 12-Sided, Stoneware, 1870-1880, 10 5/8 In. . . 50.00
Brewed, G. Kickley, Muderloh & Co., Montreal, Tan, Cream, 7 3/4 In. 60.00
Charles Wilson, Toronto, Bug-Eyed Squirrel, Stoneware, Cream, 7 In. . . . . .110.00 to 130.00
Clark Bros., Trademark, Toronto, Winged Wheel, Pottery, Cream, Blob Top, 6 3/4 In. . . . 100.00
E. Carley, Windsor, Ont., Tan, Cream, Blob Top, Stopper, Wire, 10 In. 400.00
E.S. Shapley & Sons, Stoneware, Lighthouse Pictorial, 7 In. 35.00
E.S. Shapley & Sons, Torquay Pure Home Made, Stoneware, 6 1/2 In. 35.00
English Stone Ginger, Toronto Pure Ginger Beer Co., Brown, Cream, 6 3/8 In. 50.00
English Stone Ginger, Toronto Pure Ginger Beer Co., Brown, Tan, 6 1/2 In. 70.00
Frisco Soda Water Coy., Montreal, Que., Eagle, Stoneware, Brown, Gray, 8 1/4 In. 100.00
Gaskins Brewed, Alliance Beverage Company Limited, Tan Cream 100.00
Glass Bros. & Co., London, Ont., In Oval, Stoneware, Cream, Stopper, 8 1/2 In. 260.00
Goulds, Carisbrooke Brewed, One Penny, Donkey, Stoneware, Honey Glaze 22.00
Gurd's, 3 Feathers, Stoneware, Brown, Cream, Crown Top, 9 1/8 In. 35.00
Harston & Co., Leeds & Harrogate, Corkscrew Picture, Stoneware, 7 In. 50.00
Hennessey & Nolan, Albany, N.Y., Hoxie, Vertical Letters, Red Amber 35.00
Hibberd Co., Est. 1868, Ventnor, Stoneware, Honey Glaze, White, Stencil 18.00
Howel's Stone Ginger, Stoneware, Tan, Cream, Canada, c.1920, 8 3/8 In. 75.00
Hughes & Poticher English Brewed, Johnstown, Pa. 190.00
Ireland's, Salt Glaze, Tan Brown Glaze, Cobalt Slip, 1855-1875, 7 5/8 In. 90.00
J.C. Mills, Cobalt Blue, Blob Top, Qt. 130.00
John Verner, Trademark, Toronto, Maple Leaf, Stoneware, Cream, Blob Top, 7 In. 90.00
John's English Brew, Southern English Ginger Beer Co., Jacksonville, Fl. 25.00
King & Dalton, Stone Ginger, Toronto, Tan, Cream, 8 1/4 In. 105.00
Latter's Home Brewed, Sacramento, Cal., Brown, Gray, Crown Top, 1900s 45.00
Lawrance & Sons, Yarmouth, Beccles, Ipswich, Stoneware, Oatmeal, Yellow 26.00
Lee & Green, English Brewed, Syracuse, N.Y., Pottery, Brown, Gray . . . . .20.00 to 35.00

London Ginger Beer Co., Stone Ginger Beer, Brown, Cream, Stopper, Canada, 7 In. . .   205.00
O'Keefe's Beverages, Ltd., Toronto, Canada, Stoneware, 1900s 45.00
Old Homestead, International Drug Co., Cream, Blob Top, Stopper, 7 In. 60.00
Old Homestead, International Drug Co., Cream, Crown Top, 7 In. 45.00
Orange Crush Of Truro, Nova Scotia, Ye Old English Ginger Beer In Stone, 8 Oz. 70.00
Pink's Ltd., None Nicer Brand, Guaranteed Brewed, Chichester, Stoneware, Pt. 35.00
Rycroft's Old Fashioned Ginger Beer, Honolulu, T.H., Crown Top, 9 Oz. 175.00
Salisbury Ginger Beer Co., Stone Ginger, Old Country Home Brewed, 6 7/8 In. 90.00
Smith & Clody, Brewed, Buffalo, N.Y., Amber, Crown Top, Squat 40.00
Smith & Clody, Buffalo, N.Y., Stoneware, Cream 25.00
Tamplin & Co., Liverpool, Bird With Twig In Beak, Stoneware, Black, 7 1/2 In. 95.00
W.H. Donovan, Halifax, N.S., Diamond, Stoneware, Cream, Blob Top, 6 3/4 In. 45.00
Whelan & Ferguson, Halifax, N.S., Pottery, Cream, Blob Top, c.1890, 6 7/8 In. 45.00
Wm. Robertson, Toronto, Trade Mark, G.B., Stoneware, Tan Glaze, Blob Top, 6 3/4 In.   85.00
Ye Old Country Stone Ginger Beer, Stoneware, Crown Top, Canada, 1920s, 7 3/8 In.   25.00
Ye Old Country Stone Ginger Beer, Stoneware, Crown Top, Canada, c.1925, 7 In. . . .   15.00

--------------------------------------- GLUE ---------------------------------------

Glue and paste have been packaged in bottles since the nineteenth century. Most of these bottles have identifying paper labels. A few have the name embossed in the glass.

GLUE, A. Richard's Glue & Cement, Cylindrical, Aqua, 2 1/2 In. 35.00
Boyers Mucilage, Cone, Label, Contents 20.00
Diamond Sticking Adhesive, Diamond Ink Co., Crock, Lid, Closure, 1 Gal. 100.00
H.W. & Co., Mucilage, Deep Aqua, 8-Sided, Wide Mouth, OP, 1860, 3 1/4 In. 90.00
Henry C. Hoffman's Extra Heavy Mucilage, 10-Sided, Label 35.00

------------------------------------- GRENADIER -------------------------------------

The Grenadier Spirits Company of San Francisco, California, started making figural porcelain bottles in 1970. Twelve soldier-shaped fifths were in Series No. 1. These were followed by Series 2 late in 1970. Only 400 cases were made of each soldier. The company continued to make bottles in series, including the 1976 American Revolutionary Army regiments in fifths and tenths, and many groups of minibottles. They also had series of club bottles, missions, foreign generals, horses, and more. The brothel series was started in 1978 for a special customer, Mr. Dug Picking of Carson City, Nevada. These are usually sold as *Dug's Nevada Brothels.* The Grenadier Spirits Company sold out to Fleishmann Distilling Company and stopped making the bottles about 1980. Jon-Sol purchased the remaining inventory of bottles.

GRENADIER, Horse, Appaloosa, 1978 . . . .*Illus*   50.00
Horse, Arabian, 1978 . . . .   50.00
Horse, Saddle Bred, 1978 . . . .   50.00
Horse, Tennessee Walker, 1978 . . . .   50.00
Horse, Thoroughbred, 1978 . . . .   60.00
Mission San Francisco De Asis, 1978 . . . .*Illus*   29.00
Mr. Spock, Bust, 1979 . . . .   70.00
Pancho Villa, Standing 10.00

Grenadier, Horse,
Appaloosa, 1978

Grenadier, Mission
San Francisco De
Asis, 1978

Pontiac Trans Am, 1979	50.00
San Fernando Mfg. Co., 1976	66.00
Santa Claus, Blue Sack, 1978	33.00
Santa Claus, Green Sack, 1978	30.00
Soldier, 1st Pennsylvania, 1970	30.00
Soldier, 1st Regiment, Virginia Volunteers, 1974, Miniature	14.00
Soldier, 3d Guard	27.00
Soldier, 6th Regiment, Wisconsin, 1975, Miniature	14.00
Soldier, 11th Regiment, Indiana	14.00
Soldier, Billy Mitchell, 1975	38.00
Soldier, Comte DeRochambeau, 1978	30.00 to 40.00
Soldier, Count Pulaski, 1978	54.00
Soldier, General MacArthur, 1975	26.00
Soldier, Jeb Stuart, 1970	28.00 to 30.00
Soldier, Napoleon, 1969	34.00
Soldier, Ney, 1969	21.00
Soldier, Officer, 1st Guard Regiment, 1971	25.00
Soldier, Robert E. Lee, 1976	36.00 to 40.00
Soldier, Scots Fusilier, 1971	21.00 to 25.00
Soldier, Scots Fusilier, 1975	22.00 to 25.00
Soldier, Teddy Roosevelt, 1976	30.00 to 40.00
Soldier, Teddy Roosevelt, 1977	30.00 to 40.00
Soldier, Texas Ranger, 1977	35.00 to 38.00
Soldier, Texas Ranger, 1979	33.00
Soldier, Wisconsin, 6th, 1975	13.00
Washington Blue Rifles, Miniature	13.00
Washington On Horse, 1974	24.00 to 30.00

HAIR PRODUCTS, see Cosmetic; Cure
HAND LOTION, see Cosmetic; Medicine

──────────────── **HOFFMAN** ────────────────

J. Wertheimer had a distillery in Kentucky before the Civil War. Edward Wertheimer and his brother Lee joined the business as young men. When Edward Sr. died at age 92, his son Ed Wertheimer Jr., became president. Edward Jr.'s sons, Ed Wertheimer III and Thomas Wertheimer, also worked in the family company. L. & E. Wertheimer Inc. made the products of the Hoffman Distilling Company and the Old Spring Distilling Company, including Old Spring Bourbon, until 1983 when the company was sold to Commonwealth Distillery, a company still in existence. Hoffman Originals, later called the Hoffman Club, was founded by the Wertheimers in 1971 to make a series of figural bottles. The first was the Mr. Lucky series, started in 1973. These were leprechaun-shaped decanters. Five series of leprechauns were made. Other series include wildlife, decoy ducks (1977-1978), Aesop's fables, C.M. Russell (1978), rodeo (1978), pool-playing dogs (1978), belt buckles (1979), horses (1979), Jack Richardson animals, Bill Ohrmann animals (1980-1981), cheerleaders (1980), framed pistols (1978), political (1980), and college football (1981-1982). The miniature Hoffman bottles include series such as leprechauns (1981), birds (1978), dogs and cats (1978-1981), decoys (1978-1979), pistols on stands (1975), Street Swingers (musicians, 1978-1979), pistols (1975), wildlife (1978), and horses (1978). Hoffman decanters are no longer made.

HOFFMAN, Aesop's Fables, Hare & The Tortoise, 1978	17.00
Alaska Pipeline, 1975	24.00
Animal, Bear & Cub Fishing, 1978	40.00 to 50.00
Animal, Bobcat & Pheasant, 1978	47.00 to 50.00
Animal, Doe & Fawn, 1975	45.00
Animal, Falcon & Rabbit, 1978	65.00
Animal, Fox & Eagle, 1978	45.00 to 50.00
Animal, Fox & Rabbit, 1981	44.00
Animal, Jaguar & Possum, 1978	28.00
Animal, Lion & Crane, 1979	20.00
Animal, Lion & Dall Sheep, 1977, 3 Piece	175.00
Betsy Ross, Music Box, 1974	40.00 to 48.00
Big Red Machine, 1973	44.00
Bird, Blue Jay, 1979	36.00 to 40.00
Bird, Canada Geese, 1980	20.00

Hoffman, College, Tennessee
Volunteers, Helmet, 1981

Hoffman, Jack The Ripper,
Pool Hustler, 1979

Hoffman, Mr.
Policeman, 1975

Bird, Dove, Open Wing, 1979		15.00
Bird, Egret, Baby, 1979		17.00
Bird, Love, 1979		16.00
Bird, Swan, Closed Wing, 1980		18.00 to 20.00
Bird, Titmice, 1979		27.00 to 29.00
College, Auburn Tigers, Helmet, 1981		24.00
College, Clemson Tigers, Helmet, 1981		35.00
College, Georgia Bulldogs, Helmet, 1981		35.00 to 37.00
College, Kansas State Wildcats, Helmet, 1981		20.00 to 22.00
College, Kentucky Wildcats, Helmet, 1981		24.00
College, Missouri Tiger, Helmet, 1981		22.00
College, Nebraska Cornhusker, Helmet, 1981		39.00
College, Oklahoma Sooners, Helmet, 1981		40.00
College, Tennessee Volunteers, Helmet, 1981	*Illus*	31.00
Convention, Barrel		40.00
Convention, Leprechaun On Barrel, 1982		42.00
Cowboy & Puma, 1978		360.00
Duck, Decoy, Blue Bill, 1978, Miniature, Pair		12.00
Duck, Decoy, Blue Wing Teal, 1978, Pair		17.00
Duck, Decoy, Canada Goose, 1977		18.00
Duck, Decoy, Canvasback, 1978, Miniature, Pair		14.00
Duck, Decoy, Golden Eye, 1978, Miniature, Pair		14.00
Duck, Decoy, Loon, 1978		35.00
Duck, Decoy, Mallard, 1977, Miniature, Pair		14.00
Duck, Decoy, Merganser, 1978		20.00
Duck, Decoy, Merganser, Hooded, 1978, Miniature, Pair		13.00
Duck, Decoy, Merganser, Red Breast, 1978, Miniature, Pair		12.00
Duck, Decoy, Pintail, 1977, Miniature, Pair		13.00
Duck, Decoy, Redhead, 1977, Miniature, Pair		13.00
Duck, Decoy, Ruddy Duck, 1978, Miniature, Pair		13.00
Duck, Decoy, Swan, White, 1978		22.00
Duck, Decoy, Widgeon, 1978		28.00
Duck, Decoy, Wood Duck, 1977		36.00
Duck, Mallard, Open Wing, 1980		20.00
Jack The Ripper, Pool Hustler, 1979	*Illus*	125.00
Lady Godiva, 1974		40.00
Mascot, Kentucky, Basketball, 1979		35.00
Mascot, Kentucky, Football, 1979		40.00
Mascot, LSU Tiger, 1978		38.00
Mascot, LSU Tiger, No. 2, 1981		28.00
Mascot, Miss. Southern, 1962		43.00
Mascot, Miss. State, Bulldog, 1977		42.00
Mascot, Miss. University, Rebel, 1977		48.00

Mascot, Nevada, Wolfpack, 1979 .... 50.00
Mr. & Mrs. Retired, Set 60.00
Mr. Baker, 1978 .... 36.00
Mr. Barber, 1980 .... 31.00
Mr. Bartender, 1975 .... 32.00
Mr. Blacksmith, 1976 .... 20.00
Mr. Butcher, 1979 .... 28.00
Mr. Carpenter, 1979 .... 31.00
Mr. Charmer, 1974 .... 20.00
Mr. Cobbler, 1973 .... 20.00
Mr. Dancer, 1974 .... 20.00
Mr. Dentist, 1980 .... 25.00
Mr. Doctor, 1974 .... 32.00
Mr. Electrician, 1978 .... 35.00
Mr. Farmer, 1980 .... 26.00
Mr. Fiddler, 1974 .... 22.00
Mr. Fireman, 1976 .... 70.00
Mr. Guitarist, 1975 .... 24.00
Mr. Harpist, 1974 .... 19.00
Mr. Lucky, 1973 .... 40.00
Mr. Lucky, 1974, Miniature 10.00
Mr. Lucky, Mini Set, No. 1, 1980 .... 75.00
Mr. Lucky, Mini Set, No. 2 .... 75.00
Mr. Lucky, Mini Set, No. 3 .... 100.00
Mr. Lucky, Mini Set, No. 4 .... 75.00
Mr. Lucky, Mini Set, No. 5 .... 80.00
Mr. Lucky & Rockwell, 1980, Miniature 75.00
Mr. Mailman, 1976 .... 34.00
Mr. Mechanic, 1979 .... 32.00
Mr. Organ Player, 1979 .... 29.00
Mr. Photographer, 1980 .... 28.00
Mr. Pilot, Miniature 20.00
Mr. Plumber, 1978 .... 28.00
Mr. Policeman, 1975 ....*Illus* 38.00
Mr. Policeman, Retired, 1986, Miniature 20.00
Mr. Railroad Engineer, 1980 .... 29.00
Mr. Salesman, 1982, Miniature 15.00
Mr. Sandman, 1974 .... 20.00
Mr. Saxophonist, 1975 .... 30.00
Mr. Stockbroker, 1976 .... 40.00
Mr. Tailor, 1979 .... 29.00
Mr. Teacher, 1976 .... 22.00
Mr. Tourist, 1980 .... 25.00
Mrs. Lucky, 1974 .... 19.00
Penguins, 1979 .... 50.00
Pistol, Civil War Colt, Framed, 1978 .... 28.00
Pistol, Civil War Colt, With Stand, 1975, Miniature 16.00
Pistol, Colt 45 Automatic, Framed, 1978 .... 28.00
Pistol, Colt 45 Automatic, With Stand, 1975, Miniature 17.00
Pistol, Derringer, Silver, Framed, 1979 .... 25.00
Pistol, Dodge City Frontier, Framed, 1978 .... 29.00
Pistol, Dodge City Frontier, With Stand, 1976, Miniature 17.00
Pistol, German Luger, Framed, 1978 .... 18.00
Pistol, German Luger, With Stand, 1975, Miniature 14.00
Pistol, Kentucky Flintlock, With Stand, 1975 .... 27.00
Pistol, Lawman, With Stand, 1978, Miniature 27.00
Pistol, Tower Flintlock, 1975 .... 25.00
Pistol, Tower Flintlock, With Stand, 1975 .... 27.00
Political Donkey, 1980 .... 16.00
Political Elephant, 1980 .... 16.00
Rodeo, All Around Clown, 1978 .... 45.00
Rodeo, Bareback Rider, 1978 .... 43.00
Rodeo, Belt Buckle, Saddle Bronc, 1979 .... 70.00

Rodeo, Bull Rider, 1978 .... 70.00
Rodeo, Calf Roping, 1978 .... 60.00
Rodeo, Saddle, 1978 .... 60.00
Rodeo, Steer Wrestler, 1978 .... 60.00
Russel, Buffalo Man, 1976 .... 45.00
Russel, Bust, 1978 .... 30.00
Russel, Cowboy, 1978 .... 34.00
Russel, Flathead Squaw, 1976 .... 45.00
Russel, Half Breed Trader, 1978 .... 45.00
Russel, I Rode Him, 1978 .... 40.00
Russel, Indian Buffalo Hunter, 1978 ....44.00 to 45.00
Russel, Last Of 5000, 1975 .... 20.00
Russel, Northern Cree, 1978 .... 40.00
Russel, Prospector, 1976 .... 27.00
Russel, Red River Breed, 1976 .... 42.00
Russel, Scout, 1978 .... 43.00
Russel, Stage Coach Driver, 1976 .... 35.00
Russel, Stage Robber, 1978 .... 50.00
Russel, Trapper, 1976 ....35.00 to 38.00
Soldier, Concord, 1973 .... 25.00
Soldier, Queen's Ranger, 1978, Miniature, 4 Piece 55.00
Street Swingers, Bass Player, 1979, Miniature 12.00
Street Swingers, Train, I Think I Can, 1981 .... 90.00
Truck Distillery, 1981 .... 60.00

———————————————————— HOUSEHOLD ————————————————————

Many household cleaning products have been packaged in glass bottles since the nineteenth century. Shoe polish, ammonia, stove blacking, bluing, and other nonfood products are listed in this section. Most of these bottles have attractive paper labels that interest the collector.

HOUSEHOLD, Ammonia, Mnfd. By S.F. Gaslight Co., Blue Aqua, Qt. 25.00
Ammonia, Unembossed, Light Lime Green, Bubbles, Qt. 75.00
Beau Peep Baby Shoe Cleaner, Chicago, Beau Peep Shape, 1920-1930, 6 1/4 In. 50.00
Berry Bros. Varnish Mfgrs., Detroit, Amber, Wavy, Bubbles, Cork, 9 1/4 In. 5.00
Browns Liquid Dressing, B.F. Browns Co., Boston, Mass., Aqua, Label, BIMAL 10.00
Butler IXL Oil Blacking, Hingemold, Aqua 25.00
California Toothwash, 4 1/2 In. 40.00
Eagle Brand Shoe Polish, 5 In. 15.00
Eastman, Rochester, N.Y., Amethyst, 4 Beveled Corners, Rectangular, 6 1/4 In. 5.00
Easybright Polishes, B.F. Stinson Co., Buffalo, N.Y., 6 1/4 In. ....*Illus* 9.00
Eclipse French Satin Gloss Dressing, Blacking, Olive Amber, Square 9.00
Edison Battery Oil, Thomas A. Edison, Inc., Bloomfield, N.J., 4 In. ....*Illus* 15.00
Energine Shoe White, Cummer Prod. Co., Tin Lid, Box, 1935 .... .25
Eureka Mending Liquid, Cork, 1900s, 4 In. 15.00
Fly Trap, Blown, Applied Footed & Collar, 6 1/2 In. 120.00

Household,
Easybright Polishes,
B.F. Stinson Co.,
Buffalo, N.Y., 6 1/4 In.

Household, Edison
Battery Oil,
Thomas A. Edison, Inc.,
Bloomfield, N.J., 4 In.

Household, Urinal, Embossed Ounces, Qt.

Household, White Sail
Liquid Blue, Great
Atlantic & Pacific Tea
Co., N.Y., 6 1/2 In.

Griffin Dycote & ABC Liquid Wax, Nude Woman Holding Shoe, Tin Top, Box	2.00
Griffin Shoe Creme, Nude Woman, Holding Shoe, Tin Lid, Box, 1930-1939	2.00
Handy Oiler, Danville, Indiana, Qt.	35.00
Hub Shoe Dressing, H.A. Bartlett & Co., Philada., Barrel, Aqua, 4 3/4 In.	30.00
I. Rokeach & Sons, Oil Refiners, Brooklyn, N.Y., 6-Pointed Star, Crown, 6 1/2 In.	35.00
Larkin Soap Co., Aqua, Monogram, 8 In.	20.00
Liquid Veneer, Buffalo Specialty Co., 4 Sided, Cork, 1915-1935, Box	2.00
Mercitan Caulk, Mercitan Fluid On Label, Ground Lip	10.00
Mufti Shoe White, Plough, Art Deco Type, Tin Lid, Box, 1935	.75 to 1.00
Osborn's Liquid Polish, Yellow Olive Amber, Rolled Lip, OP, 1855, 4 In.	355.00
Osborn's Liquid Polish, Yellow Olive, Tubular Pontil, 1840-1860, 3 5/8 In.	525.00
Platt's Chlorides, Household Disinfectant, Aqua, Cylindrical, Cork, 8 1/2 In.	3.00
Plynine Ammonia, Stoneware, Lid, Qt.	235.00
Premium Griffin Allwite, Tin Lid, Box, 1935	6.00
Price's Patent Candle Company, Cobalt Blue, Rectangular Wedge, England, 1860, 7 In.	130.00
Price's Soap Company, Cobalt Blue, Rectangular Wedge, England, 1870, 7 3/8 In.	100.00
Race & Sheldon Magic Boot Polish, Deep Blue Green, 8-Sided, 5 In.	1050.00 to 1650.00
Scribblers Snow White Paste, Seattle, USA, Gal.	125.00
Seabury's Laundry Blueing, Blue Green, Rolled Lip, 1840-1855, 3 7/8 In.	90.00
Seabury's Laundry Blueing, Light Green, Pontil, Rolled Lip, 1855, 3 7/8 In.	175.00
Shoe Blacking, Blue Green, Infolded Lip, Square, Pontil, 1860, 4 5/8 In.	200.00
Shulife For Shoes, RM Hollingshead Co., Camden, N.J., Olive Green, Cork, 3 3/4 In.	15.00
Smokey City Ammonia, Monogram	15.00
Sunshine Furniture Polish, Label, Contents, 6 1/2 In.	40.00
Urinal, Embossed Ounces, Qt.	7.50
Varnish, Lithrop & Spooner, Worcester, Mass., Portraits On Label	20.00
White Sail Liquid Blue, Great Atlantic & Pacific Tea Co., N.Y., 6 1/2 In.	4.00
Wycoff & Co., Union Bluing, Aqua, Star, Crude Mouth, Interior Stain, Oval, 8 In.	4.00
Wycoff & Co., Union Bluing, Blue Aqua, Star, Cork, Interior Stain, 7 In.	2.00
Yankee Shoe Polish, Whitemore, Embossed, Label, Tin Lid, 1925	3.50
Zanzibar Polish For Pianos Portes & Furniture, Label Only, 12-Sided, Light Aqua	20.00

INK

Ink was first used about 2500 B.C. in ancient Egypt and China. It was made of carbon mixed with oils. By the fifteenth century, ink was usually made at home by the housewife who bottled it for later use. In the late eighteenth century, ink was sold by apothecary shops and bookstores. The first patented ink was made in England in 1792. Ink bottles were first used in the United States about 1819. Early ink bottles were of ceramic and were often imported. Small ink bottles were made to be opened and used with a dip pen. Large ink bottles, like the cathedral-shaped Carter's inks, held a quart of ink to be poured into small bottles with dips. Inks can be identified by their shapes. Collectors have nicknamed many and the auctions often refer to *teakettles, cones, igloos,* or *umbrellas.*

Ink bottles were made to be hard to tip over. Some inks, especially English examples, were made with *bust-off* tops. The glass was cracked to open the bottle and the rough edge remained. In general the shape tells the age. Cones and umbrellas were used from the early 1800s to the introduction of the automatic bottle machine in the early 1900s. Hexagonal and octagonal bottles were preferred from about 1835 to 1865. Igloos, or turtles, were introduced in 1865 and were very popular for schools until about 1895. Barrels were made from 1840 to 1900. Square bottles became popular after 1860. Rectangular was the shape chosen in the 1900s. Figural bottles, especially ceramic types, were also made.

For further research, consult the book *Ink Bottles and Inkwells* by William E. Covill Jr. There is a national club, The Society of Inkwell Collectors, 5136 Thomas Avenue South, Minneapolis, MN 55410.

INK, 8-Sided, Aqua, Rolled Lip, 1 1/2 In.	.60.00 to 65.00
8-Sided, Black Amber, Ring Around Neck, Sheared Lip, Blown, 1760-1800, 2 3/8 In.	170.00
8-Sided, Deep Chocolate Amber, Sheared Lip, 1845, France, 2 1/4 In.	100.00
8-Sided, Forest Green, Amber Swirls, 3 1/2 In.	18.00
8-Sided, Lime Green, Elongated Neck, Pontil, 1840-1860, 2 3/8 In.	125.00
10-Sided Dome, Blown, Rayed Base, 1860, 2 3/8 In.	200.00
12 Ribs, Cobalt Blue, OP, 2 3/4 x 2 1/4 In.	200.00
12 Vertical Panels, Light Green, Fluted Shoulder, IP, 1860, 9 1/8 In.	123.00
12-Sided, Aqua, Fluted Shoulders, IP, Qt.	130.00
12-Sided, Aqua, OP, 1840-1850, 2 1/2 In.	100.00
12-Sided, Aqua, OP, 2 1/2 In.	40.00
12-Sided, Blue Aqua, Ribs Shoulder, IP, Qt.	80.00
12-Sided, Blue Aqua, Rolled Lip, Ring OP, 3 In.	35.00
12-Sided, Deep Green, Rolled Lip, OP, 2 In.	155.00
12-Sided, Deep Olive Amber, Pontil, Sheared Lip, 1845-1855, 2 In.	660.00
12-Sided, Deep Purple Amethyst, Blown, Onion Shaped Neck, Pittsburgh, 3 x 3 7/8 In.	280.00
12-Sided, Emerald Green, 2 1/16 In.	180.00
12-Sided, Light Clear Green, IP, 9 1/8 In.	240.00
12-Sided, Medium Blue Green, Infolded Lip, OP, 1840-1850, 1 15/16 In.	235.00
12-Sided, Medium Emerald Green, Infolded Lip, 1840-1860, 2 1/8 In.	145.00
12-Sided, Medium Emerald Green, Long Neck, Pontil, 2 1/8 In.	325.00
12-Sided, Olive Green, Applied Spout, IP, 1850-1860, 8 3/4 In.	1650.00
18-Sided, Cobalt Blue, 10 1/2 In.	95.00
24 Vertical Ribs, Clear, Tooled & Pressed In Funnel Lip, Pontil, 1 1/2 In.	240.00
32 Vertical Ribs, Amber, Funnel Type Opening, Blown, Mantua, Oh., 1820-1830, 2 In.	2970.00
36 Vertical Ribs, Funnel Type Opening, Blown, 1860, 1 3/4 In.	170.00
A.B. Laird's, 8-Sided, Blue Green, Infolded Lip, OP, 1840-1850, 2 1/8 In.	2530.00
A.B. Laird's, Aqua, Infolded Lip, OP, 1840-1850, 2 1/4 In.	290.00
A.M. & Co., N.Y., Building, Beveled Roof, Narrow Rectangular Body, 1860, 4 In.	280.00
A.M. Bertinguiot, 12-Sided, Sapphire Blue, Infolded Lip, Pontil, 1830-1850, 2 1/2 In.	840.00
A.M. Bertinguiot, Dark Brown Amber, Olive Tone, Sheared Lip, 1840-1850, 2 1/2 In.	200.00
Adrien Maurin, Depose, Basket Shape, Sapphire Blue, Sheared Lip, France, 1860, 3 In.	535.00
Alling's, Pat. April 25, 1871, Triangular, Blue Green, 1870-1871, 1 7/8 In.	255.00
Alling's Ink, Triangular, Aqua, 2 1/2 In.	40.00
Alling's Lilac Ink, Rochester, N.Y., Aqua, Spout, 1870, 7 1/4 In.	135.00
Amber, Disc Mouth, Coventry Glass Works, Blown, 3-Piece Mold, Pontil, 2 1/8 In.	175.00
American Standard, Frederick, Md., Grass Green, Spout, Qt.	240.00
Amethyst, Tooled Lip, Cork, 2 3/4 In.	5.00
Aqua, 2 Pen Rests, Sheared Neck, Square, 2 1/4 In.	7.00
Aqua, Bell Top, Round, Flared Lip, 3 In.	55.00
Aqua, Blown, Applied Foot, Midwestern, 4 1/2 In.	220.00
Aqua, Horse & Rider On Either Side, Disc Top, 2-Piece Mold, 1840-1850, 1 3/8 In.	13200.00
Atr Bocquet Propeiete, France, Tan, Peach, Fuchsia Glaze, 1840-1860, 3 In.	220.00
B.B. & Co., Umbrella, 8-Sided, Cornflower Blue, Embossed On 4 Sided, OP, 1 13/16 In.	450.00
Ball, Iridescent, Enameled Flowers, Brass Hinged Cover, 4 1/4 In.	230.00
Barrel, Pat. March 17, 1870, Tooled Collar, Smooth Base, 2 1/16 In.	50.00
Barrel, Pat. Oct. 17, 1865, 2 1/6 In.	80.00
Barrel, Pat. Oct. 17, 1865, Blue Aqua, Ground Lip, 1865-1875, 5 1/8 In.	330.00
Barrel, Pat. Oct. 17, 1865, Zinc Lid, 5 1/2 In.	395.00
Berlin Black Ink, Berlin, N.H., Umbrella, Aqua Green, OP, Label, Wax Sealed Cork	325.00
Bertinguiot, Aqua, Tooled Lip, Embossed, Round, France, 1840-1850, 2 1/2 In.	125.00
Bertinguiot, Domed, Olive Amber, Sheared Mouth, Pontil, 1820-1860, 2 In.	100.00
Bertinguiot, Round, Light Olive Amber, Sheared Lip, Embossed, Pontil, 1850, 2 1/4 In.	365.00
Bertinguiot, Yellow Olive, Sheared Lip, Pontil, 1835-1855, 2 In.	160.00
Billing's Mauve, Aqua, Ground Top, 2 3/4 In.	75.00

Ink, Blake & Herring, Umbrella, 8-Sided, Light Green, Pontil, 3 1/8 In.

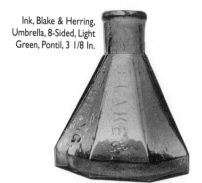

Ink, Bradford's Fine Blue Writing Fluid, Olive Amber, OP, 2 1/2 In.

Bixby, Cone, Tooled Lip, Open Bubble, Cork, 2 1/2 In.	15.00
Black Glass, Blown, 3-Piece Mold, OP, 1 1/2 x 2 3/8 In.	50.00
Black Glass, Ink, Residue Inside, Round, OP, 2 1/2 In.	150.00
Blackwood & Co., London, 1880, Dome, Cobalt Blue, Fluted Sides, Sheared Lip, 2 In.	270.00
Blackwood & Co., Patent London, Green, Dome, 2 In.	35.00
Blake, N.Y., 8-Sided, Pale Aqua, Infolded Lip, OP, 1840-1850, 2 15/16 In.	145.00
Blake & Herring, Brooklyn, N.Y., 8-Sided, Aqua, Infolded, Pontil, 1850, 3 In.	365.00
Blake & Herring, Umbrella, 8-Sided, Light Green, Pontil, 3 1/8 In. ....*Illus*	784.00
Blue Green, Blown, Tapered Lip, OP, New England, 1775-1810, 2 3/8 In.	720.00
Boat, Moss Green, Sheared Top, 2 Pen Rests, 2 1/2 In.	28.00
Boss Patent, 6-Sided, Aqua, Infolded Lip, OP, 1840-1850, 2 3/8 In.	305.00
Boss Patent, Green, Rolled Lip, OP, 2 1/2 In.	440.00
Bradford's Fine Blue Writing Fluid, Olive Amber, OP, 2 1/2 In. ....*Illus*	448.00
Brown Amber, Blown, 3-Piece Mold, Mt. Vernon Glassworks, N.Y., OP, 2 In.	475.00
Buchanan & Huggins, Wellsburg, W. Va., Uncle Sam Bust, Milk Glass, 1870-1880, 3 In.	505.00
Building, Centennial Exposition, Factory Ground Lip, Smooth Base, 1876, 3 1/2 In.	590.00
Burglar, Man, Scowling, Holding Club, Light Aqua, England, 1850-1870, 3 3/8 In.	245.00
Butler's, Cincinnati, O., 12-Sided, Aqua, OP, 1840-1850, 2 7/8 In.	305.00
Butler's, Cincinnati, O., 12-Sided, Aqua, Rolled Lip, OP, 1845-1855	95.00
Butler's, Cincinnati, O., Aqua, Vertical Embossed, OP, 1850, 3 In.	170.00
Butler's, Cincinnati, O., Cone, Aqua, Sheared Lip, Pontil, 2 In.	390.00
Butler's, Cincinnati, O., Cylindrical, Yellow Green, Infolded Lip, OP, 1850, 5 1/4 In.	590.00
Butler's, Cincinnati, O., Pale Green, Elongated Neck, Infolded Lip, 1850, 2 1/2 In.	155.00
Butler's, Cincinnati, O., Round, Aqua, Infolded Lip, OP, 2 7/8 In.	225.00
Butler's, Cincinnati, Yellow Olive, 12 Panels, OP, 2 1/2 In. ....*Illus*	6875.00
C. Blackman, Providence, R.I., Medium Green, Infolded Lip, OP, 1850, 3 In.	305.00
Cabin, Deep Gold Amber, Sheared Lip, Windows Both Sides, 1860-1870, 2 3/4 In.	2015.00
Cabin, Front & Back Doors, Tooled Square Collar, 1870, 2 1/2 In.	310.00
Cabin, Ground Mouth, Smooth Base, Rectangular, 1860-1890, 3 1/8 In.	410.00
Cabin, Heavy Flint Glass, Tooled, Ground Lip, 1860, 3 1/4 In.	645.00
Cabin, Rectangular, Ground Mouth, 3 3/8 In.	550.00
Cabin, Smooth Base, Tooled Mouth, 1865-1875, 2 1/4 In.	245.00
Cabin, Tooled Mouth, Smooth Base, 1860-1890, 2 3/8 In.	210.00
Cabin, Tooled Square Collar, Smooth Base, 1870, 2 5/16 In.	480.00
Caldwell's Flo-Eesi Inks, Aqua, Master	30.00
Carter's, 6-Sided, Cathedral, Pale Yellow, ABM, 1920, 10 In.	770.00
Carter's, 6-Sided, Cobalt Blue, 2 13/16 In.	150.00
Carter's, 6-Sided, Cobalt Blue, Clover Leaf, ABM, 1920s, 2 7/8 In.	120.00
Carter's, Cabin, Turtle, Aqua, Embossed, 2 In.	335.00
Carter's, Cathedral, 6-Sided, Cobalt Blue, 9 1/2 In.	118.00
Carter's, Cathedral, Cobalt Blue, 6 1/4 In.	220.00
Carter's, Cathedral, Cobalt Blue, ABM, 1925-1935, 6 1/4 In.	210.00
Carter's, Cathedral, Cobalt Blue, ABM, 9 3/4 In. ....90.00 to	120.00
Carter's, Cathedral, Cobalt Blue, ABM, Label, 1930, 9 3/4 In.	155.00
Carter's, Cathedral, Cobalt Blue, ABM, Qt.	100.00

Carter's, Cathedral, Cobalt Blue, Pt., 8 In. 40.00
Carter's, Cathedral, Cobalt Blue, Qt. 90.00
Carter's, Cathedral, Deep Cobalt Blue, ABM, 1920-1925, 7 7/8 In. ....110.00 to 145.00
Carter's, Cathedral, Deep Cobalt Blue, ABM, 6 1/4 In. 230.00
Carter's, Cathedral, Label, Neck Seal, Qt. 175.00
Carter's, Cathedral, Medium Cobalt Blue, ABM, 7 7/8 In. 145.00
Carter's, Clover Leaf, 8-Sided, Sapphire Blue, ABM, 2 3/4 In. 165.00
Carter's, Clover Leaf, Cobalt Blue, 6-Sided, ABM, 1920-1930, 2 7/8 In. ....100.00 to 155.00
Carter's, Cobalt Blue, Smooth Base, ABM, 1920-1930, 6 1/4 In. 175.00
Carter's, Cobalt Blue, Smooth Base, ABM, 1920-1930, 7 7/8 In. 155.00
Carter's, Cone, Aqua, 1897, Cork, 2 1/4 In. 15.00
Carter's, Cone, Blue Aqua, Double Ring Collar, Cork, 2 1/2 In. 15.00
Carter's, Cylindrical, Aqua, Cork, 2 1/2 In. 5.00
Carter's, Cylindrical, Honey Amber, Ring, Spout, 10 In. 230.00
Carter's, Cylindrical, Light Aqua, Tooled Lip, Ink, Embossed Base, Cork 5.00
Carter's, Deep Blue Green, Applied Mouth, Original Front, Back Labels, 1880, 8 In. ... 360.00
Carter's, Dome Offset Neck, Front Door, 4 Windows, 1890, 2 In. 715.00
Carter's, Dome, 16 Panels, 2 1/8 In. 150.00
Carter's, Domed Offset Neck Shape, Front Door & 4 Windows, 1860-1890, 1 5/8 In. 230.00
Carter's, Fountain Pen, Red, No. 578, 2 1/2 In. ....*Illus* 14.00
Carter's, Fountain, Ground Mouth, 2 1/4 In. 75.00
Carter's, Green, Applied Top, 7 3/4 In. 65.00
Carter's, Green, Embossed, Spout, 6 1/8 In. 85.00
Carter's, Jug, Stoneware, White & Brown, Blue Letters, Gal. 100.00
Carter's, Light Yellow Amber, Pour Spout, 9 7/8 In. 200.00
Carter's, Ma & Pa Carter, Pat'd Jan. 6, 1914, Germany, 3 1/2 In., Pair ....145.00 to 175.00
Carter's, Ma & Pa Carter, Porcelain, Multicolor, Germany, 1914, 3 3/4 In., Pair 175.00
Carter's, Semi-Cathedral, Cobalt Blue, ABM, Spout, Bakelite Lid, 9 3/4 In. 50.00
Carter's, Square, Aqua, Hinged Top, 2 1/2 In. 75.00
Carter's Sunset Brown, Clipper Ship, Tin Lid 3.00
Carter's-70, Cone, Blue Aqua, 2 1/2 In. 7.00
Cathedral, Cobalt Blue, Original Label, ABM, 1920-1935, 6 1/4 In. 265.00
Cathedral, Cobalt Blue, Original Label, ABM, 1920-1935, 7 7/8 In. 175.00
Cathedral, Medium Cobalt Blue, Original Label, ABM, 1920-1935, 9 3/4 In. 75.00
Caw's Black Fluid Ink, Deep Blue Green, Spout, Applied Top, 9 1/4 In. ....300.00 to 325.00
Caw's Ink, New York, Light Green, BIMAL, 1 13/16 In. 45.00
Cherry Puce, Burnt Orange, 3-Piece Mold, 1865-1870, 7 1/2 In. 400.00
Chicken, W.R. & Co., Akron, Ohio, Pat'd April '85, Stoneware, 2 1/2 x 4 1/2 In. 200.00
Chicken Design, 24 Ribs, Swirled To Right, Sea Green, Sheared Lip, 1830, 3 x 3 5/8 In. 16500.00
Chinese Black Ink, Shaw & Co., Boston, Olive Amber, Label, Pontil, 1840, 4 1/2 In. 35.00
Clarke & Co., N.O., Utility, 12-Sided, Aqua, Infolded Lip, OP, 1850, 4 7/8 In. 280.00
Cobalt Blue, Double Graduated Top, Rounded Sides, Sheared Lip, Brass Lid, Square, 2 In. 75.00
Commercial Ink, London, Barrel, Cobalt Blue, 1860-1870, 5 1/8 In. 300.00
Commercial Ink, London, Barrel, Cobalt Blue, Swirls, Double Spout, Canada, 5 1/8 In. . 45.00
Commercial Superior Black Ink Manufactured, Olive Amber, OP, 1830, 3 7/8 In. .. 245.00

Ink, Butler's, Cincinnati,
Yellow Olive, 12 Panels,
OP, 2 1/2 In.

Ink, Carter's, Fountain
Pen, Red, No. 578,
2 1/2 In.

Cone, Aqua, 2 Rings Around Neck, Cork, 3 In. 5.00
Cone, Aqua, Inward Folded Lip, OP, 1840-1850, 2 1/2 In. 95.00
Cone, Aqua, Rolled Lip, OP, 1835-1855, 3 1/4 In. 200.00
Cone, Blue Green, Infolded Lip, Pontil, 1845-1855, 2 1/2 In. 245.00
Cone, Blue Green, OP, New York, 1840-1850, 1 3/8 In. 245.00
Cone, Deep Olive Green, Amber Tone, Pontil, Sheared Lip, 1835-1855, 2 3/8 In. 130.00
Cone, Deep Yellow Olive, Sheared Mouth, 1860, 2 3/8 In. 185.00
Cone, Draped, Sapphire Blue, Applied Double Collar, OP, 1840-1850, 3 7/8 In. 4125.00
Cone, E.L. Foulton Druggist & Apothecary, Medium Green, OP, 1840-1850, 2 1/2 In. . . . 280.00
Cone, Green Aqua, Tooled Lip, Cork, 2 1/2 In. 15.00
Cone, L.H. Thomas, Aqua, BIMAL, 2 5/8 In. 95.00
Cone, Light Aqua, Ring Around Shoulder, Cork, 2 1/4 In. 7.00
Cone, Light Emerald Green, Rolled Lip, OP, 2 1/4 In. 100.00
Cone, Light Sapphire Blue, Rolled Inward, Pontil, 1840-1850, 2 3/4 In. 365.00
Cone, Medium Cobalt Blue, 2 3/16 In. . . . . .70.00 to 90.00
Cone, Medium Cobalt Blue, Tooled Mouth, 1860, 2 1/2 In. 880.00
Cone, Medium Olive Green, Pontil, Sheared Lip, 1835-1855, 2 3/8 In. 145.00
Cone, Medium Root Beer Amber, Sheared Lip, Pontil, 1835-1855, 2 3/8 In. 130.00
Cone, Olive Amber, Pontil, 1846-1860, 2 1/4 In. 200.00
Cone, Olive Amber, Pontil, 1846-1860, 2 3/8 In. 165.00
Cone, Olive Amber, Sheared Lip, OP, 1855-1865, 2 1/2 In. 450.00
Cone, Olive Green, Sheared Lip, 1850-1860, 2 3/8 In. 280.00
Cone, Pink Amethyst, Cork, Tooled Lip, 2 1/2 In. 20.00
Cone, Red Brown, Dark Brown Accents, Flared Lip, 1840-1850, 2 1/2 In. 170.00
Cone, Ribs, Aqua, OP, Flared Lip, 1835-1855, 2 1/8 In. 120.00
Cone, Root Beer Amber, Sheared Lip, 1835-1855, 2 1/4 In. 190.00
Cone, Sapphire Blue, Drape, Double Applied Collar, Pontil, 1840-1850, 2 1/4 In. 1980.00
Cone, Sapphire Blue, Rolled Inward, OP, 1840-1850, 2 5/8 In. 290.00
Cone, Yellow Amber, Sheared Lip, 1835-1855, 2 1/4 In. 245.00
Cone, Yellow Green, Infolded Lip, OP, 1840-1850, 2 3/8 In. 505.00
Cone, Yellow Green, X On Base, Sheared Lip, Pontil, 2 1/4 In. 345.00
Cone, Yellow Olive, Sheared Mouth, Pontil, 1860, 2 1/2 In. 220.00
Cone, Yellow, Olive Tone, Sheared Lip, Pontil, 1845-1855, 2 1/8 In. 330.00
Corona, No. 286, Porcelain, Dark Green, Hand Painted Flower Design, Holland, 2 Piece . 225.00
Corset, Cobalt Blue, 3-Piece Mold, Blown, Sandwich Glassworks, 22 In. 7150.00
Cut Glass, Canary Yellow, 3 Pen Shelves, Brass Hinged Collar, 1880-1900, 2 1/2 In. 415.00
Cylindrical, Amethyst, Spout, 1860-1880, 7 5/8 In. 120.00
Cylindrical, Cobalt Blue, Flared Lip, OP, 3 In. 40.00
Cylindrical, Cobalt Blue, Vertical Ribs, Sheared Rim, Pontil, 2 1/4 In. 100.00
Cylindrical, Deep Purple Amethyst, Spout Collar, 1860-1865, 6 1/2 In. 365.00
Cylindrical, Emerald Green, Applied Spout Mouth, IP, 8 3/4 In. 100.00
Cylindrical, Gold Amber, Funnel Type Opening, Blown, Pontil, 1840-1850, 2 1/8 In. 270.00
Cylindrical, Robin's Egg Blue, White Striped Latticinio, Metal Lid, Closure, Blown, 1890 770.00
Cylindrical, Yellow Olive Amber, Spout, New England, 1855-1875, 9 5/8 In. 85.00
Cylindrical, Yellow Olive, Spout, Pontil, 1840-1850, 6 1/2 In. 180.00
Dark Olive Amber, Disc Top, 3-Piece Mold, Pontil, Coventry, Ct., 1 7/8 In. 245.00
Dark Olive Green, Disc Top, 3-Piece Mold, Pontil, Coventry, Ct., 1830, 2 In. 290.00
Davids', Blue Green, Embossed, c.1870, 1 7/8 In. 2200.00
Davids', Turtle, Aqua, 1 3/4 In. 80.00
Davids', Turtle, Aqua, Dome, Tooled Lip, 1865-1875, 2 In. 25.00
Davids', Turtle, Deep Blue Green, Offset Neck, Tooled Lip, 1780, 1 7/8 In. 70.00
Davids', Turtle, Gold Amber, Dome, Tooled Collar, Smooth Base, 1865-1875, 2 In. 295.00
Davids', Turtle, Teal, Tooled Lip, 1870-1880, 1 3/4 In. 415.00
Davids' & Black, Emerald Green, Ring, Pour Spout, Pontil, 9 In. 185.00
Davids' & Black, Light Green, OP, 4 1/2 In. 95.00
Davids' & Black, N.Y., Blue Green, Tubular Pontil, 1860, 4 7/8 In. 145.00
Davids' & Black, N.Y., Cylindrical, Light Green, Embossed Shoulder, Pontil, 1850, 4 In. 60.00
Davids' & Black, N.Y., Deep Blue Green, Pour Spout, IP, 1860, 8 13/16 In. 245.00
Davids' & Black, N.Y., Emerald Green, Applied Tapered Collar, OP, 1840-1850, 5 7/8 In. 420.00
Davids' Electro Chemical Ink, Label, Cobalt Blue, Box, 8 3/4 In. 185.00
Davis & Miller, Umbrella, 8-Sided, Light Aqua, Wide Vertical Flutes, 1850, 2 In. 200.00
De Halsey, Dome, Dense Yellow Olive, Tooled Mouth, Pontil, 3 1/8 In. 90.00
De Halsey, Olive Amber, Dome Shape, Embossed, Sheared Lip, 2-Piece Mold, 1830, 3 In. 645.00

Deep Olive Green, Tooled Disc Mouth, 3-Piece Mold, Pontil, 1840, 1 15/16 In. 230.00
Dessauer's, Cone, Aqua, Side Embossed, 3 In. 95.00
Dessauer's Jet Black Ink, Turtle, Aqua, Ground Lip, 1870, 1 7/8 In. 80.00
Dessauer's Jet Black Ink, Turtle, Blue Aqua, Ground Lip, 1870-1880, 2 In. 150.00
Diamond Ink Co., Milwaukee, Wis., Patented April 13, 1875, Blue Green, 7 1/2 In. 120.00
Dome, Aqua, BIMAL, 1 5/8 In. 50.00
Dome, Bird On Branch, Aqua, Embossed Bird Standing On Tree Branch, 1875, 1 In. 90.00
Dome, Black Amber, Blown, Beveled Edges, Flared Lip, Pontil, 1820, 2 3/8 In. 210.00
Dove Brand Brilliant Green Ink For Rubber Stamps, Square, Aqua, Contents .40.00 to 55.00
Dovell's Inks & Fluids, Bell, Aqua, Tooled Collar, 1870-1880, 7 3/8 In. 155.00
Dr. A. Sheet's Writing Fluid, Dayton, O., 6-Sided, Aqua, Corset, OP, 1850, 3 In. 785.00
Dunbar, Taunton, Mass., Cylindrical, Aqua, 7 1/2 In. 20.00
E. Eichele, 12-Sided, Aqua, Infolded Lip, OP, 1840-1850, 2 3/4 In. 245.00
E. Waters, A, Aqua, Vertical Ribs, Embossed A On Back, OP, 1850, 3 In. . . . .*Illus*   180.00
E. Waters, B, Aqua, Vertical Ribs, Embossed B On Back, OP, 1850, 3 In. 145.00
E. Waters, Troy, N.Y., Aqua, Applied Mouth, OP, 1845-1855, 2 5/16 In. 210.00
E. Waters, Troy, N.Y., Aqua, Applied Mouth, OP, 1845-1855, 3 In. 415.00
E. Waters, Troy, N.Y., Aqua, Applied Mouth, OP, 1845-1855, 5 1/4 In. . . . . .420.00 to 605.00
E. Waters, Troy, N.Y., Aqua, Applied Mouth, Pontil, 1845-1855, 6 3/4 In. 440.00
E. Waters, Troy, N.Y., Aqua, Fluted Shoulders, 1850, 2 5/16 In.   200.00
E. Waters, Troy, N.Y., Aqua, Fluted Shoulders, OP, 1850-1860, 4 1/8 In. 420.00
E. Waters, Troy, N.Y., Blue Green, Fluted Shoulders, Flange Collar, IP, 1860, 5 5/8 In. . . .   1210.00
E. Waters, Troy, N.Y., Cylindrical, Aqua, Fluted Shoulders, 1850, 7 In. 235.00
E. Waters, Troy, N.Y., Cylindrical, Light Green, Fluted Shoulder, Pontil, 5 1/2 In. 470.00
E. Waters, Troy, N.Y., Cylindrical, Light Green, Fluted Shoulders, 1860, 3 7/8 In. 365.00
E. Waters, Troy, N.Y., Dark Yellow Olive, Rolled Over Lip, 1860-1865, 6 In. 2750.00
E.S. Curtis Indelible Ink, Yellow Green, Applied Square Collar Lip, OP, 1850, 6 1/4 In.   190.00
Electric Blue, Opalescent, Square, 1770-1795, OP, 1 3/4 In. 795.00
Estes, N.Y., 8-Sided, Aqua, Applied Ring Lip, OP, 1840-1850, 7 In. 365.00
Estes, N.Y., 8-Sided, Aqua, Elongated Neck, Applied Collar, 1840-1850, 5 9/16 In. 315.00
Estes, N.Y., 8-Sided, Green, Cone, Umbrella, OP, 1840-1850, 3 3/8 In. 2310.00
Estes, N.Y., 8-Sided, Medium Blue Green, Unusual Applied Collar, OP, 1840-1850, 6 In.   785.00
Estes, N.Y., 8-Sided, Umbrella, Aqua, Cone, OP, 1840-1850, 3 3/8 In. 280.00
F. Klett & Co. Superior Ink, Aqua, Embossed, OP, 1830-1840, 4 1/4 In. 190.00
F.H. Metzger, Cylindrical, Aqua, Infolded Lip, OP, 1840-1850, 1 15/16 In. 123.00
Fahnestock's Neutral, 6 Concave Panels, Aqua, Inward Rolled Lip, OP, 1850, 4 In. 315.00
Farley's, 8-Sided, Olive Amber, Orange Label, Tooled Collar, OP, 1840-1850, 3 In. 895.00
Farley's, 8-Sided, Olive Amber, Replaced Lip, Pontil, 1840-1850, 3 5/8 In. 325.00
Farley's, Gold Olive Amber, S On Next Panel, 1 3/4 In. 625.00
Farley's, Medium Gold Amber, Sheared Mouth, Pontil, 1846-1860, 1 3/4 In. 330.00
Farley's, Olive Amber, Sheared Mouth, Pontil, 1846-1860, 1 3/4 In. 250.00
Farley's, Yellow Amber, Octagonal Sheared Lip, Pontil, 1840-1850, 1 7/8 In. 1010.00
Field's Blue-Black Ink, Jug, Brown, Handle, Label, Stoneware, 1915, 13 1/8 In. 55.00
Flat Round Body, Cobalt Blue, Wide-Mouth Rim, Blown, Interior Lid, 2 In. 245.00
Forest Green, Spout, Applied Top, Pontil, 9 1/2 In. 140.00
Fountain, Dome, 12-Sided, 2 1/2 In. . . . . .35.00 to 55.00
Fountain, Dome, 12-Sided, Light Amethyst, 2 1/2 In. 65.00
Fountain, Snail, Light Electric Blue, Ornate Brass Stand, 1850-1890, 4 1/4 In. 220.00
Funnel, Amber, Bubbles, OP, 1 13/16 In. 85.00
Funnel, Rubber Stopper, Polished Base, BIMAL, 2 3/8 x 2 3/4 In. 15.00
G. & R. American Writing Fluid, Cone, Aqua, OP, 1840-1850, 2 5/8 In. 400.00
G. & R. American Writing Fluid, Cone, Aqua, Rolled Mouth, Pontil, 2 1/2 In. 550.00
G.A. Miller, Quincy, Ill., 8-Sided, Aqua, Applied Collar, 1860, 2 1/2 In. 290.00
Gaylord's Superior Record Ink, Boston, Olive Green, Pontil, 1835-1850, 5 In. 895.00
Geo. H. Baker Co. Pharmaceutise, Barrel, Aqua, Infolded Lip, 1870-1880, 3 3/4 In. . .   390.00
Geometric, Applied Disc, 3-Piece Mold, Pontil, 1815-1830, 2 In. 2530.00
Geometric, Deep Olive Amber, Applied Disc Mouth, Pontil, 1820s, 1 7/8 In. 145.00
Geometric, Deep Olive Amber, Tooled Disc Mouth, OP, 1815-1830, 1 7/8 In. 90.00
Geometric, Deep Olive Green, Applied Disc, 3-Piece Mold, 1815-1830, 2 In. 200.00
Geometric, Deep Root Beer Amber, Applied Disc, 3-Piece Mold, OP, 1830, 2 In. 440.00
Geometric, Medium To Light Amber, Disc Top, 3-Piece Mold, Pontil, 1 7/8 In. 670.00
Geometric, Yellow Olive Amber, Applied Disc, 1815-1830, 2 In. 155.00
Geometric, Yellow Olive Amber, Applied Disc, Pontil, 1810s, 1 1/2 In. 140.00

George A. Moss, Turtle, Aqua, Letter On Each Panel, Label Panel, 1870, 1 1/2 In. 270.00
George A. Moss, Umbrella, 8-Sided, Aqua, Rolled Lip, 1865-1880, 2 7/16 In. 65.00
Golden Treasure, Barrel, Aqua, Applied Square Collar, 1870, 3 5/8 In. 100.00
Goodwin & Leonard, Lowell, Mass., Utility, Olive, 1840-1850, 4 3/4 In. 960.00
Gross & Robinson's, Auburn, N.Y., Aqua, Applied Mouth, OP, 1845-1855, 4 1/4 In. 550.00
Gross & Robinson's American Writing Fluid, Aqua, Flared Mouth, Pontil, 4 In. 770.00
Gross & Robinson's American Writing Fluid, Aqua, IP, 1860, 6 In. 815.00
Gross & Robinson's American Writing Fluid, Aqua, Pontil, 1850, 7 In. 1010.00
H & T Red, Cone, Pale Aqua, Tooled Lip, 1840-1850, 2 In. 125.00
Hall & Parishall, Lyons, N.Y., Cobalt Blue, 3-Piece Mold, 1860-1870, 10 3/8 In. 190.00
Harrison's Columbian, 8-Sided, Aqua, Infolded Lip, OP, 1850, 2 In. 95.00
Harrison's Columbian, 8-Sided, Aqua, OP, 3 1/4 In. 110.00
Harrison's Columbian, 8-Sided, Aqua, OP, Rolled Lip, 1845-1855, 1 7/8 In. ..... 65.00 to 120.00
Harrison's Columbian, 8-Sided, Blue Aqua, Applied Mouth, 1845-1855, 6 1/8 In. 200.00
Harrison's Columbian, 8-Sided, Blue Aqua, Applied Mouth, OP, 1845-1855, 3 5/8 In. ... 145.00
Harrison's Columbian, 8-Sided, Blue Aqua, Pontil, Rolled Lip, 1845-1855, 2 In. 155.00
Harrison's Columbian, 8-Sided, Blue Green, Inward Rolled Lip, 1850, 1 7/8 In. 765.00
Harrison's Columbian, 8-Sided, Light Blue Green, Rolled Lip, OP, 1 7/8 In. 120.00
Harrison's Columbian, 8-Sided, Light Yellow Green, OP, 1850, 1 15/16 In. 895.00
Harrison's Columbian, 8-Sided, Medium Yellow Olive, OP, 1 1/2 In. 2035.00
Harrison's Columbian, 8-Sided, Yellow Green, Pontil, 1840-1850, 1 3/4 In. 260.00
Harrison's Columbian, 12-Sided, Apple Green, Flared Mouth, Pontil, 7 In. 330.00
Harrison's Columbian, 12-Sided, Aqua, Embossed Patent On Shoulder, 1850, 7 In. 145.00
Harrison's Columbian, 12-Sided, Aqua, Flange Collar, 1850, 7 1/2 In. 420.00
Harrison's Columbian, 12-Sided, Aqua, Flange Collar, Pontil, 12 In. 2310.00
Harrison's Columbian, 12-Sided, Aqua, Pontil, 1840-1860, 7 In. 265.00
Harrison's Columbian, 12-Sided, Aqua, Pontil, 1845-1860, 7 1/4 In. 280.00
Harrison's Columbian, 12-Sided, Aqua, Square Collar, Pontil, 5 7/8 In. 275.00
Harrison's Columbian, 12-Sided, Blue Aqua, OP, 5 3/4 In. 175.00
Harrison's Columbian, 12-Sided, Light Blue Green, Flange Collar, Pontil, 1850, 10 In. .. 670.00
Harrison's Columbian, 12-Sided, Medium Blue, Flange Collar, IP, 1850, 11 1/2 In. 25300.00
Harrison's Columbian, Aqua, Large Applied Top, OP, 4 1/2 In. 190.00
Harrison's Columbian, Aqua, OP, Rolled Lip, 1840-1855, 1 3/4 In. 145.00
Harrison's Columbian, Cobalt Blue, Applied Mouth, Pontil, 1845-1855, 7 In. 580.00
Harrison's Columbian, Cobalt Blue, Flange Collar, OP, 1840-1850, 4 1/8 In. 800.00
Harrison's Columbian, Cobalt Blue, Flange Collar, OP, 1840-1850, 5 In. 1100.00
Harrison's Columbian, Cobalt Blue, Flange Collar, OP, 1840-1850, 7 7/16 In. 365.00
Harrison's Columbian, Cobalt Blue, Infolded Lip, OP, 1850, 2 1/16 In. 560.00
Harrison's Columbian, Cobalt Blue, Infolded Lip, OP, Glassborrow, N.J., 3 In. 560.00
Harrison's Columbian, Cobalt Blue, Inward Folded Lip, 1840-1850, 2 1/4 In. 395.00
Harrison's Columbian, Cobalt Blue, OP, 4 5/8 In. ....275.00 to 470.00
Harrison's Columbian, Cobalt Blue, Rolled Lip, OP, 1845-1855, 2 1/8 In. 745.00
Harrison's Columbian, Cobalt Blue, Sloping Shoulders, 1840-1850, 7 3/8 In. 505.00
Harrison's Columbian, Cobalt Blue, Unembossed Variant, OP, 7 1/2 In. 365.00
Harrison's Columbian, Cylindrical, Aqua, Right-Sided, Flange Collar, 2 9/16 In. 100.00
Harrison's Columbian, Cylindrical, Cobalt Blue, Flared Mouth, Pontil, 1840-1860, 6 In. 150.00
Harrison's Columbian, Cylindrical, Cobalt Blue, OP, 1845-1855, 2 1/16 In. ....200.00 to 360.00
Harrison's Columbian, Cylindrical, Sapphire Blue, Tubular Pontil, 2 1/8 In. 525.00
Harrison's Columbian, Deep Cobalt Blue, Applied Mouth, OP, 1845-1855, 5 In. 1020.00
Harrison's Columbian, Deep Cobalt Blue, Applied Mouth, Pontil, 1845-1855, 7 In. 605.00
Harrison's Columbian, Deep Cobalt Blue, Rolled Lip, OP, 1840-1855, 2 In. 230.00
Harrison's Columbian, Igloo, 8-Sided, Aqua, Flattened Dome, 1860, 2 In. 420.00
Harrison's Columbian, Igloo, Aqua, Sheared Lip, 1850-1860, 1 7/8 In. 550.00
Harrison's Columbian, Light Blue, Infolded Lip, New Jersey, OP, 1840-1850, 2 1/8 In. .. 530.00
Harrison's Columbian, Prussian Blue, Flange Collar, OP, 1840-1850, 7 1/4 In. 2860.00
Harrison's Columbian, Sapphire Blue, Flange Collar, OP, 1840-1850, 4 1/8 In. 1100.00
Harrison's Columbian, Sapphire Blue, Infolded Lip, Tubular Pontil, 2 In. 275.00
Harrison's Columbian, Sapphire Blue, Rolled Mouth, Pontil, 2 In. 550.00
Harrison's Columbian Blue Black Writing Fluid, c.1840, 4 1/8 In. 1100.00
Harrison's Columbian Perfumery, Pink Tone, Ground Lip, 1850-1860, 2 5/8 In. 110.00
Harrison-Tippecanoe, Cabin, Tooled Flared Lip, OP, 1840, 4 In. 14850.00
Herron's, Newville, Pa., Aqua, Sloping Shoulders, Infolded Lip, OP, 3 5/16 In. 530.00
Herron's, Newville, Pa., Blue Aqua, Conical Shoulders, Embossed, OP, 1850, 3 In. 560.00

Higgs, 12-Sided, Aqua, Infolded Lip, Key Mold Base, 1840-1850, 2 7/8 In. 180.00
Hockey Puck Shape, Dark Olive Green, 2-Piece Mold, Pontil, 1790-1830, 2 1/8 In. 145.00
Hockey Puck Shape, Gold Amber, Flared Lip, 2-Piece Mold, France, 1830, 2 1/8 In. 125.00
Hodgson's, Phila., Pa., Cone, Clear, Original Label, Tooled Mouth, 1855, 1 7/8 In. 305.00
Hodgson's, Phila., Pa., Cone, Flint Glass, Flared Lip, Pontil, 1830-1840, 2 In. 95.00
Hohenthal Brothers & Co. Indelible Writing, Cylindrical, Yellow Olive, 9 1/4 In. 355.00
Hohenthal Brothers & Co. Indelible Writing, N.Y., Olive Amber, 1850, 9 In. .615.00 to 690.00
Hookers, Aqua, 3 Crossed Pen Ledges, Corner Domed, New England, 1870, 2 In. 235.00
House, Aqua, Sheared Lip, Embossed Roof Panel, 1870-1880, 2 5/8 In. 700.00
House, Aqua, Smooth Base, Tooled Mouth, 1880-1890, 3 1/2 In. 210.00
House, Aqua, Tooled Square Collar, 1870-1880, 2 5/8 In. 125.00
House, Aqua, Windows On 4 Sided, Tooled Collar, 1870-1880, 2 3/8 In. 290.00
Hover, Phila., 8-Sided, Light Blue Green, Infolded Lip, OP, 1840-1850, 2 1/4 In. 390.00
Hover, Phila., 8-Sided, Light Blue Green, OP, 1840-1850, 2 3/8 In. 895.00
Hover, Phila., 12-Sided, Blue Green, Rolled Lip, OP, 1840-1850, 1 3/4 In. 325.00
Hover, Phila., Cobalt Blue, Tooled Lip, OP, 1845, 2 5/8 In. 150.00
Hover, Phila., Cylindrical, Green, Flared Mouth, Tubular Pontil, Cleaned, 1840-1860, 6 In. 175.00
Hover, Phila., Cylindrical, Medium Green, Tapered Collar, IO, 1840-1850, 5 1/2 In. 200.00
Hover, Phila., Dome, Aqua, Sheared Lip, OP, 1840-1850, 1 5/8 In. 225.00
Hover, Phila., Green, Applied Spout, IP, 1860, 9 1/2 In. 280.00
Hover, Phila., Olive Green, Thin Flared Lip, OP, 1845-1855, 2 3/4 In. 200.00
Hover, Phila., Sapphire Blue, Flared Lip, OP, 1840-1850, 5 1/4 In. 755.00
Howe's Unchangeable Blue, Boston, Deep Green, Spout, Pontil, 1850, 7 3/8 In. 560.00
Hyde, London, Cylindrical, Cobalt Blue, Spout, 6 In. 58.00
Hyde, London, Square, Cobalt Blue, Spout, Cleaned, 5 1/2 In. 60.00
Igloo, Cobalt Blue, Ground Lip, 1875-1890, 2 In. 1320.00
Igloo, Deep Purple Amethyst, Sheared Lip, 1870-1880, 2 In. 1375.00
Igloo, Dome, Amber, High Back, Embossed Star On Base, 1865-1875, 2 In. 215.00
Igloo, Dome, Aqua, High Back, Tooled Lip, Albany, N.Y., 1865-1875, 2 1/8 In. 50.00
Igloo, High Dome, Aqua, Ground Lip, Smooth Base, 1870, 2 In. 40.00
Igloo, Red Amber, Ground Lip, 1870-1880, 2 In. 240.00
Internal Funnel Design, German Half-Post Neck, Blown, 1830, 2 7/8 In. 95.00
J. & I.E.M., Dome, Root Beer Amber, Offset Neck, 1880, 1 5/8 In. 130.00
J. & I.E.M., Domed, Yellow, Amber Tone, Tooled Mouth, 1860-1880, 2 In. 55.00
J. & I.E.M., Igloo, Aqua, 1 7/8 In. 480.00
J. & I.E.M., Igloo, Citron, Tooled Mouth, 1875-1890, 1 5/8 In. 605.00
J. & I.E.M., Igloo, Cobalt Blue, Domed Form, Offset Neck, Tooled Mouth, 1 3/4 In. 1980.00
J. & I.E.M., Igloo, Medium Amber, 1 13/16 In. 290.00
J. & I.E.M., Igloo, Medium Yellow Amber, Ground Lip, 1 5/8 In. 210.00
J. & I.E.M., Turtle, Amber, Ground Lip, 1875-1895, 1 5/8 In. .... 105.00 to 175.00
J. & I.E.M., Turtle, Blue Green, Ground Lip, c.1870-1880, 1 3/4 In. 255.00
J. & I.E.M., Turtle, Dome, Aqua, Ground Lip, 1865-1875, 1 3/4 In. .... 65.00 to 730.00
J. & I.E.M., Turtle, Dome, Aqua, Pat. Oct. 31 1865, Factory Ground Lip, 2 In. 15.00
J. & I.E.M., Turtle, Dome, Aqua, Tooled Lip, Smooth Base, 1865-1875, 2 In. 40.00
J. & I.E.M., Turtle, Dome, Aqua, Tooled Lip, Square Base, 1865-1875, 1 3/4 In. 20.00
J. & I.E.M., Turtle, Dome, Blue Green, Embossed, 1865-1875, 1 3/4 In. 3575.00
J. & I.E.M., Turtle, Dome, Blue, Factory Ground Lip, 1865-1875, 1 3/4 In. 365.00
J. & I.E.M., Turtle, Dome, Deep Amber, Factory Ground Lip, 1865-1870, 1 7/8 In. 260.00
J. & I.E.M., Turtle, Dome, Honey Amber, Factory Ground Lip, 1875, 1 3/4 In. 305.00
J. & I.E.M., Turtle, Dome, Lime Citron, Tooled Lip, Smooth Base, 1865-1875, 2 In. 590.00
J. & I.E.M., Turtle, Dome, Teal, Factory Ground Lip, 1875, 1 3/4 In. 1485.00
J. & I.E.M., Turtle, Dome, Yellow Green, Embossed, 1865-1875, 1 3/4 In. 85.00
J. & I.E.M., Turtle, Gray Variant, Dome, Embossed, Ground Lip, 1865-1875, 1 3/4 In. ... 260.00
J. & I.E.M., Turtle, High Dome, Gold Amber, Offset Neck, 1865-1875, 2 In. 125.00
J. & I.E.M., Turtle, Light Yellow, Green, Sheared Lip, 1875-1890, 1 3/4 In. 825.00
J. & I.E.M., Turtle, Sapphire Blue, Tooled Lip, c.1870-1880, 1 5/8 In. 1540.00
J. Gundry, Cincinnati, O., 12-Sided, Aqua, Rolled Lip, OP, 1845-1855, 3 In. 385.00
J. Gundry, Cincinnati, O., 12-Sided, Blue Aqua, OP, 1840-1850, 3 1/2 In. 365.00
J. Kidder Improved Indelible Ink, Square, Aqua, Rolled Lip, OP 95.00
J. Raynald, Globe, Aqua, Square Collar, Embossed, 1870-1880, 2 5/16 In. 315.00
J. Raynald, Globe, The World, Aqua, Footed, Tooled Mouth, 2 1/8 In. 110.00
J. Sargant, 10-Sided, Aqua, Tooled Lip, OP, Pittsburgh, Pa. 130.00
J.A. Williamson Chemist, Blue Green, Spout, 1870-1880, 6 7/16 In. 200.00

Ink, E. Waters,
A, Aqua, Vertical Ribs,
Embossed A On Back,
OP, 1850, 3 In.

Ink, Jared Holt's, Black
Ink, Dark Olive Amber,
Label, 3 1/8 In.

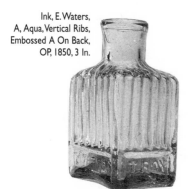

J.A. Williamson Chemist, Deep Blue Green, Spout, 1870-1880, 9 1/2 In.	255.00
J.B. Fondersmiths, 8-Sided, Aqua, Embossed Dome Shoulders, Pontil, 1850, 3 In.	125.00
J.B.C. Co., Aqua, BIMAL, 2 7/16 In.	55.00
J.C. Swearingens Inks, Pittsburg, Screw Top, Spout, Pt.	35.00
J.J. Butler, Cin., Cabin, Aqua, Rolled Lip, OP, 1845-1855, 2 3/4 In.	85.00
J.J. Butler, Cin., O., Cylindrical, Aqua, Rolled Lip, OP, 1845-1855, 2 5/16 In.	230.00
J.J. Butler, Cincinnati, O., Teakettle, 8-Sided, Aqua, Infolded Lip, OP, 1850, 1 5/8 In. . . .	270.00
J.J. Butler, Cincinnati, O., Teakettle, 8-Sided, Aqua, Sheared Lip, 1850-1860, 1 7/8 In. . .	560.00
J.J. Butler, Cincinnati, O., Teakettle, 12-Sided, Yellow Olive, OP, 1850, 2 9/16 In.	6875.00
J.J. Butler, Cincinnati, O., Teakettle, Aqua, Beveled Shoulders, Pontil, 1850, 3 In.	75.00
J.J. Butler, Cincinnati, O., Teakettle, Aqua, Sloping Shoulders, OP, 1850, 2 5/8 In.	95.00
J.J. Butler, Cincinnati, O., Teakettle, Cone, Aqua, Sheared Lip, 1850, 2 3/8 In.	280.00
J.J. Butler, Cincinnati, O., Teakettle, Cylindrical, Aqua, OP, 1850, 5 1/8 In.	215.00
J.L. Thompson, Troy, N.Y., Light Straw Yellow, Bold Embossed, 1840-1850, 5 7/8 In. . .	2530.00
J.M. & S., Dome, Aqua, Offset Neck, Ground Mouth, 1 7/8 In.	55.00
J.R. Nichols & Co., Boston, Apple Green, Druggist, Square Collar Lip, 7 In.	65.00
J.S. Dunham, 8-Sided, Blue Aqua, Rolled Lip, OP, 1845-1855, 2 5/8 In.	130.00
J.S. Dunham, 8-Sided, Blue Green, Infolded Lip, OP, 1840-1850, 2 3/8 In.	615.00
J.S. Dunham, 8-Sided, Light Green, Embossed Panels, Pontil, 1840-1850, 2 5/8 In.	180.00
J.S. Dunham, St. Louis, 12-Sided, Aqua, OP, Rolled Lip, 1845-1855, 2 7/8 In. . . .105.00 to 385.00	
J.S. Dunham, Umbrella, 8-Sided, Aqua, 2 3/8 In.	250.00
J.S. Dunham & Co., St. Louis, Aqua, 12-Panels, Infolded Lip, Pontil, 1850, 2 3/4 In. . . .	180.00
J.S. Mason, Phila., Pa., Aqua, Applied Tapered Collar, OP, 1840-1850, 6 In.	125.00
J.W. Pennell, 8-Sided, Dome, Blue Green, 2 1/8 In.	55.00
J.W. Seaton, Louisville, Ky., Umbrella, 10-Sided, Green, OP, 1840-1850, 2 3/16 In.	670.00
J.W. Seaton, Umbrella, 10-Sided, Green, Tubular Pontil, 2 1/4 In.	935.00
James P. Scott's, Aqua, Beveled Shoulders, OP, 1840-1850, 2 5/8 In.	125.00
James S. Mason & Co., 8-Sided, Aqua, Infolded Lip, Pontil, 1840-1850, 2 1/2 In.	125.00
James S. Mason & Co., Umbrella, 8-Sided, Aqua, Pontil, Rolled Lip, 1845-1855, 2 3/8 In.	140.00
Jared Holt's, Black Ink, Dark Olive Amber, Label, 3 1/8 In. . . . . *Illus*	952.00
Jet Black Ink, Scholars Choice, Little Brown Jug, Brown Glaze, 1860-1900, 2 7/8 In. . .	145.00
Jones' Empire, N.Y., 12-Sided, Emerald Green, Flange Collar, IP, 1860, 7 1/2 In.	1010.00
Jones' Empire, N.Y., 12-Sided, Olive, Applied Collar, Pontil, 7 1/4 In.	880.00
Jones' Empire, N.Y., 12-Sided, Yellow Olive, IP, 7 1/4 In.	1100.00
Jones' Empire, N.Y., Cylindrical, Emerald Green, 12-Sided, IP, 1860, 5 13/16 In.	3300.00
Joy's, Cobalt Blue, Flared Lip, 1885-1895, 2 1/4 In.	210.00
Keller Detroit, Amethyst, Tooled Lip, BIMAL, 2 In. .20.00 to 35.00	
Kirkland's Writing Fluid, Poland, O., Aqua, Rolled Lip, OP, 1845-1855, 2 1/4 In.	330.00
Kirkland's Writing Fluid, Poland, O., Round, Aqua, Dome Shape, 1840-1850, 3 In. . . .	390.00
Kosmian Safety, Medium Smoky Emerald Green, Smooth Base, 7 In.	145.00
L.C. Bordeau, Blood Red Amethyst, Infolded Collar, Pontil, France, 1790-1830, 2 1/8 In.	280.00
L.H. Thomas, Aqua, Applied Top, 8 In.	55.00
L.H. Thomas, Cone, Aqua, Embossed, 2 3/4 In.	35.00
Lancaster Glass Works, Light To Medium Blue Green, Rolled Lip, OP, 4 5/8 In.	165.00
Laughlin's & Bushfield, Wheeling, Va., 8-Sided, Aqua, Infolded, OP, 1850, 2 7/8 In. . . .	190.00

Laughlin's & Bushfield, Wheeling, Va., Aqua, Infolded Lip, 1840-1860, 3 In. 330.00
Levison's Inks, St. Louis, Gold Amber, Pen Rest Roof, Tooled Lip, 1870-1880, 1 7/8 In. 560.00
Levison's Inks, St. Louis, Modified Cabin, Honey Amber, Double Pen Rests, 2 3/4 In. .. 240.00
Lime Green, Spout, IP, 10 1/2 In. 125.00
Locomotive, American, Aqua, Ground Mouth, 2 1/8 In. 1100.00
Locomotive, Aqua, Ground Mouth, 1860-1890, 2 In. 880.00
Locomotive, Aqua, Ground Mouth, 1870-1880, 2 x 2 In. 220.00
Locomotive, Pale Green Aqua, Sheared Lip, 1870, 2 3/4 In. 1430.00
Locomotive, Pat. Oct., 1874, Aqua, Sheared & Ground Lip, 2 3/16 In. 125.00
M & P, New York, Cone, Light Blue Green, Infolded Lip, OP, 1840-1850, 2 7/16 In.135.00 to 390.00
Mason's Black Ink, Phila., 12-Sided, Emerald Green, Infolded Lip, 1 7/8 In. 330.00
Mathews & Bro's., Albany, Ia. N., 8-Sided, Aqua, Rolled Lip, OP, 1850, 2 1/2 In. 475.00
Maynard & Noyes, Boston, Yellow Olive Amber, Flared Lip, OP, 1855, 5 In. 175.00
Moncrieff Scottish Ink, Dark Cobalt Blue, Embossed, 2 1/2 In. 50.00
Monument, Cobalt Blue, Beveled Edges, N.A. Paris, Depose, 1880, 2 11/16 In. 125.00
Morgan's Patent July 16, 1867, Fountain, 2 5/16 In. 75.00
Morgan's Patent July 16, 1867, Igloo, 12-Sided, 3 13/16 In. 70.00
National Ink Co., Umbrella, 8-Sided, Aqua, Rolled Lip, 1845-1855, 2 7/16 In. 55.00
Newburgh Glass Co., Dark Green, Applied Spout, Embossed Base, 9 3/4 In. 1650.00
North & Warrins, Baltimore, Slag, Green Gray, Tapered Lip, OP, 1840-1850, 4 In. 615.00
Olive, Swirled Ribs, Blown, 2 3/8 In. 605.00
Olive Amber, Stylized Dome Shoulder, 2-Piece Mold, OP, 1820-1850, 5 1/2 In. 390.00
Olive Green, Applied Top, IP, 9 1/4 In. 75.00
Opdyke Bros., Barrel, Aqua, Tooled Collar, Smooth Base, 1860-1870, 2 1/2 In. 235.00
P & J Arnold London, Pottery, Tan, 1/2 Pt. 15.00
Parker Quink, Tin Lid, Box, 1940, 1 1/4 In. 15.00
Parker Quink, Washable Blue, Tin Lid, Box, 1940 . . . . .1.50 to 4.00
Parker Quink, Micro Film Black, World War II V-Mail Ink, Ribs, Tin Lid 6.00
Paul's Inks, New York & Chicago, Light Blue, 5 7/8 In. 130.00
Payson's Indelible, 6-Sided, Aqua, 2 Labels, Feb. 1854, 2 1/2 x 1 1/2 In. 340.00
Perine Guyot & Cie, Square, Dark Amethyst, Sheared Lip, Pontil, France, 1830, 2 1/4 In. . 280.00
Pitkin Type, 26 Vertical Ribs, Olive Green, Pontil, Keene, 1830, 1 3/4 In. 2090.00
Pitkin Type, 36 Broken Ribs, Cone, Funnel Lip, Dark Olive Green, Pontil, 1830, 2 In. . . 645.00
Pitkin Type, 36 Ribs, Swirled Left, Cone, Olive Green, Pontil, 1 3/4 x 2 7/16 In. 895.00
Pitkin Type, 36 Ribs, Swirled Left, Cone, Olive Yellow, Funnel Lip, 1830, 1 3/4 In. 1650.00
Pitkin Type, 36 Ribs, Swirled Left, Cone, Yellow Olive, Squat, 1830, 1 5/16 In. 280.00
Pitkin Type, 36 Ribs, Swirled Left, Cylindrical, Forest Green, 1 5/8 In. 440.00
Pitkin Type, 36 Ribs, Swirled Left, Deep Olive Amber, Tooled Disc Mouth, 1 1/2 In. . . . 85.00
Pitkin Type, 36 Ribs, Swirled Left, Deep Yellow Olive, Pontil, 1830, 2 x 3 In. 577.00
Pitkin Type, 36 Ribs, Swirled Left, Medium Olive Green, Beveled Edges, 1830, 1 1/2 In. 1485.00
Pitkin Type, 36 Ribs, Swirled Left, Olive Green, 1790-1815, 1 1/2 In. 580.00
Pitkin Type, 36 Ribs, Swirled Left, Square, Forest Green, Disc Lip, 1830, 2 In. 1210.00
Pitkin Type, 36 Ribs, Swirled Left, Yellow Olive, Tooled Disc Mouth, 1 1/2 In. 470.00
Pitkin Type, 36 Ribs, Swirled Right, Cylindrical, Yellow Olive, Pontil, 1 7/8 In. 330.00
Pitkin Type, 36 Ribs, Swirled Right, Dark Forest Green, Pontil, 1 3/4 In. 660.00
Pitkin Type, 36 Ribs, Swirled Right, Dark Yellow Olive, Funnel Lip, 1830, 1 5/8 In. . . . 505.00
Pitkin Type, 36 Ribs, Swirled Right, Forest Green, Tooled Mouth, Pontil, 1 7/8 In. 185.00
Pitkin Type, 36 Ribs, Swirled Right, Funnel Lip, Cone, Dark Olive Green, 1830, 1 1/2 In. 325.00
Pitkin Type, 36 Ribs, Swirled Right, Olive Green, Funnel Lip, Pontil, 1830, 1 3/4 In. . . . 5775.00
Policeman, Pale Aqua, Sheared Lip, 1850-1870, 4 In. 155.00
Pressed Glass, Square, Cobalt Blue, Faceted Diamond, Applied Metal Lip, 3 In. 125.00
Pumpkin, Yellow Olive Amber, Sheared Lip, Pontil, 1790-1830, 2 1/4 In. 672.00
Pyramid, Aqua, Elongated Neck, Infolded, Embossed Circle, 1840-1850, 2 1/8 In. 180.00
R.B. Snow, St. Louis, Mo., 12-Sided, Aqua, Infolded Lip, Pontil, 1840, 2 1/16 In. 280.00
R.F., Jet Black, Round, Sheared Lip, OP, France, 1790-1830, 2 In. 225.00
Ramsay's Ink, Nov. 7, '93, Williams' Label, Aqua, 2 1/2 In. 40.00
Ross's Excelsior Ink, 12-Sided, Deep Emerald Green, Flange Collar, Pontil, 1850, 7 In. . 3575.00
Round, Ice Blue, Ribbed Pattern, Sheared Lip, China, 3 3/4 In. 45.00
S. Fine Blk. Ink, Cylindrical, Light Green, Flared Lip, OP, 1840-1850, 3 1/4 In. 215.00
S. Fine Blk. Ink, Green, Rolled Lip, OP, 1845-1855, 3 1/16 In. 440.00
S. Fine Blk. Ink, Light Olive Green, Infolded Lip, Pontil, 1840-1850, 3 1/8 In. 235.00
S. Fine Blk. Ink, Yellow Green, Infolded Lip, Pontil, 1840-1860, 3 In. . . . . .305.00 to 425.00
S.I. Comp., Barrel, Milk Glass, Tooled Collar, Smooth Base, 1870-1880, 2 9/16 In. 420.00

S.I. Comp., Cottage, Blue Aqua, Tooled Mouth, c.1885-1895, 2 1/2 In. 185.00
S.I. Comp., House, Aqua, Half-Story, Tooled Mouth, 3 In. 330.00
S.I. Comp., House, Blue Aqua, Tooled Mouth, 1880-1890, 2 3/4 In. . . . . .130.00 to 280.00
S.I. Comp., House, Milk Glass, BIMAL, Tooled Square Collar, 1870-1880, 2 5/8 In. 365.00
S.I. Comp., House, Milk Glass, Mansard Roof, 1860-1880, 2 3/4 In. 605.00
S.I. Comp., House, Tooled Lip, Smooth Base, 1870-1880, 2 5/8 In. . . . . .155.00 to 305.00
S.J.P., Green, Monogram, Applied Top, 9 In. 45.00
S.O. Dunbar, Taunton, Mass., 8-Sided, Aqua, Flared Lip, 1840-1850, 2 5/8 In. 315.00
S.O. Dunbar, Taunton, Mass., 8-Sided, Aqua, Infolded Lip, Pontil, 1840-1850, 2 3/8 In. . 125.00
S.O. Dunbar, Taunton, Mass., 12-Sided, Aqua, Infolded Lip, Pontil, 1850, 2 1/4 In. 125.00
S.O. Dunbar, Taunton, Mass., Aqua, Spout, OP, 1840-1850, 9 In. 125.00
S.O. Dunbar, Taunton, Mass., Fluid Magnesia, Label, Aqua, Applied Mouth, 5 3/4 In.55.00 to 90.00
S.O. Dunbar, Umbrella, Taunton, 8-Sided, Aqua, Rolled Lip, OP, 1845-1855, 2 3/8 In. . . 65.00
S.S. Stafford's Inks, Made In USA, Cobalt Blue, Partial Label, 6 1/8 In. 40.00
S.S. Stafford's Inks, Made In USA, Cobalt Blue, Pour Spout, 5 3/4 In. 45.00
S.S. Stafford's Inks, Made In USA, Cobalt Blue, Spout, Qt. 60.00
Sanford's, Boat, Aqua, 2 3/16 In. . . . . .20.00 to 40.00
Sanford's, Square, ABM, 2 3/16 In. 8.00
Sanford's, Stamp Pad, Red, No. 584, 2 1/8 In. . . . .*Illus* 3.00
Sanford's Fountain Pen Ink, ABM, 2 1/16 In. . . . . .18.00 to 25.00
Sanford's Inks One Pint & Library Paste, 7 3/8 In. 7.00
Sanford's Inks One Quart & Library Paste, Amber, 9 1/2 In. 15.00
Sanford's Premium Writing Fluid, Label, Amber, Qt. 55.00
Schoolhouse, Aqua, Square Collar, Back Label Panel, 1870, 2 7/10 In. 245.00
Schoolhouse, Aqua, Windows & Door On Side, Applied Lip, 1871, 2 3/4 In. 390.00
Schoolhouse, S.F., Cal. Ink Co., San Francisco, Amber, Tooled Square Collar, 1880, 2 In. 6600.00
Ship's, Cone, Aqua, 2-Piece Mold, 1840-1850, 2 1/2 x 4 In. 270.00
Shoe Going Into Ridged Box, Amber, Germany, 5 x 2 1/2 In. 295.00
Simonds, Lawrence, Mass., 12-Sided, Cone, Aqua, 1850, 7 1/2 x 4 1/2 In. 1485.00
Skrip Chemopure, Permanent Blue Black, Label, Sheaffer, Box, 1940, 4 Oz. . . . . . . .2.00 to 3.00
Snail, 5-Panels, Aqua, Ground Lip, 1860-1870, 1 1/2 x 5 In. 115.00
Snail, Amethyst, Double Spouted, Pontil, 1780-1820, 1 3/4 x 3 1/4 In. 840.00
Snow & Quirk, St. Louis, 12-Sided, Aqua, Infolded Lip, OP, 1840-1850, 2 3/16 In. 235.00
Soc. G. Rizzo, Honey Yellow, Double Ring Around Neck, Embossed, England, 1860, 3 In. 115.00
Square, Amber, Cut Glass, Hinged Brass Mounts On Cover, 1880-1900, 1 1/16 In. 190.00
Square, Blue, Chinese Letters On Shoulder, Tooled Top, China, 3 3/4 In. 100.00
Square, Milk Glass, Opalescent Powder Blue, Pontil, c.1810-1820, 1 3/4 In. 220.00
Square, Olive Green, 4 Pen Ledges On Top, Flared Lip, 1860-1870, 2 1/2 In. 170.00
Square, Red Amber, Spout, 8 1/4 In. 235.00
Stafford's, Aqua, Spout, 6 1/2 In. . . . . .20.00 to 25.00
Stafford's Ink, Made In USA, Blue Aqua, Spout, Cork, 6 1/2 In. 20.00
Stafford's New Indelible Ink For Marking, Cork, Wrap Around Label, 2 In. 35.00
Stoddard, Cone, Olive Amber, Infolded Lip, OP, 1850, 2 3/4 In. . . . . .105.00 to 125.00
Stoddard, Inverted Cone, Yellow Olive, Tooled Mouth, Pontil, 2 1/2 In. 220.00
Stoddard, Umbrella, 16-Sided, Deep Olive Green, Sheared Lip, OP, 1840-1850, 2 1/16 In. 365.00
Stuart & Harrison, Toledo, Iowa, Aqua, Repaired Lip, 2 7/8 In. 280.00
Stuart & Harrison, Toledo, Iowa, Semi-Cottage, Deep Blue Aqua, 1860-1870, 3 In. . . . 200.00
Superior Blue Ink, Goodwin & Leonard, Olive, OP, 4 3/4 In. 560.00
Superior Violet Ink, Reading Ink Co., Reading, Mich., Cone, Aqua, 1890, 2 13/16 In. . . 80.00
T & M, Rolled Lip, Tubular Pontil, 2 1/2 In. 35.00
T.A. Dunbar, Taunton, Mass., 12-Sided, Aqua, Burst Bubble, 2 1/4 In. 165.00
Teakettle, 5-Sided, Milk Glass, Opalescent, Flower & Leaf Design, 2 In. 255.00
Teakettle, 6-Sided, Ceramic, Frog Finial, Cream Ground, 3 1/4 In. 440.00
Teakettle, 6-Sided, Milk Glass, Raised Floral, Ground Lip, Brass Ring, 2 1/4 In. 385.00
Teakettle, 6-Sided, Milk Glass, Yellow Floral Design, 2 3/8 In. 305.00
Teakettle, 6-Sided, Pottery, Teal Green, France, 1830-1860, 3 In. 75.00
Teakettle, 7-Sided, Puce Amethyst, Debossed Star Design On Base, 1860, 2 1/4 In. 330.00
Teakettle, 8-Sided, Amethyst, Sheared Lip, Sandwich Glassworks, 1860, 2 In. 1065.00
Teakettle, 8-Sided, Cobalt Blue, Ground Mouth, 2 5/8 In. 355.00
Teakettle, 8-Sided, Dome, Light To Dark Amber Swirls, Olive Tone, 1860, 2 1/2 In. 530.00
Teakettle, 8-Sided, Emerald Green, Starpoint Edges Top, Base, Sheared Lip, 2 In. 1100.00
Teakettle, 8-Sided, Grape Amethyst, Brass Collar, Sheared Lip, 1850-1860, 2 In. 390.00
Teakettle, 8-Sided, Indented, Deep Sapphire Blue, Stylized Vertical Ribbed Edges, 2 In. . 315.00

Teakettle, 8-Sided, Light Amethyst, Sheared Lip, Brass Collar, 1850-1860, 2 In. 1010.00
Teakettle, 8-Sided, Sapphire Blue, Ground Mouth, Brass Collar, 1860, 2 In. . . . . .265.00 to 305.00
Teakettle, 8-Sided, Yellow Amber, Tapered Ribs, Sheared, Ground Lip, 1860, 2 1/8 In. . .   390.00
Teakettle, 8-Sided, Olive, Amber Striations, Sheared Lip, 2-Piece Mold, 1860, 2 In. 600.00
Teakettle, 10-Sided, Corset, Milk Glass, Vine, Floral, Turquoise, 1890, 3 In. 300.00
Teakettle, 10-Sided, Opalescent, Raised Floral & Leaf, 2 1/2 In. 330.00
Teakettle, 10-Sided, Opalescent, Raised Floral & Leaf, 3 1/8 In. 360.00
Teakettle, 10-Sided, Sapphire Blue, Ground Mouth, Silver Hinged Lid, 2 In. 230.00
Teakettle, 10-Sided, Turquoise, Raised Floral, 1895, 3 In. 330.00
Teakettle, 11-Sided, Aqua, Embossed Base, Sheared Lip, 1860, 2 In. 75.00
Teakettle, 11-Sided, Emerald Green, Hinged Crown Top, 1830-1860, 3 In. 1760.00
Teakettle, 12-Sided, Sapphire Blue, Brass Medallion On Top, 1850-1860, 2 In. 700.00
Teakettle, Amethyst, Brass Collar, Sheared Lip, 1860, 2 1/4 In.   1485.00
Teakettle, Amethyst, Hinged Lid, Ground Mouth, 1860, 2 x 3 7/8 In. 355.00
Teakettle, Aqua, Pat. July 13 1880, Tooled Mouth, 1880-1890, 2 In. 120.00
Teakettle, Barrel, Cobalt Blue, Brass Collar, Hinged Lid, 2 1/8 In. 1045.00
Teakettle, Barrel, Cobalt Blue, Gilt, Floral Design, 1830-1860, 2 1/4 x 3 1/4 In. 635.00
Teakettle, Barrel, Cobalt Blue, Ground Mouth, Brass Collar & Lid, 2 1/4 In. 1540.00
Teakettle, Barrel, Deep Cobalt Blue, 2 5/16 In. 1150.00
Teakettle, Barrel, Deep Sapphire Blue, Brass Collar, 1860, 2 3/16 In. 475.00
Teakettle, Barrel, Medium Amethyst, Hinged Cap, 1860, 2 1/16 x 3 3/8 In. 825.00
Teakettle, Beehive, 5-Sided, Cobalt Blue, Embossed Floral, Ground Mouth, 2 In. 660.00
Teakettle, Ben Franklin, Bust, Aqua, Sheared Lip, 1880-1895, 2 3/4 In. 210.00
Teakettle, Ben Franklin, Bust, Cobalt Blue, Ground Lip, Metal Band, 2 3/4 In. 1485.00
Teakettle, Ben Franklin, Bust, Deep Sapphire Blue, 1875-1895, 3 In. 210.00
Teakettle, Clambroth, Ground Lip, Brass Neck Ring, Lid, 1875-1895, 2 3/8 In. 165.00
Teakettle, Cobalt Blue, Gilt, Flowers, Brass Lid, Sandwich, Mass., 1860, 2 In. 1375.00
Teakettle, Cobalt Blue, Hinged Lid, Ground Lip, Brass Neck Ring, 1875-1895, 2 1/8 In.   525.00
Teakettle, Cobalt Blue, Stylized Flowers At Top, Sheared, Ground Lip, 1860, 2 3/8 In. . .   1010.00
Teakettle, Dark Purple Amethyst, Ground Lip, 1875-1895, 2 In. 350.00
Teakettle, Deep Cobalt Blue, Debossed Star On Base, Ground Lip, 1895, 2 1/8 In. 230.00
Teakettle, Deep Cobalt Blue, Ground Lip, 1880-1890, 2 In. 210.00
Teakettle, Deep Cobalt Blue, Hinged Lid, Ground Lip, 1875-1895, 2 In. . . . . . . .550.00 to 660.00
Teakettle, Deep Forest Green, Vertially Ribs, Ground Mouth, 2 In. 385.00
Teakettle, Deep Sapphire Blue, Metal Lid, 2 3/16 In. 600.00
Teakettle, Double Font, Milk Glass, Powder Blue, Pontil, Glass Stopper, 1895, 4 In. 305.00
Teakettle, Gray Clambroth, Vertical Rib, Flower On Dome, Ground Lip, 3 In. 440.00
Teakettle, Handle, Embossed Base, Sheared Lip, England, 1860, 2 3/8 In. 215.00
Teakettle, Lime Green, Vertical Ribs, Hinged Lid, England, 1830-1860, 2 In. 415.00
Teakettle, Milk Glass, Lime Green, Polished Base, Lip, 1875-1895, 2 In. 880.00
Teakettle, Milk Glass, Opalescent, Enamel, Multicolor Flowers, 2 In. 440.00
Teakettle, Milk Glass, Opalescent, Raised Flowers, Brass Ring, Lid, 2 1/2 In. 470.00
Teakettle, Milk Glass, Powder Blue, Opalescent, Flowers, 2 3/8 In. . . . . .305.00 to 350.00
Teakettle, Milk Glass, Silver Neck Band, Silver Lid, 1875-1895, 1 5/8 In. 330.00
Teakettle, Multicolor Flowers, White, Brass Hinged Lid, 1895, 3 In. 630.00
Teakettle, Opalescent Flowers, Orange, Blue, Lavender, Pink Vines, 1860, 2 1/2 In. 505.00
Teakettle, Pale Aqua, Raised Panels With Indented Edges, 1850-1860, 1 3/4 In. 145.00

Ink, Sanford's,
Stamp Pad, Red,
No. 584, 2 1/8 In.

Ink, Turtle, Davids,
Deep Blue Green,
Embossed, 1 7/8 In.

Teakettle, Pottery, Hand Painted Flowers, Birds & Symbols, Japan, 3 In. 600.00
Teakettle, Pottery, Mottled Dark Green Glaze, France, 1880-1900, 2 1/4 In. 130.00
Teakettle, Pottery, White Mottled Glaze, France, 1830-1870, 2 1/8 x 4 In. 90.00
Teakettle, Purple Amethyst, Ground Lip, 1880-1895, 2 In. 230.00
Teakettle, Ribbed Pear, Milk Glass, Opalescent, Ground Lip, 1875-1895, 3 In. 385.00
Teakettle, Sapphire Blue, Long Curved Spout, Metal Lid, 2 In. 495.00
Teakettle, Sheared, Ground Lip, Tapered Beveled Edges, 1860, 1 5/8 In. 115.00
Teakettle, Snail, 2 5/8 In. 250.00
Teakettle, Straw Topaz, Fluted Sides, Beaded Top, Uncapped Spout, 1860, 2 1/8 In. 590.00
Teakettle, Tapered Cylinder, Opalescent, Flowers & Leaf, Brass Lid, 2 3/4 In. 360.00
Teakettle, Yellow Lime Green, Polished Lip, Smooth Base, 1875, 2 3/8 In. 465.00
Tent, Aqua, Ribs, 1 Sided Pen Rest, 2 1/2 In. 55.00
Tippecanoe, Cider Barrel, Tooled Collar, Pontil, 1840, 1 7/8 In. 895.00
Titcomb, Umbrella, 8-Sided, Aqua, Pontil, 1840-1850, 2 5/8 In. 560.00
Titcomb's, Cincinnati, O., 12-Sided, Aqua, Infolded Lip, OP, 1840-1850, 2 7/8 In. 365.00
Tree Stump, Green, Pigeon Blood Striations, Pat. Jan, 17, 1871, 1 7/8 In. 200.00
Turtle, 12-Sided, Deep Cobalt Blue, Dome, Factory Ground Lip, 1 3/4 In. 955.00
Turtle, 12-Sided, Gold Amber, Dome, Factory Ground Lip, 1865-1875, 1 1/2 In. 125.00
Turtle, 12-Sided, Light Aqua, Factory Ground Lip, 1865-1875, 1 3/4 In. 30.00
Turtle, A.C. Thompson, Chemist, Cobbleskill, N.Y., Aqua, Dome, 1875, 2 In. 190.00
Turtle, Aqua, Stylized Cross On Base Panel, Tooled Lip, 1870, 1 7/8 In. 170.00
Turtle, Davids, Deep Blue Green, Embossed, 1 7/8 In. . . . . *Illus* 2200.00
Turtle, Dome, Plain Sides, Factory Ground Lip, 1865-1875, 1 3/4 In. 135.00
Turtle, Lemon Citron, Dome, Sheared Lip, 1865-1875, 1 5/8 In. 305.00
Umbrella, 6-Sided, Aqua, Infolded Lip, OP, 1840-1860, 3 1/8 In. 280.00
Umbrella, 6-Sided, Corset, Blue Green, Infolded Lip, OP, 1850, 3 In. 530.00
Umbrella, 6-Sided, Gold Amber, 2 1/2 In. . . . . .120.00 to 130.00
Umbrella, 6-Sided, Light Blue Green, OP, Rolled Lip, 1845-1855, 2 1/2 In. 150.00
Umbrella, 6-Sided, Light Blue Green, Pontil, 1830-1850, 2 1/4 In. 75.00
Umbrella, 6-Sided, Light Lime Green, Rolled Mouth, 2 5/8 In. 155.00
Umbrella, 6-Sided, Green, Tooled Square Collar, Smooth Base, Embossed, 1885, 3 In. . . 215.00
Umbrella, 6-Sided, Olive Yellow, Infolded Lip, Pontil, 2 1/2 In. 185.00
Umbrella, 8-Sided, Amber, Infolded Lip, Pontil, 1860-1865, 2 5/8 In. 390.00
Umbrella, 8-Sided, Amber, Sheared Lip, 1855-1865, 2 3/4 In. 130.00
Umbrella, 8-Sided, Amethyst, Infolded Lip, Smooth Base, 1860-1870, 2 3/4 In. 715.00
Umbrella, 8-Sided, Apricot Amber, Olive Tone, Infolded Lip, OP, 1840-1860, 2 1/2 In. . . 245.00
Umbrella, 8-Sided, Aqua, Infolded Lip, Pontil, 3 1/8 In. 165.00
Umbrella, 8-Sided, Aqua, Rolled Lip, OP, 1845-1855, 2 1/8 In. 550.00
Umbrella, 8-Sided, Aqua, Sheared Lip, OP, 1850-1860, 3 1/4 In. 325.00
Umbrella, 8-Sided, Chocolate Amber, Tooled Lip, Brooklyn, N.Y., 1870-1880, 2 1/2 In. . . 65.00
Umbrella, 8-Sided, Citrine, Infolded Lip, OP, 1840-1850, 2 3/8 In. 245.00
Umbrella, 8-Sided, Citron, Infolded Lip, Pontil, 1840-1850, 2 1/2 In. 590.00
Umbrella, 8-Sided, Cobalt Blue, Infolded Lip, Pontil, 1850-1860, 2 9/16 In. 1210.00
Umbrella, 8-Sided, Cobalt Blue, OP, Rolled Lip, 1840-1855, 2 3/8 In. 495.00
Umbrella, 8-Sided, Cobalt Blue, Sheared Mouth, Sheared Mouth, Pontil, 2 3/8 In. 800.00
Umbrella, 8-Sided, Cobalt Blue, Tooled Square Collar, 1875-1885, 2 1/8 In. 505.00
Umbrella, 8-Sided, Cobalt, Amber, Infolded Lip, Pontil, 1840-1850, 2 5/8 In. 125.00
Umbrella, 8-Sided, Concave, Medium Blue, Star Point, Sheared Lip, OP, 1850, 2 5/8 In. . . 1100.00
Umbrella, 8-Sided, Concave, Olive Green, Pontil, Baltimore Glassworks, 1855, 2 In. . . . 1375.00
Umbrella, 8-Sided, Concave, Sapphire Blue, Starpoint, Pontil, 1850, 3 In. 1870.00
Umbrella, 8-Sided, Dark Olive Amber, Short Neck, Sheared Lip, Pontil, 1850, 2 5/16 In. . 245.00
Umbrella, 8-Sided, Davids, Olive Green, Paper Label, 3 In. . . . . *Illus* 213.00
Umbrella, 8-Sided, Deep Aqua, Rolled Lip, OP, 1845-1855, 2 1/2 In. 165.00
Umbrella, 8-Sided, Deep Blue Green, Tooled Lip, N.Y., 1840-1850, 2 3/4 In. 700.00
Umbrella, 8-Sided, Deep Cherry Puce, Rolled Lip, 1845-1855, 2 5/8 In. 770.00
Umbrella, 8-Sided, Deep Emerald Green, Tooled Collar, OP, 1840-1850, 2 3/16 In. 530.00
Umbrella, 8-Sided, Deep Olive Amber, Sheared Lip, Pontil, 1845-1855, 2 1/2 In. .130.00 to 155.00
Umbrella, 8-Sided, Deep Olive Yellow, Infolded Lip, Pontil, 1840-1850, 2 5/8 In. 260.00
Umbrella, 8-Sided, Deep Royal Blue, Infolded Lip, 1865-1875, 2 3/4 In. 645.00
Umbrella, 8-Sided, Deep Yellow Olive, Infolded Lip, OP, 1850-1860, 2 5/8 In. 390.00
Umbrella, 8-Sided, Emerald Green, Infolded Lip, 1840-1850, 2 7/16 In. . . . . .290.00 to 450.00
Umbrella, 8-Sided, Emerald Green, Pontil, Rolled Lip, 2 1/2 In. 385.00
Umbrella, 8-Sided, Forest Green, Infolded Lip, OP, 1850-1860, 2 1/2 In. 155.00

Ink, Umbrella, 8-Sided,
Davids, Olive Green,
Paper Label, 3 In.

Ink, Water's Ink,
Umbrella, 6-Sided,
Aqua, OP, 2 7/8 In.

Umbrella, 8-Sided, Forest Green, Sheared Lip, Key Mold Base, Pontil, 1850, 2 1/2 In. . .	315.00
Umbrella, 8-Sided, Gold Amber To Yellow, Wide Mouth, Pontil, 2 3/8 In.	295.00
Umbrella, 8-Sided, Gold Amber, Sheared Mouth, Pontil, 1840-1860, 2 1/4 In.	175.00
Umbrella, 8-Sided, Green, Tooled Lip, Embossed Trademark Design, 1880, 4 9/16 In. . .	225.00
Umbrella, 8-Sided, Light Blue Green, OP, 2 3/8 In.	65.00
Umbrella, 8-Sided, Light Citron, Tooled Square Collar, 1865-1875, 2 1/8 In.	450.00
Umbrella, 8-Sided, Light Gold Amber, Pontil, 1840-1860, 2 1/8 In.	160.00
Umbrella, 8-Sided, Light Green, Infolded Lip, 1870-1880, 2 1/2 In.	170.00
Umbrella, 8-Sided, Light Green, Infolded Lip, Pontil, 1850-1860, 2 3/16 In.	420.00
Umbrella, 8-Sided, Light Green, Infolded Lip, Pontil, 1850-1860, 3 1/4 In.	700.00
Umbrella, 8-Sided, Light Olive Green, OP, Rolled Lip, 1845-1855, 2 5/8 In.	465.00
Umbrella, 8-Sided, Light Powder Blue, Tooled Square Collar, 1870-1880, 2 1/2 In.	100.00
Umbrella, 8-Sided, Light To Medium Emerald Green, OP, 2 1/2 In.	145.00
Umbrella, 8-Sided, Lime Green, Rolled Lip, 1860-1870, 2 5/8 In.	465.00
Umbrella, 8-Sided, Midnight Blue, OP, 1840-1850, 2 1/2 In.	1485.00
Umbrella, 8-Sided, Olive Amber, Infolded Lip, Pontil, 1840-1860, 2 1/2 In.	125.00
Umbrella, 8-Sided, Olive Amber, Sheared Lip, Pontil, 1850, 2 5/8 In.	85.00
Umbrella, 8-Sided, Olive Amber, Sheared, Tooled Lip, OP, 1840-1855, 2 1/2 In.	55.00
Umbrella, 8-Sided, Orange Amber, Sheared Lip, OP, 1840-1855, 2 1/2 In.	265.00
Umbrella, 8-Sided, Pale Yellow Green, Sloping Shoulders, Flared Neck, 1860, 2 3/16 In.	315.00
Umbrella, 8-Sided, Peacock Blue, Square Collar, Smooth Base, 1880-1890, 2 7/8 In. . . .	615.00
Umbrella, 8-Sided, Purple Amethyst, Tooled Collar, 1865-1875, 2 1/2 In.	420.00
Umbrella, 8-Sided, Red Amber, Raised Dots On 2 Panels, Pontil, 1840-1850, 2 5/8 In. . .	235.00
Umbrella, 8-Sided, Red Amber, Sheared Lip, Pontil, 1840-1850, 2 1/2 In.	180.00
Umbrella, 8-Sided, Red Amber, Sheared Lip, Pontil, 1840-1850, 2 5/8 In.	305.00
Umbrella, 8-Sided, Salmon Puce, Tooled Lip, Pontil, 1850-1860, 2 5/8 In.	1375.00
Umbrella, 8-Sided, Sapphire Blue, Infolded Lip, 1865-1875, 2 3/4 In.	645.00
Umbrella, 8-Sided, Sapphire Blue, Infolded Lip, Pontil, 1860, 2 3/8 In.	770.00
Umbrella, 8-Sided, Sapphire Blue, Infolded Lip, Pontil, 1860, 2 5/8 In.	1045.00
Umbrella, 8-Sided, Sapphire Blue, OP, Rolled Lip, 1855, 2 1/4 In.	470.00
Umbrella, 8-Sided, Sapphire Blue, Tooled Mouth, 1860-1880, 2 In.	230.00
Umbrella, 8-Sided, Sapphire Blue, Tooled Mouth, 1860-1880, 2 5/8 In.	120.00
Umbrella, 8-Sided, Steel Blue, Infolded Lip, OP, 1840-1850, 2 1/2 In.	840.00
Umbrella, 8-Sided, Straw Yellow, Infolded Lip, OP, 1840-1860, 2 3/8 In.	675.00
Umbrella, 8-Sided, Striated Amber, Sheared Lip, Pontil, 1840-1850, 2 7/16 In.	235.00
Umbrella, 8-Sided, Teal Blue, Applied Mouth, 1870-1880, 2 5/8 In.	220.00
Umbrella, 8-Sided, Yellow Amber Topaz, Pontil, 1845-1855, 2 1/2 In.	155.00
Umbrella, 8-Sided, Yellow Amber, Rolled Mouth, 1830-1860, 2 1/2 In.	145.00
Umbrella, 8-Sided, Yellow Brown, Olive Tone, Sheared Lip, Pontil, 1850-1860	245.00
Umbrella, 8-Sided, Yellow Green, Tooled Lip, Pontil, 1840-1850, 2 1/2 In.	560.00
Umbrella, 8-Sided, Yellow Olive Amber, Rolled Lip, OP, 1840-1855, 2 1/2 In.	145.00
Umbrella, 8-Sided, Yellow Olive, Infolded Flared Lip, Pontil, 1840-1850, 2 3/4 In.	730.00
Umbrella, 8-Sided, Yellow, Infolded Lip, Pontil, 1840-1850, 2 3/8 In.	390.00
Umbrella, 8-Sided, Yellow, Infolded Lip, Pontil, 1860, 2 5/8 In.	1320.00
Umbrella, 12-Sided, Blue Green, Rolled Lip, OP, 1845-1855, 2 1/8 In.	145.00
Umbrella, 12-Sided, Emerald Green, OP, 1 15/16 In.	220.00
Umbrella, 12-Sided, Forest Green, Infolded Lip, Pontil, 1835-1850, 1 7/8 In.	450.00

Umbrella, 12-Sided, Gold Amber, OP, Rolled Lip, 1835-1855, 2 1/8 In. 200.00
Umbrella, 12-Sided, Sapphire Blue, Infolded Lip, Pontil, 1860, 2 1/8 In. 1045.00
Umbrella, 16-Sided, Chocolate Amber, Rolled Lip, Pontil, 1845-1865, 2 1/8 In. 525.00
Umbrella, 16-Sided, Olive Green, Sheared Lip, Key Mold, 1840-1860, 2 1/4 In. 1100.00
Umbrella, 16-Sided, Root Beer Amber, OP, Rolled Lip, 1855, 2 In. 440.00
Umbrella, 16-Sided, Yellow Brown, Olive Tone, OP, 1840-1850, 2 3/8 In. 450.00
Umbrella, Amethyst, Infolded Lip, OP, 1840-1850, 2 3/4 In. 2640.00
Umbrella, B.B. & Co., 8-Sided, Light Sapphire Blue, Rolled Lip, Pontil, 1 3/4 In. 770.00
Umbrella, Blue Green, Infolded Lip, Pontil, Embossed S On Base, 1850-1860, 2 5/8 In. . 305.00
Umbrella, C.F., 8-Sided, Dark Amethyst, Infolded Lip, Pontil, 1830, 2 1/2 In. 560.00
Umbrella, Citron Yellow, Infolded Lip, Pontil, 1840-1850, 2 1/2 In. 245.00
Umbrella, Emerald Green, Applied Double Collar, Long Neck, OP, 2 5/8 In. 1430.00
Umbrella, Lime Green, Sheared Top, Yellow Striations, 3 In. 100.00
Umbrella, Pale Smoky Puce, Infolded Lip, 1840-1850, 2 1/4 In. 3300.00
Umbrella, Stoneware, Brown Glaze, England, 1880-1900, 2 5/8 In. 165.00
Umbrella, Yellow Olive Green, OP, 2 1/2 In. 300.00
Umbrella, Yellow Olive, Tubular Pontil, 1830-1860, 2 1/4 In. 230.00
Umbrella, Yellow, Olive Tone, Infolded Lip, 1830-1860, 2 1/4 In. 55.00
Underwood's Ink, Cobalt Blue, Qt. ....75.00 to 150.00
W. Felton & Co., Brattleboro, Vt., Umbrella, 8-Sided, Aqua, 1865-1880, 3 1/8 In. 85.00
W.E. Bonney, Aqua, Applied Spout, 1860-1870, 7 1/4 In. 325.00
W.E. Bonney, Aqua, Tooled Collar, 1860-1870, 2 5/8 In. 145.00
W.E. Bonney, Barrel, Aqua, Applied Mouth, Spout, 1855-1865, 5 1/8 In. 165.00
W.E. Bonney, Barrel, Aqua, Applied Spout, 1860-1870, 5 15/16 In. 325.00
W.E. Bonney, Barrel, Aqua, Rolled Lip, 1850-1860, 2 5/8 In. 55.00
W.E. Bonney, Barrel, Pale Blue Aqua, Partially Rolled Lip, Label, 3 In. 95.00
W.E. Bonney, Violet Ink, Square, 3-Color Reverse Label, 2 1/4 In. 150.00
W.E. Lewis, Mfr., Fountain, Pat. June. 30-91, Corry, Pa., Ground Mouth, 2 1/2 In. 110.00
Ward's, Boston, Mass., Cylindrical, Green, Applied Spout, Smooth Base, 1880, 8 In. 112.00
Warren's Congress, 8-Sided, Aqua, Infolded Lip, Pontil, 1840-1850, 4 15/16 In. 170.00
Warren's Congress, 8-Sided, Olive Yellow, OP, 1840, 2 7/8 In. 1980.00
Warren's Congress, 8-Sided, Yellow Olive, Applied Spout, IP, 7 In. 1870.00
Water's Ink, Umbrella, 6-Sided, Aqua, OP, 2 7/8 In. ....*Illus* 672.00
Waterman's, Cylindrical, Embossed On Base, Bubbles, Cork, 2 1/2 In. 3.00
William A. Davis, Boston, Mass., Fountain, Ground Mouth, 2 3/8 x 4 1/8 In. 75.00
Williams Black Empire Ink, N.Y., Umbrella, Lime Green, Tooled Mouth, 1890, 2 5/8 In. 175.00
Williamson, Chemist, Blue Green, Embossed Books & Quill Pen, 6 7/16 In. 275.00
Wm. C. Badeau & Co., Troy, N.Y., Aqua, Beveled Edges, OP, 1840-1850, 4 In. 325.00
Wood's Black Ink, Cone, Dark Root Beer Amber, OP, 1840-1850, 2 1/2 In. 1375.00
Wood's Black Ink, Portland, Cone, Aqua, Pontil, 2 7/16 In. ....175.00 to 395.00
Worden & Hyatt's Ink, Square, Partial Label, BIMAL, 2 13/16 In. ....40.00 to 60.00
Zieber & Co's Excelsior Ink, 12-Sided, Deep Yellow Olive, IP, 1860, 7 7/16 In. 3575.00
Zieber & Co's Excelsior Ink, 12-Sided, Emerald Green, Flange Collar, IP, 1860, 6 In. ... 3850.00
Zierlein, St. Louis, 12-Sided, Blue Aqua, Rolled Lip, Pontil, 2 1/4 In. 300.00

JAR

Jar is the name for a container of a special shape. It has a wide mouth and almost no neck. Today we see jars of cold cream, but in earlier days jars made of glass or ceramic were used for storage of home-canned produce and for many commercial products. Jars are also listed in the Stoneware category in this book.

JAR, 4 Engraved Floral & Castle Panels, Ground Mouth, Pewter Lid, Square, 10 In. ... 240.00
Amethyst, Bear Pomade, 3 3/4 In. 192.00
Antiseptic, Frosted Glass, White Cross In Red Circle, Metal Lid, 10 In. 60.00
Antiseptic, Milk Glass, Lion Design, Smooth Lip, Metal Screw Lid, 1930, 7 x 6 In. 165.00
Aqua, Blown, Flared Mouth, Pontil, Cylindrical, 1800-1850, 10 1/2 In. 110.00
Aqua, Petals & Flutes On Base, Rolled Mouth, IP, 1845-1860, 12 1/2 In. 100.00
Battery, Aqua, Cylindrical, Shoulders, Slug Plate, Ground Top, Carbon Insert 15.00
California Fish & Poultry Market, Phoenix, Ariz., SCA, 1915, 8 In. 165.00
Cigar, Belfast Cigars, United Cut Plug, 8-Sided, Gold Yellow Amber, Metal Lid, 6 3/4 In. 75.00
Counter Top, Clear, Ground Lip, Metal Mouth Band, Lid, 1890-1910, 9 1/4 In. 70.00
Lab, Pat. June 11th, 1895 On Lid, Metal Clamp, Wheel 50.00
Mercantile Cigar, St. Louis, Mo., Amber, Screw Lid 145.00
Otline Double Strength For Treatment Of Freckles, Label, Contents, Tax Stamp, Box 12.00

Porcelain, Apothecary, Black, Gold, Pink, Green Enamel, Germany, 1870, 6 In. 70.00
R. Hemingray Co., Cincinnati, O., Unembossed, Cobalt Blue, Ground Lip, 1885-1895, Qt. 265.00
Sour Cream, Deposit Bottle, Embossed, ISP, Round, Pt. 10.00
Storage, 3-Piece Mold, Cornflower Blue, Rolled Mouth, 1860-1880, 10 3/4 In. 65.00
Storage, Aqua, Blown, Single Collar, OP, 1770-1800, 7 In. 30.00
Storage, Aqua, Wide Mouth, Pontil, 1830-1870, 11 1/8 In. 175.00
Storage, Blue Aqua, Outward Rolled Mouth, Pontil, 14 In. 265.00
Storage, Blue Aqua, Wide Rolled Lip, 1820-1860, 10 1/2 In. 90.00
Storage, Blue Green, Tapered Lip, OP, 6 1/2 In. 45.00
Storage, Blue Green, Wide Mouth, Wide Double Folded Rim, Pontil, 1860, 13 In. 90.00
Storage, Brown, 5 Pointed Star On Shoulder, Tin Lid, Pottery, 1890-1910, Qt. 50.00
Storage, Cylindrical, Olive Green, Rolled Mouth, Pontil, 1850, 13 7/8 In. 305.00
Storage, Green, Applied Crimped Rim, Wide Sheared Mouth, Globular, 14 In. 230.00
Storage, Green, Wide Mouth, Tooled Flared Lip, Square, 1860-1880, 10 1/4 In. 140.00
Storage, Mass Glass Co., Aqua, Embossed, Tooled Mouth, 5 1/4 In. 40.00
Storage, Olive Amber, Cone, Tooled Mouth, Pontil, 1840, 8 3/8 In. 1210.00
Storage, Olive Amber, Sheared Mouth, Applied String Rim, 7 7/8 In. 55.00
U.S.T. Co., Turquoise, Petal Shape, Ground Lip, Metal Lid, 6 1/4 In. 185.00
JIM BEAM, see Beam

JUG

A jug is a deep container with a narrow mouth and a handle. It is usually made of pottery. Jugs were often used as containers for liquor. Messages, mottoes, and the name of the distillery or bar are often printed on the jug. Jugs are also listed in the Stoneware category in this book.

JUG, 32 Ribs, Vertical, Applied Foot & Mouth, Handle, Midwest, 1830, 5 1/2 In. 3850.00
A. Moll, St. Louis, 2-Tone, 1/2 Gal. 50.00
Alter Norhauser, C.G. Kuntzer Korn Branntwein, Brown Transfer, Qt. 145.00
Amber, Applied Rib Handle, Flared Lip, Midwest, Pontil, 1830, 5 1/8 In. 465.00
Bon Bros., San Francisco, Calif., Handle, Pt. 125.00
Bon Look, 16th & Blake, Denver, Colorado, 1 Gal. 75.00
Chas. Grove, Boston, Ma., 1 Gal. 115.00
Cigar Labels, Decoupage, c.1990, 10 1/4 In. ....*Illus* 35.00
Creamery Pkg. & Supplies, Chicago, Ill., Gal. 125.00
E.M. Arnold, The Cash Store, Belle Fourche, South Dakota, Gal. 140.00
East India Tea Co., Staten Island, Pottery, Stencil, Gal. 175.00
Frank Schaetzel, Chicago, Ill., Gal. 145.00
From John McDonald, Foster's New Building, Sussex Street, Ottawa, Gray, 3 Gal. 240.00
G.I. Lazier, Picton, C.W., 2, Gray Salt Glaze, Double Floral Design, Canada, 13 1/4 In. ... 230.00
Geo. Dulling Grocery Co., San Antonio, Tex., 1/2 Gal. 700.00
H. Schuler, Paris, Ont., 2, Cream, Double Flower, Canada, 12 3/4 In. 430.00
I.M. Wilson & Son, Laurel, Miss., 1/2 Gal. 65.00
J.L. Moffit, Holyoke, Mass., Brown, Tan Glaze, Handle, 1860-1890, 8 1/2 In. 110.00

Jug, Cigar Labels,
Decoupage,
c.1990, 10 1/4 In.

Jug, N.A. White & Son, Blue
Orchid Design, c.1885, 2 Gal.

Jug, Whites Utica, Blue
Running Bird, LAW, 2 Gal.

Jacob Sanders & Sons, Trinidad, Colorado, 1/2 Gal. 100.00
Jos. Rauer, St. Louis, Mo., Gal. 145.00
Leon Sparicio, New Orleans, Stenciled, Gal. 135.00
N.A. White & Son, Blue Orchid Design, c.1885, 2 Gal. ....*Illus* 962.00
N.R. Bianchi, Calumet, Michigan, Gal. 245.00
Olsen & Co., Bakersfield, Ca., Cream, Dark Brown Top, Applied Handle, 1910, 4 1/2 In. 130.00
R.H. Jones, Reading, Pa., Salt Glaze, Tan, Blue Incised Letters, Egg Shape, Gal. 160.00
Return To A. Beattie & Co., Stratford, Ont., Tan, Incised Cobalt Letters, 1/2 Gal. 110.00
Richard & Sons, Mobile, Ala., 1/2 Gal. 125.00
W.E. Welding, Brantford, Ont., Cream, Long-Stemmed Flower, Canada, Gal. 195.00
Whites Utica, Blue Running Bird, LAW, 2 Gal. ....*Illus* 350.00
Wm. Brogman, Louisville, Ky., Gal. 135.00
Wm. Schneider, St. Louis, Mo., Gal. 135.00
Ziegler & Behrend, The Big Mail Order House, Huntington, W. Va., Gal. 100.00

──────────────────────────── **LACEY** ────────────────────────────

Haas Brothers of San Francisco, California, was established in 1851. They made W.A. Lacey and Cyrus Noble bottles in the 1970s. The firm discontinued its ceramic business about 1981 and destroyed all of the molds. Lacey bottles include the log animal series (1978-1980) and the tavern series (1975). Also see the Cyrus Noble category.

LACEY, Bank Exchange, Exterior, 1976 .... 22.00
Bank Exchange, Interior, 1976 .... 22.00
Continental Navy, 1976 .... 15.00
Fargo Bank, 1975 .... 20.00
Harold's Club, 1970, Miniature 21.00
Rabbit, Log, 1978... 29.00
Rabbit, Log, 1980... 29.00
Raccoon, Log, 1978 .... 35.00
Raccoon, Log, 1980 .... 35.00
Squirrel, Log, 1979 .... 29.00
Tennis Player, 1976, Pair... 33.00
Tun Tavern, No. 1, 1975... 10.00
Tun Tavern, No. 2, U.S. Marines, 1975 .... 25.00
Willits Frontier, 1976 .... 116.00

──────────────────────────── **LEWIS & CLARK** ────────────────────────────

Lewis & Clark bottles were created by Alpha Industries of Helena, Montana. The first bottles, full-length representations of historical figures, were made from 1971 to 1976. The pioneer series of 1977-1978 was released in two-bottle sets. Each bottle was 13 inches high and two placed together created a scene. For example, one was an Indian (bottle) offering to sell some furs to a white man (bottle). A set of six troll bottles was made in 1978-1979.

LEWIS & CLARK, Barnyard Clown, 1981 .... 38.00
Bighorn, 5 Piece 97.00
Blinking Owl, 1981 .... 40.00
Charbonneau, 1973 .... 60.00
Cook, 1977 .... 48.00
Cousin, 1979... 20.00
Cowboy, 1977 .... 42.00
Curlee Indian Scout, 1974 .... 42.00
Daughter Troll, 1978 .... 24.00
Family, 1978, Pair.. 115.00
General Custer, 1974 .... 30.00
Grandfather, 1978 .... 17.00
Grandmother, 1979 .... 17.00
Hobo, 1981 .... 38.00
Indian, 1978 .... 68.00
John Lennon 185.00
Lewis & Clark, Miniature, 5 Piece 100.00
Major Reno, 1976 .... 27.00
Meriwether Lewis, 1971 .... 48.00
Montana, 1976 .... 50.00

Mr. & Mrs., 1978	20.00
Mr. & Mrs., 1979	20.00
Plaque Peace Pipe, 1978	44.00
Prowling Panther, 1982	44.00
Sacajawea, 1972	76.00
Sheepherder	44.00
Sitting Bull, 1976	95.00
States, 1981, Miniature	8.00
States, 1984, Miniature	8.00
Trader, 1978	64.00
Trooper, 1976	33.00
William Clark, 1971	49.00
York, 1972	44.00

--------------------------------- **LIONSTONE** ---------------------------------

Lionstone Distilleries Inc. of Lawrenceburg, Kentucky, started making porcelain figural bottles to hold their whiskey for national sale in 1969. The first bottles were Western figures, each with a black label that told the historical facts about the figure. About 15,000 bottles were made for each of the first six subjects, the cowboy, proud Indian, casual Indian, sheriff, gentleman gambler, and cavalry scout. About half of the bottles were never filled with liquor because they leaked. These *leakers* were used by bars as display items on shelves and were clearly labeled with decals stating that they were for display only. More bottles were made for the series, about 4,000 of each. The set had 16 bottles. Lionstone then made a series of race cars (1970-1984), more Western figures (1970-1976), a Western bar scene (1971), birds (1970-1977), circus figures (1973), dogs (1975-1977), European workers (1974), oriental workers (1974), Bicentennial series (1976), clowns (1978-1979), sports series (1974-1983), and others. They also made many miniature bottles. Lionstone was sold to Barton Brands in December 1979. It was sold back to Mark Slepak, the original owner, in December 1983. The whiskey was distilled in Bardstown, Kentucky, but the bottles were made in Chicago. Over 800 styles were made. No decanters were made after 1995.

LIONSTONE, AMVET Riverboat, 1983	12.00
Baseball Players, 1974	80.00
Bass, No.1, 1983	50.00
Betsy Ross, 1975	22.00
Bird, Blue Jay, 1971	20.00
Bird, Canada Goose, 1980	50.00
Bird, Cardinal, 1973	27.00
Bird, Eastern Bluebird, 1972	24.00
Bird, Robin, 1975, Miniature	10.00
Bird, Western Bluebird, 1972	24.00
Bird, Woodhawk, 1969, Miniature	23.00
Bird, Woodpecker, 1975	24.00
Bird, Woodpecker, 1975, Miniature	11.00
Bird, Yellow Head, 1974, Miniature	42.00
Blacksmith, 1973	26.00
Buccaneer, 1973	23.00
Car, Corvette, 1984 Model, 1984	65.00
Car, Corvette, 1984 Model, Black, 1984	110.00
Car, Duesenberg, 1978, Miniature	15.00
Car, Jaguar, 1936 Model, 1978	18.00
Car, Johnnie Lightning, No. 1, Gold, 1972	110.00
Car, Johnnie Lightning, No. 2, Silver, 1973	100.00
Car, Mercedes, 1978, Miniature	15.00
Car, Olsonite Eagle, No. 6, 1970	100.00
Car, Stutz Bearcat, 1978, Miniature	15.00
Car, Turbo Car STP, Gold, 1972	150.00
Car, Turbo Car STP, Platinum, 1972	150.00
Car, Turbo Car STP, Red, 1972	60.00
Cherry Valley, 1971, Gold	50.00
Cherry Valley, 1971, Silver	50.00
Circus, Burmese Girl, 1973, Miniature	12.00
Circus, Fire Eater, 1973, Miniature	12.00

Circus, Snake Charmer, 1973, Miniature 12.00
Circus, Strongman, 1973, Miniature 12.00
Circus, Sword Swallower, 1973, Miniature 12.00
Circus, Tattooed Lady, 1973, Miniature 12.00
Clown, No. 1, Monkey Business, 1978 .... 36.00
Clown, No. 1, Monkey Business, 1978, Miniature 21.00
Clown, No. 2, Sad Sam, 1978 .... 38.00
Clown, No. 2, Sad Sam, 1978, Miniature 21.00
Clown, No. 3, Say It With Music, 1978 .... 38.00
Clown, No. 3, Say It With Music, 1978, Miniature 21.00
Clown, No. 4, Salty Tails, 1978 .... 38.00
Clown, No. 4, Salty Tails, 1978, Miniature 19.00
Clown, No. 5, Pie Face, 1979 .... 31.00
Clown, No. 5, Pie Face, 1979, Miniature 19.00
Clown, No. 6, Lampy, 1979 .... 38.00
Clown, No. 6, Lampy, 1979, Miniature 19.00
Dog, Afghan, 1977, Miniature 18.00
Dog, Alaskan Malamute, 1977, Miniature 15.00
Dog, Beagle, 1977, Miniature 15.00
Dog, British Pointer, 1975, Miniature ....15.00 to 20.00
Dog, British Rough Collie, 1975, Miniature 14.00
Dog, Cocker Spaniel, 1975, Miniature 15.00
Dog, Collie 15.00
Dog, Doberman, 1977, Miniature 15.00
Dog, French Poodle, 1975, Miniature 15.00
Dog, German Boxer, 1975, Miniature 18.00
Dog, German Dachshund, 1977, Miniature 15.00
Dog, German Shepherd, 1975, Miniature 18.00
Dog, Golden Retriever, 1977, Miniature 15.00
Dog, Great Dane, 1977, Miniature 18.00
Dog, Irish Setter, 1977, Miniature 15.00
Dog, Labrador Retriever, 1977, Miniature 15.00
Dog, Schnauzer, 1977, Miniature 16.00
Dog, Scottish Terrier, 1977, Miniature 16.00
Dog, St. Bernard, 1977, Miniature 15.00
Duck, Canvasback, 1981 .... 36.00
Duck, Mallard, 1981 .... 30.00
Duck, Pintail, 1981 .... 35.00
Duck, Wood, 1981 .... 40.00
European Worker, Cobbler, 1974 .... 30.00
European Worker, Horseshoer, 1974 .... 30.00
European Worker, Potter, 1974 .... 30.00
European Worker, Silversmith, 1974 .... 30.00
European Worker, Watchmaker, 1974 .... 30.00
European Worker, Woodworker, 1974 .... 30.00
F.O.E. Eagle, Las Vegas, 1982 .... 32.00
F.O.E. Eagle, Nashville, 1983 .... 33.00
F.O.E. Eagle, White, 1983 .... 20.00
Firefighter, Fire Alarm Box, Red, 1983 .... 120.00
Firefighter, Fire Equipment, 1976, Miniature, 3 Piece 70.00
Firefighter, Fire Extinguisher, No. 9, 1983 .... 75.00
Firefighter, Fire Hydrant, No. 6, 1981 .... 95.00
Firefighter, Fireman No. 1, Red Hat, 1972 .... 95.00
Firefighter, Fireman No. 1, Yellow Hat, 1972 .... 135.00
Firefighter, Fireman No. 2, With Child, 1974 .... 85.00
Firefighter, Fireman No. 3, Down Pole, 1975 .... 90.00
Firefighter, Fireman No. 4, Emblem, 1978 .... 30.00
Firefighter, Fireman No. 5, Emblem, 1979 .... 35.00
Firefighter, Fireman No. 7, Hat, 1982 .... 95.00
Firefighter, Fireman No. 8, Fire Alarm Box, 1983 .... 120.00
French Poodle, 1975 .... 20.00
God Of War, 1978 ....20.00 to 22.00
Goddess Of Love, 1978 ....20.00 to 22.00

Goldfinch, 1972	24.00
Horse, Cannonade, 1976	135.00
Horse, Secretariat, 1977	178.00
Horse, Secretariat, 1977, Miniature	17.00
Lantern, Brass, 1983	60.00
Mailman, 1974	30.00
Oil Filter, Delco	65.00
Old West, Annie Christmas, 1969	18.00
Old West, Annie Oakley, 1969	18.00 to 20.00
Old West, Backpacker, 1980	28.00
Old West, Bar Scene & Nude, With Frame, 1970	500.00 to 640.00
Old West, Barber, 1976	40.00
Old West, Barber, 1976, Miniature	14.00
Old West, Bartender, 1969	70.00
Old West, Bartender, 1969, Miniature	14.00 to 27.00
Old West, Bath, 1976	70.00
Old West, Bath, 1976, Miniature	16.00
Old West, Belly Robber, 1969	12.00 to 18.00
Old West, Buffalo Hunter, 1973	30.00
Old West, Calamity Jane, 1973	25.00
Old West, Camp Cook, 1969	18.00
Old West, Camp Follower, 1969	22.00
Old West, Cavalry Scout, 1969	10.00
Old West, Cavalry Scout, 1970, Miniature	13.00
Old West, Chinese Laundry Man, 1969	14.00
Old West, Country Doctor, 1969	12.00
Old West, Cowboy, 1969	10.00
Old West, Cowboy, 1970, Miniature	12.00
Old West, Cowgirl, 1973	28.00
Old West, Custer's Last Stand, 1979	500.00
Old West, Dancehall Girl, 1973	50.00
Old West, Frontiersman, 1969	*Illus* 20.00
Old West, Gambler, 1969	10.00 to 30.00
Old West, Gambler, 1969, Miniature	12.00
Old West, Gold Panner, 1969	48.00
Old West, Highway Robber, 1969	13.00
Old West, Indian, Bust, No. 1, 1980	45.00
Old West, Indian, Bust, No. 2, 1980	35.00
Old West, Indian, Casual, 1969	18.00
Old West, Indian, Casual, 1970, Miniature	15.00
Old West, Indian, Proud, 1969	20.00
Old West, Indian, Proud, 1970, Miniature	15.00
Old West, Indian, Squaw, 1973	24.00

Lionstone, Old West, Frontiersman, 1969

Lionstone, Old West, Mountain Man, 1969

Lionstone, Old West, Stage Driver, 1969

Lionstone, Oriental Worker, Basket Weaver, 1974

Old West, Indian, Squawman, 1969 . . . . .24.00 to 28.00
Old West, Indian, Tribal Chief, 1973 . . . . .22.00 to 24.00
Old West, Jesse James, 1969 . . . . 16.00
Old West, Judge Roy Bean, 1973 . . . . 20.00
Old West, Judge, Circuit Riding, 1969 . . . . 10.00
Old West, Lonely Luke, 1974 . . . . 25.00
Old West, Lonely Luke, 1975, Miniature 10.00
Old West, Lucky Buck, 1974 . . . . 25.00
Old West, Lucky Buck, 1975, Miniature 10.00
Old West, Madame, 1969 . . . . 42.00
Old West, Molly Brown, 1973 . . . . 18.00
Old West, Mountain Man, 1969 . . . . *Illus* 15.00
Old West, Photographer, 1976 . . . . 60.00
Old West, Photographer, 1976, Miniature 15.00
Old West, Professor, 1973 . . . . 45.00
Old West, Railroad Engineer, 1969 . . . . 23.00
Old West, Rainmaker, 1976 . . . . 30.00
Old West, Rainmaker, 1976, Miniature 14.00
Old West, Renegade Trader, 1969 . . . . 19.00
Old West, Riverboat Captain, 1969 . . . . .10.00 to 22.00
Old West, Sheepherder, 1969 . . . . 40.00
Old West, Sheepherder, 1975, Miniature 16.00
Old West, Sheriff, 1969 . . . . 20.00
Old West, Sheriff, 1970, Miniature 14.00
Old West, Shootout At OK Corral, 1971 . . . . 410.00
Old West, Shootout At OK Corral, 1971, Miniature 250.00
Old West, Sodbuster, 1969 . . . . 20.00
Old West, Stage Driver, 1969 . . . . *Illus* 22.00
Old West, Telegrapher, 1969 . . . . 25.00
Old West, Tinker, 1974 . . . . 26.00
Old West, Trapper, 1976 . . . . 22.00
Old West, Vigilante, 1969 . . . . 20.00
Old West, Wells Fargo Man, 1969 . . . . 20.00
Oriental Worker, Basket Weaver, 1974 . . . . *Illus* 30.00
Oriental Worker, Egg Merchant, 1974 . . . . 30.00
Oriental Worker, Gardener, 1974 . . . . 30.00
Oriental Worker, Sculptor, 1974 . . . . 30.00
Oriental Worker, Tea Vendor, 1974 . . . . 30.00
Oriental Worker, Timekeeper, 1974 . . . . 30.00
Police Association Convention, 1980 . . . . 30.00
Prima Donna Club, 1978, 5 Piece 315.00
Professor, 1973, Miniature 9.00
Professor, 1975, Miniature 12.00
Rose Parade, 1973 . . . . 18.00
Safari, Buffalo, 1977, Miniature 15.00
Safari, Elephants, 1977, Miniature 16.00
Safari, Gazelles, 1977, Miniature 15.00
Safari, Giraffes, 1977, Miniature 15.00
Safari, Hippos, 1977, Miniature 15.00
Safari, Kangaroos, 1977, Miniature 15.00
Safari, Koala Bear, 1977, Miniature 15.00
Safari, Leopards, 1977, Miniature 15.00
Safari, Lion & Cub, 1977 . . . . 30.00
Safari, Lion & Cub, 1977, Miniature 10.00
Safari, Mona Monkeys, 1977, Miniature 15.00
Safari, Rhinos, 1977, Miniature 16.00
Safari, Zebras, 1977, Miniature 15.00
Shamrock, 1983 . . . . 30.00
Sport, Backpacker, 1980 . . . . 28.00
Sport, Baseball Players, 1974 . . . . 55.00
Sport, Basketball Players, 1974 . . . . .48.00 to 55.00
Sport, Boxers, 1974 . . . . 60.00
Sport, Brooks Robinson, 1983 . . . . 71.00

Sport, Fisherman, 1983		.37.00 to 39.00
Sport, Football Players, 1974		.55.00 to 65.00
Sport, Golfer, 1974		42.00
Sport, Hockey Players, 1974		65.00
Sport, Johnny Unitas, 1983		175.00
Sport, Sahara Invitational, 1976		52.00
Sport, Sahara Invitational, 1977		50.00
Sport, Tennis Player, Male, 1980		28.00
Sport, Tennis Players, Female, 1980		28.00

──────────── MCCORMICK ────────────

It is claimed that the first white men to find the limestone spring near Weston, Missouri, were Lewis and Clark on their famous expedition. Over 20,000 gallons of fresh water gush from the spring each day. An Indian trading post was started near the spring by a man named McPhearson about 1830. His friend Joseph Moore decided to establish a town and paid a barrel of whiskey for the land. Bela Hughes and his cousin Ben Holladay came to the new town in 1837. They soon had a dry goods store, a drugstore, a tavern, and a hotel. They even built a Pony Express station. In 1856, Ben Holladay and his brother David started a distillery to make bourbon using the spring water. David's daughter later married a man named Barton and the distillery was renamed Barton and Holladay. It was sold in 1895 to George Shawhan but closed from 1920 to 1936. The property became a cattle and tobacco farm.

In 1936, after the repeal of Prohibition, Isadore Singer and his two brothers purchased the plant and began making Old Weston and Old Holladay bourbon. About 1939 they bought the name *McCormick* from a nearby distillery founded years before by E.R. McCormick. Legend says that Mrs. McCormick would not allow her husband to reopen the distillery because she had "gotten religion." The Singer brothers' new distillery used part of the grain for the mash, and their cattle feed lot used the leftover parts.

During World War II, alcohol was needed by the government and Cloud L. Cray bought the distillery to make industrial alcohol at a company he called Midwest Solvents. After the war, Bud and Dick Cray, sons of Cloud Cray, started making bourbon at the old plant by old-fashioned methods, producing about 25 barrels a day. The bourbon was sold in Missouri, Kansas, Iowa, and Oklahoma. The old plant, listed in the National Register of Historic Sites, is open for tours. In about 1980 the company, under the direction of the new president, Marty Adams, started marketing on a national instead of a local scale, and it is now selling in all of the states. They have a full line, including wine, beer, and many alcoholic beverages such as rum, tequila, vodka, dry gin, blended whiskey, and brandy that are now sold under the McCormick name.

McCormick Distilling Company, now a subsidiary of Midwest Grain Products, has created many types of figural bottles for their bourbon, ranging from a bust of Elvis Presley (made in 1979) to a musical apple (1982). The company discontinued making decanters in 1987.

MCCORMICK, Air Race, Pylon, 1970	*Illus*	10.00
Alabama		50.00
Arizona Wildcat		40.00
Baylor Bear, 1972		40.00
Belle Jug		34.00
Betsy Ross, 1975		25.00
Betsy Ross, 1976, Miniature		30.00
Bing Crosby, Golf		54.00
Blue Bird, 1971		16.00
California Bears		40.00
Capt. John Smith, 1977		19.00
Chair, Queen Anne, 1979		35.00
Christmas House, 1984		44.00
Cowboy Hall Of Fame, 1983		90.00
Deer Trophy Plaque, 1983		92.00
Eleanor Roosevelt, 1977		23.00
Elvis, 25th Anniversary, 1980		135.00
Elvis, 50th Anniversary, 1986		397.00
Elvis, Christmas Tree		200.00

Elvis, Graceland Gate 215.00
Elvis, Hound Dog 550.00
Elvis, Karate, 1982 .... 300.00
Elvis, Memories 525.00
Elvis, On Rising Sun, 1984 .... 650.00
Elvis, Sargeant, 1983 .... 302.00
Elvis, With Teddy Bear 700.00
Fire Extinguisher, 1983 .... 45.00
FOE, 1984 .... 75.00
FOE, 1985 .... 50.00
FOE, 1986 .... 25.00
Frontiersman Davy Crockett, 1975 .... 25.00
Georgia Tech 50.00
Hank Williams Jr., Bocephus, 1980 .... 80.00
Hank Williams Sr., 1980 ....85.00 to 140.00
Henry Ford, 1977 .... 30.00
Ice Box, 1983 .... 35.00
Iowa Hawkeye, 1974 .... 100.00
Iowa Northern Panther, 1974 .... 50.00
Jimmy Durante 55.00
Johnny Rogers, No. 1, 1972 .... 180.00
Joplin Miner, 1972 .... 20.00
Jug, Bourbon, 1967 .... 14.00
Jug, Gin, 1967 .... 10.00
Jug, Vodka, 1967 .... 10.00
Julia Bullette, 1974 .... 97.00
Kansas City Chiefs, 1969 .... 25.00
Kansas City Club, 1982 .... 27.00
Kansas City Royals, 1971 .... 14.00
King Arthur, 1979 ....40.00 to 42.00
Kit Carson, 1975 .... 25.00
Meriwether Lewis, 1978 .... 22.00
Merlin, 1979 .... 34.00
Michigan Wolverine, 1974 .... 43.00
Minnesota Gopher, 1974 .... 50.00
Mississippi Rebel, 1974 .... 50.00
Missouri, China, 1970 .... 12.00
Missouri, Glass, 1971 .... 7.00
Muhammad Ali, 1980 .... 160.00
Nebraska Football Player, 1972 .... 40.00
New Mexico Lobo, 1973 .... 40.00
Old Holiday, 1956 .... 16.00
Oregon Duck, 1974 .... 43.00
Oregon St. Beaver, 1974 .... 50.00
Packard, Hood Ornament, 1985 .... 30.00
Packard, Model 1937, Black, 1980 .... 46.00
Packard, Model 1937, Cream, 1980 .... 46.00
Packard, Model 1937, Gold 79.00
Packard, Model 1937, Silver 79.00
Paul Bunyan, 1979 .... 32.00
Pendleton Roundup 54.00
Pony Express, 1978 .... 50.00
Pony Express, 1980 .... 50.00
Quail Gamal, 1982 .... 50.00
Quail Gamal, 1984 .... 50.00
Queen Guinevere, 1979 .... 22.00
Robert E. Lee, 1976 .... 58.00
Robert Peary, 1977 .... 26.00
Rose Garden, 1980, Miniature 20.00
Samuel Houston, 1977 .... 27.00
Seal With Ball 54.00
Shriner, Noble, 1976 ....Illus 24.00
Sir Lancelot, 1979 .... 25.00

McCormick, Air Race, Pylon, 1970

McCormick, Shriner, Noble, 1976

McCormick, Washing Clothes, 1980

Skibob, 1971	13.00
Skier Club Of Kansas City	77.00
Spirit Of '76, 1976	47.00
Spirit Of '76, 1977, Miniature	10.00
TCU Horned Frogs, 1972	45.00
Telephone Operator, 1982	57.00
Texas 150th Anniversary	22.00
Texas Long Horns, 1972	40.00
Texas Tech Raider, 1972	42.00
Thelma Lu	30.00
Tom Sawyer, 1980	27.00
Tom T. Hall, 1980	90.00
Train, Locomotive, 1969	25.00
Train, Mail Car, 1969	35.00
U.S. Marshall, 1979	36.00
Victorian, 1984	20.00
Washing Clothes, 1980 ....*Illus*	35.00
Washington, 1975	24.00
Washington, 1976	24.00
Weston, 1856, Miniature	150.00
Will Rogers, 1978, Miniature	10.00
Willie Weary, 1981	92.00
Woman Feeding Chickens, 8 Piece	28.00
Wood Duck, 1980	35.00
Wood Duck, 1984	35.00
World's Greatest Fan	18.00

———————— MEDICINE ————————

If you have friends with scrofula or catarrh, they probably can find a medicine from the nineteenth century. The extravagant claims for cures and the strange names for diseases add to the fun of collecting early medicine bottles. Bottles held all of the many types of medications used in past centuries. Most of those collected today date from the 1850-1930 period. An early bottle often had a pontil. Some of the names, like Kickapoo Indian Oil, Lydia Pinkham's Female Compound, or Wahoo Bitters, have become part of the slang of America. Bitters, cures, sarsaparilla, and a few other types of medicine are listed under their own headings in this book. Apothecary and other drug store bottles are listed here. Collectors prefer early bottles with raised lettering. Labeled bottles in original boxes are also sought. For more information, look for *The Bottle Book, A Comprehensive Guide to Historic, Embossed Medicine Bottles* by Richard E. Fike. Related bottles may be found in the Bitters, Cure, Sarsaparilla, and Tonic categories.

MEDICINE, A. Eaton's Vegetable Universal Restorative Medicine, Phila., 7 1/2 In.	80.00
A. Griggs & Co. Druggist, Visalia, Cal., Variant, 6 In.	23.00
A.K. Mulford Co., Cold Laxative, Waxpaper Wrapped, 1885-1910	16.00
A.M. Cole Apothecary, Virginia City, Nev., Tooled Top, 5 In.	35.00
A.M. Rock Rose, New Haven, Blue Green, Indented Panels, IP, 1860, 9 3/8 In.	1210.00

Abigail M. Littlefield, Pharmacist, A.M.L.C., Troy, N.Y., Cobalt Blue, 5 5/8 In. 145.00
Abraham & Straus, Brooklyn, N.Y., Tooled Lip, Cork, 4 In. 3.00
Acid, Con Acid Hydrochloric HCL, Wheaton, No-Sol-It, U.S.A., 5 1/4 In. . . . .*Illus* 20.00
Alden's Extract Of Coffee, Blue Green, IP, 1855, 6 In. 855.00
Alexander's Silameau, Sapphire Blue, Pontil, 1845-1855, 6 1/8 In. 120.00
Alexander's Silameau, Violin Shape, Blue, Bulbous Neck, Pontil, 1860, 6 In. . . .470.00 to 690.00
Alexander's Tricobaphe, R. & G.A. Wright, Philada., 6-Sided, Aqua, OP, 3 In. 65.00
Allan's Anti Fat Botanic Medicine Co., Buffalo, N.Y., Cobalt Blue, 8 In. . . . .415.00 to 470.00
Allen's Lung Davis & Lawrence Co., Balsam, New York, Aqua, 6 3/4 In. 10.00
Alvas Brazilian Specific Co., Pat. June 10 1890, Acorn Squash Shape, 10 In. 20.00
Amegin Pyorrhea Liquid, For Gums, Karlin Labs., N.Y., 4 1/4 In. . . . .*Illus* 8.50
American Expectorant, Green Aqua, Outward Rolled Mouth, 1860, 5 In. 470.00
American Medicinal Oil, Burkesville, Kentucky, Blue Aqua, OP, 6 1/4 In. 595.00
Anderson's Cough Drops, Prepared By I. Mellen, Aqua, Raised Panels, OP 120.00
Anderson's Dermador, Cylindrical, Aqua, Pontil, 4 1/2 In. 30.00
Andrew's Herpetic Lotion, Olive Amber, Applied Seal, 1750-1770, 5 1/2 In. 2750.00
Apothecary, 2 Tiers, Tooled Mouth, Green Ground Glass Stopper, 11 In. 165.00
Apothecary, 2K, Partial Label, Purple Amethyst, Pontil, England, 10 3/4 In. 110.00
Apothecary, Benzine Rect., Yellow Green, Red, White, Gold, England, 1900, 8 1/8 In. . . . 175.00
Apothecary, Black Amethyst, Red, White, Black Label, 1840-1860, 11 3/4 In. 440.00
Apothecary, Cobalt Blue, Pontil, England, 1840, 6 1/4 In. 100.00
Apothecary, Cobalt Blue, Square, Rounded Corners, Recessed Panel, Stopper, Qt. 70.00
Apothecary, Cobalt Blue, White, Orange Enamel Label, Ground Glass Stopper, 7 In. . . . 120.00
Apothecary, Cobalt Blue, White, Orange Enamel Label, Ground Glass Stopper, 9 In. . . . 185.00
Apothecary, Cocaine, Pottery, Blue, Gold Leaf Design, 1880s, 6 In. 660.00
Apothecary, Deep Cobalt Blue, Red, Gold, Black Label, 1850-1870, 7 In. 135.00
Apothecary, Deep Cobalt Blue, Red, Gold, Black Label, Glass Stopper, 1840-1860, 9 In. . 245.00
Apothecary, Deep Purple Amethyst, White, Red, Gray, Globular, 1850-1870, 13 In. 1320.00
Apothecary, Diamond Dust, Label Under Glass, Jar, Stopper, Square, 1900, 8 In. 165.00
Apothecary, Green, White, Orange Enamel Label, Ground Glass Stopper, 8 In. 305.00
Apothecary, Jar, Pat. 14th Aug 1866, Tooled Lip, Applied Knob On Lid, 11 1/4 In. 100.00
Apothecary, Liq. Ars. Hyd. Iod., 7 In. . . . .*Illus* 120.00
Apothecary, Milk Glass, Ground Pontil, Ground Glass Stopper, 11 3/4 In. 120.00
Apothecary, Olive Green, Worn Painted Ships & Coat Of Arms, Globular, 10 1/2 In. . . . 650.00
Apothecary, Pillar Mold, 8 Ribs, Applied Finial Lid, Pittsburgh, 17 3/4 In. 1265.00
Apothecary, Pink Amethyst, Black, Red Label Under Glass, Glass Stopper, 12 In. 635.00
Apothecary, Pulv. Canthar, 15 1/4 In. . . . .*Illus* 120.00
Apothecary, Purple Amethyst, White, Black Original Label, 1870, 11 In. 275.00
Apothecary, Purple Amethyst, White, Red, Gray, England, 1850-1870, 13 In. 415.00
Apothecary, Ruby Red, BIMAL, Stopper, Marked Pyrex 29, 1910-1920, 8 3/4 In. 40.00
Apothecary, Strong, Cobb & Co., Druggists, Cleveland, 5 In. . . . .*Illus* 10.00
Apothecary, Turquoise, Gold, Black Porcelain Label, 1860-1880, 9 1/2 In. . . . . . .100.00 to 155.00
Apothecary, Turquoise, Gold, Black, Porcelain Label, France, 1880, 10 In. 220.00

Medicine, Acid, Con Acid
Hydrochloric HCL,
Wheaton, No-Sol-It,
U.S.A., 5 1/4 In.

Medicine, Amegin
Pyorrhea Liquid, For
Gums, Karlin Labs., N.Y.,
4 1/4 In.

Medicine,
Apothecary, Liq. Ars.
Hyd. Iod., 7 In.

Medicine,
Apothecary, Pulv.
Canthar, 15 1/4 In.

Apothecary, Turquoise, Gold, Wide Mouth, Black Porcelain Label, 9 In. 305.00
Apothecary, W.T. Co., Tinct. Cannab. Ind., Label Under Glass, Stopper, Square, Pt. 220.00
Apothecary, Yellow Green, Gold, Black, Red Label Under Glass, Glass Stopper, 8 In. . . . 135.00
Arnold Drug Co., Hartford, Ct., Tooled Lip, Cork, 5 In. 3.00
Aromatic Salts, Baltimore, Green, Sheared, Polished Lip, 1855-1865, 2 In. 210.00
Arthur's Renovating Syrup, Blue Green, Applied Mouth, IP, 1845-1860, 9 In. 1045.00
Aspen Pharmacy, Aspen, Colo, 2 1/2 In. 40.00
Athlophoros, Searles Remedy For Rheumatism, Aqua, Labels, Contents, 6 1/2 In. 28.00
Avan Hoboken & Co., Olive Green, Applied Seal, 11 In. 55.00
Ayer's Cherry Pectoral, Lowell, Mass., OP, 7 In. 35.00
B. Paul, New York, Amber, 1890, 4 3/4 In. 15.00
B.M. Keeney & Co., Brooklyn, N.Y., Honey Balm, Aqua, 1845-1855, 5 3/8 In. 85.00
Bach's American Compound, Auburn, N.Y., Aqua, OP, 1840-1855, 7 1/2 In. . . . .95.00 to 150.00
Baker's Blood Remedy, Jug, Stoneware, Cream, 6 1/2 In. 65.00
Baker's Specific, R.H. Hurd, Prop., Red Amethyst, Uncle Sam On Box, 4 1/4 In. 55.00
Ballard's Horehound Syrup, Label, 4 Oz. 6.00
Balm Of Thousand Flowers, Fetridge & Co., New York, Blue Aqua, IP, 4 3/4 In. 75.00
Barrett's Mandrake Embrocation, Duck With Bearded Mans Head, Aqua, 5 In. 35.00
Bastian's Life Animator, Dansville, N.Y., Amber, 10 1/2 In. 250.00
Beach & Clarridge, Boston, Mass., Aqua, Gal. 25.00
Benbow's Dog Mixture, 8-Sided, 5 3/4 In. 10.00
Bench's Mixture Of Cannabis Indica, Phila., Aqua, OP, 1855, 7 5/8 In. 2035.00
Benjamin Green, Portsmouth, N.H., Cobalt Blue, Tooled Lip, 7 1/4 In. 165.00
Billings Capp & Co. Chemists, Boston, Mass., Aqua, 10 1/2 In. 25.00
Bishop's Granular Citrate Of Lithia For Gout, Aqua, Rectangular, 6 In. 10.00
Bishop's Granular Citrate Of Lithia For Gout, Cornflower Blue, Rectangular, 6 In. . 75.00
Bolton's Chest & Lung Mixture, Aqua, Rectangular, 5 1/2 In. 10.00
Bon Opto For The Eyes, 1890s, 3 1/4 In. 7.00
Bonheur Co., Inc., Syracuse, N.Y., Green, Cylindrical, 7 5/8 In. 15.00
Bonpland's Fever & Ague Remedy, New York, Blue Aqua, Applied Top, OP, Error . . . 45.00
Bonpland's Fever & Ague Remedy, New York, Pontil, 5 In. 38.00
Bouvier Buchu Gin, For The Kidneys & Bladder, Louisville, Ky., 11 3/4 In. . . . . . .*Illus* 20.00
Bowman's Drug Stores, Cobalt Blue, 1 Oz. 150.00
Brandriff's Vegetable Antidote For Ague, Piqua, Ohio, Blue Aqua, Rectangular, 7 In. 45.00
Brant's Indian Pulmonary Balsam, 8-Sided, Aqua, Applied Mouth, Pontil, 6 3/4 In. . . 165.00
Brant's Indian Pulmonary Balsam, J.W. Brant Co., Albion, Mich., Aqua, 6 1/4 In. . . . 15.00
Brant's Indian Pulmonary Balsam, J.W. Brant, Hillsdale, Mich., Aqua, 6 1/2 In. 35.00
Brant's Indian Pulmonary Balsam, Mt. Wallace, Proprietor, Aqua, Pontil, 7 In. 110.00
Brant's Purifying Extract, M.T. Wallace & Co., Aqua, OP, 10 1/8 In. 265.00
Brehrens Drug Co. Rubbing Alcohol, Hourglass, Label, Tin Lid, 1920-1929 . . . . 3.00
Bromo Caffeine, Light Cobalt Blue, 3 In. 6.00
Bromo Seltzer, Cobalt Blue, Label, No Screw Cap, 1910, 2 1/2 In. 6.00
Bromo Seltzer, Cobalt Blue, Medium Size 25.00
Bromo-Seltzer, Emerson Drug Co., Baltimore, Md., Cobalt, ABM, 2 1/2 In. . . . . .3.00 to 6.00
Bromo-Seltzer, Emerson Drug Co., Baltimore, Md., Cobalt, Tooled Lip, 4 In. . . . . . . .5.00 to 6.00
Brown's Castillian, Cannon, Amber, 11 In. 145.00
Budwell's Emulsion Of Norwegian Cod Liver Oil, Lynchburg, Va., Amber, 8 In. 35.00
Bumstead's Worm Syrup, Children Cry For More, Philada., Aqua, 4 1/2 In. 8.00
Burchall & Marlow Veterinary Surgeons Eddy St., Egg Shape, Stoneware 1000.00
Burnett's Cocoaine, Burnett, Boston, Aqua . . . . .20.00 to 25.00
By A.A. Cooley, Hartford, Con., Olive Green, Sheared Lip, OP, 1840-1855, 4 5/8 In. . . . 470.00
C. Heimstreet & Co., Troy, N.Y., 8-Sided, Blue, Double Collar, OP, 7 In. . . . . . .120.00 to 355.00
C.C. Case Druggist, North Yakima, Wash., Jug, Stoneware, Blue Glaze, 1/2 Gal. 825.00
C.C. Jadwin's Subduing Liniment, Honesdale, Pa., Aqua, 1890s, 4 In. 5.00
C.C. Liniment, W.H. Bone Co., San Francisco, Ca., U.S.A., Aqua, 6 1/4 In. 100.00
C.H. Graves & Sons, Boston, Mass., Hub Punch, Gold Amber, 1885, 8 7/8 In. 190.00
C.W. Atwell, Portland, Me., Aqua, Oval, 7 3/4 In. . . . . .15.00 to 35.00
C.W. Snow & Co. Druggists, Syracuse, N.Y., Cobalt Blue, 1895, 8 1/4 In. 470.00
Calder's Dentine, CLA Monogram, Oval Panel, Round, 3 In. 5.00
California Fig Syrup, San Francisco, Cal., Syrup Of Figs, Side Panels, Rectangular, 7 In. 3.00
California Fig Syrup Co., Sterling Products Inc., 1900, 6 7/8 In. 7.00
California Fig Syrup Co., Wheeling, W.V., 7 In. 10.00
Capudine For Headache, Amber, ABM, 3 1/4 In. 5.00

Medicine, Bouvier
Buchu Gin, For
The Kidneys &
Bladder, Louisville,
Ky., 11 3/4 In.

Medicine, Apothecary,
Strong, Cobb & Co.,
Druggists, Cleveland,
5 In.

Medicine, Chase's
Healer, For Man
Or Beast, Lynn
Curtiss, Chardon,
Oh., 5 3/4 In.

Carter's Cascara Compound, Aqua, 7 1/2 In. 22.00
Carter's Ext. Of Smart Weed, Erie, Pa., Aqua, 5 1/4 In. 22.00
Carter's Spanish Mixture, Olive Green, Graphite Pontil, 8 In. 350.00
Carter's Spanish Mixture, Yellow Olive Green, Double Collar, OP, 8 In. 800.00
Caswell & Massey Chemists & Druggists, New York, Stopper, Round, Qt. 28.00
Caswell Hazard & Co., Cobalt Blue, Square, 7 In. 35.00
Caswell Hazard & Co., Elixir Of Calisaya Bark, Cobalt Blue, Square, 7 1/2 In. ... 125.00
Celery Compound, Embossed Celery, Yellow Amber, Label, 9 In. 140.00
Celery Nervine, Amber, Label, BIMAL, Contents, Square, 9 1/2 In. 15.00
Celro-Kola Co., Portland, Oregon, Amber, ABM, Square, 8 3/4 In. 40.00
Chamberlain's Cough Remedy, Des Moines, 5 3/4 In. 7.00
Chamberlain's Cough Remedy, Des Moines, Iowa, Aqua, Rectangular, Cork, 7 In. 10.00
Chamberlain's Cough Remedy, Des Moines, Iowa, Aqua, Sunken Panels, Cork, 6 In. . 7.00
Chamberlain's Immediate Relief, A.N. Chamberlain, Elkhart, Ind., Aqua, OP . . .90.00 to 120.00
Chapman's Genuine, No. 4, Salem St., Boston, Olive Amber, 1846-1860, 8 In. 4070.00
Charles E. Hires Co., Malvern, Pa., Aqua, 4 1/4 In. 25.00
Chas. C. Schrader, Druggists, Louisville, Ky., Jar, Salve, White, Gilt, 1880, 2 1/2 In. 120.00
Chas. H. Fletcher's Castoria, Aqua, Cork, 5 3/4 In. 2.00
Chase's Healer, For Man Or Beast, Lynn Curtiss, Chardon, Oh., 5 3/4 In. ....*Illus* 10.00
Chelf's Celery-Caffein, Comp'd, Richmond, Va., Cobalt Blue, 4 In. 10.00
Chesebrough Mfg. Co. Vaseline, Amber, Cork, 2 3/4 In. ....1.00 to 8.00
Christie's Magnetic Fluid, Aqua, Crude Lip, Rectangular, Pontil, 4 3/4 In. ....40.00 to 46.00
Citrate Magnesia, Light Blue, Banner, Cylindrical, 8 In.......................... 50.00
Citrate Of Magnesia, Amethyst, Cork, 9 In............................ 15.00
Citrate Of Magnesia, Boysen's Pharmacy, San Francisco, Blue, Stopper, Bail, Dose Cup 715.00
Citrate Of Magnesia, H.B. Wakelee, Cobalt Blue, Applied Mouth, 1880, 7 5/8 In. 145.00
Citrate Of Magnesia, Porcelain, Lightning Stopper, 7 1/2 In. 7.00
Clark Stanley's Snake Oil Liniment, 4 In. 40.00
Clark Stanley's Snake Oil Liniment, For Rheumatism & Neuralgia, 6 1/2 In. . . . .25.00 to 100.00
Clark's Drug Store, Ely-McGrill, Graduations, 4 1/4 In. 45.00
Clarks' Anti-Bilious, R.C. & C.S. Clark Chemists Compound, Aqua, Label 15.00
Cleaveland's Dermaline, Triangular, Beveled Corners, Aqua, IP, 7 5/8 In. 305.00
Compound Fluid Extract Of Manzanita, Sacramento, Ca., Aqua, OP, 1853, 4 1/2 In. . 1210.00
Comstock & Brother, Turkish Balm, Aqua, OP, 1855, 7 1/4 In. 260.00
Condie & Hunt Chemists & Druggists, New York, Tooled Lip, Cork, 6 1/2 In. 2.00
Costar's N.Y., Smoky Pink Puce, Rolled Lip, 1855-1865, 4 In. 90.00
Crotzer's Bromo, Philadelphia, Amber, Label, Contents, 7 3/4 In. 45.00
Curtis & Perkins' Cramp & Pain Killer, Bangor, Me., Aqua, Rolled Lip, OP, 5 In. ... 75.00
Cuticura System Of Curing Constitutional Humors, Aqua, BIMAL, 9 In. ....10.00 to 15.00
Cuticura Treatment For Affections Of The Skin, Aqua, ABM, Contents, 9 In. . .35.00 to 40.00
D. Vollmer Druggist, Ft. Wayne, Ind., Cobalt Blue, 1885, 7 1/2 In. 550.00
Daily's Pain Extractor, Louisville, Ky., Blue Aqua, Applied Mouth, Pontil, 1855, 7 In. . 605.00
Daily's Pain Extractor, Louisville, Ky., Blue Aqua, OP, Rolled Lip, 1855, 5 1/2 In. 385.00
Dallimores Celebrated Brandy, N.Y., 12-Sided, Olive Green, IP, 7 1/8 In. 2860.00
Davis & Miller Druggists, Baltimore, Emerald Green, OP, 4 In. 220.00
Davis & Miller Druggists, Baltimore, Md., Sapphire Blue, IP, 1845-1860, 7 In. 1980.00
Davis Drug Company, Rexall Store, Leadville, Colo., Paneled, 9 In. 95.00

Davis Drug Rexall Store, Leadville, Colo., Amber, 5 1/4 In. 45.00
Davis Vegetable Pain Killer, Aqua, Applied Top, OP, 5 In. 75.00
Davis Vegetable Pain Killer, Aqua, OP, 4 In. ....20.00 to 25.00
Derlachs, Apricot To Puce Amber, 2 Fish Picture Front, Applied Seal, 6 3/4 In. 90.00
DeWitt's Witch Hazel Salve, Reverse The Great Pile Cure, 1 1/4 Qt. 15.00
Dickey Pioneer Chemist, Mortar & Pestle, Teal Aqua, 5 3/4 In. 90.00
Dickey Pioneer Chemist, S.F., Mortar & Pestle, Cobalt Blue, Tooled Lip, 5 3/4 In. 35.00 to 45.00
Doct. Marshall's Snuff, Aqua, Rolled Lip, OP, 3 In. 45.00
Doctor Pierce Extract Of Smart Weed, Buffalo, N.Y., Aqua, 5 1/2 In. 15.00
Doctors Feller's & Ireland's Eclectic Liniment, 8-Sided, Aqua, Pontil, 4 5/16 In. ... 230.00
Dr. A.L. Adam's Liver Balsam, Aqua, IP, 1855, 7 1/4 In. 165.00
Dr. Baker's Pain Panacea, Aqua, Rectangular, Pontil, 5 In. 45.00
Dr. Baker's Turkish Liniment, Keokuk, Ia., Aqua, 7 3/4 In. 15.00
Dr. Barlow J. Smith's Caloric Vita Oil, Light Amethyst, Tooled Top, 5 In. 35.00
Dr. Bell's Anti-Pain, Paducah, Ky., Tooled Top, Label, Box, 5 In. 25.00
Dr. Bell's Pine Tar Honey For Coughs & Colds, Aqua, ABM, 5 1/2 In. 5.00
Dr. Birmingham's Antibilious Blood Purifier, Teal Blue Green, 1865-1875, 9 In. 685.00
Dr. Bouviers Buchu, Square Bottom, Case, 4 1/2 In. 55.00
Dr. Bowman's Indian Ointment, 8-Sided, Aqua, Applied Mouth, OP, 6 In. 300.00
Dr. Browder's Compound Syrup Of Indian Turnip, Aqua, OP, 10 In. 200.00
Dr. Browder's Compound Syrup Of Indian Turnip, Aqua, OP, 1850, 7 In. ...175.00 to 190.00
Dr. Brunet's Pulmonary Syrup, Snap Case, Applied Top, c.1860, 7 1/2 In. 40.00
Dr. C. Grattan's Diptheria Remedy, Aqua, Tooled Top, 7 In. ....65.00 to 125.00
Dr. C.F. Basford's Home Guard Medicine, Cincinnati, O., Aqua, 5 In. 105.00
Dr. Cavanaugh's Pile Salve, St. Louis, Mo., Aqua, Tubular Pontil, 2 In. 305.00
Dr. Chapman's Cholera Syrup, Geo. Moore, Proprietor, Aqua, BIMAL, 6 1/2 In. 4.00
Dr. Collin's Indian Pain Killing Remedy, Reading, Penna., 1870s, 5 1/4 In. 20.00
Dr. Cooper's Ethereal Oil For Deafness, Aqua, OP, 1840-1855, 2 5/8 In. 240.00
Dr. Crooks Wine Of Tar, Aqua, 8 3/4 In. 45.00
Dr. Cummings' Vegetine, Embossed, Oval, Aqua, 9 1/2 In. ....15.00 to 20.00
Dr. D. Jayne's Ague Mixture, Philadelphia, Aqua, OP, 7 In. 305.00
Dr. D. Jayne's Alterative, 84 Chest. St., Phila., Oval, Aqua, Pontil, 6 3/4 In. 40.00
Dr. D. Jayne's Expectorant, Philada., Flask, Aqua, Strapside, BIMAL, 6 3/4 In. 8.00
Dr. D. Jayne's Expectorant, Philadelphia, Rectangular, Trail Size, 4 1/8 In. 10.00
Dr. D. Jayne's Indian Expectorant, Phila., Aqua, Pontil, 5 In. ....80.00 to 175.00
Dr. D. Jayne's Liniment Or Counter Irritant, Philada., Aqua, OP, 5 In. 30.00
Dr. D. Jayne's Tonic Vermufuge, Embossed, Aqua, ABM, 6 1/2 In. ....8.00 to 18.00
Dr. D. Kennedy's Favorite Remedy, Kingston, N.Y., Aqua, Rectangular, Cork, 8 1/2 In. 8.00
Dr. D.C. Kellinger's Remedies, New York, Aqua, OP, 8 3/4 In. 220.00
Dr. David Rober's Milk Fever Remedy For Treating Cows, Contents, 3 1/2 In. 45.00
Dr. Davis's, Depurative, Phila., Aqua, Blue Green, IP, 1855, 9 1/2 In. 1705.00
Dr. Davis's Compound Syrup Of Wild Cherry & Tar, Green Aqua, 6 In. 45.00
Dr. E. Champlain's Ligneous Extract, Patented, Aqua, 5 1/4 In. 170.00
Dr. E.D. Hudson Veterinary Surgeon, Gettysburg, Pa., 8 1/2 In. 40.00
Dr. E.E. Burnside's Purifico, BIMAL, 9 1/2 In. 15.00
Dr. Elmore's Rheumatine Coutaline, Amber, 9 1/2 In. 110.00
Dr. Evans' Camomile Pills, Green Aqua, Flared Lip, OP, 3 In. 50.00
Dr. Flint's Remedy, Mack Drug Co., New York, Amber, Flask, Strapside, 7 1/4 In. 25.00
Dr. Friend's Cough Balsam, Morristown, N.J., Aqua, Beveled Corners, 6 In. 155.00
Dr. G. Barber's Instantaneous Relief From Pain, Aqua, OP, 4 7/8 In. 175.00
Dr. G.W. Phillips' Cough Syrup, Cincinnati, O., Aqua, IP, 7 In. 260.00
Dr. G.W. Phillips' Cough Syrup, Cincinnati, O., Blue Aqua, Pontil, 1845-1855, 7 In. 175.00
Dr. Gandy's Cough Syrup, Gandy Medical Co., Reading, Pa., Aqua, 6 1/2 In. 20.00
Dr. Grattan's Diptheria Remedy, Aqua, Rectangular, 6 3/4 In. ....115.00 to 125.00
Dr. Grave's Worm Syrup, Louisville, Ky., Cabin, Tooled Mouth, 4 In. 105.00
Dr. Greene's Nervura, Aqua, 9 1/8 In. 12.00
Dr. H. James' Cannibus Indica, Craddock & Co., SCA, 7 3/4 In. 210.00
Dr. H. Swayne's Compound Syrup Of Wild Cherry, Aqua, Flared Lip, OP, 6 In. 75.00
Dr. H.A. Ingham's Nervine Pain Extractor, Aqua, Labels, Bubbles, 4 1/2 In. ....25.00 to 40.00
Dr. Ham's Aromatic Invigorating Spirits, N.Y., IP, 8 3/8 In. 165.00
Dr. Hand's Astringent Mixture, Philadelphia, Contents, 5 3/8 In. ....*Illus* 18.00
Dr. Harter's Fever, Ague & Neuralgia Specific, Aqua, 1870-1875, 6 In. 55.00
Dr. Hayne's Arabian Balsam, Providence, R.I., Aqua, 4 1/8 In. 20.00

Dr. Henley's Celery, Beef & Iron, 1870, Gold Amber, 11 1/2 In. . . . . .100.00 to 115.00
Dr. Henley's Celery, Beef & Iron, CB&I Extract Co., S.F., Cal., Amber, 9 1/4 In. 220.00
Dr. Hitzfeld, Denver, Colo., Cobalt Blue, 3 In. 150.00
Dr. Irish's Indian Bone Ointment, Aqua, Crude, Rectangular, 6 1/2 In. 195.00
Dr. J. Clawson Kelley's Antiseptic Detergent, N.Y., Pale Blue Aqua, 9 In. 355.00
Dr. J. Moore's Essence Life, Cylindrical, Aqua, Rolled Lip, OP, 3 3/4 In. 90.00
Dr. J. Webster's Cerevisia, Angilicana Duplex, Green, 1840, 7 1/8 In. 1430.00
Dr. J. Webster's Cerevisia, Angilicana Duplex, Olive Green, OP, 1840, 8 In. 1980.00
Dr. J. Webster's Cerevisia, Angilicana Duplex, Yellow Green, 1860, 7 In. 1430.00
Dr. J.B. Marchisi, Utica, N.Y., Aqua, 6 In. 40.00
Dr. J.F. Churchill's Specific Remedy For Consumption, J. Winchester, N.Y., 7 In. . . . 165.00
Dr. J.H. Bull's Cough Syrup, Aqua, BIMAL, 6 In. 10.00
Dr. J.J. McBride, King Of Pain, Aqua, Applied Top, 6 In. .80.00 to 90.00
Dr. J.S. Wood's Elixir, Albany, N.Y., Tombstone, Emerald Green, IP, 9 In. 2530.00
Dr. J.W. Hawks Universal Stimulant, Manchester, N.H., Aqua, Emblem, 4 In. 75.00
Dr. John Bull's Compound Pectoral Wild Cherry, Aqua, IP, 1855, 7 In. 230.00
Dr. Jone's Sangvin For Blood & Nerves, Albany N.Y., Yellow Green, 7 In. 50.00
Dr. Jug's Medicine For Lungs, Liver & Blood, Jug, Pottery, Canada, 1880, 6 1/4 In. . . . 180.00
Dr. Kaiser's German Elixer, Applied Top . . . . .170.00 to 185.00
Dr. Kelling's Pure Herb Medicines, Aqua, Applied Disc Mouth, OP, 6 1/2 In. 90.00
Dr. Kennedy's Medical Discovery, Aqua, BIMAL, Wide Band Lip, 8 1/2 In. . . . . .13.00 to 20.00
Dr. Kennedy's Medical Discovery, Roxbury, Mass., Aqua, Applied Top, 8 1/2 In. .90.00 to 130.00
Dr. Kennedy's Rheumatic Dissolvent, Roxbury, Mass., Aqua, 9 1/2 In. 10.00
Dr. Kennedy's Rheumatic Liniment, Roxbury, Mass., Aqua, 6 1/2 In. 20.00
Dr. Kilmer's Female Remedy, Binghamton, Rectangular, Aqua, 8 1/2 In. . . . . . . .55.00 to 120.00
Dr. Kilmer's Herbal Extract For Uterine Injection, 4 1/2 In. 35.00
Dr. Kilmer's Indian Cough Remedy Consumption Oil, 5 1/2 In. 30.00
Dr. Kilmer's Ocean Weed Heart Remedy, Aqua, Tooled Mouth, 1895, 9 In. 175.00
Dr. Kilmer's Ocean Weed Heart Remedy, Binghamton, N.Y., Aqua, 8 1/2 In. 80.00
Dr. Kilmer's Ocean Weed Heart Remedy, Binghamton, N.Y., Cylindrical, 4 3/8 In. . . 12.00
Dr. King's New Discovery For Consumption, Aqua, 8 1/8 In. . . . . .10.00 to 12.00
Dr. King's New Life Pills, 2 1/2 In. 8.00
Dr. Lane's Headache & Liver Regulator, Louisville, Ky., Aqua, Pontil, 1855, 5 In. . . . 60.00
Dr. Larookah's Indian Vegetable Pulmonic Syrup, Partial Label, Contents, 8 5/8 In. . 145.00
Dr. Lepper's Mountain Tea, W.T. & Co., Aqua, 8 1/2 In. . . . . .55.00 to 100.00
Dr. Lepper's Oil Of Gladness, Justin Gates, Sacramento, Aqua, 5 In. 155.00
Dr. Lepper's Oil Of Gladness, Sacramento, Aqua, 8 1/2 In. 375.00
Dr. Liebig's German Invigorator, 400 Geary St., S.F., Amber, 8 1/2 In. . . . . .34.00 to 75.00
Dr. Liebig's Wonderful German Invigorator No. 1, S.F., Cal., Aqua, 7 3/4 In. . .45.00 to 90.00
Dr. M.L. Lewis, Louisville, Ky., Blue Aqua, IP, 1855, 9 3/8 In. 80.00
Dr. M.M. Fenner's Peoples Remedies, Aqua, 8 1/2 In. 20.00
Dr. M.M. Fenner's Peoples Remedies, Fredonia, N.Y., Amber, 10 1/4 In. 30.00
Dr. M.M. Fenner's Peoples Remedies, Fredonia, N.Y., Amber, Neck Seal, 8 1/2 In. . . . 50.00
Dr. Magnin's Lucina Cordial, Elixer Of Love, Paris, Aqua, Rectangular, Pontil, 6 In. . . 465.00
Dr. McLane's American Worm Specific, OP, 4 In. 15.00
Dr. McMunn's Elixir Of Opium, OP . . . . .25.00 to 35.00
Dr. Mintie's Nephreticum, San Francisco, Aqua, Applied Top, 6 1/2 In. . . . . . . .210.00 to 225.00
Dr. Moore's Venereal Antiseptic, Honey Amber, Rectangular, Pat. Jan. 5, 1892, 8 In. . . 195.00
Dr. N.M. Nutt's Cough Mixture, Aqua, Beveled Corner Panels, OP, 6 In. 230.00
Dr. Norton's Tasteless Worm Destroyer, Amber, 4 1/8 In. 20.00
Dr. Oreste Sinanide's Medicinal Preparations, Coffin, Cobalt Blue, 4 In. 155.00
Dr. P. Hall's Catarrh Remedy, Erie, Pa., Wide Mouth, 1880s, 2 1/2 In. 10.00
Dr. Perkins' Syrup, Albany, Aqua, Sloping Collar Mouth, 1855, 9 In. 690.00
Dr. Perkinson's Pain Killer, Baltimore, Md., Aqua, Rolled Lip, 1845-1855, 3 7/8 In. . . . 330.00
Dr. Perry's Last Chance Liniment, Aqua, Applied Top, 5 3/4 In. . . . . .75.00 to 170.00
Dr. Peter's Blood Vitalizer, 10 In. 12.00
Dr. Pierce's Anuric Tablets For Kidneys & Backache, 3 In. 20.00
Dr. Pierce's Golden Medical Discovery, Aqua, BIMAL, 8 3/4 In. 15.00
Dr. Pinkham's Emmenagogue, Aqua, OP, Applied Mouth, 1855, 5 3/4 In. 100.00
Dr. Roback's Swedish Remedy, Aqua, Applied Mouth, Pontil, 1840-1860, 6 In. 175.00
Dr. Roback's Swedish Remedy, Aqua, Pontil, Octagonal, 1860, 4 In. 120.00
Dr. Robbins Tecumseh Rheumatic Drops, Boston, Cobalt Blue, 5 In. 415.00
Dr. Roger's Liverwort, Tar & Canchalagua, Aqua, IP, 8 In. 95.00

Dr. Rookes Pale Newfoundland Cod Liver Oil, Cobalt Blue, Oval, 7 In. 20.00
Dr. Rookes Rheumatic Lixile, Cobalt Blue, 3 Sunken Panels, 5 In. 48.00
Dr. S. Pitcher's Castoria, Aqua, Double Collar, Cork, 5 3/4 In. . . . . .3.00 to 5.00
Dr. S.A. Weaver's Canker & Salt Rheum Syrup, Aqua, IP, 9 1/8 In. 105.00
Dr. Sage's Catarrh Remedy, Buffalo, N.Y., Green, Tooled Mouth, 2 1/4 In. . . . .220.00 to 230.00
Dr. Seth Arnold's Balsam, Aqua, OP, 4 In. 30.00
Dr. Seth Arnold's Cough Killer, Aqua, 4 Sunken Panels, Bubbles, Cork, OP, 4 3/4 In. . 3.00
Dr. Seymour's Balsam Of Wild Cherry & Comfrey, Aqua, 1860, 6 In. 520.00
Dr. Shoop's Family Medicines, Racine, Wis., Aqua, 7 In. 3.00
Dr. Shoop's Rheumatic Remedy, Labels, Aqua, Contents, Square, 7 In. 45.00
Dr. Simmons Squaw Vine Wine Compound, Aqua, 8 7/8 In. 40.00
Dr. Stanley's Double Strength Jamaica Ginger, Cookshine, Quebec, 6 1/2 In. 15.00
Dr. T. Delaney's Emerald Isle Embrocation, New York, Aqua, Pt. 35.00
Dr. T. McGown's Ess. Tar, Aqua, Rolled Lip, OP, 1835-1845, 5 1/4 In. 100.00
Dr. T.W. Graydon's, Cincinnati, O., Diseases Of The Lungs, Amber, 7 1/2 In. 25.00
Dr. Taft's Asthmalene, New York, Aqua, 8 In. 5.00
Dr. Taylor's Eczema Lotion, Philadelphia, Pa., Amber, Rectangular, 7 1/2 In. 15.00
Dr. Thatcher's Liver & Blood Syrup, Amber, 7 In. 15.00
Dr. Thatcher's Liver & Blood Syrup, Chattanooga, Tenn., Yellow Amber, 3 1/4 In. . . . 10.00
Dr. Thatcher's Liver & Blood Syrup, Honey Amber, Seed Bubbles, 7 In. 15.00
Dr. Thatcher's Worm Syrup, Chattanooga, Tenn., 4 In. 14.00
Dr. Tobias, New York, Venetian Liniment, Aqua, Oval, Pontil, 4 In. . . . . .40.00 to 42.00
Dr. Tobias Venetian Horse Liniment, New York, Aqua, 8 1/8 In. . . . . .20.00 to 25.00
Dr. Tobias Venetian Liniment, Crude, 6 In. 22.00
Dr. True's Elixir Worm Expeller, Estab. 1851, Auburn, Me., Aqua, 5 5/8 In. 15.00
Dr. Urban's Anti-Bacchanalian Elixir, Louisville, Ky., Blue Aqua, 7 In. 990.00
Dr. Velpau's French Pills, Aqua, 2 3/4 In. 40.00
Dr. W.H. Gregg, Constitution Water, New York, Aqua, c.1870s, 6 1/2 In. 30.00
Dr. Ward's Medical Co., Winona, Minn., Amber, Tooled Top, Contents, 1856 . . . . 35.00
Dr. Wheeler's Nerve Vitalizer, Aqua, 7 3/4 In. 20.00
Dr. Wistar's Balsam Of Wild Cherry, Cincinnati, O., Blue Green, 1860, 6 In. 230.00
Dr. Wistar's Balsam Of Wild Cherry, Philada, 8-Sided, Aqua, Pontil, 6 1/4 In. 50.00
Dr. Wistar's Balsam Of Wild Cherry, Philada., Aqua, Paneled, 4 In. . . . . .10.00 to 20.00
Dr. Wistar's Balsam Of Wild Cherry, Sanford & Park, Cinci, Aqua, OP, 6 1/4 In. 60.00
Dr. Wistar's Balsam Of Wild Cherry, Sanford & Park, Dark Aqua, IP, 6 1/4 In. 85.00
Dr. Wistar's Balsam Of Wild Cherry, Seth W. Fowle & Sons, Aqua, 3 1/2 In. 15.00
Dr. Wood's Aromatic Spirit, Bellow Falls, Vt., Aqua, IP, 1860, 7 3/8 In. 230.00
Drs. H. Van Vleck's & W.G. Johnson's Ague Conqueror, Aqua, OP, 5 In. 175.00
Drs. Ivans & Hart, N.Y., 8-Sided, Aqua, Applied Mouth, Pontil, 1860, 7 In. 330.00
Drs. S. Feller's Eclectic Liniment, 8-Sided, Aqua, OP, 4 1/4 In. 90.00
Dudley's Emulsion Pure Cod Liver Oil, Pancreatine & Lime, Blue, 10 1/4 In. 160.00
Durand & Tourtelot Pharmaceutists, Philadelphia, Pa., 5 1/2 In. 130.00
E. Hartshorn & Sons, Boston, Mass., 1850, Rectangular, Cork, 5 In. 3.00
E.A. Buckhout's Dutch Liniment, Deep Blue Aqua, OP, 1845, 4 3/4 In. 440.00
E.A. Buckhout's Dutch Liniment, Saratoga Co., N.Y., Aqua, OP, 1840-1860, 5 In. 440.00
E.A. Sherwin Pharmacist, Ashland, Or., Amethyst, 4 1/4 In. 8.00
E.C. Dewitt & Co., One Minute Cough Cure, Aqua, BIMAL, 3 1/2 In. 15.00
E.H. Flagg's Instantaneous Relief, Phila., Aqua, Beveled Corners, 1860, 4 In. 145.00
E.I. Smith Presc. Druggist, Visalia, Cal., Emerald Green, 5 1/4 In. 34.00
E.M. Parmelee, Manufacturing Chemist, Dansville, N.Y., Aqua, 8 1/4 In. . . . . .20.00 to 25.00
E.N. Lightner & Co., Detroit, Mich., Milk Glass, Stopper, 7 1/2 In. 100.00
E.S. Reeds, Atlantic City, N.Y., Milk Glass, Jersey Dragon, Stopper 128.00
E.V. Stoddard & Co., Apothecaries, New London, Conn., Square, Cork, 4 In. 3.00
Eau Lustrale Guerlain, Yellow Olive Amber, String Lip, Rectangular, France, 6 In. . . . 275.00
Edward A. Mueller, Brooklyn, N.Y., Tooled Lip, Cork, 5 1/2 In. 4.00
Edward Wilder's Compound Extract Wild Cherry, Cabin, 7 In. 210.00
Elliman's Royal Embrocation For Horses Manufactory, Aqua, Round, 7 3/8 In. . . . 10.00
Elmer's Great French Remedy, Northfield, Mass., Rectangular, 7 1/4 In. 32.00
Elmer's Great French Remedy, Providence, R.I., USA, Aqua, Rectangular, 8 In. 38.00
Ely's Wild Cherry Phosphate, W.T. Ely & Co., San Francisco, Clear, 1880s, 6 1/4 In. . . 90.00
Elysian Mfg. Co. Chemists & Perfumers, Detroit, U.S.A., Cobalt Blue, 6 In. 90.00
Emil Cermak, Pharm., 1266 So. 13th St., Omaha, Neb., 4 1/2 In. 8.00
Empire State Drug Co., Aqua, 6 3/8 In. 12.00

Medicine, Fritola,
Pinus Medicine Co.,
Monticello, Ill., Oil
Laxative, 6 1/4 In.

Medicine, Dr. Hand's
Astringent Mixture,
Philadelphia,
Contents, 5 3/8 In.

Medicine, Mrs.
M.G. Brown's
Scalp Renovator,
Metaphysical,
N.Y., 4 3/8 In.

Empire State Drug Co. Laboratories, Buffalo, N.Y., Aqua Panels, 1880, 5 In. 10.00
England's Balsam Of Honey Tar Wild Cherry Liverwort, Aqua, BIMAL 7.00
Epping's Buchu, Manufactured By L. Pierce, Aqua, Pontil, Double Collar, 8 3/8 In. 715.00
Evans & Sons & Mason Ltd., Medium To Light Cobalt, Canada, c.1890, 8 In. 50.00
F. Brown's Ess. Of Jamaica Ginger, Philada., Aqua, 5 1/2 In. 7.00
F.T. Maynard Druggist, Petaluma, Ca., Eagle On Mortar & Pestle, Clear, 1910, 7 In. ... 30.00
Fahnestock's Vermifuge, Pontil, 3 1/2 In. 28.00
Farmer's Horse Medicine, S.F., Cal., Aqua, 6 3/4 In. 25.00
Farmer's Horse Medicine, S.F., Cal., Aqua, Tooled Top, 8 1/4 In. 65.00
Fellows & Co., Chemist, St. Johns, N.B., Aqua, BIMAL, 3-Piece Mold, 7 1/2 In. 15.00
Fellows Laxative Tablets, Embossed, 2 3/4 In. 8.00
Field's Cattle Oils, Rectangular, 6 3/8 In. 10.00
Fink's Magic Oil, Springdale, Pa., Aqua, Indented Panels, 1890s, 5 1/2 In. 10.00
Flagg's Good Samaritan's Immediate Relief, Cincinnati, 5-Sided, Aqua, 3 3/4 In. ... 145.00
Fleming's Pharmacy, Denver, Colo., Gold Amber, 5 In. 175.00
Floraplexion, Cures Dyspepsia Liver Complaint, Franklin Hart, Aqua, 1890s, 6 In. 10.00
Foley Cathartic Tablets, Label Under Glass, Glass Stopper, 8 1/4 In. 330.00
Foley's Kidney Pills, Reversed Label, Ground Fancy Top, 12 In. 550.00
Francis H. Leggett & Co., New York, Rectangular, 4 5/8 In. 15.00
Frank Baker & Son Pharmacists, Winchester, Va., Oval, 7 In. 70.00
Franklin Hart Remedy Co., New York City, Amber, 8 1/2 In. 15.00
Fred Rogers Druggist, Willimantic, Ct., SCA, Mortar & Pestle, 8 1/4 In. 4.00
Fritola, Pinus Medicine Co., Monticello, Ill., Oil Laxative, 6 1/4 In. ....*Illus* 10.00
Fritzsche Schimmell & Co., Cobalt Blue, Applied Mouth, 1880-1890, 14 In. 120.00
From Pittsburgh Sanitary Committee, Blue Aqua, 1860-1865, 7 1/4 In. 360.00
Frost's Liniment, Blue Aqua, Applied Mouth, OP, 1845-1855, 4 7/8 In. 70.00
G. Hornung Apothecary, Marysville, Cal., Tooled Top, 6 In. 22.00
G. Watt's, Aromatic Salts, Baltimore, Milk Glass, Polished Lip, 1855-1865, 2 In. 145.00
G. Watt's, Aromatic Salts, Baltimore, Purple Amethyst, 1855-1865, 2 1/8 In. 210.00
G.C. Bristol, Buffalo, N.Y., 6-Sided, Blue Aqua, OP, Sheared Lip, 1855, 4 1/2 In. 20.00
G.C. Taylor, Liniment Or Oil Of Life, Fairport, N.Y., Aqua, Rectangular, Cork, 7 1/8 In. . 10.00
G.W. Merchant, Chemist, Lockport, N.Y., Aqua, Sloping Collar, OP, 4 7/8 In. 100.00
G.W. Merchant, Chemist, Lockport, N.Y., Aqua, Sloping Collar, Pontil, 5 3/8 In. .165.00 to 185.00
G.W. Merchant, Chemist, Lockport, N.Y., Blue Green, IP, 1855, 7 In. ....105.00 to 330.00
G.W. Merchant, Chemist, Lockport, N.Y., Blue Green, LO Inside Square, IP, 5 1/2 In. ... 205.00
G.W. Merchant, Chemist, Lockport, N.Y., Emerald Green, Star, Sloping Collar, OP, 5 In. 175.00
G.W. Merchant, Chemist, Lockport, N.Y., Emerald Green, Applied Top, OP, 5 In. 165.00 to 285.00
G.W. Merchant, Chemist, Lockport, N.Y., Emerald Green, Rectangular, 5 1/2 In. 110.00
G.W. Merchant, Chemist, Lockport, N.Y., Green, Rectangular, Tubular Pontil, 5 1/8 In. . 100.00
G.W.H., Sapphire Blue, Applied Lip, Cylindrical, 7 1/2 In. 40.00
Gargling Oil, Lockport, Green, Crooked Neck, 5 1/4 In. 30.00
Gargling Oil, Lockport, N.Y., Blue Green, 5 1/8 In. 30.00
Gargling Oil, Lockport, N.Y., Blue Green, 7 1/2 In. ....80.00 to 125.00
Gargling Oil, Lockport, N.Y., Emerald Green, 5 1/2 In. ....15.00 to 30.00
Gargling Oil, Lockport, N.Y., Yellow Green, 5 1/2 In. 45.00
Gay's Compound Extract Of Canchalagua, N.Y., Aqua, OP, 7 In. 95.00
Genuine Essence, Aqua, Flat Rectangular, OP, 5 In. 15.00

Genuine J. Russell Spaulding, Boston, Mass., Aqua, Oval, Pontil, 5 In. 45.00
Genuine Swaim's Panacea, Philada., Aqua, Pontil Base, 1840-1850, 7 3/4 In. . .800.00 to 1100.00
Geo. C. Thaxter Druggist, Carson City, Nev., 4 In. 22.00
Geo. Haskins, Medford, Ore., 6 In. 10.00
Geo. W. Lougee Md., Freedom, N.H., Druggist, Oval, 6 1/2 In. 45.00
Geo W. Laird & Co., Oleo Chyle, Cobalt Blue, Tooled Mouth, 1880, 9 7/8 In. . . . .80.00 to 145.00
George V. Dressner, Brooklyn, N.Y., Cork, 5 1/4 In. 3.00
George W. Sisson Druggist, Glens Falls, N.Y., Aqua, Applied Lip, 5 1/2 In. 25.00
Georgia Pharmacy, Vancouver, B.C., 6 In. 10.00
Gibb's Bone Liniment, 6-Sided, Olive Amber, OP, 6 1/4 In. . . . . .1100.00 to 1155.00
Gibson's Syrup, Medium Green, Square, Beveled Corners, 1860, 9 3/4 In. 305.00
Girolamo, Pagliano, Lime Green, Tooled Top, Rectangular, 4 In. 25.00
Glyco-Thymoline, Kress & Owens, Clear, 2 1/4 In. 3.00
Glyco-Thymoline, Kress, Deep Amethyst, Square, 4 In. 30.00
Golden Gate Bottling Works, San Francisco, Deep Red Amber, 1880-1900, 7 1/2 In. .   55.00
Golden State Liniment, B.F. Hewlett, Label, 5 In. 15.00
Gouraud's Oriental Cream, New York, BIMAL, 4 1/4 In. 7.00
Graetenberg Co., Children's Panacea, N.Y., Aqua, Beveled Corners, 3 3/4 In. 110.00
Green's Lung Restorer, Santa Abie Abietine Medical Co., Cal., Green, 7 3/4 In. . .40.00 to 100.00
Griswold's Malarian Antidote, Blue Aqua, Flared Lip, OP, 6 In. 45.00
Groders Botanical Dyspepsia Syrup, Waterville, Me., Label, Aqua, 8 1/2 In. 30.00
Gun Wa's Chinese Remedy, Warranted Entirely Vegetable, Yellow Amber, 8 In. .330.00 to 525.00
H. Lake's Indian Specific, Aqua, Beveled Corners, 8 3/8 In. 245.00
H.A. Elliott Pharmacist, Idaho Springs, Colo., Tooled Top, 4 1/4 In. 55.00
H.G. Farrell's Arabian Liniment, Peoria, Aqua, Cylindrical, 4 In. 10.00
H.G. Farrell's Arabian Liniment, Peoria, Blue Aqua, OP, Tooled Lip, 1855, 5 In. 50.00
H.G. Hotchkiss, Oil Of Spearmint, Lyons, N.Y., Cobalt Blue, Applied Top, 8 7/8 In. . . .   70.00
H.H. Warner & Co., Tippecanoe, Rochester, N.Y., Log, Amber, 1875, 9 In. . . . . . .80.00 to 120.00
H.H.H. Horse Medicine, D.D.T. 1868, Aqua, 8 1/4 In. 35.00
H.H.H. Horse Medicine, D.D.T. 1868, Pale Yellow, Tooled Mouth, 6 In. 120.00
H.J. Sperry Apothecary, New Haven, Conn., 4 Beveled Corners, Square, 4 In. 3.00
H.K. Mulford Co., Utros, Paper Wrapped, 1890-1910, Pt. 22.00
H.M. Parchen, Helena, Mt., 5 In. 70.00
H.P. Wakelee, San Francisco, Green Aqua, Applied Top, 7 1/4 In. 35.00
H.T. Helmbold Genuine Fluid Extracts, Philadelphia, Aqua, Rectangular, 6 3/8 In. . . .   37.00
Hagan's Magnolia Balm, Milk Glass, 5 1/8 In. 25.00
Hales Honey Of Horehound & Tar, C.N. Crittenten, New York, Aqua, 5 1/2 In. 5.00
Hales Honey Of Horehound & Tar, C.N. Crittenten, New York, Aqua, 6 3/4 In. 5.00
Hall Pulmonary Balsam, J.R. Gates & Co., Proprietors, S.F., Aqua, 6 1/2 In. 85.00
Hall's Balsam For The Lungs, A.L. Scovill & Co., Cinti & N.Y., Aqua, 7 1/2 In. . .25.00 to 30.00
Hall's Balsam For The Lungs, J.F. Henry Curran & Co., Medium Cobalt Blue, 8 In. . . .   75.00
Hall's Pulmonary Balsam, J.R. Gates, S.F., Crooked Neck, Tool Top, Hazy, Aqua .20.00 to 30.00
Hall's Pulmonary Balsam, Shepherdson & Gates, Deep Blue Aqua, 6 1/2 In. 100.00
Hampton's V Tincture, Mortimer & Mowbray, Balto., Dark Amber, OP, 6 In. . . .300.00 to 435.00
Hampton's V Tincture, Mortimer & Mowbray, Balto., Deep Olive Amber, OP, 6 In. . . .   1210.00
Hampton's V Tincture, Mortimer & Mowbray, Balto., Copper, Striations, OP, 6 1/4 In. .   435.00
Hampton's V Tincture, Mortimer & Mowbray, Bright Olive Green, OP, 7 In. 1870.00
Hampton's V Tincture, Mortimer & Mowbray, Yellow Amber, OP, 6 In. 1925.00
Hanna's Electro Silicon Liniment, Aqua, Flattened Oval, 2 7/8 In. 15.00
Hanna's Electro Silicon Liniment, Embossed Vertically, Flask Shape, Aqua, 6 1/2 In. .   6.00
Hanna's Electro Silicon Liniment, Flask Shape, Aqua, 1/2 Pt., 6 In. 10.00
Harper's Cuforhedake Brain Food, Washington, D.C., Aqua, Dug, 5 In. 30.00
Haviland & Co., Druggists, Mortar & Pestle, Aqua, Double Collar, 10 1/4 In. 95.00
Hayman's Balsam Of Horehound, Ice Blue, Embossed Panel, Rectangular, 5 In. 20.00
Haynes & Co. Blue Bottle Extracts, Montour Falls, N.Y., Cobalt Blue, 6 3/4 In. 40.00
Healy & Bigelow Kickapoo Indian Sagwa, Aqua, BIMAL, 8 1/2 In. 100.00
Healy & Bigelow Kickapoo Indian Sagwa, Aqua, Indian With Headdress, 8 3/4 In. . .   40.00
Healy & Bigelow's Kickapoo Indian Oil, Aqua, 5 1/2 In. 20.00
Heller Bros. & Co., Baltimore, Md., Aqua, 4 1/4 In. 10.00
Henry M. Bishop Prescription Drug Store, New Haven, Conn., Cork, 3 3/4 In. 4.00
Henry's Calcined Magnesia, Manchester, Clear, OP, 4 1/4 In. 20.00
Hobsun's Mange Treatment For Dogs, Cattle, Pfeiffer Chemical Co., 8 In. 38.00
Hollenback & Raker Pharmacists, Shamokin, Pa., 4 3/4 In. 10.00

Honorable Lady Hill, Aqua, Cylindrical, Pontil, 3 1/2 In. 52.00
Hooper & Co., Chemists, Crown, Canada, c.1895, 8 1/4 In. 10.00
Hopkins Chalybeate, Baltimore, Blue Grass, Pt. 70.00
Hotchkiss, Lyons, N.Y., Label, Hotchkiss Oil Of Wintergreen, Cobalt Blue, 1/2 Gal. 50.00
Houck's Patent Panacea, Baltimore, Aqua, Pontil, 1845-1855, 6 3/4 In. 120.00
Huff's Pulmonic Balsam, Cincinnati, Aqua, OP, 1840, 5 3/4 In. 355.00
Humphrey's Chem. Co., N.Y., Bromated Pepsin, 3 1/4 In. 20.00
Humphrey's Homeopathic No. 20 Whooping Cough, Large Logo, Wrapped 18.00
Humphrey's Homeopathic No. 29 Fever Blisters, Large Logo, Wrapped 15.00
Humphrey's Homeopathic Vet. Prep, AA For Simple Fevers, Horse, Label, 3 1/2 In. . 10.00
Humphrey's Marvel Of Healing, Strapside 8.00
Humphrey's New York & Rio De Janeiro, Embossed, Screw Cap, 1910 .... 10.00
Hunnewell's Universal Cough Remedy, Boston, Mass., Aqua, OP, 5 In. 110.00
Hunt's Liniment, G.E. Stanton, N.Y., Aqua, Pontil, 1840-1860, 5 1/2 In. 40.00
Huntoon & Lovelace Druggists, Visalia, Cal., Dug, 5 1/2 In. 26.00
Hyatt's Infallible Life Balsam, N.Y., Green, IP, 1860, 10 1/4 In. ....305.00 to 770.00
Hyatt's Pulmonic Balsam, N.Y., Aqua, IP, 1845-1855, 9 3/4 In. 470.00
Hydrogen Peroxide, Parke-Davis, Amber, Tin Lid, 1930-1939, 4 Oz. .... .75
Hydroleine, Physicians, Oval, Sample, 5 1/8 In. 10.00
I. Covert's Balm Of Life, Yellow Olive, Tubular Pontil, Rectangular, 5 7/8 In. 605.00
I. Newton's Panacea Purifier Of The Blood, Vt., Yellow Olive Amber, 7 In. 3190.00
I. Newton's Panacea Purifier Of The Blood, Vt., Yellow Olive, 8 In. 2090.00
I.L. St. John's Cough Syrup, Deep Aqua, 8-Sided, OP, 6 3/8 In. ....150.00 to 250.00
Iceland Balsam For Pulmonary Consumption, Yellow Olive, 1830-1850, 6 1/2 In. .. 6050.00
Improved Magnesia, Bolton Drug Co., Brooklyn, N.Y., Cobalt Blue, 1900, 7 In. 165.00
Indian, see also Medicine, Healy & Bigelow
Indian Cough Syrup, Warm Springs, Ore., Clear, Tooled Lip, 1890-1900, 6 3/4 In. 55.00
Indian Medicine Inhaler, Labeled Vial, Contents 12.00
Indian Wigwam Remedies, Compounded, Denver, Colo., Amber, OP, 1890, 7 7/8 In. .. 715.00
Indian Wigwam Remedies, Compounded, Mineral Springs, Denver, Amber, 9 3/4 In. .. 55.00
J. & C. Maguire Chemists & Druggists, St. Louis, Cobalt Blue, IP, 8 In. 2145.00
J. & C. Maguire Chemists & Druggists, St. Louis, Cobalt Blue, OP, 1865, 7 In. 330.00
J. Milhau Druggist, N.Y., Dark Brown Glaze, Stoneware, 1820, 6 1/2 In. 150.00
J.A. Calvins, Celery Compound Mold, Cobalt Blue, 9 3/4 In. 650.00
J.B. Wheatleys Compound Syrup, Dallasburgh, Ky., Aqua, IP, 6 In. ....120.00 to 175.00
J.D. McGann Co., Hornellsville, Ky., Widemouth, 2 In. 5.00
J.D. Morgan Druggist, Pittsburgh, Pa., Aqua, Rolled Lip, 1845-1855, 5 In. 120.00
J.J. Hunt's Modern Remedy, Aqua, OP, 1845-1855, 6 1/2 In. 90.00
J.L. Hamilton Preparation, Root Beer Amber, IP, 1855, 7 In. 5830.00
J.L. Leavitt, Boston, Deep Yellow Olive, Sloping Collar, Ring, IP, 8 1/4 In. ......200.00 to 305.00
J.M. Henry & Sons, Waterbury, Vt., Vermont Liniment, Pontil, 5 In. 220.00
Jacobs' Pharmacy, Atlanta, Ga., Eagle, Mortar, Pestle, Amber, Tooled Mouth, 2 1/2 In. . 75.00
Jaffe's Electric Pain Expeller, Aqua, 7 1/4 In. 40.00
Jar, Inhaler, Chemist's, Dark Green, Wide Mouth, Glass Stopper, 6 1/2 In. 50.00
JCH The Great Disinfectant, Trademark, Yellow, Rectangular, 8 1/2 In. 70.00
Jermyn Drug Store, Always The Best Of Everything, Scranton, Pa., Yellow Green, 8 In. 195.00
Jewett's Liniment For Fever, Aqua, OP, Rolled Lip, 1840-1855, 4 In. 440.00
Jno. Sullivan, Pharmacist, Boston, Milk Glass, 5 In. 58.00
John Gilbert & Co. Druggists, Phila., Aqua, Pontil, 12 1/2 In. 120.00
John M. Winslow, Compound Balsam Of Hoarhound, Rochester, N.Y., Aqua, 5 1/4 In. .. 220.00
John W. Cope Co., Stockton, Ca., Yellow Amber, Tooled Lip, 1900, 9 In. 330.00
John Wyeth & Bro., Cobalt Blue, Square, Dose Cap, 4 1/2 In. ....25.00 to 45.00
John Wyeth & Bro., Cobalt Blue, Square, Dose Cap, 6 1/4 In. 22.00
John Wyeth & Bro., Philada, Amber, 8 In. 20.00
John Wyeth & Bro., Philada, Cobalt Blue, Flared Lip, Strap Side, Oval, 3 1/4 In. 15.00
John Youngson, Extract Of American Oil, Aqua, Rolled Lip, OP, 1855, 5 In. 155.00
Johnson & Johnson, New York, Jar, Amber, Ground Top, No Lid, Qt. 40.00
Johnson's American Anodyne Liniment, Aqua, Cylindrical, Pontil, 4 1/2 In. .....5.00 to 30.00
Jones & Elmes Veterinary Surgeons, London, Cornflower Blue, 1896, 9 In. 50.00
Joy's Anti Dyspeptic Elixir, Aqua, Flared Mouth, 1840-1860, 5 1/2 In. 275.00
Jozeau-Pharmacien, Olive Green, Rolled Lip, Pontil, 1840, 4 1/2 In. 155.00
Jr. Nichols & Co., Chemists, Boston, Cobalt Blue, Tooled Mouth, 9 1/4 In. 200.00
Keeler, Cobalt Blue, c.1890, 4 In. 7.00

Kemp's Balsam For Throat & Lungs, Aqua, 8 In. 18.00
Kickapoo Oil, see Medicine, Healy & Bigelow
Kilmer's U & O Ointment, Lid, 3 In. 20.00
Kimball Bro's & Co., Enosburg Falls, Vt., Rectangular, Cork, 4 1/2 In. 4.00
Koop's Cure A Cough, York, Pa., Aqua, 1890s, 5 In. 9.00
Kopp's Atlas Liniment, Asheville, N.C., Aqua, Indented Panels, 1880s, 5 1/2 In. 10.00
L. Pantanberger Pharmacient, Paris, Cobalt Blue, Label, Square, 8 In. 70.00
L.P. Dodge, Rheumatic Liniment, Newburgh, Amber, OP, 6 In. ....255.00 to 825.00
L.P. Dodge, Rheumatic Liniment, Newburgh, Blue Green, OP, 1855, 5 In. 275.00
Lactopeptine, Best Remedial Agent, Cobalt Blue, Panels, Square, 8 In. 50.00
Lactopeptine, The Best Remedial Agent, Digestive Disorders, Cobalt Blue, 7 3/4 In. 45.00
Lambert Pharmacal Company, Listerine, Tooled Lip, Cylindrical, Cork, 6 3/4 In. 2.00
Langley's Ess. Jamaica Ginger, San Francisco, Etched, 5 1/4 In. 65.00
Langley's Red Bottle Elixir Of Life, Pontil, 5 In. 225.00
Laubach Apothecary, Philadelphia, Cobalt Blue, Applied Top, 1880s, 4 In. 65.00
Laughlin & Bushfield Wholesale Druggists, Wheeling, Va., Aqua, Pontil, 9 1/2 In. . . 400.00
Laxol, A.J. White, New York, Laxol, Cobalt Blue, 5 In. 75.00
Lederle Labs., Amber, Bakelite Lid, Box, 1935-1945, 8 Oz. 5.00
Lee & Butler Liquid Opodeldoc, Long Crooked Neck, Thin Flared Lip, 4 7/8 In. 55.00
Lee's Crea-Lyptos, Consolidated Royal Chemical Corp, Tin Lid, Box, 1939, 8 Oz. 4.00
Lennex Cough Syrup, Chloroform & Formaldehyde, Bakelite Lid, Box 10.00
Lents Drug Store, Portland, 1880s, 8 1/2 In. 20.00
Levan & Rotheremel Druggist, Embossed, 10 1/2 In. 15.00
Licorice Lozenges, Jar, Adlams Patent On Base, Round Slug Plate, Ground Lip, Gal. ... 65.00
Liebig's Beef, Wine & Iron, 9 In. 15.00
Life Plant Trademark, Bird Emblem, Amber, 8 1/2 In. 35.00
Lindsey's Blood Searcher, E.E. Sellers & Co., Pittsburgh, Aqua, 9 In. 60.00
Liquid Opodeldoc, Light Green Aqua, Flared Lip, OP, 4 1/2 In. 55.00
Little's Eureka Specific, Portland, Or. ....70.00 to 90.00
Log Cabin Cough & Consumption Remedy, Sept. 6, 1887, Amber, 9 In. 150.00
Log Cabin Extract, Rochester, N.Y., Amber, 3 Embossed Panels, 1860, 8 1/8 In. . .65.00 to 115.00
Log Cabin Hops & Buchu Remedy, Sept. 6, 1887, Amber, 1885-1895, 10 In. . .200.00 to 350.00
Log Cabin Scalpine, Rochester, N.Y., Pat. Sept. 6, 87, Amber, 8 3/4 In. 400.00
Longley's Panacea, Olive Green, Beveled Corners, 1870, 6 In. 245.00
Loomis's Cream Liniment, 6-Sided, Emerald Green, Tooled Mouth, Pontil, 4 3/4 In. .. 305.00
Lord's Opoldeldoc, Man Throwing Away Crutches, Aqua, Tooled Top, 5 In. 75.00
Louden & Co. Alternative, Philada., Aqua, OP, 6 1/2 In. 45.00
Louis A. Mansbach, Veterinary Surgeon, Philadelphia, 8 1/4 x 3 1/4 In. 15.00
Louis Daldlin Co., Worcester, Mass., Blood Wine, Rectangular, Sample, 3 1/2 In. 25.00
Louis Taussig & Co., San Francisco, Ca., Amber, Applied Lip, 1875-1885, 9 1/4 In. 255.00
Lucien Pratt, Le Renovateur De La Femme, Waterbury, Conn., Cobalt, 9 1/2 In. .200.00 to 385.00
Lull's Anti Spasmodic For Coughs, San Francisco, Aqua, 1895, 5 In. ....110.00 to 390.00
Lunnon Hospital Liniment, Sullivan's Drug Store, Yellow Olive, Pontil, 8 In. 230.00
Luscomb's Lavender Salts, Teal Blue, 1 3/4 In. 12.00
Lutted's S.P. Cough Drops, Log Cabin, Feet, 20th Century, 7 1/8 In. 100.00
Lydia E. Pinkham's Blood Purifier, Aqua, 8 1/4 In. ....15.00 to 18.00
Lydia E. Pinkham's Vegetable Compound, Aqua, 8 1/4 In. ....12.00 to 15.00
Lyon's Powder, B & P, N.Y., Deep Red Puce, Rolled Lip, OP, 1855, 4 3/8 In. 105.00
M.B. Robert's Vegetable Embrocation, Blue Green, Pontil, 5 1/2 In. 120.00
M.B. Robert's Vegetable Embrocation, Medium Golden Amber, Pontil, 5 In. 120.00
M.E. Doe, Phillipsburg, Mont., 5 1/2 In. 10.00
M.K. Paine Druggist & Apothecary, Windsor, Vt., Milk Glass, 1870-1880, 6 1/2 In. .. 120.00
M.L. Lewis' Mother's Friend, Louisville, Ky., Aqua, IP, 1855, 9 In. 1210.00
M.W. Bartholomew Presc. Specialist, Hanford, Cal., 3 1/2 In. 17.00
Macamoose, Rev. J.R. Gates, Philada., Cathedral Windows, Hinge Mold, Aqua, 8 1/2 In. 60.00
MacKenzie's Ague & Fever, Cleveland, O., Aqua, 1860, 7 In. 440.00
Maguire Druggist, St. Louis, Mo., Citron, 1845-1855, 5 3/4 In. 630.00
Manchester Wilds Gout & Rheumatic Mixture, Aqua, Sunken Panels, 6 In. 18.00
Marchand's Peroxide Of Hydrogen, New York, Amber, Cork, 5 1/2 In. 5.00
Masonic Hall Infirmary, For Lung Complaints, Aqua, Pontil, 5 In. 145.00
Masta's Indian Pulmonic Balsam, Aqua, Rectangular, 5 3/4 In. 75.00
Matthews Medicine Co., Peruvian Celery, Indianapolis, Ind., Amber, 8 3/4 In. ....28.00 to 45.00
McClellan's Diptheria Remedy, Curved R, Aqua, Tooled Top, 8 In. 225.00

McKesson's Liquid Petrolatum, McKesson & Robbins, Tin Lid, Box, 1935 . . . . . . .2.00 to 3.00
McKesson's Milk Of Magnesia, 10-Sided, Cobalt Blue, Ribbed, Box, 1925-1930, Pt. . .   12.00
McLean's Volcanic Oil Liniment, Aqua, Applied Top, 1860s, 4 In. . . . . .8.00 to 15.00
McMillan & Kester's Ess Of Jamaica Ginger, S.F., Deep Blue Aqua, Applied Top 65.00
Melvin & Badger Apothecaries, Boston, Mass., 6-Sided, Cobalt Blue, 6 1/8 In. 140.00
Mentholated Spirits, C. Lewis, Pharmaceutical Chemist, T. Eaton Drug Co., 8 In. 10.00
Merrell's Milk Of Magnesia, Cobalt Blue, Tin Lid, Cellophane, 1935, Pt. 10.00
Merrell's Milk Of Magnesia, Taste That Please, Cobalt, Tin Lid, 1935, Box, 6 Oz. . . .7.00 to 8.00
Mexican Mustang Liniment, Aqua, 4 In. 50.00
Mexican Mustang Liniment, Aqua, Cylindrical, Red IP, 7 3/4 In. . . . . .155.00 to 250.00
Mexican Mustang Liniment, Aqua, Rolled Lip, 7 3/4 In. . . . . .55.00 to 75.00
Mexican Mustang Liniment, Lyons Mfg. Co., New York, 1865, 7 1/2 In. 100.00
Meyer Milk Of Magnesia, Cobalt Blue, Ribbed, Tin Lid, 8 Oz. 8.00
Mitchell's Liniment, Pittsburgh, Pa., Aqua, Rolled Lip, 1855, 4 7/8 In. 355.00
Modern Pharmacy, Pasadena, Cal., Amethyst, 9 In. 20.00
Moore's Revealed Remedy, Monogram In Shield, Amber, Tooled Top, 1890s, 9 In. 45.00
Moroline, Plough, Petroleum Jelly, 8-Sided, Tin Lid, 1930-1939, 4 Oz. . . . . .1.00 to 2.00
Mortimer's Rheumatic Compound & Blood Purifier, Yellow Green, 6 3/4 In. 2750.00
Mother's Friend, Atlanta, Ga., Aqua, BIMAL, 7 In. 8.00
Mother's Worm Syrup, Edward Wilder & Co., Tooled Mouth, 1880-1890, 4 3/4 In. . . .   145.00
Moxie Nerve Food, Lowell, Mass., Aqua, 11 In. . . . . .10.00 to 45.00
Mrs. Dr. Secor, Boston, Mass., Cobalt Blue, Tooled Mouth, 1880-1890, 9 5/8 In. .145.00 to 275.00
Mrs. M.G. Brown's Scalp Renovator, Metaphysical, N.Y., 4 3/8 In. . . . .*Illus*   35.00
Mrs. Winslow's Soothing Syrup, Curtis & Perkins, Aqua, OP, 5 In. 45.00
Munyon's Germicide Solution, Green, 1890, 3 In. 10.00
Munyon's Paw Paw, Amber, Rectangular, 4 In. 18.00
Myers' Rock Rose, New Haven, Emerald Green, IP, 9 1/4 In.   175.00
N.E. Wilson Co., Inc., Pharmacist, Reno, Nevada, 5 In. 30.00
N.L. Clark & Co. Peruvian Syrup, Aqua, Sunken Panel, Cork, 8 In. 15.00
N.T. Brown, Chemist & Druggist, Battleford & N. Battleford, BIMAL, Canada, 6 In. . . .   15.00
N.Y. Pharmacal Association, Lactopeptine, Cobalt Blue, 7 1/2 In. 45.00
National Remedy Co., N.Y., Aqua, 5 1/2 In. 10.00
Nerve Bone Liniment, Pontil, 3 3/4 In. 25.00
New York Medical University, Cobalt Blue, Rectangular, 7 In. 140.00
New York Pharmacal Association, Cobalt Blue, 12 In. 110.00
Newell's Pulmonary Syrup, Redington & Co., Aqua, 1865-1875, 7 5/8 In. . . . . . . .65.00 to 90.00
Nichols' Infallible Injection, Aqua, Applied Top, 7 1/4 In. 80.00
None Genuine Without This Trademark, Man On Horse, Serpent, Amber 220.00
Norman's Chalybeate Cough Syrup, St. Louis, Aqua 45.00
Norwich, Pepto-Bismol, Bakelite Lid, 1935-1940, Box, 4 Oz.   3.00
Norwich, Pepto-Bismol, Embossed Shoulder, Bakelite Lid, Box, 1935-1940, 10 Oz. 4.00
Norwich Cod Liver Oil, 3-Sided, Amber, 1938-1945, 6 Oz. 3.00
Norwich Tancro-Cough Syrup, Tin Lid, 1930-1939, 8 Oz. 1.25
Nubian Tea, Man, Wearing Hat, Amber, 4 In. 25.00
O.O. Woodman, New Orleans, Aqua, Applied Sloping Collar, 1865-1870, 9 In. 85.00
Oakland Chemical, Yellow Amber, 4 1/2 In. 15.00
Oakland Chemical Company, Amber, Tooled Lip, Cylindrical, Cork, 5 3/4 In. 5.00
Odol, White Stoneware, Olive Green Label, Sample 35.00
Oliveine Emulsion, In English & French, Unopened Box, 8 1/2 In. 35.00
Olympene, Antiseptic Liniment, Athletes, Label, Contents, Box, Canada, 1950s, 4 3/8 In.   10.00
One Minute Cough Cure, Aqua, 6 3/4 In. 15.00
Optrex Safe Guards Sight, Cobalt Blue, With Eyecup, 5 In.   40.00
Oregon Blood Purifier, Embossed Baby's Face, Amber, Tooled Lip, 7 1/2 In. 65.00
Oregon Blood Purifier, Portland, Or., Baby Face, Amber, Tooled Lip, 7 1/2 In. 60.00
Orrick's Vermifuge Worm Destroyer, Baltimore, Md., Aqua, Flared Lip, 5 In. 120.00
Osgood's India Cholagogue, New York, Aqua, 5 1/16 In. . . . . .12.00 to 20.00
Owl Drug Co., 1-Wing Owl, Amber, 4 1/2 In. 110.00
Owl Drug Co., 1-Wing Owl, Milk Glass, Square, BIMAL, 4 1/2 In. . . . . .15.00 to 75.00
Owl Drug Co., 2-Wing On Mortar & Pestle, Cobalt Blue, 6 1/4 In. 240.00
Owl Drug Co., 2-Wing On Mortar & Pestle, Peroxide, Amber, Round, 8 In. 60.00
Owl Drug Co., 2-Wing Owl, Peroxide, Amberon Mortar & Pestle, 8 In. 60.00
Owl Drug Co., 2-Wing Owl, Witch Hazel, Amethyst, Partial Label, Square, 8 In. 35.00
Owl Drug Co., Celluloid Cap, Duraglas, 6 Oz. 12.00

Owl Drug Co., Glycerine, Embossed, Label, 5 1/2 In. 45.00
Owl Drug Co., Owl On Mortar & Pestle, SCA, 1915, 10 In. 145.00
Owl Drug Co., San Francisco, Citrate, Teal Green, Tooled Top, 9 1/2 In. ....100.00 to 145.00
P.J. McCormick College Pharmacy, Rectangular, Cork, 5 In. 3.00
P.T. Wright & Co. Pectoral Syrup, Philada., Green Aqua, Applied Top, OP 110.00
Page's Vegetable Syrup For Females, Aqua, Applied Mouth, Pontil, 8 1/2 In. 440.00
Paine's Celery Compound, Amber, Sunken Panels, Square, 9 1/2 In. 10.00
Palmer, Green, 5 1/4 In. 22.00
Parchen & D'Acheul, Butte, Mt., 5 7/8 In. 65.00
Paris Injection Brou, Amethyst, 7 1/2 In. 10.00
Patterson Block Pharmacy, Fresno, Emerald Green, 3 1/2 In. 26.00
Pawnee Indian Balm, Clear, 4 1/2 In. 25.00
Pearl's White Glycerine, Cobalt Blue, 4 In. 22.00
Peptenzyme, Reed & Carnrick, New York, Cobalt Blue, Rectangular, 3 1/4 In. 18.00
Pepto Bismol Relieves Sour Stomach, Stopper, Square, 1900s, 7 1/2 In. 80.00
Perry's Magnetic Wine Of Iron, Manchester, N.H., Cobalt Blue, 1880, 7 In. ...230.00 to 305.00
Peruvian Syrup, Aqua, Cylindrical, Label, 10 In. ....35.00 to 50.00
Peruvian Syrup, Cylindrical, Aqua, Flared Lip, 9 In. ....69.00 to 75.00
Pharmacal Association, Cobalt Blue, Square, Ring Lip, 7 3/4 In. 18.00
Phelp's Arcanum, Worcester, Mass., Olive Amber, 1830, 8 3/4 In. 920.00
Phelp's Rheumatic Elixir, Scranton, Pa., Amethyst, BIMAL, 5 1/2 In. 15.00
Phelp's Rheumatic Elixir, Scranton, Pa., Aqua, 5 1/2 In. 15.00
Phillip's Milk Of Magnesia, Aqua, 3 1/4 In. 30.00
Phillip's Milk Of Magnesia, Aug. 21, 1906, Blue, Cork, 1906, 6 3/4 In. 10.00
Phillip's Milk Of Magnesia Skin Cream, Cobalt Blue, Tin Lid, 1940, 2 3/4 Oz. 13.00
Phillip's Phospho-Murisate Of Quinine, 8 In. 5.00
Phospho-Caffein Comp., Arlington Chemical Co., Yonkers, Amber, 4 7/8 In. 8.00
Phychine For Consumption & Lung Troubles, T.A. Slocum Co., Aqua, 9 1/2 In. 20.00
Pinkstone's Curechiline Cures Cattle Diseases, Aqua, 7 1/2 In. 28.00
Pinol Quinine Tonic Promotes Hair Health, Tooled Mouth, 1925, 6 3/4 In. 220.00
Powell's Pharmacy, Opp. Temple Hotel, Redding, Cal., Man & Pick, 4 1/2 In. 75.00
Pratt's Abolition Oil For Abolishing Pain, Aqua, Flared Lip, 5 7/8 In. 55.00
Pratt's New Life, 7 3/4 In. 40.00
Prepared By William Coe, Worcester, Mass., Yellow Olive, Ring, Pontil, 2 3/4 In. 2200.00
Prepared Only By W.F. Gray, Nashville, Tenn., Aqua, Double Collar, IP, 7 1/2 In. 880.00
Prescribed By R.V. Pierce, M.D., Horizontal Lines On Reverse, Aqua, BIMAL, 7 In. .. 7.00
Prices Patent Candle Co., Diamond, Monogram, Blue, IP, 1865-1875, 7 1/8 In. 145.00
Prof. DeGrath's Electric Oil, Philada., OP, 2 3/4 In. 55.00
Prof. Elmer's Great French Remedy, Northfield, Mass., Aqua, 7 1/2 In. 40.00
Protonuclein, R & C, N.Y., Amber, 3 1/8 In. 10.00
Pulv. Sucrosum, Pharmacy, Cobalt Blue, Label, Cork Stopper 60.00
Queru's Cod Liver Oil Jelly, Aqua, Rolled Rim, Pontil, 1840-1860, 5 1/4 In. 200.00
R.D. Porter's Genuine Oriental Life Liniment, Aqua, OP 140.00
R.E. Woodward's Vegetable Tincture, South Reading, Mass., Aqua, OP, 6 In. 65.00
R.H. Lackey Pharmacies, Philada., Stoneware, Spout, 7 1/2 In. 165.00
R.R.R. Radway & Co., New York, Aqua, Pontil, 4 1/2 In. ....25.00 to 32.00
Raney's Drug Store, Hanford, Cal., 3 In. 17.00
Red Arrow Extra Heavy Mineral Oil, Red Arrow Labs, Tin Lid, 1930-1939, Qt. 2.00
Red Arrow Extra Heavy Mineral Oil, Red Arrow Labs, Tin Lid, 1935, Pt. 1.00
Red Arrow Milk Of Magnesia, Cobalt Blue, Tin Lid, Cellophane, 1935, 6 Oz. 4.00
Reddington & Co., Ess Of Jamaica Ginger, San Francisco, Aqua, Applied Top, 5 1/2 In. 45.00
Reed, Carnrick & Andrus, Pure Cod Liver Oil, Cobalt Blue, 1868-1874, 9 1/4 In. 305.00
Reese Chemical Co., Infection 1000 External Use 4 Times Daily, Cobalt, 5 1/2 In. 55.00
Reese Chemical Co., Thoxine, Screw Lid, Box, 1935 .... 3.00
Remedy Of Dr. Josephus, Great Shoshonees, Blue Aqua, Tooled Mouth, 1885, 6 In. ... 75.00
Renne's Magic Oil, Sample, 2 In. 10.00
Renne's Pain Killing-Magic Oil-It Works Like A Charm, Aqua, Cork, 5 In. 12.00
Renwar Salts, 6-Sided, Cobalt Blue, 2 Labels, ABM 20.00
Reuter's Life Syrup, New York, Aqua, 9 3/8 In. 15.00
Rev. N.H. Downs' Vegetable Balsamic Elixer, Aqua, 5 1/2 In. 8.00
Rheumatic Syrup, 1882, R.S. Co., Rochester, N.Y., Trademark, Amber, 9 1/2 In. 160.00
Rhodes' Fever & Ague Cure, 2 Indented Body Panels, Light Green, 9 In. 355.00
Richard's Golden Balsam, San Francisco, Applied Top, Aqua, 5 1/2 In. 100.00

Robert Clarkson Modern Druggist, Springfield, Ill., Oval 10.00
Robert Turlington, By The Mings Royal Patent, Aqua, Pontil, Flared, 2 1/2 In. 110.00
Roger's Vegetable Worm Syrup, Aqua, 4 1/2 In. 10.00
Rohrer's Expectoral Wild Cherry Tonic, Lancaster, Pa., Amber, IP, 10 1/2 In. .265.00 to 275.00
ROL Co., Prussian Blue, Tooled Sloping Collar, 1870-1890, 4 5/8 In. 55.00
Rouzer Funeral Home, Smelling Salts, Box 20.00
Rowlands Macassar Oil, The Original & Genuine, London, Flared Lip, Aqua, 3 1/2 In. . 10.00
Rubifoam For The Teeth, Put Up By E.W. Hoyt & Co., 4 1/2 In. 10.00
Rush's Buchu & Iron, Aqua, Hinge Mold, 8 5/8 In. 20.00
Rushton's Cod Liver Oil, N.Y., Light Green, Applied Top, OP, 10 In. 90.00
Ryker & Hegeman Co., Mortar & Pestle, Rectangular, Cork, 3 1/2 In. 3.00
Ryker-Jaynes Drug Stores, You Are Safe When You Buy At 5.00
S & D Milk Of Magnesia, Sharp & Dohme, Cobalt Blue, Label, Sealed Lid, 1935 . . . . 4.00
S. Maw Son & Sons, London, England, Jar, Inhaler, White Stoneware, 6 1/2 In. 45.00
S. Smith Green Mountain Renovator, East Georgia, Vt., Aqua, Oval, 7 3/8 In. 100.00
S.A. Palmer, Druggist, Santa Cruz, Cal., Amber, 6 In. 45.00
S.C. Dispensary, Jo-Jo Flask, 1/2 Pt. 75.00
S.C. Dispensary, Palm Tree, Flask, Light Amber, Banded, Tooled Lip, 9 In. 1430.00
S.D. Baldwin's Liniment, Marysville, Cal., Applied Top 110.00
S.O. Richardson's Pectoral Balsam, Aqua, Flared Lip, OP, 1840-1855, 5 7/8 In. 90.00
S.R. VanDuzer, New York, Origanum, Label, Amber 15.00
S.S. Seely & Co., Morris', Otsego County, N.Y., Aqua, Rectangular, Pontil, 4 5/8 In. 46.00
S.S. Seely & Co., Morris', Otsego County, New York, Yellow Green, OP 35.00
San Diego Drug, Ferris & Ferris, 6 1/8 In. 20.00
SanAnco Mineral Oil, Russian, Gem Cut Type, Tin Lid, 1930-1940 . . . . .1.50 to 3.00
Sanderson's Blood Renovator, Vt., Aqua, Applied Mouth, 1860, 8 In. 715.00
Sanford's Extract Of Hamamelis, Cobalt Blue, Panels, Rectangular, 9 1/2 In. . .245.00 to 250.00
Sanford's Extract Of Witch Hazel, Cobalt Blue, 1880-1895, 9 1/4 In. . . . . .155.00 to 185.00
Sanford's Genuine Ginger, Aqua 15.00
Sangsues, J. Mourier & Cie. , Leech Jar, Porcelain, France, 12 3/4 In. 3960.00
Saratoga Aperient, Cobalt Blue, Tooled Mouth, 5 7/8 In. 85.00
Save-The-Horse Spavin Remedy, Aqua, BIMAL, 6 1/2 In. 6.00
Schenck's Pulmonic Syrup, Philad., 8-Sided, Aqua, 7 In. . . . . .10.00 to 18.00
Scott & Bowne, Cherry Malt Phosphate, Lady's Leg, Amber, Round 55.00
Scott & Stewart, United States Syrup, N.Y., Ice Blue, IP, 9 3/8 In. 1320.00
Scott's Emulsion, Cod Liver Oil, With Lime & Soda, Aqua, Sunken Panels, Cork, 9 In. . 15.00
Scovill's Blood & Liver Syrup, Cin. & N.Y., Aqua, 10 In. . . . . .35.00 to 40.00
Seaside Drugstore, San Pedro, Cal., Sailing Ship, Tooled Top, 5 1/2 In. 45.00
Shaker Cherry Pectoral Syrup, Canterbury, N.H., No. 1, Aqua, OP, 5 1/2 In. . . .85.00 to 165.00
Shaker Family Pills, A.J. White, Dose 2 To 4, Amber, Tooled Lip, 1900, 2 1/4 In. 130.00
Shaker Fluid Extract Valerican, Aqua, OP, 3 3/4 In. . . . . .50.00 to 95.00
Shaker's Aromatic Elixir Of Malt, Pleasant Hill, Ky., Aqua, 8 1/2 In. 355.00
Sharp & Dohme, Cremo-Carbonates, Cobalt Blue, Tin Lid, 1935-1945 . . . . 15.00
Sharp & Dohme, Ficus, Amber, Embossed, 1890-1900, Box, 2 1/2 In. 9.00
Shecutts Southern Balm For Coughs Colds Consumption, Aqua, Pontil, 6 1/8 In. . 275.00
Sheldon's Cough Remedy, J.H. Widber, San Francisco . . . . .100.00 to 115.00
Sherrin & Co., Druggists, Souris, Man., BIMAL, Canada, c.1895, 6 In. 10.00
Sherry & Iron Company, Stockton, Cal., Aqua, Monogram, Applied Top, 11 1/4 In. . . . 230.00
Silver Pine Healing Oil, International Food Co., Minneapolis, Minn., 8 1/4 In. . . . .10.00 to 20.00
Simmon's Liver Regulator, J.H. Zeilin & Co., Philadelphia, Macon, Aqua, 9 In. 15.00
Smith, Kline & French, Box, 1930-1940 . . . . 9.00
Smith & Davis Druggist, Portland, Ore., Aqua, Applied Mouth, 1865-1875, 7 In. 210.00
Smith's Anodyne Cough Drops, Montpelier, Vt., Aqua, Pontil, 1860, 6 In. 150.00
Smith's Green Mountain Renovator, East Georgia, Vt., Blue Green, 1870, 7 In. 120.00
Smith's Green Mountain Renovator, Light Green, Applied Mouth, Oval, 1870, 7 In. . . 360.00
Smith's Green Mountain Renovator, Olive Amber, IP, 1846-1850, 7 In. . . . .465.00 to 1430.00
Smith's Sex-O-Tine, The Great Tonic For Men, Tooled Mouth, 1890-1905, 6 5/8 In. . . . 330.00
Snake Oil, Millers Antiseptic Oil, Herb Juice Medicine Co., ABM 20.00
South Carolina Dispensary, Blue Aqua, Tooled Mouth, 6 7/8 In. 465.00
South Carolina Dispensary, Palm Tree, Amber, 1885-1900, Pt. 1045.00
South Carolina Dispensary, Palm Tree, Blue, 7 1/2 In. .175.00 to 305.00
South Carolina Dispensary, Palm Tree, Green, Tooled Mouth, 7 1/2 In. 165.00
Spurlock-Neal Co., Nashville, Tenn., Label, Strap Side, Contents, 8 1/2 In. 30.00

Squibb, Aromatic Spirit Ammonia, Bakelite Top, Box, 1930-1939 .... 4.00
Squibb, Milk Of Magnesia, 8-Sided, Embossed Squibb, 1935 .... 7.00
St. John's Cough Syrup, 8-Sided, Aqua, Contents, OP, 5 1/2 In. 145.00
St. Joseph's Mineral Oil, Plough, Label, 1940 .... 2.00
Stearn's Chemist, Detroit, Mi., Cobalt Blue, Mortar & Pestle, 1900, 4 1/2 In. 200.00
Stewart D. Howe's Arabian Milk-Cure For Consumption, New York, Aqua, 7 1/2 In. 55.00
Stockton Drug Co., Stockton, Cal., Emerald Green, Round, 7 3/4 In. 43.00
Stoever's, Phil'a., Aqua, BIMAL 5.00
Strong, Cobb & Co., Wholesale Druggists, Cleveland, O., Cobalt Blue, 6 1/4 In. 110.00
Strong, Cobb & Co., Wholesale Druggists, Cleveland, O., Cobalt Blue, 11 In. ...120.00 to 155.00
Sun Drug Co., Amber, Embossed, 4 1/2 In. 20.00
Sun Drug Co., Emerald Green, 1 Oz. 225.00
Sun Drug Co., Los Angeles, Amethyst, Tooled Lip, 1890-1910, 9 1/4 In. 105.00
Sutcliffe & Hughes Druggists, Louisville, Ky., Aqua, IP, 1855, 10 1/4 In. 175.00
Swaim's Panacea, Phila., Pa., Olive Green, 1860, 8 In. ....255.00 to 440.00
Swaim's Panacea, Philada., Light To Medium Olive Green, Pontil, 1845, 8 In. 525.00
Swaim's Panacea, Philada., Olive Amber, Applied Sloping Collar, 7 5/8 In. 470.00
Swaim's Panacea, Philadelphia, Pa., Aqua, Tooled Mouth, 7 3/4 In. ....35.00 to 50.00
Swift's Syphilitic Specific, Cobalt Blue, Applied Mouth, Oval, 1890, 9 In. 1100.00
Syrup Of Tar & White Pine Compound, Norwich, 3-Sided, Tin Lid, 1940 .... 3.00
T & R Timmerman, Chemists, New York, Cylindrical, Gold Amber, Cork, 6 3/4 In. 3.00
T.E. Jenkins & Co., Chemists, Louisville, Ky., Aqua, OP, 1840, 6 5/8 In. 60.00
T.H. Bailey, Pharmacist, Haverhill, Mass., Semi-Oval Shape, Panel, Cork, 3 1/4 In. 3.00
T.H. Taylor, Brattleboro, Vt., Aqua, Applied Mouth, 1840-1860, 8 1/8 In. 210.00
T.O.D. Co., Cobalt Blue, Tooled Mouth, 1890-1915, 9 3/8 In. 385.00
Taylor's Cherokee Remedy Of Sweet Gum & Mullien, Aqua, 4 3/4 In. 20.00
Telephone Liniment, Charles W. Horn, Slatington, Pa., 6 1/2 In. 20.00
Telssier Prevost A Paris, Embossed Bell, Emerald Green, Rectangular, 7 1/4 In. 525.00
Terp-Heroin, Foster's, Amber, Tooled Lip, 1906-1910, 8 5/8 In. 175.00
Terp-Heroin, Foster's, W.T. & Co., U.S.A., Pat. Dec. 11 1894, Amber, 6 3/4 In. 60.00
Thompson's Original Hygeia Wild Cherry Phosphate, Aqua, 8 In. 15.00
Three In One, 8-Sided, Aqua, 2 Panels, Sample, 2 7/16 In. 15.00
Tilden & Co., New Lebanon, N.Y., Square, Amber, 7 In. 245.00
Tilden & Co., New Lebanon, N.Y., Square, Olive Amber, Striations, 7 In. 135.00
Tittle's Petroleum Ointment For Horses, Peabody, Mass., 50 Cents Per Bottle 30.00
Tonsiline, Embossed Giraffe, Clear, 6 3/4 In. 10.00
Tr. Cannab. Ind., Cobalt Blue, Label Under Glass, Tooled Lip, 7 3/4 In. 330.00
Tristram Pharmacy, Oil Of Coconut, Puce Amber, 1900s-1920s, 6 In. 11.00
Trommer Extract Of Malt Co., Freemont, Ohio, Amber, 8 In. 6.00
Trommer's Evergreen, Brooklyn, N.Y., Green, Ceramic Stopper 70.00
True Daffy's Elixir, Ice Blue, England, 1850, 4 5/8 In. 100.00
True Daffy's Elixir, Olive Green, Beveled Corners, Pontil, 1850, 4 5/8 In. 185.00
True Daffy's Elixir, Yellow Olive, IP, England, 1835-1855, 4 3/8 In. ....550.00 to 605.00
Trunk Bros., Denver, Colo., Trunk Picture, Tooled Top, 5 1/2 In. 35.00
U.S.A. Hosp. Dept., Amber, Applied Mouth, 1860-1870, 9 3/8 In. 690.00
U.S.A. Hosp. Dept., Aqua, Applied Mouth, 1860-1875, 8 7/8 In. ....85.00 to 210.00
U.S.A. Hosp. Dept., Aqua, Rolled Wide Mouth, 1860-1870, 7 5/8 In. ....330.00 to 470.00
U.S.A. Hosp. Dept., Cobalt Blue, Applied Mouth, 1860-1875, 9 1/8 In. 1595.00
U.S.A. Hosp. Dept., Cobalt Blue, Tooled Lip, 1870-1880, 2 1/2 In. ....300.00 to 690.00
U.S.A. Hosp. Dept., Cobalt Blue, Tooled Mouth, 1865-1880, 7 1/4 In. 1650.00
U.S.A. Hosp. Dept., Emerald Green, Applied Mouth, 1860-1875, 6 In. ....660.00 to 935.00
U.S.A. Hosp. Dept., Lavender Blue, Tooled Lip, 1860-1870, 3 In. 330.00
U.S.A. Hosp. Dept., Lavender Blue, Tooled Lip, Oval, 1860-1875, 6 7/8 In. 855.00
U.S.A. Hosp. Dept., Medium Yellow Olive Green, Applied Mouth, 1860-1870, 9 In. 530.00
U.S.A. Hosp. Dept., Medium Yellow Olive Green, Applied Mouth, 1860-1870, 10 In. ... 600.00
U.S.A. Hosp. Dept., Yellow Amber, Applied Mouth, 9 3/8 In. 530.00
U.S.A. Hosp. Dept., Yellow Amber, Double Collar, 1860-1870, 9 1/8 In. ....495.00 to 605.00
U.S.A. Hosp. Dept., Yellow Green, Applied Mouth, 1860-1870, 9 1/2 In. 660.00
U.S.A. Hosp. Dept., Yellow Olive, Cylindrical, 9 1/4 In. 355.00
Uberts Tar, Bone Set & Honey, Aqua, Tooled Lip 20.00
Umatilla Indian Relief, Campbell & Lyon, Detroit, Mich., Aqua, 5 In. 35.00
United Drug Co., Boston, Emerald Green, Oval Coin Shape, Pedestal, 5 3/4 In. 35.00
United Drug Co., Boston, U.S.A., Cadueus, Blue Green 80.00

University Of Free Medicine, Philada., 6-Sided, Aqua, 6 In. 130.00
Use Pritchards Teething Powders, Baby Medicine, Aqua, Rectangular, 3 1/2 In. 12.00
Vanderveer's Medicated Gin, Schiedam Schnapps, Amber Black, IP, 6 7/8 In. 935.00
Vapo-Cresolene, Milk Glass Chimney, Cast Iron Stand, Box, 1899-1915, 6 1/4 In. 190.00
Vermont Spring Saxe & Co., Medium Yellow, Olive Tone, 1880, 9 In. 440.00
Vicks Va-Tro-Nol, Vicks Chemical Co., Cobalt Blue, Tin Screw Lid, Box, 1945, 2 1/2 In. 5.00
Vicks Vapo Rub, Vicks Chemical Co., Cobalt Blue, Screw Lid, Box, 1945 . . . . 2.00
Victor Liniment, Frederick, Md., 6 In. 15.00
Voldner's Aromatic Schnapps Schiedam, Green, Applied Top, 10 In. 90.00
W. Day Pharmacist, Hopkinton, Mass., Amber, 5 In. 25.00
W. Henderson, Druggist, Pittsburgh, Aqua, Rolled Lip, OP 100.00
W. Olmstead & Co., Constitutional Beverage, New York, Golden Yellow, 10 In. 315.00
W. Peets, Salem, Mass., Deep Olive Amber, Pontil Base, 1830-1845, 7 In. 385.00
W. Sawen's Med. Co., Celebrated Oil Liniment, Utica, N.Y., Aqua 8.00
W.B. French, Camden, N.J., Aqua, Applied Mouth, 1840-1855, 5 5/8 In. 40.00
W.F. Lawrences Genuine Preparations, Epping, N.H., Aqua, Rectangular, OP, 8 3/4 In. 175.00
W.H. Hooker, Cobalt Blue, Front & Side Embossed, Tooled Lip, 4 3/4 In. 22.00
W.M. Bunch Pharm., Brookfield, Mo., 3 In. 10.00
W.M.M. Gordon Pharmaceutist, Cincinnati, Oh., Aqua, Cylindrical, IP, 7 1/4 In. 60.00
W.R. Warner & Co.'s Soluble Coated Pills, Globe Form, Folded Base Rim, 3 1/8 In. . 175.00
W.S. Whitehead Prescription Druggist, Boise, Idaho 25.00
W.T. Co., Pat. 1889, Jamaica Ginger, Label Under Glass, Stopper, 5 3/4 In. 80.00
W.T. Wenzell, San Francisco, Aqua, Applied Top, 5 1/2 In. 55.00
W.W. Huff's Liniment, Light Green, Applied Mouth, OP, 4 1/2 In. 220.00
Wakefield's Blackberry Balsam Compound, Aqua 30.00
Wakelee's Camelline, Cobalt Blue 45.00
Wakelee's Pharmacies, San Francisco, Citrate Of Magnesia, Green, 7 1/4 In. 605.00
Wampole's Syrup Hypo Comp., Philadelphia, Aqua 10.00
Ware's Bermingham Nasal Douche, Philadelphia, Box 18.00
Warner's Safe Diabetes Remedy, Rochester, Light Golden Amber, 16 Oz. 90.00
Warner's Safe Kidney & Liver Remedy, Rochester, N.Y., 16 Fl. Oz., Clear, 9 1/2 In. . 120.00
Warner's Safe Nervine, 4 Cities, Amber, Blob Top, 9 3/4 In. 350.00
Warner's Safe Nervine, A. & D.H.C. Amber, Applied Top, 9 1/2 In. . . . . .60.00 to 130.00
Warner's Safe Nervine, Copper, Yellow Shoulders, England, 1895, 7 3/8 In. 95.00
Warner's Safe Nervine, Double Crown Top, 7 1/2 In. 55.00
Warner's Safe Nervine, Red Amber, Applied Mouth, 7 3/8 In. 500.00
Warner's Safe Nervine, Rochester, N.Y., Honey Amber, Tooled Mouth, 7 1/2 In. . .55.00 to 65.00
Warner's Safe Nervine, Trademark, Rochester, N.Y., A. & D.H.C., 7 3/8 In. . . . .110.00 to 145.00
Warner's Safe Remedies Co., Rochester, 12 1/2 Oz. 60.00
Warner's Safe Remedies Co., Rochester, Amber, Label, ABM, 6 Oz. . . . . .45.00 to 85.00
Warner's Safe Remedies Co., Rochester, N.Y., U.S.A., 12 1/2 Oz. 45.00
Warner's Safe Rheumatic Remedy, Rochester, Light Amber, Pt. 85.00
Warner's Safe Yeast Dominoes, Label, Box 125.00
Warner's Wine Of Life, Amber, Qt. 145.00
Watt's Nervous Antidote, 12-Sided, Aqua, 5 1/2 In. . . . . .10.00 to 25.00
Wentz's The Place To Buy Your Drugs, Gilroy, Cal., Tooled Top, 6 1/2 In. 22.00
White's Pharmacy, Pensacola, Fl., 5 1/4 In. 20.00
White's Prairie Flower, Toledo, O., Blue Aqua, Applied Top, 7 1/2 In. 90.00
Whittemore's Vegetable Syrup For Diarrhoea, Essex, Ct., Aqua, 5 In. 195.00
Whitwell's Patent Volatile Aromatic & Headache, Aqua, Pontil, 1860, 4 In. 220.00
Wilder's Vermifuge, Blue Aqua, OP, Rolled Lip, 1840-1855, 5 7/8 In. 175.00
Willes & Horne Drug Co., Desert New Bldg., Salt Lake, Utah 20.00
William Brown, Druggist & Chemist, 481 Washington St., Boston, 8 3/4 In. 195.00
Williams' Balsamic Cream Of Roses, S.F. PGW On Base, Light Blue, Tooled Top 145.00
Williams' Magnetic Relief, Frenchtown, N.J., Rectangular, Aqua, 6 1/2 In. 15.00
Williamson & Son, Phila., Deep Emerald Green, 1840-1855, 8 3/8 In. 330.00
Wintersmith, Louisville, Ky., Deep Amber, 5 3/4 In. 25.00
Wisdom's Robertine, Embossed, Cobalt Blue, Ring Lip, Square, 5 In. 25.00
Wises Triturations, Amber, Contents, 8 1/2 In. 10.00
Wm. H. Keith & Co., San Francisco, Green Aqua, Applied Top, 6 1/4 In. 35.00
Wm. H. Keith Apothecaries, San Francisco, Cylindrical, Applied Top . . . . .50.00 to 75.00
Wm. Pfunders Oregon Blood Purifier, Face, Amber 85.00
Wm. R. Warner & Co., Philadelphia, Cobalt Blue, Dose Cup, Cylindrical, 7 In. 65.00

Wm. Radam's Microbe Killer, Label On 4 Sides, Directions, Amber, Square, 12 In. 200.00
Wm. Radam's Microbe Killer, Medium Amber, Tooled Mouth, 1900, 10 1/4 In. ..85.00 to 130.00
Wm. S. Dunham Mfg., N.Y., Medium Emerald Green, 1855, 9 3/4 In. 500.00
Wolfe Drug, San Rafael & Larkspur, California, Clear, Yellow Tint 25.00
Wolfstim's Rheumatic & Gout Remedy, Hoboken, N.H., Aqua, Rectangular, 5 In. ...   4.00
Wonderfluff After Clip Lotion, For Dogs, 1960s 18.00
Woodcock, Schroeder's Med. Co., Rectangular, Amber, 8 In. 80.00
Woodward Chemist, Nottingham, Cobalt Blue, Oval, 6 1/4 In. 20.00
Worm Mixture, Stabler, 6-Sided, Aqua, Sheared & Tooled Lip, 1845, 4 In. 145.00
Wyeth's Liniment, Bakelite Lid, Round, Box, 1920-1930 ....   4.00
Yerba Santa, San Francisco, California, Embossed Cross, Aqua, Tooled Top, 8 1/2 In. ..   200.00
Zoeller's Kidney Remedy, The Zoeller Medical Co., Pittsburg, Pa., Amber, 9 In. 155.00

-------------------- MICHTER'S --------------------

Michter's claims to be America's oldest distillery, established in Schaefferstown, Pennsylvania, in 1753, before it was even the state of Pennsylvania. The building was named a national historic landmark in 1980. Special ceramic jugs were first made in 1955 and figural decanters were made beginning in 1977. One of the most famous series was King Tut (1978-1980). About 3,000 were made of the large size. Miniature bottles were also made. Production ended in 1989.

MICHTER'S, 230th Anniversary, 1983 ....   30.00
 Amish Buggy 57.00
 Auto, York Pulman, 1977 ....   100.00
 Barn, Daniel Boone, 1977 ....   30.00
 Canal Boat, 1977 ....22.00 to 26.00
 Casinos, 1980 ....   27.00
 Christmas, Bell, 1983 ....   53.00
 Christmas Ornament, 1984 ....   25.00
 Christmas Tree, 1978 ....   50.00
 Christmas Wreath, 1980 ....   34.00
 Conestoga Wagon, 1976 ....   62.00
 Covered Bridge, 1984 ....   47.00
 Doughboy, 1979 ....   23.00
 Easton Peace Candle, 1979 ....   20.00
 Football On Tee, Pennsylvania, 1979 ....*Illus*   20.00
 Goddess Selket, 1980 ....*Illus*   32.00
 Halloween Witch, 1979 ....*Illus*   55.00
 Hershey Trolley, 1980 ....   48.00
 Ice Wagon, 1979 ....   19.00
 Indian Kneeling 50.00
 Jug, 1955 ....   60.00
 Jug, 1957, 1/2 Gal. 68.00
 Jug, 1957, Qt. 20.00

Michter's, Football On Tee,
Pennsylvania, 1979

Michter's, Goddess Selket,
1980

Michter's, Halloween Witch,
1979

Jug, Sheridan, 1970, Qt. . . . . .20.00 to 22.00
Jug, Sheridan, 1976, Qt. 10.00
Jug, Sheridan, 1978, Qt. 10.00
King Tut, 1978 . . . . 60.00
King Tut, Miniature 17.00
Knights Of C, 4th Degree 100.00
Liberty Bell, Brown, 1976 . . . . 43.00
Liberty Bell, With Cradle, 1976 . . . . 14.00
Liberty Brown, Bisque, 1975 . . . . 75.00
Packard, Fleetwood, 1979 . . . . 36.00
Penn State Nittany Lion, 1978 . . . . 48.00
Pennsylvania, Keystone State, 1980 . . . . 20.00
Pennsylvania Hex, 1977 . . . . 12.00
Pitt Panther, 1977 . . . . 53.00
Policeman, New York, 1980 . . . . 30.00
Reading, Pagoda, Pa., 1977 . . . . 24.00
Stagecoach, 1978 . . . . 17.00
USC Trojan 35.00

MILK

The first milk bottle we have heard about was an earthenware jar pictured on a Babylonian temple stone panel. Evidently, milk was being dipped from the jar while cream was being churned into butter.

Milk came straight from the cow on early farms; but when cities started to grow in America, a new delivery system was needed. The farmer put the milk into large containers. These were taken to the city in horse-drawn carts and delivered to the consumer. The milkman took a slightly dirty dipper and put it into the milk, ladling a quantity into the customer's pitcher.

Flies, dirt, horse hairs, and heat obviously changed the quality of the milk. By the 1860s iceboxes were developed. One type of milk can claimed to keep milk from becoming sour in a thunderstorm. In 1895, pasteurization was invented and another source of disease from milk was stopped. The first milk bottle patent was issued in the 1880s to the Warren Glass Works Company. The most famous milk bottle was designed in 1884 by Dr. Harvey D. Thatcher, a physician and druggist from Potsdam, New York. His glass bottle had a *Lightning* closure and a picture on the side of a cow being milked. In 1889 The Thatcher Company brought out the bottle with a cap that is still used.

The characteristic shape and printed or embossed wording identify milk bottles for collectors. The round bottle was the most popular until 1936, when the squat round bottle was invented. In 1940 a square squat bottle became the preferred shape. A slug plate was used in the manufacture of a special type of round milk bottle. The manufacturer would change the name embossed on the bottle by changing a metal plate in the glass mold. The letters *ISP* seen in some publications mean *inserted slug* plate. In the following list of bottle prices, the words *slug plate* are used. Amber-colored glass was used for a short time. Makers claimed it resisted spoiling. A green bottle was patented in 1929. *Pyro* is the shortened form of the word *pyroglaze,* an enameled lettering used on milk bottles after the mid-1930s. Before that, the name had been embossed. Some bottle collectors now refer to these as *ACL,* Applied Color Label. In this listing, color refers to the applied color of the label not to the color of the glass.

Cop the top, babyface, toothache, and *cream top* are some of the terms that refer to the shapes of bottle necks popular in the 1930s. Near the top of the bottle there was an indentation so the cream, which separated from the standing milk, could be poured off with little trouble. Today, with homogenized milk, few children realize that the cream on natural milk will rise to the top. The glass bottle was displaced by cartons by the 1960s. There are two newsletters for collectors,The Milk Route, 4 Ox Bow Road, Westport, CT 06880-2602 and The MOOSletter, 240 Wahl Avenue, Evans City, PA 16033.

MILK, 2 Cent Deposit, Amber, Black, Square, Qt. 15.00
A. George Jewske Home Dairy, N. Braddock, Embossed, Qt. 30.00
A.J. Spring & Son, Mother, Green & Red, Round, Pt. 25.00
Abbotts Alderney Dairies, Vertical Stripes, Pt. 8.00
Absolutely Pure Milk, Milk Protector, Man Milking Cow, 6 1/2 In. 145.00
Absolutely Pure Milk, Milk Protector, Man Milking Cow, Glass Lid, 7 In. 275.00

Absolutely Pure Milk, Milk Protector, Tooled Lip, 1886-1890, Pt. 305.00
Acadia Dairies, Aqua, BIMAL, 1/2 Pt. 6.00
Adderholdt Bros. Creamery, Gainesville, Ga., Uncle Sam, U.S.A., Red, Qt. .....60.00 to 65.00
Adderholdt Bros. Creamery, Rich Jersey Milk, Red, Square, Qt. 12.00
Adhor, Reg. Cal., Red, Square, Pt. 15.00
Alameda County Milk Dealers Assn., Oakland, Great Champions, Orange, 1/2 Gal. .. 45.00
Alex Bolin & Son, Bradford, Pa., Embossed, 1/2 Pt. 30.00
Alex Pike, Salisbury, Mass., Embossed, Qt. 20.00
Allegheny Dairy, Cow, ABM, Pt. 70.00
Alpen Rose Homogenized Milk, Portland, Oregon, Amber, White, Square, Qt. 12.00
Alta Crest Farms, Spencer, Mass., Green, Qt. 150.00
Alton Moore, Matteawan, N.Y., Whiteman, 144 Chambers St., N.Y., Tin Top, Pt. 50.00
Amador Goat Dairy, Glendale, Arizona, Brown, Square, Qt. 40.00
Anderson's Dairy, Auburn, Calif., Milkman Carrying Bottles, Amber, White, Square, Qt. 12.00
Anderson's Dairy, Pecatonica, Ill., Embossed, Qt. 12.00
Athens Co-Operative Creamery, Athens, Ga., Orange, Square, Qt. 25.00
Athens Co-Operative Creamery, War Bonds For Victory, Green, Round, Qt. 55.00
Augusta Dairies Inc., Staunton, Va., Milk For Health, Children Playing, Black, Qt. 32.00
Averill, Akron, Ohio, Drive Safely, There Is Health In Milk, Red Label, Pt. ....*Illus* 75.00
Averill, Akron, Ohio, We Cherish Liberty And Health, Red Label, Qt. ....*Illus* 75.00
B.A. Mason, T.B. Tested, Delight Farm Dairy, Embossed, Pt. 10.00
B.M.S. Indianapolis, On Base, Cream, 1/2 Pt. 5.00
Bacon Creamery, Loudon, Tennessee, Red, Round, Qt. 60.00
Bacon Creamery, Properly Past., Loudon, Tenn., Red, Tall Round, Qt. 45.00
Baker & Son Dairy, Guernsey Products, Atlanta, Michigan, Cow, Orange, Qt. .....24.00 to 25.00
Barker's Dairy, Curry, W. Va., Embossed, Qt. 18.00
Bartholomay Buttermilk, Rochester, N.Y., Amber, Round, Qt. 85.00
Batchelder's Dairy, Hampton Falls, N.H., Orange, Round, Qt. 22.00
Baywood Farm Dairy, Hollister, Calif., Baby Sitting Next To Bottle, Magenta, Round, Qt. 40.00
Beetz's Dairy, Raw Milk, Palmerton, Pa., Red, Qt. 25.00
Bellview Dairy, Himrod, N.Y., Amber, Shield With Letters BFDC, White, Square, Qt. .. 12.00
Ben Jansing Farm Dairy, Licking Pike, Newport, Ky., Family, Red, Round, Qt. 45.00
Bentley & Rendkens Dairy, Thatcher, 3-26-1957, Orange, Square, 1/3 Qt. 5.00
Bentley & Sons Farm Dairy, Fairbanks, Standing Cow, Red & Brown, Round, Pt. 70.00
Bentley's Farm Products, Fairbanks, De Laval Slug Plate, Embossed, Round, Pt. 125.00
Bentley's Farm Products, Fairbanks, Slug Plate, Embossed, Round, Pt. 100.00
Benware Creamery, Malone, N.Y., Qt. 25.00
Better Dairy Products, Inc., Dayton, Pa., Embossed, Qt. 30.00
Better Maid Dairy Prod., Athens, Gainesville, Ga., ABCDG, Orange, Square, 1/2 Pt. .. 12.00
Better Maid Dairy Prod., Athens, Gainesville, Ga., Orange, Square, Qt. 15.00
Bieber's Mill Creek Farm Dairy, Woodworth, Ohio, 2-Color, Qt. 70.00
Big Elm Dairy Company, Slug Plate, Amber, Neck Grips, 1934, Qt. 65.00
Birleys, Hollywood, Calif., June 1926, 6 3/4 Oz. 23.00
Bison Buffalo Milk, Embossed, Pt. 20.00
Blake's Creamery, Manchester, N.H., Round, Qt. .... .28.00 to 30.00
Blankeney Dairy, Poplar Bluff, Mo., Baby On Phone, Black, Round, Qt. 50.00
Blue Boy Sparkle, Vitamin-Mineral Fortified, Fairy, Amber, Label, Qt. 25.00
Blue Ribbon Dairy, Circleville, Ohio, Embossed, 1/2 Pt. 33.00
Bolder Brook Farm, Milan, Pa., Qt. 25.00
Bolger Farms, Embossed, 1/2 Pt. 5.00
Bolton Dairy, Good News Travels Fast, Bolton, Conn., Man On Horse, Green, 1/2 Pt. .. 10.00
Borden Company, Southern Division, Gail Borden, Amber, Qt. 29.00
Borden's, Circle, 1/2 Pt. 10.00
Borden's, Condensed Milk Company, 6-Sided, Flint, Milk Glass Lid, Metal Band, Pt. ... 45.00
Borden's, Eagle, 1/2 Pt. 15.00
Borden's, Eagle, Tin Top, Qt. 45.00
Borden's, Elsie Head, Red, Square, Plastic Bail, Gal. 55.00
Borden's, Gail Borden's Silhouette, Signature, Amber, Square, Qt. 20.00
Borden's, Niagara, 1/2 Pt. 20.00
Borden's, Sealed, Registered, One Quart Liquid 4.00
Borden's, Squat, 1/2 Pt. 10.00
Borden's Milk & Cream, Red, Square, 1/2 Pt. 25.00
Borden's Phoenix Store, Cactus, Jug, Brown, Large Mouth, Round, 1/2 Gal. 45.00

Borden's Quality, Embossed, ACL, Canada, 1930-1940, 1/2 Pt. 20.00
Bowman Farm Dairy, Embossed, Qt. 8.00
Boyles' Dairy, Topeka Kansas, Amber, White, Square, Qt. 8.50
Brighton Place Dairy, Rochester, N.Y., Green, Machined Mouth, 20th Century, Qt. 495.00
Brookfield, Baby Face, Red, 1/2 Pt. 75.00
Brookfield, Baby Face, Red, Qt. 75.00
Brookfield Baby Top, Double Baby Face, Embossed, Square, Qt. 50.00
Brookfield Dairy, Hellertown, Baby Face, Embossed, 1/2 Pt. 50.00
Brookfield Dairy, Hellertown, Pa., Babyface, Embossed, Round, Pt. 100.00
Brookville Dairy Prod. Co., Brookville & Clarion, Pa., Cream Top, Orange, Qt. 75.00
Burch Dairy Co., Health In Every, Florence, S.C., Orange, Round, Qt. 40.00
Buzzelli Sons, Embossed Cow, 1/2 Pt. 20.00
Buzzelli Sons, Niagara Falls, Babyface, Qt. 40.00
C. Wierson Dairy, Killdeer, N.D., Embossed, Round, Qt. 190.00
Canham's Dairies, Fresno, Cal., Paper Cover, 1/4 Pt. 27.00
Cape Cod Creamery Co., Hyannis, Mass., Embossed, Qt. 30.00
Carnation, Shoulder Logos, Red, Square, 1/2 Gal. 40.00
Case Dairy, Rochester, Mich., From Cow To Your Door, Cow, Orange, Round, Qt. 32.00
Cedar Grove Dairy, Wilfong & Son, Memphis, Tenn., Cedar Tree & Pirates, Green, Qt. . 50.00
Cedar Hill Dairy, Galt, Ont., Delicious Creamed Cottage Cheese, Red, 1/2 Pt. 60.00
Cedar Valley Co-Op Dairies, Cedartown, Ga., Woman Shopping, Red, Square, 1/3 Qt. . 15.00
Central Dairy, Rockford, Ill., Embossed, Qt. 9.00
Challenge Milk, Deer, Tooled Top, Pt. 65.00
Chapman's Dairy, Cows Milked In Parlor, Greenville, S.C., Red, Round, Qt. 65.00
Chas. A. Hoak's Modern Sanitary Dairy, Embossed, Cream Top, Round, Pt. 40.00
Chemung Valley Farms, Z, Elmira, N.Y., Thatcher Mark, Crown Top, 1911, 1/2 Pt. 40.00
Chenar Farm Guernsey Milk, Easton, Md., Embossed, Round, Qt. 14.00
Chestnut Ridge Dairy, Ellet, Ohio, Embossed, Qt. 33.00
City Dairy, Harbor Beach, Michigan Slug Plate, Embossed, Round, Pt. 3.00
City Dairy, Mullan, Idaho, Round, Squat, Qt. 40.00
Clark's Dairy, Sutton, Mass., Embossed, Pt. 12.00
Clifton Springs Sanitarium Dairy, Clifton Springs, N.Y., Slug Plate, Round, 1/2 Pt. .. 50.00
Cline's Pasteurized Dairy Products, Cream Top, With Spoon, Embossed, Pt. 29.00
Clover Dairy Products, 3-Leaf Clover, Embossed, Round, 1942, Qt. ....17.00 to 22.00
Coble, Dande Process, General Mills Laboratories, Amber, White, Square, Qt. 10.00
Cranford Dairy, Cranford, N.J., Embossed, Round, 1/4 Pt. 10.00
Creamer, Cranford Dairy, Cranford, N.J., 1/4 Pt. 25.00
Creamer, Crowley's, Fresh-Fresh Dairy Foods, Maroon 13.00
Creamer, Dairylea, Family On Back, Red, Round, 1 Oz. ....15.00 to 20.00
Creamer, Dallas Dairy, Script, Red, 3/4 Oz. 14.00
Creamer, Dart's Dairy, Manchester, Conn., Orange, Round, 3/4 Oz. 25.00
Creamer, Dean's Dairy, Red, 3/4 Oz. 27.00
Creamer, Exner Dairy, Niles, Mich., Phone 780-W, Black, 3/4 Oz. 25.00
Creamer, Hillview Dairies Cream, Pouring Lip, Handle, 3 5/8 In. 15.00
Creamer, Honolulu Dairymen's Assn., Honolulu, T.H., 1/4 Pt. 125.00
Creamer, Lancashire Hygienic Dairies Ltd., Churn Shape, 2 7/8 In. 30.00

Milk, Averill,
Akron, Ohio,
Drive Safely,
There Is Health
In Milk, Red
Label, Pt.

Milk, Averill,
Akron, Ohio, We
Cherish Liberty
And Health, Red
Label, Qt.

Milk, Hancock Co.
Creamery, Ellsworth,
Me., Kone Shape, Red
& White, I Qt., 10 In.

Creamer, Northampton Sanitary Dairy, Northampton, Pa., 3/4 Oz. 40.00
Creamer, Old's Dairy, Maroon, 3/4 Oz. 15.00
Creamer, R. Barden Cream Co., Dorchester, Mass., 1/2 Pt. 28.00
Creamer, Wm. Hyde Rice, Lihue, Kauai, 1/4 Pt. 150.00
Crisp County Dairies, Cordele, Ga., Red, Round, Qt. 45.00
Crystal, Marietta, Ohio, Qt. 12.00
Crystal Creamery, Adams, Ma., Round, Qt. 23.00
Crystal Springs Dairy, Chatham, Va., Embossed, Qt. 45.00
Dairy Products Co., Morristown, Tenn., Trophy, Red, Round, Qt. 30.00
Dairymen's Co-Op Assn., Includes Deposit, Embossed, Qt. 15.00
Dairymen's Meadow Gold, Honolulu, Hawaii, Red & Orange, Square, Qt. 45.00
Dairymen's Meadow Gold, Honolulu, Hawaii, Red, Orange, Square, 1955, 1/2 Pt. 10.00
Dalton Dairy, Nogales, Ariz., Embossed, Qt. 23.00
Darrow Dairy, Embossed, 1/2 Pt. 10.00
Dash Dairy, Springville, N.Y., Qt. 10.00
Dellinger Dairy Farm, Gold Medal, Jeffersonville, Ind., Orange & Black, Qt. 60.00
Denver Retail Dairymen's Association, Train & Bottle, Buy War Bonds, Orange, Qt. . 75.00
Denver Retail Dairymen's Association, War Motto, Qt. 45.00
Diamond Dairy, Olympic 2620, Oakland, Calif., Round, Qt. 25.00
Diamond Dairy Farms, Salem, N.H., Orange, 1/2 Pt. 30.00
Diamond Dairy Farms, Salem, N.H., Orange, Pt. 30.00
Dixie Dairy Co., Gary, Ind. & Beecher, Ill., Dixie, Pt. 8.00
Dixieland Dairy, Montgomery, Ala., Qt. 15.00
Dougan's Guernsey Farm, Beloit, Wis., Embossed, 1/2 Pt. 8.00
Driscoll's Dairy, Yantic, Ct., Fresh Cream For Your Coffee, Red, Round, 1/2 Pt. 13.00
Dublin Co-Op Dairies, 5 Cent Deposit, Red, Round, Squat, Qt. 25.00
Dublin Co-Op Dairies, You Owe It To Your Country, Buy War Bonds, Red, Pt. 20.00
Dunnville Dairy, Dunnville, Ont., 1/2 Pt. 10.00
Dunnville Dairy, Economize On Your Food Bill, Red, Canada, c.1949, Pt. 70.00
Dunnville Dairy, No One Ever Outgrows The Need, Red, Canada, 1940s, Qt. 70.00
Dunnville Dairy, Yes Sir It's Good For Grown Ups Too, Red, Qt. 30.00
E.A. Warwick, Willowdale Dairy, Keyser, W.V., Emblem, Qt. 25.00
E.F. Mayer, 289 Hollenbeck St., Amber, Embossed, Round, Qt. 75.00
E.S. Dairy Magic Milk Bottle, B.G. Co., Balto, Md., ABM Mouth, c.1920, Qt. 120.00
E.W. Woolman's, 4709 Lancaster Ave., Lightning Stopper, Pt. 35.00
Edelweiss Dairy, San Jose, Cal., 3 Edelweiss Flowers, Green, Tall Round, Qt. 40.00
Eden Plains, Hagerstown, Md., 1/2 Gal. 40.00
El-Fre Nubian Goat Farm, Ebenezer, N.Y., All Our Goats Are Registered, Blue, Qt. 40.00
Elberon Dairy, E.P. Davison, Elberon, N.J., T. Mfg. Co., Metal Lid, ABM Lip, Pt. 50.00
Elmore's Creamery, Elwood, Cream, 1/2 Pt. 8.00
Elry S. Leasure, Zanesville, Ohio, Embossed, Slug Plate, Pt. 15.00
Embassy Dairy Inc., Washington, DC, Baby Face, Embossed, Square, Qt. 55.00
Evergreen Dairy Farm, Kannapolis, N.C., Child On Bike, Orange, Round, Qt. 45.00
F.E. Walker Dairy, Cleveland, Ohio, Embossed, Qt. 33.00
F.H. Robinson & Son, Lexington, Mass., Embossed, Qt. 30.00
F.W. Elliott, Petersham, Mass., Dairy Farm Scene, Black & Orange, Round, Qt. 25.00
Fairfield Creamery Co., Fairfield, Ill., Embossed, 1/2 Pt. 12.00
Fairfield Western Maryland Dairy, 1/4 Pt. 15.00
Fairfield Western Maryland Dairy, Health Dept. Permit Triangle, Embossed, 1/2 Pt. .. 10.00
Fairlea Farms, Newport, New Hampshire, Orange, Square, Qt. 10.00
Fairview Dairy Quality Products, Antigo, Wis., Painted Label, 1/2 Pt. 14.00
Farmer's Co-Op Milk Co. Inc., Poughkeepsie, Embossed, 1/2 Pt. 12.00
Farmer's Dairy Products Co. Inc., Cumberland, Md., Embossed, Pt. 10.00
Farmers Fairfield Dairy Co., Reading, Pa., Wild Folk Bill Beaver, Squat, Red, Qt. 60.00
Ferndale Dairy, J. Williams, White Haven, Aqua, BIMAL, Qt. 20.00
Florida Universal, Pt. 10.00
Forest City Dairy, Rockford, Ill., Embossed, Qt. 15.00
Frazier's Down On The Farm, Cream, Snap-On Cap, 1/2 Pt. 5.00
Fredericktown Ice & Dairy Co., Ohio, Embossed, 1/2 Pt. 33.00
Fredrick's Farm Dairy, Conyngham, Pa., Ayrshire Cow, Brown, Round, Qt. 35.00
Garst Bros. Dairy Inc., Plan Meals To Avoid Waste, Orange, Round, Qt. 40.00
Glendale Dairy, Decatur, Ala., Milking Parlor, Orange, Tall Round, Qt. 80.00
Gold Spot Dairy, Enid, Okla., Enjoy Our Ice Cream, Orange, Square, Qt. 26.00

Golden Guernsey Co-Op Dairy, Phoenix, Arizona, Pitchers, Amber, White, Qt. 12.00
Golden Guernsey Table Milk, Honolulu, Hawaii, Orange & Red, Square, Qt. 45.00
Goodrich Milk Co., Endicott, N.Y., Orange, 1/2 Pt. 20.00
Goodrich Milk Co., Endicott, N.Y., Orange, Pt. 20.00
Gosselin's Dairy Inc., Embossed G On Shoulder, 1/2 Pt. 4.00
Gracefield Dairy, Perth, Embossed, Slug Plate, Round, 1943-1950, 1/4 Pt. 20.00
Grady Farms, Waterloo, Iowa, Red, Gal. 25.00
Gratzer Dairy, Syracuse, N.Y., Deposit, Amber, Square, Qt. 25.00
Great Lakes Creamery, Buffalo, N.Y., Embossed, 1/2 Pt. 11.00
Greendale Farm, West Lebanon, N.H., Embossed, Round, Qt. 14.00
Grimm's Dairy Products, Mount Carroll, Ill., Red, Qt. 9.00
Guernsey Dairy, Boise, Idaho, Round, 1/2 Gal. 40.00
Guernsey Dairy, Stockton, Ill., Embossed, 1/2 Pt. 8.00
Guilford Dairy, Greensboro, N.C., Milk—Perfect Food, Red, Round, 1/2 Pt. 20.00
H-B Dairy Products., Frankfort, Ky., Boy & Dog, Let Them Play, Red, Qt. 40.00
H.E. Britton Cream, Sandwich, Ill., Embossed, 1/2 Pt. 8.00
H.G. Williams Co., Norfolk, Va., Embossed, 1/2 Pt. 15.00
H.L. Green, Golden Guernsey Products, Chester, New York, Stork, Baby, Orange, Qt. 30.00
H.P. Hood & Sons, Dairy Experts, Hood, Embossed, 1939, Qt. 18.00
Haleakala Dairy, Makawao, 1 Ring, Embossed, 1/2 Pt. 12.00
Haleakala Dairy, Makawao, 1 Ring, Embossed, Qt. 25.00
Haleakala Dairy, Makawao, 1/2 Pt. 38.00
Haleakala Dairy, Makawao, 3 Rings, Embossed, Pt. 125.00
Haleakala Dairy, Makawao, 4 Rings, Embossed, 1/2 Pt. 150.00
Haleakala Dairy, Orange, Gray, Square, 1959, Qt. 20.00
Haleakala Dairy, Orange, Gray, Square, 1964, Pt. 8.00
Hampden Creamery Co., Everett, Mass., Tin Top, Slug Plate, 1/2 Pt. 40.00
Hancock Co. Creamery, Ellsworth, Me., Kone Shape, Red & White, 1 Qt., 10 In. . .*Illus* 10.00
Happy Valley Farms, Inc., Rossville, Georgia, Steer Head, Cap Seat, ABM Lip, Qt. 105.00
Haskell's Grade A Guernsey Milk, Children Really Enjoy, Dacro, Aqua, Square, Qt. .. 20.00
Haskell's Guernsey Milk, Rhyme, Dacro, Aqua, Round, Qt. 27.00
Hawaii Dairy, Hilo, Hawaii, Embossed, Qt. 125.00
Hershey's Chocolate Corp., Hershey, Pa., 1/2 Pt. 35.00
Hershey's Dairy Products, Hershey, Pa., 1/2 Pt. 15.00
Hi Acre Milk Farms, Globe Of The World, Cow, Orange, Squat, Qt. ....25.00 to 30.00
Highland Dairy, Baby Face, Qt. 75.00
Hill Crest, Eddington, Pa., Square, Qt. 12.00
Hill Top Dairy, N.Y., Deposit, Green & Orange, Square, Qt. 25.00
Hillcrest, Adults, Babies, They All Need Milk, Hill, Green, Orange, Round, Qt. 40.00
Hillcrest Dairy Farm, San Mateo, Pt. 30.00
Hilo Dairymen's Center, Mickey & Minnie Mouse, Black, 1/2 Pt. 125.00
Hoak's, Harrisburg, Pa., Minute Man, War Bonds, Cream Top, Qt. 85.00
Hollands Quality Dairy, Madera, Cal., Gripper Neck, Qt. 30.00
Home Dairy, Nursery Rhyme, 1/2 Pt. 15.00
Homes & Wadington, Amethyst, Pt. 65.00
Honey Brook Dairy, W.L. Frankhouser, Embossed, Qt. 35.00
Howard Zink Dairy, Bradford, Pa., Embossed, 1/2 Pt. 30.00
Howertown Sanitary Dairy, 1/2 Pt. 5.00
Hygienic Dairy Co., Red, Embossed, Round, 1/4 Pt. 10.00
I.M. Smith's Dairy, Kinards, Red, Round, 1/3 Qt. 25.00
Ideal Dairies Co., Painesville, Ohio, Green, 1/2 Pt. 30.00
Independent Creamery & Ice Cream Co., Los Gatos, Calif., 1/2 Pt. 25.00
Indian Hill Farm Dairy, Greenville, Me., Indian With Headdress, Orange, Qt. .....25.00 to 30.00
Iris Farms, Franconia, N.H., Embossed, Round, Qt. 14.00
Irvindale Farms, Atlanta, Ga., Red, Square, Qt. 15.00
J.D. Poole & Sons, Minford, Ohio, Red, Square, Qt. 33.00
J.H. Belle, Long Ridge Dairy, Stamford, Conn., Embossed, 1/2 Pt. 22.00
J.N. Thatcher Homestead, Martinsburg, W. Va., Qt. 50.00
Janeazeks, Orange & Green, Qt. 15.00
Jersey Farm Dairy, Fresno, Cal., 1/4 Pt. 22.00
Joceda Farm, Marlboro, N.J., 5 Cent, Embossed, Qt. 16.00
Johnstown Bottle Exchange, 5 Cents Dep., 1/2 Pt. 15.00
Jordan's Dairy Ltd., Kentville, N.S., Yellow & Black, ABM, Canada, 1940s, Qt. 30.00

Julius' Dairy, York, Penna., Julius' Milk & Ice Cream, Man & Woman, Red, Round, Qt. .   35.00
K. Yamashita Newfair Dairy, Phone 7473, 6 Rings, Embossed, Pt. 40.00
Keeler Homestead, Inc., Titicos Farm, North Salem, N.Y., Orange, Pt. 9.00
Keewadin Dairy, Tillsonburg, Swing To Our Quality Dairy Products, Orange, 1/2 Pt. . . .   20.00
Kenny's Creamery, West Rutland, Vt., Cream Top, Red, Square, Qt. 24.00
Kenolie Dairy, Newfane, Black, Square, Qt. 25.00
Kenolie Dairy, Newfane, Maroon, Square, Qt. 20.00
Keystone Dairy Goat Farm, Bridgeville, Pa., Embossed, Round, Qt. 50.00
King Farm Dairy, Rockford, Ill., Embossed, Qt. 15.00
Kishwaukee Dairy, Embossed, 1/2 Pt. . . . . .6.00 to 8.00
Kishwaukee Dairy, Embossed, Pt. 12.00
Kleen Kwality Cream, Fairbanks, Rising Sun, Red, Round, 1/4 Pt. 66.00
Klondike Farm, Elkin, N.C., Golden Guernsey Logo, Green, Round, 1/2 Pt. 25.00
Lake View Dairies Inc., Ithaca, N.Y., Star, Embossed, Lip Roll, 1/2 Pt. 22.00
Lakeview Farm Dairy, Ticonderoga, N.Y., Embossed, Round, Pt. 15.00
Lang's Creamery, Buffalo, N.Y., Green, Qt. 400.00
Lassig's Dairy, Rhinelander, Wis., Square, 1/2 Pt. 8.00
Lassig's Dairy, Rhinelander, Wis., Square, Pt. 8.00
Lassig's Dairy, Rhinelander, Wis., Square, Qt. 8.00
Lenkerbrook Farms, Red & Orange, Square, Pt. 30.00
Lewis Kelso, Louden, N.H., Embossed, Round, Qt. 18.00
Liberty Dairy, Shillington, Pa., Embossed, Qt. 30.00
Liberty Milk Co., Cumberland, Md., Embossed, Qt. 15.00
Lima Dairy, J.L. Slaughter, Danville, Va., Embossed, Qt. 32.00
Lindsay Creamery, Safford, Arizona, Burgundy & Orange, Tall Pt. 50.00
Lions Club, Your Cows Will Keep Blind Family From Want, Red Pyro, 1/2 Pt. 25.00
Little Falls Dairy Co., Qt. 14.00
Little's Dairy, Hanover, Pa., Thank You For Returning Bottles Promptly, Red Paint, Pt. .   12.00
Long Hill Farm, Leon & Roger Anstett, Goshen, Ct., Black, Round, 1/2 Pt. 15.00
Long Hill Farm, Leon & Roger Anstett, Goshen, Ct., Black, Round, Qt. 35.00
Louise Farming Company, Toccoa, Ga., Round, Slug Plate, Qt. 40.00
Lowry's Clover Hill Farm, Williamstown, Ma., Maroon, Round, Qt. 30.00
Lyon Brook Dairy, Aerated, E.L. Haynes, Tooled Mouth, Cap Seat, Metal Lid, 1/2 Pt. . .   100.00
M. & W. Dairy, Liberty Ky., Blindfolded Woman, Red, Round, Squat, Qt. 25.00
M.C. Warren & Sons Dairy, Hot Springs, Va., Embossed, Pt.   42.00
M.H. Laipson & Co., Mass., Seal, Vertical Ribs, Embossed, Tall Round, Qt. 22.00
M.P. Curry, A.V. Whiteman, T. Mfg. Co., 144 Chambers St., Wash & Return, Amethyst, Qt.   250.00
M.W. Dairy Co., New Martinsville, W.V., Qt. 30.00
Magic City Ice & Milk Co., Endicott, N.Y., Graduate Cream Top, Sunrise, Red, Qt. 95.00
Manchester Dairy, Red & Black, Round 30.00
Mansfield Caughey Co., Madison, Wis., Embossed, 1/2 Pt. 5.00
Mansfield Dairy, Stowe, Vermont, Cow Skiing, Green, Round, Qt. 195.00
Maola Milk & Ice Cream Co., New Bern, N.C., Baby Holding Bottle, Orange, Qt. 45.00
Maple Lane Dairy, LaPlume, Pa., Embossed Maple Leaf, Slug Plate, Cap, Round, Qt. . .   20.00
Maple Moor Farms, Galax, Va., Embossed, Round, Qt. 12.00
Maplewood Dairy, Fair Haven, Vt., Round, Qt. 22.00
Marion Center Creamery, Indiana, Pa., Geppetto W.D.P., 1/2 Pt. 225.00
Matanuska Maid-Pasteurized Grade A Milk, Anchorage Dairy, Orange, Round, Qt. .   92.00
McAllister's Little Farm Boy, Warren, Ohio, Farm Boy, Wagon, Red, Handle, Gal. 18.00
McVeigh Dairy Co., Stork Carrying Baby, Round, Qt. 20.00
Meadow Glen Dairy, San Francisco, Calif., Milk Builds Great Champions, Qt. 75.00
Meadow Gold, Embossed, 1/2 Pt. 8.00
Meadow View Dairy, Johnstonville, Reg. Cal., Red, Round, Qt. 25.00
Medosweet Dairies, Tacoma, Wash., Embossed, Round, Qt.   14.00
Melrose Dairy, Ormand, Fla., Milk Bottle Jumping, Blue, Tall Round, Qt. 35.00
Melville Dairy, Buy War Bonds, Airplane, Red, Round, Qt. 42.00
Merry's Dairy, Ben Avon, Penn., Superior Quality, Red & Green, Qt. . . . . *Illus*   20.00
Messer's Dairy, New London, N.H., Guernsey Milk, Round, Qt. 35.00
Metzcer's, Embossed Boy's Face, Qt. 35.00
Miller Bros. Creamery, Red, 1/2 Pt. 20.00
Miller Flounders Safe Milk, Chester, Pa., Cream Top, Aqua, Qt. 15.00
Minard & Barclay, Harbor Beach, Mich., Embossed, Round, Pt. 4.00
Minton's Dairy, New Smyrna, Fla., Emblem, 1/2 Pt. . . . . .15.00 to 25.00

Mitchel, Bridgeport, Ct., Qt. 4.00
Moanalau Dairy, Star Of Quality, Brown, Round, Pt. 35.00
Modern Dairy Products Co., Rhinelander, Wis., Pasteurized In Glass, Embossed, Qt. . 10.00
Monson Milk Co., Est. 1921, Cow & Barn Scene, Orange & Red, Round, Qt. 25.00
Mountain View Dairy, Capreol, Pasteurized Milk, Orange, Canada, 1934-1950, Qt. 160.00
Mueller Dairy, Harbor Beach, Michigan, Slug Plate, Embossed, Round, Pt. 3.00
Munson Milk Company, Embossed, Round, 1/4 Pt. 10.00
New Ulm Dairy, Minnesota, 50th Anniversary, Iwo Jima, Feb. 23, 1995, Qt. 25.00
Newson's Pride Dairy, Albany, Ga., Boxer, Black, Round, Pt. 25.00
Norris Creamery Inc., Harriman, Tennessee, Phone 330, Slug Plate, Round, Qt. 30.00
Northwestern Creamery, Ltd., Please Return Daily, Fresh Cream, Red, Canada, 1/2 Pt. 15.00
O.K. Dairy, Geo. S. Turner, Canon City, Colo., Orange, Qt. 35.00
Oak Grove Dairy Products, Jackson, Mich., Robert Jenkins, Windmill, Barn, Pt. 10.00
Oak Grove Farm, Boston, Slug Plate, Embossed, Tall Round, 1/2 Pt. 15.00
Oak Hill Dairy, Asheville, N.C., Embossed, Round, Qt. 14.00
Oakhurst Dairy Co., Bath, Me., Embossed, Round, Pt. 40.00
Old Forge Farm, Spring Grove, Pa., Forge Scene, Embossed, Qt. 30.00
Old Homestead Dairy, Windsor, Baby Face, Orange 85.00
Palm Milk & Cream, Red Circle, Green Border, Round, 1 1/2 Liter 24.00
Park Farms Milking Parlor, San Antonio, Tex., Black, Round, Qt. 45.00
Parker Pennsylvania Centennial, Ecology Flag, 9 Colors, Square, Qt. 32.00
Parker Ranch Dairy, Red, Qt. 125.00
Parkers Dairy, Nichols, Conn., Calf, My Name Is Dawn, 1/2 Pt. 8.00
Parkview Dairy, 339 Perth Ave., Slug Plate, Embossed, Round, Qt. 12.00
Parkview Woodlawn Dairies, Pt. 15.00
Patterson Bros., Grasmere Dairy, Slug Plate, Embossed, Round, Canada, 1/4 Pt. 25.00
Peckham's Dairy, North Adams, Mass., Embossed, Round, Pt. 8.50
Pensacola Dairy, Pasteurized, Ribbed, 1923, Pt. 40.00
People's Milk Company, 7078 East Ferry St., Reed, Slug Plate, Amber, Round, Qt. 53.00
People's Milk Company, New York, Amber, Round, Qt. 45.00
Perry Creamery Co., Tuscaloosa, Ala., Emblem, 1/2 Pt. 15.00
Pet Pasteurized Milk, Grade A Laboratory Controlled, Red, Square, Pt. 10.00
Phelp's Dairy, Waycross, Ga., Phone 708-J, Orange, Round, Qt. 25.00
Pilleys Fine Dairy Products, Lion On Shield, Red, Round, Qt. 22.00
Pine Grove Dairy, Skaneateles, N.Y., Pine Trees, Green & Orange, Tall Round, Qt. 28.00
Pinehurst Farms Dairy, Rockford, Illinois, Bottled On The Farm, Green, 1/2 Pt. 18.00
Pinehurst Farms Dairy, Rockford, Illinois, Embossed, Qt. 8.00
Poplar Hill Dairy, Frederick, Md., Embossed, Round, Qt. 14.00
Portland Milk Producers Assn., Red, Round, Qt. 20.00
Pratt's Dairy, Visalia, Cal., 1/4 Pt. 38.00
Premier Creamery, Coalings, Qt. 43.00
Price's Dairy, Mt. Albert, Here's To You, For Health, Happiness, Vitality, Red, 1/2 Pt. .. 15.00
Producer's Dairy, Nashua, N.H., Cream Top, Square, Qt. 30.00
Producer's Past. Milk, Greenville, Texas, Red, Qt. 85.00
Property Of Altman's Dairy, Baby Riding Stork, Cream Jar, Tooled Top, 1/2 Pt. 55.00
Puritan Dairy Farm, Decatur, Georgia, Famous For Flavor, Cow's Head, Orange, Qt. .. 12.00
Quality Control, Red & Turquoise, Qt. ....*Illus* 10.00
Queen City Dairy Inc., Cumberland, Md., Embossed Cream Top, Round, Pt. 52.00
Queen City Dairy Inc., Cumberland, Md., Embossed, 1/2 Pt. 17.00
R.A. Cook, Bridgeton, R.I., Orange, Pt. 15.00
R.L. Mathis Certified Milk, Decatur, Ga., Dacro, Orange, Square, Qt. 10.00
Ravetta Dairy, Rockford, Ill., Embossed, Qt. 18.00
Reiter & Harter All Star Dairies, Red & Blue Shield, 1/2 Gal., 10 In. ....*Illus* 15.00
Rider Dairy Co., Cream When You Want It, Hand Pouring Cream, Qt. 8.00
Rieck's Milk & Cream, Amber, Qt. 85.00
Riverdale Creamery Co., Deep Cream Line, Embossed, Qt. 30.00
Riverview Dairy, Caledonia, A.C. Phipps, Always A Hit, Baseball Player, Red, Pt. 20.00
Roanoke Dairy & Ice Cream Co., Roanoke, Va., Baby With Bottle, Black, Qt. ...24.00 to 55.00
Roberts, Leaf Design, Cream Top, Red, Square, Qt. 6.50
Robinson Dairy, Square, Qt. 10.00
Rochester Farm Pure Milk, Baby On Back, Round, Qt. 36.00
Rock Castle Heavy Whipping Cream, Lynchburg, Va., Green, Round, 1/4 Pt. 15.00
Rock River Farms, Byron, Ill., Holstein Cow, 1/2 Pt. 12.00

Milk, Merry's Dairy, Ben Avon, Penn., Superior Quality, Red & Green, Qt.

Milk, Quality Control, Red & Turquoise, Qt.

Milk, Reiter & Harter All Star Dairies, Red & Blue Shield, 1/2 Gal., 10 In.

Milk, Sealtest, Store Bottle, Red Logo, Plastic Handle, 1/2 Gal., 10 In.

Round House Dairy, A. Stewart & Son, Blue, 1/2 Pt.	10.00
Round Tree Farms, Damariscotta, Embossed, 1/2 Pt.	10.00
Royale Dairy, Hanover, Pa., Milk Products Fit-For-A-King, Crossing Guard, Qt.	25.00
Ruff's Dairy, St. Clair, Mich., Embossed, 10 Oz.	5.00
Ruff's Dairy, St. Clair, Mich., Girl, Building Blocks, Round, Qt.	8.50
S. End Dairies, Kline Bros., Cumberland, Md., Embossed, 1/2 Pt.	25.00
Sanitary Market, Bethlehem, N.H.	15.00
Saskatchewan Co-Operative Creamery Assn., Ltd., Consult Your Doctor Annually, Pt.	40.00
Saskatchewan Co-Operative Creamery Assn., Ltd., Please Return Our Bottles, 1/2 Pt.	15.00
Schmidt's Dairy, Monticello, Iowa, Embossed, 1/2 Pt.	8.00
Schoonover's Dairy, Knoxville, Pa., Orange, Round, Pt.	20.00
Scream Crest Milk Products, Troy, N.Y., Cream Top, Embossed, Qt.	35.00
Sealtest, Store Bottle, Red Logo, Plastic Handle, 1/2 Gal., 10 In. ....*Illus*	18.00
Seeger's, North Adams, Mass., Good Morning With Baby, Black, Round, 1/2 Pt.	13.00
Seely Dairy, Embossed, 1/2 Pt.	5.00
Seneca Syracuse Dairy Inc., Indian Head, Orange, Round, Pt.	22.00
Serve Producers Ice Cream, Delicious, Crawfordsville, Ind., Black, Round, Qt.	31.00
Seward Dairy, Seward, Alaska, Embossed, Round, Pt.	125.00
Seward Dairy, Seward, Alaska, Embossed, Round, Qt.	110.00
Shaker Grove Dairy, Cleveland, Ohio, Embossed, 1/2 Pt.	33.00
Shaw's Dairy, Brattleboro, Baby Face, Orange	80.00
Shrodes Dairy, N. Irwin, Pa., 1/2 Pt.	15.00
Silverwood Dairy, Cream Top, Canada, Qt.	25.00
Sky-Royal, Front Royal, Va., Sky-Line Drive, Qt.	75.00
Skyline Farms Grade A, Lincoln, Neb., Milk Bottle, Red, Round, Qt.	35.00
Slades Dairy, Santa Fe, New Mexico, Cow's Head, Qt.	40.00
Smalley, This Bottle To Be Washed & Returned, Tin Top, Metal Bands, Handle, Pt.	265.00
Smalley, Tin Top, Handle, 1/2 Gal.	120.00
Smalley, Tin Top, Handle, Pt.	135.00
Smalley, Tin Top, Handle, Qt.	95.00
Smith & McNell, Hudson, N.Y., Tooled Mouth, 1885-1900, 9 5/8 In.	55.00
Smith's Dairy, Verda, Kentucky, Pure Bred Herds, Cow & Calf, Black, Round, Qt.	50.00
Smooth Dairy Jersey Creamline Milk, Centerville, Utah, Orange, 1/2 Pt.	20.00
Snyder's Dairy, Hazelton, Pa., Red, Round, Pt.	12.00
Sokei Dairy, Kapaa, Kauai, A Business With A Heart, Orange, 1950, Pt.	40.00
Sokei Dairy, Kapaa, Kauai, A Business With A Heart, Orange, 1951, Qt.	80.00
Standard Dairy Co., Rockford, Ill., Ribbed Top, Embossed, Pt.	15.00
Star Dairy, Galveston, Texas, You Buy Only Milk In Glass, Green, Square, 1/2 Gal.	40.00
Starland Creamery, Savannah, Ga., Embossed, Round, Qt.	17.00
Statham's Dairy, Cordele, Ga., Cartoon Cow, Rhyme, Tall Round, Qt.	60.00
Stephens Bros. Dairy, Carbondale, Pa., Aqua, 1/2 Pt.	10.00

Steward's, The Best Milk, Thermopolis, Wyo., Black, Tall Round, Qt. 40.00
Stokes Northwest Dairy, Manitowoc, Wis., Milk That Is Milk, Black, Pt. 18.00
Strathroy Creamery, Embossed, Slug Plate, Round, 1/2 Pt. 8.00
Sunlight Dairy, Rockford, Ill., Embossed, 1/2 Pt. 7.00
Sunny Hill Dairy, Cape Girardeau, Mo., Red, Round, Squat, Qt.   25.00
Sunnycrest, Niagara Falls, Cop The Cream, Qt. 150.00
Sunset Milk, Tucson, Ariz., Square, Pt. 20.00
Sunshine Dairy, Peabody, Mass., Embossed, Round, Qt. 14.00
Sunshine Milk, Bridgeport, Conn., Barn Scene, Orange, Round, Qt. 24.00
Supreme, Atlanta's Finest Milk, Irvindale, Minnie, Amber, White, Square, Qt. 20.00
Swanson's Dairy, Manistee, Mich., Qt. 35.00
Sweet Jersey, Westfield, Vermont, Black, Square, Pt. 15.00
T.A. Beale & Sons, Milk & Cream, 1/2 Pt. 7.00
T.E. Horn, Raw & Pasteurized Milk, Baby With Milk Bottle, Orange, Tall Round, Qt. . . .   18.00
Terrace Farm Dairy Co., Telephone Connections, 51 In. Seal, Slug Plate, Qt. 35.00
Thatcher Farm, Milton, Cream Top, Square, Qt. 30.00
Three People's, 70-78 Ferry St., Bowling Pin, Qt. 75.00
Three People's, 70-78 Ferry Street, Amber, Qt. 55.00
Tonopah, Nevada, Tooled Top, Pt. 65.00
Tri-County, 2 Cents Deposit, Black, Square, Qt. 10.00
Tro-Fe Dairy, Gadsden, Ala., Woman In Kitchen, Food Fights Too, Red, Round, Qt. 42.00
Tulare Creamery, Tulare, Cal., 1/4 Pt. 42.00
Turner Centre System, Bottle Not Sold But Lent On Deposit, 5 Cents, Embossed, 1/2 Pt.   10.00
Two Echo Farm Dairy, H.F. Sandelin, Brunswick, Maine, Red, Round, Qt. 40.00
Uecke Dairy Co., Eau Claire, Wis., Embossed, 1/2 Pt. 12.00
Universal Store Bottle, 5 Cent, Embossed Vertical Ribbing, 1/2 Pt. 9.00
Universal Store Bottle, 5 Cent, Embossed, Qt. 15.00
University Of Georgia, George Washington, Nature's Best Food, Red, Round, Squat, Qt.   80.00
Vaca Valley Creamery, 5 Cts., Cap, Qt. 85.00
Vaca Valley Creamery, Store Bottle, Qt. 65.00
Valley Dairy, Syracuse, N.Y., Graduate Cream Top, Cup Graduations, Embossed, Qt. . . .   55.00
Van's Dairy, Hudson, N.Y., Cream Top, Embossed, Square, Qt. 35.00
Vezina Dairy, Telluride, Embossed, Qt. 45.00
Vita-Rich Goat Milk, Vita-Rich Dairy, Phoenix, Arizona, Amber, White, Square, Qt. . . .   50.00
W.H. Shipman Ltd., 6 Rings, Embossed, Pt. 150.00
W.J. Kennedy Dairy Co., Token, Baby, Pat. Sept. 22, 1925, 1/4 Pt. 400.00
W.L. Flory Dairy, Dayton, Va., Qt. 15.00
W.O. Clark, Peru, N.Y., Yellow, Round, Qt. 40.00
W.S. Fenn, Westminster, Vt., Embossed, Round, Pt. 15.00
Waihee Dairy, Quality Plus Service, Cow's Head, Red, Square, Qt. 40.00
Waihee Dairy, Quality Plus Service, Red, Square, 1956, Pt. 20.00
Waihee Dairy, Quality Plus Service, Red, Square, 1964, 1/2 Pt.   10.00
Waihee Dairy, Quality Plus Service, Red, Square, 1964, Qt. 20.00
Wakefield, Cop The Cream, Qt. 75.00
Walnut Crest Farm, Clinton F. Rines & Sons, Westbrook, Maine, Guernsey Milk, Qt. . . .   30.00
Wash & Return, Amethyst, Round Raised Panel For Label, Qt. 4.00
WAWA Dairy, Flower, Embossed, Cap, 1/2 Pt. 8.00
Weckerle, Amber, Qt. 80.00
Weckerle, Green, Qt. 525.00
Weir-Cove Dairy Co., Hollidays Cove, W. Va., Emblem, 1/2 Pt. . . . . .25.00 to 28.00
Welland Dairy, Tenpin Shape, Qt. 20.00
West Side Dairy, Ann Arbor, Mich., Orange, Round, Qt. 22.00
Western Creamery, Butte, Mont., Baby & Flower, Brown, 1/2 Pt. 28.00
Western Lynn Creamery, Embossed, Pt. 10.00
Western Maryland Dairy, Health Dept. Permit Triangle, Embossed, Pt. 10.00
Western United, Embossed, Qt. 6.00
Westmoreland, Queen Of Quality, Cow's Head, Orange, Red, Plastic Bail, Square, Gal.   45.00
Westmoreland St., 1/2 Pt. 5.00
Westmount Dairy, I.S. Higgins, Prop., W On Base, Slug Plate, Embossed, Round, 1/4 Pt.   15.00
Whartons Dairies, Escondido & Oceanside, Qt. 50.00
Whartons Dairies, Inc., Reg. Cal., Escondido, California, Round, Squat, Qt. 15.00
White Belt Dairy, Registered Standard Milk, Lemon City, Fla., Slug Plate, Round, 1/2 Pt.   35.00
White Oak Dairy, Tree, Cows, Frosted Diamond Design, Tapered, Orange, 1/2 Pt. 6.00

Willow Brook Creamery, Oakland, Cal., Pt. 30.00
Willow Brook Dairy, Mt. Vernon, N.Y., Emblem, 1/2 Pt. .25.00 to 28.00
Windale Farms, Galena, Ohio, Orange, Round, 1/2 Pt. 30.00
Wiseman Dairy, Crooksville, Ohio, Embossed, Qt. 33.00
Wm. Kelly, 1204 Pine St., Amethyst, BIMAL, Pt. 20.00
Wood's, Peterburg-Hopewell, Va., Baby Face, Orange, Square, Qt. 135.00
Woodhall's Dairy Limited, Elves Baking In Top Hat, Black, Canada, 1936-1950, Pt. . . 115.00
Worcester Farm, Keene, N.H., Red & Black, Round 30.00
Worthmore Farms, Chelmsford, Ma., Round, 1/2 Gal. 15.00
Worthmore Ice Cream Com., Lake Worth, Fla., 5 Cent Deposit, Embossed, Qt. 24.00
Wright Farm, Concord, Ma., Embossed, Round, Qt. 17.00
Yasgur Farms Dairy, Bethel, N.Y., Red, 1950s, Qt. 150.00
Yasgur Farms Dairy, Bethel, N.Y., Woodstock 25th Anniversary, Brown & Yellow, Qt. . 25.00
York Sanitary Milk Company, Amethyst, BIMAL, Pt. . . . . .25.00 to 28.00
Zenda Farms, Clayton, N.Y., 1/4 Pt. 17.00

MILK GLASS

It makes perfect sense to think that white milk-colored glass is known as *milk glass* to collectors. But not all milk glass is white, nor is all white glass milk glass, so the name may cause a little confusion.

The first true milk glass was produced in England in the 1700s. It is a semi-opaque glass, often with slight blue tones. The glass reached the height of its popularity in the United States about 1870. Many dishes and bottles were made. Both new versions of old styles and new styles have been made continuously since that time, many by the Westmoreland and the Kemple glass companies. These pieces, many very recent, often appear at antiques sales.

Westmoreland Glass Company worked from 1890 to 1984. In the early years, they made figural milk glass bottles to hold food products, especially mustard. Later they made reproductions of earlier pieces of tableware. Today it is considered correct to talk about blue milk glass or black milk glass. This is glass made by the same formula but with a color added. It is not correct to call a glass that is white only on the surface *milk glass*. Bottles made of milk glass may also be found in this book in the Cologne, Cosmetic, and Figural categories. There is a newsletter for collectors, The Original Westmoreland Glass Collector's Newsletter, P.O. Box 143, North Liberty, IA 52317.

MILK GLASS, Apothecary, W.T. Co., Opalescent, Lilacs, Flowers, Stopper, 8 1/2 In. 120.00
Apothecary, W.T. Co., Opalescent, Roses, Flowers, Stopper, 8 1/2 In. 100.00
Aromatic Salts, Baltimore, Opalescent, 1855-1865, 2 1/8 In. 165.00
Champlin's Liquid Pearl 15.00
Dresser, Victorian Girl & Puppies, Label, Stopper 140.00
Good Night, Man In Night Cap, Metal Screw Cap, 1910, 4 In. 95.00
Humpty Dumpty, Christmas 65.00
Jar, Flaccus Design, Pt. 40.00
McNeill & Libby, Chicago, 1890, 4 In. 10.00
Multicolored Floral Design, Enameled, Germany, 1778, 5 In. 500.00
Owl, Tin Screw Cover, Embossed Eagle Glass Insert, 6 In. . . . . *Illus* 70.00
S.B. Rothenberg, Applied Seal On Shoulder, 1891-1896, 7 1/2 In. 130.00

Milk Glass, Owl, Tin
Screw Cover,
Embossed Eagle Glass
Insert, 6 In.

Be sure a copy of lists of valuables, photographs, and other information can be found in case of an insurance loss. Give a copy to a trusted friend. Do not keep them in the house. If you keep them in a safe deposit box, be sure you have a key off site. The key could be lost in a house fire.

Sanitol, Blue	15.00
Sheared Ground Lip, 4 1/2 In.	7.00
Tapered Case Type, 9 1/8 In.	10.00
W.T. & Co., Rectangular, Beveled, 5 In.	15.00
World's Fair, 1939, Map Of World	35.00

MINERAL WATER

Although today it is obvious which is soda water and which is mineral water, the difference was not as clear in the nineteenth and early-twentieth centuries. Mineral water bottles held the fresh natural spring waters favored for health or taste. Even though some had a distinct sulfur or iron taste, the therapeutic values made them seem delicious. Some mineral waters had no carbonation, but many were naturally carbonated. Soda water today is made with artificial carbonation and usually has added flavor.

Mineral water was mentioned by the ancient Greeks, and the Romans wrote about visiting the famous springs of Europe. Mineral springs were often the center of resorts in nineteenth-century America, when it was fashionable to "take the waters." Often the water from the famous springs was bottled to be sold to visitors. Most of the mineral water bottles collected today date from the 1850-1900 period. Many of these bottles have embossed lettering and blob tops. The standard shape was cylindrical with thick walls to withstand the pressure of carbonation. Most were made in a snap case mold although a few can be found with open or iron pontils. Common colors are clear, pale aqua, and light green. More unusual are dark green, black, and amber bottles, while cobalt blue ones are rare. The bottles were sealed with a cork. A few places, like Poland Springs and Ballston Spa, made figural bottles. Related bottles may be found in the Seltzer and Soda categories.

MINERAL WATER, A. Bartunes & Co., 135 Dauphin St., Mobile, 1840-1850, 7 1/4 In.	2420.00
A. Dearborn & Co., N.Y., Deep Cobalt Blue, IP, 1845-1855, 7 1/4 In. ....90.00 to 110.00	
A. Hain & Son, Lebanon, Pa., Cobalt Blue, Blob Top, IP, 1855, 7 1/4 In.	275.00
A. Hain & Son, Lebanon, Pa., Sapphire Blue, Cleaned, 1855-1865, 7 3/8 In.	175.00
A. Ritter, Cincinnati, Light Green, 10-Sided, IP, Applied Mouth, 7 1/4 In.	175.00
A.D. Schnackenberg & Co., Brooklyn, N.Y., Golden Amber, Pt.	385.00
A.L. Edic, Utica Bottling Establishment, Superior, Cobalt Blue, IP, 7 1/2 In.	1150.00
A.P. Smith, Charleston, S.C., Deep Sapphire, IP, Applied Mouth, 1845-1855, 7 In.	265.00
A.P. Smith, Charleston, S.C., Medium Cobalt Blue, IP, 1845-1855, 7 1/2 In.	110.00
A.R. Cox, Norristown, Pa., Emerald Green, IP, 6 7/8 In.	175.00
A.R. Cox, Norristown, Pa., Squat	15.00
A.W. Cudworth & Co., San Francisco, Cal., Green, Embossed, 1850s	110.00
A.W. Cudworth & Co., San Francisco, Cal., Green, IP, 1859-1861, 7 1/4 In.	65.00
A.W. Cudworth & Co., San Francisco, Emerald Green, Blob Top, IP, 1861, 7 In.	120.00
A.W. Meyer, Savannah, Ga., Teal Blue, Hutchinson, 1885-1890, 7 3/8 In.	85.00
Abilena Natural Cathartic Water, Amber, Round, 1890-1900	12.00
Adirondack Spring, Westport, N.Y., Emerald Green, Qt. ....375.00 to 395.00	
Adirondack Spring, Whitehall, N.Y., Emerald Green, Pt.	315.00
Adirondack Spring, Whitehall, N.Y., Emerald Green, 1875, 10 In.	1100.00
Aetna Mineral Spouting Springs, Saratoga, N.Y., Aqua, Pt.	2550.00
Alburgh A Springs, Vt., Emerald Green, Ring Collar, Cylindrical, Qt.	120.00
Alburgh A Springs, Vt., Gold Amber, Ring Mouth, 1860-1880, Qt.	250.00
Alburgh A Springs, Vt., Golden Yellow, Cylindrical, Qt.	440.00
Alburgh A Springs, Vt., Honey Amber, Ring Mouth, Cylindrical, Qt.	605.00
Alburgh A Springs, Vt., Red Amber, Ring Collar, Qt.	275.00
Alburgh A Springs, Vt., Yellow Amber, Cylindrical, Qt.	355.00
Alburgh Springs, Vt., Apricot Amber, Cylindrical, 1860-1880, Qt.	1100.00
Alburgh Springs, Vt., Gold Yellow, Applied Mouth, Cylindrical, 1880, Qt.	880.00
Alpena Magnetic Spring Co., Red Amber, 1875-1885, Qt., 8 3/4 In.	580.00
American Mineral Water Co., S.F., Flag, Light Green, Tooled Top, 1899-1906	145.00
American Spa Spring Co., N.J., Green, Blob Top, 1870-1880, 7 1/2 In.	440.00
Armia Mineral Water, In English & Chinese, Light Emerald, Crown, 9 1/2 In.	8.00
Artesian Spring Co., Ballston Spa, N.Y., Deep Emerald Green, 1875, 8 In.	155.00
Artesian Spring Co., Ballston, N.Y., Green, Pt.	100.00
Artesian Spring Co., Ballston, N.Y., Medium Green, Applied Mouth, Pt.	80.00
Ashton Mineral Water Co., Ashton-U-Lyne, England, Green, Stopper	35.00
Avon Spring Water, Aqua, Applied Double Collar, 1865-1875, Qt., 9 5/8 In.	385.00

Avon Spring Water, Olive Green, Bubbles, 1865-1875, Qt., 9 1/2 In. 935.00
B. & G. Superior, Superior, San Francisco, 10-Sided, Peacock Blue, IP, 1852-1856 . . . . .   255.00
B. & G. Superior, San Francisco, 10-Sided Base, Cobalt Blue, IP, Saucer Top 360.00
B. & G. Superior, San Francisco, 10-Sided Base, Cobalt Blue, Mug Base, Graphite 305.00
B. & G. Superior, San Francisco, Cobalt Blue, Blob Top, IP, 1860, 6 7/8 In. 175.00
B. Bick, Cincinnati, Cobalt Blue, Blob Top, IP, 7 1/2 In. 130.00
B. Bick, Cincinnati, Cobalt Blue, IP, Applied Mouth, 7 1/2 In.   275.00
B. Bick & Co., Cincinnati, Aqua, 10-Sided, IP, Applied Mouth, 7 3/8 In. 175.00
B. Bick & Co., Cincinnati, Cobalt Blue, 10-Sided, IP, 1845-1855, 7 1/4 In. 635.00
B.R. Lippincott & Co., Stockton, Cobalt Blue, Mug Base, IP 1500.00
Babb & Co., San Francisco, Green, Applied Mouth, IP, 1845-1855, 7 3/8 In. 120.00
Backus & Pratt, Bing Hampton, N.Y., Aqua, Applied Mouth, IP, 7 3/4 In. 190.00
Ballston Spa, N.Y., Deep Blue Aqua, Applied Mouth, 1875, 7 3/4 In. 465.00
Bartlett Spring, California, Aqua, Blob Top, 12 In. 25.00
Bear Spring Water, Walking Bear, Aqua, Tooled Blob Top, Closure, 10 1/2 In. 125.00
Blount Springs, Natural Sulphur Water, BS, Trademark, Cobalt Blue, 7 3/8 In. . . .70.00 to 100.00
Blount Springs, Natural Sulphur Water, Cobalt Blue, 9 In. 185.00
Blount Springs, Natural Sulphur Water, Trademark, Cobalt Blue 130.00
Blue Lick Co., Ky., Deep Emerald Green, IP, 1850-1865, 8 In. 2200.00
Blue Lick Water Co., Ky., Deep Blue Green, Applied Mouth, IP, 1865, 8 In. 685.00
Boardman, Deep Sapphire Blue, Red IP, Applied Mouth, 1855, 7 1/4 In. 210.00
Bolen Waack & Co., New York, Emerald Green, Saratoga Type, 1/2 Pt., 6 3/4 In. 120.00
Boley & Co., Sac City, Cal., Cobalt Blue, 1850-1862, IP 165.00
Boley & Co., Sac City, Cal., Union Glass Works, Philad., Small C, Cobalt Blue, IP 220.00
Boley & Co., Sac. City, Cal., Cobalt Blue, Large C In Sac, IP, 7 1/4 In. 255.00
Boston & Co., London, Deep Olive Amber, 1820-1830, 6 5/8 In. 635.00
Buffalo Lithia, Medium Emerald Green, Applied Mouth, 1885-1895, 9 5/8 In. 275.00
Buffalo Lithia, Nature's Materia Medica Trademark, Blue Green, 1/2 Gal. 200.00
Buffalo Lithia, Woman, Seated Holding Pitcher, Blue, Green, Disc, 1885, 10 In. 255.00
Buffalo Lithia Spring Water, Virginia, Blue Green, Cylindrical, 9 1/4 In. 495.00
Buffums Porter, Aqua Green, Blob Top, IP, 7 3/8 In. 45.00
Byron Acid Spring Water, Medium Blue Green, Sloping Collar, Ring, IP, Qt. 2310.00
C. Clark, Deep Emerald Green, IP, Applied Mouth, 1845-1855, 7 1/4 In. 230.00
C. Clark, Deep Olive Amber, Applied Sloping Collar Mouth, 1855, 7 1/8 In. 175.00
C. Cleminshaw, Troy, N.Y., Teal Blue, IP, 1845-1860, 1/2 Pt., 4 5/8 In. . . . . .150.00 to 200.00
C. Lomax Congress Water, Chicago, Cobalt Blue, IP, Blob Mouth, 7 In. 205.00
C. Snider, J. Konig & Co., Fulton, Aqua, Blob Top, 1855, IP, 7 3/8 In. 230.00
C.A. Cole, Baltimore, Md., Yellow Olive, Squat, 1845-1860, 7 1/2 In. 935.00
C.A. Cole, C.F. Brown, Baltimore, Sapphire Blue, Ten-Pin, 8 1/2 In. 230.00
C.A. Reiners, 723 Turk St., S.F., Improved, Moon, Stars, Aqua, 1875-1882 . . . .   55.00
C.A. Reiners & Co., San Francisco, Improved, Moon, Stars, Blue Aqua, 1873-1875 . . . .   525.00
C.B. Owen & Co. Bottlers, Cincinnati, Sapphire Blue, IP, 7 5/8 In. . . . . .85.00 to 175.00
C.W. Weston & Co., Saratoga, N.Y., X On Base, Deep Olive Green, 1860s, Pt. 100.00
Caladonia Spring, Wheelock, Vt., Gold Amber, Applied Mouth, 1860-1880 . . . .   140.00
Caladonia Spring, Wheelock, Vt., Medium Yellow Amber, Qt. 195.00
Caladonia Spring, Wheelock, Vt., Yellow Amber, Olive Tone, Qt. 495.00
Cambridge Springs, Jug, Miniature 110.00
Cape Cod Pilgrim Mineral Spring Co., South Wellfleet, Mass. 5.00
Carl H. Schultz, Aerated Distilled Water, Aqua, 6 Pt. 40.00
Castalian Springs, Amber, Pt. 20.00
Catell's Superior, 10-Sided, Sapphire Blue, IP, 1845-1855, 6 In. 1595.00
Ch. Gloeser, Phila., Deep Blue Green, IP, Slug Plate, 1845-1855, 7 3/8 In. 275.00
Chalybeate Water, American Spa Spring Co., Blue Green, Pt. . . . . .440.00 to 495.00
Champion Spouting Spring, Saratoga Springs, N.Y., CSS On Reverse, Aqua, Pt. 485.00
Champion Spouting Spring, Saratoga, N.Y., Aqua, Pt. . . . . .375.00 to 395.00
Champion Spouting Spring, Saratoga, N.Y., Blue Aqua, 1875, 8 In. 70.00
Champion Spouting Spring Co., Saratoga Springs, N.Y., Aqua, Pt. 445.00
Champlain Spring, Alkaline Chalybeate, Forest Green, 1860-1880, Qt. 200.00
Champlain Spring, Alkaline Chalybeate, Highgate, Vt., Emerald Green, Qt. . . . .275.00 to 290.00
Champlain Spring, Highgate, Vt., Emerald Green, 1860-1880, Qt. 230.00
Champlain Spring, Highgate, Vt., Emerald Green, 1870-1880, Qt. 80.00
Champlain Spring, Highgate, Vt., Emerald Green, Applied Mouth, Qt. 220.00
Charles Clark, Charleston, S.C., Deep Cobalt Blue, IP, 1845-1855, 7 In. 470.00

Charles Clark, Charleston, S.C., Green, Applied Mouth, IP, 1845-1855, 7 3/4 In. 120.00
Chase & Co., San Francisco, Cal., Emerald Green, 1853-1855, IP 75.00
Chase & Co., San Francisco, Stockton, Marysville, Cal., Green, IP, 7 1/4 In. 550.00
Chemung Spring Water, Indian At Well, Rocks, Trees, Yellow Amber, 1/2 Gal. 395.00
Clarke & Co., New York, Blue Green, IP, 1850-1860, 7 3/4 In. ....140.00 to 385.00
Clarke & Co., New York, Forest Green, Pontil, Qt. 190.00
Clarke & Co., New York, Forest Green, Pt. ....180.00 to 190.00
Clarke & Co., New York, Olive Amber, Applied Mouth, 1840-1860, Qt. 185.00
Clarke & Co., New York, Olive Green, Ring Collar, Cylindrical, Qt. 100.00
Clarke & Co., New York, X On Base, Deep Olive Green, Pt. 75.00
Clarke & Co., New York, Yellow Olive Amber, Sloping Double Collar, Pt., 7 5/8 In. 50.00
Clarke & Co., New York, Yellow Olive, Cylindrical, 1860-1880, Qt. 180.00
Clarke & White, C, New York, 5 On Base, Olive Green, Pt. 45.00
Clarke & White, C, New York, Dark Green, Qt. 65.00
Clarke & White, C, New York, Dark Olive Green ....65.00 to 75.00
Clarke & White, C, New York, Dark Yellow Olive, Cylindrical, Qt. 45.00
Clarke & White, C, New York, Deep Olive, Bubbles, Qt. 70.00
Clarke & White, C, New York, Forest Green, Pt. ....70.00 to 75.00
Clarke & White, C, New York, Olive Green, Qt. 70.00
Clarke & White, C, New York, Olive Green, Sloping Collared Mouth, 1860, Qt. 55.00
Clarke & White, New York, Deep Emerald Green, Applied Top, Qt. 55.00
Clarke & White, New York, Olive Green, Applied Top, Pt. 55.00
Clarke & White, New York, Olive Green, Pontil, 1855-1865, Qt. 100.00
Clarke & White, New York, Yellow Olive Amber, OP, Pt. 150.00
Clarke & White, New York, Yellow Olive, Applied Collar Mouth, Qt. 100.00
Clarke & White, New York, Yellow Olive, Cylindrical, Collared Mouth, Qt. 65.00
Clarke & White, Olive Green, Pt. 45.00
Clarke & White, Olive Green, Qt. ....50.00 to 60.00
Congress & Empire Spring Co., C, Saratoga, N.Y., Yellow Olive, Ring, Qt. 220.00
Congress & Empire Spring Co., E, Empire Water, Emerald Green, Qt. 130.00
Congress & Empire Spring Co., E, Saratoga, N.Y., Deep Olive Green, 1875 .... 55.00
Congress & Empire Spring Co., E, Saratoga, N.Y., Golden Amber, Ring, Qt. 470.00
Congress & Empire Spring Co., E, Saratoga, N.Y., Olive Green, Pt., 7 3/4 In. 140.00
Congress & Empire Spring Co., E, Saratoga, N.Y., Olive Green, Ring Mouth, Qt. 305.00
Congress & Empire Spring Co., E, Saratoga, N.Y., Yellow Olive, Ring Mouth, Pt. 415.00
Congress & Empire Spring Co., Hotchkiss' Sons, C, Forest Green, Ring, Qt. 175.00
Congress & Empire Spring Co., Hotchkiss' Sons, C, Light Yellow Olive, Pt. 145.00
Congress & Empire Spring Co., Hotchkiss' Sons, C, Medium Olive Yellow, Pt. 240.00
Congress & Empire Spring Co., Hotchkiss' Sons, C.W., Dense Olive Green, Pt. 100.00
Congress & Empire Spring Co., Hotchkiss' Sons, C.W., Emerald Green, Qt. 135.00
Congress & Empire Spring Co., Hotchkiss' Sons, C.W., Olive Green, Ring, 1/2 Pt. ... 415.00
Congress & Empire Spring Co., Hotchkiss' Sons, E, Golden Amber, Pt. 525.00
Congress & Empire Spring Co., Hotchkiss' Sons, E, Yellow Olive, Ring, Qt. 470.00
Congress & Empire Spring Co., Hotchkiss' Sons, Emerald Green, 1/2 Pt. 470.00
Congress & Empire Spring Co., Hotchkiss' Sons, Emerald Green, Pt. 25.00
Congress & Empire Spring Co., Hotchkiss' Sons, Emerald Green, Qt. ....45.00 to 85.00
Congress & Empire Spring Co., Hotchkiss' Sons, New York, Honey Yellow, Pt. 465.00
Congress Spring Co., Saratoga, N.Y., Emerald Green, Ring Collar, Cylindrical, Qt. 65.00
Congress Spring Co., Saratoga, N.Y., Yellow Green, 1870-1885, Pt. 60.00
Cooper's Well Water, Miss., Orange Amber, Double Collar, Pt., 8 In. 130.00
Cooper's Well Water, Miss., Orange Amber, Double Collar, Qt., 9 5/8 In. 120.00
Cooper's Well Water, Miss., Red Amber, Applied Mouth, 1870-1880, 9 3/4 In. 165.00
Cosgrove & Kernan, Charleston, S.C., Deep Blue Green, IP, 1845-1855, 7 In. 200.00
Cottle, Post & Co., Portland, Ore., Eagle, Outstretched Wings, Teal, 1887, 7 In. 440.00
Coxe & McPherson, New Orleans, La., Light Yellow Green, IP, 1855, 7 In. 825.00
Coxe & McPherson, New Orleans, Light Yellow Green, IP, 1845-1855, 7 1/2 In. 550.00
Crane & Brigham, San Francisco, Cal., Yellow Olive, Amber Hue, 1890, 10 In. 800.00
Curo Mineral Springs, South Omaha, Neb., Aqua, Light Haze, Hutchinson 12.00
D.A. Knowlton, Saratoga, N.Y., Deep Olive Green, High Shoulders, Qt. 220.00
D.A. Knowlton, Saratoga, N.Y., Forest Green, High Shoulders, Qt. 220.00
D.A. Knowlton, Saratoga, N.Y., Green, Applied Top, Qt. 65.00
D.A. Knowlton, Saratoga, N.Y., Olive Green, Cylindrical, Qt. 85.00
D.A. Knowlton, Saratoga, N.Y., Olive Green, Ring Collar, Cylindrical, 1880, Pt. 70.00

D.A. Knowlton, Saratoga, N.Y., Olive Green, Sloping Collar, Ring, Pt. 175.00
D.A. Knowlton, Saratoga, N.Y., Yellow Olive, Cylindrical, Qt. 205.00
Darien Mineral Springs, Tifft & Perry, Darien Centre, N.Y., Aqua, Pt. 550.00
Dawson & Blackman, Charleston, S.C., Deep Cobalt Blue, IP, 1845-1855, 7 In. 550.00
Dawson & Blackman, Charleston, S.C., Medium Teal, IP, Blob Mouth, 8 In. 825.00
Deep Rock Spring, Oswego, N.Y., Blue Aqua, Monogram, 1880, 7 3/4 In. 85.00
Dove & Co., Richmond, Va., Blue Aqua, Applied Disc Mouth, 1865, 9 1/4 In. 135.00
Dr. Thornton, Superior, Lewisburg, Pa., Cobalt Blue, Blob Top, IP, 6 3/4 In. 740.00
Drink Howe's Distilled Water, Be On The Safe Side, Green, 5 Gal. 40.00
E.W. Reynal, Troy, N.Y., Sapphire Blue, Blob Top, 1855-1865, 7 3/8 In. 850.00
Electrical Febrifuge, A. Kendall Co., New Orleans, Aqua, 8-Sided, OP, 4 In. 145.00
Empire Spring Co., E, Saratoga, N.Y., Emerald Green, Sloping Collar, Ring, Pt. 145.00
Empire Spring Co., E, Saratoga, N.Y., Emerald Green, Sloping Shoulders, Qt. ....80.00 to 92.00
Empire Spring Co., Emerald Green, Qt. 45.00
Excelsior Spring, 8-Sided, Emerald Green, Blob Top, IP, 1855, 7 In. 330.00
Excelsior Spring, Saratoga, N.Y., Emerald Green, Pt. 50.00
Excelsior Spring, Saratoga, N.Y., Teal Blue, Applied Mouth, 1880, 8 In. 190.00
Excelsior Spring, Saratoga, N.Y., Yellow Green, 1885, 10 1/8 In. 205.00
Excelsior Spring, Saratoga, N.Y., Yellow Olive Green, 1875, 7 5/8 In. 135.00
Excelsior Spring, Saratoga, N.Y., Yellow Olive Green, 1880, 7 3/4 In. 70.00
Excelsior Springs, Mo., Jug, Gray, Stoneware, Bail Handle, Qt. 255.00
F. Gleason, Rochester, N.Y., 10-Pin Shape, Blue Aqua, Collar Mouth, 8 1/4 In. 175.00
F. Gleason, Rochester, N.Y., 10-Pin Shape, Sapphire Blue, Outside Stained, 1860, 8 In. .. 800.00
F. Scrader, Scranton, Pa., Medium Blue Green, IP, Blob Mouth, 1855, 7 In. 685.00
Farrel & Co., Evansville, Ice Blue, IP, Blob Mouth, 1845-1855, 7 3/8 In. 795.00
Friederich Rau, Phila., Deep Emerald Green, IP, Applied Mouth, 1855, 7 In. 95.00
Frost's Magnetic Spring, Eaton Rapids, Mich., Blue Aqua, Qt., 9 1/2 In. ......230.00 to 415.00
G. Ebberwein, Savannah Ga., Aqua, Monogram, Blob Top 20.00
G.A. Kohl, Lambertville, N.J., Deep Emerald Green, IP, 1845-1855, 7 1/8 In. 80.00
G.A. Kohl, Lambertville, N.J., Emerald Green, Blob Top, IP, 7 5/8 In. 165.00
G.P. Fey & Co., Green Aqua, 10-Sided, Pontil, Applied Mouth, 7 3/8 In. 200.00
G.W. Weston & Co., Saratoga, N.Y., Deep Olive Green, Qt. 140.00
G.W. Weston & Co., Saratoga, N.Y., Medium Yellow Olive, Pontil, Qt. ....100.00 to 120.00
G.W. Weston & Co., Saratoga, N.Y., Yellow Olive, Cylindrical, 1860, Pt. 415.00
Geo. Eagle, Twisted Rib Around Whole Bottle, Blue Green, 1845-1855, 7 In. 635.00
Gettysburg Katalysine Water, Emerald Green, Qt. ....60.00 to 110.00
Gettysburg Katalysine Water, Gettysburg, Pa., Teal, Embossed G.K.W., Qt. 100.00
Gettysburg Katalysine Water, Olive Green, Partial Label, Qt. 100.00
Gettysburg Katalysine Water, Yellow Green, Ring Mouth, Cylindrical, Qt. 70.00
Gettysburg Katalysine Water, Yellow Olive, 1866-1870, Qt. 260.00
Geyser Spring, Saratoga Springs, N.Y., Deep Blue Aqua, 1875, 7 3/4 In. 60.00
Geyser Spring, Spouting Springs, Saratoga, Aqua, Pt. 85.00
Gossmann & Verhage, Cincinnati, G & V, Blue Aqua, 10-Sided, IP, 7 1/4 In. 210.00
Great Radium Spring Water Co., Pittsfield, Mass., Ice Blue, 10 In. 25.00
Guilford Mineral Spring Water, Guilford, Vt., Blue Green, 1880, Qt. 330.00
Guilford Mineral Spring Water, Guilford, Vt., Forest Green, Ring Mouth, Qt. ....90.00 to 155.00
Guilford Mineral Spring Water, Guilford, Vt., Medium Olive Green, Qt. 55.00
Guilford Mineral Spring Water, Guilford, Vt., Yellow Green, Cylindrical, Qt. ..80.00 to 110.00
Guilford Mineral Spring Water, Guilford, Vt., Yellow Olive, Ring Mouth, Qt. ..385.00 to 520.00
H. Borgman, Cumberland, Md., 10-Pin, Blue Green, IP, 8 1/2 In. 1320.00
H. Verhage, Cincinnati, Ohio, Light Cobalt Blue, Applied Mouth, 7 3/8 In. 165.00
Haskin's Spring Co., H, Shutesbury, Mass., Emerald Green, Pt., 7 3/8 In. 100.00
Haskin's Spring Co., Shutesbury, Mass., Green, 1885, 8 3/8 In. 275.00
Hathorn Spring, Black Amber, Qt. 60.00
Hathorn Spring, Emerald Green, Pt. ....35.00 to 45.00
Hathorn Spring, Saratoga, N.Y., Amber, Applied Top, Qt. 45.00
Hathorn Spring, Saratoga, N.Y., Black, Pt. 60.00
Hathorn Spring, Saratoga, N.Y., Deep Emerald Green, Qt. 95.00
Hennessey & Nolan, Albany, N.Y., Deep Red Amber, 1855-1870, Pt. 80.00
Henry Winkle, Sac. City, Light Green, Graphite, IP, 1850s 190.00
Highrock Congress Spring, 1767, C & W, Saratoga, N.Y., Golden Amber, Pt. ...315.00 to 330.00
Highrock Congress Spring, 1767, C & W, Saratoga, N.Y., Yellow Brown, Pt. 240.00
Highrock Congress Spring, C & W, Saratoga, N.Y., Light Yellow Olive, Ring, Pt. 385.00

Highrock Congress Spring, C & W, Saratoga, N.Y., Medium Olive Green, Pt. 210.00
Highrock Congress Spring, C & W, Saratoga, N.Y., Teal Blue, Pt., 7 3/4 In. . . . .440.00 to 875.00
Highrock Congress Spring, C & W, Saratoga, N.Y., Yellow Green, Ring, Pt. 265.00
Highrock Congress Spring, Saratoga, N.Y., Gold Yellow, Ring Mouth, Pt. 240.00
Highrock Congress Spring, Saratoga, N.Y., Yellow Amber, Pt. 265.00
Highrock Congress Spring, Saratoga, N.Y., Yellow Olive Green, 8 In. . . . . .165.00 to 230.00
Highrock Congress Spring, Teal Blue, 1860-1880, Qt. 660.00
Hoffman & Berry, Phila., Deep Blue Green, IP, Slug Plate, 7 In. 185.00
Hopkins Chalybeate, Baltimore, Dense Amber, IP, Pt. 140.00
Hopkins Chalybeate, Baltimore, Olive Amber, Sloping Double Collar, IP, 7 In. 155.00
Hopkins Chalybeate Water, Baltimore, Yellow Green, IP, Pt. 150.00
Howell & Smith, Buffalo, N.Y., Sapphire Blue, IP, 1855, 7 1/2 In. 165.00
Hulshizer & Co. Premium, Emerald Green, 8-Sided, IP, 1845-1855, 7 1/2 In. 770.00
Humboldt Artesian, Eureka, Cal., Blue Aqua, Tooled Lip, 1897, 6 7/8 In. 65.00
Iodine Spring, Vt., Brilliant Gold Amber, 1860-1880, Qt. 1320.00
J. & A. Dearborn, N.Y., Cobalt Blue, Blob Top, IP, 6 7/8 In. 135.00
J. & A. Dearborn, N.Y., Philada., Cobalt Blue, Blob Top, IP, 7 1/4 In. 120.00
J. & A. Dearborn, New York, Cobalt Blue, 8-Sided, IP, 1845-1855, 7 In. 275.00
J. & A. Dearborn, New York, Star, Sapphire Blue, 8-Sided, Blob Top, IP, 6 7/8 In. 220.00
J. & A. Dearborn, New York, Star, Sapphire Blue, 8-Sided, Blob Top, IP, 7 In. 75.00
J. Boardman, New York, Cobalt Blue, 8-Sided, Applied Mouth, 7 3/8 In. 190.00
J. Bodine & Sons, Deep Blue Green, IP, Applied Mouth, 1855, 7 1/4 In. 305.00
J. Cosgrove, Charleston, S.C., Aqua, Blob Top, 1855-1870, 7 1/4 In. 100.00
J. Dowdall, Phila., Superior, Cobalt Blue, Mug Base, Blob Top, IP, 1855, 7 1/2 In. 205.00
J. Lamppin, Utica Bottling Establishment, Cobalt Blue, Blob Top, IP, 6 7/8 In. 440.00
J. McLaughlin, Phila., Deep Emerald Green, IP, Slug Plate, 1855, 6 1/2 In. 120.00
J. Postell, Cincinnati, P, Green Aqua, 10-Sided, IP, Applied Mouth, 7 1/2 In. 185.00
J. Price's, Improved, Light Blue Green, Rolled Lip, Pontil, 1855, 7 3/4 In. 155.00
J. Reynolds & Co., Philadelphia, Emerald Green, OP, 1855, 6 7/8 In. 330.00
J. Reynolds Bottlers, Phila., Deep Blue Green, IP, Slug Plate, 1855, 7 1/8 In. 130.00
J. Simonds, Boston, Medium Green, Applied Mouth, IP, 1855, 7 1/8 In. 60.00
J. Sloan, Phila., Medium Blue Green, IP, Slug Plate, 1845-1855, 7 In. 130.00
J. Steel, Easton, Pa., Cobalt Blue, IP, Applied Mouth, 1845-1855, 7 1/4 In. 120.00
J.A. Farrell, Grass Valley-F, Deep Aqua, Green Tone, Blob Top, 1867, 7 In. 80.00
J.A. Lomax, Chicago, B.F.G. Co., Cobalt Blue, Blob Top, 1875, 6 7/8 In. 65.00
J.H. Yale, Middletown, Conn., Cobalt Blue, Blob Top, IP, 1855, 7 1/4 In. 670.00
J.M. Flurshut, Torpedo, Light Blue Green, Sloping Collar Mouth, 1850, 9 In. 1540.00
J.N. Gerdes, S.F., Aqua, 8-Sided 40.00
J.N. Gerdes, S.F., Light Aqua, 8-Sided, Applied Top, 1873-1877 . . . . 110.00
J.R. Donaldson, Newark, N.J., Superior, Reverse J, 10-Sided Mug Base, Blue, IP 200.00
James L. Bispham, Philada., Teal Blue, 8 1/4 In. 65.00
Jean Hornig, Danbury, Conn., Honey Amber, Tooled Mouth, 1890, 7 3/4 In. 50.00
John Clark, New York, 3-Piece Mold, Olive Amber, Pontil, Qt. 150.00
John Clarke, Deep Olive Amber, Pontil, 1855-1865, Pt. 145.00
John Clarke, N.Y., Olive Amber, Applied Mouth, Pontil, 1860, Qt. 110.00
John Clarke, New York, Dark Olive Amber, Cylindrical, Qt. . . . . .55.00 to 100.00
John Clarke, Yellow Olive, Cylindrical, Qt. 415.00
John Ogden's, Pittsburg, Aqua, IP 150.00
John Ryan, Excelsior, Savannah, Ga., 1859, Cobalt Blue, Blob Top, 7 1/8 In. . . . .105.00 to 120.00
John Ryan, Excelsior, Savannah, Ga., Medium Cobalt Blue, Blob Top, 7 In. 135.00
John Ryan, Excelsior, Union Glass Works, Sapphire Blue, IP, Blob Top 95.00
John S. Baker, 8-Sided, Blue Aqua, IP, 1840-1855, 7 1/2 In. 135.00
Johnston, Philadelphia, Green, IP 50.00
Keach, Torpedo, Deep Green, Applied Sloping Collar Mouth, 1850, 8 1/2 In. 855.00
Kissingen Water, Hanbury Smith, Olive Green, 1/2 Pt. 55.00
Kissingen Water, Hanbury Smith, Yellow Olive, Sloping Collar, 1/2 Pt. 145.00
Kissingen Water, Patterson & Brazeau, Olive Green, Cylindrical, Pt. 145.00
Kissingen Water, The Spa, Phila., Amber, 1870-1880, 7 3/4 In. 155.00
L. Fisher, Phila., Deep Blue Green, IP, 1845-1855, 7 1/4 In. 130.00
L. Gahre, Bridgeton, Medium Emerald Green, Blob Top, 1860, 7 1/4 In. 140.00
Lake Como, Lithia Water, Richmond, Va., Aqua, Applied Square Collar, 1/2 Gal. 230.00
Langley & Michael's, San Francisco, Aqua, Florida Water, 8 3/4 In. 25.00
Langley & Michael's, San Francisco, Florida Water, Aqua 25.00

Lansing Mineral & Magnetic Well, Amber, High Shoulder, 9 3/4 In.	440.00
Lippencott & Vaughn, Stockton, 1852-1857, Cleaned	165.00
Lithia Mineral Spring Co., Gloversville, Blue Aqua, 1865-1880, Pt.	825.00
Litton's, Healdsburg, Light Blue Green, Applied Top, 1870s	360.00
Liverpool Mineral Water Co., Ltd., Blue Aqua, Crown Top, BIMAL	15.00
Lover's Leap Spring Water Co., Trademark Purity, Lynn, Mass., U.S.A., Crown Top . .	12.00
Lynch & Clarke, N.Y., Deep Olive Amber, Applied Mouth, 1865, 8 In.	1815.00
Lynch & Clarke, N.Y., Deep Yellow Olive Amber, Pontil, 1865, 7 In.	230.00
Lynch & Clarke, N.Y., Yellow Olive, Applied Mouth, 1840-1860, Pt.	300.00
Lynch & Clarke, Yellow Olive, Pt.	40.00
Lynde & Putnam, San Francisco, Blue Green, Blob Top, IP, 1860, 7 1/8 In.	205.00
Lynde & Putnam, San Francisco, Cal., Cobalt Blue, c.1850	305.00
Lynde & Putnam, San Francisco, Cal., Teal Green, Blob Top, Graphite Pontil	275.00
Lynde & Putnam, San Francisco, Union Glass Works, Aqua, IP, 7 In.	130.00
Lyon's Powder, B. & P., N.Y., Medium Red Puce, OP, 1845-1855, 4 3/8 In.	100.00
M. & J.S. Perrine Importers, Phila., Pa., Orange Amber, 1855-1865, Qt.	855.00
M. Altenbaugh's, Pittsbg., 10 Panels, Medium Blue Aqua, Blob Top, IP, 8 In.	220.00
M.T. Crawford, Hartford, Conn., Deep Sapphire Blue, IP, 1845-1860, 1/2 Pt.	470.00
M.T. Crawford, Hartford, Ct., Cobalt Blue, Cylindrical, Mug, IP, 1845, 1/2 Pt.	175.00
M.T. Crawford, Hartford, Ct., Cobalt Blue, Mug Base, Blob Top, IP, 7 1/2 In.	415.00
M.T. Crawford, Springfield, Cobalt Blue, Cylindrical, Mug Base, IP, 1/2 Pt.	415.00
M.T. Quinan, Savannah, Ga., Deep Cobalt Blue, Tooled Mouth, 1885, 8 In.	80.00
Magnetic Spring, Henniker, N.H., Gold Yellow, Red Amber, 1880, Qt.	550.00
Massena Spring Water, Gold Amber, Tooled Mouth, 1880-1890, Qt.	130.00
Massena Spring Water, Golden Yellow Amber, Qt., 1885-1895, 9 7/8 In.	200.00
Massena Spring Water, Monogram, Teal Blue, 1875-1890, Qt.	175.00
McEwin, San Francisco, Cal., 10-Sided, Blue Aqua, 1863-1870, 6 7/8 In.	120.00
McKinney & Co., Phila., Medium Teal Blue, IP, Applied Mouth, 1855, 7 In.	120.00
Middletown Healing Springs, Grays & Clark, Middletown, Vt., Amber, 9 In.	55.00
Middletown Healing Springs, Light Gold Amber, 1860, Pt.	85.00
Middletown Healing Springs, Middletown, Vt., Apricot Amber, Qt.	660.00
Middletown Healing Springs, Middletown, Vt., Emerald Green, Qt.	825.00
Middletown Healing Springs, Middletown, Vt., Yellow Amber, Qt.	155.00
Middletown Healing Springs, Vt., Yellow Apricot Amber, 1880, Qt.	1320.00
Middletown Mineral Spring Co., Middletown, Vt., Blue Green, Ring Mouth, Qt.	430.00
Middletown Mineral Spring Co., Middletown, Vt., Emerald Green, Qt.	275.00
Milton Aerated Water Works, Queens Co., N.S., Aqua, Codd Stopper, 8 In.	105.00
Minnehaha Natural Springs, Light Aqua, 13 1/2 In. . . . . *Illus*	50.00
Missisquoi A Springs, Apricot Amber, Applied Mouth, 1860-1880, Qt.	165.00
Missisquoi A Springs, Gold Amber, Applied Mouth, 1880, Qt.	110.00
Missisquoi A Springs, Olive Green, Yellow Tone, Magnum	135.00
Missisquoi A Springs, Olive Yellow, Cylindrical, Ring Mouth, Qt.	385.00
Missisquoi A Springs, Reverse Indian Squaw, Ground Outside Oval, Green, Qt.	660.00
Missisquoi A Springs, Squaw & Papoose, Yellow Green, 1880, Qt.	770.00
Missisquoi A Springs, Squaw With Papoose, Yellow, Lime Green, Qt.	140.00
Missisquoi A Springs, Yellow Olive, Cylindrical, 1880, Qt.	100.00
Missisquoi A Springs, Yellow Olive, Sloping Mouth, 1880, Qt. . . . . .55.00 to 75.00	
Mohican Spring Water, Aqua, BIMAL, 9 In.	20.00
Mountain Valley, Painted Print Design, Residue Inside, 2 Qt.	15.00
Mt. Tamalpais Natural Mineral Water Co., Light Blue Aqua, Tooled Top, 1906	470.00
Oak Orchard, Acid Springs, G.W. Merchant, Lockport, N.Y., Emerald Green, Qt. 100.00 to 120.00	
Oak Orchard, Acid Springs, Lockport, N.Y., Blue Green, 1855-1870, 9 1/4 In.	45.00
Oak Orchard, Acid Springs, Lockport, N.Y., Green, 1875, 9 In.	85.00
Ogden & Gibson, Pittsburgh, Blue Aqua, Blob Top, IP, 7 In.	30.00
P. Babb, Baltimore, Md., Blue Green, IP, 1845-1855, 8 1/4 In.	495.00
P. Latterner, Cincinnati, Light Blue Green, 12-Sided, IP, 1845-1855, 7 1/2 In.	120.00
Pacific Congress Water, Aqua, Applied Top, 1869-1876	65.00
Pacific Congress Water, Blue Green, Blob Top, 1869-1876, 7 In.	90.00
Pacific Congress Water, P. Caduc, Aqua, Applied Top	55.00
Pacific Congress Water, Sage's Pacific, Running Deer, Emerald Green, 8 In.	990.00
Pacific Congress Water, Saratoga, California, Deer, Olive, Pt.	4400.00
Pavilion & United States Spring Co., Saratoga, N.Y., Emerald Green, Pt.	210.00
Philip Young & Co., Savannah, Ga., Eagle & Shield, Teal Blue, 8 In.	550.00

Poland Mineral Springs Water, Aqua, Moses, 1880-1890, 11 In. 180.00
Poland Water, H. Ricker & Sons Proprietors, Blue Aqua, 1875, 11 1/8 In. 80.00
Poland Water, H. Ricker & Sons, Moses, Light Honey Amber, 11 In. 305.00
Poland Water, Lime Green, Screw Top, ABM, 6 In. 125.00
Poland Water, Moses, Aqua, Applied Top 120.00
R.K. Duffield, Philadelphia, Pa., Emerald Green, IP, Qt. 230.00
R.P.T.L., Blue Green, Applied Mouth, IP, 1845-1855, 6 7/8 In. 910.00
Rice & McKinney, Philada, Aqua, Blob Top, IP, Squat 40.00
Rice & McKinney, Philada, Light Green, Applied Top, IP 50.00
Rock Spring, Oswego, N.Y., Apple Green, Cylindrical, Qt. 495.00
Rock Spring, Oswego, N.Y., Aqua, Cylindrical, Pt. 230.00
Rock Spring, Oswego, N.Y., Reddish Amber, Cylindrical, 1860, Pt. 145.00
Rockbridge Alum Water, Rockbridge Co., Va., Aqua, 1/2 Gal. 85.00
Roussel's, Green, IP 45.00
Roussel's, Silver Medal 1847 Awarded, Emerald Green, IP, 7 3/8 In. 130.00
Royal Springs Table Water, Aqua, 1/2 Gal. 25.00
Rutherford's Premium, Cincinnati, Cobalt Blue, 10-Sided, IP, 1845-1855, 7 1/4 In. ... 330.00
Rutherford's Premium, Cincinnati, Deep Ice Blue, 10-Sided, IP, 7 1/4 In. 204.00
Rutherford's Premium, Cincinnati, Sapphire Blue, 10-Sided, IP, 7 3/8 In. 525.00
S. Smith, Auburn, N.Y., Cobalt Blue, 10-Sided, Blob Top, IP, 1855, 7 1/8 In. 300.00
S. Smith, Auburn, N.Y., Sapphire Blue, 10-Sided, Blob Top, IP, 1856, 7 3/8 In. 230.00
S. Smith, Auburn, N.Y., Sapphire Blue, Blob Top, IP, 7 1/2 In. 385.00
Saint Leon Spring Water, Earl W. Johnson, Boston, Mass., Blue Green, Pt. 500.00
Saratoga A Spring Co., N.Y., Jet Black, Pt. ....280.00 to 335.00
Saratoga A Spring Co., N.Y., Yellow Green, Pt. ....245.00 to 260.00
Saratoga High Rock Spring, Saratoga, N.Y., Medium Green, 1880, Pt. 935.00
Saratoga Red Spring, 5-Pointed Star, Red Amber, 1865-1875, Qt. 90.00
Saratoga Red Spring, Deep Blue Green, 1865-1875, Qt. 110.00
Saratoga Red Spring, Emerald Green, Applied Mouth, 1880, Pt. .... 90.00 to 100.00
Saratoga Red Spring, Saratoga, N.Y., Deep Blue Green 60.00
Saratoga Red Spring, Saratoga, N.Y., Emerald Green, Qt. 180.00
Saratoga Star Spring, Dark Olive Green, Applied Mouth, 1880, Pt. 330.00
Saratoga Star Spring, Deep Olive Green, Applied Mouth, 1875, 9 In. 145.00
Saratoga Star Spring, Emerald Green, Applied Mouth, 1880, Qt. 300.00
Saratoga Star Spring, Emerald Green, Sloping Collar, Ring, Qt. 75.00
Saratoga Star Spring, Gold Olive Amber, Cylindrical, 1880, Qt. 110.00
Saratoga Star Spring, Golden Amber, Ring Mouth, Cylindrical, 1880 .... 90.00
Saratoga Star Spring, Golden Amber, Sloping Collared Mouth, Pt. 155.00
Saratoga Star Spring, Medium Orange Amber, 1865-1875, 9 3/8 In. 120.00
Saratoga Star Spring, Olive Amber, Applied Mouth, 1880, Qt. 220.00
Saratoga Vichy Spouting Spring, Saratoga, N.Y., Blue Aqua, 1/2 Pt. 60.00
Schultz & Warner, N.Y., Kissingen, Gold Amber, Cylindrical, Pt. 175.00
Seitz & Bro., Easton, Pa., 8-Sided, Cobalt Blue, IP, 1845-1855, 7 5/8 In. 255.00
Seitz & Bro., Easton, Pa., Premium, Cobalt Blue, 8-Sided, IP, 7 1/4 In. 440.00
Seitz & Bro., Premium, Easton, Pa., Cornflower Blue, 7 1/4 In. 110.00
Seymour & Co., Buffalo, N.Y., Cobalt Blue, IP, Applied Mouth, 7 1/8 In. 70.00
Sheldon A Spring, Red Amber, Applied Mouth, 1860-1880, Qt. 635.00
Sheldon A Spring, Sheldon, Vt., Gold Red Amber, Ring Mouth, Qt. 1100.00
Sno Top Spring, Boonville, N.Y., Green Aqua, Full Label, 1900, 1/2 Gal. 150.00
Southwick & Tupper, New York, Cobalt Blue, 10-Sided, IP, 7 1/2 In. 185.00
Southwick & Tupper, New York, Medium Green, 10-Sided, IP, 7 3/8 In. ....135.00 to 175.00
St. Regis Water, Massena Springs, Teal Blue, Applied Collar Mouth, 10 In. 55.00
Star Spring Co., Saratoga, N.Y., Deep Black Amber, 1875, Pt., 8 In. 360.00
Star Spring Co., Saratoga, N.Y., Emerald Green, Cylindrical, 1860-1880, Pt. 305.00
Star Spring Co., Saratoga, N.Y., Golden Amber, Pt. ....190.00 to 220.00
Star Spring Co., Saratoga, N.Y., Olive Amber, 8 In. 210.00
Star Spring Co., Saratoga, N.Y., Red Amber, Ring Collar, Cylindrical, Pt. 130.00
Star Spring Co., Saratoga, N.Y., Root Beer Amber, Sloping Collar, Ring, Pt. ....120.00 to 155.00
Strumatic, Deep Red Amber, Applied Mouth, 1870-1880, 7 3/8 In. 550.00
Summit Mineral Water, J.H., Light Green Aqua, Applied Top 65.00
Superior, Union Glass, Bright Green, Mug Base, Cylindrical, IP, 1/2 Pt. 215.00
Superior Mineral Water, Union Glassworks, Mug Base, Light Teal Blue, Pontil 165.00
Syracuse Springs, Excelsior, Amber, Applied Collar, 1875, 9 In. 220.00

Mineral Water, Minnehaha
Natural Springs, Light
Aqua, 13 1/2 In.

Mineral Water, Vichy
Water, Green, Paper
Label, 10 1/2 In.

Mineral Water, Waukesha
Imperial Spring Co.,
Green, 9 1/2 In.

Mineral Water,
White Rock, Brown,
9 1/2 In.

Syracuse Springs, Excelsior, Amber, Bubbles, Applied Top, 9 1/2 In. 155.00
Syracuse Springs, Excelsior, Amber, Sloping Double Collar, Pt., 8 In. 175.00
Syracuse Springs, Excelsior, Golden Amber, Cylindrical, Qt. 240.00
Syracuse Springs, Excelsior, Yellow Amber, Pt., 7 5/8 In. 265.00
Syracuse Springs, N.Y., Deep Red Amber, Applied Mouth, 1880, Pt. 145.00
Syracuse Springs, N.Y., Gold Yellow Amber, 1870-1880, Pt. 440.00
T. Kellett, Newark, N.J., Light To Medium Green, Heavy Collar, IP, 1/2 Pt. 175.00
T.H. Muller's, Cincinnati, Cobalt Blue, IP, Applied Mouth, 7 In. 800.00
Tahoe Soda Springs, Natural, Aqua, Tooled Top, 1880s 230.00
Tarr & Smith, Boston, Emerald Green, Blob Top, IP, 7 3/8 In. 210.00
Torpedo, Amber Olive, Applied Ring, Light Interior Stain, 1850-1860, 8 1/4 In. 205.00
Tweddle's Celebrated, New York, Cobalt Blue, IP, 1855, 7 1/2 In. 175.00
Twitchell, Superior, Philada, Green ....35.00 to 38.00
Union Glass Works, Phila., Cobalt Blue, Blob Top, IP, 7 In. 440.00
Union Glass Works, Phila., Deep Blue Aqua, IP, 1845-1855, 7 1/4 In. 605.00
Vermont Spring, Saxe & Co., Dark Olive, Sloping Collar, 1860, Qt. 90.00
Vermont Spring, Saxe & Co., Sheldon, Vt., Blue Green, Cylindrical, Qt. 155.00
Vermont Spring, Saxe & Co., Sheldon, Vt., Citron, Cylindrical, Ring Mouth, Qt. 75.00
Vermont Spring, Saxe & Co., Sheldon, Vt., Emerald Green, Ring Mouth, Qt. ..100.00 to 185.00
Vermont Spring, Saxe & Co., Sheldon, Vt., Forest Green, Yellow, Qt. 100.00
Vermont Spring, Saxe & Co., Sheldon, Vt., Yellow Green, Ring Mouth, Qt. .....165.00 to 175.00
Vichy Water, Green, Paper Label, 10 1/2 In. ....*Illus* 10.00
Vichy Water, Hanbury Smith, Blue Green, 1/2 Pt. 60.00
Vichy Water, Hanbury Smith, N.Y., Blue Green, 1890, Pt. 110.00
Vichy Water, Patterson & Brazeau, N.Y., Forest Green, 1/2 Pt. 220.00
Victoria Springs, Deep Blue Aqua, Applied Mouth, Canada, 1885, Qt. 935.00
W. & B. Shasta, Union Glass Works, Phila., Cobalt Blue, IP, Blob Top, 7 3/8 In. 8250.00
W. Heiss Jr., Philadelphia, Medium Cobalt Blue, IP, 1855, 7 1/4 In. 440.00
W. Wilke & Co., Cin., O., Aqua, 12-Sided, IP, Applied Mouth, 7 1/2 In. 130.00
W. Wilke & Co., Cin., O., Medium Green, Olive Striations, 12-Sided, IP, 7 1/2 In. 470.00
Washington Lithia Well, Ballston Spa, Aqua, Pt. 325.00
Washington Lithia Well, Ballston Spa, N.Y., Aqua, Tooled Mouth, 8 In. 120.00
Washington Spring, Saratoga, N.Y., Emerald Green, 1870-1880, 8 In. 220.00
Washington Spring, Saratoga, N.Y., Yellow Green, Single Collar, Pt. ....340.00 to 385.00
Waukesha Imperial Spring Co., Green, 9 1/2 In. ....*Illus* 10.00
WEM In Oval, S.F. On Both-Sided, Aqua, Applied Top, 6 3/4 In. 45.00
Whann Lithia Water, Franklin, Pa., 11 3/4 In. 20.00
White Rock, Brown, 9 1/2 In. ....*Illus* 10.00
Williams & Severance, Sapphire Blue, Blob Top, IP, 1852-1854, 7 1/4 In. 385.00
Wm. Goldstein, IXL, Florida Water, Aqua, Applied Top, 9 In. 65.00
Wm. H. Weaver, Hackettstown, Emerald Green, Blob Top, 1855, 7 1/4 In. 1075.00
Wm. P. Davis & Co., Excelsior, Brooklyn, Cobalt Blue, 8-Sided, IP, 7 1/2 In. 195.00

Wolf, Phila., Blue Emerald Green, Blob Top, ABM, 7 In. 155.00
Yampah, Glenwood Springs, Colo., Cylindrical, Amber, Pt. 65.00
York Springs, Lime Green, ABM, Crown Top, Canada, c.1915, 9 1/8 In. 20.00
Young's Natural, Vichy Springs, Napa Co., Cal., Lime Green, Tooled Top, c.1900 . . . . . 110.00

MINIATURE

Most of the major modern liquor companies that make full-sized decanters and bottles
quickly learned that miniature versions sell well too. Some modern miniatures are listed
in this book by brand name. There are also many older miniature bottles that were made
as give-aways. Most interesting of these are the small motto jugs that name a liquor or
bar, and the comic figural bottles. Collectors sometimes specialize in glass animal
miniatures, beer bottles, whiskey bottles, or other types. Interested collectors can join
the Lilliputian Bottle Club, 54 Village Circle, Manhattan Beach, CA 90266-7222; or
subscribe to Miniature Bottle Collector, P.O. Box 2161, Palos Verdes, CA 90274.

MINIATURE, Baird Daniels Co. Dry Gin, Aqua, BIMAL, 3 1/8 In. 10.00
Bardinet Apricot Liqueur, Amber, Labels, 4 In. 10.00
Baxter's Old Nauvoo Brand Wines, Jug, Stoneware, 4 In. 35.00
Best Is At J.H. Pinnell's, 1268 Market St., Chattanooga, Tenn., Jug, Stoneware, 3 In. . . 470.00
Blown, Chestnut, Blue Green, Outward Rolled Mouth, Pontil, 3 1/4 In. 210.00
Blown, Chestnut, Olive Amber, Sheared Mouth, String Rim, Pontil, 1830, 4 In. 1100.00
Blown, Chestnut, Yellow Green, Sheared Mouth, String Rim, Pontil, 1830, 3 1/2 In. 230.00
Blown, Globular, Aqua, Sheared Mouth, Pontil, 2 1/2 In. 145.00
Blown, Globular, Olive Amber, Tooled Flared Mouth, Pontil, 3 5/8 In. 690.00
Blown, Globular, Red Amber, Outward Rolled Mouth, 1840, Pontil, 3 1/4 In. 935.00
Blue Delft's, Made For Henke Distilleries, KLM, Holland, 3 3/8 In. . . . . *Illus* 65.00
British Navy Prussers Rum, White, Dark Blue, Pottery 15.00
Bullivants Grocery, Jug 75.00
Cigar, Whiskey Nip, Amber, 5 In. 40.00
Clark, Stoneware, 6 In. 30.00
Clifford Bros., Chicago, Ill., Brown & White, Jug, 4 In. 150.00
Compliments Of Bistling & Hodson, Carthage, Mo., Jug, Incised, 3 In. 250.00
Compliments Of Bulwinkle Cannon & Rulledge, Charleston, Stoneware Brown, 3 In. 275.00
Compliments Of Dickson Beaton & Co., Jug, Stoneware, Dark Brown, Incised, 3 In. . . 690.00
Compliments Of F. Vonoven, 237 King St., Jug, Stoneware, Tan, Brown, 3 1/2 In. 120.00
Compliments Of F.W. Meise, Maple River Jct., Ia., Jug, Pottery, Brown, Tan, 3 In. 385.00
Compliments Of J.D. Holland & Sons, Mt. Vernon, Tex., Jug, Cream, Brown, 3 In. . . . 800.00
Compliments Of McGinley Bros., Sedalia, Mo., Jug, Incised, 3 In. 250.00
Compliments Of Peter Koch, Jug, Tan, Dark Brown Glaze, Stoneware, 3 3/8 In. 165.00
Compliments Of T.R. Walton, Jug, Stoneware, Dark Brown Albany Slip, Incised, 3 In. 260.00
Compliments Of Tom S. Esres Co., Hanford, Cal., Jug, Gold Trim, 3 In. 125.00
Dewar's Scotch Whisky, Embossed On Base, Amber, BIMAL, Dug, 4 1/8 In. 15.00
Dr. Cronk, Stoneware, 7 In. 30.00
Dry Sack Sherry, Amber, Paper Label, Spain 4 1/2 In. . . . . *Illus* 15.00
Dubonnet, Embossed Vertically, Light Aqua, BIMAL, 4 1/4 In. 15.00
Duffy Malt Whiskey, Amber, 4 In. 30.00
Flask, Pumpkinseed, BIMAL, 3 3/8 In. 8.00

Miniature, Blue Delft's,
Made For Henke
Distilleries, KLM,
Holland, 3 3/8 In.

Miniature, Dry Sack
Sherry, Amber,
Paper Label, Spain
4 1/2 In.

Gin, Case, Crosshatch Sides, Medium Cobalt Blue, Blown, Flared Lip, OP, 3 In. 935.00
Gin, Case, Medium Cobalt Blue, Blown, Flared Lip, OP, 2 1/2 In. 1430.00
Gin, Case, Olive Amber, Flared Lip, OP, 2 3/4 In. 330.00
Greybeard Heather Dew Whiskey, Jug, Stoneware, Cream, Brown, 4 3/8 In. 55.00
Harry Watt, Phila, Amethyst, BIMAL 4.00
Henry Bosquet's Old Rye House So. Kenna Whiskey, Jug, Tan, White, Brown, 3 In. 75.00
House Of Koshu Plum Wine, Light Amber, Labels, 5 In. 8.00
I.W. Harper Nelson Co. Kentucky Whiskey, Jug, White 85.00
J. Rieger & Co., Dist., Kansas City, Mo., 4 1/2 In. 15.00
Jno. W. Hicks, 416 Ohio St. Sedalia, Mo., Jug, Incised, 3 In. 250.00
Jones Bros. & Co., Manufacturers Of Blue Grass Belle Vinegar, Stoneware, 3 3/8 In. 40.00
Jug, Bauer Saloon, Peoria, Pt. 100.00
Jug, Four Roses, Amber, Embossed, 4 In. 10.00
Jug, From Breers Cash Grocery, Red Key, Ind., Stoneware, 3 In. 175.00
Jug, New York Pottery Co., 3 In. 150.00
Jug, Old Duck Whiskey, Wright & Young, Pottery, Cream, Blue Transfer, 3 1/4 In. 525.00
Jug, Victoria Rye, 3 In. 95.00
Jug Of Joy, Germa-Vici Cures, Jug, Pottery, Cream, Gray Glaze, 2 5/8 In. 305.00
Karl's, Washington, D.C., Gent On Bar Stool, German, Nip 200.00
Kiwanis Moonshine, Asheville, N.C., Oct. 1922, Jug, Stoneware, Tan, Brown, 4 In. 130.00
Kola, Jug, Stoneware, Blue Letters, 5 1/2 In. 25.00
Kord Blackberry Liqueur, Horn Of Plenty Shape, Labels, 4 In. 20.00
Kord Creme De Menthe Glacial, Label, 3 1/2 In. 10.00
L.P. Frobe & Co. Liquor Dealers, Try Our Phil Whiskey, Jug, Pottery, 3 1/4 In. 525.00
Lapp Goldsmith & Co., Jug, Stoneware, Brown Albany Glaze, Incised, 3 In. 60.00
Little Brown Jug, Brown Glaze, 3 In. ....40.00 to 68.00
Loomis Hind Skol Raspberry, Amber, Labels, 6 In. 10.00
M.S. Herlihy & Co., Jug 75.00
Meredith's Diamond Club Pure Rye, Jug, White, Blue Green Letters, 4 1/2 In. 90.00
Meredith's Malt Whiskey, East Liverpool, Ohio, Amber, 9 In. 8.00
Meridith's Diamond Club, Jug, 4 In. 100.00
Merry Xmas, Chas. Blum Co., Jacksonville, Fla., Jug, Stoneware, Cream, 3 1/8 In. 145.00
Metropolitan Club Whiskey Blend, Freiberg & Kahn, Cincinnati, Jug, Gray, 3 In. ... 55.00
Michter's Whiskey, White, Blue Letters, 1/2 Pt. 25.00
Mohawk Coffee, Labels, Jug, Pottery, 3 In. 30.00
Old Continental, Jug, Stoneware, Cream, Black Stencil, 4 In. 40.00
Old Continental Sour Mash, Incised, 4 In. 80.00
Old Kentucky Tavern, Diamond Pattern, Labels, 3 3/4 In. 10.00
Old Pepper Whiskey, Ja. E. Pepper & Co. Distillers, Amber, Wicker Cover, 4 In. 40.00
Old Scotch, Man Tipping Glass, 3348 On Reverse, Brown, White, Stopper, Nip, 4 In. ... 30.00
Old Taylor Bourbon Whiskey, Labels, 4 In. 10.00
Parker Rye, Phil Kelly, Richmond, Va., Bulb Type Decanter 35.00
Paul Mason, Cream Sherry Labels, Amber, Heart Shape, 4 In. 8.00
Pensacola Golden Corn, Jug, 3 In. 150.00
Radium Water From Sequoyah Hotel, Claremore, Okla., Jug, Brown, Cream, 4 1/2 In. 120.00
Ridgeway Straight Corn, H.G. Sprinkle Dist., Co., Jug, Stoneware, Tan, 3 1/4 In. ... 95.00
Sandeman Founders Porto, Green, Black & Gold Paper Label, 4 In. .... *Illus* 5.00

Miniature, Sherry,
Nectar, Gonzalez
Byass Jerez, 5 1/4 In.

Miniature, Sandeman
Founders Porto, Green,
Black & Gold Paper
Label, 4 In.

Miniature, Whiskey,
Hiram Walker's Old
Fashioned, United Air
Lines, 4 1/4 In.

Miniature, Whiskey, Joke, Davey Crocked, Hydrated Bear Grease, Paper Label, 4 In.

Miniature, Whiskey, Joke, Old Croak Kentucky Embalming Fluid, Dead Crow, 4 In.

Miniature, Whiskey, Old Crow, Kentucky Straight Bourbon, 4 1/4 In.

Sherry, Nectar, Gonzalez Byass Jerez, 5 1/4 In. . . . .*Illus*	12.00
Souvenir Riverton Park, Portland, Me., Jug, Stoneware, Brown, Cream, 3 In.	25.00
Sweet Mash Corn, Atlantic Coast Distilling Co., Jug, Stoneware, 3 In.	120.00
Use Jos. L. Friedman Co. Paducah Ky. Vinegar, Jug, Stoneware, Brown, Incised, 3 In.	160.00
W.H. Co. Pride Of Kentucky, Cleveland, Ohio	35.00
Whiskey, 800 On Base, Dark Green, BIMAL, 4 1/2 In.	10.00
Whiskey, B8004 On Base, BIMAL, 4 5/8 In.	6.00
Whiskey, Ball's 8 Blend Scotch, Amber, Ball Shape, Labels, 3 3/4 In.	10.00
Whiskey, Benedictine, Emerald Green, BIMAL, 2 3/8 In.	15.00
Whiskey, Black & White Scotch, Amber, Label, 5 In.	15.00
Whiskey, Bretzfelder & Bronner, Louisville, Ky., Square, 5 In.	45.00
Whiskey, Chas. Grove Co. Liquor Merchants, Boston, Jug	90.00
Whiskey, Continental Hotel, Script, Mug Base, 3 In.	30.00
Whiskey, Dachshund, 1976	65.00
Whiskey, Duffy Malt Whiskey, Amber, 4 In.	20.00
Whiskey, Father Marquette 1866 Pure Rye, F.F. Gluck Co., Jug, Stoneware, 3 In.	85.00
Whiskey, H.B. Kirk, Trademark, Amber, 4 3/8 In.	20.00
Whiskey, Hall Luhrs & Co. Snowflake Whiskey, Golden Amber, 5 3/4 In.	360.00
Whiskey, Hiram Walker's Old Fashioned, United Air Lines, 4 1/4 In. . . . .*Illus*	25.00
Whiskey, J. Reiger & Co., Kansas City, 3 In.	12.00
Whiskey, J.F. Callahan, Diagonal Script, 4 3/4 In.	15.00
Whiskey, Joke, Davey Crocked, Hydrated Bear Grease, Paper Label, 4 In. . . . .*Illus*	5.00
Whiskey, Joke, Old Croak Kentucky Embalming Fluid, Dead Crow, 4 In. . . . .*Illus*	5.00
Whiskey, Kellerstrass, Fluting, 4 3/8 In.	35.00
Whiskey, L 539 On Base, BIMAL, 4 In.	6.00
Whiskey, Lady's Leg, 6208 On Base, Dark Green, BIMAL, 5 1/2 In.	10.00
Whiskey, Lady's Leg, 8178 On Base, Dark Green, BIMAL, 5 1/4 In.	10.00
Whiskey, Mount Vernon, Square, Lady's Leg Neck, Amber, Contents, 3 1/8 In.	25.00
Whiskey, N.M. Uri, Rectangular, Amber, 3 1/2 In.	20.00
Whiskey, Old Crow, Kentucky Straight Bourbon, 4 1/4 In. . . . .*Illus*	10.00
Whiskey, Paul Jones, Amber, Labels, 4 1/2 In.	35.00
Whiskey, Petts Bald Eagle, 4 1/2 In.	40.00
Whiskey, PM 219 On Base, Lady's Leg, BIMAL, 5 1/8 In.	6.00
Whiskey, Torrey's, Trademark, Amber, 5 In.	30.00
Whiskey, Tullamore Dew, 90 Years Old, Irish Whisky, Jug, Green, Cream, Ireland, 3 In. .	75.00
Wine, Champagne, Teal Green, Tooled Top	55.00

MR. BOSTON, see Old Mr. Boston

——————————————————— **NAILSEA TYPE** ———————————————————

The intricate glass called *Nailsea* was made in the Bristol district of England from 1788 to 1873. The glass included loopings of white or colored glass worked in patterns. The characteristic look of Nailsea was copied and what is called Nailsea today is really Nailsea type made in England or even America. Nailsea gemel bottles are of particular interest to collectors.

NAILSEA TYPE, Bar, Pink, White Swirled Stripes, Sheared Mouth, Pontil, 1870-1900, 11 In.	415.00
Cone, Olive Green, Sheared Lip, 1840-1850, 4 In.	730.00

Cone, Olive Green, White, Blue, Red Specks, Pontil, N.Y., 1840-1850, 4 5/8 In.	365.00
Decanter, Globular, Green Aqua, White Opaque Loop Pattern, Pontil, 9 In.	1485.00
Flask, Amber, Milk Glass & White Opalescent Loopings, Flared Mouth, 4 In.	265.00
Flask, Chestnut, Green Aqua, Red & White Splotches, Sloping Double Collar, 8 In.	130.00
Flask, Clear, Milk Glass, Red & White Loops, Berry Rigarees, Sheared Lip, 7 1/4 In.	145.00
Flask, Flattened Teardrop, Cranberry, 16 Diamond Pattern, Pontil, 8 In.	385.00
Flask, Milk Glass Looping, Canary Yellow, Sheared Lip, 1840-1870, 7 1/4 In.	255.00
Flask, Milk Glass, Blue Band Trim, Yellow Green, Sheared Lip, 20th Century, 7 In.	90.00
Flask, Pocket, Amber, Milk Glass Loopings, Sheared Mouth, 1850, 5 In.	220.00
Flask, Pocket, Forest Green, Milk Glass Loopings, Sheared Mouth, 6 1/2 In.	210.00
Flask, Red, White, Blue Looping, Sheared Lip, Pontil Foot, 1850-1860, 6 1/2 In.	130.00
Flask, Ruby, White Herringbone Loopings, Double Collar, Pontil, 1880, 7 1/8 In.	440.00
Flask, Teardrop, Cranberry Body, Milk Glass Loopings, 1880, 7 7/8 In.	120.00
Flask, Teardrop, Gold Amber, Milk Glass Loopings, Ring, Pontil, 7 3/4 In.	440.00
Flask, Teardrop, Milk Glass, Blue & Rose Loopings, Pontil, 1880, 7 3/4 In.	330.00
Flask, Teardrop, Teal Green, White Loopings, Sheared Mouth, Pontil, 8 3/4 In.	255.00
Flask, Teardrop, White Loops On Clear, 4 Lines Of Rigaree, 7 In.	160.00
Flask, Teardrop, Yellow Amber, White Looping, Ring Mouth, Pontil, 7 1/2 In.	330.00
Flask, White Herringbone Looping, Teal Green, Pontil Foot, 1830-1860, 6 3/4 In.	200.00
Flask, Yellow Olive, White & Fiery Opalescent Milk Glass Loopings, 5 3/8 In.	255.00
Jug, Pale Green, Milk Glass Splotches, Sloping Collar, Ring, Pontil, 6 1/2 In.	55.00

NURSING

Pottery nursing bottles were used by 1500 B.C. If a bottle was needed, one was impro-
vised, and stone, metal, wood, and pottery, as well as glass bottles were made through
the centuries. A glass bottle was patented by Charles Windship of Roxbury, Massachusetts, in 1841. Its novel design suggested that the bottle be placed over the breast to try
to fool the baby into thinking the milk came from the mother. By 1864 the most common nursing bottle was a nipple attached to a glass tube in a cork that was put into a
glass bottle. Unfortunately, it was impossible to clean and was very unsanitary. The
nursing bottle in use today was made possible by the development of an early 1900s
rubber nipple.

Nursing bottles are easily identified by the unique shape and the measuring units that
are often marked on the sides. Some early examples had engraved designs and silver
nipples but most are made of clear glass and rubber. There is a collectors club, The
American Collectors of Infant Feeders, 1849 Ebony Drive, York, PA 17402-4706, and
a publication called *Keeping Abreast*. A reference book, *A Guide to American Nursing
Bottles* by Diane Rouse Ostrander, is also available.

NURSING, 3 Little Pigs, 8 Nursery Rhyme Characters, ABM, Canada, c.1930, 8 Oz.	50.00
16 Diamond, Blue Aqua, Sheared Lip, Pontil, 9 1/2 In.	240.00
16 Ribs, Vertical, Green Aqua, Sheared Mouth, Pontil, 1835	100.00
20 Ribs, Vertical, Yellow Green, Midwest, Pontil, 7 1/2 In.	330.00
28 Ribs, Vertical, Yellow Green, Sheared Lip, Midwest, Pontil, 6 In.	120.00
Albert Hygienic Feeder, Banana Shape, Embossed Top	29.00
Allenbury's Feeder, Ploughshare Picture	40.00
Aqua, 15 Diamond, 5 7/8 In.	50.00
Baby Bunting, Embossed Rabbit, Narrow Mouth	7.00 to 15.00
Baby's Delight, Turtle, Child Drinking From Nursing Bottle Picture	90.00
Best Feeding Bottle, Tooled Lip, Metal Filling Cap, Box, Japan, 1900-1920, 7 1/4 In.	45.00
Blown, Vertical Ribs, Aqua, Midwest, 6 3/8 In.	80.00
Chestnut, 16 Ribs, Vertical, Blue Aqua, Midwest, Pontil, 4 5/8 In.	275.00
Clark Drug Co., Petaluma, Cal., Graduation On Reverse, Tooled Top, 6 1/2 In.	100.00
Crown Feeder, Turtle, Aqua, 1880, 5 1/2 In.	45.00
Ding Dong Bell, Pussy's In The Well, Child Holding Cat, Well, ABM, 8 Oz., 6 1/2 In.	40.00
Doll's, 2 3/4 In.	4.00
Duck Shape, Graduated Scale, Chinese Characters, ABM, Asia, 20th Century, 8 In.	255.00
Embossed Baby, 6 3/4 In.	10.00
Embossed Baby, On Stomach, Marked Ounces, 6 1/2 In.	*Illus* 12.00
Flask, 12 Diamond, Green Aqua, Pontil, 1820-1830, 6 1/2 In.	165.00
Flask, 14 Diamond, Blue Aqua, Flared Lip, Pontil, 1820-1830, 7 3/8 In.	165.00
Flask, Blown, Light Green, OP, Nipple Top, 7 1/2 In.	60.00
Grimes, Fredericksburg, Pa., Baby Top, ACL, Qt.	275.00

Nursing, Hazel-Atlas
Glass, Embossed
Elephant, Faultless
Wonder Nipple,
8 Oz.

Nursing, Embossed
Baby, On Stomach,
Marked Ounces,
6 1/2 In.

**To dry a small necked
bottle, give it a last
rinse with alcohol.**

Griptight, Banana Shape, Embossed 24.00
Happy Baby, Seated Baby, 8 Oz. 10.00
Hazel-Atlas Glass, Embossed Elephant, Faultless Wonder Nipple, 8 Oz. .... *Illus* 80.00
Hey Diddle Diddle, The Cat & The Fiddle, Cat, Dog, Cow, ABM, c.1930, 8 Oz., 6 1/2 In. 35.00
Horizontal Ribs, Graduations, Plastic Screw Cap, Blue Rubber Nipple Protector 12.00
Hygeia, Embossed, Ball, Instructions, 4 Oz. 8.00
Hygienic Feeder, 2 Mouths 40.00
Hygienic Feeder, Banana Shape, Hole At Both Ends .... 20.00 to 24.00
Milk Glass, Hard Rubber Nipple, France, 11 1/2 In. 120.00
Miniature Hygienic Feeder, Leather Cap, England, c.1900, 5 1/4 x 2 1/8 In. 30.00
Olive Green, OP, 1840-1860, Pt. 60.00
Our Little Beauties, WH Monogram, Slipper Shape 35.00
Pyrex, Owens-Illinois Glass Co., Pink, Wide Mouth, 1935, 8 Oz. 6.00
Reclining Baby, 8 Oz. 7.00
Rock-A-Bye Baby On The Treetop, Baby In Cradle, Tree Branch, ABM, 6 1/2 In. 40.00
S. Maw & Thomson, London, England, Slipper Shape .... 30.00 to 40.00
See-Saw Margery Daw, Rhyme, Kids On See-Saw, ABM, c.1930, 8 Oz., 6 1/2 In. 40.00
Storkey, Large Mouth, 8 Oz. 8.00
Sure Feed Ltd. Cardiff, Flat Turtle, Long Neck 30.00
The Crown Feeder, Turtle Shape, Aqua, Screw Thread, 5 1/2 In. 45.00
The Graduated Nursing Bottle, 1890, 6 3/4 In. 10.00
There Was An Old Woman Who Lived In A Shoe, Woman, Kids, Shoe, 6 1/2 In. 40.00

─────────────────────────────── OIL ───────────────────────────────

Motor oil, battery oil, and sewing machine and lubricating oils were all sold in bottles.
Any bottle that has the word *oil* either embossed in the glass or on the paper label falls
in this category. A battery jar has straight sides and an open top. It was filled with a
chemical solution. The jars were usually made with a zinc plate or a copper plate plus
a suspended carbon plate. With the proper connections the chemicals and metals gen-
erated an electric current. Many companies made batteries that included glass jars, and
the jars are now appearing at bottle shows. In the Edison battery, the solution was covered with a special protective layer of oil which kept it from evaporating. Edison battery oil jars, dating from about 1889, were specially made to hold the protective oil and
can still be found.

OIL, Battery, Waite & Bartlett, N.Y. Mfg. Co., Pat. July 22, 90, Aqua, 2 Oz., 3 1/2 In. 65.00
Bears Oil, Blue Aqua, OP, Rolled Lip, 1830-1845, 2 3/4 In. 185.00
Bicycle Oil, Made In U.S.A., Indented Panels, Ringed Neck, Tooled Lip, 5 In. 25.00
Canary Gun Oil, Label 20.00
G.W. Cole & Co., Three In One, Aqua, Cork, 5 1/2 In. 2.00
Hamlin's Wizard Oil, Aqua, 6 1/4 In. 20.00
I. Rokeach & Sons, Oil Refiners, Brooklyn, N.Y., Star, Tooled Lip, Cork, 8 In. 5.00
Near's Fly Oil, Auburn, N.Y., Farm Animals, 1/2 Gal. 40.00
Pennzoil Outboard Motor Oil, Painted Label, ABM, Lid 35.00
Scotch Oil, Yellow Amber, 8 Panels, 4 3/4 In. 10.00
Standard Oil Co., Cleveland, Oh., Rectangular, 1890, 5 In. 10.00

OLD BARDSTOWN

Old Bardstown was made and bottled by the Willit Distilling Company in Bardstown, Kentucky. Figural bottles were made from about 1977 to 1980. One unusual bottle pictured Foster Brooks, the actor who is best known for his portrayal of drunks.

OLD BARDSTOWN, Affirm & Alydar	150.00
Christmas Card, 1977	16.00
Clemson Tiger	70.00
Delta Queen, 1980	38.00
Fiddle, Miniature	15.00
Fighting Gamecock	150.00
Football Player	37.00
Foster Brooks, 1978	20.00
Georgia Bulldog, 1980	145.00
Horse, Citation, 1979	175.00
Iron Worker, 1978	28.00
Keg With Stand, 1977, 1/2 Gal.	14.00
Keg With Stand, 1977, Gal.	27.00
Kentucky Colonel, No. 1, 1978	18.00
Kentucky Colonel, No. 2, 1979	55.00
Kentucky Derby, 1977	11.00
Surface Miner, 1978	20.00
Tiger, 1979	30.00

OLD COMMONWEALTH

Old Commonwealth bottles have been made since 1975 by J.P. Van Winkle and Sons, Louisville, Kentucky. They also put out bottles under the Old Rip Van Winkle label. An apothecary series with university names and other designs such as firemen, coal miners, fishermen, Indians, dogs, horses, or leprechauns was made from 1978 to the present. As few as 1,600 were made of some of these designs. Some of the decanters were made with music box inserts. A limited edition Irish decanter is made every year for St. Patrick's Day. The distillery will sell its remaining empty bottles for the apothecary series and the Irish decanters to collectors interested in completing a set. Write to 2843 Brownsboro Road, Louisville, KY 40206.

OLD COMMONWEALTH, Alabama Apothecary, 1980	27.00
Auburn Tigers, 1979	38.00
Castles Of Ireland, 1990	30.00
Chief Illini, No. 1, 1979	80.00
Chief Illini, No. 2, 1981	60.00
Clemson Tigers, 1979	45.00
Coal Miner, Coal Shooter, 1983	28.00
Coal Miner, Lump Of Coal, 1977	33.00
Coal Miner, Lump Of Coal, 1981	33.00
Coal Miner, Lunch Time, 1980 . . . .*Illus*	40.00
Coal Miner, Lunch Time, 1983, Miniature	40.00
Coal Miner, Pick, 1976	39.00
Coal Miner, Pick, 1982	39.00
Coal Miner, Shovel, 1975	70.00
Coal Miner, Shovel, 1980	70.00
Coins Of Ireland, 1979	22.00
Cottontail Rabbit, 1981	35.00
Crimson Tide, 1981	17.00
Dogs Of Ireland, 1980	19.00
Fireman, Modern Hero, 1982	62.00
Fireman, Modern No. 2, Nozzle Man, 1983	62.00
Fireman, Modern No. 3, On Call, Boots, Yellow Hat, 1983	66.00
Fireman, Modern No. 4, Fallen Comrade, 1982	70.00
Fireman, No. 1, Cumberland Valley, 75th Anniversary, 1976	115.00
Fireman, No. 2, Volunteer, 1978	74.00
Fireman, No. 3, Valiant Volunteer, 1979	76.00
Fireman, No. 4, Heroic Volunteer, 1981	80.00
Fireman, No. 5, Lifesaver, 1983	60.00
Fisherman, Keeper, 1980	46.00

Old Commonwealth, Coal Miner, Lunch Time, 1980

Old Commonwealth, Horses Of Ireland, 1981

Old Commonwealth, Lumberjack, Old Time, 1979

Flowers Of Ireland, 1983	23.00
Happy Green, 1986	25.00
Horses Of Ireland, 1981 ....*Illus*	18.00
Irish At The Sea, 1989	25.00
Irish Idyll, 1982	12.00
Irish Lore, 1988	25.00
Kansas State Wildcats, 1982	34.00
Kentucky Peach Bowl, 1977	30.00
Leprechaun, No. 1, Elusive, 1980	34.00
Leprechaun, No. 2, Irish Minstrel, 1982	30.00
Leprechaun, No. 3, Lucky, 1983	25.00
Louisville Champs, 1980	30.00
LSU Tiger, 1979	43.00
Lumberjack, Old Time, 1979 ....*Illus*	29.00
Maryland Terps, 1977	25.00
Missouri Tigers, 1979	40.00
Princeton Univ., 1976	23.00
Sons Of Erin, No. 2, 1978	25.00
Sports Of Ireland, 1987	24.00
St. Patrick's Day Parade, 1984	23.00
Statue Of Liberty, Miniature	20.00
Symbols Of Ireland, 1985	25.00
Thoroughbreds, Kentucky, 1977	40.00
Waterfowler, No. 1, Hunter, 1978	47.00
Waterfowler, No. 2, Here They Come, 1980	37.00
Waterfowler, No. 3, Good Boy, 1981	40.00
Western Boot, 1982	21.00
Western Logger, 1980	32.00

OLD CROW

Dr. James Crow of Kentucky was a surgeon and chemist from Edinburgh, Scotland. He started practicing medicine but decided to improve the quality of life by distilling corn whiskey instead. In those days, about 1835, whiskey was made by a family recipe with a bit of that and a handful of the other. The results were uneven. Dr. Crow was a scientist and used corn and limestone water to make a whiskey that he put into kegs and jugs. He used charred oak kegs, and the liquid became reddish instead of the clear white of corn liquor. More experiments led to his development of the first bourbon, named after northeastern Kentucky's Bourbon County, which had been named for the French royal family.

Old Crow became a popular product in all parts of the country and was sold to saloons. Salesmen for competing brands would sometimes try to ruin the liquor by putting a snake or nail into the barrel. In 1870, for the first time, bourbon was bottled and sealed at the distillery. The distillery was closed during Prohibition, and when it reopened in 1933, Old Crow was purchased by National Distilleries. That Old Crow would be packaged in a crow-shaped decanter was inevitable, and in 1954 National Distillers Products Corporation of Frankfort, Kentucky, put Old Crow bourbon into a ceramic crow. Again in 1974 a crow decanter was used; this time 16,800 Royal Doulton bottles were made. The bourbon was sold in the 1970s in a series of bottles shaped like light or dark green chess pieces. Jim Beam Brands bought National Distillers in 1987. Old Crow is still made, but not in figural bottles.

OLD CROW, Chess Set, Pawns	22.00
Chess Set, With Rug, 32 Piece	315.00
Crow, Red Vest, 1974	25.00
Crow, Royal Doulton	90.00

OLD FITZGERALD

In 1908, Julian P. Van Winkle, Sr., and another salesman for W.L. Weller & Sons, liquor wholesaler, bought the Weller company. Later they bought A. Ph. Stitzel Distillery, of Louisville, Kentucky, which had supplied sour-mash whiskey to W.L. Weller & Sons. The Stitzel Weller firm became known as The Old Fitzgerald Distillery. President Van Winkle, Sr., created the Old Rip Van Winkle series just before Prohibition. Van Winkle remained an active distiller until his death in 1965. His son, Julian, Jr., had become president of Stitzel-Weller in 1947. In 1968 the Old Fitzgerald decanter, "Leprechaun Bottle" carried the words *plase God.* The use of "God" was ruled objectionable under Federal law and the decanters were changed to read *prase be.* In 1972, the distillery was sold to Somerset Importers, Ltd., a division of Norton Simon Company, Inc. Somerset Importers continued to market the Old Rip Van Winkle series until 1978, when they sold to J.P. Van Winkle & Son, a distillery created by Julian Van Winkle, Jr., with his son, Julian, III, after the sale of Stitzel-Weller.

J.P. Van Winkle & Son sold whiskey under the new label, Old Commonwealth, and also the Old Rip Van Winkle series. The Van Winkle series of bottles for both brands included only 20 different bottles through 1986.

Esmark purchased Norton Simon in 1984, then sold the Old Fitzgerald label to Distillers of England in 1985, who sold it to Guinness Stout of Ireland in 1986. The last Old Fitzgerald decanter was made in 1989. Guinness Stout has since become Guinness Distillers Worldwide in Edinburgh, and its Louisville distillery is called United Distillers Mfg., Inc.

An out-of-print pamphlet, *Decanter Collector's Guide,* pictures Old Fitzgerald decanters offered between 1951 and 1971. Most are glass in classic shapes. Besides Old Fitzgerald, the distillery made Cabin Still, W.L. Weller, and Rebel Yell bourbons.

OLD FITZGERALD, America's Cup, 1970	22.00
American Sons, 1976	15.00
Around We Go, 1983	20.00
Birmingham, 1972	47.00
Birmingham, 2nd Edition	40.00

Old Fitzgerald, Cabin Still, Early American, 1970

Old Fitzgerald, Cabin Still, Hillbilly, 1954, Qt.

Old Fitzgerald, Cabin Still, Hillbilly, 1969

Old Fitzgerald, Four
Seasons, 1965

Old Fitzgerald,
South Carolina,
Tricentennial, 1970

Blarney, Irish Toast, 1970	20.00
Cabin Still, Early American, 1970 ....*Illus*	4.00
Cabin Still, Hillbilly, 1854, Gal.	80.00
Cabin Still, Hillbilly, 1954, Pt.	18.00
Cabin Still, Hillbilly, 1954, Qt. ....*Illus*	18.00
Cabin Still, Hillbilly, 1969 ....*Illus*	15.00
Candlelite, 1955	20.00
Candlelite, 1961	10.00
Classic, 1972	6.00
Colonial, 1969	5.00
Davidson, N.C., 1972	30.00
Eagle, 1973	8.00
Executive, 1960	7.00
Flagship, 1967	8.00
Four Seasons, 1965 ....*Illus*	5.00
Gallon In Cradle	16.00
Geese, 1970	9.00
Gold Coaster, 1954	12.00
Gold Web, 1953	12.00
Hostess, 1977	5.00
Huntington, W.V., 1971	25.00
Illinois, 1972	14.00
Irish Charm, 1977	20.00
Irish Counties, 1973	17.00
Irish Luck, 1972	28.00
Irish Patriots, 1971	15.00
Irish Wish, 1975	18.00
Jewel, 1951 ....9.00 to 10.00	
Memphis, 1969	15.00
Nebraska, 1972	29.00
Ohio State, 1970	20.00
Old Fitz 101, 1978	5.00
Old Ironsides	5.00
Pheasant Rising, 1972 ....8.00 to 10.00	
Pilgrim Landing, 1970	18.00
Ram, Bighorn, 1971	7.00
Rip Van Winkle, 1971	30.00
Songs Of Ireland, 1974	12.00
Sons Of Erin, 1969	10.00
South Carolina, Tricentennial, 1970 ....*Illus*	11.00
Tree Of Life, 1964	7.00
Triangle, 1976	5.00
Venetian, 1966	5.00
Vermont, 1970	18.00
Virginia, 1972	17.00
W.V. Forest Festival, 1973	30.00

OLD MR. BOSTON

It seems strange that a liquor company began as a candy factory, but that is part of the history of Old Mr. Boston. The Ben Burk Candy Company started in 1927 making nonalcoholic cordials during Prohibition. After Repeal, they became the first Massachusetts company to get a license for distilled spirits. They built a still and started making gin. One of the first brand names used was Old Mr. Boston. There was even a live Mr. Boston, an actor who made appearances for the company. In the early 1940s the company was sold to American Distilleries, but four years later Samuel Burk and Hyman Burkowitz, brothers, bought the company back. They expanded the Old Mr. Boston brand to include other beverages, such as flavored cordials and homogenized eggnog. They claim to be the first to introduce the quarter-pint size. In the mid-1960s the company began putting the liquor in decanters. No decanters were made after the early 1970s. They also made Rocking Chair Whiskey in a bottle that actually rocked. Traditionally, whiskey barrels were rolled back and forth on ships to improve the taste. Ships' captains liked the improved flavor and when they retired they would tie barrels of whiskey to their rocking chairs. A series of liquors in glass cigar-like tubes called *The Thin Man* were made in the mid-1960s. Glenmore Distillers Company acquired Old Mr. Boston in 1969. The brand name was changed to Mr. Boston about 1975. Barton Brands bought the Mr. Boston name about 1994. Mr. Boston products are still made.

The Mr. Boston trademark was redesigned in the 1950s and again in the 1970s. Each time he became thinner, younger, and more dapper. The slogan *An innkeepers tradition since 1868* was used in the 1980s. It refers to the year the Old Mr. Boston mark was first registered.

OLD MR. BOSTON, AMVETS, Iowa Convention, 1975 .... 10.00
Anthony Wayne, 1970 .... 10.00
Assyrian Convention, 1975 .... 21.00
Bart Starr, No. 15 .... 47.00
Berkley, W.V. 24.00
Bingo In Illinois, 1974 .... 13.00
Black Hills Motor Club, 1976 .... 25.00
Clown Head, 1973 .... 16.00
Clown Head, Signature, 1974 .... 25.00
Cog Railway, 1978 .... 30.00
Concord Coach, 1976 .... 26.00
Dan Patch, 1970 .... 15.00
Dan Patch, 1973 .... 15.00
Deadwood, South Dakota, 1975 ....16.00 to 19.00
Eagle Convention, 1976 .... 8.00
Eagle Convention, 75th Anniversary, 1973 .... 14.00
Eagle Convention, 78th Anniversary, 1973 .... 13.00
Eagle Convention, Atlanta, 1972 .... 14.00
Eagle Convention, Boston, 1971 .... 8.00
Green Bay, No. 87 .... 30.00
Greensboro Open, Gold Shoe, 1978 .... 37.00
Greensboro Open, Golf Bag, 1976 .... 34.00
Guitar, 1968 ....10.00 to 15.00
Illinois Capitol, 1970 .... 16.00
Lincoln, Horseback, 1972 .... 12.00
Lion Sitting, 1974 ....14.00 to 16.00
Miss Madison Boat, 1973 .... 36.00
Monticello, 1974 .... 12.00
Mooseheart, 1972 .... 12.00
Nathan Hale, 1975 .... 14.00
Nebraska, No. 1, Gold, 1970 .... 45.00
Nebraska Czechs, 1970 .... 8.00
New Hampshire, 1976 .... 17.00
Paul Revere, 1975 .... 10.00
Polish American Legion, 1976 ....15.00 to 17.00
President Inauguration, 1953 ....18.00 to 20.00
Prestige Bookend, 1970 .... 9.00
Race Car, Mario Andretti, No. 9, Yellow 45.00

Red Dog Dan, 1974 . . . . 12.00
Sherry Pitcher . . . . .4.00 to 6.00
Ship Lantern, 1974 . . . . .18.00 to 20.00
Steelhead Trout, 1976 . . . . 14.00
Tennessee Centennial 10.00
Town Crier, 1976 . . . . 12.00
Venus 15.00
W.V. Forest Festival, 1975 . . . . 50.00
W.V. National Guard, 1973 . . . . 35.00
Wisconsin Football 25.00
York, Nebraska, 1970 . . . . 13.00

--------------------------------------- OLD RIP VAN WINKLE ---------------------------------------

Old Rip Van Winkle apothecary jars and figurals shaped like Rip Van Winkle were made from 1968 to 1977. J.P. Van Winkle and Son, Louisville, Kentucky, made these bottles and others under the Old Commonwealth and Old Fitzgerald labels. Old Rip Van Winkle bourbon is still sold.

OLD RIP VAN WINKLE, Bay Colony, 1975 . . . . 13.00
Cardinal, 1974 . . . . .15.00 to 17.00
Colonial Virginia, 1974 . . . . 12.00
Kentucky, Wildcat, 1974 . . . . 28.00
Kentucky Sportsman, 1973 . . . . 25.00
New Jersey Bicentennial, 1975 . . . . 15.00
New York Bicentennial, 1975 . . . . 16.00
No. 1, Rip Van Winkle, Green, 1975 . . . . 24.00
No. 2, Rip Van Winkle, Reclining, 1975 . . . . 25.00
No. 3, Rip Van Winkle, Standing, 1977 . . . . 21.00
Sanford, N.C., Centennial, 1974 . . . . 12.00

--- PACESETTER ---

Bottles shaped like cars and trucks were made under the Pacesetter label from 1974 to about 1983.

PACESETTER, Ahrens Fox Pumper, 1983 . . . . 125.00
Camero Z-28, Gold, 1982 . . . . .46.00 to 48.00
Camero Z-28, Platinum, 1982 . . . . .53.00 to 55.00
Corvette, 1975, Moving Wheels . . . . .65.00 to 69.00
Corvette, 1978, Black, 375 Milliliter . . . . .39.00 to 42.00
Corvette, 1978, Brown, 375 Milliliter 39.00
Corvette, 1978, Gold, Milliliter 49.00
Corvette, 1978, White, 375 Milliliter 39.00
Corvette, 1978, Yellow, 375 Milliliter 39.00
Fire Truck, LaFrance, White, 1982 . . . . 68.00
Fire Truck, Snorkle, Red, 1982 . . . . 58.00
Mack, Truck, Distillery 115.00
Mack Pumper 150.00
Mack Truck, Barrel 125.00
Olsonite Eagle, No. 8, 1974 . . . . 70.00
Pirsch Pumper, Red, 1983 . . . . 69.00
Pirsch Pumper, White, 1983 . . . . 60.00
Pontiac Firebird, 1980 . . . . 40.00
Tractor, Massey Ferguson, 1939 . . . . 99.00
Tractor, No. 1, John Deere, 1982 . . . . 140.00
Tractor, No. 2, International Harvester, 1983 . . . . 105.00
Tractor, No. 3, International Harvester, 1983, Miniature 122.00
Tractor, No. 4, 4-Wheel Drive, Big Red, 1983 . . . . 120.00
Tractor, No. 4, 4-Wheel Drive, Ford, 1983 . . . . 100.00
Tractor, No. 4, 4-Wheel Drive, Green Machine, 1983 . . . . 90.00
Tractor, No. 5, Allis Chalmers, 1984 . . . . 100.00
Tractor, Steiger, 4-Wheel Drive, 1959 . . . . 180.00
Truck, Coca-Cola 158.00
Truck, Elizabethtown 127.00
Vukovich, 1974 . . . . 90.00

PEPPER SAUCE

There was little refrigeration and poor storage facilities for fresh meat in the nineteenth century. Slightly spoiled food was often cooked and eaten with the help of strong spices or sauces. Small hot chili peppers were put into a bottle of vinegar. After a few weeks the spicy mixture was called *pepper sauce*. A distinctive bottle, now known as a pepper sauce bottle, was favored for this mixture. It was a small bottle, 6 to 12 inches high, with a long slim neck. The bottle could be square or cylindrical or decorated with arches or rings. Most were made of common bottle glass in shades of aqua or green. A few were made of cobalt or milk glass. Very early examples may have a pontil mark. More information on pepper sauce can be found in the book *Ketchup, Pickles, Sauces* by Betty Zumwalt.

PEPPER SAUCE, Aqua, Paneled, Applied Collar, Impressed Pontil, 8 In.	22.00
Aqua, Roped Corners, Pontil, Applied Sloping Collar, 1855, 11 In.	240.00
Beehive, 21 Ribs, Oval, Double Collar	9.00 to 10.00
Beehive Rings, Partial Label, Aqua	30.00
Cathedral, 4-Sided, Aqua, Applied Top	45.00
Cathedral, 6-Sided, Aqua, 1860s, 8 In.	38.00
Cathedral, 6-Sided, Aqua, Applied Top, IP, 8 1/2 In.	120.00
Cathedral, 6-Sided, Aqua, Applied Top, OP, 8 1/2 In.	140.00
Cathedral, 6-Sided, Light Blue Green, OP, 1845-1860, 9 In.	145.00
Cathedral, 6-Sided, Light To Medium Blue Green, 1855-1865, 8 3/4 In.	165.00
Cathedral, 6-Sided, Medium Blue Green, OP, 8 In.	150.00
Cathedral, 10-Sided, Aqua, Double Collar, 1870, 10 1/2 In.	130.00
Cathedral, Aqua, Applied Large Top, 8 In.	65.00
Cathedral, Aqua, Applied Top, OP, 8 1/2 In.	90.00
Cathedral, Blue Aqua, IP, Applied Double Collar, 1855, 10 In.	120.00
Cathedral, Blue Green, OP, Applied Double Collar, 1855, 8 3/4 In.	495.00
Cathedral, Deep Aqua, Large Applied Top, OP, 8 In.	265.00
Cathedral, Lime Green, BIMAL, c.1880, 9 1/4 In.	25.00
Cathedral, Medium Blue Green, Double Collar, Tubular Pontil, 1860, 8 3/4 In.	575.00
Cathedral, Smoky, OP, Applied Double Collar, 1855, 10 In.	230.00
Cathedral, Yellow Green, Applied Double Collar, 1865, 10 In.	360.00
Concave Panel, Aqua, Rolled Lip, 8 In.	15.00
E.R. Durkee & Co., Light Green, Tooled Top, 7 3/4 In.	55.00
E.R.D. & Co., Pat. February, '74, Light Green, Tooled Top, 8 In.	55.00
Fluted, Ringed Neck, OP, 7 3/4 In.	30.00
Hinge Molded, Crude Applied Lip, Scalloped Sides	34.00
Pyramid Form, Roped Corners, Deep Aqua, 1845-1860, 11 1/4 In.	385.00
Ribbed, Teal Green, 8 In.	22.00
S & P, 6-Sided, Teal Blue, Spiral Ridges, 8 In.	35.00
S & P, Pat. App. For, On Base, Spiral Rings, Deep Blue Aqua, Tooled Top, 8 In.	65.00
S & P, Pat. App. For, On Base, Spiral, Green, Cap, 8 In.	45.00
S & P, Pat. App. For, On Base, Spiraled Ridges, Blue Green, 8 In.	50.00
S & P, Pat. Appl. For, Emerald Green, 8 In.	75.00
Scalloped Sides, Paneled Shoulder, Hinge Molded, Applied Lip, 8 In.	35.00
Teal Blue, 9 In.	20.00
W.K.L. & Co., Cathedral, Aqua, Double Collar, Pontil, 1860, 10 In.	120.00
Wells Miller & Provost, 8-Sided, Petal Shape, Ring Neck, Aqua, Pebbled, Pontil	125.00
Wells Miller & Provost, No. 217 Front St., New York, Aqua, OP, 8 In.	100.00

PEPSI-COLA

Caleb Davis Bradham, a New Bern, North Carolina, druggist, invented and named Pepsi-Cola. Although he registered the trademark, the word *Pepsi-Cola* in calligraphy script, in 1903, he claimed that it had been used since 1898. A simpler version was registered in 1906. The bottle is marked with the name. The name in a hexagonal frame with the words *A Sparkling Beverage* was registered in 1937. This logo was printed on the bottle. The bottle cap colors were changed to red, white, and blue in 1941 as a patriotic gesture. Until 1951, the words Pepsi and Cola were separated by 2 dashes. These bottles are called *double dash* by collectors. In 1951 the modern logo with a single hyphen was introduced. The simulated cap logo was used at the same time. The name *Pepsi* was started in 1911, but it was not until 1966 that the block-lettered logo was registered. Both names are still used. A few very early Pepsi bottles were made of amber glass. Many other Pepsi bottles with local bottlers' names were made in the early 1900s. Modern bottles made for special events are also collected. There is a club, Pepsi-Cola Collectors Club, P.O. Box 817, Claremont, CA 91711. The company has archives at One Pepsi Way, Somers, NY 10589.

PEPSI-COLA, 2 Full Glasses, Double Dash, 10 In. ....*Illus*	55.00
Bennettsville, S.C., Red Label, 1954	15.00
Bethlehem, Pa., Drum, 8 In.	50.00
Chamberlain, S.D., Blue & Red Label, 1946	20.00
Charlottesville, Va., Blue Aqua, 1923-1924	75.00
Chillin', Shaq, Long Neck, 9 In. ....*Illus*	10.00
Diet Pepsi, 10 In. ....*Illus*	6.00
Do Not Drink Novelty, Applied Color Label, Cap, 1950s, 3 1/2 In.	25.00
Durham, N.C., Amethyst, 1910	150.00
Durham, N.C., Aqua, 1928	70.00
Elko, Nev., Blue & Red Label, 1946	25.00
Exmore, Va., Aqua, 1920-1922	75.00
Fayetteville, N.C., Blue Aqua, 1908	85.00
Long Island City, 10 In. ....*Illus*	45.00
Los Angeles, Calif., Red Label, 1955	15.00
Lufton, Texas, Blue & Red Label, 1946	20.00
Merced, Cal., Blue & Red Label, 1947	15.00
Mount Airy, N.C., Green Aqua, ABM, 1920-1924	75.00
Nashville, Tenn., Blue & Red Label, 1947	20.00
New York, N.Y., 418 Back Of Neck, Red Label, 1954	15.00
New York, N.Y., Red Label, 1957	10.00
Norfolk, Va., Aqua, 1920	75.00
Norfolk, Va., Blue Aqua, ABM, 1918	75.00
Oroville, Cal., Red Label, 1950	20.00
Patio Diet Cola, Red Label, 1963, 16 Oz.	8.00
Patio Pepsi-Cola Company, Red Label, 1961	10.00
Redding, Cal., Red Label, 1953	15.00
Refreshing Healthful, Grace Bros., Santa Rosa, Cal., Label, 1926-1928	50.00
Refreshing Healthful, New Century Beverage Co., San Francisco, Label, 1926-1928 ...	50.00
Rocky Mount, N.C., Green Aqua, 1920	95.00
Roseburg, Ore., Red Label, 1955	12.00
Sacramento, Cal., Red Label, 1956	10.00
San Francisco, Cal., Red Label, 8 Oz.	15.00
Santa Rosa, Cal., Red Label, 1949, 8 Oz.	8.00
Soda Fountain Syrup, 10 In. ....*Illus*	25.00
Suffolk, Va., Aqua, 1908	85.00
Suffolk, Va., Aqua, 1914	95.00

Pepsi-Cola, 2 Full Glasses, Double Dash, 10 In.	Pepsi-Cola, Chillin', Shaq, Long Neck, 9 In.	Pepsi-Cola, Diet Pepsi, 10 In.	Pepsi-Cola, Long Island City, 10 In.	Pepsi-Cola, Soda Fountain Syrup, 10 In.

Twin Falls, Idaho, Blue & Red Label, 1947	20.00
Wenatchee, Wash., Red Label, Contents, 1953	20.00
Woodland, Cal., Light Blue Label, 1948	25.00
Woodland, Cal., Light Blue Label, 1952	15.00

-- **PERFUME** --

Perfume is a liquid mixture of aromatic spirits and alcohol. Cologne is similar but has more alcohol in the mixture so it is not as strong. Perfume bottles are smaller than colognes and usually more decorative. Most perfume bottles today are from the twentieth century. Some were made by famous glass makers such as Lalique or Webb, and some held expensive perfumes such as Schiaparelli, Nina Ricci's Coeur de Joie, or D'Orsay's Le Lys D'Orsay. DeVilbiss is a manufacturer of the spray tops used on perfume bottles and the name sometimes appears in a description. The word *factice,* which often appears in ads, refers to store display bottles. The International Perfume Bottle Association publishes a newsletter (3314 Shamrock Rd., Tampa, FL 33629). Related bottles may be found in the Cologne and Scent categories.

PERFUME, Ahmed Soliman, Egyptian Queen, Enamel, Cloth Stopper, 3 3/4 In., Box	2855.00
Baccarat, Christian Dior, Miss Dior, Clear & Frosted, Obelisk, 8 In.	795.00
Baccarat, City Of Paris, Ah!! Paris, Clear & Frosted, Coat Of Arms, Stopper, 3 3/4 In. . .	2065.00
Baccarat, Coty, Ambre Antique, Chinese Dragon, Gilt, Square Stopper, 4 In.	1585.00
Baccarat, D'Orsay, Bouquet D'Orsay, Heart Shape, Floral, Gilt Label, Stopper, 3 1/2 In. .	555.00
Baccarat, D'Orsay, Roses D'Orsay, Brass Lower Band, Inner Stopper, 5 1/4 In.	2380.00
Baccarat, Guerlain, Ode, Amphora Shape, Frosted, Rosebud Stopper, Box, 7 3/4 In.	2220.00
Baccarat, Houbigant, Parfum D'Argeville, 12-Sided, Apothecary Style, Stopper, 4 In. . . .	315.00
Baccarat, Les Parfums De Rosine, Poiret, Black Oval Stopper, Ribbon, 4 5/8 In.	1180.00
Baccarat, Lubin, Kismet, Elephant Shape, Frosted Mahout Stopper, 4 1/4 In.	6740.00
Baccarat, Tresor De Muguet, Engraved & Filt, Stopper, 1908, 5 In.	595.00
Benoit, Merry Christmas, Black, Gilt Nativity Scene, Mary & Jesus Stopper, 4 3/4 In. . . .	3015.00
Blown, 3-Piece Mold, Sapphire Blue, Plume, Round Collar, Pontil, 6 7/8 In.	7700.00
Bolton & Neely, Perfumery Dept., New Haven, Ct., Tooled Lip, Cork, 3 3/8 In.	5.00
Bourjois, Evening In Paris, Cobalt Blue, Hotel Door Presentation, Box, 3 7/8 In.	910.00
Bourjois, Kobako, Allover Molded Oriental Floral, Stopper, Box, 3 1/4 In.	675.00
Bourjois, Two For You, Cobalt Blue & Clear, Fitted Box, 3 1/4 & 1 1/4 In., 2 Piece	240.00
Breidenbach & Cie., Jockey Club, Ribbon Neck, Presentation, c.1880, 5 1/2 In., Pair . . .	1030.00
Christian Dior, Miss Dior, Amphora Shape, Teardrop Stopper, Box, 3 1/2 In.	360.00
Christmas Tree Shape, Germany, 1920, 3 3/4 In.	75.00
Ciro, Chevalier De La Nuit, J. Viard, Clear, Frosted, Medieval Knight Stopper, 7 3/4 In. . .	1030.00
Cobalt Blue, Sheared Top, Inside Blob Of Glass, 3 In.	65.00
Corday, Le Renard, Fame, Brass Screw Cap, With Toy Fox On Faux Powder Box, 2 In. . .	205.00
Coty, L'Origan, Inner Stopper, Black Leather Traveling Case, 3 3/4 In., 3 Piece	595.00
Croret, Societe Parisienne De Verreries, Butterfly Front, Daisy Stopper, 2 3/4 In.	1425.00
Cruselashoyca Perfumistas, Habana, Cuba, 12 In.	55.00
Cut Glass, Hexagonal Design, Sterling Silver Hinged Cap, Ground Stopper, 3 1/2 In. . . .	30.00
Cut Glass, Rectangular, Small Ground Stopper, 3 In.	10.00
D'Amboise, Mimosa, H. Saumont, Plant Design, Square, 1925, 1 1/2 In.	1430.00
D'Izia, J. Viard, Molded Vertical Stripes, Frosted Button Stopper, Box, 3 1/2 In.	715.00
D'Orsay, Le Chevalier A La Rose, Gilt, 4 Lobed Shape, Stopper, 1912, 12 1/2 In.	950.00
D'Orsay, Le Dandy, Milord, Trophee, Belle De Jour, Display Stand, 2 3/4 In., 4 Piece . . .	1030.00
Dabrook, Art Nouveau Woman On Label, No Stopper, 2 1/2 In. . . . .*Illus*	3.50
Dabrook's Perfumes, Detroit, 3 1/2 In.	10.00
Dark Cobalt Blue, Sheared Top, Cork, 1890, 2 1/2 In.	75.00
De Vigny, Le Golliwogg, Black Head Shaped Stopper, Black Fur Hair, 3 1/2 In.	1110.00
DeVilbiss, Black, Oval, Vertical Gilt Stripes, Gilt Pedestal, Round Foot, c.1920, 9 In. . . .	255.00
Dubarry, Apres La Pluie, Depinoix, Flower & Fruit Design, Frosted Stopper, 3 1/2 In. . .	1110.00
Dubarry, Golden Morn, Clear & Frosted, Baroque Masks, Square Stopper, 5 In.	2380.00
Elizabeth Arden, Memoire Cherie, Woman's Head & Torso, Clear & Frosted, 3 In.	635.00
Elysian Chemists & Perfumers, Detroit, Cobalt Blue, 6 1/2 In.	30.00
End Of Day, Pink, Red, Blue, White, Pewter Atomizer, 6 1/2 In.	130.00
F. Wolff & Sohn, J. Viard, Flattened Round Shape, Black Star Stopper, 1 3/4 In.	395.00
Faberge, Straw Hat, 8-Sided, Bakelite Screw Cap, Flower Shaped Card, 1 1/4 In.	280.00
Fern & Scroll, Embossed All Sides, Aqua, Label, Fluted Neck, OP, 5 1/2 In.	125.00
Fragonard, Moment Vole, Zizanic, Gardenia Royal & Belle De Nuit, 2 In., 4 Piece	555.00
G.W. Laird, Perfumer, New York, Rectangular, Milk Glass, 4 1/2 In.	15.00

Ganna Walska, Divorcons, Labels, Rectangular, Brass Screw Cap, Box, 1927, 2 1/4 In. . . 140.00
Gelle Freres, Lila Supreme, Clear, Frosted, Molded Flowers Around, Stopper, 4 1/4 In. . . . 715.00
George Lorenz Perfumers, Emerald Green, Floral Design, Ball Stopper, Label, 7 3/8 In. 20.00
Germay Embossed On Base, 8-Sided, Long Glass Dauber, 2 In. 15.00
Gi. Vi. Emme, Contessa Azzura, Label, Blue Button Stopper, Round Box, 1 1/2 In. 400.00
Gueldy, Vision D'Orient, A. Jollivet, Oriental Mask 2 Sides, Black Stopper, 4 In. 1190.00
Guerlain, Caravelle, Black, Sailing Ship Shape, Gilt Stopper, 5 1/8 In. 2380.00
Guerlain, Chant D'Aromes, Black, White & Gold Label, 2 7/8 In. 240.00
Guerlain, Eau De Verveine, Pochet Et Du Courval, Label, Classic Stopper, 6 3/4 In. 875.00
Guerlain, Esprit De Fleurs De Cedrat, Flacon, Mushroom Stopper, 8 1/2 In. 1190.00
Guerlain, Muguet, Vase Shape, Hollow Stopper, Ribbon Neck, 3 3/4 In. 1110.00
Guerlain, Pavillon Royal, Gilt, Presentation 1924, Stopper, 4 In. 1505.00
Guerlain, Vol De Nuit, Smoky Gray, Square, Stopper, Box, 4 3/4 & 3 5/8 In., 2 Piece . . . 1190.00
Guyla, Caresse Parisienne, Upside Down Cone Shape, Orange Flowers, 5 3/4 In. 7535.00
Harriet Hubbard Ayer, Muguet, Heart Shape, Braid Shoulders, Pouch, 2 In. 380.00
Helena Rubinstein, Heaven Sent, Eau De Parfum, New York, 5 1/2 In. . . . . *Illus* 8.00
Honore Payan, Real Parfum, J. Viard, Oval, Labels, Fan Shaped Stopper, 3 7/8 In. 795.00
Houbigant, Chantilly, Amphora Shape, On Metal Ice Cream Parlor Chair, 2 In. 160.00
Isabey, Bleu De Chine, Bobin Freres, 8-Sided, Enameled Floral, Aqua, 2 3/4 In. 2060.00
Isabey, Le Collier D'Isabey, 6 Different Flacons, Ball Stopper, Case, 2 1/2 In., 6 Piece . . . 5550.00
Isabey, Le Gardenia D'Isabey, Art Deco Label, Bakelite Screw Cap, Box, 2 In. 135.00
Jean Patou, Moment Supreme, Tester, Raspberry Shape, Sealed, Box, 2 1/4 In. 555.00
Lalique, Carre Hirondelle, Clear & Frosted, Swallows, Rectangular Stopper, 3 5/8 In. . . . 3175.00
Lalique, Colgate, Night, Clear & Frosted, Floral Design, Button Stopper, 3 1/4 In. 3570.00
Lalique, Coty, Chypre, Curved Pyramid Shape, Thistle Stopper, 3 In. 1110.00
Lalique, Coty, Jacinthe, Gilt Label, Tall Rectangular, Frosted Stopper, 5 1/4 In. 515.00
Lalique, Coty, L'Effleurt, Gray Glass Plaque, Faceted Ball Stopper, 5 3/4 In. 5950.00
Lalique, D'Heraud, Marjolaine, Square, Molded Face Each Side, 1925, 3 3/4 In. 1905.00
Lalique, D'Heraud, Phalene, Butterfly Shape, Sienna Patina, Flower Stopper, 3 In. 9520.00
Lalique, D'Orsay, Chypre, Clear & Frosted, Daisy Design, Stopper, 2 1/2 In. 795.00
Lalique, D'Orsay, Leurs Ames, Large Tiara Stopper With Nudes, 5 In. 15860.00
Lalique, De Vigny, D'Ou Vient-Il, Clear & Frosted, Butterfly Stopper, 3 3/4 In. 7930.00
Lalique, De Vigny, L'Ambre, Floral, Vase Shape, Clear, Frosted, Conical Stopper, 6 In. . . 5155.00
Lalique, Fioret, Chose Promise, Clear, Frosted, Woman's Figure Stopper, 5 In. 12690.00
Lalique, Fougeres, Fern Molded Design, Woman Busts Center, Stopper, 3 7/8 In. 14275.00
Lalique, Gabilla, La Violette, Stylized Violet Design, Button Stopper, 3 1/2 In. 5155.00
Lalique, Lalo, Flat Flower Shape, Shaped Petals, Flat Round Stopper, 1 1/2 In. 5155.00
Lalique, Lepage, Clear & Frosted, Nudes & Floral, Stopper, 4 5/8 In. 10300.00
Lalique, Meplat, Medallion 1 Side, Nudes Other, Frosted Stopper, 5 1/8 In. 10300.00
Lalique, Nina Ricci, Coeur-Joie, L'Air Du Temps, Stopper, 4 3/8 & 5 1/4 In., Pair 595.00
Lalique, Quatre Soleils, 4 Floral Medallions, Button Stopper, 2 3/4 In. 9515.00

Perfume, Dabrook, Art
Nouveau Woman On
Label, No Stopper,
2 1/2 In.

Perfume, Helena
Rubinstein, Heaven
Sent, Eau De Parfum,
New York, 5 1/2 In.

Perfume, Revlon,
Intimate, Eau De
Toilette, Spray
Mist, 6 In.

Perfume, Roger &
Gallet, Bouquet
Nouveau, L. Chalon,
Green, 4 3/8 In.

Lalique, Rene, Vaporizer, Molded Women Figures Around, 3 5/8 In. 555.00
Lalique, Roger & Gallet, Pyska, Triangular, Clear & Frosted Stopper, 4 In. 2538.00
Lalique, Serpent, Molded Coiled Snake, Frosted Snake's Head Stopper, 3 1/2 In. 5155.00
Lalique, Spirales, Ionic Column Shape, Clear & Frosted, 3 7/8 In. 3015.00
Lanvin, Colonne Morris, Kiosk Shape, Ceramic, Store Display, 10 7/8 In. 395.00
Lighting Perfumes Heliotrophy, Label Under Glass 150.00
Loulette, Femme Divine, Depinoix, Gilt Drapery & Floral, Stopper, 3 1/8 In. 2060.00
Lubin, Magda, J. Viard, 8 Round Panels, Woman's Head Stopper, 1921, 5 In. 3965.00
Lubin Parfumeur Paris, Cylindrical, Embossed, Ground Stopper, 3 3/4 In. 5.00
Lucien LeLong, Opening Night, Stepped Pyramid, Box, Gold Cap, 1 1/2 In. 1745.00
Lucien LeLong, Perfume Album, Tailspin, Indiscret, Sirocco, Orgueil, Box, 5 Piece 1905.00
Lucien LeLong, Tailspin, 8 Vertical Panels, Stopper, Label, Box, 3 5/8 In. 715.00
Lucien LeLong, White Bakelite Tassel Shaped Covering, 2 3/4 In. 395.00
Marquay, Prince Douka, Figural, Satin Cape, Frosted Hindu Stopper, 3 5/8 In. 435.00
Mary Chess, Elizabethan, George VI & Queen Elizabeth, 1 1/8 In. 475.00
Mary Chess, Rainbow Sextette, Chess Piece Shape, Brass Cap, Box, 2 3/8 In., 6 Piece . . 675.00
Mary Dunhill, White Hyacinth, Ball Shape Stopper, Box, 2 1/2 In. 355.00
Myrurgia, Embrujo De Sevilla, J. Viard, Urn Shape, 8-Sided, Label, 2 7/8 In. 475.00
Palmer, Script, Embossed Diagonally, Green, Oval, 5 5/16 In. 20.00
Phalon & Sons, New York, Cylindrical, Ground Stopper, 4 In. 15.00
Potter & Moore, Mitcham Lavender, Silver Jubilee, Brass Cap, Gilt Box, 4 3/4 In. 635.00
Prince Matchabelli, Duchess Of York, Eau De Toilette, Cross Stopper, Box, 6 3/4 In. . . 315.00
Prince Matchabelli, Wind Song, Stradivari, Added Attraction, 1 5/8 In., 3 Piece 555.00
Princess Pat, Eau De Toilette, Black, Button Stopper, Box, 3 1/2 & 6 1/4 In., 2 Piece . . . 595.00
Raffy, Voici Paris, Lentil Shape, Opaque Green Stopper, Ribbon, Box, 2 3/8 In. 515.00
Reboux, Clear & Frosted, Cub Shape, Clear Stepped Stopper, 2 3/8 In. 395.00
Revlon, Intimate, Eau De Toilette, Spray Mist, 6 In. . . . . *Illus* 10.00
Richard Hudnut, Deauville, J. Viard, Pear Shape, Aphrodite Rising Stopper, 3 7/8 In. . . 4750.00
Richard Hudnut, R.S.V.P., Rectangular, Label, Clear Ball Stopper, 3 In. 715.00
Rickseckers, N.Y., Cylindrical, 3 1/8 In. 5.00
Robj, Le Secret De Robj, Amphora Shape, Clear Flame Stopper, 6 1/2 In. 475.00
Rodo, Lance Parfum, A. Mucha, Vial, 1900s, 4 3/4 In. 795.00
Roger & Gallet, Bouquet Nouveau, L. Chalon, Green, 4 3/8 In. . . . . *Illus* 2379.00
Roger & Gallet, Innuendo, Pear Shape, Flame Stopper, Label, 3 1/2 In. 715.00
Roger & Gallet, Le Jade & Fleurs D'Amour, Frieze Shoulders, 4 1/4 & 3 1/2 In., Pair . . 515.00
Roger & Gallet, Le Jade, Flattened Pear Shape, Flame Stopper, 3 1/2 In. 755.00
Roger & Gallet, Peau D'Espagne, 4 Molded Women, Stopper, 5 3/4 In. 3805.00
Roger & Gallet, Shake Glass Top 20.00
S. Palmer Perfumer, New York, 2 1/4 In. 5.00
Saville, June, Sundial Shape Casing Bottle, Cardboard Backdrop, Box, 3 1/4 In. 715.00
Schiaparelli, Bulbous, Pink Metal Cap, With 1961 Calendar, 3 In., 2 Piece 200.00
Toilet Water, Matching Undertray, Pomegranate Form, 1860, 8 In. 770.00
Violet, Compliment, Diamond Cut Stopper, Label, 4 3/4 In. 595.00
Violet, L. Gaillard, Brosse, Flattened Oval Shape, Clear & Frosted, 3 3/4 In. 3490.00
Vivaudou, Lady Mary, Dragonfly Design, Frosted Gothic Stopper, 8 1/8 In. 435.00
Volnay, Perlinette, Pink Pearlized Finish, Label, Stopper, 2 In. 355.00
Wil Furs, Padisha, Clear & Frosted, Minaret Stopper, Presentation Box, 3 5/8 In. 2220.00

-------------------------------- **PICKLE** --------------------------------

Pickles were packed in special jars from about 1880 to 1920. The pickle jar was usually large, from one quart to one gallon size. They were made with four to eight sides. The mouth was wide because you had to reach inside to take out the pickle. The top was usually sealed with a cork or tin cover. Many pickle jars were designed with raised gothic arches as panels. These jars are clear examples of the Victorian gothic revival designs, so they are often included in museum exhibitions of the period. Their large size and attractive green to blue coloring make them good accessories in a room. Bottle collectors realize that pickle jars are examples of good bottle design, that they are rare, and that a collection can be formed showing the works of many glasshouses. Pickle bottles are so popular that they are being reproduced. For more information on pickle jars, see *Ketchup, Pickles, Sauces* by Betty Zumwalt.

PICKLE, 6-Sided, Green Aqua, Beaded Neck, 8 1/2 In. 20.00
Albany Glass Works, Cathedral, Aqua, Rolled Lip, IP, 1850, 8 5/8 In. 990.00
Amber, Applied Mouth, Midwest, 13 1/2 In. 330.00

Anchor Pickle & Vinegar Works, Blue Aqua, 1880-1890, 8 In. 45.00
Aqua, Applied Mouth, 13 1/2 In. 185.00
Arrow Brand Pickles, Chicago, Il., Aqua, Tooled Lip, 1890-1900, 7 1/4 In. 165.00
Barrel, Green, Gal. 60.00
Cathedral, 4 Embossed Panels, Leaf Design, Beveled Corners, 1860-1880, 11 In. 175.00
Cathedral, 4-Sided, OP, 9 In. 230.00
Cathedral, Amber, 6-Sided, Tooled Mouth, 1880-1890, 13 3/8 In. 1265.00
Cathedral, Aqua, 11 In. 100.00
Cathedral, Aqua, 6-Sided, 13 1/2 In. 200.00
Cathedral, Aqua, 6-Sided, 13 In. 100.00
Cathedral, Aqua, 6-Sided, Rolled Lip, 1865-1875, 13 1/4 In. 120.00
Cathedral, Aqua, Applied Mouth, 1860-1875, 11 3/4 In. 210.00
Cathedral, Aqua, Applied Mouth, OP, 1850-1860, 7 3/8 In. 145.00
Cathedral, Aqua, Beveled Corners, Fancy Arches, Rolled Mouth, IP, 1860, 11 3/4 In. . . . 525.00
Cathedral, Aqua, Beveled Corners, Tooled Square Mouth, 1845-1860, 11 3/4 In. 185.00
Cathedral, Aqua, Rolled Lip, 1855-1870, 14 In. 330.00
Cathedral, Aqua, Rolled Mouth, Square, 11 3/4 In. 55.00
Cathedral, Arrow Brand, Chicago, Yellow Amber, Tooled Mouth, 1880, 8 5/8 In. 355.00
Cathedral, Clock Face On 2 Sides, Aqua 325.00
Cathedral, Crisscross Design, OP, 6 3/8 In. 85.00
Cathedral, Deep Blue Aqua, Green, Rolled Lip, 1855-1865, 11 3/4 In. 255.00
Cathedral, Deep Blue Green, Rolled Lip, IP, 1865, 11 3/4 In. 1265.00
Cathedral, Deep Emerald Green, Rolled Lip, IP, 1860, 11 1/2 In. 2530.00
Cathedral, Deep Emerald Green, Yellow Tone, Applied Mouth, IP, 1850-1860, 9 In. . . . 690.00
Cathedral, Deep Grass Green, Olive, IP, 1865, 8 1/2 In. 2365.00
Cathedral, Deep Green Aqua, Rolled Lip, Petal Style, Large IP, 1865, 10 5/8 In. 330.00
Cathedral, Deep Olive Yellow, Embossed Leaf Pattern, Rolled Lip, 1865-1880, 8 1/2 In. 1265.00
Cathedral, Emerald Green, Rolled Collar, 1860-1880, 7 1/4 In. 1210.00
Cathedral, Emerald Green, Rolled Lip, IP, 11 3/4 In. .800.00 to 1200.00
Cathedral, Gothic, Green Aqua, Applied Top, 11 1/2 In. 330.00
Cathedral, Green Aqua, Applied Mouth, 1855-1870, 11 1/2 In. 110.00
Cathedral, Green Aqua, Applied Mouth, IP, 1850-1865, 11 1/2 In. 330.00
Cathedral, Green Aqua, Tooled Rolled Mouth, 1860-1880, 11 1/2 In. 150.00
Cathedral, Green, Applied Lip, 13 1/2 In. 187.00
Cathedral, Green, Tooled Rolled Mouth, Square, 15 In. 355.00
Cathedral, Light Blue Green, Applied Mouth, IP, 1855-1865, 11 3/4 In. 165.00
Cathedral, Light Blue Green, Rolled Lip, 1855-1865, 11 3/4 In. 440.00
Cathedral, Light Green, 6-Sided, Applied Mouth, IP, 1855-1865, 9 In. 360.00
Cathedral, Light Green, Bubbles, 11 3/4 In. 325.00
Cathedral, Light Green, Square, 1845-1860, 9 In. 265.00
Cathedral, Light To Medium Apple Green, Applied Mouth, 1855-1865, 10 7/8 In. 440.00
Cathedral, Light To Medium Blue Green, Applied Mouth, 11 3/4 In. 195.00
Cathedral, Light To Medium Blue Green, Rolled Lip, 1855-1865, 11 In. 220.00
Cathedral, Light Yellow Citron, Applied Mouth, 1855-1865, 11 5/8 In. 465.00
Cathedral, Medium Blue Green, 6-Sided, Rolled Lip, Bubbles, 1855-1870, 13 In. 440.00
Cathedral, Medium Blue Green, Applied Mouth, 1855-1870, 11 1/2 In. 220.00
Cathedral, Medium Blue Green, Applied Mouth, Bubbles, 1855-1870, 13 1/2 In. 305.00
Cathedral, Medium Emerald Green, Applied Mouth, 1855-1870, 8 7/8 In. 330.00
Cathedral, Medium Emerald Green, Applied Mouth, Bubbles, 1855-1870, 8 3/4 In. 360.00
Cathedral, Medium Emerald Green, Rolled Lip, 1855-1870, 13 3/8 In. 305.00
Cathedral, Medium Emerald Green, Rolled Lip, OP, 1850-1860, 9 1/4 In. 580.00
Cathedral, Medium Emerald Green, Tooled Rolled Mouth, IP, 1845-1860, 11 1/4 In. . . . 1045.00
Cathedral, Medium Green, 4-Sided, Tooled Mouth, 1860-1880, 10 5/8 In. 715.00
Cathedral, Medium Green, Fancy Arches, Tooled Mouth, 1860-1880, 11 3/4 In. 305.00
Cathedral, Medium To Deep Blue Green, Applied Mouth, Bubbles, 1855-1870, 12 In. . . 580.00
Cathedral, Medium To Deep Blue Green, Rolled Lip, Pontil, 1850-1860, 14 1/2 In. 800.00
Cathedral, Medium To Deep Emerald Green, Rolled Lip, 1865, 11 7/8 In. 855.00
Cathedral, Medium To Deep Emerald Green, Rolled Lip, 1870, 13 3/4 In. 145.00
Cathedral, Molded Flower Baskets & Scrolls, 10 In. 11.00
Cathedral, Pale Blue Green, Rolled Lip, OP, 1860, 7 1/2 In. 165.00
Cathedral, R. & F. Atmore, Blue Aqua, Pontil, c.1865-1875, 11 1/2 In. 525.00
Cathedral, R. & F. Atmore, Blue Aqua, Rolled Lip, c.1855-1865, 11 3/8 In. 255.00
Cathedral, Teal Blue Green, 6-Sided, Base Marked W.T. & Co., Gal., 13 1/2 In. 1295.00

Pickle, H.J. Heinz Co.,
Preserved Sweet
Gherkins, Guaranteed
Pure, 6 1/4 In.

Pickle, Watson Pickle
& Vinegar Works,
Ulam & Co, Paper
Label, 7 In.

Cloverleaf, Aqua, 8-Leaf Shape, Outward Rolled Mouth, Pontil, 8 In.	305.00
Cloverleaf, Medium Orange Amber, Applied Mouth, 1870, 8 3/8 In.	605.00
Cloverleaf, Red Amber, Irregular Square Form, Applied Mouth, 1860-1870, 8 1/8 In.	520.00
Cloverleaf, Sun-Colored Amethyst, 5 1/2 In.	18.00
E.D. Pettengill & Co., Portland, Me., Shaker Brand, Golden Yellow, 5 In.	935.00
E.H.V.B., N.Y., Emerald Green, Applied Top, IP, 8 3/4 In.	4840.00
Fruit Growers Trade, Trademark, Light Blue, Oval, Tooled Top, Pt.	90.00
Goofus, Design, Ground Top, 14 In.	185.00
H.J. Heinz Co., Aqua, Embossed, Rectangular, Cork, 7 1/4 In.	5.00
H.J. Heinz Co., Preserved Sweet Gherkins, Guaranteed Pure, 6 1/4 In. *Illus*	55.00
Heinz, Barrel, Pickle & Keystone Picture, Frosted, Bunghole, Gal.	180.00
Heinz, Keystone, Barrel, Frosted, Ground Top, Gal.	90.00
High Grade Spiced Pickles, Anderson Canning Co., Keokuk, Ia., Label, Glass Lid	35.00
J. McCollick & Co., N.Y., Cathedral, Aqua Teal, Rolled Lip, IP, 9 In.	1650.00
J.K. & S., 2000, 8-Sided, Aqua, Seed Bubbles	20.00
Jar, W.D.S., N.Y., Pale Green Aqua, Rolled Lip, IP, 1855-1865, 7 3/4 In.	200.00
Lea's Celebrated Pickles & Condiments, Mustard, Labels, Rectangular, 7 5/8 In.	25.00
Light Green, 2 Oval Panels, Rounded, Footed, Applied Top	230.00
Light Green, Large Fern Design, Applied Top, 13 In.	145.00
Milwaukee Pickle Co., Wauwatosa, Wis., Amber, Applied Mouth, 1895, 9 3/4 In.	100.00
Pioneer Pickle Works, Sacramento, Ca., Mixed Pickles, Blue Aqua, Label, 10 3/4 In.	55.00
Rectangular, Fluted Corners, Square, 5 1/4 In.	15.00
Richmond Pickle, Richmond, Va., 8 1/4 In.	22.00
Skilton Foote & Co.'s, Bunker Hill Pickles, Aquamarine, Yellow Amber, 1890, 11 In.	210.00
Skilton Foote & Co.'s, Bunker Hill Pickles, Trademark, Yellow, Applied Top, 7 3/4 In.	55.00
Skilton Foote & Co.'s, Bunker Hill, Cathedral, Olive, Tooled Mouth, 1885, 8 In.	175.00
Skilton Foote & Co.'s, Bunker Hill, Citron, Variant, With Trees, Qt.	65.00
Skilton Foote & Co.'s, Bunker Hill, Gold Orange Amber, Square, 6 3/4 In. 135.00 to	195.00
Skilton Foote & Co.'s, Bunker Hill, Light Amber, Qt. 50.00 to	100.00
Skilton Foote & Co.'s, Bunker Hill, Lime Green, Barrels & Monument, Pt.	180.00
Square, Light Green, Ring Around Neck, Tapered Sides	40.00
Stoddard, Medium Amber, Applied Mouth, 1855-1870, 8 1/4 In.	230.00
T. Smith & Co., Cathedral, Aqua, 6-Sided, Rolled Lip, OP, 9 1/2 In.	690.00
T.B. Smith & Co., Philada, Aqua, 9 1/2 In.	550.00
Vase, 3-Piece Mold, Gold Amber, Allover Flower & Beaded, Ground Top, 9 3/4 In.	130.00
W. Numsen & Son, Baltimore, Aqua, Rolled Lip, 1850-1860, 10 1/2 In.	715.00
W.D. Smith, N.Y., Light Green Aqua, Square, 9 In.	305.00
W.K. Lewis & Co., Boston, Aqua, Lobe Sided, IP, 9 In.	475.00
W.K. Lewis & Co., Boston, Mass., Aqua, Rolled Lip, IP, 1850-1865, 10 1/2 In.	495.00
Watson Pickle & Vinegar Works, Ulam & Co, Paper Label, 7 In. *Illus*	48.00
William Numsen & Sons, Baltimore, Cathedral, Citron, Rolled Lip, Pontil, 1860, 9 In.	385.00
William Underwood & Co., Cathedral, Aqua, Rolled Lip, IP, 1860, 12 1/2 In.	190.00
Wm. Bodmann, Baltimore, Arches Below Swirled Neck, Cylindrical, Pontil, 11 1/2 In.	330.00

─────────────────── **POISON** ───────────────────

Everyone knows you must be careful about how you store poisonous substances. Our
ancestors had the same problem. Nineteenth-century poison bottles were usually made
with raised designs so the user could feel the danger. The skull and crossbones symbol

was sometimes shown, but usually the bottle had ridges or raised embossing. The most interesting poison bottles were made from the 1870s to the 1930s. Cobalt blue and bright green glass were often used. The bottle was designed to look different from any type of food container. One strange British poison bottle made in 1871 was shaped like a coffin and was often decorated with a death's head. Another bottle was shaped like a skull. Poison collectors search for any bottle that held poison or that is labeled poison. Included are animal and plant poisons as well as dangerous medicines. A helpful reference book is *Poison Bottle Workbook* by Rudy Kuhn.

POISON, A.C. Meyer & Co., Death Dust, Embossed, 1890, 5 In. 10.00
  Acid Carbolic, WT & Co., Cobalt Blue, Crosshatch, White Enameled Label, 7 In. 150.00
  Amber, 12 Vertical Grooves, Cylindrical, 7 In. 15.00
  Amber, Round, Qt., 9 In. 35.00
  Ammonia, Mnfd. By S.F. Gaslight Co., Circle On Shoulder, Yellow Green, 9 1/4 In. 1870.00
  Ammonia, Poisonous, Not To Be Taken, Bars, Dots, Aqua, Oval, England, 6 1/8 In. 15.00
  Ammonia, Poisonous, Not To Be Taken, Cylindrical, Ribbed, 6 1/2 In. 40.00
  Ammonia, San Francisco Gaslight Co., Gold Amber, Tooled Mouth, 9 In. 120.00
  Apothecary, Methyl-Hydrate, Poison, Mullins Pharmacy, Label, Stopper, 6 In. 8.00
  Apothecary, Nitrate Owl Poison, Glass Stopper, Skull & Crossbones Top, 8 In. 85.00
  Apothecary, Tinct. Cannab. Ind. Poison, Cobalt Blue, Horizontal Ribs, 1/2 Pt. 135.00
  Aqua, Ribbed, Porcelain Stopper, 10 In. 15.00
  Bernard P. Christ, XXXX, Skull & Crossbones, Label Under Glass, Qt. 250.00
  Birmingham Work House, Not To Be Taken, 6-Sided, Green, 3 Panels, 6 In. 90.00
  Bolic Disinfectant, Aqua, Cylindrical, Sheared Top, 5 In. 14.00
  Bottled By Jeyes, Green, Embossed, Oval, 6 In. ....10.00 to 25.00
  Bowker's Pyrox, Jar, Lid & Clamp, 4 1/2 In. 25.00
  Bowker's Pyrox, The One Best Spray, Embossed Poison, Jug, Gal. 70.00
  Bowman's Drug Store, C.L.G. Co., Cobalt Blue, 1910, 4 In. 220.00
  Bowman's Drug Store, Cobalt Blue, 1890-1910, 6 1/4 In. 770.00
  Bowman's Drug Store, Cobalt Blue, Tooled Lip, 3 3/8 In. ....175.00 to 280.00
  Bowman's Drug Store, Deep Cobalt Blue, Tooled Lip, 1890-1910, 2 3/4 In. 175.00
  British Household Ammonia, Poisonous, Not To Be Taken, Aqua, Oval, 6 1/2 In. 20.00
  Burdall's LTD Manufacturing Chemist, Sheffield, Not To Be Taken Internally, Aqua . 35.00
  C.L.G. Co., Cobalt Blue, 7 1/2 In. 205.00
  C.L.G. Co., Patent Applied For, Cobalt Blue, 7 1/2 In. 205.00
  Carbolic Acid, Booker, Richmond, Va., Poison On Label, Kelly Green, 7 1/2 In. 12.00
  Carbolic Acid, Cobalt Blue, Embossed Warnings, Oval, 7 1/2 In. 10.00
  Carbolic Acid, Schieffelin, Waxpaper Around Bottle, 1930, 7 1/2 In. 2.50
  Carbona-Marshal Chemical Co., Carbona, 12-Sided, Aqua, Cork, 6 In. 5.00
  Champion Chemical Co., Springfield, Ohio, Embalming Fluid, 56 Oz. 185.00
  Chemical Cat, Chases Rats & Mice, St. Louis, Mo., 8 Oz. ....*Illus* 10.00
  Chester A. Baker, Boston, Mass., Cobalt Blue, Tooled Lip, 1890-1910, 5 In. ....275.00 to 305.00
  Clarks Ammonia, Aqua, Contents Stain, BIMAL, 8 In. 30.00
  Cobalt Blue, 3-Sided, 3 In. 35.00
  Cobalt Blue, Arrow, 6-Sided, 10 1/2 In. 150.00
  Cobalt Blue, Cylindrical, Quilted, 7 In. 90.00
  Cobalt Blue, Latticework, Label, Stopper, 5 1/2 In. 95.00
  Cobalt Blue, Pat. Appl'd. For, Tooled Mouth, 1894-1910, 3 1/2 In. 3080.00
  Cobalt Blue, Pat. Appl'd. For, Tooled Mouth, 1894-1910, 4 1/4 In. 2035.00
  Cobalt Blue, Patented June 26 1894, 1890-1910, 3 5/8 In. 330.00
  Cobalt Blue, Quilted, 5 1/2 In. 65.00
  Cobalt Blue, Ribbed, Glass Stopper, Tooled Top, 8 1/4 In. 75.00
  Cobalt Blue, Tooled Lip, Pat. June 26 1894, 1890-1910, 2 7/8 In. 1925.00
  Coffin, Amber, 5 In. 900.00
  Coffin, Cobalt Blue, Tooled Lip, 1890-1910, 3 3/8 In. 220.00
  Coffin, Irregular 6-Sided, Emerald Green, Glass Stopper, 3 In. 28.00
  Coffin, Medium Cobalt Blue, Tooled Mouth, Original Label, Norwich, 8 In. 965.00
  Coffin, Medium Yellow Amber, 3 1/2 In. 290.00
  Compressed Antiseptic Tablets, Amber, ABM Lip, 1910-1920, 2 In. 525.00
  Davis & Geck, Brooklyn, N.Y., Cobalt Blue, Tooled Mouth, 1890-1910, 3 1/4 In. 1760.00
  Davis & Miller Worm Destroyer, Remedy For Worms, 6-Sided, Aqua, 4 In. 60.00
  Dead Shot Sure Death To Insects, Dr. Traeger & Son, Scranton, Pa., Aqua, Label ... 100.00
  Dead Stuck For Bugs, Bug Stuck With Pin, Aqua, 7 In. 20.00
  Dead Stuck For Bugs, Cottle B. Marshall & Co., Cassel Germany & Philadelphia, Aqua 45.00

Dead Stuck For Bugs, Gottlieb Marshall, Philadelphia 8.00
Dioxogen, Oakland Chemical, Amber, Round, 7 In. 5.00
Doctor Oreste Sinanide's Medicinal Preparations, Coffin, Cobalt Blue, 4 In.   275.00 to 330.00
Dr. Hobson's Larkspur Lotion, Pfeiffer Co., Skull & Crossbones, Label, Lid, 1930s   . .   5.00
Dr. Stonebraker's Rat Killer, Baltimore, Md., Aqua, Rolled Lip, 1850-1865, 3 In. 145.00
Dr. Trager's Dead Shot Sure Death To All Bugs 20.00
Durfee Embalming Fluid Co., Grand Rapids, Tooled Lip, Label, 1910, 8 5/8 In. 145.00
Dutchers Dead Shot For Bed Bugs, St. Albans, Vt., Aqua, 1860, 5 In. 440.00
E.R. Squibb & Son's, N.Y., Cobalt Blue, Glass Stopper, 1890-1910, 5 In. 465.00
E.R.S. & S. Co., Deep Cobalt Blue, Sawtooth Edge Stopper, 1910, 5 In. 440.00
Eastman, Rochester, N.Y., Graduation Marks, 5 In. 7.00
Eastman Kodak, Amber, Label, Partial Contents, BIMAL, 3 In. 10.00
Eastman Kodak Co., Rochester, N.Y., Light Amber 16.00
Eastman Kodak Co., Rochester, N.Y., Sulphite Of Soda, Amber, 1890s, 6 1/4 In. 12.00
Eastman Kodak Tested Chemicals, Rochester, N.Y., 5 In. 10.00
Embalming Fluid, National Casket Co., Blob Top, Square, 1890, 1/2 Gal. 60.00
Embossed Not To Be Taken, Aqua, Cylindrical, Applied Top, 8 1/2 In. 60.00
Embossed Not To Be Taken, B.F.G. Co., Cobalt Blue, 6-Sided, Canada, 5 1/2 In. 55.00
Embossed Not To Be Taken, Carbolic Acid, Cobalt Blue Label, England, 6 3/4 In. 60.00
Embossed Not To Be Taken, Cobalt Blue, 2 Panels, 3 5/8 In.   12.00
Embossed Not To Be Taken, Cobalt Blue, 3 Ribbed Panels, BIMAL, 4 1/4 In. 65.00
Embossed Not To Be Taken, Cobalt Blue, 6-Sided, 3 In. 9.00
Embossed Not To Be Taken, Cobalt Blue, 6-Sided, 4 Oz., 5 1/2 In. 15.00
Embossed Not To Be Taken, Cobalt Blue, 6-Sided, 5 In. 16.00
Embossed Not To Be Taken, Cobalt Blue, 6-Sided, 6 3/4 In. 30.00
Embossed Not To Be Taken, Cobalt Blue, 6-Sided, BIMAL, 7 In. 35.00
Embossed Not To Be Taken, Cobalt Blue, 6-Sided, Ribbed, England, 1 Oz. 15.00
Embossed Not To Be Taken, Cobalt Blue, 6-Sided, Vertical Ribs, 2 5/8 In. 12.00
Embossed Not To Be Taken, Cobalt Blue, 6-Sided, Vertical Ribs, 3 5/8 In. 12.00
Embossed Not To Be Taken, Cobalt Blue, Pulv Opii On Painted Label, 1900, 6 In. 150.00
Embossed Not To Be Taken, Cobalt Blue, Ribbed, 3 1/4 In. 22.00
Embossed Not To Be Taken, Cobalt Blue, Ribbed, 7 1/4 In. 60.00
Embossed Not To Be Taken, Cobalt Blue, Ribbed, BIMAL, 6 5/8 In. 35.00
Embossed Not To Be Taken, Cobalt Blue, Ribbed, Oval, England, 8 In. 20.00
Embossed Not To Be Taken, Cobalt Blue, Tooled Mouth, England, 1890-1915, 13 In. . .   185.00
Embossed Not To Be Taken, Dark Green, 6-Sided, 2 3/4 In. . . . . *Illus*   15.00
Embossed Not To Be Taken, Deep Cobalt Blue, Tooled Lip, England, 6 3/4 In. 110.00
Embossed Not To Be Taken, Giftig, Olive Emerald Green, South Africa, 1 Oz. 50.00
Embossed Not To Be Taken, Green, 6-Sided, BIMAL, 5 In. 25.00
Embossed Not To Be Taken, Irregular, Yellow Green, 6-Sided, X Design 30.00
Embossed Not To Be Taken, Jug, Amber, Lattice Ribbing Front, 6 1/2 In. 24.00
Embossed Not To Be Taken, K-8912 On Base, Ribbed, Cobalt Blue, BIMAL, 5 5/8 In.   25.00
Embossed Not To Be Taken, Poisonous, Aqua, Oval, 7 Ribs On Front, 6 1/2 In. 28.00
Embossed Not To Be Taken, Poisonous, Cobalt Blue, Oval, Vertical Ribs, 7 3/8 In. . . .   25.00
Embossed Not To Be Taken, Poisonous, Cobalt Blue, Ribbed, England, 5 7/8 In. 25.00
Embossed Not To Be Taken, Poisonous, Oval, Vertical Ribs, Aqua, 7 In. 28.00

Poison, Embossed
Not To Be Taken,
Dark Green,
6-Sided, 2 3/4 In.

Poison, Chemical
Cat, Chases Rats
& Mice, St. Louis,
Mo., 8 Oz.

Poison, Ku-Rill
Germicide, A.C.
Hynd Corp., Buffalo,
N.Y., 1936, 10 In.

Embossed Not To Be Taken, Prison, Cobalt Blue, 6-Sided, 5 1/2 In. 100.00
Embossed Not To Be Taken, Ribbed, Lightening Type, No Stopper, ABM, 11 1/2 In. . . . 125.00
Embossed Not To Be Taken, RIGO On Base, Cobalt Blue, 6-Sided, Canada, 6 5/8 In. . 90.00
Embossed Not To Be Taken, Usage Externe, Use With Caution, 6-Sided, Cobalt, 5 In. . 115.00
Embossed On 2 Sides, Amber, Tooled Lip, 1890-1910, 10 In. 120.00
Embossed On 3 Panels, Cobalt Blue, 6-Sided, Stopper, 5 1/2 In. 65.00
Embossed Poison, 2 Rows Of 13 Dots, Light Cobalt Blue, BIMAL, 3 1/2 In. 25.00
Embossed Poison, 6-3 On Base, Amber, ABM, 3 1/2 In. 8.00
Embossed Poison, Amber, 4 In. 65.00
Embossed Poison, Amber, Contents, 3 In. 25.00
Embossed Poison, Amber, Triangular, Round Back, 10 1/8 In., Qt. 200.00
Embossed Poison, Astiseptic Disks, Yellow Amber, Tooled Mouth, 1910, 4 7/8 In. 185.00
Embossed Poison, Carbolic Acid, Use With Caution, O.C.P., Cobalt Blue, 6-Sided, 5 In. 35.00
Embossed Poison, Clear, Raised Skull Face, Tooled Lip, 1875, 4 1/8 In. 4730.00
Embossed Poison, Cobalt Blue, Label, 3 1/4 In. 30.00
Embossed Poison, Cobalt Blue, Quilted, 3 7/8 In. 25.00
Embossed Poison, Cobalt Blue, Quilted, 4 7/8 In. 35.00
Embossed Poison, Cobalt Blue, Tooled Lip, Original Label, 1910, 3 1/4 In. 90.00
Embossed Poison, Golden Amber, Tooled Lip, 1910, 3 3/8 In. 55.00
Embossed Poison, Light Blue, Cobalt Blue Neck & Base, 4 1/2 In. 160.00
Embossed Poison, Mercury Bichloride, Tooled Lip, Label, Contents, 1910, 2 5/8 In. . . . 45.00
Embossed Poison, Rows Of Dots, Cobalt Blue, Rectangular, BIMAL, 4 3/8 In. 40.00
Embossed Poison, Triangular, Tooled Lip, Original Label, 1890-1910, 5 1/2 In. 180.00
Embossed Poison 2 Sides, Horizontal Lines, 4 On Base, Cobalt Blue, ABM, 3 In. 25.00
Embossed Poison Be Careful, E Inside Diamond, Toronto, 6-Sided, Cobalt, 8 1/2 In. . . 55.00
Embossed Poison On 1, Cross Stitching, Cobalt Blue, 3 1/8 In. 40.00
Embossed Poison On 2 Sides, 66 On Base, Amber, BIMAL, 4 3/4 In. 15.00
Embossed Poison On 2 Sides, Amber, 3 3/4 In. 6.00
Embossed Poison On 2 Sides, Amber, 4 7/8 In. 30.00
Embossed Poison On 2 Sides, Amber, Label, 10 1/2 In. 155.00
Embossed Poison On 2 Sides, Amber, Label, Pill Contents, 3 3/4 In. 30.00
Embossed Poison On 2 Sides, Cobalt Blue, 6-Sided, 4 In. 50.00
Embossed Poison On 2 Sides, Cobalt Blue, 6-Sided, 4 3/8 In. 75.00
Embossed Poison On 2 Sides, Cobalt Blue, C.L.G. Co., Pat. Applied For, 4 1/2 In. . . . 70.00
Embossed Poison On 2 Sides, Master 225.00
Embossed Poison On 2 Sides, Medium Amber, Tooled Mouth, 8 In. 130.00
Embossed Poison On 2 Sides, P.D. & Co.-295 On Base, Ribbed, Amber, 2 3/8 In. 10.00
Embossed Poison On 2 Sides, Strychnine Sulfate, Label, Amber, 2 3/4 In. 20.00
Embossed Poison Vergif, Amber, Rectangular, Ribbed, South Africa, c.1920, 1/2 Oz. . . 15.00
Embossed Poison Vergif, Amber, Rectangular, Vertical Ribs, South Africa, c.1920, 1 Oz. 15.00
Embossed Poison Vergif, Amber, Rectangular, Vertical Ribs, South Africa, c.1920, 4 Oz. 30.00
Embossed Poisonous, Aqua, Cylindrical, Vertical Ribs, BIMAL, 5 5/8 In. 15.00
Embossed Poisonous, BIMAL, c.1895-1910, 2 7/8 In. 35.00
Embossed Poisonous, Not To Be Taken, Aqua, Ribbed, England, 4 7/8 In. 8.00
Emerald Green, Jug, 4 In. 22.00
ERS Poison, Stopper, 3 1/4 In. 120.00
F.A. Thompson & Co., Detroit, Poison, Coffin, Yellow Amber, Tooled Lip, 3 1/8 In. 1210.00
Farmer's Rat Paste, On Base, Aqua, Jar, 1 1/2 In. 25.00
Figural, Skull, Cobalt Blue, Quilted, Cylindrical, Stopper, 7 In. 90.00
Figural, Skull, Cobalt Blue, Quilted, Poison Stopper, Master, 5 1/2 In. 115.00
Figural, Skull, Cobalt Blue, Tooled Lip, 1910, 4 In. 715.00
Figural, Skull, Cobalt Blue, Tooled Mouth, 1880-1900, 2 7/8 In. 520.00
Figural, Skull, Cobalt Blue, Tooled Mouth, 1880-1900, 4 1/4 In. 935.00
Figural, Skull, Embossed Poison, Pat. Appl'd. For, Cobalt Blue, 4 1/4 In. 265.00
Figural, Skull, Medium Cobalt Blue, Tooled Mouth, 1885-1910, 2 7/8 In. 855.00
Figural, Skull, Medium Cobalt Blue, Tooled Mouth, 1885-1910, 3 5/8 In. 745.00
Figural, Skull, Medium Cobalt Blue, Tooled Mouth, 1885-1910, 4 1/4 In. 1265.00
Flask, Allover Waffle Design, Sapphire Blue, Inward Rolled Mouth, Pontil, 1/2 Pt. 880.00
Flask, Blown, Half Post Type, Applied Mouth, Pontil, 6 1/2 In. 95.00
Flask, Cobalt Blue, Quilted, Tooled Lip, OP, 5 5/8 In. 880.00
Flask, Diamond, Blue Aqua, Tooled Lip, Pontil, 4 1/4 In. 75.00
Flask, Overall Hobnail, Medium Oliver Green, Sheared Lip, 1855, 5 1/4 In. 580.00
Foulstons Crescent, Not To Be Taken, Cobalt Blue, Rectangular, 5 In. 60.00

Gordon Brand Lysol, Not To Be Taken, Jug, Amber, Crosshatching, 5 In. 32.00
Hobson's Carbolic Acid Ointment Treatment, 1900-1920 .... 10.00
Hobson's Lark Spur Lotion, Standard Laboratories & Lark Spur, Screw Lid, Box 2.50
Honey Amber, 3-Sided, Ribbed, Rows Of Bumps On Corners, England, 1 Oz. 15.00
Hunter Edinburgh Domestic Cleansing Ammonia, Stoneware, Stencil 100.00
Inmans Household Ammonia, Edinburgh, Newcastle, Stoneware, 11 In. 90.00
Iodinol, Manor Remedies Co., Ltd., Newcastle, Aqua, 6-Sided, 6 1/4 In. 15.00
J. Wilson Bonesetter, Light Cobalt Blue, Rectangular 55.00
J.F. Hartz Co. Limited, Toronto, Embossed Hearts, Cobalt Blue, BIMAL, 6 1/4 In. 535.00
J.T.W. & Co., Amber, Tooled Lip, 1890-1910, 3 In. 65.00
J.W. McBeath Kimberley, W.T. & Co., Pat. Dec 11.1894, Cobalt Blue, Dug, 5 3/8 In. .. 635.00
Jacobs' Bed Bug Killer, Skull & Crossbones, Amber, Tooled Mouth, 5 1/4 In. ...570.00 to 855.00
Jar, Medium Amber, ABM Lip, 20th Century, 5 3/4 In. 685.00
Kil Lol Electric Bug Killer, 7 1/4 In. 35.00
Kil-A-Roach Poison, Skull & Crossbones, Roach, Amber, ABM, Label, Canada, 7 1/2 In. 10.00
Kill Pest, Non Poisonous Disinfectant, Aqua, 6-Sided, 5 In. 16.00
Kilner Bros., Poison On 2 Shoulders, Ribbed, Cobalt Blue, 9 1/2 In. 68.00
Knowle's Insect Destroyer, C.N. Crittenton, New York, Aqua, Etched 40.00
Ku-Rill Germicide, A.C. Hynd Corp., Buffalo, N.Y., 1936, 10 In. ....*Illus* 20.00
Larvex, Embossed, Cobalt, 7 3/8 In. ....*Illus* 10.00
Lattice, Cobalt Blue, 5 1/2 In. 130.00
Lattice & Diamond, Aqua Ammonia, Label, Cobalt Blue, Poison Stopper, 5 1/2 In. 60.00
Lattice & Diamond, Cobalt Blue, Original Poison Stopper, 1890-1910, 9 In. ....355.00 to 385.00
Lattice & Diamond, Cobalt Blue, Poison Stopper, 1890-1910, 5 1/2 In. ....55.00 to 120.00
Lattice & Diamond, Cobalt Blue, Poison Stopper, 1890-1910, 7 1/8 In. ....85.00 to 205.00
Lattice & Diamond, Cobalt Blue, Stopper, 1890-1910, 11 In. ....470.00 to 635.00
Lattice & Diamond, Cobalt Blue, Tooled Mouth, 1890-1910, 13 1/8 In. ....965.00 to 1760.00
Lattice & Diamond, Cobalt Blue, Tooled Mouth, Stopper, 1890-1910, 4 3/4 In. 105.00
Lattice & Diamond, Deep Cobalt Blue, Tooled Lip, 1890-1910, 5 1/2 In. 110.00
Lattice & Diamond, Deep Cobalt Blue, Tooled Lip, 1890-1910, 10 7/8 In. 470.00
Lattice & Diamond, Hydrochloric Acid, Label, Cobalt Blue, Poison Stopper, 4 5/8 In. .. 75.00
Lattice & Diamond, Medium Amber, Tooled Lip, Original Label, 1890-1910, 5 In. 465.00
Lattice & Diamond, Nitric Acid, Label, Cobalt Blue, Poison Stopper, 5 1/2 In. 145.00
Lattice & Diamond, Potassium Hydroxide, Label, Cobalt Blue, Poison Stopper, 3 3/4 In. 55.00
Lime Green, Ribbed, Rectangular, ABM, South Africa, c.1920, 1/2 Oz. 8.00
Liquid Dead Shot Insect Destroyer, Ft. Wayne, Ind., 7 In. 18.00
Lysol, Boots All British, Jug, Yellow Amber, 5 In. 24.00
Lysol, Hobnail, Cobalt Blue 45.00
Lysol, Jug, Black Glass, Dates To 1914, 6 1/2 In. 50.00
Lysol, Lehn-Fink, Skull & Crossbones, Box, 1930-1935 .... 7.00
Lysol, London, Amber, ABM, 4 1/2 In. 18.00
Lysol Boots All British, Jug, Amber, ABM, 6 1/2 In. 20.00
Manchester Royal Infirmary, Cobalt Blue, 6-Sided, Embossed, 4 In. 25.00
Melvin & Badger Apothecaries, Boston, Mass., Cobalt Blue, Rectangular, 6 In. 150.00
Melvin & Badger Apothecaries, Boston, Mass., Cobalt Blue, Ribbed, 5 In. 90.00
Mercury Bichloride, Cobalt Blue, Tooled Lip, 8 1/8 In. 275.00
Mercury Bichloride, E.R. Squibb & Son's, Cobalt Blue, Sawtooth Edge Stopper 160.00
Mercury Bichloride, Rexall Drug Co., Original Label, 1890-1910, 5 1/4 In. 155.00
Mercury Bichloride, Sharp & Dohme, Amber, Ribbed, Label, Box, 4 In. 45.00
Mercury Bichloride, Sharp & Dohme, Ribbed, Red Label, Box, 1915, 4 In. 30.00
Mercury Bichloride, Sharp & Dohme, Wm. R. Warner, Triangular, 1900, 4 In. 45.00
Mercury Bichloride, Yellow Amber, Tooled Mouth, Original Label, 1910, 5 In. 390.00
Nafis Automatic Acidity Test, Amber, Round, Long Neck, 1870-1880 .... 40.00
National Ammonia, Not To Be Taken, Cobalt Blue, Cleaned, Oval, 6 1/2 In. 48.00
Norwich Coffin, Cobalt Blue, Tooled Lip, 7 1/2 In. 1800.00
Norwich Coffin, Label, Cobalt Blue, 3 1/2 In. 135.00
Norwich Coffin, Medium Amber, Tooled Lip, 1890-1910, 4 7/8 In. 935.00
Oakland Chemical Co., Amber, 4 3/4 In. 10.00
Oakland Chemical Co., Dioxogen, Amber, Tooled Lip, Amber, 5 In. 5.00
Olive Green, Vertical Ribs Front, Oval, 7 In. 25.00
Owbridge's Embrocation Hull, Cobalt Blue, 6-Sided, Bent Neck, 3 Panels, 5 In. 35.00
Owbridge's Embrocation Hull, Medium Blue, 6-Sided, 4 1/2 In. 15.00
Owl Drug Co., 1-Wing Owl, Cobalt Blue, Triangle, Mold, 3 5/8 In. 125.00

| Poison, Larvex, Embossed, Cobalt, 7 3/8 In. | Poison, Rat-Nip, Kills Rats, Wartime Package, 3 In. | Poison, Strychnia, Philadelphia, 2 1/2 In. | Poison, Triloids-Poison, Cobalt Blue, Triangular, Hobnail Corners, 3 1/2 In. |

Owl Drug Co., 1-Wing Owl, Label, 4 7/8 In. 245.00
Owl Drug Co., 1-Wing Owl, Triangle, Cobalt Blue, BIMAL, 3 5/8 In. 125.00
Owl Drug Co., 1-Wing Owl On Pestle, Aqua, Tooled Lip, 1890-1910, 10 In. 110.00
Owl Drug Co., 1-Wing Owl On Pestle, Milk Glass, Tooled Lip, 1890-1910, 6 In. 130.00
Owl Drug Co., Bright Yellow Green, Tooled Mouth, 1890-1915, 9 5/8 In. 100.00
Owl Drug Co., Cobalt Blue, ABM Lip, 1890-1910, 5 In. 110.00
Owl Drug Co., Cobalt Blue, ABM Lip, 1900-1920, 4 In. 100.00
Owl Drug Co., Cobalt Blue, ABM Lip, Original Label, 1915-1925, 6 In. 220.00
Owl Drug Co., Cobalt Blue, Original Label, 1910, 4 1/2 In. 210.00
Owl Drug Co., Cobalt Blue, Tooled Lip, 1890-1915, 7 7/8 In. . . . . .255.00 to 360.00
Owl Drug Co., Cobalt Blue, Tooled Mouth, Original Label, 1890-1915, 5 1/8 In. .120.00 to 185.00
Owl Drug Co., Cobalt Blue, Tooled Mouth, Original Label, 1890-1915, 6 1/4 In. 305.00
Owl Drug Co., Cobalt Blue, Tooled Mouth, Original Label, 1915, 9 5/8 In. 605.00
Owl Drug Co., Cobalt Blue, Tooled Mouth, Smooth Base, 1890-1915, 3 1/2 In. 55.00
Owl Drug Co., Light Teal Blue, Tooled Mouth, 1890-1915, 9 1/2 In. 210.00
Owl Drug Co., Medium Yellow Amber, Tooled Lip, 1890-1910, 7 In. 880.00
Owl Drug Co., Owl, Cobalt Blue, ABM Lip, 5 3/4 In. 90.00
Owl Drug Co., Owl, Embossed Poison, Cobalt Blue, 3 1/4 In. 150.00
Owl Drug Co., Owl On Mortar & Pestle, Chloroform Liniment USP, Label, Cobalt, 6 In. 145.00
Owl Drug Co., Owl On Mortar & Pestle, Cobalt Blue, 1890-1915, 2 7/8 In. 95.00
Owl Drug Co., Owl On Mortar & Pestle, Cobalt Blue, 6 1/4 In. 110.00
Owl Drug Co., Owl On Mortar & Pestle, Cobalt Blue, 8 In. 360.00
Owl Drug Co., Owl On Mortar & Pestle, Cobalt Blue, 9 1/4 In. 715.00
Owl Drug Co., Owl On Mortar & Pestle, Cobalt Blue, Tooled Lip, 4 3/4 In. 65.00
Owl Drug Co., Owl On Mortar & Pestle, Collodion Flexible Poison, Label, Cobalt, 3 In. 75.00
Owl Drug Co., Owl On Mortar & Pestle, Deep Cobalt Blue, Triangular, 8 In. 385.00
Owl Drug Co., Owl On Mortar & Pestle, Denatured Alcohol, Label, Cobalt Blue, 9 1/2 In. 525.00
Owl Drug Co., Owl On Pestle, Cobalt Blue, 1890-1910, 3 1/2 In. 105.00
Owl Drug Co., Owl On Pestle, Cobalt Blue, 1890-1910, 6 In. 220.00
Owl Drug Co., Owl On Pestle, Embossed, Yellow Green, Tooled Lip, 1890-1910, 10 In. . 130.00
Owl Drug Co., San Francisco, Cobalt Blue, Tooled Mouth, 1890-1910, 6 1/2 In. 265.00
Owl Drug Co., San Francisco, Cobalt Blue, Tooled Mouth, 1890-1910, 9 1/2 In. 470.00
Owl Drug Co., San Francisco, Cobalt Blue, Tooled Mouth, 1920, 3 1/2 In. 135.00
Owl Drug Co., San Francisco, Cobalt Blue, Tooled Mouth, 1920, 7 7/8 In. 605.00
Owl Drug Co., San Francisco, Green, Tooled Mouth, 1915, 9 1/2 In. 155.00
Owl Drug Co., San Francisco, Sun Colored Amethyst, Tooled Lip, 1910, 10 In. 135.00
Owl Drug Co., San Francisco, Teal Blue, Tooled Mouth, 1900-1915, 9 1/2 In. 100.00
Poison, Amber, Cylindrical, Stopper, 7 1/2 In. 50.00
Poison, Amber, Label, 10 1/4 In. 170.00
Poison, Bi-Chloride Of Mercury, Mays Drug Co., Label, Coffin, Cobalt Blue, 3 1/2 In. . . 90.00
Poison, Orange Amber, 3-Sided, Rounded Back, Tooled Mouth, 1890-1910, 10 1/8 In. . . 110.00
Poison Tinct. Iodine, Skull & Crossbones, Cobalt Blue, 3 1/8 In. 70.00
Poisonous, Sheared Lip, Cylindrical, 4 In. 12.00
Quick Death, Insect, Embossed, Label 60.00
Rat-Nip, Kills Rats, Wartime Package, 3 In. . . . .*Illus* 7.00

Red Amber, Tooled Lip, Smooth Base, 1890-1910, 10 1/4 In. 120.00
Red Amber, Tooled Top, 10 In. 65.00
Reese Chemical Co., Cleveland, Oh., Green, Tooled Mouth, 1910, 6 In. 80.00
Registered No. 336907, Submarine, Cobalt Blue, Tooled Mouth, 3 x 2 In. 415.00
Ribbed, Oval, Amber, Tooled Top, 3 5/8 In. 15.00
Royal Germetuer, Atlanta Chemical Co., KRG, Medium Amber, Tooled Mouth, 8 3/4 In. 35.00
S.E. Massengill Co., Bristol, Tenn., Amber, Rolled Lip, 1890-1910, 3 1/8 In. 690.00
Ser C Sol Elliott, Not To Be Taken, Medium Gold Amber, Embossed Crown, 5 In. 200.00
Sharpe & Dohme, Baltimore, 6-Sided, Medium Amber, 2 1/2 In. ....7.00 to 10.00
Sharpe & Dohme, Baltimore, Amber, 1 7/8 In. 15.00
Sharpe & Dohme, Baltimore, Md., Amber, Crosshatches, 1890, 3 In. 20.00
Sharpe & Dohme, Baltimore, Md., Triangular, Rounded Back, Cobalt Blue, 3 1/4 In. ... 15.00
Sharpe & Dohme, Philadelphia, Pa., Strychnine, Embossed, Amber, Screw Cap 10.00
Skull, Embossed Poison, Pat. Appl'd. For, Cobalt Blue, Tooled Mouth, 2 7/8 In. 2420.00
Skull, Figural, Embossed Poison, Cobalt Blue, Pat. June 26, 1894, 3 1/2 In. 1210.00
Skull & Crossbones, 5-Pointed Star Above Crossbone, Yellow Amber, 5 In. 630.00
Skull & Crossbones, 6-Sided, Medium Citron, ABM Lip, 1910, 10 3/4 In. 1540.00
Skull & Crossbones, 6-Sided, Pale Yellow Green, ABM Lip, France, 10 In. 1705.00
Skull & Crossbones, Antiseptic Tablets, Cobalt Blue, 2 In. 230.00
Skull & Crossbones, Cobalt Blue, Tooled Mouth, 1890-1910, 4 1/2 In. 4070.00
Skull & Crossbones, Cobalt Blue, Tooled Mouth, Canada, 1910, 6 1/2 In. 3850.00
Skull & Crossbones, De-Dro Gifflesche, Medium Yellow Green, ABM Lip, 10 In. 550.00
Skull & Crossbones, Demert Drug & Chemical Co., Cobalt Blue, 1910, 6 In. 2750.00
Skull & Crossbones, Demert Drug & Chemical Co., Spokane, Cobalt Blue, 5 In. 4070.00
Skull & Crossbones, DP Poison, Coffin, Cobalt Blue, Tooled Lip, 1910, 3 In. 660.00
Skull & Crossbones, Dr. Trager's Fata Roach Powder, Scranton, Pa., Red, White, 3 In. . 40.00
Skull & Crossbones, Medium Amber, 8-Sided, Tooled Mouth, 1890-1910, 2 In. 880.00
Skull & Crossbones, Star Above, Below Skull, Yellow Amber, 1910, 4 3/4 In. 690.00
Skull & Crossbones, Star, Yellow, Amber Tone, 1890-1910, 4 3/4 In. 825.00
Stabler Worm Mixture, Pale Green Aqua, 6-Sided, OP, 1834-1850, 3 3/4 In. 55.00
Star, Cobalt Blue, Narrow Neck, 4 1/2 In. 290.00
Star, Cobalt Blue, Wide Mouth, 4 1/2 In. 290.00
Star, Deep Cobalt Blue, Wide Mouth, 4 1/2 In. 290.00
Strychnia, Philadelphia, 2 1/2 In. ....Illus 275.00
Strychnine, Tooled Mouth, Original Label, 1890-1910, 2 1/2 In. 185.00
Strychnine, Upjohn, Amber, Cork, 6 In. 16.00
Submarine, Cobalt Blue, Tooled Mouth, England, 1890-1910, 2 1/2 In. ....120.00 to 330.00
Submarine, Cobalt Blue, Tooled Mouth, England, 1890-1910, 4 5/8 In. 440.00
Submarine, Deep Cobalt Blue Center, Light Blue Ends, 1910, 2 3/8 x 4 In. 360.00
Submarine, Registered No. 336907 On Base, Cobalt Blue, Tooled Lip, 3 x 2 In. ..200.00 to 415.00
Sulpholine, Cobalt Blue, Embossed, Rectangular, 4 1/2 In. 12.00
Sulpholine, Rectangular, 4 In. 10.00
Swift's Arenate Of Lead, 5 Lbs., Crock, Cream, Black Stencil, Repaired Lid 85.00
T. Eaton Drug Co. Limited, Toronto, Ont., Wood Alcohol, Poison, Flint, 9 1/4 In. 75.00
T.O.D. Co. Trade Mark, Owl On Mortar & Pestle, 1890-1915, 11 In. 120.00
T.O.D. Co. Trade Mark, Owl On Mortar & Pestle, Cobalt Blue, 1890-1915, 6 1/4 In. ... 200.00
T.O.D. Co. Trade Mark, Owl On Mortar & Pestle, Tooled Lip, 1890-1915, 8 In. 85.00
T.O.D. Co. Trade Mark, W.T. Co. U.S.A., Cobalt Blue, 9 1/2 In. 220.00
The Martin, Aqua, Tooled Mouth, England, 1890-1915, 4 1/2 In. 145.00
The Martin, Aqua, Tooled Mouth, England, 1890-1915, 6 1/2 In. 175.00
The Paine Drug Co., Rochester, N.Y., Green, Tooled Mouth, 1890-1910, 3 In. 230.00
The Paine Drug Co., Rochester, N.Y., Green, Tooled Mouth, 1890-1910, 7 In. 880.00
Thornton & Ross, Milnsbridge, Aqua, Oval, 7 1/2 In. 46.00
Tinct, Cannab, Ind., Embossed, Cobalt Blue, White & Orange Lettering, 7 In. 240.00
Tinct Iodine, Skull & Crossbones, Cobalt Blue 95.00
Tinct Nucis Vom. Dose For Horses & Cattle, Cobalt Blue, Cylindrical, 11 In. 125.00
Tincture Of Iodine, Skull & Crossbones, Amber, ABM, 1 1/2 In. 12.00
Tincture Of Iodine, T. Eaton Co., 6-Sided, Cobalt Blue, Label, Stopper, 2 Oz. 40.00
Triangular, Amber, ABM, Contents, Pills Imprinted With Skull & Crossbones, 3 1/2 In. . 25.00
Triangular, Red Amber, 5 In. 40.00
Triloids-Poison, Cobalt Blue, Triangular, Hobnail Corners, 31/2 In. ....Illus 30.00
Tristram Pharmacy, Pharmacist Heineke, Rubber & Screw Lid, 1920-1929 .... 7.00
United Drug, Triangle, Quilted, 5 1/4 In. 160.00

Vapo Cresolene Co., Deep Cobalt Blue, Pat. July 17, 1891, Tooled Mouth, 4 In.	175.00
Vasogen, Amber, 6-Sided, Embossed, 3 3/4 In.	12.00
Vasogen Glass, Amber, 6-Sided, Vertical Ribs On 2 Panels, 4 1/4 In.	45.00
Verminicide Paste, On Base, Honey Amber, Jar, 1 1/2 In.	20.00
Vertical Ribs On Front, Light To Medium Olive Green, Oval, 7 In.	25.00
Victory Chemical Co., Philada., Quick Death Insecticide & Disinfectant, Amethyst	15.00
Vorsicht, Skull & Crossbones, Light Turquoise, Hexagonal, Germany, 8 1/4 In.	165.00
Whiskey, Caspers, Made By Honest North Carolina People, Cobalt Blue, Qt.	300.00
Wm. Radam's Microbe Killer, Chicago No. 1, Cream, Stoneware, 1 Gal.	130.00
Wm. Radam's Microbe Killer, Gold Amber, Man Beating Skeleton, Embossed, 10 In. .	145.00
Wm. Radam's Microbe Killer, Jug, Cream, Brown, Embossed Daisy Pattern, 10 3/4 In.	110.00
Wm. Radam's Microbe Killer, Jug, Stoneware, Salt Glaze, Cobalt Blue Incised, Gal. ..	140.00
Wm. Radam's Microbe Killer No. 2, Jug, Stoneware, Partial Label, Gal.	80.00

POTTERY

Many bottles were made of pottery. In this section we have included those that have no brand name and do not fit into another category. Many figural flasks, such as those made at the Bennington, Vermont, potteries or the Anna pottery, are listed. Another section lists stoneware bottles.

POTTERY, Bartender, Figural, Glazed, With 4 Black Shot Glasses, c.1930s, 9 In., 5 Piece .	85.00
Jar, Glass Bros., London, Ont., Chocolate Glaze, Wire Bail, c.1886, Imperial Qt., 7 In.	35.00
Jug, — & Boynton, Burlington, Vt., Applied Handle, Gray Tan, Floral, 17 In.	275.00
Jug, City Of Hamburg Co., San Francisco, Calif., Gal.	115.00
Jug, Face, Dark Brown Slip, Applied Eyes, Ears, Mouth, Handle, c.1940, 7 In.	580.00
Jug, Face, E.J. Flowers, Almond, N.C., Dark Brown, Olive, 20th Century, 9 5/8 In.	90.00
Jug, J. Norton & Co., Gray Tan, Cobalt Floral, Applied Handle, 16 In.	330.00
Jug, Redware, Egg Shape, Green, Yellow Orange Spots, 7 1/4 In.	440.00
Monk, Figural, Cork In Base Of Head, Western Germany, 8 In.	40.00
N. Eberhardt, Toronto, O., 6, Mottled Cream, Brown Interior, Sunflower, 13 1/2 In.	240.00
Pot, Holloways Ointment For Cure Of Gout & Rheumatism, London, 1900, 1 1/2 In.	40.00

PURPLE POWER

Purple power is the Kansas State University slogan. A series of bottles was made from 1970 to 1972 picturing the wildcat at a sporting event. They were distributed by Jon-Sol.

PURPLE POWER, Football Player, 1972	15.00
On Basketball, 1971	15.00
Wildcat Walking, 1970	17.00
SANDWICH GLASS, see Cologne; Scent	

SARSAPARILLA

The most widely distributed syphilis cure used in the nineteenth century was sarsaparilla. The roots of the smilax vine were harvested, cleaned, dried, and sold to apothecaries and drug manufacturers. They added alcohol and other flavorings, such as the roots of yellow dock, dandelion, or burdock or the bark from prickly ash, sassafras, or birch trees. A few makers also added fruit or vegetable juice and clover blossoms. All of this was mixed to make the medicine called *sarsaparilla*. It was claimed to cure many diseases, including skin diseases, boils, pimples, piles, tumors, scrofulous conditions including king's evil (a swelling of the neck), and rheumatism. It could cleanse and purify the blood, a process doctors thought should take place regularly for good health.

The first labeled sarsaparilla was made in the early 1800s. Some bottled products called sarsaparilla are still made today. The bottles were usually rectangular with embossed letters, or soda-bottle shaped. Most were light green or aqua but some amber and cobalt bottles were made. Later bottles had paper labels.

SARSAPARILLA, A.D. & C. Co's Best Extract Sarsaparilla, Rectangular, Aqua, 9 1/2 In.	50.00
A.H. Bull's Extract, Hartford, Conn., Aqua, Rectangular, Pontil, 7 In.	50.00
Allen's Sarsaparilla, Oval, Deep Aqua, 8 1/4 In.	40.00
Ayer's Concentrated Extract, Aqua, Rectangular, Pontil, 8 1/2 In.	90.00
B.F. Williams, Syrup Of Sarsaparilla, Louisville, Ky., Aqua, IP, 10 In.	1375.00
Billy Baxter, Red Raven, Pa., Paper Label, Contents, Cap, 7 In. ....*Illus*	15.00
Bristol's Extract Of Sarsaparilla, Buffalo, Aqua, Applied Top, OP, 5 1/2 In.	145.00
Bristol's Extract Of Sarsaparilla, Buffalo, Aqua, Pontil	50.00

| Sarsaparilla, Billy Baxter, Red Raven, Pa., Paper Label, Contents, Cap, 7 In. | Sarsaparilla, Gooch, McCullough Drug Co., Paper Label, 9 1/2 In. | Sarsaparilla, Sands, New York, 10 In. | Sarsaparilla, Yager's Compound Extract, Gilbert Bros. & Co., Baltimore, 8 1/2 In. |

C.D. Co.'s Sarsaparilla Resolvent, Amber, 8 1/2 In. 120.00
Cantrell's Compound Medicated Syrup Of Sarsaparilla, Aqua, OP, 6 In. 945.00
Cha's Cable & Son, Pokeepsie Premium & Lemon Soda, Dark Green, 7 1/4 In. 715.00
Charles Joly, Philadelphia, Jamaica Sarsaparilla, Amber, Crown Top, 10 In. 45.00
Chas. Langley & Co. Compound Extract Sarsaparilla, San Francisco, Aqua, 9 In. .. 225.00
Dana's Sarsaparilla, Aqua, 9 In. 15.00
Dr. B.W. Hair's, Deep Aqua, OP, 1845-1855, 9 3/4 In. 580.00
Dr. Channing's Sarsaparilla, Aqua, 10 In. 80.00
Dr. Cronk's Sarsaparilla Beer, Stoneware, 12-Sided, Gray Glaze, 9 3/4 In. 50.00
Dr. De Andries, New Orleans, Amber, 1875, 10 In. 605.00
Dr. Greene's, Sarsaparilla, Aqua, 9 In. ....8.00 to 15.00
Dr. Guysott's Compound Extract Of Yellow Dock, Aqua, 10 In. ....120.00 to 255.00
Dr. Henry's Sarsaparilla, Aqua, 9 1/4 In. 65.00
Dr. Ira Baker's Honduras Sarsaparilla, Aqua, 10 1/4 In. 50.00
Dr. J. Townsend's, New York, Emerald Green, Square, Pontil, 9 3/4 In. 425.00
Dr. J.S. Rose's, Philadelphia, Aqua, IP, Applied Mouth, 9 1/2 In. 5390.00
Dr. Stillman's, New Orleans, Deep Olive Green, Double Collar, 8 In. 2250.00
Dr. Townsend's, Albany, N.Y., Blue Green, IP, 9 3/4 In. 415.00
Dr. Townsend's, Albany, N.Y., Blue Green, OP, 1855, 9 7/8 In. 550.00
Dr. Townsend's, Albany, N.Y., Blue Green, Square, Beveled Corners, IP, 10 In. 155.00
Dr. Townsend's, Albany, N.Y., Deep Emerald Green, IP, 1845, 9 1/2 In. 495.00
Dr. Townsend's, Albany, N.Y., Deep Olive Green, 1855, 9 3/8 In. ....390.00 to 415.00
Dr. Townsend's, Albany, N.Y., Deep Yellow Amber, 10 In. 550.00
Dr. Townsend's, Albany, N.Y., Emerald Green, IP, 9 3/4 In. ....235.00 to 345.00
Dr. Townsend's, Albany, N.Y., Emerald Green, IP, 9 5/8 In. ....305.00 to 385.00
Dr. Townsend's, Albany, N.Y., Green, IP, 9 1/4 In. 345.00
Dr. Townsend's, Albany, N.Y., Light Green, IP, 4 1/2 In. 365.00
Dr. Townsend's, Albany, N.Y., Medium Blue Green, IP, 9 5/8 In. 185.00
Dr. Townsend's, Albany, N.Y., Medium Green, IP, 1845-55, 9 1/4 In. 255.00
Dr. Townsend's, Albany, N.Y., Medium Yellow Olive Amber, 9 1/2 In. 330.00
Dr. Townsend's, Albany, N.Y., Olive Amber, Pontil, 1855, 9 1/8 In. ....130.00 to 255.00
Dr. Townsend's, Albany, N.Y., Olive Green, Pontil, 1855, 9 1/2 In. 75.00
Dr. Townsend's, Albany, N.Y., Olive Green, Tapered Collar, Pontil, 9 3/4 In. 220.00
Dr. Townsend's, Albany, N.Y., Teal Blue, IP, 1845-1855, 9 3/8 In. 415.00
Dr. Townsend's, Albany, N.Y., Yellow Olive, Square, Pontil, 9 3/8 In. 305.00
Dr. Townsend's, Albany, N.Y., Yellow Olive Amber, 1865, 10 In. ....130.00 to 155.00
Dr. Townsend's, Albany, N.Y., Yellow Olive Green, Embossed, Square, 9 3/4 In. 245.00
Dr. Webster's, Ithaca, Blue Aqua, Sloping Collar, OP, 6 1/2 In. 330.00
Dr. Winslow's Compound & Iodine Potash, Howard Drug, 9 In. 60.00
E.N. Lewis Sarsaparilla Beer, Blue Aqua, Applied Mouth, 1880, 7 In. 120.00
Edward Wilder's Sarsaparilla & Potash, Louisville, Ky., Building 140.00
Edward Wilder's Sarsaparilla & Potash, Semi-Cabin, 1865-1875, 8 1/4 In. 60.00
Edward Wilder's Sarsaparilla & Potash, Semi-Cabin, 1880-1890, 8 3/4 In. 85.00

Edwin W. Joy Co., San Francisco, Aqua, Square, 8 3/4 In. 35.00
F. A. Richter & Co., Rotterdam, N.Y., Green Aqua, Tooled Lip, 1900, 9 In. 150.00
Foleys, Amber, Label, Contents, 9 In. 65.00
Genuine Phoenix, Louisville, Ky., Aqua, IP, 1855, 9 In. ....1375.00 to 1430.00
Genuine Sands', New York, Aqua, OP, 1855, 10 In. 185.00
Gooch, McCullough Drug Co., Paper Label, 9 1/2 In. ....*Illus* 40.00
Hall's, J.R. Gates & Co., San Francisco, Aqua, Applied Mouth, 1880, 9 1/2 In. ....55.00 to 100.00
Hood's, London, England, Aqua, Sunken Panel, 5 1/2 In. 12.00
Hood's, Lowell, Mass., Aqua, BIMAL, 9 In. 5.00
Hoonduras Cos. Compound Extract, Abrams & Carroll, Sole Agents, S.F. 380.00
Irwin M. Gray & Co., Montrose, Pa., Blue Aqua, Tooled Mouth, 8 1/2 In. 120.00
John Bull, Louisville, Ky., Medium Emerald Green, IP, 1840-1860, 9 In. 2585.00
John Bull Extract Of Sarsaparilla, Blue Aqua, OP, 1845-1855, 9 3/4 In. 140.00
John Bull Extract Of Sarsaparilla, Green, Aqua, 1865, 9 In. 85.00
John Bull Extract Of Sarsaparilla, Louisville, Ky., Yellow Green, 8 5/8 In. 385.00
John Bull's Extract Of Sarsaparilla, Aqua, OP, 1855, 6 In. 275.00
John Bull's Extract Of Sarsaparilla, Deep Blue Aqua, IP, 9 In. 190.00
Joy's Sarsaparilla, Edwin W. Joy Co., San Francisco, Aqua, Applied Ring Lip, 9 In. 35.00
King's Sarsaparilla Celery & Compound, Amber, 10 In. 120.00
Log Cabin, Rochester, N.Y., Amber, 9 In. ....70.00 to 135.00
Masury's Compound, Aqua, OP, 8 1/4 In. 220.00
Masury's Sarsaparilla Cathartic, Aqua, Pontil, 1845-1855, 6 1/2 In. 45.00
Old Dr. J. Townsend's, N.Y., Emerald Green, IP, 9 1/2 In. ....145.00 to 305.00
Old Dr. Townsend's, N.Y., Blue Green, IP, 1855, 9 1/2 In. 440.00
Old Dr. Townsend's, N.Y., Blue Green, IP, Applied Mouth, 9 1/2 In. ....425.00 to 635.00
Old Dr. Townsend's, N.Y., Ice Blue, IP, 1835-1860, 9 1/2 In. ....300.00 to 525.00
Old Dr. Townsend's, N.Y., Ice Blue, IP, 1855, 9 1/2 In. 880.00
Rackley's Sarsaparilla, B.F. Rackley Apothecary, Dover, N.H., Aqua, 9 1/4 In. 110.00
Rush's Sarsaparilla & Iron, A.H. Flanders, New York, Aqua, 8 3/4 In. ....7.00 to 20.00
Sand's, N.Y., Aqua, Applied Double Collar Mouth, 1845-1855, 10 In. 210.00
Sand's, New York, Aqua, Pontil, 1855, 6 1/4 In. 55.00
Sands, New York, 10 In. ....*Illus* 210.00
Sand's Sarsaparilla Genuine, New York, Aqua, OP, 1848-1858, 10 In. 150.00
Shaker Syrup, No. 1, Canterbury, N.H., Aqua, Rectangular, Pontil, 1840, 7 In. ...125.00 to 265.00
Skoda's, Concentrated Extract, Amber, 9 In. 60.00
Thos. A. Hurley's Compound Syrup, Louisville, Ky., Aqua 375.00
Thos. A. Hurley's Compound Syrup, Louisville, Ky., Medium Amber, 10 In. 415.00
Turner's, Deep Aqua, Applied Sloping Collar Mouth, 1865, 12 In. ....440.00 to 525.00
Yager's Compound Extract, Gilbert Bros. & Co., Baltimore, 8 1/2 In. ....*Illus* 35.00

SCENT

Perfume and cologne are not the same as scent. Scent is smelling salts, a perfume with ammonia salts added for a sharp vapor that could revive a person who was feeling faint. Because our female ancestors wore tightly laced corsets and high starched collars, the problem of feeling faint was common. Scent bottles were sometimes small mold-blown bottles in the full spectrum of glass colors. Sometimes the bottles were free blown and made in elaborate shapes to resemble, perhaps, a seahorse. By the mid-nineteenth century molded scents were made, usually of dark green, cobalt, or yellow glass. These were rather squat bottles, often with unusual stoppers. There is much confusion about the difference between cologne and scent bottles because manufacturers usually made both kinds. Related bottles may be found in the Cologne and Perfume categories.

SCENT, 19 Vertical Ribs, Citron, Sheared Mouth, Pontil, 1840-1860, 2 7/8 In. 255.00
 20 Vertical Ribs, Cobalt Blue, OP, 3 In. 100.00
 26 Ribs, Cobalt Blue, Tooled Lip, 1840-1855, 3 In. 100.00
 Acanthus Leaf Design, Sapphire Blue, Sheared Lip, Europe, 3 1/8 In. 175.00
 Allover Diamond & Sunburst Pattern, Lavender Blue, Metal Screw Cap, 3 5/8 In. .. 140.00
 Chamfered Corner Panels, Multicolored Floral Design Germany, 1830, 7 7/8 In. 635.00
 Cobalt Blue, Ground & Polished Lip, Pewter Screw Cap, Sandwich, 1860-1870, 3 1/8 In. 165.00
 Cogglewheel Rigaree, Sheared Lip, 1820-1830, 3 1/8 In. 120.00
 Concentric, Coin, Corrugated Edges, Light Blue Tint, Sheared Mouth, Pontil, 2 1/4 In. .. 265.00
 Copper Wheel Cut Design, Medium Grape Amethyst, 1865-1880, 2 7/8 In. 40.00
 Crown & Plumage Design, Pontil, Cobalt Blue, Sheared Lip, 1830-1855, 2 7/8 In. 305.00
 Cut Glass, Medium Purple Amethyst, Polished Mouth, Screw Cap, 1885, 2 7/8 In. 120.00

Flattened Pumpkin Seed Shape, 20 Ribs, Yellow Green 100.00
Football Form, Amber, Metal Screw Cap, Sandwich, 1865-1875, 1 7/8 In. 100.00
Long Teardrop Shape, Swirled Ribs, Emerald Green 200.00
Opaque White Swirls, Gray, Blue, Pewter Cap, 2 1/2 In. 220.00
Pinwheel, Aqua, 2 1/8 In. 110.00
Pinwheel, Aqua, Open Pontil, 1830-1850 .... 450.00
Plume & Crown Design, Deep Cobalt Blue, Purple Tone, Sheared Lip, Pontil, 2 7/8 In. . 255.00
Ribbed, Deep Grass Green, Slag Striations Throughout, Dug, 1860, 2 3/4 In. 155.00
Ribbed, Emerald Green Swirl, 2 7/8 In. 99.00
Seahorse, Cobalt Blue, Applied Rigaree, Sheared Mouth, 1835-1855, 4 In. 230.00
Shell Shape, Cobalt Blue, 2 3/8 In. 467.50
Stiegel Scent, Vertical Ribs, Blue, Pontil, 1815-1835 .... 125.00
Sunburst, Barrel, Rigaree Trailings Around Body, Yellow Olive Green, Pontil, 4 7/8 In. . 495.00
Sunburst, Clear, Sheared & Tooled Lip, Pontil, 1840-1855, 2 1/2 In. 110.00
Sunburst, Emerald Green, 2 In. 495.00
Sunburst, Emerald Green, 3 In. 412.50
Sunburst, Light Cobalt Blue, Darker Striations, Sheared Lip, Pontil, 1845-1855, 2 7/8 In. 210.00
Sunburst, Light Ice Blue, OP, 1845-1860, 2 1/8 In. 110.00
Sunburst, Purple Cobalt Blue, Pontil, Sheared Lip, 1830-1855, 2 7/8 In. 330.00
Sunburst, Shield Form, 14 Ribs, Cobalt Blue, Sheared Mouth, Pontil, 2 3/4 In. 465.00
Teardrop, 24 Vertical Ribs, Deep Yellow Green, Sheared Mouth, Pontil, 3 1/4 In. 230.00
Violin Shape, Hearts & Fleur-De-Lis Design, Embossed Crown, Pontil, 3 In. 55.00
White Slag, Waisted, Cobalt Blue, No Screw Cap, 2 3/8 In. 20.00

--------------------------------- **SEAL** ---------------------------------

Seal or sealed bottles are named for the glass seal that was applied to the body of the bottle. While still hot, this small pad of glass was impressed with an identification mark. Seal bottles are known from the second century but the earliest examples collectors can find today date from the eighteenth century. Because the seal bottle was the most popular container for wine and other liquids shipped to North America, broken bottles, seals alone, or whole bottles are often found in old dumps and excavations. Dutch gin, French wine, and English liquors were all shipped in large seal bottles. Seal bottles also held rum, olive oil, mineral water, and even vinegar. It is possible to date the bottle from the insignia on the seal and from the shape of the bottle.

SEAL, A.S.C.R., Cylindrical, Black Glass, Yellow Olive, Sheared Mouth, Pontil, 10 5/8 In. . 120.00
A.S.C.R., Dark Olive Green, Applied Mouth, Pontil, England, 1820-1840, 11 1/2 In. 110.00
A.S.C.R., Wine, 3-Piece Mold, 1830s, 11 1/2 In. 130.00
Black Glass, Deep Olive Green, Pontil, England, 1783, 10 5/8 In. 910.00
Black Glass, Deep Olive Onion, Applied String Lip, England, 1709, 6 1/8 In. 6875.00
Black Glass, Deep Olive Onion, Applied String Lip, Pontil, England, 1785, 9 1/2 In. 1650.00
Black Glass, Lime Juice, 3-Piece Mold, English Navy, 1840 .... 165.00
Border Maid, 1877, 3-Piece Mold, Black Glass, Dark Olive Green, 11 5/8 In. 360.00
C.A. Richards, Boston, Deep Yellow Green, Applied Mouth, 1860-1890, 10 1/8 In. 305.00
C.H.H. Sillaton, Black Glass, Deep Yellow Olive, String Rim, Pontil, 1789, 8 7/8 In. ... 825.00
C.H.H. Sillaton, Deep Yellow Amber, England, 1789, 9 In. 605.00
Class Of 1846, W. Dyottville Glass Works, IP, Yellow Olive Amber, 11 In. 580.00
Class Of 1846, W. Dyottville Glass Works, Phila., Black Glass, Olive, IP, 11 1/2 In. 305.00
Crown, Monogram, Onion, Yellow Olive Green, String Lip, OP, Europe, 7 3/8 In. 1210.00
Crown, P, 3-Piece Mold, Olive Amber, Applied Mouth, 1850-1870, 11 3/8 In. 155.00
Deep Olive Amber, Applied Collar Mouth, 1830-1840, 10 1/2 In. 200.00
Deep Olive Amber, Applied Collar Mouth, 1870-1880, 10 1/2 In. 110.00
Deep Olive Amber, Applied Mouth, 1790-1810, 10 In. 1070.00
Deep Olive Amber, Applied Mouth, Pontil, England, 1800-1820, 12 In. 525.00
Deep Olive Amber, Applied Mouth, Pontil, England, 1805, 10 1/4 In. 660.00
Deep Olive Amber, Applied Mouth, Pontil, England, 1830, 10 1/4 In. 495.00
Deep Olive Amber, Applied String Collar, Pontil, 1745-1760, 9 1/4 In. 1070.00
Deep Olive Green, Amber Tone, Applied String Lip, 1758, 9 1/8 In. 4070.00
Deep Yellow Olive Amber, Tooled Collar Lip, England, 1820-1835, 11 In. 150.00
Doneralle House, H.H. Rickett & Co. Glass Works, Olive Green, 11 1/8 In. 175.00
Dyottsville Glass Works, Phil., Deep Yellow Olive Amber, 1846, 11 1/8 In. 685.00
Earl Of Mt. Edgecomb, Coat-Of-Arms, Deep Olive Amber, 1800, 11 1/8 In. 200.00
English Onion, Williamson Alford, 1723, Yellow Olive Green, 6 1/2 In. 7700.00
Fritzsche Bros., N.Y., Deep Amber, 3-Piece Applied Seal, 1870-1890, 13 In. 145.00

Fritzsche Bros., N.Y., Deep Cobalt Blue, Tooled Mouth, 1870-1890, 13 In. 255.00
Grommes & Ullrich, Chicago, In., Cylindrical, Olive Green, Fifth 35.00
Grommes & Ulrich, Chicago, Cylindrical, Black Glass 60.00
H. Rickett's Glass Works, Bristol, Lanoyd, Patent, Olive Amber, 1830s, 11 1/8 In. 75.00
H. Rickett's Glass Works, Bristol, Yellow Olive Green, 1825-1840, 10 5/8 In. 215.00
I. Hennefsy Park 1774, Olive Amber, String Lip, Pontil, Magnum, 13 1/8 In. 1540.00
I. Watson, Esqr., Bilton, Black Glass, Yellow Olive, String Rim, Pontil, 9 1/4 In. 660.00
I.T. 1787, Olive Amber, Applied String Lip, Pontil, 10 1/2 In. 855.00
Inner Temple, Wine, Dark Olive Green, 1845, 9 1/2 In. 50.00
J. Bell, Black Glass, Cylindrical, Yellow Olive, Tooled Sloping Collar, Pontil, 12 In. 385.00
J.N., Cylindrical, Black Glass, Deep Yellow Olive, Tooled Mouth, Ring, Pontil, 10 1/8 In. 120.00
John Key, English Mallet, 1726, Olive Green, String Lip, Pontil, 7 1/2 In. 4070.00
Medium Olive Amber, Applied Mouth, Pontil, England, 1810-1830, 11 In. 100.00
Medium Olive Amber, Pontil, England, 1780-1810, 10 1/4 In. 110.00
Meijer's East India Schnapps, Clear, Blue Seal, Case Gin Type, Thin Glass, 9 1/4 In. . 145.00
Napa Valley Wine Co., S.F., Amber, Applied Top, Kick Up Base, 9 1/2 In. 75.00
Old Colony, 1620, Black Glass, Yellow Olive, Sheared Mouth, String Rim, Pontil, 9 In. . 825.00
Olive Amber, Applied Mouth, England, 1784, 10 1/2 In. 1540.00
Olive Green, Applied Mouth, Germany, 1894, 23 In. 1265.00
Picton Castle, 1827, 3-Piece Mold, Black Glass, Deep Olive Amber, Pontil, 11 1/4 In. . . 360.00
R. Green, 1765, English Mallet, Olive Amber, Applied String Lip, England, 8 7/8 In. 2035.00
Revd. J.B. Melhuish, 3-Piece Mold, Black Glass, Dark Yellow Olive, 11 1/8 In. 305.00
Revd. J.B. Melhuish, 3-Piece Mold, Ring Mouth, Pontil, Black Glass, England 11 In. . . . 120.00
RHC, 1815, Black Glass, Yellow Olive, Tooled Mouth, String Rim, Pontil, 11 In. 305.00
Ribbon, Olive Amber, OP, Applied Handle, 1800-1835, 9 3/4 In. 385.00
Rousdon Jubilee 1887, Olive Amber, Applied Mouth, England, 11 3/4 In. 145.00
T W, English Onion, Bell, 1707, Olive Green, String Lip, Pontil, 6 1/4 In. 4070.00
Tabac De A. Delpit, Nouvelle Orleans, Deep Olive Amber, Applied Double Collar, 11 In. 935.00
TB, English Mallet, Olive Green, Applied String Lip, Pontil, 1735-1745, 7 In. 660.00
W. Meuschel Sehr, Castle, Deep Blood Red, Applied Mouth, Handle, 1895, 6 3/8 In. . . . 130.00
Yellow Olive Green, Applied Mouth, England, 1790-1830, 8 7/8 In. 360.00
Yellow Olive Green, Pontil, England, 1811, 9 1/8 In. 440.00

─────────────────────────── **SELTZER** ───────────────────────────

The word *seltzer* was first used for mineral water with medicinal properties at Selters, Germany. Seltzer was thought to be good for intestinal disorders. The word soon was used for any of the artificially carbonated waters that became popular in the nineteenth century. Seltzer bottles were advertised in Philadelphia by 1816. *Soda* and *seltzer* mean the same thing. Some collectors want the bottles that say *seltzer* and the special pump bottles that dispensed it. These pump bottles were usually covered with a metal mesh to keep glass from flying in case of an explosion. The top of the bottle was a spigot and carbonation was added to the water when the spigot was pressed. Related bottles may be found in the Coca-Cola, Mineral Water, Pepsi-Cola, and Soda categories.

SELTZER, B. Nierenberg Bottling Co., Phila., Pa., Made In Czechoslovakia, Blue, 11 In.   20.00
Barrett & Co. Mineral Water, Ashton U Lyne, Forest Green, 6 1/2 In. 35.00

Seltzer, New York Seltzer, Detroit, Mich., Bright Blue, Czechoslovakia, 11 In.

Seltzer, Pat-Ra-Cola Beverage Co., Chicago, Ill., Over Excelsior Label, 11 In.

Brinton & Brosius Standard Mineral Waters, Philadelphia, Etched, c.1920, 11 In. . . . 7.00
Bronx Beverage Co., Bronx, N.Y., Honey Amber, Ribbed 100.00
C.C.B.Co., Greensburg, Pa., Cont. 28 Fl. Oz., 10 Ribbed Panels, Deep Blue, 12 1/4 In. . . . 125.00
C.D. 257 F. Hemingray R., 2 Dates, Electric Blue 700.00
C.Z. Seelie Co., Wallace, Idaho 75.00
Commarano Crystal Springs, Tacoma, Seattle, ACL 70.00
Delaney & Young, Eureka, Cal., Pewter Top, Glass Straw 55.00
Eagle Bottling Works, Tacoma, Wash. 75.00
Everett Bottling Works, Lithilated Sparkling Water, Everett, Wash., ACL 60.00
Henry Krick Co., Santa Fe, New Mex. 110.00
Hollister Soda Works, Hollister, Cal. 50.00
Imperial Beverage Co., Oakland, Cal., Bears Drink From Bottle In Circle, Qt. 80.00
Independent Bottling Co., Ice Blue 75.00
Irwins Beverages, Phila., Pa., Made In Austria, Light Blue, BIMAL, c.1900, 11 In. 15.00
J. & B. Jewsbury & Brown, Manchester, Cobalt Blue, Chrome Top 100.00
J.H. Bryant, Sherbrooke, Que., Silver Spring Bottling Works, Medium Blue, 12 In. 40.00
John R. Shaw Aerated Waters, Alexandria, Ont., Monogram, BIMAL, 11 3/4 In. 35.00
Michael Beck, Phila., Pa., Made In Czechoslovakia, Peacock Blue, BIMAL, 11 1/8 In. . . . 30.00
Moran Beverages, St. Catharines, Ont., Art Deco Fountain, Paneled Sides, 12 In. 8.00
Mumby & Co. Ltd., Portsmouth, Lion, Unicorn, Emerald Green, England, 9 1/2 In. 95.00
New York Seltzer, Detroit, Mich., Bright Blue, Czechoslovakia, 11 In. . . . .*Illus* 48.00
Pat-Ra-Cola Beverage Co., Chicago, Ill., Over Excelsior Label, 11 In. . . . .*Illus* 23.00
Royal Windsor Beverages, 1471 Park Ave., N.Y., Shield, Lion, Unicorn, Blue, 11 In. . . . 15.00
Saratoga Seltzer Water, Teal Green, Gloppy Top, Haze 60.00
South Bend Bottling Works, South Bend, Wash, Sings 45.00
Tulip Bottling Co., Johnstown, Pa., Yellow Green, Pewter Top, 44 Oz. 60.00
W. Nichols, Lindsay, Ontario, Light Blue, 1930s, 30 Oz., 12 In. 55.00
W.C. Cooke Cross Street Kettering, Pink Champagne, Ribbed, 13 In. 295.00
W.T. Wagern's Sons Co., Cincinnati, Oh., Dark Green 75.00

―――――――――――――――――――― **SKI COUNTRY** ――――――――――――――――――――

Ski Country bottles are issued by The Foss Company of Golden, Colorado. These decanters are sold empty and filled by various distillers. The first bottles were made in 1973. By 1975 the company was making about 24 different decanter designs in each size each year, plus one decanter in the gallon size. They made 3 designs in 1995. The firm has marketed many series of decanters. The National Ski Country Bottle Club, at 1224 Washington Avenue, Golden, CO 80401, will send lists and information.

SKI COUNTRY, Animal, Antelope, Pronghorn, 1979 . . . . 60.00
Animal, Badger Family, 1981 . . . . 60.00
Animal, Basset Hound, 1978 . . . . 50.00
Animal, Bear, Brown, 1974 . . . . 36.00
Animal, Bobcat, 1981 . . . . 62.00
Animal, Buffalo, Stampede, 1982 . . . . 65.00
Animal, Buffalo, Stampede, 1982, Miniature 16.00
Animal, Bull Rider, 1980 . . . . 80.00
Animal, Bull, Charolais, 1974 . . . . 50.00
Animal, Circus, Tiger, On Ball, 1975 . . . . 45.00
Animal, Cow, Holstein, 1973 . . . . 75.00
Animal, Coyote, Family, 1978 . . . . 50.00
Animal, Deer, White-Tailed, 1982 . . . . 140.00
Animal, Elk, American, 1980 . . . . 200.00
Animal, Ferret, Blackfooted, 1976, Miniature 55.00
Animal, Giraffe, Circus Wagon, 1977 . . . . 47.00
Animal, Goat, Mountain, 1975 . . . . 80.00
Animal, Kangaroo, 1974 . . . . 37.00
Animal, Moose, Bull, 1982 . . . . 104.00
Animal, Otter, River, 1979 . . . . 70.00
Animal, Raccoon, 1975 . . . . 55.00
Animal, Sheep, Dall, Grand Slam, 1980 . . . . 180.00
Animal, Sheep, Desert, Grand Slam, 1990 . . . . 115.00
Animal, Sheep, Rocky Mountain, 1981 . . . . 70.00
Animal, Skunk, Family, 1978, Miniature . . . . .45.00 to 48.00
Animal, Walrus, Alaskan, 1985 . . . . .50.00 to 60.00

Bird, Blackbird, Red Wing, 1977 .... .42.00 to 44.00
Bird, Blue Jay, 1978 .... .82.00 to 85.00
Bird, Cardinal, 1977 .... 75.00
Bird, Cardinal, 1979, Miniature 35.00
Bird, Cardinal, Holiday, 1991 .... 65.00
Bird, Chickadee, 1981 .... 70.00
Bird, Condor, California, 1973 .... 55.00
Bird, Dove, Peace, 1973 .... 60.00
Bird, Duck, Blue Wing Teal, 1976 .... 80.00
Bird, Duck, Canvasback, 1981 .... 40.00
Bird, Duck, Green Wing Teal, 1985 .... 180.00
Bird, Duck, Mallard Drake, 1973 .... 60.00
Bird, Duck, Mallard Family, 1977 .... 75.00
Bird, Duck, Mallard, Banded, 1980 .... 60.00
Bird, Duck, Merganzer, Female Hooded, 1981 .... 50.00
Bird, Duck, Merganzer, Male Hooded, 1983 .... .76.00 to 80.00
Bird, Duck, Pintail, 1978 .... 100.00
Bird, Duck, Pintail, 1979, 1/2 Gal. 200.00
Bird, Duck, Red Head, 1974 .... 70.00
Bird, Duck, Widgeon, 1979 .... 51.00
Bird, Duck, Wood Duck, Banded, 1982 .... 95.00
Bird, Duck, Wood, 1974 .... 170.00
Bird, Eagle, Bald, On Water, 1981 .... 140.00
Bird, Eagle, Birth Of Freedom, 1976 .... 105.00
Bird, Eagle, Birth Of Freedom, 1976, Miniature 70.00
Bird, Eagle, Birth Of Freedom, 1977, Gal. 2000.00
Bird, Eagle, Harpy, 1973 .... 125.00
Bird, Eagle, Majestic, 1971 .... 325.00
Bird, Eagle, Majestic, 1973, Gal. 1650.00
Bird, Eagle, Mountain, 1973 .... 104.00
Bird, Eagle, On A Drum, 1976 .... 130.00
Bird, Flycatcher, 1979 .... 135.00
Bird, Goose, Canada, 1973 .... 100.00
Bird, Grouse, Ruffled, 1981 .... .55.00 to 65.00
Bird, Grouse, Ruffled, 1981, Miniature 33.00
Bird, Grouse, Sage, 1974 .... 75.00
Bird, Kestrel, Plaque, 1986 .... 75.00
Bird, Meadowlark, 1980 .... 55.00
Bird, Oriole, Baltimore, 1977 .... 60.00
Bird, Owl, Barn, 1979 .... .80.00 to 85.00
Bird, Owl, Barred, 1981 .... *Illus* 130.00
Bird, Owl, Great Gray, 1985 .... 55.00
Bird, Owl, Great Horned, 1974 .... 85.00
Bird, Owl, Saw Whet, 1977, Miniature 60.00
Bird, Owl, Screech, Family, 1977 .... 105.00
Bird, Peacock, 1973 .... 105.00

Ski Country, Bird,
Owl, Barred, 1981

Ski Country, Indian,
Ceremonial, No. 2,
Buffalo, 1980

Bird, Pelican, Brown, 1976 . . . . .55.00 to 57.00
Bird, Pelican, Brown, 1976, Miniature 35.00
Bird, Pheasant, Golden 54.00
Bird, Pheasant, In Corn, 1982 . . . . 70.00
Bird, Prairie Chicken, 1976 . . . . 63.00
Bird, Seagull, Plaque, 1985 . . . . 50.00
Bird, Swallows, Barn, 1977 . . . . 46.00
Bird, Swan, Black, 1974 . . . . 50.00
Bird, Turkey, 1976 . . . . .80.00 to 100.00
Bird, Whooping Crane, 1983 . . . . 50.00
Bird, Woodpecker, Gila, 1972 . . . . 75.00
Bird, Woodpecker, Ivory Billed, 1976 . . . . 50.00
Bonnie, Customer Specialty, 1974 . . . . 35.00
C.S.M. Burro, Customer Specialty, 1973, Miniature 70.00
Caveman, Customer Specialty, 1974 . . . . 26.00
Christmas, Cardinal, 1990 . . . . 67.00
Christmas, Cedar Waxwing, 1985 . . . . 65.00
Christmas, Woodland Trio, 1980 . . . . 70.00
Circus, Elephant, 1974 . . . . .37.00 to 44.00
Circus, Horse, Lipizzaner, 1976 . . . . 60.00
Circus, Horse, Palomino, 1976 . . . . 60.00
Circus, Jenny Lind, Blue, 1976 . . . . 80.00
Circus, Jenny Lind, Yellow, 1976 . . . . 130.00
Circus, Jenny Lind, Yellow, 1976, Miniature 185.00
Circus, P.T. Barnum, 1976 . . . . 50.00
Circus, Tom Thumb, 1974 . . . . 32.00
Circus, Clown, 1974 . . . . 67.00
Clyde, Customer Specialty, 1974 . . . . 37.00
Fire Engine, 1923 Ahrens-Fox, 1981 . . . . 185.00
Fish, Salmon, 1977 . . . . 42.00
Fish, Trout, Rainbow, 1976 . . . . 65.00
Indian, Ceremonial, No. 1, Eagle, 1979 . . . . 230.00
Indian, Ceremonial, No. 2, Buffalo, 1980 . . . .*Illus* 210.00
Indian, Ceremonial, No. 3, Deer, 1980 . . . . 125.00
Indian, Ceremonial, No. 4, Wolf, 1981 . . . . 85.00
Indian, Ceremonial, No. 5, Antelope, 1982 . . . . 80.00
Indian, Ceremonial, No. 6, Falcon, 1983 . . . . 135.00
Indian, Ceremonial, Rainbow Dancer, 1984 . . . . 50.00
Indian, Cigar Store, 1974 . . . . .40.00 to 45.00
Indian, End Of Trail, 1976 . . . . 240.00
Indian, Great Spirit, 1976 . . . . 105.00
Indian, Lookout, 1977 . . . . 55.00
Indian, North American, Tribes, 1977, 6 Piece 225.00
Indian, North American, Tribes, 1977, 6 Piece, Miniature 120.00
Indian, South West Dancers, 1975 . . . . 350.00
Indian, Warrior, Hatchet, Chief, No. 1, 1975 . . . . 140.00
Indian, Warrior, Lance, Chief, No. 2, 1975 . . . . 140.00
Phoenix Bird, Customer Specialty, 1981 . . . . 60.00
Political Donkey, Customer Specialty, 1976 . . . . 45.00
Political Elephant, Customer Specialty, 1981 . . . . 42.00
Rodeo Barrel Racer, 1982 . . . . 80.00
Skier, Blue, Customer Specialty, 1972 . . . . 40.00
Skier, Gold, Customer Specialty, 1972 . . . . .70.00 to 80.00
Skier, Red, Customer Specialty, 1972 . . . . .25.00 to 40.00
Submarine, Customer Specialty, 1976, Miniature 30.00
U.S. Ski Team, Olympic, 1980 . . . . 40.00

SNUFF

Snuff has been used in European countries since the fifteenth century, when the first tobacco was brought back from America by Christopher Columbus. The powdered tobacco was inhaled through long tubes. The French ambassador to Portugal, Jean Nicot, unknowingly made his name a household word when he sent some of the powdered tobacco to his queen, Catherine de Medici. The stuff became known as *nicotine*.

Tobacco was at first considered a remedy and was used in many types of medicines. In the sixteenth and seventeenth centuries, royalty enjoyed snuff and kept it in elaborate gold and silver snuffboxes. Snuff was enjoyed by both royalty and laboring classes by the eighteenth century. The nineteenth-century gentleman no longer used snuff by the 1850s, although poor Southern women used snuff by dipping, not sniffing, and putting it in the mouth, not the nose. Snuff bottles have been made since the eighteenth century. Glass, metal, ceramic, ivory, and precious stones were all used to make plain or fancy snuff holders. Commercial bottles for snuff are made of dark glass, usually shaped more like a box or a jar than a bottle. Snuff was also packaged in stoneware crocks. Most oriental snuff bottles have a small stick with a spoon end as part of the closure. The International Chinese Snuff Bottle Society, 2601 North Charles Street, Baltimore, MD 21218, has a colorful, informative publication.

SNUFF, Agate, Leave, Vine Design, Red, Green Stone Stopper, 1900, 1 3/4 In. 154.00
  Agate, Mask, Mock Ring Handles, Coral Stopper, 2 In. 70.00
  Agate, Moss, Green, Red, Gray Ground, Green Stone Stopper, 2 1/8 In. 121.00
  Agate, Puddingstone, Carved Flower & Mask, Mock Ring Handle, 1 3/4 In. 785.00
  Agate, Puddingstone, Spade Shape, Carved Ducks, Green Stone Stopper, 2 In. 210.00
  Agate, Soochow, Fruit Form, Carved Insect & Leaves, Coral Stopper, 1 3/4 In. 4114.00
  Amber, Mask & Mock Ring Handles, Stopper, 3 1/4 In. 330.00
  Carnelian, Flat Sides, Plum Blossoms, Jade Stopper, 2 3/4 In. 103.00
  Chalcedony Agate, Brown, White Ground, Egg Shape, Pink Glass Stopper, 2 In. 275.00
  Cinnabar, Bird, Floral Landscape, Red, Overlay Neck, Stone Stopper, 2 1/2 In. 28.00
  Coral, Branch Form, Flower, Leaf Design, Jadeite Stopper, 1 3/4 In. 176.00
  Coral, Relief Floral Design, Stopper, Early 20th Century, 2 1/4 In. 231.00
  Glass, A. Delpit, No. 16, St. Louis St., New Orleans, Amber, Tall, Thin, 4 1/4 x 2 In. 480.00
  Glass, E. Roome, Troy, N.Y., Green, Amber Tone, Sheared & Flared Lip, Label, 4 3/8 In.   495.00
  Glass, E. Roome, Troy, N.Y., Yellow Olive Amber, Sheared & Flared Lip, Pontil, 4 1/8 In.   255.00
  Glass, E. Roome, Troy, N.Y., Yellow Olive, Tooled Mouth, Pontil, 4 1/8 In. 230.00
  Glass, Eagle, Flat Reverse, Green Aqua, Ground Top, 4 3/4 In. 110.00
  Glass, Erotic Scene Inside, Man & Woman, Chinese Calligraphy, 1 1/4 x 2 3/4 In. 225.00
  Glass, Flora & Fauna Interior, Sloping Shoulders, Jade Stopper, 2 7/8 In. 35.00
  Glass, Flowering Branch Front, Spade Shape, Jade Stopper, 2 1/4 In. 460.00
  Glass, Forest Green, F On Base, Concave Beveled Corners, Pontil, 4 1/4 In. 110.00
  Glass, Forest Green, Flared Mouth, Square, Pontil, 4 1/4 In. 35.00
  Glass, Gourd, Sage In A Landscape Design, Agate Stopper, Late 19th Century, 1 1/4 In. . .   440.00
  Glass, Helme's Railroad Mills, Medium Amber, Ground Lip, Lid, 7 1/2 In. 45.00
  Glass, Jar, Blown, Yellow Olive, Square, Sheared Mouth, Pontil, 1830, 3 1/2 In. 605.00
  Glass, Jar, Deep Cobalt Blue, Tooled Lip, Square, 1870-1890, 7 In. 200.00
  Glass, Jar, Deep Red Amber, Rolled Lip, 1860-1880, 8 1/2 In. 80.00
  Glass, Jar, Emerald Green, Sheared Mouth, Square, Pontil, 1860, 6 In. 1320.00
  Glass, Jar, Olive Amber, Tooled Mouth, Rectangular, Beveled Corners, Pontil, 4 1/4 In. . .   165.00
  Glass, Jar, Puce, Crude, Bubbles, 4 In. 130.00
  Glass, Jar, S On Base, Green, Bubbles, 5 In. 55.00
  Glass, Jar, Scotch Snuff, E. Goodwin & Brother, Gold Amber, Pontil, 1860, 4 1/8 In. 200.00
  Glass, Jar, Yellow Olive, Square, Beveled Corners, Sheared Mouth, Pontil, 1840, 5 5/8 In.   465.00
  Glass, Levi Garrett & Son, 2nd Quality, Gold Yellow, Mouth Chips, Square, Pontil, 4 In. .   210.00
  Glass, Light Yellow Olive Green, Sheared Lip, Pontil, Bubbles, 1790-1820, 5 1/4 In. 155.00
  Glass, Medium Olive Amber, Wide Chamfered Panels, Flared Lip, 1850-1870, 7 1/4 In. . .   165.00
  Glass, Medium Olive Amber, Wide Rolled Lip, Pontil, Paddle Marks, 6 1/4 In. 305.00
  Glass, Medium Olive Green, Amber Tone, Rolled Mouth, 1770-1800, 5 1/4 In. 110.00
  Glass, Medium Red Amber, Wide Mouth, Rolled Lip, 1860-1880, 8 1/2 In. 80.00
  Glass, Medium Yellow Olive Green, Sheared, Tooled Lip, Pontil, 1780-1810, 4 1/2 In. . . .   360.00
  Glass, Olive Amber, Tooled Lip, Pontil, 1790-1825, 5 In. 190.00
  Glass, Olive Green, Bar On Base, Concave Beveled Corners, Pontil, 4 1/4 In. 75.00
  Glass, Railroad Mills Scotch Snuff, Amber, 1870, 3 3/4 x 2 3/8 In. 45.00
  Glass, Reverse Painted Vase Of Flowers & Butterflies, Black Stopper, 2 1/4 In. 46.00
  Glass, Ruby, Pear Shape, Stopper, Early 19th Century, 2 1/4 In. 55.00
  Glass, Sage Under Pine Tree, Spade Shape, Horn Stopper, 1900, 2 In. 385.00
  Glass, True Cephalick, By The King's Patent, Blue Green, Cylindrical, Pontil, 3 7/8 In. . . .   75.00
  Hornbill, Figural Carving On Natural Ground, 1920s, 1 3/4 In. 968.00
  Horsehide, 2 Side Handles, Scotland, c.1780, 2 1/2 x 1 In. 595.00
  Inkstone, Carved Dragon Design, Coral Stopper, 2 1/4 In. 484.00
  Ivory, Figure Seated Beneath Tree One Side, Bird On Other, Stopper, 2 3/4 In. 195.00

Snuff, Lorillard's
Maccoboy, Tin Top

Snuff, Scotch &
Rappee, Brown, 4 In.

Ivory, Flattened Urn Form, Etched Flowering Trees & Bushes, 1 3/4 In. 105.00
Ivory, Gardeners, Man With Paper, Removable Top With Spoon, Brass Base, 2 1/2 In. . . .   110.00
Ivory, Leaping Carp Design, Stopper, 2 3/4 In. 121.00
Ivory, Repeated Shou Design, Jade Stopper, 18th Century, 2 1/2 In. 5082.00
Ivory, Swimming Carp Form, Conforming Stopper, c.1900 . . . .   1452.00
Jade, Black, Flattened Egg Shape, Simulated Coral Stopper, 2 In. 605.00
Jade, Celadon Green, Butterfly & Vine, Double Gourd Form, Stopper, 2 3/4 In. 220.00
Jade, Crouching Mouse Eating Coral Kernel Of Rice, 2 1/2 In. 3630.00
Jade, Man On Bull Near Rock, Amethyst Top, Brown Stone, 2 3/4 In. 575.00
Jade, Man On Bull Near Rock, Orange Top, Blue, Handles, 2 3/4 In. 144.00
Jade, Raised Calligraphic Design, 19th Century, 2 1/4 In. 121.00
Jade, White, Rectangular, Raised Panel Sides, Green Jade Stopper, 2 1/4 In. 110.00
Jadeite, Apple Green, Silver Mounts, Jadeite Stopper, 19th Century, 2 3/4 In. 1210.00
Jadeite, White, Spade Shape, Mock Ring Handles, Lapis Lazuli Stopper, 7/8 In. 121.00
Lapis Lazuli, Lion & Peonies, Pear Shape, Conforming Stopper, 3 3/8 In. 155.00
Lapis Lazuli, Relief Peony Design, Spade Shape, Stopper, 1900, 2 1/4 In. 88.00
Lapis Lazuli, Spade Shape, Blue Accents, Gray, Spade Shape, Agate Stopper, 2 In. 66.00
Lorillard's Maccoboy, Tin Top . . . .*Illus*   50.00
Malachite, Leaping Carp Shape, Coral Stopper, 2 3/4 In. 220.00
Mother-Of-Pearl, Gold Design, Brass Chain, 3 In. 200.00
Mother-Of-Pearl, Woman With Lute, Spade Shade, Conforming Stopper, 3 In. 110.00
Porcelain, 5-Claw Green Dragon Design, Tiger's Eye Stopper, Cylindrical, 3 In. 522.00
Porcelain, Blue, Gilt Bird, Floral Design, Agate Stopper, 20th Century, 2 1/4 In. 44.00
Porcelain, Dark Green & Black Dragon, Jade Stopper, 3 In. 115.00
Porcelain, Dragon Panels, Mask Handles, Bell Form, Coral Stopper, 1 7/8 In. 297.00
Porcelain, Green, 3-Legged Frog, Teardrop Shape, Glass Stopper, Early 20th Century, 2 In.   220.00
Porcelain, Herdboy & Water Buffalo, Ivory Stopper, 18th Century, 2 7/8 In. 133.00
Porcelain, Magpie Design, Cylindrical, Coral Stopper, 1880, 2 1/2 In. 605.00
Porcelain, Mask, Mock Ring Handles, White, Coral Stopper, 19th Century, 2 In. 187.00
Porcelain, Pilgrim Flask Form, Lapis Lazuli Stopper, 1 1/4 In. 66.00
Porcelain, Pilgrim Flask Form, Pearl & Coral, Silver, Stopper, 19th Century, 2 5/8 In. . . .   465.00
Porcelain, Relief Gold Dragons, Turquoise Ground, Jadeite Stopper, 2 1/4 In. 121.00
Porcelain, Sage, Double Gourd On His Back, Blue, White, Lapis Lazuli Stopper, 2 In. . . .   38.00
Porcelain, Salmon Red, Black Ground, Teardrop Shape, Coral Stopper, 2 3/4 In. 264.00
Porcelain, Shoulder Dog Masks, Musician 1 Side, 2 Women Other, Agate Stopper, 2 3/4 In.   92.00
Pottery, Yi Hsing, Fret Design, Agate Stopper, 2 1/4 In. 1935.00
Pressed Burl, Little Milkmaid On Lid, France, 1820, 3 x 1 In. 300.00
Puddingstone, Egg Shape, Jadeite Stopper, Late 19th Century, 2 In. 465.00
Rock Crystal, Cameo Carved Bird, Prunus & Lotus, 19th Century, 2 1/4 In. 513.00
Rock Crystal, Carved Carp & Sea Grass, 19th Century, 2 1/4 In. 363.00
Rock Crystal, Women In Winter Landscape, Interior Painted, 1915, 2 1/2 In. 484.00
Scotch & Rappee, Brown, 4 In. . . . .*Illus*   20.00
Tortoiseshell, Crane & Pheasant Design, Stopper, Rectangular, 2 1/2 In. 265.00
Tourmaline, Pink, Flower & Vine Design, Spade Shape, Stopper, 2 3/4 In. 2640.00
Turquoise, Double Gourd Shape, Silver-Mounted, Coral Stopper, 2 1/4 In. 825.00
Turquoise, Flattened Egg Shape, Glass Stopper, 2 1/4 In. 135.00
Turquoise, Spade Shape, Butterfly, Floral Design, Stopper, 2 1/2 In. 440.00

Turquoise, Spade Shape, Sage, Meijin Design, Stopper, 2 5/8 In. 220.00
Turquoise, Temple Jar Shape, Bird, Flower Design, Stopper, 1 5/8 In. 165.00
Wooden, Seal Scene, Calligraphy, Spade Shape, Jadeite Stopper, 2 In. 1980.00

--------------------------------------- **SODA** ---------------------------------------

All forms of carbonated drink—naturally carbonated mineral water, artificially carbonated and flavored pops, and seltzer—are forms of soda. The words are often inter-
changed. Soda bottles held some form of soda pop or carbonated drink. The early soda
bottle had a characteristic thick blob top and heavy glass sides to avoid breakage from
the pressure of the carbonation. Tops were cleverly secured; the Hutchinson stopper and
Coddball stopper were used on many early bottles. The crown cap was not developed
and used until 1891. The cork liner inside the crown cap was outlawed in 1969. The
first soda was artificially carbonated in the 1830s by John Matthews. He used marble
chips and acid for carbonation. It is said he took all the scrap marble from St. Patrick's
Cathedral in New York City to use at his plant, which made, so they say, 25 million gallons of soda water. In 1839 a Philadelphia perfume dealer, Eugene Roussel, had the
clever idea of adding flavor to the soda. Soon colors were added and the soft drink
industry had begun. The late 1800s saw the beginning of Coca-Cola (1886), Pepsi-Cola
(1898), Moxie (1876), Dr Pepper (1885), and others. The English brand Schweppes was
already established, but they added artificially carbonated sodas as well. Collectors
search for the heavy blob top bottles and the newer crown top sodas with embossed lettering or silk-screened labels. Collectors refer to *painted label bottles* as *ACL* or
Applied Color Label. Recent commemorative bottles are also in demand. In this book,
the soda bottle listing includes modern carbonated beverage bottles as well as the older
blob tops, Hutchinsons, and other collectible soda bottles. Coca-Cola, Pepsi-Cola, mineral water, sarsaparilla, and seltzer bottles are listed in their own sections. Collector
clubs with newsletters include Painted Soda Bottle Collectors Association, 9418 Hilmer
Drive, LaMesa, CA 91942; Dr Pepper Collectors Club, 3100 Monticello, Suite 890,
Dallas, TX 75205; and the clubs listed in this book in the Coca-Cola and Pepsi-Cola
sections. Related bottles may be found in the Coca-Cola, Mineral Water, Pepsi-Cola,
Sarsaparilla, and Seltzer categories.

SODA, 7-Up, Indianapolis 500, 1978 . . . . 35.00
A-Treat Beverage, Factory Scene, Red & White, ACL, Allentown, Pa., 12 Oz. 85.00
A. & W. Burns, 406 Yonge St., Toronto, Beaver Soda Water Works, Aqua, 7 3/4 In. 30.00
A. & W. Burns, 406 Yonge St., Toronto, Beaver, Deep Aqua, Blob Top, Variant, 7 3/8 In. 45.00
A. & W. Burns, Toronto, Beaver, Aqua, Blob Top, Putnam Cork Fastener, 7 3/4 In. 175.00
A. Jimason, Parksburg, Pa. . . . . .35.00 to 55.00
A. Nicholson, Pittsburg, Aqua, Blob Top, IP, 7 3/8 In. 45.00
A.M. Hanna Prop., City Bottling Works, Kosciusko, Miss. 100.00
A.W. Cudworth & Co., San Francisco, Green Blue, Blob Top, Slug Plate 45.00
A.W. Fisher, Reading, Pa., Blob Top, Squat 15.00
A.W. Fisher, West End Bottling Works, Reading, Pa., Hutchinson 12.00
A.W.K. Co., Auburn, Calif., Aqua, Crown Top, BIMAL 10.00
Acme Soda Mfg. Co., Pittsburgh, A.S.M. On Reverse, Hutchinson 8.00
Acme Soda Water Co., Pittsburgh, Pa., Hutchinson 10.00
Acme Soda Works, Ventura, Cal., Green Aqua, Hutchinson 95.00
Advance Bottling Co., Peoria, Ill., Crown Top 3.00
Alameda Soda Water Co., Oakland, Cal., Clasped Hands, Hutchinson 45.00
Albert Krumenaker, Monogram, Aqua, Blob Top, Cork, 7 In. 8.00
Alkalaris Water, St. Matthews, Kentucky, Indian Drinking, Red & Yellow, ACL 40.00
American Soda Fountain Co., Amber, Blob Top, 12 In. 22.00
American Soda Fountain Co., Qt. 20.00
Arctic Beverages, Polar Bears, Label 10.00
Arctic Soda Works, Honolulu, H.T., Crown Top 20.00
Arizona Bottling Works, Aqua, Applied Crown 12.00
Arizona Bottling Works, Phoenix, Ariz., 4-Piece Mold, Oval Slug Plate, Hutchinson . . 150.00
Arizona Bottling Works, Phoenix, Ariz., Crown Top, BIMAL 16.00
Arny & Shinn, Georgetown, D.C., Blue Green, Applied Mouth, Cylindrical, 1870, 1/2 Pt. 150.00
Arny & Shinn, Georgetown, D.C., Yellow Green, Squat, Cylindrical, 1870, 1/2 Pt. 140.00
Ashland Bottling Works, Ashland, Wis., Blue Aqua, 8 Oz. 20.00
Aspinock Beverages, Indian Head, ACL, 1940s-1950s 40.00
Athens Bottling Works, Athens, Pa., Yellow Green, Crown Top 45.00
Aug. J. Lang, San Francisco, Medium Yellow Amber, Tooled Lip, 1880-1900, 5 1/2 In. . . 275.00

Soda, Billy Baxter
Root Beer, Red
Raven, Pa., Paper
Label, Contents,
Cap, 7 In.

Soda, Brough Co.,
Cleveland, Ohio,
Eagle, Trademark
Registered,
Embossed, 6 1/2

Soda, Canada
Dry, Carnival
Finish, 9 1/2 In.

August Hohl, Catasauqua, Pa., Blob Top, Pony 10.00
August Hohl, Catasauqua, Pa., Crown Top 3.00
B, Aqua, Blob Top 40.00
Baldwin Bottle Co., Bay Minette, Ala., Aqua, Crown Top, 8 In. 125.00
Barrett & Co., Aldershot, Aqua, Embossed, Codd, 9 1/4 In. 35.00
Bay City Soda Water Co., S.F., Sapphire Blue, Applied Mouth, 1860-1870, 7 1/4 In. .. 130.00
Bay City Soda Water Co., San Francisco, Cobalt Blue, Large Embossed Star, Blob Top 90.00
Bay City Soda Water Co., San Francisco, Blue, Applied Mouth, 1871-1880, 7 In. 100.00
Bayshore Bottling Co., Long Island, Blob Top 15.00
Beaver, A. & W. Burns, Yonge St., Toronto, Aqua, Blob Top, 7 3/4 In. 40.00
Belfast Ginger Ale, C.C. Dows & Co., Boston, Aqua, Round Base 20.00
Belfast Ginger Ale, San Francisco, Aqua, Hutchinson 30.00
Berle & Padderatz, Trenton, N.J., Blob Top 5.00
Biedenharn Candy Co., Vicksburg, Miss., Pale Blue Aqua, Tooled Blob Top, 1900, 7 In. 265.00
Big Bot'l., Flower City Beverage Co., Crown Top, ABM 20.00
Big Chief, Indian, Orange & Yellow, ACL, Ely, Nevada, 9 Oz. 85.00
Big Chief, Indian, Red & White, ACL, Price, Utah, 9 Oz. 85.00
Big Chief, Indian, White & Red, ACL, Beatrice, Nebraska, 9 Oz. 50.00
Big Chief, Indian, White & Red, ACL, Raton, N.M., 6 1/2 Oz. 40.00
Big Shot Beverage, Cartoon, Man With Cigar, Red & White, ACL, 12 Oz. 35.00
Billy Baxter Root Beer, Red Raven, Pa., Paper Label, Contents, Cap, 7 In. ......*Illus* 15.00
Birdsboro Bottling Works, Birdsboro, Pa., Pony 35.00
Black Kow Co., McKeesport, Pa., ACL, 1950s, 12 Oz. 7.00
Blatz Brewing, Milwaukee, Embossed, 7 1/2 Oz. 8.00
Bludwine Bottling Co., West Point, Ga., Crown Top, 7 1/2 In. 20.00
Boehret, Roxborough, Pa., Aqua, Squat ....12.00 to 20.00
Bolger & Co., Toronto, Aqua, Blob Top, Fat Boy, 1876-1881, 7 3/8 In. 30.00
Bowling Green Bottling Works, Bowling Green, Ohio, Aqua, Hutchinson 14.00
Boyer's Bottling Works, Lebanon, Pa., Wire Bail, BIMAL, Slug Plate, 9 In. 60.00
Boyle & Libby, Arm Holding Scale, Trade Mark Registered, Toronto, Amber, 7 5/8 In. .. 185.00
Breig & Schafer, S.F., Fish, Deep Blue Aqua, Green Streaks, Applied Top 145.00
Bremkampf & Regli, Eureka, Nev., Aqua, Blob Top 75.00
Broadway Dry, New York City Skyline, Emerald Green, Crown Top 35.00
Bronx Co., Mt. Vernon, N.Y., Owl & Crescent Moon, Light Amethyst, Pt. 25.00
Brough Co., Cleveland, Ohio, Eagle, Trademark Registered, Embossed, 6 1/2 In. ...*Illus* 24.00
Brown Stout, Kensington, Green, Sloping Ring Mouth, Cylindrical, IP, 1/2 Pt. 45.00
Brownell & Wheaton, New Bedford, Teal Blue, Heavy Mouth, Cylindrical, 1/2 Pt. 90.00
Brownie Club Beverage, Little Brownie, R.I., White & Red, ACL, 12 Oz. 85.00
Bryces Beverage, Butlers Holding Tray, Troy, N.Y., 7 Oz. 45.00
Buffalo Bottling, Redding, Cal., Selenium Tint, Crown Top, ABM, 1920-1930 .... 10.00
Burgin & Sons, Philada Glass Works, Blue Green, Applied Mouth, IP, 7 1/4 In. 110.00
Burgin & Sons, Philada Glass Works, Green Aqua, Blob Top, IP 45.00
Burke Mountain, Mountain, Blue & White, ACL, 1940s-1950s 10.00
Burr & Water Bottlers, Buffalo, N.Y., Smoky Sapphire Blue, 8-Sided, IP, 7 1/4 In. 360.00
C. & J. Dithmar's Bottling Establishment, No. 453 N. 3rd St., Green, Pontil 85.00
C. Abel, St. Louis, Mo., 10-Sided, Aqua, Blob Top, Pontil 45.00
C. Alfs, Charleston, S.C., 8-Sided, Yellow Olive Green, IP, 1845-1855, 7 1/4 In. 8525.00

C. Clark, Charleston, S.C., Deep Grass Green, IP, Slug Plate, 1845-1855, 7 1/2 In. 305.00
C. Freeman, Buffalo, N.Y., To Be Returned, Amber, Sloping Double Collar, IP, 6 1/2 In. .. 780.00
C. Leary Root Beer, Newburyport, Mass. 40.00
C. Nusbaum, Dark Green, IP 60.00
C. Schlieper & Co., St. Louis, Mo., Aqua, Blob Top 20.00
C. Wittemore, New York, Emerald Green, Tapered, Cylindrical, 8 In. 135.00
C.A. Kohl, Lambertville, N.J., Deep Emerald Green, OP, Tapered Top 240.00
C.A. Scheidemantal, Denver, Col., Blue Aqua, Applied Top 75.00
C.B. Owen, Cincinnati, Root Beer, Cobalt Blue, 12-Sided, Applied Mouth, IP, 8 3/8 In. ... 1155.00
C.B. Owen & Co. Bottlers, Cincinnati, Deep Blue, IP 200.00
C.B. Owen's Root Beer, Cincinnati, Sapphire Blue, 12-Sided, IP, 8 1/2 In. 935.00
C.C. Dows & Co., Boston, Belfast Ginger Ale, Aqua, Round Bottom, Squat 20.00
C.C. Soda, Berkshire Coca-Cola, Pittsfield, Mass., 11-6-23, Shaped To Fit Hand, 6 Oz. ... 65.00
C.F. Riley Soda Works, Aqua, Eagle, Tooled Top 65.00
C.H. Haeberle, Philada., Forest Green, Double Collar, IP, Squat 60.00
California Cub Bear, Crown Top, ABM 15.00
California Gazosa Works, Blue Aqua, Codd 90.00
California Soda Works, Eagle, Aqua, Tooled Top, 7 In. 35.00
California Soda Works, H. Ficken, San Francisco, Ca., Aqua, 1879, 7 In. 275.00
California Soda Works, H. Ficken, San Francisco, Deep Aqua, Blob Top, 6 7/8 In. 45.00
California Soda Works, San Francisco, Blue Aqua, Applied Mouth, 1878-1879, 7 In. ... 210.00
California Sweet, California Soda Works, Stockton, Cal., Walking Bear, Crown Top ... 50.00
Calistoga Bottling Wks., G. Musante, Calistoga, Cal., Crown Top, ABM 12.00
Calumet Bottling Works, Wm. Stein, Blue Island, Ill., Hutchinson 25.00
Canada Dry, Carnival Finish, 9 1/2 In. ....*Illus* 29.00
Canada Dry, Iridized, Paper Labels, 1920s 80.00
Canster & Fessler, Reading, Pa., Hutchinson 20.00
Cantrell & Cochran, Dublin & Belfast, Round Bottom, Crown Top 7.00
Capital City Bottlers, Harrisburg, Pa., Amber 20.00
Capital City Bottlers, Harrisburg, Pa., Wire Bail, Slug Plate, BIMAL, 9 1/2 In. 60.00
Carl H. Schultz, Pat. 1868, N.Y., Ten-Pin, Blob Top 15.00
Carl H. Schultz, Pat. May 1868, New York, Ten-Pin, Aqua, Blob Top 60.00
Carolina Moon Beverage, Green, Red & Yellow Sunrise, ACL, 12 Oz. 75.00
Casey & Cronan, Eagle Soda Works, Pale Blue, Gravitating Stopper, Hutchinson 25.00
Catawissa, Catawissa, Pa., Sexy Lady, White & Red, ACL, 12 Oz. 35.00
Celro-Kola Co., Portland, Ore., Celro-Kola In Script, Light Amber, ABM, 9 In. 35.00
Champagne Mead, Light Blue Green, 8-Sided, Applied Top 110.00
Charles Wilson, Squirrel, Light Aqua, Stopper, Hutchinson, Fat Variant, Canada, 6 1/2 In. 35.00
Chas. Grove, Cola, Pa., Brown Stout, Emerald Blue Green, IP, Squat 160.00
Chas. Wilson, Toronto, Ont., Squirrel, Gray Cornflower Blue, Blob Top, 7 1/2 In. 40.00
Chas. Zech, Lancaster, Pa., Aqua, Hutchinson 12.00
Chas. Zech, Lancaster, Pa., Light Apple Green, Hutchinson 35.00
Chattanooga Ice & Beer Co., Chattanooga, Tenn., Hutchinson, Amber, 7 In. 1375.00
Chero Cola, Columbus, Ga., Crown Top, 7 1/2 In. 10.00
Chero Cola, Harrison, N.Y., Pat. Pending, Diagonal Ribs, 6 Oz. 25.00
Chero Cola, Jacksonville, Fla., Script, Crown Top, 8 In. 15.00
Chero Cola, Pensacola, Fla., Aqua, Crown Top, 7 1/2 In. ....10.00 to 15.00
Chero Cola, Rocky Mount, N.C., Aqua, Quilted, Crown Top, Hutchinson, 7 1/2 In. 15.00
Cherry Malt Phosphate, Scott & Browne, N.Y., Amber, Round, Lady's Leg, 1890-1895 55.00
Cherry Nectar, West Point, Ga., Crown Top, 7 1/2 In. 10.00
Chester Bottling Works, Chester, Ill., Aqua 20.00
Chester Club, Poughkeepsie, N.Y., Green, Golfer, Red & White, ACL, 8 Oz. 40.00
Chester Club, Poughkeepsie, N.Y., Red, White, ACL 25.00
Chicago Consolidated Bottling Co., Aqua, Large 12.00
Chief, Chief's Head, Pat'd. Dec. 29, 1928, Crown Top, ABM 20.00
Chocolate Soldier, Toy Soldier, Deep Amber, Crown Top 35.00
Chuk Ker, Cowboy On Horse, Green, White Logo, Bottled By Dr. Pepper, 6 Oz. 50.00
Citro, The Thirst Quencher, Baltimore, Md., ABM, Cobalt Blue 90.00
City Bottling Works, Toledo, O., Sapphire Blue, Applied Top, Hutchinson 250.00
City Ice & Bottling Works, Georgetown, Tex. 20.00
Clark & White, New York, Medium To Dark Green, Bubbles, Pt. 60.00
Clark & White, New York, Olive Green, Qt. ....65.00 to 70.00
Clark Bros., Toronto, Winged Wheel, Aqua, Blob Top, Wire Closure, 7 1/2 In. 35.00

Classen & Co., San Francisco, Ca., Light To Medium Green, Blob Mouth, 1868, 7 In. .. 80.00
Classen & Co., San Francisco, Pacific Soda Works, Green 55.00
Clicquot Club, Eskimo Boy, Red & White, 12 Oz. 6.00
Clicquot Club, Millis, Mass., Klee Ko Face Shape, Pt. 5.00
Clinton, Woodbridge, Conn., Emerald Green, Blob Top, IP, 7 3/8 In. 100.00
Coca-Cola Bottling Co., Green Aqua, Tooled Lip, Hutchinson, 1885-1895, 7 1/8 In. ... 1150.00
Coeur D'Alene Bottling Works, Coeur D'Alene, Idaho, Aqua, Crown Top, BIMAL ... 30.00
Cole & Henderson, St. Thomas, Steam Locomotive, Aqua, Blob Top, Canada, Qt., 11 In. 155.00
Cole & Southey, Washington, D.C., Aquamarine, Applied Mouth, Squat, 1880, 1/2 Pt. .. 120.00
Columbia Soda Works, S.F., C.C. Dall, Seated Liberty, Aqua, Applied Top 155.00
Comstock Cove & Co., Aqua, Ten-Pin, Applied Blob Top, 1855-1865, 7 1/8 In. 130.00
Concord Bottling Co., Concord, N.H., Star, Hutchinson 30.00
Congress & Empire Spring, Green, Pt. ....35.00 to 40.00
Congress & Empire Spring Co., Green, Qt. 55.00
Connell & Tallon, Bordentown, N.J., Emerald Green, Sloping Double Collar, 7 1/2 In. .. 90.00
Conner & McQuaide, J.C. Buffum & Co., Pittsburgh, Pa., Aqua, Squat 15.00
Connolly & Bro., S.F., Yellow Lime Green 40.00
Cottle Post & Co., Portland, Motif Of Eagle, Blue, Blob Top, 1877-1887, 7 In. ..110.00 to 145.00
County Squire, Man In Top Hat, Red, ACL, 8 Oz. 30.00
Crandall & Baker Bottling Works, Elk Point, S.D., Aqua, Hutchinson 85.00
Cream Ale, A. Templeton, Louisville, Black Amber, Saratoga Mug Base 70.00
Cream Soda, N.Y., Deep Aquamarine, Applied Mouth, 1860-1880, 5 3/4 In. 140.00
Cream Soda, Taylor & Wilson, 127 Reade St., Aqua, Blob Top, 6 In. 80.00
Cressona Bottling Works, Cressona, Pa 15.00
Cripple Creek Bottling Works, Cripple Creek, Colo., Light Aqua 90.00
Crone & Co., St. Louis, Mo., Blob Top 20.00
Crown Bottling Works, De Funiak Springs, Fla., Aqua, Slug Plate, 7 1/2 In. 20.00
Crystal Palace Premium, W. Eagle, New York, Deep Blue, IP, 7 1/4 In. 1265.00
Crystal Soda Water Co., Light Aqua, Blob Top, 1873-1886 .... 110.00
Crystal Soda Water Co., Medium Cobalt Blue, Blob Top, 1873-1886 .... 175.00
Crystal Soda Water Co., Patented Nov. 12, 1872, Aqua, Amber Streak, Pt. 100.00
D. Fuelscher, Central City, Col., This Bottle To Be Returned To, Aqua, Hutchinson 120.00
D. McCoy, Cincinnati, Root Beer, Deep Cobalt Blue, Applied Mouth, IP, 8 1/8 In. 6400.00
D. McCullin, Wilmington, Del., Aqua, Blob Top, Pony 10.00
D. McCurdy, Phila., 6-Pointed Star, Medium Blue Green, Wide Mouth, IP, 5 In. 305.00
D. Strecker, Phila., Medium Teal Blue Green, IP, Applied Mouth, 1845-1855, 7 In. 185.00
D.G. Hall, Green, Push-Up Base, Graphite Pontil 125.00
D.L. Ormsby, New York, Cobalt Blue, Cylindrical, IP, 1/2 Pt. 55.00
D.L. Ormsby, New York, Electric Cobalt Blue, Blob Top, IP, 7 3/8 In. 255.00
D.L. Ormsby, New York, Union Glass Works, Philada., Light Ice Blue, IP 105.00
D.L. Ormsby, Union Glass Works, New York, Aqua, IP 100.00
D.S. & Co., San Francisco, Slugplate, Green Aqua, Applied Top, 1861-1864 .... 110.00
D.T. Cox, Port Jervis, N.Y., Blue Green, Blob Top, IP, 1845-1855, 7 1/8 In. 145.00
Dad's Old Fashioned Root Beer, Los Angeles, Calif., Junior Size, ACL 25.00
Daniel Boone Mix, Green, Daniel, Indian, Dog, White, ACL, 7 Oz. 50.00
Daniel J. Toohey, Chester, Pa., Blob Top 4.00
Deamer, Grass Valley, Aqua, Blob Top 35.00
Delaney & Young, Eureka, Calif., Aqua, Crown Top, BIMAL 15.00
Dextrose-O-So-Grape-Oh, So Good, Flat River, Mo., White, ACL, 8 In. 6.00
Dillon Beverages, Pocatello, Idaho, ACL 10.00
Distilled Soda Water Co., Alaska, Aqua, Mug Base, Hutchinson 700.00
Distilled Soda Water Co., Alaska, Light Green Aqua, 12-Sided Mug Base 605.00
Dixon & Carson, 41 Walker St., N.Y., Blue Green, Blob Top, Squat 40.00
Donahoe & Robinson, Wilm., Del., Aqua, Blob Top, Pony 10.00
Donald Duck Cola, Walt Disney Product, Donald Duck Face, ACL 20.00
Double Cola, Oval Shield, Red & White, 1950s, 12 Oz. 7.00
Dr Pepper, 10-2-4, 6 1/2 Oz. 15.00
Dr Pepper, A.M.B. Co., Waco, Texas, St. Louis, Mo., Aqua 75.00
Dr Pepper, Good For Life, 10-2-4 Clock On Reverse, 6 1/2 Oz. 30.00
Dr Pepper Seltzer, Etched 450.00
Dr. Swett's Root Beer, Boston 40.00
Dragon, San Antonio, Tex., Crown Top 20.00
Dwight Brinton, Falls Village, Conn., Blob Top 40.00

Dyottville Glass Works, Light Sapphire, Blob Top, 1855-1865, 7 In. 90.00
Dyottville Glass Works, Philada., Emerald Green, BIMAL, Pony 25.00
E. Duffy & Son, No. 44 Filbert St., Deep Emerald Green, IP, Slug Plate, 7 In. 55.00
E. Ottenville, E.O., Nashville, Tenn., Deep Amber, Applied Mouth, Qt., 8 3/4 In. 85.00
E. Postens, Philadelphia, Pa., Yellow Green, Blob Top, Squat 70.00
E. Roussel, Philada., Dyottville Glass Works, Sapphire Blue, IP, 1845-1860, 1/2 Pt. 65.00
E. Sherwood, Bridgeport & New Haven, Teal Blue, Cylindrical, IP, 1/2 Pt. 145.00
E. Wagner, Manchester, N.H., Yellow, Original Lightning Stopper 50.00
E. Young, Pitts., Aqua, Applied Top, IP, 7 5/8 In. 55.00
E.A. Post, Portland, Ore., Eagle, Aqua, Blob Top 125.00
E.E. Sprenger, Lancaster, Pa., Hutchinson 12.00
E.F. Sutton, Holland, Mich., Hutchinson 10.00
E.G. Cullin & Bro., Chester, Pa., Aqua, BIMAL 6.00
E.J. Heffernan, Saratoga, N.Y., Squat 15.00
E.K.B. Aerated, Cobalt Blue, Blob Top, IP, 1855, 7 1/2 In. 130.00
E.K.B. Aerated, Opalescent Cobalt Blue, Blob Top, Graphite Pontil 225.00
E.L. Billings, Sac City, Geyser Soda, Aqua, Blob Top 35.00
E.L. Billings, Sac City, Geyser Soda, Cobalt Blue, Blob Top 55.00
E.L. Billings, Sac City, Geyser Soda, Lime Green, Applied Top, 1872-1879 .... 275.00
E.L.B. Co., T.F. Murphy, Brookfield, Mass., Elk 15.00
E.S & H. Hart, Superior, Cobalt Blue, Blob Top, IP, 1845-1855, 7 5/8 In. 220.00
E.W. Zeis, Winthrop, Calif., Crown Top, BIMAL 50.00
Eagle & Flags, On Banner, Blue Green, Applied Mouth, IP, Cylindrical 190.00
Eagle Bottling Works, Tacoma, Wash., Aqua, Eagle On Branch & Badge 30.00
Eagle Design, Light Blue Green, IP, Applied Blob Top, 1845-1855, 7 In. 130.00
Eagle Premium, Vestal Varick & Canal Sta., Aqua, Pt. 45.00
Eagle Steam Soda Works, San Francisco, Cal., Eagle, Etched, Blue 110.00
Eastern Cider Co., Golden Amber, Applied Top, 1877-1882 .... 165.00
Eastern Cider Co., Honey Amber, Blob Top 95.00
Eastern Cider Co., Red Amber, Applied Top, 1877-1882 .... 110.00
Eaton S. Hall, Warwick, N.Y., Hutchinson 45.00
Edgar B. Jones, Peekskill, N.Y., Vertical Embossed, Gravitating Glass Stopper, Gasket .. 40.00
Elk Club, Elk Head, Green, 7 Oz. 8.00
Elk Club, Elkton, Va., Black Elk, Red, ACL, 9 Oz. 100.00
Ely Bottling Works, Ely, Minn., Hutchinson 30.00
Empire Bottling Co., Lancaster, Pa., Crown Top 5.00
Empire Bottling Works, Reading, Pa., Amber, Blob Top, Squat 20.00
Empire Soda Works, Alameda, Cal., Blue Aqua, Hutchinson 65.00
Empire Soda Works, Vallejo, Aqua 45.00
Empson's, Cincinnati, Ohio, Aqua, Mug Base, 10 In. 30.00
Eureka California Soda Water Co., S.F., Eagle On Branch, Hutchinson 50.00
Eureka Soda Works, San Francisco, Dark Aqua, Hutchinson, 7 In. 45.00
Excelsior Bottling Co., Reading, Pa., Light Green, Hutchinson 12.00
Excelsior Bottling Co., Reading, Pa., Thou Shalt Not Steal 15.00
Excelsior Spring, Green, Pt. 125.00
F. Engle, Lancaster, Pa., Aqua, Pony, 1860 ....10.00 to 20.00
F. Gleason, Mineral Water, Rochester, N.Y., Sapphire Blue, Ten-Pin, 1850-1860, 8 1/2 In. 800.00
F. Horlacker, Allentown, Pa., Aqua, Blob Top, Pony 10.00
F. McKinney, Philad., Aqua, Blob Top, 7 In. 15.00
F. McKinney, Philada., Teal, BIMAL, Pony 20.00
F. O'Neill, Downingtown 35.00
F. Riddell, Toronto, Hamilton Glassworks, Aqua, Slug Plate, Arrow Neck, 7 1/2 In. 45.00
F. Schmidt, Leadville, Colo., Blue Aqua, Tombstone, Hutchinson 50.00
F. Sherwood, Bridgeport, New Haven, Blue Green, Cylindrical, IP, 1/2 Pt. 175.00
F.A. Conant, 252 Girod St., N.O., C, Blue Aqua, Applied Drip Top, OP 3300.00
F.A. Conant, Deep Emerald Green, IP, Applied Sloping Collar, 7 1/8 In. 175.00
F.J. Cutter, Burlington, N.J., Blob Top 7.00
Fett & Son, Blob Top, Squat 10.00
Fields Superior, Charleston, S.C., Cobalt Blue, 8-Sided, IP, 1845-1855, 7 In. 350.00
Fields Superior, Charleston, S.C., Cobalt Blue, 8-Sided, IP, 1845-1855, 7 5/8 In. 415.00
Fr. Goosmann & Co., Cincinnati, Root Beer, Cobalt Blue, 12-Sided, IP, 8 3/4 In. 2475.00
Francis Bros., Doylestown, Pa., Light Green, Squat 10.00
Frank McKeone, Phoenixville, Pa., Blob Top 7.00

Frank McKeone, Phoenixville, Pa., Hutchinson 15.00
Fred Schmidt, Hopkinsville, Ky., Hutchinson 40.00
Fries & Croessant, Reading, Pa., Aqua, Squat ....15.00 to 35.00
Frost King, Jackson, Miss., Snowman & Sports Figures, Blue, ACL, 7 Oz. 45.00
G. Field, Union Glass Works, Teal Green, Sloping Collared Mouth, IP, 1845, 1/2 Pt. 170.00
G. Lomax, Chicago, Cobalt Blue, Hutchinson 80.00
G. Norris & Co., A. & D.H.C. City Bottling Works, Detroit, Mich., Blue, 7 1/2 In. 100.00
G. Sollar, Philada., Green, Squat, 3-In. Base 50.00
G. Upp Jr., Light Blue Green, Sloping Collar, IP, 1845-1855, 7 3/8 In. 275.00
G. Van Shouton, Bridgeport, Conn., Brown Stout, Teal, Squat 250.00
G.A. Kohl, Lambertville, N.J., Bright Green, IP, 1/2 Pt. 230.00
G.A.K., Nevada, Green Aqua, Coddball, Tooled Top 65.00
G.A.P., Norwich, Ct., Amber, Blob Top, 1881, Qt. 20.00
G.P. Morrill, Light To Medium Green, Aqua Tone, 1855-1865, 7 1/2 In. 470.00
G.S. Smith, Towanda, Pa., Patented Favorite Stopper, Applied Lip 35.00
G.W. Brandt, Carlisle, Deep Emerald Green, IP 240.00
G.W. Epler, Oregon, Hutchinson 50.00
G.W. Otto & Co., Blue Green, Blob Top, Squat 50.00
Gardner, Elmira, Aqua, Squat 30.00
Garner & Auch, Conshohocken, Pa., Aqua, Hutchinson 10.00
Geo. Bennett, Rockaway Beach, L.I., Blob Top 15.00
Geo. Eagle, Spiral Rib, Medium Blue Green, IP, 1845-1855, 6 7/8 In. 935.00
Geo. Gemenden, Savannah, Geo., Eagle, Crossed Flags, Green, IP, 1855, 7 In. ....155.00 to 220.00
Geo. Spreitzer & Co., 1887, Paterson, N.J., Eagle 40.00
Geo. Van Benschoten, Bridgeport, Conn., Teal Blue, Blob Top, IP, 7 1/4 In. 460.00
Geo. W. Hoffman, Allentown, Pa., Emerald Green, 8-Sided, 1865, 7 1/4 In. 100.00
Geo. Weller, Schenectady, N.Y., Blue Aqua, Applied Sloping Collar Mouth, 6 3/4 In. ... 85.00
Geo. Weller, Schenectady, N.Y., Emerald Green, Applied Mouth, 6 3/4 In. 100.00
George A. Kiehl, Lancaster, Pa., Blue Green 40.00
Gesundheidt, Adolph Buehler, 435 W. Girard Ave., Philadelphia, Pa., Blob Top 15.00
Ghirardelli's Branch, Oakland, Ca., Deep Cobalt Blue, Blob Top, 7 3/8 In. 120.00
Gilhully's Bottling Works, New Haven, Conn., Hutchinson, Aqua, Blob Top, 6 1/2 In. . 20.00
Gilhuly & Bohen, New Haven, Conn., Hutchinson, Green Aqua, Blob Top, Cork, 6 3/4 In. 20.00
Gill's Beverage, Beeville, Texas, Boys At Table, White & Red, ACL, 10 Oz. 35.00
Ginger Ale, Green, White Felix The Cat Picture, 1958 .... 198.00
Glacier Beverage, Kalispell, Mont., Bear Drinking From Bottle, ACL, 7 Oz. 175.00
Gold-En Cola, Refreshing As Coffee, Sun-Drop Cola Co., Amber, 12 Oz., 9 1/2 In. *Illus* 5.00
Golden Gate, Brilliant Green, Heavy Collared Mouth, 1/2 Pt. 160.00
Golden Valley, Gone With The Wind Scene, Red & White, ACL, 12 Oz. 30.00
Graba Gazzosa Beverage, Weird Hand, Pa., Green, White, ACL, 7 Oz. 35.00

Soda, Gold-En Cola,
Refreshing As Coffee,
Sun-Drop Cola Co.,
Amber, 12 Oz., 9 1/2 In.

Soda, Hill Billy Brew,
Hillbilly & Still, Green
& Red Paper Label,
10 Oz., 9 1/2 In.

Soda, Holly, Orange Pop,
Girl In Shorts,
Youngstown, Oh.,
Original Cap, 7 Oz., 8 In.

Soda, Howel's, Elf
With Tray & Bottle Of
Pop, Blue & White,
7 Oz., 8 In.

Graf's Zep Soda, John Graf Co., Milwaukee, Aqua 11.00
Grumback & Schumacher, Santa Ana, Cal., Blue Aqua, Hutchinson 65.00
Gwinn Bottling Works, Gwinn, Mich., Light Amethyst, Stopper, Hutchinson, Qt. 150.00
H. & C. Overdick, Cincinnati, Cobalt Blue, 12-Sided, Applied Mouth, IP, 1865, 8 5/8 In. 4500.00
H. Denhalter & Son, Salt Lake City, Aqua, Tombstone Slug Plate, Pony Blob, 6 In. 225.00
H. Denhalter & Son, Salt Lake City, Ut., Blue Aqua, Tooled Top 65.00
H. Maillard, Lead City, S.D., Slug, Aqua, Hutchinson 55.00
H. Mau & Co., Eureka, Nevada, Aqua, Blob Top 75.00
H. Nash & Co. Root Beer, Cincinnati, 12-Sided, Blue, IP, 1845-1855, Qt., 8 3/8 In. 415.00
H. Sproatt, Sapphire Blue, Torpedo, Blob Top, Canada, 1850-1865, 7 7/8 In. 1760.00
H.A. Elliott, Idaho Springs, Colo., E On Base, Hutchinson 185.00
H.A. Elliott, Idaho Springs, Colo., Tooled Top 110.00
H.B. Kilmer, New York, Philada., Porter & Ale, Green, Pontil, Squat 90.00
H.L. & J.W. Brown, Hartford, Ct., Yellow Olive, Heavy Collar, Cylindrical, IP, 1/2 Pt. . . 175.00
H.M. Lochen, West Bend, Wis., Hutchinson 10.00
Haas Bro's Natural, Napa Soda, Light To Medium Blue, 1873-1877 . . . . 165.00
Hamilton Glass Works, N.Y., Green Aqua, Applied Top, IP 45.00
Hamilton Glass Works, N.Y., Light Blue Green, Blob Top, Bubbles, IP, 7 In. 70.00
Hanford Soda Works, Aqua, Hutchinson 27.00
Harmony Club, Cleveland, Ohio, Pin-Up Girl, Blue & White, ACL, 7 Oz. 10.00
Hathorn Spring, Amber, Qt. 38.00
Hathorn Spring, Black Amber, Pt. 45.00
Hathorn Spring, Green, Pt. 35.00
Hedlund, Chicago, Ill., Sapphire Blue, Blob Top, IP, 7 1/8 In. 65.00
Hennessy Nolan, 1879, Albany, Monogram On Reverse, Aqua, Metal Cork Retainer . . . 35.00
Henrich, Mt. Carmel, Pa., Aqua, Pony, Blob Top 25.00
Henry Kuck, Savannah, Ga., Deep Blue Green, Blob Top, 1860-1870, 7 1/4 In. 55.00
Henry Kuck, Savannah, Ga., Deep Teal Blue, Tooled Mouth, 1855-1865, 7 1/4 In. 60.00
Henry Kuck, Savannah, Ga., Yellow Olive Green, Blob Top, 1860-1870, 7 1/8 In. 80.00
Henry Lubs & Co., Savannah, Ga., Deep Blue Emerald Green, Blob Top, 1865, 7 1/4 In. 85.00
Henry Sierichs, Rockaway Beach, 3 Embossed Bottles In Shield, Blob Top 20.00
Herman Floto, Reading, Pa., Blue Green, Squat 460.00
Hi Ho, Plymouth, Wis., Cartoon Of Boy, White & Red, ACL, 7 Oz. 50.00
Highland Ginger Ale, San Mateo, Ca., Aqua, Crown Top 30.00
Hill Billy Brew, Hillbilly & Still, Green & Red Paper Label, 10 Oz., 9 1/2 In. . . . . . . *Illus* 8.00
Hires, Amber, Crown Top 25.00
Hires, Improved Root Beer, Charles E. Hires Co., Philadelphia, Aqua, Cork, 4 1/2 In. . . . 5.00
Hires, On Base, Aqua, Tooled Lip, Hutchinson, 9 In. . . . . .15.00 to 20.00
Hires, Straight Sides, Crown Top, 9 3/4 In. 5.00
Hollister & Co., Honolulu, Ice Blue, Applied Top, Round Base, 8 1/4 In. 175.00
Hollister & Co., Honolulu, Light Green Aqua 55.00
Hollman & Stoll, Phoenixville, Pa., Hutchinson 12.00
Holly, Orange Pop, Girl In Shorts, Youngstown, Oh., Original Cap, 7 Oz., 8 In. . . . . . *Illus* 22.00
Holt & Co., Aqua, Embossed, Codd, 9 1/4 In. 54.00
Home Soda Works, Chas. Peverley, Hutchinson, Light Aqua, Round Slug Plate 600.00
Hosmer Mountain Beverage, House, Mountain, Red & White, ACL, 8 Oz. 50.00
Howel's, Elf With Tray & Bottle Of Pop, Blue & White, 7 Oz., 8 In. . . . . *Illus* 6.00
Howel's Beverages, Pittsburgh, Pa., Elf With Tray, Blue & White, ACL, 8 In. 8.00
Howell & Smith, Buffalo, Sapphire Blue, Applied Mouth, IP, 1845-1855, 7 1/2 In.105.00 to 230.00
Hubert Jacks Up, Gillespie, Ill., Green, 3 Jacks, 2 Aces, Qt. 65.00
Hugh A. Bonner, West Phila., Aqua, Blob Top, Tall 12.00
Hugh Casey, Eagle Soda Works, Sacramento, Cal., Blue Aqua, Hutchinson, Tooled Top . 35.00
Hugh McFadden, South Bethlehem, Pa., Hutchinson 5.00
Hygeia Bottling Works, Pensacola, Fla., Aqua, Crown Top, 8 In. 15.00
Hygeia Bottling Works, Pensacola, Fla., Green Aqua, Hutchinson 50.00
I. Brownell, New Bedford, Cobalt Blue, Applied Mouth, IP, 7 1/4 In. 100.00
I. Brownell, New Bedford, Cobalt Blue, Blob Top, 7 1/4 In. 185.00
I. Brownell, New Bedford, Sapphire Blue, Blob Top, Metal Closure, 7 1/8 In. 210.00
I. Brownell, New Bedford, This Bottle Never Sold, Deep Blue, IP 200.00
I. Sutton, Cincinnati, Medium Cobalt Blue, IP, Applied Mouth, 7 1/2 In. 525.00
I.E. Rabold, Lebanon, Pa., Aqua, Hutchinson 7.00
Independence Bottling Works, Independence, Ia., Hutchinson 30.00

Indian Head Beverages, Indian Chief, Paneled, Textured, ACL 55.00
Indian Rock Ginger Ale, Script, Ten-Pin, 7 3/4 In. 20.00
Ingalls Bros., Portland, Me., Pale Green, Double Collar Mouth, 1855-1870, 6 7/8 In. ... 35.00
Iroquois, Trademark, Buffalo, Indian Head, Amber, Blob Top 20.00
Iroquois Bev. Corp., Buffalo, Indian In Circle, Aqua, Crown Top, Tall 6.00
Italian Soda Water Manufactory, San Francisco, Cobalt Blue, Graphite, Blob Top ... 275.00
Italian Soda Water Manufactory, San Francisco, Green, IP, 1856-1863 .... 145.00
Italian Soda Water Manufactory, San Francisco, Union Glass Works, Teal Green, GP 185.00
J. & A. Boyce, Chester, Pa., Aqua, BIMAL, Pony 15.00
J. & A. Dearborn, N.Y., Albany Glass Works, D, Deep Blue, OP 400.00
J. & A. Dearborn, N.Y., Albany Glass Works, D, New York, Sapphire Blue, Pontil 205.00
J. & A. Dearborn & Co., New York, Cobalt Blue, Heavy Mouth, Cylindrical, IP, 1/2 Pt. . 155.00
J. & J.W. Harvey, Norwich, Conn., Cobalt Blue, H On Reverse, Applied Top, IP 110.00
J. & W. Shields, Braddock, Pa., Hutchinson 10.00
J. Andrews, Philada., Blob Top, Pony 5.00
J. Cairns & Co., St. Louis, Aqua, Blob Top, Pontil 75.00
J. Casper, Lancaster, Pa., Aqua, c.1860 .... 20.00
J. Cosgrove, Charleston, S.C., Cobalt Blue, Blob Top, 1855-1865, 7 1/4 In. 90.00
J. Cummings, Easton, Pa., Squat 15.00
J. Edwards, Chester, Pa., Aqua, BIMAL, Pony 10.00
J. Edwards, Chester, Pa., Brown Stout, Aqua, Blob Top, Pony 20.00
J. Edwards, Chester, Pa., Green, Squat 10.00
J. Eves Soda Water, Manufr., Bottle Never Sold, 1862, Light Aqua, Canada, 7 1/2 In. .. 75.00
J. Eves Soda Water, Manufr., Light Jade Green, Blob Top, Brass Fastener, 7 3/8 In. 220.00
J. Eves Soda Water, Manufr., Nectar Cream, Pat. 1867, Aqua, 7 3/8 In. 105.00
J. Harley, West Chester, Pa., Slug Plate, Green, Squat ....50.00 to 60.00
J. Harvey & Co., Providence, R.I., Deep Yellow Olive, Heavy Collar Mouth, IP, 1/2 Pt. . 145.00
J. Harvey & Co., Providence, R.I., Medium Green, Blob Top, IP, 7 3/4 In. 130.00
J. Hindle's Pop, Stoneware 75.00
J. Lusch, Altoona, Pa., Deep Green 190.00
J. Manke & Co., Savannah, Emerald Green, Blob Top, Slug Plate, 1855-1865, 7 1/8 In. ... 70.00
J. McLaughlin, Philada., Teal, IP, Pony 50.00
J. McLaughlin, Teal, BIMAL, Pony 20.00
J. Monteith, F. Road, Phila., Blue Green, Ring Mouth, Cylindrical, IP, 1/2 Pt. 110.00
J. Ogden, Pittsburgh, Blue Green, Blob Top, IP, 7 1/2 In. 45.00
J. Robinson, Salem, N.J., Deep Green, IP, Blob Top, Squat 100.00
J. Strassner, Phila., Aqua, Mug Base, Hutchinson 15.00
J. Trebilcock, G.B., Toronto, Amber, Blob Top, Arrow Neck, Squat, Wire Closure, 7 3/4 In. 210.00
J. Tune & Son, Trademark Registered, London, Ont., Stag, Red Amber, Stopper, Bail, Qt. 810.00
J. Tweddle Jr.'s Celebrated, 41 Barclay St., Reverse J, Aqua 50.00
J. Wise, Allentown, Pa., Deep Cobalt Blue 90.00
J. Wise, Allentown, Pa., This Bottle Belongs To James Wise, Midnight Blue 60.00
J.A. Blaffer, New Orleans, Amber, Applied Double Collar Mouth, 1870-1875, 6 3/8 In. .. 85.00
J.A. Keeler & Co., Stoneware, Salt Glaze, Cobalt Wash On Shoulders, Mushroom Top .. 150.00
J.A. Lomax, Light Cobalt Blue, Hutchinson 35.00
J.A. Seitz, Easton, Blob Top, Pony 10.00
J.A. Seitz, Easton, Pa., Blue Green, Squat 40.00
J.A. Seitz, Easton, Pa., Dark Green, Squat 30.00
J.A. Wallis, Bangor, Maine, Blob Top 50.00
J.B. Cohen, 132 E. Gay St., West Chester, Pa., Aqua, Squat 15.00
J.B. Moser, Pottstown, Pa., Mug Base, Hutchinson ....20.00 to 25.00
J.C. Buffum, Pittsburgh, Blue Aqua, Blob Top, Squat 40.00
J.C. Buffum & Co., Pittsburgh, Pa., Squat 15.00
J.C. Parker & Son, Cobalt Blue 40.00
J.C. Parker & Son, New York, Medium Blue, Applied Top, IP 75.00
J.C. Parker & Son, New York, Periwinkle Blue, Blob Top 55.00
J.D. Ludwick, Pottstown, Pa., Dark Green 40.00
J.F.I., Tucson, Aqua, Hutchinson, Applied Top 65.00
J.G. Gilbert, Pottstown, Pa., Blob Top 12.00
J.G. Leber, Ephrata, Pa., Blob Top, Squat 20.00
J.G. Schoch, Philada., Cobalt Blue, IP 195.00
J.H. Fett & Son, Reading, Pa., Light Green, Hutchinson 10.00
J.H. Yale, Middletown, Conn., Apple Green, Blob Top, IP, 7 3/8 In. 575.00

J.J. McLaughlin, Toronto, Hygeia Waters, Mortar & Pestle, Aqua, Round Bottom, 9 1/2 In.   35.00
J.J. McLaughlin, Toronto, Mortar & Pestle On Base, Ruby, Blob Top, c.1890, 7 1/2 In. ..   95.00
J.J. McLaughlin, Toronto, Mortar & Pestle, Light Aqua, Blob Top, Torpedo 880.00
J.J. Steinhilber, Flushing, Pa., Blob Top, 9 In. 15.00
J.M. Roseberry & Co., Alexandria, Va., Eagle Wreath & Shield, Yellow Green, IP, 1860   880.00
J.N., Boise, Idaho, Green Aqua 25.00
J.O. Pomeroy & Bros., Cadillac, Mich., Aqua, Hutchinson, Pt. 50.00
J.R. Ettinger, Blue Green, Double Collar, IP, Squat 80.00
J.T. Brown, Chemist, Boston, Double Soda Water, Green, Torpedo, Blob Top, 8 1/2 In. ..   220.00
J.T. Brown, Chemist, Boston, Double Soda Water, Teal Blue Green, Torpedo 325.00
J.T. Nusbaum & Brothers, Deep Green, Swirl Lines Throughout, IP, 1855, 7 In. 105.00
J.V. Dellicker, Richmond, Va. & Columbus, O., Blue Aqua, Applied Blob Top, IP, 7 In. ..   330.00
J.W. Harris's, New Haven, Conn., Light Sapphire Blue, IP, 1845-1860, 1/2 Pt. 465.00
J.W. Pew & Co., Gloucester, N.J., Blue Green, Applied Mouth, IP, 1845-1855, 6 3/4 In. .   1705.00
J.W. Sutherland, Trademark, Hamilton, Scales, Aqua, Codd Stopper, Canada, 9 In. 95.00
Jackson's Springs, Napa Soda, Natural, Aqua, Blob Top 20.00
Jackson's Springs, Napa Soda, Natural, Teal Cobalt Blue, Green Striations 660.00
Jacob Voelker, Cleveland, Oh., Deep Cobalt Blue, Tooled Mouth, 1870, 8 In. 150.00
James M. Banghart & Co., Strathroy, Ontario, Hamilton Glassworks, Aqua, 7 1/2 In. ..   60.00
James Ray, Ginger Ale, Deep Cobalt Blue, Applied Mouth, 1870-1885, 7 5/8 In. 95.00
James Ray, Ginger Ale, Embossed Vertically, Deep Electric Blue, Blob Top 280.00
James Ray, Ginger Ale, Savannah, Cobalt Blue, Tooled Mouth, 1870-1890, 7 3/4 In. 190.00
James Walsh, Toronto, Aqua, Beaver Over Crown, Arrow Neck, Blob Top, 7 1/4 In. 20.00
Jersey Creme Co., Toronto, 12 Ribbed Panels, Emerald Green, Crown Top, ABM, 8 In. .   15.00
Jet, Waco, Texas, Red Airplane, White, ACL, 8 Oz. 40.00
Jimbo Pure, Mule's Head, Aqua 20.00
John B. Cohen, West Chester, Pa., Blob Top 10.00
John Clancy, New Haven, Hutchinson, Aqua, 6 1/2 In. 20.00
John Coles, Coatesville, Pa., Mug Base, Hutchinson 12.00
John Deitrich, Pottstown, Pa., Blue Green, Slug Plate, Double Collar, Squat 100.00
John Graf, Milwaukee, This Bottle Not To Be Sold, Paneled, Red Amber, Blob Top 20.00
John Heydt, Indian Leap Hotel, Indian Orchard, Mass., Amethyst, Slug Plate, 9 1/4 In. ..   100.00
John Moran, 343 West 38th, N.Y., Blob Top 20.00
John Ogden & Co., No. 187 First Street, Aqua, Blob Top, IP, 7 1/4 In. 45.00
John Ryan, Augusta & Savannah, Ga., Excelsior Bottling Works, Cobalt Blue, 7 1/8 In. .   185.00
John Ryan, Excelsior Soda Works, Savannah, Ga., Cobalt Blue, Blob Top, 1865, 7 In. ..   100.00
John Ryan, XXX Porter & Ale, Philada., Cobalt Blue, IP, Applied Mouth, 6 7/8 In. 175.00
John Schroth, Trenton, N.J., Aqua, Squat 20.00
John W. Stone, Roebling, N.J., Blob Top 5.00
Johnson Bottling Works, Montgomery, Ala., Hutchinson 20.00
Johnston & Co., Phila., Green, Squat 60.00
Johnston & Co., Philada., Aqua, Blob Top 15.00
Jolly Beverage, Fitchburg, Ma., Boy & Glass, Green & White, ACL, 12 Oz. 35.00
Jumbo, Elephant Picture, Embossed, Trunk In Air, 13 1/2 In. 35.00
Jumbo, Embossed Elephant, 60 Oz. 60.00
Jurgens & Price Bottlers, Helena, Mont., Aqua, Blob Top 90.00
K.C., Muskogee, Okla., Cowboy On Horse, White & Red, ACL, 10 Oz. 50.00
Kalispell Liquor & Tobacco Co., Kalispell, Mont., Aqua, Hutchinson, 1890-1910, 7 In.   305.00
Karl E. Katz, York, Pa., Lime Citron, Hutchinson, 1896 ....   295.00
Keach-Balt., Green, Torpedo, Applied Sloping Collar Mouth, 1850-1860, 8 5/8 In. 468.00
Keach-Balt., Yellow Topaz, Torpedo, Applied Sloping Collar Mouth, 1855-1865, 9 In. ..   880.00
Keenan & Gaffney, Union Mfg. Co., Leadville, Colo., Aqua, Mug Base, Hutchinson ...   235.00
Kehl & Keefer, Lancaster, Pa., Blob Top 12.00
Kennedy & Hassett, Elmira, N.Y., Golden Amber, Metal Stopper & Wire, 7 In. 110.00
Kenneth Campbell & Co., Medical Hall, Montreal, Round Bottom, Blue, 9 In. 55.00
Kenoza Club, Methuen, Ma., Castle Scene, White, ACL, 7 Oz. 50.00
Kimball & Co., Cobalt Blue, 1853-1856, 6 5/8 In. 355.00
Krebs & Knorr, Wilkes-Barre, Pa., Aqua, Blob Top, Smooth Base, 7 1/4 In. 25.00
Kroger Bros., Butte, Mt., Aqua, Tooled Top 110.00
L & B, B Over V, Light Green, Applied Top, 1857-1870 ....   90.00
L & V, Green, IP, 1852-1857 ....   220.00
L. Gahre, Bridgeton, N.J., Yellow Green, Squat 50.00
L. Maggio & Co., Buffalo, N.Y., Tombstone, Hutchinson 12.00

L.D. Clauss, Allentown, Hutchinson 9.00
L.J. Felder, Braddock, Pa., Hutchinson 10.00
La Orange Cola, St. Louis, Mo., French Girl, White & Red, ACL, 9 1/2 Oz. 35.00
Lahaina Ice Co. Ltd., Lahaina, Maui, 4-Piece Mold, Hutchinson, Stopper 245.00
Lancaster Glass Works, Blue, Applied Top, IP 130.00
Lancaster Glass Works, N.Y., Sapphire Blue, IP 150.00
Lancaster Glass Works, N.Y., X On Front, XX On Reverse, Blue, Applied Top, IP 110.00
Lancaster Glass Works, N.Y., Yellow Green, Applied Top, IP 70.00
Leigh & Sons, Salford, Olive Amber, Codd, 7 1/2 In. 30.00
Leominster Home Beverages, House, Green, Red & White, ACL, 8 In. 8.00
Lewellen & McMullin, Philada., Teal Blue, IP, 1845-1855, 7 1/8 In. 190.00
Liberty Soda Works, DWVSF, Eagle 25.00
Lincoln Beverage, Chicago, Ill., Blue & Red, ACL, 7 Oz. 350.00
Little Chute Bev., Indian, Canoe, Teepee, Label 10.00
Little Rock Bottling, Ark., Hutchinson 30.00
Livermore Soda Works, Livermore, Cal., Green Aqua, Tooled Top, Hutchinson 35.00
Los Gatos Soda Works, Los Gatos, Cal., Wildcat Face, Crown Top, ABM 40.00
Lotta Cola, Yellow & White, Pittsburgh, 18 Pa., Original Cap, 16 Oz., 11 In. ...... *Illus* 15.00
Luke Beard, Medium Green, Ten-Pin, IP, Applied Mouth, 1845-1855, 7 In. 255.00
Luke Beard, Teal Blue, Ten-Pin, Applied Mouth, 6 7/8 In. 240.00
M. McCormack's, Celebrated Ginger Ale, Light Cobalt Blue, Applied Mouth, 8 1/8 In. .. 605.00
M. Wishcum, Philada. 5.00
M.J. Ryan, Mahonoy City, Pa., Amber, Blob Top, Contents, Stopper, Squat 55.00
M.R., Sacrimento, Union Glass Works, Phila., Teal, IP, 1850s, Error 1430.00
M.T. Crawford, Hartford, Conn., Cobalt Blue, Mug Base, IP 550.00
M.T. Crawford, Teal, IP, Squat 300.00
Mahaska, Oskaloosa, Iowa, Indian, Red & White, ACL, 10 Oz. 100.00
Maicks & Phillipson, Reading, Pa., Green, Squat 45.00
Manhattan Beverages, Picture Of Manhattan, Green, Red & White, ACL, 8 In. ...10.00 to 20.00
Manila, Emerald Green, Round, Crown Top, 9 1/2 In. 5.00
Mansfield Bottling Works, Mansfield, Ark., Hutchinson 25.00
Martin Coda, West Orange, N.J., Blob Top 6.00
Martin Rancich, Union Glass Works, c.1858 .... 2750.00
Mason, Sausalito, Cal., Aqua, Crown Top 30.00
Mason & Burns, Richmond, Va., Medium Yellow Green, IP, Applied Mouth, 7 3/8 In. .. 2860.00
Matewan Bottling Co., Matewan, W.Va., Crown Top, ABM, Embossed Base 10.00
Maui Soda Works, Aqua, Crown Top 25.00
Maui Soda Works, Aqua, Hutchinson, 7 3/4 In. 45.00
McCarthy & Moore, Waterbury, Conn., Hutchinson 30.00
McGregor Springs Bottling Works, Springhill, Ala., Aqua, Crown Top, Slug Plate ... 60.00
McGrudden & Campbell, Philada., Blob Top 40.00
McKay & Clark, Balto-B, Emerald Green, IP, 1845-1855, 7 3/8 In. 120.00
McKeon, Washington, D.C., Medium Emerald Green, Torpedo, 1855-1865, 8 5/8 In. 3520.00
McLaughlin, Philadelphia, Blue Grass, Blob Top, IP 45.00
McManus & Meade Bottlers, Nasonville, R.I., Aqua 2000.00
Meamber's Beverages, Yureka, Calif., Mt. Shasta, Red & White, ACL, Crown, 7 3/4 In. 12.00
Meincke & Ebberwein, Ginger Ale, Savannah, Ga., Amber, Blob Top, 1875-1885, 8 In. 95.00
Meriam's, Cobalt Blue, Applied Mouth, IP, 1852-1856, 7 3/8 In. 5500.00
Meridian Steam Bottling Co., Meridian, Miss., Light Amethyst, Tooled Top, Hutchinson 35.00
Merrit & Co., Helena, Mont., Blob Top 65.00
Michl. McGrann, Lancaster, Deep Emerald Green, Sloping Double Collar, IP, 6 7/8 In. .. 150.00
Michl. McGrann, Lancaster, Pa., Green, IP, Qt. 75.00
Mills Seltzer Springs, Aqua, Applied Top, 1874-1885 .... 55.00
Millville Glass Works, L.M. & Co., Green, Applied Top, IP 155.00
Mingo, Williamson, W.Va., Indian Princess, Red & Black, ACL, 9 Oz. 135.00
Mission Of California, Los Angeles, Calif., Crown Top, ACL 10.00
Montezuma Bottling Works, Montezuma, Ind., Light Aqua 175.00
Mooo-Cho, Ridgefield Park, N.J., Cartoon Of Cow's Face, Red Letters, 7 Oz. 65.00
Moroney & Conner, Philada., Aqua, BIMAL 10.00
Mountain Dew, Green, Hillbilly With Gun, 10 Oz. 7.50
Mountain Dew, Hillbilly, ACL 6.00
Moxie Nerve Food, Light Apple Green, Cylindrical, Applied Mouth, 9 3/4 In. 175.00

Mt. Hood Soda Water, Portland, Ore., Lion, Aqua, 10-Sided Mug Base, Tooled Top ...   75.00
Mt. Jewett Bottling Works, Mt. Jewett, Pa., Hutchinson ....10.00 to 12.00
Mt. Lassen Beverages, Susanville, Calif., Faded Crown, Red & White, 1920s, 8 1/2 In. .   25.00
Mt. Washington Mfg. Co., Cold Spring, Boston, Mass. 80.00
Mug Root Beer, San Francisco, Three Color Mug, White & Red, ACL, 6 Oz. 75.00
Napa, A. Ludwig, Green Aqua, Tooled Mouth, Hutchinson, 1890-1910, 6 7/8 In. 45.00
Napa, Emerald Green, Applied Mouth, 1861-1862, 7 1/4 In. 120.00
Napa, Louis Leloy, Natural Mineral Water, Blue Aqua, Applied Top, 1881-1884 ....   55.00
Napa, Phil Caduc, Natural Mineral Water, Cobalt Blue, Applied Top, 1873-1881 ....   275.00
Napa, Phil Caduc, Natural Mineral Water, Deep Ice Blue, Applied Top 75.00
Napa, Phil Caduc, Natural Mineral Water, Light Aqua, Bent Neck 75.00
Napa, Phil Caduc, Natural Mineral Water, Light Green, Applied Top, 1873-1881 ...65.00 to 110.00
Napa, Phil Caduc, Natural Mineral Water, Teal To Steel Blue, Applied Top 825.00
Napa, Phil Caduc, Natural Mineral Water, Teal, Applied Mushroom Top 165.00
Napa Natural, Cobalt Blue, Blob Top, Metal Closure, 1855-1865, 7 1/4 In. 190.00
Nashua Bottling Works, Sun & Mountains, Brown & White, ACL, 1940s-1950s 6.00
Natural, Priest, Lime Green 45.00
Natural Up, Highland, Ill., Green, 4 Dice, Qt. 24.00
Nevada City Bottling, Nevada City, Ca., Embossed, Crown, 1920s, 9 1/2 In. 25.00
Nevada City Soda Works, E.I.R., Powell, Aqua, Hutchinson 45.00
New England Soda Water, Yellow Olive Amber, Pontil Base, 1830, 5 7/8 In. 525.00
New Holland Bottling Works, New Holland, Pa., Blob Top 15.00
New Liberty Soda W. Co., S.F., Aqua, Woman Picture, Tooled Top, Hutchinson 90.00
New Orleans Seltzer Co, Etched, Logo 50.00
Newman Steam Bottling Works, Helena, Ark., Hutchinson 25.00
Nick Rothecker, Devils Lake, N.D., Hutchinson 90.00
None Shall Surpass, Lucky Strike Beverages, Red, White & Green, ACL, 1940s-1950s .   15.00
Nonpareil Soda Water Co., S.F., Star On Base, Aqua, Tooled Top, 1881-1887 ....   75.00
Northwestern Bottling Co., Butte, Mont., Aqua, Hutchinson 35.00
NuGrape, Hattiesburg, Miss., Crown Top, 8 In. 10.00
O'Kane, Dyottville Glass Works, Philada., Pontil 110.00
O'Tullman's Mineral Water Works, S.L.O., Cal., Hutchinson 35.00
Oakland Bottling Co., Aqua, Wooden Marble, Tooled Large Top 110.00
Oceanview Bottling Works, N & B. Props., Mendocino, Cal., Aqua, Hutchinson 125.00
Ogden's, Porter, Aqua, Blob Top, IP, 7 1/8 In. 45.00
Ogden's, Porter, O., Green Aqua, Pontil 155.00
Ohio Bottling, Clvd. O. Works, Ten-Pin, Shooting Cork, Aqua, 7 3/8 In. 95.00
Ohio Cider, Jos. Werner & Co., St. Louis, Mo., Deep Chocolate Amber, Blob Top, 7 In. .   55.00
OK Bottling Works, Ontario, Cal., Embossed, Aqua, Crown, ABM, 7 1/2 In. 8.00
Old Homemade Root Beer, From Hires Extract, Stoneware, Crown Top 95.00
Olyphant Bottling Works, Hutchinson 4.00
Orange Crush, ACL, 8 3/4 In. 10.00
Orange Crush, Black, Unopened, Paper Label, Gold Foil Seal, 1920-1930 ....   260.00
Orange Crush, Do Not Drink Novelty, ACL, 1950s, 3 1/2 In. 20.00
Ortonville Bottling Co., Ortonville, Minn., Hutchinson 30.00
Owen Casey, Eagle Soda Works, Sac City, Aqua, Blob Top 45.00
Owen Casey, Eagle Soda Works, Sac City, Blue, Blob Top 100.00
Owen Casey, Eagle Soda Works, Sac City, Blue, Green Streaks, Applied Top 90.00
Owen Casey, Eagle Soda Works, Sac City, Green, Applied Top, 1867-1871 ....   175.00
Owen Casey, Eagle Soda Works, Sac City, Teal Blue, Blob Top 55.00
Owen Casey & James Kelly, Cobalt Blue, Blob Top ....100.00 to 145.00
Owl Drug Co., 2-Wing Owl, S.F., N.Y., Chicago, Green, Crown, ABM, 9 3/4 In. 40.00
Owl Drug Co., Green, Crown Top, Machine Made, 9 3/4 In. 40.00
P. Babb, Balto., Blue Aqua, Blob Top, 1845-1855, 7 1/8 In. 100.00
P. Ebner, Bottler, Wil., Del., Aqua, Hutchinson 15.00
P. Ebner, Bottler, Wil., Del., Aqua, Mug Base, Hutchinson 10.00
P. Ertel, P.E., Brown Stout, Emerald Green, IP, Squat 110.00
P. Hall, Phila., Applied Top, Contents, Squat 35.00
P. Seashultz, Pottstown, Pa., Light Green, Squat 40.00
P. Twohig, Memphis, Root Beer Amber, Applied Mouth, 1875-1885, Qt., 8 7/8 In. 55.00
P.H.J. Tholey, Philada., Yellow Green, Squat 50.00
Pacific & Puget Sound Soda Works, Seattle, Hutchinson, Blue, Stopper, 7 In. 475.00

Soda, Lotta Cola, Yellow & White, Pittsburgh, 18 Pa., Original Cap, 16 Oz., 11 In..	Soda, Polka Dot Beverages, Blue & Clear Dots, Paris, Texas, King Size, 9 1/2 In.	Soda, Spur, Canada Dry, Green, White & Red Label, Philadelphia, Pa., 9 1/2 In.	Soda, Squeeze, Boy & Girl On Bench, Klee & Coleman, Indianapolis, Ind., 9 1/2 In.

Pacific Bottling Works, Tacoma, Wash., Aqua, Hutchinson 35.00
Pacific Soda Works, Hilo, Hawaii, Embossed, Crown, 1920s, 8 1/2 In. 25.00
Pacific Soda Works, Santa Cruz, Hutchinson 55.00
Pacific Soda Works, Santa Cruz, Light Aqua, Large R Center, Tooled Top, Hutchinson . 22.00
Park City Bottling Works, Ed. McPolin, Utah, Crown, ABM, Embossed, 7 Oz. 18.00
Parker, Sapphire Blue, Blob Top, Teardrop Bubbles, 6 7/8 In. 70.00
Pelican Beverages, Red & White Textured Glass, 2 Pelicans, ACL, 1940s-1950s 40.00
Pelican Beverages, Red, ACL, 10 Oz. 25.00
Pellisier & Sons, Beaver On Base, Aqua, Crown Top, BIMAL, Canada, c.1900, 9 In. . . . 40.00
Pensacola Bottling Works, Pensacola, Fla., Aqua, Crown Top, Hutchinson 75.00
Pep-Up, Green, Pixie Walking, Red & White, ACL, Sandusky, Ohio, 7 Oz. 65.00
Pepsi, Commemorative, Amber, Base Marked A204, 1970s 85.00
Perko, Elyria, Ohio, Green, Jockey On Horse, Yellow & Red, ACL, 6 1/2 Oz. 85.00
Peter S. Joerg, West Chester, Pa., Blob Top, Squat 20.00
Philada. & Reading Bottling Works, 6th & Franklin, Rdg., Pa. 12.00
Phillip Brown, Haverstraw, N.Y., Slug Plate, Tooled Lip, Hutchinson 15.00
Phillips Soda Water Co., San Francisco, Cal., Blue Aqua, Hutchinson 350.00
Phoenix Bottling Works, Phoenix, Az., Deep Aqua Hutchinson, 1900-1910, 6 7/8 In. . . 85.00
Phoenix Soda Water Co., Phoenixville, Pa., Hutchinson 15.00
Pilgrim Bros. & Co., Hamilton, Ont., Eagle, SCA, BIMAL, Crown Top, Split, 5 3/4 In. . 40.00
Pioneer Bottling Works, Victor, Colo., Hutchinson 100.00
Pioneer Soda Water Co., S.F., Club Soda, Bear, Light Aqua, Tooled Top, 1897-1906 . . 230.00
Pioneer Soda Works, San Francisco, Initials In Shield, Aqua, Applied Top, 1877-1896 . 130.00
Pioneer Soda Works, Smith & Brian Co., Reno, Nev. 750.00
Pittsburgher Beverage, Green, Street Scene, Red, ACL, 7 Oz. 85.00
Polar Cola, Salem, Mass., Owl, Red, ACL, 12 Oz. 40.00
Polar Pak Beverage, San Diego, Cartoon Bear, White & Green, ACL, 7 Oz. 45.00
Polka Dot Beverages, Blue & Clear Dots, Paris, Texas, King Size, 9 1/2 In. . . . . . . *Illus* 9.50
Pomeroy Bottling Works, Manistee, Amber, Pt. 75.00
POPland Beverage, Yellow & Green, ACL, 12 Oz. 30.00
Popular Soda Water Co., San Francisco, Blue Aqua, Hutchinson, Bubbles 50.00
Portland Soda Works, Eagle, Aqua, Hutchinson 40.00
Prescott Bottling Works, Prescott, A.T., Light Aqua, Crown Top, 7 3/4 In. 185.00
Priest, Napa Valley, Priest Picture, Aqua, Crown Top 40.00
Priest Natural, Troll, Blob Top, Squat 50.00
R. Riddle, Philada., Green, Squat 20.00
R. Riddle, Philada., R On Back, Teal Green, Blob Top, Smooth Base, 7 1/4 In. 50.00
R.C. & T., New York, Blue Green, IP, 7 1/4 In. 35.00
R.C. & T., New York, Brown Stout, Blue Green, IP, Squat .65.00 to 70.00
R.C. Co., Teal Green 10.00
Ramona Bottling Works, Los Angeles, Calif., Blue Aqua, Crown Top, BIMAL 25.00
Rancho, Glendale, Ca., Cowboy On Horse, Black & White, ACL, 10 Oz. 75.00

Reasbeck, Martins Ferry, Ohio, Aqua, 10-Sided, Hutchinson 15.00
Reichart & Bro., Wilkes-Barre, Pa., Aqua, Blob Top, Squat 40.00
Reilly Bros., Fulton St., Brooklyn, Mortar & Pestle, Aqua, Iridescent Satin Finish 75.00
Reno Bottling Works, Reno, Blue Aqua, 4-Piece Mold, Crown Top 20.00
Ritz Beverage, St. Louis, Mo., Man In Top Hat, Green, White, ACL, 12 Oz. 45.00
Ritz Lemon-Lime, St. Louis, Mo., Man In Top Hat, Green, Red, ACL, 12 Oz. 45.00
Rob Roy, Canada, Green, Scottish Warrior, White & Red, ACL, 12 Oz. 85.00
Robinson & Moore, Bottlers, Wilmington, Del., Blob Top, 9 In. 10.00
Robinson, Wilson & Legalee, 102 Sudbury St., Boston, Emerald Green, Applied Top, IP 100.00
Roche, Scranton, Pa., Aqua, Hutchinson 6.00
Roseville Ice & Soda Company, Crown Top, ABM 20.00
Roussele, Philada., Dark Green, IP, Squat 50.00
Ryan Bottling Works, Chicago, Hutchinson 12.00
S. Charlton Soda Water, Toronto, Aqua, Blob Top, Torpedo, 1862-1874, 8 5/8 In. 385.00
S. Cummings, Philada., Emerald Green, Blob Top, 7 1/8 In. 50.00
S. Cummings, Philada., Pa., Aqua, Gravitating Stopper, 6 1/2 In. 25.00
S. Cummings, Philada., Pa., Pony 20.00
S. Grumman, 1887, Norwalk, Conn., Aqua, Blob Top 20.00
S. Pablo, No. 70, New Orleans, Yellow Green, Applied Mouth, 1845-1855, 7 1/4 In. 910.00
S. Shapiro Bottling Works, Chester, Pa., Aqua, Hutchinson 15.00
S.B. Wolf, Roxborough, Pa., Aqua, Squat 10.00
S.C.O.N.M.W. Ass'n., Sacramento, Cal., Hutchinson 25.00
S.S. Knicker Bocker Soda Water, Blue, 10-Sided, Applied Top, Graphite, IP 360.00
Sacramento, Eagle, In Slug Plate, Deep Teal Green, Pontil 155.00
Salt Lake City Soda Water Co., Red Seal, Monogram, Amethyst 75.00
Sam. Verner, Trademark Registered, Toronto, Tree, S On Base, Hutchinson, Aqua, 7 In. . 25.00
Sammons Bros., Jamestown, Green Aqua, 4-Piece Mold, Tooled Top, Hutchinson 90.00
San Diego Soda Works, Crown Top 25.00
San Francisco Glass Works, Ice Blue, Applied Top, 1870-1876 .... 525.00
Sandberg Bros., Hibbing, Minn., Hutchinson 30.00
Saybrook Bottling Works, Aqua, Blob Top, Hutchinson, 6 3/4 In. 10.00
Schick & Fett, Reading, Pa., Green, Squat 35.00
Schmidts Tiger Brand Cream Ale, Philadelphia, Pa., Amber, Crown Top, ABM, Label 10.00
Seal Rock Springs, Saco., Maine, Green, Seal On Rocks Label, Qt. 22.00
Seisler Beverage, St. Charles, Mo., Eskimo, Blue & White, ACL, 10 Oz. 100.00
Seitz & Bro., Easton, Pa., Cobalt Blue, Double Collar Mouth, IP, 7 1/4 In. 120.00
Seitz & Bro., Easton, Pa., Olive Green 100.00
Seitz & Bro., Easton, Pa., Sapphire Blue, IP, 7 3/8 In. 50.00
Seth Butler, Des Moines, Iowa, Light Amethyst, Slug Plate, Hutchinson 35.00
Seven-Up, John L. Gebhardt, Boston, Mass., Deep Green, Original Bale, Stopper 100.00
Sierra Club, Scotch Mist, Champagne Style, Crown Top, ABM 15.00
Simonton & Co., Huntingdon, Pa., Aqua, Hutchinson, Qt. 100.00
Ski Beverage, Montreal, Skier, White & Green, ACL, 12 Oz. 75.00
Skipper Beverages, In Red & White Flag, Skipper, In Red Flag, Pittsburgh, Pa., 8 In. .. 5.00
Slo Soda Water, S. Seribelli, Curved R, Aqua, Applied Top, Gravitator 55.00
Sloan's Soda Water, Boise, Ida., Aqua, Crown Top, BIMAL 30.00
Smedley & Brandt, Blue Green, Applied Sloping Double Collar, 1855, 6 1/4 In. 175.00
Smith & Co., Charleston, S.C., 8-Sided, Deep Green, IP, Blob Mouth, 1845-1855, 7 In. . 465.00
Smith & Co., Philada., Medium Green, Double Collar, Squat 30.00
Smith & Co. Premium Soda Water, Charleston, S.C., Emerald Green, 8-Sided, IP, 8 In. 65.00
Smith Bros., New Bedford, Mass., Blob Top 15.00
Sour Schnapps, Oskaloosa, Ia., Green, Lady, Red, ACL, 7 Oz. 35.00
South Bend Soda & Bottling Works, Aqua, Hutchinson, Tooled Top 35.00
Spartan, Greenville, S.C., Roman Soldier, Red & White, ACL, 12 Oz. 85.00
Spatz Beverages, Saugerties, N.Y., Sparrow, Brown & White, ACL, 1940s-1950s 40.00
Spencer's & Howorth Registered, Accrington, Leg Kicking Ball, Codd Stopper 20.00
Spring Hill Beverage, Ohio, Country Scene, Green & White, ACL, 7 1/2 Oz. 35.00
Spur, Canada Dry, Green, White & Red Label, Philadelphia, Pa., 9 1/2 In. .... *Illus* 8.00
Squarey & Sons, Salisbury, Green, Applied Top, Torpedo, England 255.00
Squeeze, Boy & Girl On Bench, Klee & Coleman, Indianapolis, Ind., 9 1/2 In. ..... *Illus* 4.50
St. Helena, Cal., Crown Top 50.00
St. Louis Soda Co., Wm. McC. & Co., Pitts., Pa., Aqua, Blob Top, Pontil, 7 1/2 In. 25.00
Standard Bottling Co., Peter Orello Prop., Silverton, Colo., Aqua, Tooled Top 100.00

Star, Atlantic City, N.J., Large & Small Star, Aqua, Mug Base, Hutchinson 12.00
Star Bottling Works, Middlesburg, Ky. 30.00
Star Bottling Works, St. Paul, Minn., Aqua, Hutchinson 15.00
Star Bottling Works, Star, South Sharon, Pa., Hutchinson, 7 3/4 In. 18.00
Star Brand Super Strong, Aqua, Codd Stopper, Cobalt Blue Marble 35.00
Star Ice & Soda Works, Wailuku Maui, Star, 9 Oz. 47.00
Star Soda, Kern, Ca., Aqua, Crown Top 15.00
Star Soda Works, Kern, Cal., Crown Top 20.00
Steelton Bottling Works, E.G. Irwin, Aqua, Wire Bail, BIMAL, 10 In. 50.00
Steinke & Kornahrens, Charleston, S.C., 8-Sided, Deep Cobalt Blue, 1845-1855, 8 In. . 155.00
Steinke & Kornahrens, Return This Bottle, Charleston, S.C., Cobalt Blue, IP, 8 In. 715.00
Stockton, B, Blob Top 20.00
Strike, Bowling Ball Hitting Pins, Green, White & Yellow, ACL, 1940s-1950s 25.00
Sun Dial Beverage, Aurora, Ontario, Red & Yellow Sun Dial, ACL 65.00
Sun-Rise Soda Works, Sacramento, Calif., Green Aqua, Rising Sun, Crown Top, BIMAL 25.00
Sunset Beverage Co., Portland, Maine, Green, Girl In Bathing Suit Label, Qt. 22.00
Superior Effervescing Gingerade, Stoneware, Hamilton, Tan, England, 1855-1870, 8 In. 580.00
Superior Soda Water, Deep Yellow Olive Amber, Eagle, Crossed Flags, 1845-1855, 8 In. 470.00
Superior Soda Water, Eagle & Shield, Grass Green, IP, Applied Mouth, 1845-1855, 8 In. 275.00
Superior Soda Water, Eagle, Crossed Flags, Shield, Deep Cobalt Blue, IP, 7 5/8 In. 935.00
Superior Soda Water, Medium Cobalt Blue, Applied Mouth, IP, 1845-1855, 7 3/8 In. .. 715.00
T. Burkhardt, Braddock, Pa., Hutchinson 10.00
T. Coyle, Chester, Pa., Aqua, Tapered Top 15.00
T.D. Cummings, Chester, Pa., Aqua, BIMAL 10.00
T.L. Neff's Pop & Premium Root Beer, Amber, Round Applied Top, c.1880, Qt. 470.00
T.P. Bowman, Phoenixville, Aqua, Squat 40.00
T.W., 141 Franklin St., N.Y., Blob Top 20.00
T.W. Gillett, New Haven, 8-Sided, Deep Sapphire Teal Blue, IP, Blob Top, 7 3/8 In. 770.00
T.W. Gillett, New Haven, Conn., Medium Sapphire Blue, Applied Mouth, IP, 1/2 Pt. 330.00
T.W. Gillett, New Haven, Conn., Paneled, Light Cobalt Blue, IP 550.00
Tahoe, Famous As The Lake, Carson City, Nevada, Embossed, Crown, 1920s, 9 3/4 In. 35.00 to 40.00
Tahoe Soda Springs, Aqua 30.00
Tahoe Sparkling Water, Green, Painted Label, 1950s, 13 Oz. 9.00
Tater's Beverage, Fitchburg, Ma., Boy & Glass, White & Green, ACL, 7 Oz. 75.00
Taylor & Co., Cobalt Blue, Blob Top, Early 1850s, 6 3/4 In. 275.00
Taylor & Co., Valparaiso, Chili, Medium Green, Blob Top, IP, 7 1/8 In. 140.00
Taylor & Co. Soda Waters, San Francisco, Eureka, Blue, IP, 1850s 340.00
Taylor & Co. Soda Waters, San Francisco, Eureka, Cobalt Blue, Graphite Pontil 450.00
Taylor Soda Water Mfg. Co., Boise, Ida., Aqua, Mug Base 75.00
Thomas & Dunleavy, Troy, N.Y., Aqua, Blob Top, Squat, Pt. 75.00
Thorpe & Co. Ltd., British Columbia, Light Aqua, Internal Threaded Closure, 9 1/2 In. . 45.00
Thos. Maher, Savannah, Deep Green, Blob Top, IP, 1845-1855, 7 1/8 In. 65.00
Thos. Maher, Savannah, Light Green, Blob Top, IP, 1845-1855, 7 In. 60.00
Thrill, 8-Sided, Cap Top, c.1920 .... 5.00
Tonopah Soda Works, Nev., Aqua, Tooled Mouth, 1960s 1650.00
Torah Beverages, Paneled, Textured, Trees, Mountains, Sunset, Orange & Black, ACL . 45.00
Tulpe Hocken Spring Water, Sunbury, Pa., ACL, 1/2 Gal. 15.00
Tweddle's Celebrated Soda, N.Y., Medium Cobalt Blue, IP, 1855, 7 3/8 In. 575.00
Tweddle's Celebrated Soda Or Mineral Waters, 38 Cortland St., Blue Green, Squat . 195.00
Tweddle's Celebrated Soda Or Mineral Waters, Medium Cobalt Blue, IP, 7 1/4 In. . 360.00
Twin Lights, 2 Lighthouses, ACL 6.00
Twitchell, T., Philada, Green, Applied Mouth, 1855-1865, 7 5/8 In. ....20.00 to 50.00
U. & I.D. Clinton, Woodbridge, Conn., Emerald Green, Blob Top, IP, 7 3/8 In. 220.00
Unembossed, Aqua, Hutchinson, Qt. 10.00
Union Glass Works, E.S. & H. Hart, Deep Cobalt Blue, Blob Top, IP, 7 1/2 In. 440.00
Union Lava Works, Conshohocken, Patented 1852, Cobalt Blue, 1855, IP, 7 In. 525.00
V. Mager, Sapphire Blue, Applied Gloppy Mouth, IP, 1845-1855, 7 1/8 In. 155.00
Va. Etna Springs, Vinton, Va., Ten-Pin 10.00
Vanharten & Grogan, Savannah, Ga., Teal Blue, Applied Mouth, 1855-1865, 6 3/4 In. . 80.00
Vess, Green, Baltimore Md., 8 1/2 In. ....*Illus* 8.00
Vin Fiz, Label Under Glass, Indented Panel, Cork Stopper, Fountain, c.1900, 12 In. 130.00
Vincent Hathaway & Co., Boston, Green, Round Bottom 110.00

Soda, Whistle,
Blue & White,
ACL, St. Louis,
Missouri, 8 In.

Soda, Whistle,
Columbus, Ohio, Blue
& White Label, 10 Oz.,
Original Cap, 9 1/2 In.

Soda, Vess, Green,
Baltimore Md.,
8 1/2 In.

Virginia Dare, First Lady Of The Land, Winooski, Vermont, Red & White, Pebbly Glass	15.00
Virginia Fruit Juice Co., Norfolk, Va., Script, Ten-Pin, 7 3/4 In.	25.00
Visalia Soda Works, Crown Top	20.00
Viva Bottling Works, Birmingham, Ala., Slug Plate, Crown Top, 9 In.	45.00
W. Dean, Newark, N.J., Blue Green, Pontil, Squat	65.00
W. Eagle, New York, Crystal Palace, Teal Blue, Blob Top, IP, 7 1/4 In.	745.00
W. Eagle, Superior, Cobalt Blue, Blob Top, Pontil, 6 7/8 In.	105.00
W. Eagle, Vestry Varick, Teal Blue Green, Blob Top, Bubbles, IP, 7 3/8 In.	240.00
W. Sievers, Cincinnati, Ohio, S In Diamond	60.00
W.A. Verner, Toronto, Monogram, Pure Apple Cider On Base, Aqua, Arrow Neck, 7 7/8 In.	30.00
W.A. Verner, Trade Mark Registered, Toronto, Pure Apple Cider, Light Aqua, Blob Top, Qt.	45.00
W.E. Brockway, N.Y., Emerald Green, Blob Top, IP, 1840, 7 1/4 In.	155.00
W.E. Deamer Nevada Soda Water Co., Grass Valley, Nevada Co., Aqua, Gravitating	70.00
W.E. Whyte's Sons, Wilkes-Barre, Pa., Green, Blob Top, Pt.	75.00
W.F. Driscoll, Pottsville, Pa., Aqua, Blob Top, Pony	25.00
W.H. Buck, Norfolk, Va., Deep Green, Applied Mouth, IP, 1845-1860	260.00
W.H. Burt, San Francisco, Green, Applied Mouth, IP, 1852	110.00
W.H. Burt, San Francisco, Green, IP, 1852	165.00
W.H. Raubenhold, Hamburg, Pa., Orange Amber, Blob Top, Squat	95.00
W.H.H., Chicago, W. McC. & Co., Mug Base, Pale Ice Blue	60.00
W.K. Hartenstine, Pottstown, Pa., Blob Top	12.00
W.N. Zinn, Carlisle, Pa., Amber, Crown Top	4.00
W.P. Knicker Bocker, Cobalt Blue, 10-Sided, Blob Top, IP, 7 1/4 In.	240.00
W.P. Knicker Bocker, Medium Cobalt Blue, 10-Sided, Blob Top, IP, 7 3/8 In.	130.00
W.P. Knicker Bocker, Sapphire Blue, 10-Sided, IP, Blob Mouth, 1845-1855, 7 3/4 In.	150.00
W.R. Chipman & Co., New London, Conn., Aqua, Blob Top, Hutchinson, 6 3/4 In.	20.00
W.S. Wright, Pacific Glass Works, Light Green, Early 1860s	550.00
W.T. & Co., 49 Greene St., N.Y., Sapphire Blue, Cylindrical, Burst Bubble Neck, 1/2 Pt.	35.00
W.T. & Co., N.Y., Cobalt Blue, Blob Top, 1865-1870, 7 1/8 In.	100.00
Walkers Root Beer, Skier, ACL, 1940s-1950s, 12 Oz.	20.00
Walkers Root Beer, Skier, ACL, 1940s-1950s, Pt.	20.00
Walsh & Norton, Toronto, Beaver Over Crown, Aqua, Blob Top, Squat, c.1895, 7 5/8 In.	50.00
Walsh & Willarton, Registered, Toronto, 1869, Crown, Aqua, Blob Top, 7 1/2 In.	60.00
Walt Everett, New Haven, Conn., Blue Aqua, Blob Top, 7 1/2 In.	20.00
Walter & Brother, Reading Pa., Teal, Blue, Green, Squat	70.00 to 90.00
Walter & Brother, Reading, Pa., Blue Green, Squat	40.00 to 50.00
Watertown Bottling Establishment, N.Y., Cornflower Blue, IP, 1/2 Pt.	75.00
Weber & Snyder, Chillicothe Mo., A&DHC, Light Aqua, Blob Top	100.00
Weinstein & Kaplan, Albany, N.Y., Fancy Log, Tombstone Slug Plate, Hutchinson, Qt.	80.00
Wells Bro. & Co., Stopper Made By Albertson John Mathews New York, Blue, 7 In.	990.00
West Chester Bottling Works, Pa., Blob Top	15.00
West Chester Bottling Works, West Chester, Pa.	20.00
West Chester Bottling Works, West Chester, Pa., Blob Top	10.00
Western Soda Works, P.O., Deer's Head, Hutchinson	40.00
Westmoreland Bottling Works, Derry, Pa., Hutchinson	10.00
Wheeler Bros., Waukesha, Wis., Hutchinson	20.00

Whelan & Ferguson, Halifax N.S., Aqua, Tooled Top 35.00
Whippers Beverage, Toronto, Green, Wrestler, Yellow & Red, ACL, 7 Oz. 350.00
Whippers Beverage, Wrestler Logo, Green, Yellow & Red, ACL, Toronto, 7 In. 350.00
Whistle, Blue & White, ACL, St. Louis, Missouri, 8 In. .... *Illus* 8.00
Whistle, Columbus, Ohio, Blue & White Label, 10 Oz., Original Cap, 9 1/2 In. .... *Illus* 9.50
White Eagle, Green, Eagle Picture, Pt. & 12 Oz. 9.00
White Eagle Beverages, Eagle, Chicopee Falls, Mass., Red & White, ACL, 8 3/4 In. .. 6.00
White Rock Quinine Water, New York, Lady On Rock, Carnival Glass, ACL 10.00
White Sox, WS, Embossed Bats, Sock, Crown Top, 1930s 130.00
White Star Soda Works, Los Angeles, Cal., Amethyst, Crown Top, ABM 20.00
Wielands Bottling Works, Reno, Nev., Aqua, Tooled Crown Top, 7 7/8 In. 125.00
William Bosse, Washington, D.C., Light To Medium Green, Squat, 1860-1870, 1/2 Pt. .. 100.00
Williams & Severance, Green, Long Neck, 1852-1854, 7 In. 175.00
Williams & Severance, San Francisco, Cal., Soda & Mineral Waters, Cobalt Blue, IP .. 200.00
Williams & Severance, San Francisco, Cal., Soda & Mineral Waters, Green, IP, 1854 .. 200.00
Williams Bros., San Jose, Calif., W In Square, Crown Top, BIMAL 20.00
Wilson Mfg. Co., High Grade Carbonated Drinks, Sacramento, Cal., Aqua, Crown, 12 In. 18.00
Wilson Mfg. Co., Sacramento, Cal., Aqua, Carbonated Drinks, 11 3/4 In. 18.00
Winebergs Gold Medal, Winebergs Quality Soda, Oregon & Washington, Wasp Waist . 20.00
Winslow Junction Bottling Co., Blob Top, Hutchinson, 8 1/2 In. 12.00
Wiseola Bottling Co., Birmingham, Ala. 150.00
Wm. A Kearney, Shamokin, Pa., Dark Brown, Hutchinson, Qt. 250.00
Wm. Callahan, Philada., Tombstone Plate Mold, Applied Top, Mug Base 10.00
Wm. Callahan, Philada., Tombstone Plate Mold, Mug Base, Applied Top, Hutchinson .. 10.00
Wm. Cook, Light Blue Green, 10-Sided, IP, Canada, 7 1/8 In. 905.00
Wm. Eagle, New York, Premium, Cobalt Blue, 8-Sided, Blob Top, IP, 7 1/8 In. 200.00
Wm. H. Stoll, Phoenixville, Pa., Aqua, Blob Top, Closure, Tall 10.00
Wm. Hill, Llandudno., Bird On Crossed Arms, Aqua, Codd, C. 1890, 8 7/8 In. 35.00
Wm. Phillips, Goderich, Aqua, Crown Top, BIMAL, Canada, Qt., 11 1/8 In. 115.00
Wm. Robertson, Toronto, Trademark, G, Light Aqua, Arrow Neck, Blob Top, 8 In. 30.00
Wm. S. Ford, 65 Willoughby Street, Root Beer & Heart On Reverse, 1878, Aqua, Qt. 200.00
Wm. W. Lappeus Premium Soda, Albany, N.Y., Sapphire Blue, 10-Sided, IP, 1855, 7 In. 145.00
Wolf & Hornkohl, Manistee, Hutchinson 45.00
Wonderland Beverages, Crater Lake, Mt. Shasta-Klamath Falls, Or., Blue & White, ACL 10.00
Wood Wiltwyck Rondout, Aqua, Squat 30.00
Woodland Soda Works, Cal., Blue Aqua, Hutchinson 90.00
Worthington Bottling Works, Worthington, Minn., Mug Base, Stopper, Hutchinson .. 40.00
Yaky's Beverages, Aliquippa, Pa., Red & White, ACL, 8 In. 6.00
Yankee Beverage, R.I., Uncle Sam's Top Hat, Blue & White, ACL, 12 Oz. 45.00
Youngblood, Dark Green, Blob Top 60.00
Youngblood, Light Emerald Green, Applied Blob Top, 1855-1865, 7 1/8 In. 50.00
Yukon Club Seltzer, A & P Tea Co., ACL 25.00
Yuncker Bottling, Tacoma, Wash., Mug Base, Hutchinson 15.00
Zee Beverage, Flying Saucer, White & Blue, ACL, 7 Oz. 30.00
Zeeh's Beverages, Kingston, N.Y., 2 Terriers, Red & White, ACL, 1940s-1950s 20.00
Zeis & Sons, Redding, Cal., Light Green, Applied Top, Hutchinson 45.00
Zeis Bros., Winthrop, Cal., Blue Aqua, Crown Top 60.00
Zep Up, Wilkes Barre, Pa., ACL, Qt. 20.00
Zircon Ginger Ale, Rumford, Maine, Green, Crown Top, ABM, 1931, Pt. 7.00
SPIRIT, see Flask; Gin; Seal

———————————————————— **STIEGEL TYPE** ————————————————————

Henry William Stiegel, an immigrant to the colonies, started his first factory in Pennsylvania in 1763. He remained in business until 1774. Glassware was made in a style popular in Europe at that time and was similar to the glass of many other makers. It was made of clear or colored glass that was decorated with enamel colors, mold blown designs, or etchings. He produced window glass, bottles, and useful wares. It is almost impossible to be sure a piece is a genuine Stiegel, so the knowing collector now refers to this glass as Stiegel type. Almost all of the enamel-decorated bottles of this type that are found today were made in Europe.

STIEGEL TYPE, Amethyst, 12 Diamond, Chestnut, Sheared Lip, Pontil, 5 1/2 In. 800.00
Amethyst, 12 Diamond, Sheared Mouth, Pontil, 1763-1774, 5 3/8 In. 3300.00

Amethyst, Chestnut, Blown, Sheared Lip, Pontil, 6 In. 410.00
Amethyst, Diamond & Daisy Design, Fluted, Manheim, Pa., 1774, 5 In. 4680.00
Amethyst, Flask, Diamond Daisy, Inward Rolled Mouth, Pontil, 1774, 4 7/8 In. 3740.00
Cut Floral Design, Thumbprint Pattern On Edges, Rolled & Flared Lip, 7 1/2 In. 95.00
Enameled, 8-Sided, Floral, German Writing, Pewter Top, 5 1/2 In. 395.00

─────────────────── **STONEWARE** ───────────────────

Stoneware is a type of pottery, not as soft as earthenware and not translucent like porcelain. It is fired at such a high temperature it is impervious to liquid and so makes an excellent bottle. Although glazes are not needed, they were often added to stoneware to enhance its appearance. Most stoneware bottles also have the name of a store or brand name as part of their decoration.

STONEWARE, Bottle, J.P. Plummer, Tan Glaze, Cobalt Mouth, 1852, 9 3/4 In. 90.00
Bottle, John Howell & Sons, Cobalt Letters, 1880-1895 . . . . 40.00
Bottle, Paul Pohl, Chicago 80.00
Bottle, Rice Paterson, N.J., Gray, Brown 140.00
Bottle, Square, Green Glaze, Design In Corners & Around Neck, 9 1/4 In. 75.00
Bottle, Strong, Cobb & Co. Wholesale Druggist, Cleveland, Gal. 75.00
Canteen, Greater Cleveland, Tan Glaze, Horseshoe Both Sides, Gal. 140.00
Canteen, Tan Glaze, Sunflower, Handle, Pat. Aug. 11, 1891, 1/2 Gal. 60.00
Flask, Reform, G. Peacey, Lord Nelson, Grape Vines, Men Drinking, Tan, Brown, 5 1/2 In. 205.00
Jar, A.P. Donaghho, Parkersburg, W. Va., Cobalt Blue, Handle, 14 1/2 In. 275.00
Jar, Canning, A.P. Donaghho, Parkersburg, W. Va., Gray, Salt Glaze, Blue Slip, 5 1/4 In. . 240.00
Jar, Cobalt Blue Brushed Lines, Foliage, 11 3/4 In. 220.00
Jar, Cobalt Blue, Applied Ear Handles, Swan, Oh., 17 In. 415.00
Jar, D. Brannan, San Antonio, Salt Glaze, Brown, Tan, Gal. 200.00
Jar, Flowers, Eagle, Cobalt Blue Stenciled Label, Shoulder Handles, 20 1/2 In. 1595.00
Jar, Macomb Stoneware Co., Macomb, Ill., White, Brown Top, Pt. 65.00
Jar, Roxbury Rye Fisher Brothers Co., Baltimore, Md., Brown, Cream, 1/2 Gal. 70.00
Jar, White, Lid, Metal Clamp, Thumbscrew, Gal. 75.00
Jar, You Can't Beat This Jar For Beating Or May's Groceries For Eating, Cream, Qt. 100.00
Jug, 2 Handles, Tan Gray, Cobalt Birds On Flowering Plant, 1860s, 5 Gal., 17 1/2 In. 1540.00
Jug, Ackers, H.G. Registered Finley Acker & Co., Screw In Stencil, Qt. 120.00
Jug, Ackers, H.G., Registered Finley Acker & Co., Oyster, Wide Mouth, Qt. 140.00
Jug, B.J. Semmes & Co., Cream, Brown Slip, Applied Handle, 1885-1890, 8 3/8 In. 90.00
Jug, Batter, Wood Handle, Dark Brown Albany Slip Glaze, 1880-1900, 8 3/8 In. 90.00
Jug, Bellarmine, Orange Brown Glaze, Face On Neck, 16th Century, 16 3/4 In. 470.00
Jug, Bennington, Dark Brown Albany Slip, Applied Mouth, 1877, 3 1/8 In. 70.00
Jug, Brown County Hills, Bean Blossom, Dark Brown Albany Slip, 3 3/4 In. 75.00
Jug, Burrows, Drugs, Jewelry & Books, San Augustine, Tex., Gal. 695.00
Jug, California Wine House, Cream, Black Transfer, 1890-1910, 11 1/2 In. 70.00
Jug, City Of Hamburg Co., San Francisco, Brown Top & Tan Base, 10 In. 65.00
Jug, Cobalt Flower, Cobalt Accents, 1820-1860, 1/2 Gal. 120.00
Jug, Compliments Of John J. Stumpf Co., Cumberland, Md., Wire Handle, 1/2 Pt. 130.00
Jug, Cream, Cobalt Slip Design, Bird Over Lettering, Handle, 1890, 11 1/8 In. 965.00
Jug, Cream, Dark Brown Glaze Shoulder, Handle, Black Transfer, 1900, 3 In. 440.00
Jug, Creamery & Dairy Supply's Poions, Minneapolis, Gal. 55.00
Jug, Dark Brown Albany Slip, Handle, 1885-1910, 3 In. 100.00
Jug, Down On The Farm, Farmmato, C.W. Rodefer Co., Shadyside, Ohio, Pt. 140.00
Jug, E.L. Stork, Tucker, Ga., Incised, Olive Brown Tobacco Glaze, Gal. 170.00
Jug, Edwin T. Moul Wines & Liquors, York, Pa., Brown & Cream, Qt. 195.00
Jug, Empire Bottling Co., Denver, Tan, 1/2 Gal. 65.00
Jug, F.A. Amoes & Co., Owensboro, Ky., Dark Brown Albany Slip, Handle, 1885, 3 In. . . 255.00
Jug, F.B. Norton & Co., Worcester, Mass., 5, Gray, Blue Parrot, Foliage, 18 1/4 In. 770.00
Jug, Fort Edward Pottery Co., Dark Gray, Cobalt Slip Bird Design, 1890, 12 In. 465.00
Jug, Fort Edward Pottery Co., Gray, Cobalt Slip Bird Design, 1890, Gal. 575.00
Jug, Frank Lind, St. Louis, Mo., Dark Brown Slip Glaze, Handle, 1910, 2 5/8 In. 110.00
Jug, G.P. Sieman, Westport, S.D., Cream, Dark Brown Glaze Neck, Handle, 3 In. 440.00
Jug, Geo. A. Dickel & Co., Cream, White & Blue Rings, Applied Handle, 9 5/8 In. 215.00
Jug, Goodwin & Webster, Cobalt Blue, 12 1/2 In. 192.50
Jug, Goodwin & Webster, Hartford, Conn., Tan, Man In Hat, Incised, c.1830, 17 In. 1100.00
Jug, Gray, Salt Glaze, Blue Flower Slip Design, Incised 2, 1865-1890, 2 Gal. 175.00

Jug, Grover Cleveland Picture, Brown Slip Glaze, Handle, 1892, 1 1/2 In. 145.00
Jug, Gun Club From E.W.V. Connor, Savannah Ga., Brown Albany Slip, 3 1/8 In. 240.00
Jug, H.W. Wilson Co. Ltd., Saint John, N.B., Brown & Cream, Blue Lettering, Gal. 80.00
Jug, Handle, Strap, Cobalt Blue Slip Flower, 13 1/4 In. 247.50
Jug, Haxstun, Ottman & Co., Fort Edward, N.Y., Gray Tan, Cobalt Slip Bird, 13 In. 525.00
Jug, Hazelwood, Big Drug Store, Nacogdoches, Tex., Gal. 750.00
Jug, J. Norton & Co., Vt., Stylized Cobalt Bird On Branch, Gray Glaze, 1880, Gal. 255.00
Jug, J.D. Howard, Joplin, Mo., Cream, Brown Glaze Neck, Handle, 1910, 3 3/8 In. 360.00
Jug, J.F. Brower, 1, Inside Circle, Green Gray Ash Glaze, 1870-1880, 10 7/8 In. 240.00
Jug, J.S. Taft & Co., Keene, N.H., Cobalt Floral Design, Embossed, 1860-1880, Gal. 110.00
Jug, John Bauer, Louisville, Ky., Tan, Black Transfer, Handle, 1890, 2 1/2 In. 330.00
Jug, John Raese Davis, W. Va., Silver Brown Albany Slip Glaze, Handle, 1910, 3 In. 210.00
Jug, Johnstreet Wine Brandy Co., St. Paul, Minn., Cream, Cobalt Transfer, 1910, 3 In. .. 360.00
Jug, L. Norton & Son, Dark Gray, Dark Brown Albany Slip Flower Design, 11 In. 605.00
Jug, L.J. Cale, Brainerd, Minn., Cream, Brown Glaze Neck, Handle, 1910, 3 1/4 In. 255.00
Jug, Lambert Orchard Co., Sedalia, Col., Cream, Brown Glaze, Blue Transfer, 9 In. 145.00
Jug, Meredith's Diamond Club, East Liverpool, Oh., 7 1/2 In. 66.00
Jug, Merry Christmas, Compliments Of W.C. Hanlen, Reading, Pa., Cream, Blue, Qt. ... 195.00
Jug, Morton & Co., Brantford, C.W., 2, Gray, Floral Design, Canada, 14 In. 265.00
Jug, N. Eberhardt, Toronto, O., 2, Gray, Cream, Rust Speckles, Flower, 13 In. 210.00
Jug, Nicholas Lang, Wines & Liquors, Savannah, Ga., Cream, Brown, 1880-1900, 9 In. .. 150.00
Jug, Richard Devine Grocer, Phila., Dark Brown Slip Glaze, Handle, 1910, 3 1/2 In. 175.00
Jug, Ricksecker's Cologne, N.Y., Cream, Brown Shoulder, Handle, 1910, 3 In. 60.00
Jug, S. Hart Fulton, 2, Gray, Cobalt Blue Slip Tulip Design, 1845-1860, 12 3/4 In. 360.00
Jug, Saloon, Buckhorn, San Antonio, Tex., White, Applied Handle, 1890-1900, 2 In. 210.00
Jug, Tan Gray, Cobalt Slip Plumage Design, Handle, 1855-1870, 11 3/8 In. 550.00
Jug, Tetts, San Augustine, 2 Gal. 950.00
Jug, The Woodward Co., Roanoke Va., Cream, Black Letters, Applied Handle, 3 In. 145.00
Jug, Thos. Fielding Superior, Junction, Wis., Cream, Dark Brown Glaze, 1910, 3 In. 330.00
Jug, Toronto Pottery Co., Toronto, Blue & White Stripes, Stencil, Qt. 60.00
Jug, Try Karolina Korne, Cream, Black Transfer, Applied Handle, 3 1/8 In. 660.00
Jug, W.W. Stacy, Osage, Ia., Cream, Brown Glaze Neck, Handle, 1910, 3 In. 330.00
Jug, William Schaeffer, Wholesale Distributor, Kellogg, Idaho, Brown, Tan, 1/2 Gal. 360.00
Jug, Wm. Radam's Microbe Killer, No. 2, Cream Glaze, Label, 11 In. 130.00
Jug, Yellowstone, S.F., Twomey & Miholovich, Tan, Brown, Handle, 6 3/4 In. 185.00

———— TARGET BALL ————

Target balls were first used in England in the early 1830s. Trapshooting was a popular sport. Live birds were released from a trap and then shot as they tried to fly away. The target balls, thrown into the air, replaced the live birds. The first American use was by Charles Portlock of Boston, Massachusetts, about 1850. A mechanical thrower was invented by Captain Adam Bogardus and with this improvement, trap shooting spread to all parts of the country. Early balls were round globes but by the 1860s they were made with ornamental patterns in the glass. Light green, aqua, dark green, cobalt blue, amber, amethyst, and other colors were used. Target balls went out of fashion by 1880 when the *clay pigeon* was invented.

TARGET BALL, Black Tar-Like Substance, 2-Piece Mold, 1880-1890, 2 3/4 In. 415.00
Bogardus, Apr. 10 1877, Cobalt Blue, 2 3/4 In. ....*Illus* 1540.00
Bogardus, Pat'd Apr. 10 1877, Backwards 6, Sheared Lip, Golden Amber, 2 5/8 In. 670.00
Bogardus, Pat'd Apr. 10 1877, Gold Amber, Lattice, Sheared Mouth, 2 3/4 In. 265.00
Bogardus, Pat'd Apr. 10 1877, Hobnail, Sheared Lip, Yellow Amber, 2 3/4 In. 2970.00
Bogardus, Pat'd Apr. 10 1877, Medium Olive, 2 3/4 In. ....*Illus* 1375.00
Bogardus, Pat'd Apr. 10 1877, Yellow Amber, 2 3/4 In. 550.00
Bogardus, Yellow Amber, Diamond Pattern, Dot In 4 Panels, 2 5/8 In. 470.00
Cobalt Blue, Allover Square, Sheared, Flared Mouth, 1880-1890, 2 5/8 In. 120.00
Cobalt Blue, Diamond Pattern With Dot At Tips, Bird With Ring, France, 2 3/4 In. 220.00
Cobalt Blue, Intersecting Horizontal & Vertical Bands 75.00
Cobalt Blue, Square Band Design, Funnel Neck 90.00
Cobalt Blue, Square Pattern, Center Band, Sheared Lip, France, 1880-1890, 2 5/8 In. ... 90.00
Copper Puce, Diamond, Center Band, Ground Lip, 1880-1890, 2 5/8 In. 415.00
Diamond, Amber, No Center Band, 1880-1890, 2 5/8 In. 605.00
Diamond, Cobalt Blue, France, 1870-1900, 2 In. 185.00

Target Ball, Bogardus,
Apr. 10 1877, Cobalt Blue,
2 3/4 In.

Target Ball, Bogardus, Pat'd
Apr. 10 1877, Medium Olive,
2 3/4 In.

Target Ball, Hobnail, Ribbing
Along Seams, Yellow Amber,
c.1890, 2 3/4 In.

Diamond, Vertical Line Pattern Center Band, Sheared Mouth, Cobalt Blue, 2 5/8 In. 360.00
Diamond, Yellow Amber, Unembossed Center Band, 1880-1890, 2 3/4 In. 230.00
Diamond, Yellow Olive, Center Band, Rough Sheared Mouth, 1880-1890, 3 In. 3410.00
For Hockey's Patent Trap, Medium Green, Sheared Lip, England, 1890, 2 In. 1265.00
For Hockey's Patent Trap, Smoky Green, Sheared Lip, 1880s, 2 3/8 In. 1815.00
Glashuttenewotte Jun Charlottenburg, Diamond, Yellow Olive, 1880-1890, 3 In. 1155.00
Great Western Gun Works, Pittsburgh, Pa., Tobacco, Root Beer Amber, 1890, 2 In. . .   4620.00
Grenade Unic Extinctrice, Medium Amber, Vertical Rib, France, 5 1/2 In. 305.00
Grenades Du Progres, Grenades Extingtives, Yellow, France, 1875, 5 1/8 In. 440.00
Hobnail, Ribbing Along Seams, Yellow Amber, c.1890, 2 3/4 In. . . . .*Illus*   1430.00
Ira Paine's, Gold Yellow Amber, Pat. Oct. 23 1877, 1877-1890, 2 3/4 In. 465.00
Ira Paine's, Oct. 23, 1877, Yellow Amber, Sheared Lip, Filled Ball, 2 5/8 In. 200.00
Ira Paine's, Pat. Oct. 23, 1877, 3-Piece Mold, Gold Amber, 2 3/4 In. . . . . .240.00 to 265.00
J.H. Johnston, Great Western Gun Works, Pittsburgh 4620.00
J.H. Johnston, Pittsburgh, Pa., Root Beer Amber, Sheared Lip, 1890, 2 1/2 In. 5060.00
L. Jones Gunmaker, Blackburn, Diamond, Sheared Lip, Cobalt Blue, 2 3/4 In. 165.00
L. Jones Gunmaker, Blackburn, Diamond, Sheared Lip, Light Sapphire Blue, 2 5/8 In. .   175.00
Light Cobalt Blue, Rough Sheared Mouth, 3-Piece Mold, 1880-1890, 2 5/8 In. 175.00
Man, Shooting, Bright Yellow Green, Sheared Lip, England, 1880-1890, 2 7/8 In. 770.00
Man, Shooting, Diamond, Sheared Lip, Clear, Pink Cast, England, 2 1/2 In. 360.00
Man, Shooting, Diamond, Sheared Lip, England, 1880-1890, 2 5/8 In. 415.00
Man, Shooting, Diamond, Sheared Lip, Light Pink Amethyst, 1880-1890, 2 1/2 In. 495.00
Man, Shooting, Medium Pink Amethyst, England, 1880-1890, 2 3/4 In. 715.00
Man, Shooting, Sheared Lip, England, 1880-1890, 2 3/4 In. 440.00
Medium Cobalt Blue, Square Pattern, Center Band, 1880-1890, 2 3/4 In. 120.00
Medium Sapphire Blue, Square Pattern, Center Band, England, 1880-1890, 2 3/4 In. . .   265.00
N.B. Glass Works, Perth, Diamond, Green Aqua, England, 1880-1890, 2 5/8 In. 185.00
N.B. Glass Works, Perth, Diamond, Reversed S, Upside Down P, Sapphire Blue 230.00
N.B. Glass Works, Perth, Medium Sapphire Blue, Sheared Lip, England, 1890, 3 In. . . .   100.00
N.B. Glass Works, Perth, Pale Green Aqua, England, 1880-1890, 2 3/4 In. 105.00
N.B. Glass Works, Perth, Reverse S, Upside Down P, Light Sapphire Blue 130.00
N.B. Glass Works, Perth, Upside Down SS & P, Smoky Sapphire, Cross Hatching 175.00
Sapphire Blue, 3-Piece Mold, Sheared Lip, 1880-1890, 2 1/2 In. 100.00
Teal Green, Blown, 3-Piece Mold, Sheared Lip, 1880-1890, 2 3/4 In. 415.00
Van Cutsem, A St. Quentin, Cobalt Blue 175.00
Van Cutsem, A St. Quentin, Cobalt Blue, Lattice, Spherical, France, 1860, 2 1/2 In. . . .   110.00
Van Cutsem, A St. Quentin, Deep Cobalt Blue, Diamond, France, 1890, 2 5/8 In. 275.00
Van Cutsem, A St. Quentin, Diamond, Deep Cobalt Blue, Center Band, 1890, 3 In. 185.00
Van Cutsem, A St. Quentin, In Center Band, Cobalt Blue, 1880-1890, 2 3/4 In. . . .80.00 to 110.00
Van Cutsem, A St. Quentin, In Center Band, Deep Cobalt Blue, France, 1900 . . . .   80.00
Van Cutsem, Blue, Embossed 135.00
W.W. Greeners, Diamond, Medium Cobalt Blue, Sheared Mouth, 1890, 2 5/8 In. 305.00
W.W. Greeners, St. Mary's Works, Diamond, Cobalt Blue, 1880-1890, 2 5/8 In. 145.00
W.W. Greeners, St. Mary's Works, Diamond, Pink Amethyst, 1880-1890, 2 5/8 In. 500.00

Yellow Amber, 7 Horizontal Bands, Sheared Lip, 3-Piece Mold, 2 5/8 In. 550.00
Yellow Amber, Blown, 3-Piece Mold, Sheared Mouth, 1880-1890, 3 In. 95.00
TOILET WATER, see Cologne

─────────────────────────────── TONIC ───────────────────────────────

Tonic is a word with several meanings. Listed here are medicine bottles that have the
word *tonic* either on a paper label or embossed on the glass. In this book *hair tonic* is
listed with cosmetics or cure. There may be related bottles listed in the Cure and Medicine categories.

TONIC, Althrop's Constitutional Tonic, Chicago & N.Y., Blue Aqua, 1855-1865, 9 7/8 In.   155.00
Baldwin's Celery Pepsin & Dandelion Tonic, Amber 125.00
Bitter Apple Tonic, BIMAL 25.00
Dalton's Sarsaparilla & Nerve Tonic 8.00
Doct. Harrison's Chalybeate Tonic, Rectangular, Blue Green, 9 In. 80.00
Doct. Harrison's Chalybeate Tonic, Rectangular, Emerald Green, 9 In. 180.00
Dr. Baker's Tonic Laxative, Keokuk, Iowa, Amber 20.00
Dr. Boyce's Tonic Bitters, Henry & Co., Proprietors, Vertical, 12-Sided, Blue Aqua, 8 In.   95.00
Dr. D. Jayne's Carminative Balsam, OP 40.00
Dr. D. Jayne's Hair Tonic, Philada, Aqua, Oval, OP, 4 1/2 In. 72.00
Dr. D. Jayne's Tonic Vermifuge, Phila, Aqua, Applied Top, OP, 5 In. ....30.00 to 45.00
Dr. Flander's Diffusable Tonic, Flask, Strapside, 5 7/8 In. 15.00
Dr. Harter's Dixie Tonic, Dr. Harter Medicine Co., Medium Amber, Tooled Lip, 7 3/8 In.   195.00
Dr. Harter's Iron Tonic, Amber 30.00
Dr. Harter's Iron Tonic, Aqua 40.00
Dr. Henley's Dandelion Tonic, Amber, Tooled Mouth, 9 In. 220.00
Dr. Hul Cee's Blood Building Tonic, Louisville, Ky., Aqua 40.00
Dr. Jas. Graves Tonic, Louisville, Ky., Semi-Cabin, Aqua, 1865-1875, 9 7/8 In. 360.00
Dr. Miles' Heart Treatment, Rectangular, Tonic & Regulator, Light Aqua, Label, c.1900   35.00
Dr. Miles' Restorative Tonic, Aqua, 8 1/8 In. 15.00
Dr. Sledge's Nervous Tonic, Blue Aqua, IP, Applied Sloping Collar, 9 5/8 In. 825.00
Dr. Townsend's Aromatic Hollands Tonic, Bitters Shape 100.00
Edward Wilder's Chill Tonic, Louisville, Ky., Semi-Cabin, 1880-1890, 6 1/4 In. 210.00
Gogings Iron Tonic, Sacramento, Aqua, Tooled Top, Banded, 8 In. 75.00
Gogings Wild Cherry Tonic, Amber, Tooled Top, 9 In. 90.00
Gogings Wild Cherry Tonic, Light Amber 120.00
Gogings Wild Cherry Tonic, Square, Light Amber 100.00
Goldlen's Liquid Beef Tonic, Physicians Sample 25.00
Graves & Son, Louisville, Ky., Semi-Cabin, 5-Pointed Star, Ice Blue, 10 In. 415.00
Hop-Cel Co., San Francisco, Nerve, Blood & Brain, Amber, Tooled Top 55.00
I.O. Woodruff-Freleich's Tonic, 2 Sunken Side Panels, Cork, Rectangular, 3 In. 3.00
Invigorating & Refreshing Wisto Nerve & Brain Tonic, 1895-1915, 11 In. 305.00
Johnson's Chill & Fever Tonic, Guaranteed To Cure, Savannah, Ga., 6 In. 25.00
Johnson's Malarial Chill & Fever, 1940, 3 Oz. 9.00
Johnson's Malarial Chill & Fever, James F. Ballard, Tin Lid, 1939-1939, Box, 6 Oz. ..   12.00
Kickapoo Sage Hair Tonic, Cobalt Blue, Tooled Mouth, Cylindrical, 1870-1900, 5 In. .   175.00
Kodol Nerve Tonic, Free Sample 20.00
Mexican Tonic, Flask, Amber, Sloping Shoulders, Chamfered Corners, 10 3/4 In. 40.00
Pe-Ru-Na Tonic, Consolidated Royal Chemical Co., Box, 1940 ....   7.00
Petty's Hog Tonic, Jug, Black, 2 Gal. 750.00
Psychine, Greatest Of Tonics, For Consumption, T.A. Slocum Co., New York, Label, 9 In.   35.00
Pursang, McKesson & Robbins, Green, Screw Lid, Box, 1935 ....   6.00
Reed's Gilt Edge Tonic 1878, Amber 40.00
Risley & Co., N.Y., Orange Tonic, Lady's Leg, Amber, Applied Mouth, Whittled 65.00
Rohrer's Expectoral Wild Cherry, Lancaster, Pa., Amber, IP, 10 3/8 In. 265.00
Rohrer's Expectoral Wild Cherry, Lancaster, Pa., Amber, IP, 1865, 10 In. .....200.00 to 230.00
Rohrer's Expectoral Wild Cherry, Lancaster, Pa., Light Amber, Pontil, 10 1/2 In. 290.00
Rohrer's Expectoral Wild Cherry, Lancaster, Pa., Pyramid, Golden Amber, IP, 11 In. ..   415.00
Rohrer's Expectoral Wild Cherry, Medium To Light Amber, Pontil, 12 1/4 In. 240.00
Rowand's Tonic Mixture, 6-Sided 35.00
Schenck's Seaweed, Blue Aqua, IP, Applied Mouth, 1845-1855, 8 7/8 In. 165.00
Sim's Tonic Elixir Pyrophosphate Of Iron, Antwerp, N.Y., Medium Amber, 7 In. 120.00
Spooner's Hygeian, N.Y., 8-Sided, Deep Yellow Olive Amber, Rolled Lip, 1855, 6 In. ...   635.00

Standard Tonic, Sherry & Iron Co., Stockton, Ca., Tall Pyramid Shape, Applied Top . . .   200.00
Thorn's Hop & Burdock, Brattleboro, Vt., Amber, 8 1/4 In. . . . . .30.00 to 45.00
Thorn's Hop & Burdock, Brattleboro, Vt., Rectangular, Yellow, 5 In. 60.00
Thorn's Hop & Burdock, Brattleboro, Vt., Yellow, 6 1/4 In. 65.00
Vin Tone, The Food Tonic, Amber 45.00
W.M. Johnson's Pure Herb, Sure Cure For All Malarial Disease, Dark Amber 90.00
Wait's Wild Cherry Tonic, The Great Tonic, Bitters Shape, Amber 35.00
Warner's Safe Tonic, Amber, Slug Plate, Pt. 300.00
Warner's Safe Tonic, Rochester, Tombstone-Shaped Panel, Pt. 275.00
Web's A No. I Cathartic Tonic, Light To Medium Amber, PCGW On Base, 9 1/2 In. . .   40.00
Web's A No. I Tonic, Embossed Tree Limb, Burnt Amber 45.00
Webb's Indian, Aqua, Tenpin 30.00
Westmoreland's Calisaya, Gold Yellow Amber, Tooled Mouth, 1880-1890, 8 1/4 In. . . .   90.00
Westmoreland's Tonic, Yellow Apricot Amber, Square, Indented Panels, 8 In. 100.00

--- **VINEGAR** ---

Vinegar was and is sold in glass bottles. Most vinegar packers prefer a large glass jug-shaped bottle with a small handle, the shape used today even for modern plastic vinegar bottles. The collector wants any bottle with the name *vinegar* on a paper label or embossed on the glass. The most famous vinegar bottles were made by National Fruit Product Company for their White House Brand vinegar. Bottles with the embossed brand name and a picture of a house, the trademark, were made in the early 1900s. Jugs in three or four sizes, apple-shaped jars, canning jars, fancy decanters, cruets, a New York World's Fair bottle, rolling pins, vases, a refrigerator water jar, and other fanciful reusable shapes were used until the 1940s. The company is still in business.

VINEGAR, Buy Leo Vinegar, O.J. Gregory Vinegar Co., Rogers, Ark., 4 1/2 In. . . . . . . *Illus*   100.00
C.I. Co., L.T.D., E. Rindge, N.H., Cobalt Blue, Applied Mouth, 11 1/4 In. 880.00
C.I. Co., L.T.D., East Rindge, N.H., Deep Cobalt Blue, Tooled Mouth, 1885-1895, 11 In. .   825.00
Cabiria, Apple Cider, Stute & Co., St. Louis, 9 3/4 In. . . . .*Illus*   15.00
Chapman 45.00
Duffy's 1842 Apple Juice, 8-Sided, Amber, 10 1/2 In. 45.00
Hirsch Bros. & Co., Vinegar & Cider, Pittsburg, Pa., Jug, Miniature 165.00
Holbrook & Co. 45.00
Johnson's Pure Cider Vinegar, Kishwaukee, Ills., Jug, Salt Glaze, Gal. 175.00
Maple Sap & Boiled Cider, Deep Sapphire Blue, Tooled Mouth, 1890, 11 3/8 In. 440.00
Oklahoma Vinegar Co., Fort Smith, Ark. 225.00
White House, Decanter, 2 Handles, Rose Pattern 20.00
White House, Double Handle, Apple Jug, Pt. 195.00
White House, Green, 7 3/4 In. 9.00
White House, Jug, 6 In. . . . .*Illus*   15.00
White House, Label Only, Shield Shape, Jar, Bail, 1926, Qt. 12.00
White House, Large Apple, 1/2 Gal. . . . . .65.00 to 75.00
W.A. LACEY, see Lacey
WATER, MINERAL, see Mineral Water

Vinegar, Buy Leo Vinegar, O.J. Gregory Vinegar Co., Rogers, Ark., 4 1/2 In.

Vinegar, Cabiria, Apple Cider, Stute & Co., St. Louis, 9 3/4 In.

Vinegar, White House, Jug, 6 In.

---------------------------- **WHISKEY** ----------------------------

Whiskey bottles came in assorted sizes and shapes through the years. Any container for whiskey is included in this category. Although purists spell the word *whisky* for Scotch and Canadian and whiskey for bourbon and other types, we have found it simpler in this book to use only the spelling *whiskey*. There is also blended whiskey, which includes blended bourbon, Scotch, Irish, or Canadian. Although blends were made in Scotland and Ireland for many years, it was not a process popular in the United States until 1933. One way to spot very new whiskey bottles is by the size. The 1 3/4-liter bottle is slightly less than a half gallon, the 1-liter bottle slightly more than a quart, and the 3/4-liter bottle almost the same size as a fifth. These bottles were introduced in 1976. Several years ago there was a contest to find the oldest bourbon bottle made in America. It was thought to be one dated 1882. The contest turned up an even older bottle, a Bininger made in 1848. Bourbon was first made in 1789 in Kentucky. Rum was made in America by the mid-seventeenth century; whiskey made of corn, rye, or barley by the early 1700s. It was the tax on this whiskey that caused the so-called Whiskey Rebellion of 1794. A museum of interest to collectors is the Seagram Museum, 57 Erb St., Waterloo, Ontario, Canada. See also modern manufacturers categories by brand name, and the Figural category.

WHISKEY, 2-Piece Mold, Pear Shape, Strawberry Puce, Applied Handle, Jug, IP, 6 In. ...	175.00
3 Shore Distilling Co. Purest Liquors, Elk City, Ok., Jug, Cream, Amber Handle, 14 In.	110.00
9-Sided, Pontil, 1/2 Pt.	60.00
A. Fenkhausen & Co., San Francisco, Ca., Smoky Clear, 1893, 12 In.	330.00
A.G. Lambert, Marchand DeVins, Liquors Et Epicures, Blue, White Stripes, Jug, 1/2 Gal.	75.00
A.G. Thomson & Co., Glasgow, Jug, Tan, Brown Glaze, Blue Slip Over Medallion, 8 In.	275.00
A.P. Simms, Fine Whiskies, Natchez, Miss, Jug, Gal.	90.00
Alderney, Chris Gallagher Co., Philadelphia, Backbar, Cylindrical, 11 1/2 In.	350.00
Amber, Vertical Rib, Applied Handle, Pour Spout, 1855-1870, 8 1/2 In.	415.00
Americus Club, Henry Campe, San Francisco, Front & Back Labels, Flask	50.00
Arch Cowan Mason & Co. Leith, Apple Green, Rectangular, Blob Top, 8 In.	38.00
Auld Lang Syne, The Weideman Company, 3 Men, Poem, Jug, Pottery, 7 7/8 In.	305.00
B.F. & Co., N.Y., Jug, Pottery, Green & Cream Mottled Glaze, 7 1/4 In.	265.00
Bacardi Rum, Santiago De Cuba, 11 3/4 In. ....*Illus*	10.00
Backbar, Clear, Multicolor Enamel Design, Gold Trim, 1880-1910, 11 In.	150.00
Backbar, Figure Of A Monk, Multicolor, White Enamel Lettering, Pontil, 8 In.	110.00
Backbar, Floral Design Around Body, Copper Wheel Cut, 1885-1910, 10 5/8 In.	55.00
Backbar, Horse's Head Rye, Clear, Cut Flutes Around Shoulder, 1885-1905, 11 In.	145.00
Backbar, Multicolor Label Under Glass, Pretty Woman In Center, 1910, 11 In.	2530.00
Backbar, Multicolor, Jockey, Sitting, On Horse, Glass Stopper, 1885, 9 In.	580.00
Backbar, Multicolor, Pretty Woman, Marked, Kummel, 1902-1910, 10 7/8 In.	550.00
Backbar, Old Rolling Fork Bourbon Whiskey, Ear-Of-Corn, 1890-1905, 11 In.	255.00
Backbar, Old Rosebud, Multicolor, Jockey, Sitting On Horse, Glass Stopper, 9 In.	440.00
Backbar, Pale Yellow Green, Opalescent Stripes, Whirled To Right, 1900, 10 In.	220.00
Backbar, Pedigree, Multicolor, Jockey, Riding Horse, Glass Stopper, 8 5/8 In.	500.00
Backbar, Pinch, Clear, Multicolor Enamel Design, 1890-1910, 6 1/2 In.	110.00
Backbar, Robin's Egg Blue, Opalescent Stripes, Swirled Right, 1870-1900, 12 1/4 In. ...	110.00
Backbar, Vertical Rib, Pink, White Enamel Lettering, Tooled Mouth, 11 3/8 In.	45.00
Backbar, Yellowstone, Geo. Delporte, San Francisco, Tooled Lip, 1880-1900, 11 In.	120.00
Banner, Emerald To Olive Green, Oval, BIMAL, Imperial Quart	8.00
Barg & Kleen O.K. Rosedale Bourbon, Hollister, Coffin, 1886-1895, Pt.	200.00
Barkhouse Bros. & Co., Gold Dust Kentucky Bourbon, 1871-1874	550.00
Belle Of Anderson, Old Fashioned Hand Made Sour Mash, In Star, Purple Milk Glass ..	65.00
Bennett & Carroll, Pittsburg, Barrel, Gold Yellow Amber, IP, 1855-1865, 9 1/2 In.	770.00
Bennett & Carroll, Pittsburg, Chestnut, Olive, IP, 1855-1865, 8 1/2 In.	880.00
Bennett & Carroll, Pittsburg, Deep Amber, Applied Mouth, 1865, 8 1/4 In.	715.00
Bertin & Lepori, San Francisco, Amber, Rectangular, Fifth	26.00
Bininger, see the Bininger category	
Black & White Whiskey, Green	15.00
Bonnie Castle, Jug	110.00
Booth & Co., Sacramento, Embossed Anchor, Light Purple, Tool Top	425.00
Boulevard O.K. Bourbon, Buneman & Martinoni, S.F., Buckle	330.00
Bouquet Whiskey, Clear, White Enamel, Backbar, Qt.	30.00
Braunschweiger & Co., Tennessee White Rye, San Francisco, Amethyst, Fifth	175.00

Brown's Catalina, Spanish Cannon Shape, Amber, 11 In. 175.00
Buchanan & Co., House Of Commons Scene, Jug 565.00
Buchannan's White, Olive Green, 3-Piece Mold, Label 10.00
Buffalo Old Bourbon, Geo. E. Dierssen & Co., Sacramento, Cal. 660.00
Buffy Malt Whiskey Co., Amber, 9 3/4 In. 9.00
Bullock Lade's B.L. Scotch, Brown, Tan, Black, Red Stencil, Pouring Lip, Qt. ..160.00 to 240.00
C.A. Richards, 99 Washington St., Boston, Red Amber, Sloping Collar, 9 1/2 In. 360.00
C.A. Richards & Co., Boston, Mass., Amber, Olive Tone, 1860-1880, 9 5/8 In. ...100.00 to 130.00
C.A. Richards & Co., Boston, Mass., Dark Olive Green, Black Base, 1860-1880, 9 In. .. 165.00
C.A. Richards & Co., Boston, Mass., Red Amber, Beveled Corners, 1860-1880, 10 In. .. 140.00
C.A. Richards & Co., Boston, Mass., Yellow Green, Beveled Corners, 1860-1880, 9 In. . 605.00
C.A. Richards & Co., Boston, Mass., Yellow Green, Beveled Corners, 1860-1880, 10 In. . 88.00
C.H. Atwood, Emerald Green, 6-Sided Fluted Neck, Backbar, 11 In. 135.00
C.H. Moore Old Bourbon & Rye, Jesse More Hunt Co., San Francisco, Amber, Qt. 35.00
Campbell & McGregor, Jug, Cream, Brown Neck, Blue Transfer, Handle, 1900, 6 In. .. 190.00
Campbell & McGregor, Old Scotch Whiskey, Jug, Pottery, Cream, Brown, 7 1/4 In. 220.00
Canadian Club Whisky, Hiram Walker & Sons, Jug, Tan, Cream, Basket, Canada, 13 In. 125.00
Canteen, 1899 33rd National Encampment, Phila., Pa., Label Under Glass 225.00
Caput, Fils & Cie Wholesale Grocers & Liquors, Montreal, Jug, Cream, Bands, Gal. 100.00
Cartan, McCarthy & Co., Medium Amber, Gold Tone, Applied Mouth, 1880-1894 ..... 390.00
Casa Gallo, Monogram, Diamond Pattern, Tooled Top, 13 In. 35.00
Casey Bros., Scranton, Pa., Amber, Qt. 15.00
Casper Co., Winston-Salem, N.C., Jug, Cream, Double Ears, Bail Handle, Gal. ...150.00 to 160.00
Casper Co. Inc., Roanoke, Va., Jug, Lowest Price Whiskey House, Double Ear, Bail 135.00
Casper Co. Inc., Winston-Salem, N.C., New York, Chicago, St. Louis, 5 7/8 In. 495.00
Casper's, Made By Honest North Carolina People, Cobalt Blue, Ring Mouth, Qt. 355.00
Casper's Whiskey, Made By Honest N.C. People, Cobalt Blue, 11 7/8 In. 360.00
Casper's Whiskey, Made By Honest N.C. People, Cobalt Blue, 12 In. ....440.00 to 495.00
CC & B, San Francisco, Cobalt Blue, Blob Top, IP, 1856-1858, 6 1/2 In. 330.00
Chapin & Gore, Barrel, Federal Law Forbids, Amber, 1915-1930 .... 20.00
Chapin & Gore, Chicago, Amber, 8-Sided, Round, 1880-1885 .... 55.00
Chapin & Gore Sour Mash, 1867, Chicago, Amber, Strap Side, Cleaned, 1/2 Pt. 95.00
Charrot & Henry, Flatbush Ave., Brooklyn, Amber, Bulged Neck, Qt. 20.00
Chas. D. Moul Wines & Liquors, York, Pa., Jug, Stoneware, 1/2 Gal. 165.00
Chatfield Rye, Backbar, Cylindrical 100.00
Chatwood, Yellow Green, Applied Top, 10 1/2 In. 120.00
Cherry Bestle, Happy Birthday Music, Labels, Green, Pt. 40.00
Chestnut Grove, Amber, Applied Mouth, Handle, Seal, 1855-1865, 8 5/8 In. 145.00
Chestnut Grove, C.W. On Seal, Medium Amber, OP, Partial Labels, 8 3/4 In. 145.00
Chestnut Grove, Flask, Amber, OP 165.00
Chestnut Grove, Flattened Chestnut Shape, Handle, Gold Amber, 9 In. 120.00
Chestnut Grove, Medium Amber, Handle, OP, 1860-1870, 8 7/8 In. 155.00
Chicago Liquor House, Cor. Main & First, Pueblo, Colorado, Stoneware, Gray, 1/2 Gal. . 165.00
Clark River, Hand Made Sour Mash Whiskey, Paducah, Ky., Jug, Gal. 150.00
Clinch Mercantile Co., Grass Valley, Cal., Clear, Amethyst Tone, Tooled Top, Fifth 55.00
Connoisseur, Jug, Multicolored Glaze, Doulton Kingsware, 1930, 8 3/4 In. ......85.00 to 165.00

Whiskey, Bacardi
Rum, Santiago De
Cuba, 11 3/4 In.

Whiskey, Denison
Pure Bourbon
Whiskey, Label,
Chillicothe, Ohio,
Qt., 11 In.

Whiskey, Julius
Kessler & Co.,
G.R. Sharpe, 6 In.

Copper Distilled Cedar Valley Ky. Bourbon, Crane, Hastings & Co., Amber 660.00
Cordial, see the Cordial category
Coronation Brand Kornschnapps Style Liquor, Product Of Ohio, Jug, Stoneware .. 140.00
Crabbie Scotch, Jug 45.00
Craigard Royal Blend, MacTavish & Co., Glasgow, Jug, Cream, Black Transfer, 7 In. ... 155.00
Cream Of Irish Whiskey, Shamrock, Jug, Tan, Brown Glaze, Black Transfer, 9 In. .55.00 to 95.00
Cream Of Old Scotch Whiskey, Bonnie Castle, Jug, Tan, Brown Glaze, 1910, 8 3/4 In. 105.00
Crigler & Crigler Distiller, Covington, Ky., 4 1/2 In. 75.00
Crown Distilleries Co., Crown, Monogram, Amber, Inside Threads, Applied Top, Qt. .. 175.00
Crown Distilleries Co., Red Amber, Inside Screw Threads, Crown Monogram 330.00
Cruiskeen Lawn Mitchell's Old Irish, Belfast, Jug, Cream, Brown Glaze, Handle, 7 In. 130.00
Cruiskeen Lawn Old Irish Whiskey, Jug, 8 In. ....40.00 to 50.00
Cutter Extra Old Bourbon, Gold Amber, 11 In. 715.00
Cylindrical, Yellow, Dot On Kick-Up Base, Qt. 30.00
Davy Crockett, Hey, Grauerholz & Co., Orange Amber, 12 In. 110.00
De Tabac De Natchitoches, Louisiana, Medium Olive Green, 1875-1895, 9 3/8 In. 1045.00
Deer Park Distillery, St. Paul, Stoneware, Jug, Gal. 135.00
Denison Pure Bourbon Whiskey, Label, Chillicothe, Ohio, Qt., 11 In. ....*Illus* 30.00
Dewar's, Peace Flagon Design, Jug, Cream, Allover Brown Glaze, England, 1920, 7 In. . 230.00
Dewar's Perth Whiskey, Tan, Brown, Dark Olive Green Glaze Neck, Jug, 1915, 10 In. . 2000.00
Dewar's White Label, Jug, Kingsware, Raised Uncle Sam Design, 1907, 7 1/4 In. 360.00
Dewar's, Bonnie Prince Charlie, Jug, Kingsware, Doulton, 7 1/8 In. 100.00
Diamond City Sherry, Backbar, White Enamel, 11 In. ....70.00 to 80.00
Dimond Seymore Co. Wholesale Beer, Wine & Liquors, Windber, Pa., Jug, 1/2 Gal. . 100.00
Dog Holding Bird, Trademark, JJW Peters Hamburg On Base, Amber, Germany 45.00
Dr. Abernethy's Green Ginger Brandy, Jos. N. Souther, San Francisco, 10 3/4 In. 35.00
Dreyfuss Wail Co., Inc. Distillers, Paducah, Ky., Amber, 6 3/4 In. 15.00
Duffy Malt Whiskey, Front & Back Label, Fifth 20.00
Duffy Malt Whiskey, Pt. ....30.00 to 38.00
Duffy Malt Whiskey, Rochester, N.Y., Amber, 10 1/4 In. 15.00
Dyottville Glassworks, Light Olive Yellow, Bubbles, Fifth ....25.00 to 50.00
Dyottville Glassworks, Phila, Embossed Base, Black, Cylindrical 20.00
E. Packham Jr., Our Candidates, McKinley, Roosevelt, Label, Backbar, 10 3/4 In. 1870.00
E. Packham Jr., Our Candidates, W.J. Bryan, A.E. Stevenson, Label, Backbar, 10 5/8 In. 1870.00
E. Swasey & Co., Portland, Maine, Jug 80.00
E.G. Booz's Old Cabin, Cabin, Amber, Applied Mouth, Qt. 715.00
E.G. Booz's Old Cabin, Cabin, Amber, Straight Roof, BIMAL 125.00
E.G. Booz's Old Cabin, Cabin, Gold Amber, Sloping Collar, Qt. 440.00
E.G. Booz's Old Cabin, Deep Amber, Applied Mouth, 1855-1870, 7 5/8 In. 3100.00
E.G. Booz's Old Cabin, Phila., Medium Yellow Amber, Smooth Base, 8 In. 2255.00
E.R. Betteron & Co. Distiller's, Chattanooga, Tenn., Amber, 8 1/2 In. 20.00
Eagle Glen, 29 Market Street, S.F., Mohns & Mohns, Inc., Eagle, Shield, Fifth 495.00
Edward E. Hall, New Haven, Ct., Medium Amber, Tooled Mouth, 1842, 11 1/4 In. 175.00
El Rey, San Francisco, Backbar, Amber, 11 1/2 In. 275.00
Ellenville Glass Works, 3-Piece Mold, Olive Green, Applied Collar, Inside Haze 65.00
Elliott & Burke, Fine Whiskey, Memphis, Tenn., Jug, Gal. 125.00

If you have unopened bottles of drugs or other pharmaceuticals, be sure to check for ether or picric acid. These can explode spontaneously and are dangerous to keep.

Whiskey, Greybeard,
Heather Dew,
Blended Scotch, 9 In.

Embossed Club In Diamond, Cylindrical, Teal Green, IP, Qt. 370.00
Emerald Brand Whiskey, Steinhardt, Bros. & Co., N.Y., Jug, Cream, Brown Glaze, 7 In.   175.00
Emerald Meehan's Superior Irish Whiskey, Woman & Harp Stencil, Jug, 7 In. .80.00 to 130.00
F. Chevalier & Co., San Francisco, Ca., Medium Orange Amber, 12 In. 330.00
F. Chevalier & Co. Whiskey Merchants, Yellow, Folds In Top, Squat, Qt. 715.00
F. Zimmerman & Co. Mail Order House, Portland, Ore., Amber, Tooled Top 25.00
Fay Bros. Family Liquor Dealers, Dunkirk, N.Y., 1/2 Pt. 25.00
Flask, see the Flask category
Fleishmanns Canteen, Circular Label, Stopper, Qt. 40.00
Four Roses, Paul Jones, Louisville, Ky., Amber, 11 In. 25.00
Free's Pure Rye Whiskey, York, Pa., Amber, 12 In. 45.00
Freed's Big Liquor Store, Schenectady, N.Y., Jug, 1/2 Pt. 145.00
Freiberg Bros., 1879, Jug, Pottery, Cream, Brown, Black Transfer, 11 In. . . . . .85.00 to 100.00
Friedman Keiler & Co. Distillers Wholesale Liquor Dealers, Paducah, Ky., Amber .   40.00
Full Measure, Levinson's Our Name, Seattle, Medium Amber, 10 In. 145.00
G.A. Jourde Bordqaux, Olive Green 55.00
G.J. Ashe XXX Rye, Knoxville, Tenn., Jug, Cream, Brown, Blue Letters, 8 1/2 In. 130.00
G.O. Blake's, Bourbon Co., Ky. Whiskey, Amber, Yellow, Applied Mouth, 1880, 12 In. . . .   2750.00
G.O. Blake's, Bourbon Co., Ky. Whiskey, Yellow Amber, Sloping Collar, Label, 10 3/4 In.   265.00
G.W. Huntington, Medium Blue Green, Applied Mouth, Seal, IP, 1855-1865, 12 In. 465.00
Galway Bay, Export Old Irish, Ship, Jug, Pottery, Cream, Green Transfer, 6 3/4 In. 230.00
Garrett & Co., St. Louis, Mo., Embossed, Eagle, 11 In. 25.00
George Benz & Sons Old Days Pure Rye, Jug, Internal Screw Stopper, Qt. 110.00
Georgia Moon Corn, 90 Proof, Label, 4/5 Qt. 6.00
German Peppermint Schnapps, 4 In. 50.00
Gilbert Bros. & Co., Baltimore, Md., Flask, Pt. 12.00
Gilmore & Gibson Importer's, Baltimore, Md., Red Amber, 1870-1880, 9 3/4 In. 305.00
Gilmour Thomson's Royal Stag, Cream, Jug, Brown, Black Transfer, Handle, 8 In. . . .   70.00
Gin, see the Gin category
Glen Garry Old Highland Whisky, Jug 60.00
Glen Lake Export, Scotch, Jug, Cream, Black Transfer, 1910, 6 3/4 In. . . . . .330.00 to 495.00
Glen Lossie Old Highland Whisky, Jug, Pottery, Cream, Brown, 7 1/8 In. 470.00
Glencoe Distillery Scotch Malt Whisky, Iron Cross, Jug 80.00
Glencoe Distillery Scotch Malt Whisky, Jug, Pottery, Cream, Brown, 7 In. . . .145.00 to 175.00
Glendale Kentucky, Jug, 2 Handles 30.00
Glenmore Distilleries Co., Owensboro, Kentucky, Jug, Stoneware, Stencil, Qt. 395.00
Gold Dust, Kentucky Bourbon, N. Van Bergen & Co., Gold Dust, 1890s . . . . . . .825.00 to 935.00
Goldberg, Bowen & Co., Light Amethyst, Tooled Top, 1896-1905 . . . .   65.00
Golden Creme, Alabama, Jug, 1/2 Pt. 75.00
Golden Dome Whiskey, Honey Amber, 21 1/4 In. 50.00
Golden Eagle Distilleries Co., San Francisco, Eagle, With Crest, Yellow Amber, 11 In.   350.00
Goldie-Klenert Co., Stockton, Cal., 1916-1918, Fifth 10.00
Good Cheer, B.L. Cromwell, Metal Bird Cage Stopper, Swirl Marble, Backbar, 10 1/4 In.   165.00
Good Old Bourbon, In A Hogs..., Arrow Pointing, Pig, Amber, 1890, 6 3/4 In. 275.00
Grannie Taylor's Liqueur Whisky, Taylor Brothers Co., Jug, 1885, 8 1/8 In. . . . .95.00 to 140.00
Greeley's Bourbon Whiskey, Barrel, Medium Strawberry Puce, 9 In. 440.00
Green River, Whiskey Without Regrets, Owensboro, Kentucky, Labels, ABM, Qt. 95.00
Greenless Brothers, AC 1908, Jug, Pottery, Indian Head, Gray, Brown, 7 In. 415.00
Greenless Brothers, Sailor's Story, Jug, Kingsware, Doulton, 6 1/2 In. 880.00
Greybeard, Heather Dew, Blended Scotch, 9 In. . . . .*Illus*   75.00
Greybeard, Heather Dew, Blended Scotch, Cream, Brown Glaze, Jug, 3 In. 70.00
Greybeard, Scotch Whiskey, Jug, Single Handle, Stencil, Qt. . . . . .40.00 to 90.00
Griffith Hyatt & Co., Baltimore, Jug, Medium Yellow Amber, 7 1/4 In. 230.00
Griffith Hyatt & Co., Baltimore, Jug, Puce, Square Mouth, Pontil, 7 1/4 In. 385.00
Griffith Hyatt & Co., Baltimore, Md., Oliver Amber, OP, 1870, 7 1/4 In. 415.00
H. Bosquet, Old Blue Horse, Cream, Dark Brown Glaze, Blue Transfer Handle, 3 In. . . .   45.00
H. Brickwedel & Co. Wholesale Liquor Dealers, S.F., Amber, 1880s, Fifth 75.00
H. Free & Co. Fine Wines & Liquors, York, Pa., Jug, Stoneware, White, Tan, 1/2 Gal. .   195.00
H. Weinreich & Co., Monogram, Sacramento, Cal., Tooled Top, 1890-1898, Fifth 100.00
H.A. Graef's Son, N.Y., Canteen, Yellow Olive Green, Applied Disc Mouth, 6 5/8 In. . . .   770.00
H.W. Bauss, Wines & Liquors, Galveston, Tex., Jug, 1/2 Gal. 750.00
H.W. Gray, 1878, Jug, Tan & Brown Stencil 80.00
Hall, Luhrs & Co., Sacramento, Amber, Screw Top, 1880-1915, Pt. 35.00

Hall, Luhrs & Co., Sacramento, Clear, 1900-1910, Fifth 65.00
Hanford Liquor Store, Vucovich Bros., Clear, 1910-1915, Fifth 42.00
Happy Days Famous Old Rye, Tan, Brown Glaze, Black Transfer, Jug, 8 In. .....70.00 to 100.00
Hard To Beat Extra Old Bourbon, Loewe Bros., S.F., Cal., Amber, Horse, Rider, Fifth 935.00
Harris Wine & Liquor Co., Mail Order House, Danville, Va., Flask, Oval, 1/2 Pt. 35.00
Hawkins & Bascom Liquors & Wine, Aspen, Colorado, Jug, Gal. 650.00
Hayner Distilling Co., Dayton, Ohio, Patented Nov. 30th, 1897, 12 In. 30.00
Hayner Private Stock Pure Whiskey, Distillery, Troy, Oh., 11 1/2 In. 9.00
Henke & Pillot, Inc., Grocers Wine & Liquors, Houston, Tex., Jug, Gal. 650.00
Hirsch's Malt Whiskey, Reliable Stimulant In Circle, Amber, 10 3/4 In. 65.00
Hollywood Whiskey, Amber, Glob Top, 12 In. 20.00
Honegger Bros. Liquor Merchants, Aberdeen, South Dakota, Jug, Gal. 200.00
Honest Measure, Flask, Strapside, Qt. 20.00
Honest Measure, Garret Williams Co., Baltimore, U.S.A., 6 1/2 In. 25.00
Honest Measure, Winchell & Davis, Albany, N.Y., Amber Strap, 6 1/2 In. 160.00
I. Goldberg, 171 E. Broadway, Houston, Amber, Label, 13 In. .... .30.00 to 60.00
I. Trager Co., Amber, Pt. 10.00
I.W. Harper Nelson Co., Kentucky, Jug, Pinched Style, 3 In. 90.00
Iron City Club Pure Rye Whiskey, Gentlemen On Label, Clear, Wood-Covered, Qt. ... 100.00
J. Rieger & Co., Kansas City, Clear, Qt. 5.00
J.E. Denaher, Albany, N.Y., Amber, Square, Spiral Neck, Tooled Top, 1890s 55.00
J.F. Cutter Extra Old Bourbon, Star, Shield, Star On Base, Amber, Fifth .....185.00 to 230.00
J.F.T. & Co., Phila., Vertical Rib, Medium Amber, Jug, 1860-1870, 7 1/8 In. 580.00
J.H. Cutter O.K. Whiskey, Honey Amber, Applied Mouth, Fifth 110.00
J.H. Cutter Old Bourbon, A.P. Hotaling & Co., Chocolate Amber, Fifth 495.00
J.H. Cutter Old Bourbon, A.P. Hotaling & Co., Amber, Crown Top 45.00
J.H. Cutter Old Bourbon, A.P. Hotaling & Co., Olive Amber 660.00
J.H. Cutter Old Bourbon, Amber, Applied Mouth, 1877-1880, 12 In. ....230.00 to 525.00
J.H. Cutter Old Bourbon, San Francisco, Amber, Shoofly, Pt. 850.00
J.H. Cutter Old Bourbon, Yellow Amber, Applied Mouth, 1871-1877, 11 7/8 In. 130.00
J.H. Cutter Old Bourbon Crown, A.P. Hotaling & Co., Orange Amber, Glob Top .25.00 to 55.00
J.H. Schroeder, Louisville, Ky., Olive Amber, Qt. 100.00
J.L. Shelley, Payne Ave., Cleveland, Ohio, 1/2 Pt. 20.00
J.N. Kline & Co. Aromatic Digestive Cordial, Teardrop, Cobalt Blue, Label, 5 1/2 In. . 465.00
J.R. Rohrbach, Little Brown Jug, Oakland, Cream, Brown Handle, 1890, 6 3/4 In. 350.00
J.R.D. & Fine Old Scotch Whiskey, Wreath, Medallion, Jug, Doulton Mark, Tan, Green 170.00
Jack Daniel, Lem Motlow Prop., Inc., Lynchburg, Tenn., Amber, 1940-1955, 9 7/8 In. .. 105.00
Jack Daniel, Old Time Distillery, Lynchburg, Tenn., ABM Lip, 1910-1920, 10 7/8 In. 175.00
Jack Daniel, Old Time Distillery, Lynchburg, Tenn., Amber, Tooled Mouth, 10 7/8 In. ... 230.00
Jack Daniel, Old Time Distillery, Lynchburg, Tenn., Deep Red Amber, 1890-1900, 11 In. 580.00
Jack Daniel, Old Time Distillery, Lynchburg, Tenn., Jug, 1915-1930, 10 7/8 In. 495.00
Jack Daniel, Old Time Distillery, Lynchburg, Tenn., Jug, Cream, Black Transfer, 11 In. .. 525.00
Jack Daniel, Old Time Distillery, Lynchburg, Tenn., Tooled Mouth, Cylindrical, 9 In. ... 550.00
Jack Daniel, Old Time Distillery, No. 7, Tooled Mouth, 1890-1910, 4 3/4 In. 110.00
Jack Daniel, Old Time Distillery, Tooled Mouth, Cylindrical, 1890-1910, 9 7/8 In. 660.00
Jack Daniel's Gold Medal Old No. 7, ABM Lip, Glass Stopper, 1971, 13 In. 30.00
Jack Daniel's No. 7, W.T. & C.D. Gunter Liquor Dealers, Nashville, Tenn., Jug, 1/2 Gal. 350.00
James E. Pepper, San Francisco, Corset Waist, White Lettering, 11 1/8 In. 85.00
Jas. A. Jackson & Co.'s Cocktail, Jug, Medium Amber, 8 3/4 In. 470.00
Jas. Durkin Wines & Liquors, Spokane, Wash., Amber, Qt. 25.00
Jas. Thorp's Sons Wine & Liquors, Washington, D.C., Amber, Flask, Strap, 1/2 Pt. ... 25.00
JB Brockett Wines & Liquors, Elizabeth City, N.C., Aqua, Strapside, Square SP, 1/2 Pt. 100.00
Jesse Moore & Co., Louisville, Ky., Amber, 1876-1885, Fifth 110.00
Jesse Moore & Co., Louisville, Ky., Antlers, Gold Amber, Applied Top, Fifth 110.00
Jesse Moore Bourbon & Rye, Gold Amber, Tooled Top, 6 In. 110.00
Jesse Moore-Hunt Co., San Francisco, Cal. & Louisville, Ky., Amber, Fifth .....20.00 to 35.00
Jno. Fl. Home, Knoxville, Tenn., Amber, Strap Side, Reverse Anchor, Qt. 75.00
John Dewar & Sons, Perth, N.B., Jug, Pottery, Brown, Black, 6 In. ....120.00 to 180.00
John Dewar & Son Limited, Light Brown, Olive Green Glaze, 1915, 6 In. .....145.00 to 220.00
John J. Rainville, Wholesale & Retail Liquor Dealers, Stoneware, Gal. 50.00
Jonas F. Brown, Wines & Liquors, 216 Nicollet Avenue, Jug, Brown, Cream, 1/2 Gal. .. 125.00
Jos. A. Magnus & Co., Cincinnati, O, Embossed Lion, Amber, 1895-1900 .... 15.00
Jos. Leopold & Bros., Belleville, Ill., Jug, Step Type, Brown & Cream, Gal. 125.00

Whiskey, Lincoln Club, Non-Intoxicating Beverage, Clear, 12 In.

Whiskey, Manastirka Slivovitz Plum Brandy, Yugoslavia, 7 In.

Whiskey, Mitchell's Old Irish, Jug, Stoneware, Belfast, 7 1/2 In.

Joseph N. Galway, N.Y., Deep Amber, Applied Mouth, 1860-1870, 8 3/4 In.	175.00
Josh Melczer, Los Angeles, Light Green, Full Pint	20.00
Jug, Blown, Cylindrical Corset Shape, Applied Handle, Gold Amber, 1860, 8 In.	385.00
Jug, Blown, Flattened Chestnut Shape, Gold Amber, Applied Handle, 1860, 8 In.	520.00
Jug, Blown, Gold Amber, Cylindrical Corset Waist, Double Collar, 8 3/4 In.	355.00
Jug, Blown, Pear Shape, Red Amber, Applied Mouth, 1840-1860, 6 1/8 In.	240.00
Jug, Bulbous, Blown, Deep Strawberry Puce, Sloping Collar, Pontil, 1830-1860, 8 In. . . .	440.00
Jug, Chestnut, Blown, Sapphire Blue, Double Collar, Pontil, 1860, 7 3/4 In.	1100.00
Jug, Flattened Ewer, Yellow Amber, Spout, Whitney Glass Works, 1880, 10 In.	305.00
Jug, Tan, Brown, Dark Olive Green Glaze Neck, Handle, England, 1890-1915, 12 In.	195.00
Julius Kessler & Co., G.R. Sharpe, 6 In. . . . . *Illus*	15.00
Kellerstrass Distilling, Kansas City, Fifth . . . . .25.00 to 40.00	
Kellogg's, Cylindrical, Amber, Fifth . . . . .55.00 to 65.00	
Kellogg's Extra Bourbon, W.L. Co., Amber, Tooled Lip, 1890-1900, 5 In.	60.00
Kellogg's Nelson County Extra Kentucky Bourbon, Red Amber, Fifth	935.00
Kentucky Belle Bourbon, Jug, Cream, Brown Glaze, Black Transfer, 1910, 8 1/4 In. . .	330.00
King Edward Reserve, Barrel, Amber, Screw Threads, No Stopper, 8 1/2 In.	445.00
Klein Bros., Cincinnati, Keystone Rye, Jug, Pottery, Gold Gilt	75.00
Kreielsheimer Bros., Seattle, Wash., Amber, Tooled Top, Fifth . . . . .35.00 to 40.00	
L.M. & Co., New York, Deep Root Beer Amber, Handle, Seal, 9 5/8 In.	2090.00
L.P. Turcotte & Co., Lowell, Mass., Flask, SCA, Embossed In Circle, Cork, 1/2 Pt.	15.00
Label Under Glass, Woman Pictured, Word Whiskey, 1910, 11 1/2 In.	1595.00
Lady's Leg, Honey Amber, Deep Kick-Up Base, c.1860-1870, 12 1/4 In.	50.00
Lancaster Glass Works, Lancaster, N.Y., Barrel, Medium Puce, 9 3/4 In. . . . . . .200.00 to 440.00	
Laundrine, Sallade Mfg. Co., Pottsville, Pa., Patented, Aqua, 1880s, 9 In.	10.00
Lilienthal & Co., Medium Amber, Applied Mouth, 1878-1884, 11 1/2 In.	800.00
Lilienthal & Co. Distillers, 4-Piece Mold, Amber, Crown & Monogram . . . . . . .110.00 to 235.00	
Lilienthal Distilleries, With Crown, Amber, Tooled Screw Thread, 1890s, 14 In.	120.00
Lincoln Club, Non-Intoxicating Beverage, Clear, 12 In. . . . .*Illus*	25.00
Little Brown Jug 1884 Rye, Gerson & Seligman, Montgomery, Ala., Jug	135.00
Lowenstein & Co., Old Harvest Corn Whiskey, Statesville, N.C., Rectangular, 1/2 Pt. . .	125.00
Lyrmill-Kentucky Bourbon, M.R. Miller Co., Bristol, Va., Jug, 1/2 Pt.	250.00
M. Wollstein & Co., Whiskeys, Wines & Liquor, Omaha, Neb., Beehive, Gal.	275.00
M.R., Sacramento, Cobalt Blue, Blob Top, IP, 1851-1863, 7 1/2 In.	1320.00
Maderia, Amber, Shield Shaped Label, Backbar	95.00
Manastirka Slivovitz Plum Brandy, Yugoslavia, 7 In. . . . .*Illus*	10.00
Manhattan Club Pure Rye, Santa Barbara, Amber, 3-Leaf Clover, Tooled Top, 9 3/4 In.	90.00
Marmore, Speaks For Itself, Clear, Gilt, Amethyst Tint, Fluted Neck, Backbar, 7 1/2 In. .	75.00
Meehan's, Superior Irish Whiskey, Jug, Cream, Brown, Black Transfer, Handle, 7 In. . . .	145.00
Meredith's Diamond Club Pure Rye Whiskey, Medicinal Use, Jug, 7 1/2 In. . .120.00 to 165.00	
Meridith's Diamond Club Pure Rye 1880, Jug, Stoneware, White, Red, Qt. . .100.00 to 395.00	
Methusalem, Amber, Embossed Around Shoulder, Applied Top	40.00
Meyer Brothers Drug Co., St. Louis, Clear, Lady's Leg, Rectangular, 1885-1895	15.00
Michaelis & Lindeman, New York, Amber, Applied Top, Cylindrical, Qt.	25.00
Mike & Jim's Private Stock, Anderson, Co. Whiskey, KTK, Jug, Green Transfer	170.00
Miller's Oldest Corn, Bristol, Va., Jug, 1/2 Pt.	135.00
Miniature, see the Miniature category	

Minnehaha Laughing Water, Jug, Pottery, Squaw & Waterfall, 7 1/8 In. 580.00
Minnehaha Martindale & Johnston, Philadelphia, Jug, 2 Birds At Fountain   . . .645.00 to 910.00
Mitchell's Old Irish, Jug, Stoneware, Belfast, 7 1/2 In. . . . .*Illus*   100.00
Mitchell's Old Irish Whiskey, Belfast, Jug, Cream, Brown, Red Purple Transfer, 8 In.   .   495.00
Mohawk Pure Rye, Pat. Feb. 11 1868, Figural, Indian Queen, Gold Amber, 12 In. 2365.00
Mohawk Pure Rye, Pat. Feb. 11 1868, Figural, Indian Queen, Yellow Amber, 12 1/4 In. .   1760.00
Monk's Old Bourbon, Medicinal Purposes, Yellow Olive, 1860, IP, 9 In. . . . . . .715.00 to 1210.00
Montana Liquor Co., Butte, Amber, Cylindrical, Turn Mold 100.00
Mountain Dew Old Scotch Whiskey, Deimal Bros., N.Y., Jug, Qt. 75.00
Mt. Vernon, Square, Lady's Leg Neck, Amber, Qt., 8 5/8 In. 25.00
Mt. Vernon Pure Rye Whiskey, Gold Amber, Applied Mouth, 1870-1890, 23 In. 550.00
My Old Kentucky Home, Amber, Qt. 60.00
My Queen Jubilee Blend, Thom & Cameron, Glasgow, Jug, Pottery, Cream, 7 1/2 In. . .   305.00
Myers & Co., Pure Fulton Whiskey, Covington, Ky., Jug, Cream, Salt Glaze, 13 In. 65.00
N.C. Cannon, Wines, Liquors, Vicksburg, Miss., Jug, 2 Gal. 200.00
N.M. Uri, Rectangular, Amber, Qt., 8 5/8 In. 15.00
Nabor, Alfs & Brune Wholesale Liquor Dealers, San Francisco, Amber, 11 3/4 In. 2640.00
Nashville Pure Rye, Square, Swirl, Lady's Leg Neck, Qt. 15.00
Nordhanfen Korn Schnapps, Drinking Man, Jug, Blue Transfer, Qt.   . . . . .40.00 to 85.00
O'Donnel's Old Irish, Belfast, Jug, Cream, Brown, Green Letters, 8 In. . . . . .90.00 to 120.00
O'Keefe's Pure Malt Whiskey, Oswego, N.Y., Jug, Tan & Cream, Qt. . . . . .45.00 to 90.00
O.K. Old Bourbon Castle Whiskey, F. Chevalier & Co., Red Amber, Fifth 440.00
O.P.S. Bourbon Whiskey, A.P. Hotaling's Old Private Stock, Dark Amber, 1879-1885 . .   3575.00
Oak Valley Distilling Co. Extra Pony, Griffin In Diamond, Light Blue, Qt., Squat 90.00
Old Boone, Enamel, Corseted, Backbar, Stopper 125.00
Old Bourbon, Maysville, Ky., I. Nelson's, Barrel, Gold Amber, Disc Mouth, 1870, 8 In. .   2750.00
Old Bourbon Castle, F. Chevalier & Co., Amber, Applied Mouth, Fifth 110.00
Old Club House, N.Y., Gold Amber, Applied Handle, 1880-1895, 9 In. 70.00
Old Cyprus, Dennis Donovan, Haverhill, Mass., Stoneware, Pt. 22.00
Old Highland Whiskey, Wright & Greig Ltd., Glasgow, Jug, Cream, Brown Glaze, 8 In.   55.00
Old Joe Gideon Bros., Amber, 6 In. . . . . .8.00 to 10.00
Old Joe Gideon Whiskey, Awarded Gold Medals, St. Louis, 1904, Flask, 1/2 Pt. 40.00
Old Jug Rye, Jug, Pt. 30.00
Old Maryland 1881 Pure Rye, K.T. & K., Jug, Pottery, White, 7 3/8 In. . . . . . .360.00 to 525.00
Old Mill, Whitlock & Co., Amber, Applied Mouth, Handle, 1860-1870, 8 3/8 In. . .385.00 to 800.00
Old Monongahela Rye Whiskey, Sheaf Of Wheat, Olive Amber, 1875, 9 1/2 In. 330.00
Old Nectar Bourbon, Fritz Thies, Denver, Colo., Tooled Top 415.00
Old Orkney Scotch, Stromness Distillery, Scotland, Jug, Cobalt Over White, 7 7/8 In. . . .   95.00
Old Phil Lacy Whiskey, Treadwell & Co., S.F., Cal., Amber, Tooled Top, 1905-1906 . . .   230.00
Old Poplar Log Corn, M. Markstein, Full Quart, Aqua, Label, 1880-1890, 9 1/2 In. 95.00
Old Prentice, Enamel, Bell Shape, Backbar, Stopper 150.00
Old Quaker, Embossed, Back Label, Tax Stamp, Screw Cap, ABM 20.00
Old Scotch Liqueur, Jolly Mariners, Jug, Cream, Brown Wreath, Floral Design, 6 5/8 In.   105.00
Old Scotch Malt, Rosslyn Distillery, Jug, Tan, Light Brown Glaze, Handle, 1910, 7 In.   .   200.00
Old Silver Lake, Cylindrical, Ribbed, Backbar, Porcelain Stopper 125.00
Old Sour Mash R. Brand & Co., Toledo, Ohio, Stoneware, Blue Transfer, Qt. 60.00
Old Tarr, Sample 35.00
Old Taylor, Premier Kentucky Whiskey, Kansas City, Mo., Backbar, 1890-1900 . . . .   60.00
Old Tom Parker, Kolb & Denhard, San Francisco, Amber, Tooled Mouth, Fifth 880.00
On The Square Paducah Distilleries Co., Paducah, Kentucky, Jug, Stoneware, Gal. . .   200.00
Our Choice Old Bourbon, Hencken & Schroder, Amber, Tooled Top, Fifth 360.00
Owl Club, Lexington, Ky., Amber, Fifth 75.00
Owl Weber, Nevada City, Cal., Sun Colored Amethyst, 1900, 7 3/4 In. 145.00
P. Chlolero Wholesale Liquor, 1487 19th St., Denver, Colo., Jug, Stoneware, Gal. 150.00
P. Hogan Pure Liquors, South St. & St. Mary, Amber, Flask, Strap, 1/2 Pt. 20.00
P.H. Goldberg, N.Y., Jug, 1/2 Gal. 70.00
P.J. Desmond Pure Liquors, Part St., Lawrence, Mass., Amber, Strap Side, Qt. 135.00
P.J. Murray's Saloon, Jug, Stoneware, Tan Top, Brown Base, Screw Cap, 5 In. 305.00
Paul Jones, Amber, Bulbous, 4 1/8 In. . . . . .20.00 to 35.00
Paul Jones, Amber, Bulbous, 9 1/4 In. 10.00
Paul Jones 4 Roses, Amber, Embossed, Qt. 15.00
Pennsylvania Club Pure Rye Whiskey, Jug, Porcelain, Green Transfer, 7 In. . . .240.00 to 440.00

Pennsylvania Club Pure Rye Whiskey, KTK, Jug, Maroon Transfer 170.00
Perfection Mfg. Co., Minneapolis, Minn., Jug, Gal. 65.00
Perrine Apple Ginger, Phila., Log Cabin, Medium Amber, 1890, 9 7/8 In. 220.00
Perrine Pure Barley Malt, Philadelphia, Amber 18.00
Petts Bald Eagle, Qt., 12 1/4 In. 20.00
Phoenix Old Bourbon, Naber, Alfs & Brune, S.F., Bird, Gold Amber, 1880-1885, Fifth   1540.00
Piedmont Hotel, Atlanta, Ga., Clear, Tooled Mouth, 1890-1900, 3 3/4 In. 90.00
Pipe Major, Jug, Kingsware, Doulton, England, 1910-1925, 8 3/8 In. 155.00
Pipe Major, Jug, Kingsware, Doulton, England, 1910-1930, 8 3/8 In. 185.00
Planters Old Nectar Monongahela, N.Y., Amber, Chestnut Shape, 1846-1855, 7 In. . . .   470.00
PM Deluxe Blended Whiskey, For Display Purpose Only, Amber, Label, 24 1/2 In. . . .   55.00
Pointer, Maryland, Rye & Gottschalk Co., Baltimore, Md., Jug, Cream, Brown Transfer .   300.00
Potts & Potts, Atlanta, Ga., Medium Amber, 1870-1880, 9 1/2 In. 265.00
Pullman, Ferdinand Westheimer Sons, Jug, Pottery, Cream, Brown, 9 1/8 In. 1540.00
Pullman, Hand Made Sour Mash, 7 Years Old, Flask, Pumpkinseed, 4 1/2 In. 85.00
Pure Old Brandy For Medicinal Use, Yellow Apricot, Label, Fifth 80.00
Pure Old Maryland Rye, Jug, Limoges 250.00
Pure Rye Trade Mark, Gold Yellow Amber, Applied Mouth, 1920, 24 1/2 In. 130.00
Pure White Lily Rye, KTK, Jug 150.00
R.B. Cutter, Louisville, Ky., Gold Amber, Handle, OP, 1855-1870, 8 3/4 In. 415.00
R.B. Cutter, Louisville, Ky., Jug, Pear Shape, Amber, Pontil, 8 1/2 In. . . . . .230.00 to 255.00
R.B. Cutter Pure Bourbon, Deep Amber, Applied Handle, 1870, 8 1/2 In. . . . . .220.00 to 275.00
R.H. Parker Rye N.M., Uri & Co., Louisville, Ky., Jug, Stoneware, Brown, Tan, 1/2 Pt. .   50.00
Ramsay's Trade Mark Superior Scotch Malt, Jug, Pottery, Cream, Brown, 7 3/8 In. . .   110.00
Red Top Rye, Flask, Amber, 1/2 Pt. 15.00
Red Top Rye, Flask, Amber, Pt. . . . . .10.00 to 15.00
Red Top Rye, Flask, Amethyst, Pt. 15.00
Rheinstrom Bros., Cincinnati, USA, Amber, Cream De Cocoa 65.00
Richmond Club, White Enamel, Backbar, Pt. 30.00
Ridgeway Straight Corn Whiskey, H.L. Sprinkle Dist., Jacksonville, Fla. 110.00
Rieger & Lindley, Salt Lake City, Amber Neck, Cream Body, Handle, 1900, 9 1/2 In. . . .   180.00
Rob Roy Old Highland, K. McGregor & Co., Glasgow, Jug, Cream, 6 3/4 In. . . .105.00 to 175.00
Rocko Ryo Beverage, Cleveland, Ohio, ABM, Front & Back Label, Qt. 25.00
Roderick Dhu Old Highland Whisky, Glasgow, Jug, Pottery, Cream, 1900, 8 In. 120.00
Rohrer's, Lancaster, Pa., Amber, IP 195.00
Rooney's Malt, Vertical Script Whiskey, BIMAL, 12 In. 15.00
Rosenbaum Bros. Old Kentucky Whiskies, Louisville, Ky., Pig, Figural, Pottery 500.00
Rosslyn Distillery, Old Scotch Malt, 2 Stags On Barrel, Jug, Cream, Brown, 7 1/8 In. . .   185.00
Rosslyn Distillery, Old Scotch Malt, Jug, Cream, Brown, Cobalt Transfer, 1900, 7 In. . .   144.00
Roth & Co., San Francisco, Red Amber, Fifth 415.00
Rye, Quinn's Quality Quantity, Kansas City, Mo., Jug, Stoneware, Black, Gal. 155.00
Rye, Red Amber, Metal Inlay, Pewter-Covered Handle & Mouth, Chestnut, 6 1/4 In. 65.00
S. Grabfelder & Co. Distiller's, Louisville, Ky., Square, 7 1/4 In. 10.00
S. Perkins & Co., Barrel, Yellow Amber, Ground Lip, 1900-1920, 18 7/8 In. 195.00
S.B. Rothenberg & Co., Old Judge Kentucky Bourbon, Amber, Tooled Top 130.00
S.B. Rothenberg Old Judge Kentucky Bourbon, Red Amber, Applied Top 400.00
S.M. & Co., Old Velvet Brandy, Medium Amber, Rib, Medallion Seal, 10 In. 690.00
S.T. Suit, Suitland, Md., Little Brown Jug, Stoneware, Brown, 1880, 7 1/4 In. 220.00
Saffell's Fine Wines & Liquors, Frankfort, Ky., Jug, Cream, 1/2 Gal. 110.00
Sam Schmalhausen Wholesale Wines & Liquors, Chicago, Ill., Jug, Stoneware 140.00
Samuel Bros. & Co., Louisville, Ky., San Francisco, Orange Amber, Fifth 465.00
Schiedam Aromatic Ajentes Dominques Nueva York Schnapps, Olive Amber 220.00
Schiedam Aromatic Schnapps, Black, 9 1/2 In. 40.00
Schiedam Balsamic Schnapps, Citron 65.00
Schlesinger & Bender, Inc., Pure California Wines & Brandies, San Francisco, Cal. . . .   25.00
Scotch Whisky Long John's Celebrated Dew Of Ben-Nevis, Jug, Cream, 7 1/4 In. .   215.00
Season, Union Hotel, Angiolini & Co., Nevada City, Ca., Clear, 1900-1915, 10 1/4 In. . .   50.00
Senior & Co. Inc., Curacao, N.W.I. Curacao Liqueur, 4 In. 15.00
Shamrock, Cream Of Irish Whiskey, Jug, Pottery, Cream, Brown, 8 7/8 In. 95.00
Showell Fryer & Co., Philadelphia, Aqua, Etched, Qt. 20.00
Silkwood, Laventhal Bros., San Francisco, Ca., Amber, Tooled Lip, 12 In. 155.00
Silver Tip Whiskey, Big Spring Distilling Co., Louisville, Ky., Flask, 6 1/2 In. 20.00

Simon Lewis Wholesale Wines & Liquor, Rock Island, Ill., Gal. 230.00
Smokine, Alfred Andersen & Co., Minneapolis, Winnipeg, Cabin, Red Amber, Pt. 165.00 to 195.00
Smokine, Imported & Bottled By Alfred Andersen & Co., Log Cabin, Amber, 6 5/8 In. . .   100.00
Sontaw's Old Cabinet, Medium Amber, Applied Mouth, Seal, 1860-1870, 8 3/4 In. 180.00
Spears & Co. Old Pioneer Whiskey, Fenkhausen, Bear, Tooled 475.00
Splaine's Unmixed Parkwood Club, Haverhill, Mass., Jug, Stoneware, Cream, Qt. . . .   200.00
Spring Lake, KTK, Jug, Maroon 90.00
Spring Lake Hand Made Sour Mash, Klein Brothers, Jug, Pottery, Purple, 7 3/8 In. . .   185.00
Spring Lake Hand Made Sour Mash, Klein Brothers, Jug, Pottery, Teal Blue, 7 1/2 In.   145.00
Spruance Stanley & Co., Horseshoe, Star On Base, Red Amber, Applied Top 305.00
Spruance Stanley & Co., San Francisco, Medium Yellow Amber, 1885-1905, 12 In. . . .   195.00
Spruance Stanley Wholesale Liquor Dealers, San Francisco, 1890s, Fifth . . .210.00 to 330.00
Star, Flask, Gold Amber, Screw Top, 1885, 7 In. 45.00
Starbright, Kansas City 35.00
Stoddard Ale, 3-Piece Mold, Olive Amber 45.00
Stone Brook, 3-Piece Glob Top, Cylindrical, 12 In. 15.00
Straight Whiskey, Kansas City, Mo. 35.00
Superior Bourbon, Stoddard, Gold Amber, Gold Amber, Label, Fifth 325.00
Superior Old Pa. Pure Rye, Phila., Olive Amber, Applied Mouth, 1846, 9 3/4 In. 65.00
Swallow Bros., Norristown, Pa., 11 1/2 In. 40.00
Sweet Mash Corn, Atlantic Coast Distilling Co., Jacksonville, Fla., Jug, 1/2 Pt. 75.00
Tappit Hen Hawthorn Dew, Thom & Cameron Limited, Jug, Pottery, 7 1/2 In. 120.00
Taylor & Williams Whiskey, Louisville, Ky., Cylindrical, 4 3/4 In. 40.00
Taylor Brothers & Co., Glasgow & London, Tan, Born Glaze, Handle, Jug, 1910, 8 In. .   130.00
Teakettle Bourbon, Corset Waist, Blue, White Ground, White Lettering, 1900, 11 In. . .   415.00
Teakettle Old Bourbon, Gold Amber, Tooled Top 470.00
Theo. Blauth & Sons Co., Sacramento, Calif., Amber, Fifth 210.00
Theodore Netter, Greeting, 1232 Market St., Phila., P.A., Barrel, Cobalt Blue, 5 7/8 In.   275.00
Theodore Netter, Phil., Barrel, Cobalt Blue, 4 In. 400.00
Thomas Taylor & Co., P. Vollmers Old Bourbon, Louisville, Ky., Amber, Fifth . .220.00 to 275.00
Topic Bar, Glenwood Springs, Colo., Jug, Gal. 300.00
Torrey's, Mt. Verno, Red Amber, Qt., 12 3/8 In. 20.00
Truet Jones & Arrington Etchelberger Dew Drop, Amber, Urn Shape, Bubbles, Qt. . 1700.00
Turner Brothers, New York, Barrel, Olive Green, Applied Mouth, 9 3/4 In. 240.00
Turner Brothers, New York, Barrel, Root Beer Amber, Square Collar, 9 7/8 In. 130.00
U.S. Eagle Mail, Mailbox, Tooled Mouth, Label, 1880-1900, 9 In. 255.00
Udolpho Wolfe's Aromatic Schnapps, Amber, Applied Top, 7 1/2 In. 45.00
Udolpho Wolfe's Aromatic Schnapps, Citron, 9 1/2 In. 120.00
Udolpho Wolfe's Aromatic Schnapps, Green, IP, 7 1/2 In. 95.00
Udolpho Wolfe's Aromatic Schnapps, Lime Green, 9 In. 50.00
Udolpho Wolfe's Aromatic Schnapps, Medium Olive Amber, 1855, 9 In. . . . . .100.00 to 120.00
Udolpho Wolfe's Aromatic Schnapps, Medium Olive Green, 9 In. . . . . .25.00 to 75.00
Udolpho Wolfe's Aromatic Schnapps, Olive Amber, IP, 9 1/2 In. 85.00
Udolpho Wolfe's Aromatic Schnapps, Olive Green, 8 1/4 In. 40.00
Udolpho Wolfe's Aromatic Schnapps, Olive Green, 10 In. 80.00
Udolpho Wolfe's Aromatic Schnapps, Olive Green, Label, 9 3/4 In. 120.00
Udolpho Wolfe's Aromatic Schnapps, Pink Puce, 1870, 8 1/4 In. 525.00
Udolpho Wolfe's Aromatic Schnapps, Yellow Amber, 10 In. . . . . .50.00 to 140.00
Udolpho Wolfe's Aromatic Schnapps, Yellow Green, Square, 9 1/2 In. . . . . .30.00 to 90.00
Udolpho Wolfe's Aromatic Schnapps, Yellow Olive IP, 1845-1855, 8 In. 470.00
Udolpho Wolfe's Aromatic Schnapps Scheidam, Yellow, 8 In. . . . . .40.00 to 60.00
Van Bergen & Co., Gold Dust, Ky. Bourbon, Aqua Gold Dust, Fifth 1430.00
Van Brunt's Aromatic Schnapps, Deep Olive, Forest Green, 1860-1870, 10 In. 130.00
Vess Champagne Drylime Rickey, Green, Label, Qt. 30.00
Vess Dry, Green, Shaker Bottle, Tin Lid, Embossed, Qt. 40.00
VM & EA, Whitlock & Co., New York, Apricot Puce, 1855-1865, 9 In. 130.00
Voldner's Aromatic Schnapps, Olive Green, IP, 10 In. 90.00
Vonthofen's Aromatic Schnapps, Applied Mouth, Deep Green, 9 In. 330.00
Vonthofen's Aromatic Schnapps, Green, IP, Square, 8 In. 125.00
Vonthofen's Schnapps, Teal, Pontil 50.00
W & A Giblely, Silver Stream Schnapps, Black, 9 In. 40.00
W. & Co. Cognac, Medium Amber, Applied Mouth, Handle, 1860-1870, 5 3/4 In. 660.00

W.D. Winsop, Star, Olive Amber, Double Collar, Seal, Squat, Qt. 75.00
W.J. Van Schuyver & Co., Portland, Yellow Amber, Tooled Screw Thread, Fifth 220.00
W.N. Walton's, Pat. Sept. 23, 1862, Indented Label Panel, Etched Flowers, Backbar, Qt. . 50.00
Weeks & Gilson, Stoddard, N.H., Yellow Amber, Applied Mouth, 1873, 12 In. 265.00
Weeks Glass Works, Embossed Base, Yellow Amber, Olive Tone, 1860-1870, 11 In. . . 220.00
Weeks Glass Works, Stoddard, N.H., Gold Amber, Applied Mouth, 1870, 11 1/2 In. . . . 135.00
Weeks Glass Works, Stoddard, N.H., Red Amber, Cylindrical, Ring Mouth, 11 1/2 In. . . 230.00
Weil Bros., Standard Old Bourbon, Amber, 1878-1885, Fifth 880.00
Weller Sons Distillers, Louisville, Rectangular, Qt. 15.00
West End Wine & Spirits Co., 15-19 Leverett St., Boston, Mass., Rectangular, 8 1/4 In. 15.00
Westmoreland County Whiskey, Jug, Cream, Cobalt Letters, Applied Handle, 3 In. . . 525.00
Wharton's, Chestnut Grove, Amber, Applied Double Collar Mouth, 1865, 5 3/8 In. 205.00
Wharton's, Chestnut Grove, Flask, Teardrop, Amber, 5 1/4 In. . . . . .200.00 to 325.00
Wharton's, Chestnut Grove, Sapphire Blue, Applied Double Collar Mouth, 1870, 5 In. . . 165.00
Wharton's, Chestnut Grove, Teardrop, Cobalt Blue, Applied Mouth, 5 1/2 In. 360.00
White Lily Pure Rye, S.B. & Co., Blue, Yellow Transfer, Jug, 1910, 7 1/2 In. 144.00
White Lily Pure Rye, S.B. & Co., K.T. & K. China, Green, Yellow Transfer, 7 3/8 In. . . . 116.00
Whitney Glass Works, Orange Amber, Cylindrical Base 20.00
Wicklow Distillery, Old Irish, Cream, Light Brown, Black Transfer, Handle, Jug, 8 In. . . 305.00
Will Lea, Bristol, Tenn., Cream, Gal. 150.00
William A. Hentz & Co., Stylus Club Whiskey, Philadelphia, Pa., 12 1/4 In. 15.00
William Jameson & Co. Whisky Distillers, Dublin, Jug, Pottery, Tan, Brown, 7 3/8 In. 305.00
Wintersmith, Louisville, Ky., Oval, Strap Side, Double Collar, 1/2 Pt. 6.00
Wise's Old Irish, Cream, Brown Glaze, Black Transfer, Handle, Jug, 1900, 8 In. 105.00
Wise's Old Irish, Cream, Brown Neck, Maroon Transfer, Handle, Jug, 7 In. 144.00
Wise's Old Irish, Dragons & Shamrock Stencil . . . . .85.00 to 130.00
Wise's Old Irish, Trademark, Jug, Cream, Brown, Sepia Transfer, Ireland, 7 3/8 In. 230.00
Wise's Old Irish, White, Brown Glaze Neck, Handle, Jug, England, 1915, 7 In. 100.00
Wm. Davison Liquor Dealer, Fresno, Cal., Flask, Outside Threads, Flint Color, 1/2 Pt. . 46.00
Wm. Edwards & Co. Pure Rye, Cleveland, Oh., Cream, Black Transfer, 1910, 11 1/4 In. 190.00
Wm. H. Spears & Co., Embossed Bear, c.1890 . . . . 6270.00
Wm. H. Spears & Co., San Francisco, Pale Straw Tone, Applied Mouth, 1893, 12 In. . . . 550.00
Wm. H. Spears & Co., San Francisco, Pale Straw, Tooled Lip, 1875-1893, 12 1/8 In. . . . 385.00
Wm. Watson & Co., Oakland, Cal., Red Amber, Tooled Top, Inside Threads 35.00
Wm. White & Sons, Wholesale Straight Whiskey House, Stoneware, Gal. 65.00
Wolf, Wreden & Co., Peerless Whiskey, Medium Orange Gold, 12 In. 440.00
Wolf, Wreden & Co., San Francisco, Medium Yellow Amber, In Slug Plate, 12 In. 330.00
Wolter's Bros. & Co., Red Amber, 1880-1895, 11 1/2 In. 880.00
Wolter's Bros. & Co., San Francisco, Gold Amber, Glob Top, 1895, 12 In. . . . .2050.00 to 2260.00
Wolter's Bros. & Co., San Francisco, Medium Yellow Amber, Orange Tone, 1895, 12 In. 330.00
Yellow Olive, Stoddard Type Magnum, 11 In. 40.00
YPM, In Banner, Cylindrical, Amber 5.00

——————————————— **WILD TURKEY** ———————————————

Wild Turkey is a brand of bourbon made by Austin Nichols Distillery. The company says the bourbon was originally made as a gift for some hunting companions and so was named for their favorite gamebird. A crystal bottle with an etched flying turkey design was made in 1951. The company made turkey-shaped ceramic bottles from 1971 to 1989. The first bottle, filled with bourbon, sold for $20. In 1981 the company added miniature bottles. For a short time during the 1980s, the company marketed a line of *go-withs* such as plates and plaques. After 1989, Wild Turkey sold two limited-edition bottles: a Rare Breed Whiskey bottle in a teardrop shape, which is still made, and a Kentucky Legend decanter shaped like a violin, which is no longer in production. Since mid-1994, under the Rare Breed label, Austin Nichols & Co. Distillery has issued a Kentucky Spirit, single barrel bourbon in a distinctive bottle with a pewter-style top, available year-round in a gift box. Wild Turkey figural decanters are no longer being made.

WILD TURKEY, Decanter, Baccarat, Crystal, 1979 . . . . 226.00
  Decanter, Wedgwood, 1 Liter 215.00
  Series I, No. 1, Standing, Male, 1971 . . . . 180.00
  Series I, No. 1, Standing, Male, 1981, Miniature 1802.00
  Series I, No. 2, On Log, Female, 1972 . . . . 115.00

Series 1, No. 2, On Log, Female, 1981, Miniature 100.00
Series 1, No. 3, On Wing, 1973 .... 60.00
Series 1, No. 3, On Wing, 1982, Miniature 60.00
Series 1, No. 4, With Poult, 1974 .... 44.00
Series 1, No. 4, With Poult, 1982, Miniature 43.00
Series 1, No. 5, With Flags, 1975 .... 30.00
Series 1, No. 5, With Flags, 1983, Miniature 30.00
Series 1, No. 6, Striding, 1976 ....*Illus* 24.00
Series 1, No. 6, Striding, 1983, Miniature 26.00
Series 1, No. 7, Taking Off, 1977 ....*Illus* 32.00
Series 1, No. 7, Taking Off, 1983, Miniature 25.00
Series 1, No. 8, Strutting, 1978 .... 40.00
Series 1, No. 8, Strutting, 1983, Miniature 40.00
Series 2, No. 1, Lore, 1979 .... 30.00
Series 2, No. 2, Lore, 1980 .... 32.00
Series 2, No. 3, Lore, 1981 .... 40.00
Series 2, No. 4, Lore, 1982 .... 41.00
Series 3, No. 1, In Flight, 1983 .... 92.00
Series 3, No. 1, In Flight, 1984, Miniature 25.00
Series 3, No. 2, With Bobcat, 1983 .... 100.00
Series 3, No. 2, With Bobcat, 1985, Miniature 25.00
Series 3, No. 3, Turkeys Fighting, 1983 .... 140.00
Series 3, No. 3, Turkeys Fighting, 1983, Miniature 25.00
Series 3, No. 4, With Eagle, 1984 .... 90.00
Series 3, No. 4, With Eagle, 1984, Miniature 35.00
Series 3, No. 5, With Raccoon, 1984 .... 85.00
Series 3, No. 5, With Raccoon, 1984, Miniature 25.00
Series 3, No. 6, With Poult, 1984 ....70.00 to 78.00
Series 3, No. 6, With Poult, 1984, Miniature 20.00
Series 3, No. 7, With Fox, 1984, Miniature ....*Illus* 25.00
Series 3, No. 7, With Fox, 1985 .... 85.00
Series 3, No. 8, With Owl, 1985 .... 80.00
Series 3, No. 8, With Owl, 1985, Miniature 25.00
Series 3, No. 9, With Bear Cubs, 1985 .... 83.00
Series 3, No. 9, With Bear Cubs, 1985, Miniature 30.00
Series 3, No. 10, With Coyote, 1986 .... 80.00
Series 3, No. 10, With Coyote, 1986, Miniature 25.00
Series 3, No. 11, With Falcon, 1986 .... 90.00
Series 3, No. 11, With Falcon, 1986, Miniature 35.00
Series 3, No. 12, With Skunk, 1986 .... 95.00
Series 3, No. 12, With Skunk, 1986, Miniature 35.00
Series 4, No. 1, Habitat, Female, 1988 .... 100.00
Series 4, No. 1, Habitat, Female, 1988, Miniature 50.00
Series 4, No. 2, Habitat, 1989 .... 115.00
Series 4, No. 2, Habitat, 1989, Miniature 50.00

Wild Turkey, Series 1, No. 6,
Striding, 1976

Wild Turkey, Series 1, No. 7,
Taking Off, 1977

Wild Turkey, Series 3, No. 7,
With Fox, 1984, Miniature

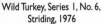

Wine, Borghini Lacrima
Christi, White Wine, Cat,
Paper Label On Back, 12 In.

Wine, Blanc D'Oro
Champagne,
Always Elvis,
12 1/2 In.

Wine, Embossed
Grapes And
Vines, Screw
Top, 1/2 Gal.

WINE

Wine has been bottled since the days of the ancient Greeks. Wine bottles have been made in a variety of sizes and shapes. Seal bottles were used from the second century and are listed in their own section in this book. Most wines found today are in the standard shapes that have been used for the past 125 years. The Bordeaux shape has square shoulders and straight sides while the Burgundy shape is broader with sloping shoulders. The German or Rhine wine flute bottle is tall and thin. Other wines, such as champagne, are bottled in slightly different bottles.

WINE, Alloa Glass Work Co., Scotland, 3-Piece Mold, Yellow Olive, 1830-1860, 8 1/2 In.	360.00
Baxter's Old Nauvoo Brand Wines, Jug, 1/2 Pt.	100.00
Blanc D'Oro Champagne, Always Elvis, 12 1/2 In. ....*Illus*	15.00
Blown, Amber, Applied Top, OP, 1760s	200.00
Blown, Dark Amber, Applied Top, Sandy Pontil, c.1810	65.00
Blown, Olive, Long Neck, Laid On Ring, Tubular Pontil, c.1760	130.00
Borghini Lacrima Christi, White Wine, Cat, Paper Label On Back, 12 In. ....*Illus*	35.00
Bowen & Schram Distributors, San Francisco, Ca., Yellow Olive, 1910, 5 In.	70.00
Champagne, Black Glass, 3-Piece Mold, Applied Top, IP	55.00
Cobalt Blue, Cone, Flat Stopper, 1840-1860, 12 In.	195.00
Decanter, 3-Piece Mold, Stopper, 8 1/2 In.	495.00
Dutch, c.1720, 7 1/2 In.	145.00
E.B. Gibson Fine Wines & Liquors, Jug, Stoneware, Cream, 1880s, 3 1/8 In.	385.00
Embossed Grapes And Vines, Screw Top, 1/2 Gal. ....*Illus*	7.00
Goldberg, Bowen & Co., San Francisco, Tooled Lip, 1905, 11 In.	120.00
H.B. Kirk & Co., New York, Blue Aqua, Label, Tooled Mouth, 1890, 7 7/8 In.	220.00
Hemmings Ales, Wines & Liquors, Tooled Mouth, 1890-1910, Pt.	145.00
J.H. Anderson, Oporto, Black Glass	25.00
Jas. Tharp's Sons Wines & Liquors, Washington, D.C., Amber Strap, Pt.	125.00
London White Dinner, Bottle In Woven Basket Shape, Applied Handle, 11 1/2 In. .15.00 to 20.00	
Madeira, Amber, Backbar, Label Under Glass	95.00
Marachino F. Droli Zara, Sea Green, Crude, Seal, Croatia, 10 1/2 In.	65.00
Marachino Magazzino Zara, 2 Headed Eagle, Seal	100.00
Middle Temple, Blown, Shoulder Seal, 1840, 11 1/2 In.	145.00
Miniature, see the Miniature category	
N.B. Jacobs, San Francisco, Yellow Amber, Applied String Lip, 1870-1890, 13 1/4 In.	415.00
Olive Amber, Applied String Lip, Gilt Letter S, Pontil, England, 1798, 8 1/8 In.	330.00
Olive Amber, Cylindrical, Tubular Pontil, Deep Kick-Up, France, 13 In.	100.00
Olive Green, Applied String Rim, Bulbous, Pontil, England, 1660, 5 1/2 In.	3300.00
Onion, Dark Olive Green, Sheared Mouth, Squat, Marked CP, 1697, 5 In.	9900.00
Onion, Yellow Olive, Painted War Ships Under Fire, Coat Of Arms, Netherlands, 9 1/4 In.	990.00
Porter Type, c.1780, 10 3/4 In.	145.00
W. Gilmore, Pavilion, N.Y., Cornflower Blue, Champagne Top, Pt.	55.00
Yellow Green, Enamel Bar Scene, Flattened Egg Shape, Long Neck, 12 3/4 In.	100.00

ZANESVILLE

The Zanesville Manufacturing Company started making glass in Zanesville, Ohio, in 1815. This glassworks closed in 1838 but reopened from 1842 to 1851. The company made many types of blown and mold blown pieces. At least one other glassworks operated in Zanesville from 1816 to the 1840s. The products of all the Zanesville factories are sometimes identified as *Midwestern* glass and are grouped with pieces made in Mantua, Kent, Ravenna, and other Ohio towns. The blown glass pieces include diamond patterned and ribbed pieces in clear, blue, amethyst, aquamarine, and amber colored glass. Collectors prize the Zanesville swirl pieces and identify them as *right* or *left* swirl.

ZANESVILLE, 24 Ribs, Swirled To Left, Deep Amber, Rolled Lip, 1820-1830, 7 7/8 In. . . .	525.00
24 Swirled Ribs, Amber, Applied Lip, 9 1/4 In.	1045.00
24 Swirled Ribs, Amber, Globular, 7 1/2 In.	550.00
24 Swirled Ribs, Aqua, 7 3/8 In.	95.00
24 Swirled Ribs, Aqua, Globular, 7 1/2 In.	155.00
24 Swirled Ribs, Aqua, Globular, 7 3/4 In.	95.00
24 Swirled Ribs, Citron, Applied Lip, 7 3/4 In.	880.00
24 Swirled Ribs, Honey Olive, Applied Lip, 7 3/4 In.	1290.00
24 Swirled Ribs, Honey Olive, Applied Lip, 8 3/8 In.	550.00
24 Vertical Ribs, Amber, Grandfather's Type, 9 In.	495.00
24 Vertical Ribs, Gold Amber, Globular, 9 In.	1155.00
Aqua, Globular, Kick-Up, 10 3/4 In.	80.00
Chestnut, 10 Diamonds, Gold Amber, 5 1/2 In.	935.00
Chestnut, 24 Vertical Ribs, Amber, 5 5/8 In.	220.00
Chestnut, 24 Vertical Ribs, Amber, Large Bubbles, 5 In.	220.00

GO-WITHS

There are many items that interest the bottle collector even though they are not bottles: all types of advertising that picture bottles or endorse bottled products like whiskey or beer, many small items like bottle openers or bottle caps, and related products by well-known companies like trays and plaques. Collectors call all of these *go-withs*. A variety of the items are listed here. Many others can be found under company names in other price lists such as *Kovels' Antiques & Collectibles Price List.* Clubs and publications that will help collectors are listed in the bibliography and club list in this book.

GO-WITHS, Ashtray, Gallagher & Burton, Philadelphia, Fine Whiskies, Bottle, Tin, 4 1/2 In.	65.00
Ashtray, Green River Whiskey, She Was Bred In Old Kentucky, Metal, 1930s	125.00
Ashtray, King George IV Whiskey, Spittoon Shape, 3-Footed, Copper, 2 3/4 In.	55.00
Bag, Snow Peak Dairy, Albany, Ore., Paper, Handle, Holds 2 Qt. Bottles	1.00
Bag Rack, Coca-Cola, Take Enough Home Today, Embossed, c.1940s, 17 x 36 In.	660.00
Bag Rack Cover, Drink Pepsi-Cola, Bigger, Better, Pepsi Cops, 13 x 24 In.	1495.00
Bank, Coca-Cola, Drink Machine, Tin, 1940s-1950s, 4 In.	65.00
Bill Of Lading, Coca-Cola Bottling Company, Newark, Ohio, For 1932 Calendars	15.00
Billfold, Dwight Soda Co., Leather	35.00
Billhead, Joseph Beckett & Co., Chemists & Druggists, Toronto, 1851, 8 1/2 x 11 In. . . .	20.00
Blotter, K.D.C., The Greatest Cure Of The Age, Canada, 1890-1910, 3 3/4 x 8 In.	25.00
Booklet, $100 Reward For Any Case Hall's Catarrh Cure Will Not Cure, 1890	15.00
Booklet, California Magic With Cottage Cheese, California Dairy Industry, 1956	6.00
Booklet, Coca-Cola, Vendorlator Model 242 Drink Machine Service Manual	15.00
Booklet, Dairying Bygones, Arthur Ingram, History Of Dairying, Pictures, 1977	3.00
Booklet, De Laval Sterling Speedway Milker, Canada, Instruction, 8 x 11 In.	10.00
Booklet, Directions, Economy King Cream Separators, 5 1/2 x 8 1/2 In.	25.00

Go-Withs, Bottle Art, Pepsi-Cola, Stretched And Filled With Colored Water, 24 In.

Go-Withs, Bottle Opener, Corkscrew, Cast Iron, Andress Tool, Pat. 1875, 5 1/2 In.

Go-Withs, Bottle Cover, Poodle, Crocheted, Pompons, Button Eyes, 7 1/2 In.

Go-Withs, Bottle Opener, Mallet, Measuring
Jigger, Chrome, 6 1/4 In.

Go-Withs, Bottle Opener,
Horse's Rear End, Pot
Metal, Rubal, N.Y., 5 1/2 In.

Go-Withs, Bottle Opener, Shady Lady
At Lamppost, Cast Iron, 4 1/4 In.

Booklet, Dr. Chase's New Receipt Book, Toronto, 1889	30.00
Booklet, Dr. Chase's Recipes Or Information For Every Body, Ann Arbor, Mich., 1881	20.00
Booklet, Dr. Chase's Third, Last & Complete Household Physician, 1895, 865 Pages	40.00
Booklet, Dr. Foote's Plain Home Talk Embracing Medical Common Sense, 1888	25.00
Booklet, Dr. Pierce's Common Sense Medical Advice	30.00
Booklet, Humphrey's Manual, 1948	25.00
Booklet, I.W. Harper Whiskey, 1914, Pocket	9.00
Booklet, Lydia E. Pinkham's Private Text-Book, Ailments Peculiar To Women, 79 Pages	30.00
Booklet, Recipe, Elsie Borden, World's Fair, 1939	22.00
Booklet, Uses Of Elliman's Embrocation, For Horses, Dogs, Birds, Cattle, 1902	35.00
Bookmark, Coca-Cola, Owl Reading Book, Celluloid, 1906, 1 1/2 x 3 1/8 In.	750.00
Bottle Art, Pepsi-Cola, Stretched And Filled With Colored Water, 24 In. ....*Illus*	10.00
Bottle Cap, 3V Cola, Red On Yellow, Cork Lined	3.00
Bottle Cap, Ace High, Red On White	2.00
Bottle Cap, Artificial Lemon-Lime Soda, Green On Yellow, Cork Lined	2.00
Bottle Cap, Canada Dry Black Cherry Beverage, CD Logo, Red, Silver, Green	2.00
Bottle Cap, Canada Dry Hi-Grape Ale, CD Logo, Green, Silver, & Red, Cork Lined	2.00
Bottle Cap, Coca Cream Soda, Brown On Cream, Corked Lined	3.00
Bottle Cap, Corky, Clown Picture, Red, Cream & Blue, Corked Lined	5.00
Bottle Cap, Cream & Milk Separator, The Derby, Round Lake, N.Y., Metal	20.00
Bottle Cap, Frostie Root Beer, Red On Silver, Cork Lined	2.00
Bottle Cap, Ginger Beer, Yellow On Red, Cork Lined	2.00
Bottle Cap, Haleakala Dairy, Kahului, Maui, Hawaii, Mountain Fresh Milk, Blue, Yellow	.10
Bottle Cap, Hires Root Beer, Brown, White & Orange, Cork Lined	3.00
Bottle Cap, Imitation Grape Soda, Cream On Purple, Cork Lined	2.00
Bottle Cap, Kist Imitation Pineapple Soda, Silver, Black & Yellow, Cork Lined	5.00
Bottle Cap, Lemmy, Yellow On Black, Cork Lined	5.00
Bottle Cap, Lemon Benzoate Soda, Horace Horsecollar, Black, Red, Yellow, 1930s	60.00
Bottle Cap, MarBert Cola, Please Daddy, Red On Yellow, Cork Lined	5.00
Bottle Cap, Scoffee Coffee Soda, Brown, Cream & Yellow, Coffee Cup Pictured	8.00
Bottle Cap, Sprite, Dark Green On Silver, Cork Lined	2.00
Bottle Cover, Poodle, Crocheted, Pompons, Button Eyes, 7 1/2 In. ....*Illus*	15.00
Bottle Opener, Corkscrew, Cast Iron, Andress Tool, Pat. 1875, 5 1/2 In. ....*Illus*	75.00
Bottle Opener, Drink B-1 & Orange Crush, Dillon-Routt Co., Jackson, Dyersburg, Tenn.	20.00
Bottle Opener, Drink Coca-Cola, Chrome, Painted Red Cap Catcher, c.1950s	55.00
Bottle Opener, Full Woman Nude, 6 3/4 In.	35.00
Bottle Opener, Horse's Rear End, Pot Metal, Rubal, N.Y., 5 1/2 In. ....*Illus*	50.00
Bottle Opener, Iroquois Bev. Corp., Buffalo, N.Y., Indian, Cast Metal, c.1950	30.00
Bottle Opener, Mallet, Measuring Jigger, Chrome, 6 1/4 In. ....*Illus*	12.00
Bottle Opener, Shady Lady At Lamppost, Cast Iron, 4 1/4 In. ....*Illus*	25.00
Bottle Opener, Teacher's Highland Cream Scotch Whiskey	25.00
Bottle Opener, The New Deal, Stamped Steel, 5 1/8 In. ....*Illus*	35.00
Bottle Topper, Dr. Pepper, Edith Luce, With Bottle	150.00
Bottle Topper, Dr. Pepper, Sandy Carleson, With Full Bottle	195.00

Bottle Topper, Hires For Finer Flavor, 5 Cents, Flowers 80.00
Bottle Topper, Hires, Healthful, Delicious, 5 Cents 80.00
Bottle Topper, Hires, So Good With Food, 5 Cents 80.00
Bottle Topper, Howdy, Reach For A Bottle, With Bottle 140.00
Bottle Topper, Mission Orange, Try This Delicious New Beverage, With Bottle 65.00
Bottle Topper, Smile, Your Favorite Beverage In Many Flavors, With Full Bottle 430.00
Bottle Topper, Thirsty Just Whistle, Smiling Girl, Holes For 3 Bottles, 1920s 265.00
Bottle Topper, Whistle, Girl's Head, Sipping Through Straw, With Bottle 175.00
Box, Borden Cheese, Wooden, 9 In. 6.00
Box, Carter's Ink, No. 11, Qt. 55.00
Box, Carter's Mucilage Ink, No. 343, 1 1/2 Oz. 30.00
Box, Hero Fruit Jar Co., Boyd's Porcelain Lined Cap & Rubbers, Wooden, 10 x 7 In. 70.00
Box, Kerr Economy Clamps 8.00
Box, Kerr Economy Lids 25.00
Box, Koontz Dairy Products, Tin, Hinged Lid, c.1950s-1960s, 12 1/2 x 13 1/2 In. 35.00
Box, Kraft Cheese, Wooden, Lettering, 2 Lb. 3.00
Box, Maynard & Noyl's Writing Ink, 3 Doz., Cone Ink, Wooden, 6 1/2 x 11 1/2 In. 130.00
Box, Mel-O-Bit, Cheese, Wooden, Great Atlantic & Pacific Tea Co., 9 In. 8.00
Box, Paul's Black Ink 40.00
Box, Sanford's Jet Black Ink, Qt. 40.00
Box, Use The Famous Granite State Spring Water & Tonics, Atkinson, N.H., Wooden ... 45.00
Box, White's Cheese, Wooden, Lettering, 3 Lb. 5.00
Box, Zoagiaine, Asthma Conqueror & Catarrh Cure, Knight, Dragon, 3 x 2 x 9 In. 15.00
Broadside, Dr. J. Bovee Dod's Imperial Remedy & Family Physician, 21 3/4 In. 65.00
Broom Holder, Land O'Lakes, Mankato Creamery Association, Metal 15.00
Brush, Hutchinson & Peterson, Bottle Stoppers & Bottlers' Supplies, Wood, 7 1/2 In. ... 25.00
Button, Golden Creme Farms, Metal, Mottled Green & Gold 1.00
Cabinet, De Laval Cream Separators, Oak, Tin, 4 Drawers, Hooks, 26 x 17 x 11 In. 550.00
Cabinet, Humphrey's Remedies, Wood, Tin, 35 Compartments, 29 x 20 x 7 In. 880.00
Cabinet, Putnam Fadeless Dye, Monroe Chemical Co., Tin Lithograph, 1930s-1940s 130.00
Cabinet, Sauer's Extracts, Wood, Glass Front, c.1910-1915, 12 x 26 x 7 In. 1065.00
Cake Chest, Avon, California Perfume Co., Cake Chest, Tin, 1938 .... 10.00
Calendar, 7-Up, Little Girl, Partial Pad, 1947, 10 x 20 In. 150.00
Calendar, Antikamnia Calendar, 1901, Heavy Paper, 24 x 18 In. 335.00
Calendar, Burnett's Floral Hand Book Ladies' Calendar, 1876, 42 Pg., 3 x 4 1/2 In. 15.00
Calendar, Coca-Cola, April 1903 Page, Matted, Frame, 7 1/4 x 10 1/8 In. 2760.00
Calendar, Coca-Cola, Betty With Bottle, June 1914 Page, Metal Strip, Loop, Frame 3795.00
Calendar, Coca-Cola, June 1908 Page, Frame, 7 x 14 In. 8280.00
Calendar, Glenshaw Glass Co., Inc., Woman Sitting By Water, 1920, 17 x 32 In. 85.00
Calendar, Hires Root Beer, 1893, 2 Girls With Cat, Complete, Unused, 9 x 7 In. 2475.00
Canister Set, Avon, Townhouse, 4 Piece 90.00
Cap, Soda Fountain, Enjoy Red Rock Cola, Cotton, White, Red & White Emblem 20.00
Card, Coca-Cola, Card Entitles You To The Contents Of One Bottle, 2 1/4 x 3 1/2 In. ... 20.00
Card, Playing, Coca-Cola, Airplane Spotter, Woman With Bottle, Deck, Box, 1943 ..... 65.00
Card, Playing, Dr. Harter's, Columbian Expo Buildings, 1892, Set 200.00
Card, Playing, Dr. Van Dyke's Holland Bitters, Box, Tax Stamp 155.00
Card, Playing, Nu-Grape Soda, 1926 .... 75.00
Card, Trade, Ayers Cathartic Pills, The Country Doctor, 1880s 20.00
Card, Trade, Bookmark, Dr. Hands Remedies, Baby's Face 15.00
Card, Trade, Burdock Blood Bitters, Kittens In Wicker Trunk 5.00
Card, Trade, C.K. Magee's Emulsion Of Pure Cod Liver Oil, c.1880, 6 1/4 x 4 3/8 In. ... 15.00
Card, Trade, Certain Cough Cure, Brookville, Ind., Winter Scene, Ducks, People 25.00
Card, Trade, Coca-Cola, Girl In Tub, Girl As Waitress, Folding, c.1907 .... 1430.00
Card, Trade, Dr. Kilmer's Indian Cough Cure Consumption Oil, Stricker & Swartz 35.00
Card, Trade, Dr. Kilmer's V. & O. Anointment 8.00
Card, Trade, Dr. Mettaurs Headache Pills 8.00
Card, Trade, Dr. Thomas Electric Oil 8.00
Card, Trade, Dr. Warner's Coraline, Corset, Pat. Nov. 1878 .... 15.00
Card, Trade, Hires Root Beer, Boy At Table, Say, Mama, I Want Another Glass 275.00
Card, Trade, Hood's Sarsaparilla, Girl, Barnum & Bailey On Reverse 7.00
Card, Trade, Hood's Sarsaparilla, Grover Cleveland, 1884 Campaign, 6 x 4 1/2 In. 15.00
Card, Trade, Hood's Sarsaparilla, James Blaine, 1884 Campaign, 6 x 4 1/2 In. 14.00
Card, Trade, Horsford Acid Phosphate 8.00

Card, Trade, Jayne's Tonic Vermifuge, Lake Preston, Dakota 20.00
Card, Trade, Masfields Capillaris 8.00
Carrier, Buy Pepsi-Cola, 6-Pack, Wooden, 1930s-40s 80.00
Carrier, Coca-Cola, 24-Pack, Individual Tubes, Cardboard, c.1940s 80.00
Carrier, Dr. Pepper, 6-Pack, Wire, Tin, 1930s-40s 605.00
Carrier, Drink Pepsi-Cola, 12 Full Glasses-72 Oz., Cardboard, 6 Bottles, 1930s 65.00
Carrier, Pepsi-Cola, Bigger, Better, Cardboard, 6 12-Oz. Bottles 80.00
Carrier, Pepsi-Cola, Hits The Spot, 6-Pack, 4 Bottles, 3 With Contents, 1930s-1940s 75.00
Carton, Kone Buttermilk, Waxed, Lid, Qt. 10.00
Case, Coussens Honey Of Tar Cough Killer, Metal, Wood, Glass, 26 x 22 In. 2200.00
Case, Milk, Oak, For 12 Qt. Bottles 25.00
Case, Milk, Oak, For 6-1/2 Gal. Bottles 15.00
Case, Sauer's Flavoring Extracts, Wood, Reverse Painted Glass, 20 x 15 In. 1430.00
Case, York Springs Water, O'Keefe's Beverages, Limited, Toronto, 20 x 12 x 12 3/4 In. .. 10.00
Chair, Coca-Cola, Metal, Folding Type 100.00
Chalkboard, Dad's Root Beer, Tastes Like Root Beer Should, Tin, 27 1/2 x 19 1/2 In. 220.00
Chalkboard, Nehi, Ice Cold, Gas Today, Tin, 1-Sided, Self-Framed, 4 1/2 x 15 In. 505.00
Chalkboard, Whistle, Elves, Tin, 1-Sided, 1948, 27 x 20 In. 825.00
Clamp, Millville, For Specimen Jar, 6 In. 20.00
Clock, 7-Up, You Like It, It Likes You, Plastic, Metal, Wood Frame, Square, 34 In. 255.00
Clock, Beverly Farms Milk, Light-Up, Metal, Glass, Square, 14 In. 165.00
Clock, Coca-Cola, Fishtail Logo, Green Ground, Square, Box, 1960s, 15 1/2 In. 460.00
Clock, Coca-Cola, Light-Up, Round Clock Face, Counter, 1950s 750.00
Clock, Coca-Cola, Neon, Rainbow Panel On Top, Plastic, 1950s, 24 In. 2300.00
Clock, Dr Pepper, Pressed Board, World War II Era, Round, 15 In. 185.00
Clock, Drink Coca-Cola In Bottles, Reverse Painted, Metal Frame, Round, 1939-1942 ... 720.00
Clock, Drink Coca-Cola, Bottle Below Hands, White Ground, Light-Up, Round, 15 In. .. 460.00
Clock, Drink Coca-Cola, Countertop, Light-Up, Metal, Reverse Glass, 19 x 9 In. 1020.00
Clock, Drink Coca-Cola, Maroon, Electric, 1951 .... 115.00
Clock, Drink Coca-Cola, Please Pay When Served, Counter, Square Clock Face, 1950s .. 865.00
Clock, Drink Dr. Pepper, Good For Life, Art Deco, Reverse-Painted Glass, 1930s 4255.00
Clock, Drink Dr. Pepper, Light-Up, Metal, Glass, Plastic Face, 15 1/2 In. 145.00
Clock, Drink Royal Crown Cola, Wood Body, Metal Face, Glass Front, 15 1/2 In. 330.00
Clock, Duquesne, Finest Beer In Town, Reverse Painted Glass, Hanging, 18 x 24 In. 470.00
Clock, Evervess Sparkling Water, Parrot With Hat, Light-Up, Round, 1940s-1950s 405.00
Clock, Gilbert Old Mr. Boston Fine Liquors, Bottle Shape, Wood, 10 x 6 x 2 3/4 In. 155.00
Clock, Green River Whiskey, 2 Men Shaking Hands, Cast Brass, 15 3/4 x 13 In. 770.00
Clock, Lewis 66 Rye, The Strauss, Pritz Co., Reverse Painted, White, Silver, Black, 12 In. 175.00
Clock, Pepsi-Cola, Bottle Cap, Yellow Ground, Light-Up, 1950s 375.00
Clock, Pepsi-Cola, The Light Refreshment, Bottle Cap, Yellow, Red, Plastic, 1950s 690.00
Clock, Royal Crown Cola, Neon, Light-Up, Metal, Plastic, Glass Insert, 34 x 37 In. 1100.00
Clock, Sugar-Free Diet Rite Cola, Light-Up, Metal, Glass, Diamond Shape, 16 In. 155.00
Clock, Sun Crest Root Beer, Bottle, Telechron, 1940s 405.00
Clock, Time For Pepsi-Cola, Double Dot Light-Up, Telechron, Square, 1940s 375.00
Clock, Walker's All-Star Dairy Products, Electric, Light-Up, Square, 15 1/2 In. 115.00
Coin, 1869 H.J. Heinz Company 1939, Bust Of Heinz, 70th Anniversary, Copper, 3 In. .. 45.00
Container, W.T. Wright, Woolwich, Maine, Pure Cream, Wax Paper, 1920, Pt. 22.00

Go-Withs, Bottle
Opener, The New
Deal, Stamped
Steel, 5 1/8 In.

Go-Withs,
Cork, Man,
Porcelain Head,
Made In
Germany Label,
3 In.

Go-Withs,
Cork, Painted
Wood Rooster,
Your Health,
Leg And Tail
Move, 4 In.

Cooler, Coca-Cola, Metal, Galvanized Interior, Tray, Box, 19 x 17 x 12 In.	420.00
Cooler, Coca-Cola, Plastic, Miniature, Promoting Sales, c.1940s	240.00
Cooler, Drink Coca-Cola, Single Case, Metal, c.1929, 27 1/2 x 17 1/2 In.	855.00
Cooler, Orange Crush, Logo, Wood, Zinc Lining, 1920s, 34 x 19 x 33 In.	455.00
Cooler Bag, Drink Coca-Cola In Bottles, Vinyl, 1950s	12.00
Cork, Man, Porcelain Head, Made In Germany Label, 3 In. *Illus*	25.00
Cork, Painted Wood Rooster, Your Health, Leg And Tail Move, 4 In. . . . . *Illus*	20.00
Cork Shaping Machine, Enterprise Mfg. Co., Phila., No. 1, Pat. Aug. 7, 1867, 9 In.	105.00
Corkscrew, Sample Dr. Harter's Wild Cherry Bitters, Iron, Mechanical, 8 5/8 In.	360.00
Coupon, Belle Plain Diary, Belle Plain, Iowa, Butter, 59 Cents Per Lb., Card Stock	.10
Coupon Book, Tri City Dairy, Durand, Wis., $1 Value, 35 Coupons, c.1950	13.00
Crate, Dr. Harter's Wild Cherry Bitters, Dayton, O., Wood, 13 x 9 x 17 In.	210.00
Crate, Pepsi-Cola, A Nickel Drink Worth A Dime, Holds 24 Bottles	38.00
Crate, St. Jacob's Oil, 1880-1899 . . . . .80.00 to 90.00
Cup, Bakers Cocoa	50.00
Cup, Borden Instant Hot Chocolate, Elsie, Yellow, Red, Brown, Plastic, 1950s, 2 1/2 In. . .	10.00
Cutout, Coca-Cola Circus, How A Circus Comes To Town, 1932, 10 x 15 In.	40.00
Cutout, De Laval, Cow, Calf, Brown, White, Tin, 2-Sided, 3 x 5 In. & 2 x 2 In., 2 Piece .	220.00
Cutout, De Laval, Cow, Calf, Tan, Tin, Die Cut, 2-Sided, 3 x 5 In. & 2 x 2 In., 2 Piece . .	205.00
Decal, Rayette Dandruff Lotion, Unused, 18 1/2 x 5 In.	65.00
Dish, Coca-Cola, Map Of World, 1960s, 6 3/4 In.	65.00
Dish, Sundae, Elsie The Cow	20.00
Dispenser, Buckeye Root Beer, Teardrop Style, Pump, 1915, 15 In.	1840.00
Dispenser, Cherry Smash, 5 Cents, Glass On Leaves, Porcelain, Pump, c.1920	3450.00
Dispenser, Drink Grape Smash, It's Delicious, Ball Pump, 1918-1922	10925.00
Dispenser, Drink Hires, It Is Pure, Hourglass Shape, Porcelain, 1920, 14 x 8 In.	1210.00
Dispenser, Keg, Drink Hires Root Beer, For Thirst & Cheer, Oak, Brass, 26 x 15 In.	990.00
Dispenser, Lyons Powder, Lyon Manufacturing Co., Brass Pushbutton Top, Red Paint . . .	65.00
Dispenser, Mint Julep, Stoneware, Glass, 8 Dispenser Perfection Cooler Co., 18 In.	440.00
Dispenser, Mission Orange, Metal, Porcelain Lid, Base, Brass Plaque, 27 x 14 In.	420.00
Dispenser, Pepsi-Cola, Soda Fountain, Countertop, 1940s, 16 x 16 x 12 In.	2185.00
Dispenser, Ward's Lemon Crush, Lemon Shape, Pump, Marked Ball, 13 1/2 In.	2645.00
Dispenser, Ward's Orange Crush, Orange Shape, Pump, Marked Ball, 14 In.	1785.00
Display, Arrow 77, The Globe's Finest Beer, Globe Shape, 2 Lenses, Glass Gill Body . . .	825.00
Display, Coca-Cola, 100, Centennial Celebration, Shadow Box, Bottles, Box	105.00
Display, Coca-Cola, Bottle, Hot Dog, 3D, Cardboard, Hanging, 1932, 10 x 20 In.	1150.00
Display, Coca-Cola, Girl's Heads, Backbar, Cardboard, 5 Pieces In Envelope, 1951	4945.00
Display, Dickinson's Witch Hazel, Cardboard, Countertop, 1923, 27 1/2 x 19 1/2 In.	140.00
Display, Dr. Morse's Indian Root Pills, Cardboard, Countertop, 1900-1915	95.00
Display, Dr. Pepper, Girl With Bottle, 3D, Cardboard, Die Cut, 1940s, 18 x 16 In.	1610.00
Display, Fitch's Dandruff Remover Shampoo, Cardboard, 24 x 17 1/2 In.	160.00
Display, Herpicide Scalp & Hair Treatment, Cardboard, 35 x 65 In.	210.00
Display, Hires For Thirst, Kids Baseball Team, Lithographed, 3D, 1914, 18 x 30 In.	5720.00
Display, Hires To You, Couple, For 3 Bottles, 8 1/2 x 11 In.	75.00
Display, Jack Daniel's Old No. 7, Silver Plate Stand, England, 1900-1915, 4 1/8 In.	65.00
Display, Mason's Old Fashioned Root Beer, At The Beach, 10 x 12 In.	50.00
Display, Newbro's Herpicide, 21 Hooks, Tin, Self-Framed, 19 x 16 In.	60.00
Display, Noonan's Morning After Rub, Stand-Up, Cardboard, 21 1/2 x 17 In.	40.00
Display, Sharples Tubular Cream Separators, Woman Sitting, Cardboard, 52 x 40 In.	415.00
Display, Whistle, Elves, Countertop, Cardboard, 1948, 16 1/2 x 8 1/4 In.	225.00
Display Rack, Duquesne Pilsner, Take Home A Six Pack, Wood, Box, 14 x 58 In.	40.00
Domino Set, Coca-Cola, For Victory Buy U.S. Savings Bonds, Box, Halsam Products Co.	65.00
Door Push, Buvez Coca-Cola Glace, Porcelain, Canada, 3 1/2 x 31 In.	40.00
Door Push, Golden Bridge Root Beer, Embossed, 1930s	40.00
Door Push, You're Next, Use Zepp's For The Hair, Tin, 10 x 3 3/4 In.	440.00
Dose Cup, Duffy Whiskey	12.00
Dose Cup, Fleet Phospho Soda	5.00
Dose Cup, Severance & Co. Druggists, Williamstown, Mass., Slug Plate	15.00
Dose Glass, George Jay Drug Co., Shenandoah, Iowa, ACL	10.00
Dose Glass, Use Dollams Great German Medicine, Slug Plate	75.00
Dose Goblet, Dr. Harter's, Crescent Moon, Trademark, 3 In., 8 Piece	95.00
Drawing, Borden's Complete Set Of Aeroplanes, World War 1 Era, Set Of 5, Mail Tube .	30.00
Drum, Pepsi-Cola, Syrup Concentrate, Tin, White, Red Lithograph, 1930s, 10 Gal.	210.00

Eyecup, Clear, Applied Stem, Foot, 1850-1870, 2 3/8 In. 85.00
Eyecup, Cobalt Blue, Applied Foot, 1850-1870, 1 7/8 In. 95.00
Eyecup, Cobalt Blue, Stem, Ring Base, England 32.00
Eyecup, Green, Ground Pontil, Applied Foot, Tooled Rim, 2 1/2 In. 55.00
Eyecup, John Bull, Pat. Aug. 14 1917, 1236597, Trademark, Olive Green, 2 3/4 In. 70.00
Eyecup, Leaf Green, Base Reservoir, England, 1920, 2 In. 30.00
Fan, Cold Spring, N.Y., Dairy, Baby In High Chair, Puppy, Paper, Wood Handle, 1940s . . 15.00
Fan, Hope Creamery Co., Hope, Kansas 3.50
Fan Pull, Dr. Pepper, Smiling Girl, Cardboard, 2-Sided, 1940s, 7 In. 140.00
Figure, Back Bar, Jack Daniel's Whiskey-90 Proof, Granite Base, 1850-1911, 11 In. 145.00
Figure, Drinking Bear, Sitting On Log, Pours Pepsi In Cup, Eyes Light Up, Japan, 9 In. . 155.00
Figure, Old Crow, Coated Papier Mache, Wire Glasses, 16 x 5 x 6 In. 110.00
Funnel, Dr. Van Dyke's Holland Bitters, Van Dyke Bitters Co., Copper, 7 3/8 In. 50.00
Funnel, Sanitary Fruit Jar, Pottery, White, Canada, c.1895, 4 3/4 x 2 1/2 In. 95.00
Game, Jayne's Expectorant, Move 2 Signs, Tin, Bottle Shape, 5 3/8 In. 145.00
Game Board, Checkers, Harry Horne Food Products, Bottles, Boxes, Storefront 20.00
Glass, Borden, Canada, Ingersol, 1899-1974, Red ACL, Gold Trim, 3 1/4 In. 35.00
Glass, Coca-Cola, Modified Flare, No Trademark, 1923-1925 . . . . 75.00
Glass, Dr. Petzold's German Bitters 40.00
Glass, Drink Hires Root Beer, c.1920s-1940s, 3 1/2 In. 125.00
Glass, Elsie The Cow, Blue & Red 15.00
Glass, Erickson's Cafe, Music Hall, Saloon, Portland, Ore., Fancy Letters 125.00
Glass, Harper Highball, Etched, Gold Rim, 4 In. 6.00
Glass, Pilsner, W.J. Lemp 50.00
Glass, Ritschler & Tiesse Malting Co., Lion, Shield, Gold Design, 4 3/4 In. 60.00
Glass, Soda, Drink Moonshine, Etched 55.00
Glass, Stemmed, Hermanhoff, Hermann, Mo.. . . . . 40.00
Grenade Rack, For 3 Hayward's Fire Grenades, Wire, 1875-1895 . . . . 60.00
Hat, Flip, Dr. Fox's Sarsaparilla, For The Blood, 1 1/2 In. 75.00
Headband, Whistle, Feathers, H. Gamse & Bro., Litho, Bato, Md., Paper, 5 1/2 x 23 In. . 45.00
Horseshoe, Simmon's Liver Regulator, Take In Time, Brass, 6 In. 65.00
Ice Chipper, Lash's Bitters, Metal 70.00
Ice Cream Cover, Meadow Gold Dairies Inc., Columbus, Ohio, Strawberry, Individual . . .10
Ice Cream Cover, Sinton's Dairy Co., Colorado Springs, Colo., Chocolate, Individual . . 1.00
Ice Cream Cover, Walsenburg Creamer, Walsenburg & Pueblo, Colo., Individual 1.00
Inkwell Filler, Toucan Shape, Copper, Tapered Body, 4 1/2 In. Pour Spout, 9 1/2 In. 95.00
Jacket, Coca-Cola, Driver's, Dark Green Twill, 2 Flap Pockets, Talon Zipper, 1950s 95.00
Key Chain, Pepsi-Cola, Bottle Cap, Metal, Cloisonne, Nickel-Plated Brass, 2 3/4 In. 15.00
Kit, Coca-Cola, V.I.P. Production Training Series, Bottle Case Shaped, Cardboard 15.00
Knife, Compliments Matthews Fine Whiskeys, Baltimore, Brass 35.00
Letter Opener, Ball Perfect Mason, Nickel-Plated Brass 150.00
Letter Opener, Canadian Club Whisky, Hiram Walker & Sons, Silver Plate, 7 1/2 In. . . . 25.00
Lid, A. Kline Pat'd Oct. 27, 1863, Aqua 3.00
Lid, Cannington Shaw & Co., St. Helens, Aqua, Pontil 3.00
Lid, Mason Milk Glass Immerser Lid, Pat. Nov. 30, 1880 . . . . 15.00
Lighter, Coca-Cola, Bottle Shape, Gold Plated, Metal, Plastic, Original Bag, 2 1/2 In. . . . 95.00
Match Holder, De Laval, Cream Separator Shape, Tin 100.00
Match Holder, Tubeless Cream Separator, Sharples Separator Co., Tin, 6 x 2 In. 315.00
Match Holder, Watson's Whisky, Dundee, England, c.1895 . . . . 60.00
Milk Bottle Cap, Broguiere's Dairy, Cow 1.50
Milk Bottle Cap, Brown Baker & Son Dairy, Chocolate Milk, Watervliet, Mich. 1.00
Milk Bottle Cap, Crescent Hill Dairy, Whole Milk, Ravenna, O., 1 5/8 In. . . . . *Illus* .35
Milk Bottle Cap, Dannheim's Chocolate, Lowfat Milk, 1 3/4 In. . . . . *Illus* .35
Milk Bottle Cap, Great Britain, Direct From The Farm, Quality Guaranteed, Cow 2.50
Milk Bottle Cap, Great Britain, Guaranteed Pure New Milk, Green 2.50
Milk Bottle Cap, Haxon Dairy Chocolate Milk, Watervliet, Mich., Plug Type, Pull Tab . 1.00
Milk Bottle Cap, Hood, Boston, Mass., Pasteurized Homogenized Sour Cream, Foil 10
Milk Bottle Cap, Kent's Dairy Farms, Olean, N.Y., 2 1/4 In. . . . . *Illus* .35
Milk Bottle Cap, Lassig's Dairy Inc., Rhinelander, Wisc., Buttermilk, Red & Green 25
Milk Bottle Cap, Meadow Brook Farms, Chocolate, Eighty Four, Pa., 2 1/2 In. . . . . *Illus* .35
Milk Bottle Cap, Notzke Bros. Grade A Milk, Peoria Ill., 1 5/8 In. . . . . *Illus* .35
Milk Bottle Cap, Pasteurized Milk, For Your Protection We Use Sealright Sanitary 25
Milk Bottle Cap, Quebec, Canada, Lavez Et Retournez Les Bouteilles, Cow & Calf 25

Go-Withs, Milk Bottle Cap, Notzke Bros. Grade A Milk, Peoria Ill., 1 5/8 In.
Go-Withs, Milk Bottle Cap, Dannheim's Chocolate, Lowfat Milk, 1 3/4 In.
Go-Withs, Milk Bottle Cap, Crescent Hill Dairy, Whole Milk, Ravenna, O., 1 5/8 In.

Milk Bottle Cap, Ricker's Dairy, Milo, Maine, Orange	.25
Milk Bottle Cap, Riverside Dairy, Homogenized Milk, Fulton, N.Y., 3 1/4 In. ..... *Illus*	.35
Milk Bottle Cap, Serendipity Farm, Upton, Maine, Guernsey Gold Raw Milk, Moose ..	.25
Milk Bottle Cap, Try Our Cottage Cheese, Girl, Green	.25
Milk Bottle Cap, Yeoman's Dairy, Ionia, Mich., Plug Type, Pull Tab	1.00
Milk Coupon, Eriksen's Dairy, Qt., Sheet Of 20	1.00
Milk Filters, Kendall Company, Walpole, Mass., Cardboard Box, 1951, 100 Piece	3.00
Milk Pail, Robinson Dairy Products, Chicago, Tin, Handle	35.00
Mirror, Coca-Cola, Woman At Beach, 1922, Pocket, 1 3/4 x 2 3/4 In.	8280.00
Mirror, Duffy's Malt Whiskey, Pocket, 1900	95.00
Mug, Anheuser-Busch, Harrisburg Bottling Works, Eagle, Shield, Stoneware, c.1900	380.00
Mug, Armour's Vigoral, Flower Design	30.00
Mug, Belfast Root Beer	50.00
Mug, Coors, Stoneware	5.00
Mug, Dr. Pepper, History	6.00
Mug, Drink Hires Root Beer, Hires Boy, Mettlach, Pot Belly, 4 1/2 In., 2 Piece	1210.00
Mug, Drink Moxie, Trademark	75.00
Mug, Figural, Soldier, M On Cap, Mustache, Custard, Avon, 5 1/2 In. .... *Illus*	.50
Mug, Hires Boy, Join Health & Cheer, Drink Hires Rootbeer, Mettlach, 5 In., 2 Piece	880.00
Mug, Hires Root Beer, Hires Boy, Join Health & Cheer, Mettlach, 5 In., Pair	880.00
Mug, Kagemeister Brewing Co., Green Bay, Wis., Stoneware	240.00
Mug, Lash's Root Beer	45.00
Mug, Leisy Brewing Co.	55.00
Mug, Moxie, Embossed, Fluted, 1915-1920, 5 In.	50.00
Mug, Pabst Milwaukee, 5 Gnomes Drinking, Thuemler Mfg. Co., Stoneware, 1880s	120.00
Mug, Pennsylvania Bottling & Supply Co., Dove Brand Ginger Ale	75.00
Mug, Shamokin Brewing Co., Rising Sun Beer, Monks, Milk Glass	80.00
Mug, Smith's Musty Ale, Philadelphia ....25.00 to 35.00
Mug, South Bend Brewing Association, Brewery Picture, Mettlach On Base, 1909	150.00
Mug, Stroh's Beer, Detroit Mich., Utica Pottery	150.00
Napkin, Hires Boy, Hires In Script Around Sides, 5 Cents, Square, 14 In.	770.00

Go-Withs, Milk Bottle Cap, Kent's Dairy Farms, Olean, N.Y., 2 1/4 In.
Go-Withs, Milk Bottle Cap, Riverside Dairy, Homogenized Milk, Fulton, N.Y., 3 1/4 In.
Go-Withs, Milk Bottle Cap, Meadow Brook Farms, Chocolate, Eighty Four, Pa., 2 1/2 In.

Novelty, Bottle, Hires, Bill's Specialty Mfg. Co., Milwaukee, 3 1/2 In. .... *Illus*   30.00
Order Form, Swihart Coca-Cola Clocks, Electric Clock & Rocking Bottle Clock 80.00
Paper Bag, Iroquois Indian Head Beer & Ale, Chief, Both Sides, Handles, 13 1/2 In. ...   7.00
Picture, H.P. Hood Ice Cream, Dairy Cows In Barn, Cloth 20.00
Pitcher, Dr. Harter's Wild Cherry Bitters, Silver Plate, Thermos, 1890-1910, 13 In. ... 305.00
Pitcher, Dr. Van Dyke's Holland Bitters, Silver Plate, Thermos, 1890-1910, 13 3/8 In. ... 275.00
Pitcher, Orange Crush 70.00
Plaque, Owl Drug Co., Round, 13 In. 125.00
Plaque, Presentation, Coca-Cola, Gold-Colored Bottle, c.1950s 100.00
Plaque, Presentation, Coca-Cola, Jamestown Bottling Co., Bronze-Colored Bottle 30.00
Plate, Avon, American Portraits Collection 25.00
Plate, Avon, Betsy Ross, 1974 .... 10.00 to 26.00
Plate, Avon, Christmas, 1974 .... 200.00
Plate, Avon, Christmas, 1991 ....   20.00
Plate, Avon, Christmas, Box, 1973 .... 200.00
Plate, Avon, Gentle Moments, 1974 ....   15.00
Plate, Avon, Mother's Day, 1975 ....   15.00
Plate, Avon, Mother's Day, 1983 ....   5.00
Plate, Avon, Singin' In The Rain, 1986 ....   15.00
Plate, Avon, Spirit Of Avon, 1986 ....   35.00
Plate, Avon, Wild Flowers, Eastern, 1926-1928 ....   40.00
Plate, Dr Pepper, Woman With Bottle, 1983, 9 1/2 In. 75.00
Pocket Knife, Have A Coke & A Smile, Truck Shape, Metal, Pearl Handle, 3 In. 55.00
Poster, List Of Poisons & Their Antidotes, J.F. Yorba & Company, Frame, 16 x 12 In. ... 265.00
Poster, Smith's Egg & Health Producer, Dr. H.M. Smith Med. Co., Paper, 13 x 21 In. ...   90.00
Pot Holder, Baby Top Milk, Pecora's, Hazelton, Pa., Bottle, Red, White 20.00
Pot Lid, Bazin's Shaving Cream x Bazin Perfumer, Cream, Red Transfer, 3 1/4 In. ..50.00 to 80.00
Pot Lid, Burgess Genuine Anchovy Paste, Toast & Biscuit, Lion, Unicorn, Black 36.00
Pot Lid, H.P. & W.C. Taylor's Saponaceous Shaving Compound, New Size, 3 3/4 In. ..   80.00
Pot Lid, Hazard, Hazard & Co., Violet Cold Cream, N.Y., White, Brown Transfer, 3 In. . 230.00
Pot Lid, Home Made Potted Meats Army & Navy, 2 Men Holding Flags, Black 36.00
Pot Lid, Jules Hauel Saponaceous Shaving Compound, White, Red Transfer, 4 In. 230.00
Pot Lid, Roussel's Premium Shaving Cream, Phila., White, Gray Transfer, 3 In. 240.00
Pot Lid, Toothpaste Deer Nagase, Picture Of Deer, Green 185.00
Rack, Coca-Cola, Sign Of Good Taste, Tin, Metal Bracket, 1950s, 16 In. 60.00
Rack, Coca-Cola, Take Home A Carton, Tin, 2-Sided, 1930s, Round, 13 In. 185.00
Rack, Drink Coca-Cola, Fishtail Logo, Plastic, Metal Bracket, 1960s, 16 In. 115.00
Rack, Serve Coca-Cola, Sign Of Good Taste, Fishtail, Bracket, Metal, 1960s, 9 In. 50.00
Radio, Coca-Cola, Bottle Shape, 1933, 24 In. 5750.00
Radio, Pepsi-Cola, Shaped Like Soda Fountain Cooler, Plastic, Red, White, Blue, 1950s . 375.00
Rationing Stamps, Queen City Dairy, Cumberland, Md., For 30 Qt. Milk 35.00
Ruler, Courtesy Of Ontario's Dairy Industry, Slogans, Wood, Red Letters, 6 In. 10.00
Salt & Pepper, Avon, Country Kitchen, Box 5.00
Salt & Pepper, Borden, Elsie The Cow, Foil Label, Stamped The Borden Co., 1943 .... 150.00
Salt & Pepper, Canada Dry, Paper Label, Box, 1930s 65.00

Go-Withs, Mug, Figural, Soldier,
M On Cap, Mustache, Custard,
Avon, 5 1/2 In.

Go-Withs, Novelty, Bottle,
Hires, Bill's Specialty Mfg.
Co., Milwaukee, 3 1/2 In.

Go-Withs, Shot Glass,
Boot, Jim Beam,
2 1/2 In.

Scale, Dr. C.H. Gitch's Prescription Scale, Pat. Sept. 29th, 1885, 3 x 1 1/2 x 3/4 In. 70.00
Scoop, Dr Pepper, 1964 .... 6.00
Scrip, Dr. Dyotts Manual Labor Bank, 10 Dollars, Glasshouse Scene, 1836 .... 50.00
Scrip, Dr. Dyotts Manual Labor Bank, 20 Dollars, Glasshouse Scene, 1836 .... 80.00
Scrip, Dr. Dyotts Manual Labor Bank, 50 Cents, Engraved Portraits, 1837 .... 80.00
Scrip, Vermont Glass Factory, 1 Dollar, Engraved Glasshouse, 1812 .... 50.00
Shopping Cart, Enjoy Coca-Cola While You Shop, 2-Bottle Rack, 1950s 70.00
Shot Glass, 12-Beveled Panels, Light Canary Yellow Green, 1865-1875, 2 1/4 In. 55.00
Shot Glass, 6- Sided, Ice Blue, 1865-1875, 2 1/2 In. 140.00
Shot Glass, 6-Sided, Cobalt Blue, 2 5/8 In. 45.00
Shot Glass, 6-Sided, Cornflower, Pontil Base, 1865-1875, 2 1/2 In. 165.00
Shot Glass, 6-Sided, Deep Green Aqua, Pontil Base, 1865-1885, 2 1/4 In. 80.00
Shot Glass, 6-Sided, Gold Yellow Amber, 1865-1875, 2 1/2 In. ....150.00 to 190.00
Shot Glass, 6-Sided, Light Turquoise Blue, 1865-1875, 2 3/4 In. 150.00
Shot Glass, 6-Sided, Lime Green, 1865-1875, 2 In. 90.00
Shot Glass, 6-Sided, Opalescent Milk Glass, Pontil, 1865-1875, 2 1/4 In. 110.00
Shot Glass, 8-Sided, Yellow Green, Pontil, 1865-1875, 2 In. 130.00
Shot Glass, Boot, Jim Beam, 2 1/2 In. ....*Illus* 8.00
Shot Glass, Delaney's Whiskey ....*Illus* 68.00
Shot Glass, Fritz Schmidt & Sons, Rock Island, Ill. 20.00
Shot Glass, Golden Eagle Liquor Dept., Denver, Colo., Tooled Rim, 1900-1915, 2 In. ... 80.00
Shot Glass, Hotel Kelly, Cambridge Spring, Pa., Etched, 3 In. 70.00
Shot Glass, Jack Daniel's 15.00
Shot Glass, Old Lexington Club, Enameled 25.00
Shot Glass, Schneider Bros. ....*Illus* 55.00
Shot Glass, Try OK Rye 35.00
Shot Glass, Voes Marigold Rye 15.00
Shot Glass, Wild Cherry Bracer, Great Appetizer 35.00
Sign, After All No Ink Like Carter's, Tin, Self-Framed, 1900, 25 x 8 1/2 In. 445.00
Sign, Be Sure & Take Welch's, The National Drink, Picnic Basket, 1920s, 15 x 15 In. ... 100.00
Sign, Buvez Coca-Cola Glace, Sprite Boy, Porcelain, France, 1954, 54 x 17 1/2 In. 230.00
Sign, Carling's Ale, Nine Pints Of The Law, Policemen, Tin, Cardboard, 13 x 20 In. 110.00
Sign, Centilivre's Nickel Plate Bottled Beer, Paper Frame, 28 x 22 1/2 In. 110.00
Sign, Coca-Cola Classic, Official Soft Drink Of Summer, Neon, 1980s, 28 In. 1380.00
Sign, Coca-Cola, 1937, 5 x 3 Ft. 475.00
Sign, Coca-Cola, AM 103, Button, Arrow, 1-Sided, Painted Metal, 20 x 12 In. 990.00
Sign, Coca-Cola, Bottle In Center, Celluloid, 1940s-1950s, Round, 9 In. 150.00
Sign, Coca-Cola, Bottle, Celluloid Over Metal, Cardboard Backing, Round, 9 In. 200.00
Sign, Coca-Cola, Bottle, Porcelain, 5 1/2 x 17 In. 125.00
Sign, Coca-Cola, Bottle, Sprite Boy, Yellow, Tin, 1-Sided, Round, 13 In. 1430.00
Sign, Coca-Cola, Fountain Service, Dual Spigots, Porcelain, 1939, 14 x 27 In. 4715.00
Sign, Coca-Cola, Ice Cold, Gas Today, Tin, 1937, 18 x 54 In. 980.00
Sign, Coca-Cola, Ice Cold, Sold Here, Arrow Shape, Tin, 2-Sided, 1927, 8 x 30 In. 2070.00
Sign, Coca-Cola, Metal Ring, Arrow, Kay Display Wood Cooler In Center, 1940s, 16 In. . 115.00
Sign, Coca-Cola, Please Pay Cashier, Glass Logo On Ends, Counter, 1950s, 18 In. 2990.00
Sign, Coca-Cola, Please Pay Cashier, Mirror, Reverse Glass, c.1920s, 11 1/4 In. 720.00
Sign, Coca-Cola, Please Pay When Served, Counter, Glass, Wood, 1948, 17 x 12 In. 1670.00
Sign, Coca-Cola, Policeman, Slow, School Zone, 2-Sided, 1961, 32 x 63 In. 2530.00
Sign, Coca-Cola, Seasons Greetings, Santa, Sleeping Boy, Cardboard, Stand-Up, 47 In. ... 215.00
Sign, Coca-Cola, Six-Pack, Regular Size Circle, Tin, Die Cut, 1958, 11 x 12 In. 2070.00
Sign, Coca-Cola, Slow School Zone, Girl, Wood, Metal Base, 2-Sided, 49 1/2 In. 715.00
Sign, Coca-Cola, Wallace Beery, Cardboard, Matted, Frame, 1934, 13 3/4 x 29 1/2 In. ... 4370.00
Sign, Coca-Cola, Woman Holding Out Glass, Tin, Oval, 1926, 13 x 19 In. 5980.00
Sign, Columbian Extra Pale Bottled Beer, Tennessee Brewing Co., Tin, 14 x 10 In. 240.00
Sign, Cork Distilleries Co. Ltd., Whisky, Tin, 1-Sided, Self-Framed, 12 1/2 x 16 1/2 In. .. 125.00
Sign, Daisy Quinine Hair Tonic, Buerger Bros. Supply Co., Denver, Tin, 9 3/4 x 9 In. ... 120.00
Sign, Dandro Solvent, Stand-Up, Countertop, Tin, Self-Framed, 9 1/4 x 13 1/2 In. 175.00
Sign, De Laval Authorized Agency, Separator, Flange, Porcelain, 26 1/2 x 18 In. 715.00
Sign, De Laval Cream Separators, Bonneted Lass, Calf, Tin, Frame, 41 x 30 In. 2640.00
Sign, Dr. B.J. Kendall's Blackberry Balsam, Dysentery, Summer Complaints, 5 x 14 In. ... 24.00
Sign, Dr. B.J. Kendall's Pectoral Elixir, Paper, 5 x 14 In. 20.00
Sign, Dr. B.J. Kendall's Tonic & Blood Purifier, Paper, 5 1/2 x 24 In. 35.00
Sign, Dr. Harter's Wild Cherry Bitters, Girl Feeding Puppy, Litho, 13 x 29 1/2 In. 1320.00

Go-Withs, Shot Glass,
Delaney's Whiskey

Go-Withs, Shot Glass,
Schneider Bros.

Go-Withs, Sign, Hostetter's
Stomach Bitters, Reverse Painted,
24 1/2 x 30 1/4 In.

Sign, Dr. Harter's Wild Cherry Bitters, Girl, Broken Bottle, Litho, Frame, 23 x 40 In. 1375.00
Sign, Dr. Harter's Wild Cherry Bitters, Girl, Crate, Litho, Frame, 23 x 40 1/4 In. 1018.00
Sign, Dr. Harter's Wild Cherry Bitters, Woman Picking Cherries, Litho, 11 1/2 x 29 In. . . . 825.00
Sign, Dr. Harter's Wild Cherry Bitters, Woman, Doves, Dr. Harter Frame, 25 x 33 In. 2750.00
Sign, Dr. Horner's Rheumatic Lightning, 500 Dollars Reward If Not Cured, 8 x 11 In. 20.00
Sign, Dr. J. Bovee Dod's Imperial Remedy & Family Physician, Frame, 21 3/4 In. 65.00
Sign, Dr. Pepper, Drink A Bite To Eat, At 10, 2 & 4, Bottle, Tin, 1938, 18 x 54 In. 3795.00
Sign, Dr. Swett's Root Beer, Woman With Glass, Cardboard, 1940s, 10 x 17 In. 65.00
Sign, Drink Cheer Up, Bottle Pouring Into Glass, Tin, 1940s-1950s, 9 x 11 In. 85.00
Sign, Drink Coca-Cola In Bottles, Bottle On Left, Tin, Embossed, 1931, 10 x 28 In. 750.00
Sign, Drink Coca-Cola, Delicious & Refreshing, Porcelain, 1932, 3 x 5 Ft. 2990.00
Sign, Drink Coca-Cola, Delicious & Refreshing, Porcelain, Canada, 1938, 4 x 8 Ft. 1250.00
Sign, Drink Coca-Cola, Fountain Service, Porcelain, 1-Sided, 12 x 28 In. 230.00
Sign, Drink Coca-Cola, Goes Good With Food, Cardboard, c.1950s, 7 x 22 In. 25.00
Sign, Drink Coca-Cola, Ice Cold, Blue, Oval, Porcelain, 1-Sided, 11 x 16 In. 360.00
Sign, Drink Coca-Cola, Ice Cold, Blue, Porcelain, 1-Sided, Round, 14 In. 360.00
Sign, Drink Coca-Cola, Ice Cold, Dispenser, Porcelain, 2-Sided, 1950s, 27 x 28 In. 1265.00
Sign, Drink Coca-Cola, Ice Cold, Red, Porcelain, 1-Sided, Round, 14 In. 110.00
Sign, Drink Coca-Cola, In Oval, Red, Green, Tin, Beveled Edges, 1930, 8 1/2 x 11 In. . . . 2415.00
Sign, Drink Dr Pepper, Chevron, Tin, Embossed, 1950s-1960s, 12 x 28 In. 105.00
Sign, Drink Dr Pepper, Good For Life, Porcelain, 1-Sided, Border, 10 1/2 x 26 1/2 In. . . . 230.00
Sign, Drink Dr Pepper, Stout Sign Co., Tin, 1-Sided, Self-Framed, 12 x 27 In. 75.00
Sign, Drink Frostie, Happiest Taste In Town, Tin, 1940s-1950s, 10 x 20 In. 85.00
Sign, Drink Hires, 2 Women Sipping Root Beer, Woman In Border, Oval, 20 x 24 In. 4675.00
Sign, Drink Hires, Delicious, Bracing, Bottle, Glass, Cardboard, Hanging, 11 x 8 In. 275.00
Sign, Drink Moxie For Extra Pep, Children Running, Cardboard, 1950s, 13 x 19 In. 40.00
Sign, Drink Moxie, Embossed Tin, 1-Sided, Wood Frame, 7 1/2 x 20 1/4 In. 230.00
Sign, Drink Pepsi-Cola, Delicious, Healthful, Peps You Up, Tin, 1910, 14 x 28 In. 2990.00
Sign, Drink Saltzman Bro's Beer, Woman In Red Dress, Tin, 1905, 19 x 13 In. 1870.00
Sign, Drink Squirt, Never An After-Thirst, Tin, Embossed, 1951, 9 x 28 In. 85.00
Sign, Dub-L-Valu Root Beer, Pin-Up Girl, Cardboard, 1940s, 11 x 17 In. 110.00
Sign, Eagle Angostura Bark Bitters, Partly Nude Woman, Canvas, c.1900, 22 x 14 In. . . . 825.00
Sign, Ed Pinaud's Eau De Quinine Hair Tonic, Paper, Frame, 1900, 27 x 22 In. 525.00
Sign, Eisemann's Klondike Head Rub, Bottle, Embossed, Cardboard, 8 1/2 x 11 In. 170.00
Sign, Enjoy Coke Ice Cold, Bottle In Snow, Die Cut, Cardboard, 2-Sided, 10 x 14 In. . . . 85.00
Sign, Enjoy Hires, Woman Smiling, Cardboard, 11 x 8 In. 770.00
Sign, Enjoy Old Colony Beverages, Celluloid, Round, 9 In. 30.00
Sign, Enjoy Orange Crush, Naturally It Tastes Better, Celluloid, Round, 9 In. 125.00
Sign, Ernest Wolf Inc. Chicago, Barber Bottles, Paper, Wood Frame, 14 1/2 x 18 In. 150.00
Sign, Evervess Table Water, Bottle, Cardboard, Easel Back, Canada, 11 x 18 In. 95.00
Sign, Fehr's Brewing, Meek Company, Coshocton, Ohio, Self-Framed, 33 x 23 In. 1870.00
Sign, Fort Pitt Beer, Thanks To Our Courageous President, Tin, 1933-1937, 25 x 22 In. . . 165.00
Sign, Fountain Service, Drink Coca-Cola, Porcelain, 1-Sided, 45 1/2 x 60 In. 2420.00
Sign, Genesee Beer & Ale, Humphrey Bogart, Lauren Bacall, Bold Venture, 18 x 15 In. . . 155.00

Sign, Get HEP For Yourself, Bottle, Flange, Metal, 2-Sided, Die Cut, 13 1/2 x 18 In. 360.00
Sign, Get The Kit Carson Kerchief, Cardboard, Easelback, 1950s, 16 x 24 In. 200.00
Sign, Gurd's Dry Ginger Ale, Green, Red, Yellow, White, Tin, Canada, 1920s, 19 x 27 In. 40.00
Sign, Hires, So Refreshing, Made In U.S.A., BN6, Flange, Metal, 2-Sided, 12 x 14 In. ... 170.00
Sign, Hostetter's Stomach Bitters, Reverse Painted, 24 1/2 x 30 1/4 In. ....*Illus* 1815.00
Sign, Ice Cold Coca-Cola Sold Here, 1923 Bottle, Tin, Embossed, 1933, 20 x 28 In. 1150.00
Sign, Japp's Hair Rejuvenator, Tin, Cardboard Back, Self-Framed, 9 1/4 x 13 In. 155.00
Sign, Jeris Antiseptic Hair Tonic, Countertop, Stand-Up, Cardboard, 24 1/2 x 18 In. 70.00
Sign, Jeris Antiseptic Hair Tonic, Couple, Stand-Up, Cardboard, 27 1/2 x 20 1/2 In. 45.00
Sign, Jeris Hair Tonic, Light-Up, Paper, Glass, Metal, Wood Frame, 13 1/2 x 16 x 6 In. .. 175.00
Sign, Malt Nutrine, A Hurry Call, Doctor In Buggy, Tin, Cardboard, 7 3/4 x 12 3/4 In. ... 120.00
Sign, Mellin's Food, Baby In Seat, Cardboard, Die Cut, Plexiglas Frame, 12 x 13 In. 85.00
Sign, Morris Evans Remedies, Fight Pain & Disease, Britain, 1915, 15 x 10 In. 110.00
Sign, Nehi, Square Deal Service, You Get What You Call For, Paper, 8 x 10 In. 60.00
Sign, Old Continental Whiskey, Bernhem Bros. Distillers, Chalk, Relief, 27 x 31 In. 305.00
Sign, Old Overholt Pennsylvania Rye, Reverse Glass, Frame, 1880-1910, 25 x 33 In. 1430.00
Sign, Orange Crush, Bottle, Tin, 2-Sided, Semitriangular, 1936, 17 1/2 x 23 1/2 In. 750.00
Sign, Orange Crush, Refreshment For Workers & Fighters, Eagle, Cardboard, 7 x 10 In. . 195.00
Sign, Pepsi-Cola, Bottle Cap Shape, Porcelain, 1-Sided, 19 In. 305.00
Sign, Pepsi-Cola, Bottle Cap, White Ground, Tin, Embossed, 48 x 42 In. 155.00
Sign, Pepsi-Cola, Cold Beverages, Light-Up, Metal, Plastic, 12 x 24 x 4 In. 165.00
Sign, Pepsi-Cola, Fluorescent, Light-Up, Mirrored, 2-Sided, c.1970s, 12 x 20 In. 65.00
Sign, Pepsi-Cola, Pepsi Cop Chasing Butterfly, Cardboard, Frame, 1930s, 10 x 18 In. ... 1150.00
Sign, Pilaster, Coca-Cola, Refresh Yourself, 1949 Button, Tin, 1950, 16 x 52 In. 1610.00
Sign, Royal Crown Cola, So Bubbly Fresh, RC, People In Boat, Cardboard, 27 x 40 In. .. 120.00
Sign, Royal Crown Cola, Take Home A Carton, Die Cut, Tin, Metal Bracket, 24 x 29 In. . 525.00
Sign, Sharples Tubular Cream Separators, Tin, Die Cut, 2-Sided, 27 x 19 In. 605.00
Sign, Snider's Catsup, Black On Yellow, Embossed, Tin, 20 x 7 In. 65.00
Sign, Step Up To Spur, Woman In Evening Gown, Stand-Up, Cardboard, Die Cut, 62 In. . 95.00
Sign, Straight Whiskies, Light-Up, Wood, Glass Face, Metal Frame, 9 1/2 x 34 x 4 In. ... 145.00
Sign, Sunshine Beer, Since 1861, Porcelain, 2-Sided, Metal Loops, Round, 32 x 38 In. ... 275.00
Sign, Surge, Cleaner Milk, Faster Milking, Orange, Navy Blue, Black, Metal, 12 x 19 In. . 30.00
Sign, There's Only One Orange Crush, Tin, 1-Sided, Diamond Shape, 16 In. 200.00
Sign, Things Go Better With Coke, Tin, 1960s, Vertical, 12 x 30 In. 85.00
Sign, Tuborg, Cerveza Boy, 2 Men Drinking, Germany, 1940s-1950s, 29 x 19 In. 1430.00
Sign, Vigorator Foaming Hair Tonic & Head Rub, Man Washing Hair, Tin, 5 x 9 In. 50.00
Sign, Whistle, 12 Ounces, 5 Cents, Bottle, Cardboard, 1939, 9 x 31 In. 60.00
Sign, Whistle, Vertical Letters, Bottle, Elves, Cardboard, 1948, 3 x 23 In. 30.00
Sign, White Rock Sparkling Dispenser, Stand-Up, Cardboard, 3-D Effect, 30 x 22 In. 75.00
Sign, Zepp's Dandruff Cure, Celluloid Over Metal, Cardboard Back, Diamond, 6 In. 275.00
Spoon, Avon, Hospitality Spoon Series, American Pineapple, Box 20.00
Spoon, Avon, Hospitality Spoon Series, German Maiden, Box 20.00
Spoon, Avon, Hospitality Spoon Series, Italian Grapes, Box 20.00
Spoon, Avon, Hospitality Spoon, Scottish Thistle, Box 20.00
Spoon, Borden's, Elsie, Yellow, Plastic, 1950s, 5 In. 7.00
Spoon, Serving, Duffy's Pure Malt Whiskey, 4 In. Handle 30.00
Stereo Card, Baker & Record Congress Springs & Three Grand Hotels 15.00
Stereo Card, Baker & Record Geyser Spring Mineral Fountain, Saratoga Springs, N.Y. . 15.00
Stopper Injector, Hutchinson, Finished Maple, 1890-1910, 12 5/8 In. 75.00
Straw Holder, Pepsi-Cola, Woman In Hat Holding Glass, Tin, Lithographed, c.1909 .... 5980.00
T-Shirt, Milk Cap Collectors, Cotton, 6 Color Caps Front, Large 5.00
Tap Knob, Peter Barmann Brewery, Kingston, N.Y., Bakelite, Monogram & Wings 12.00
Theater Slide, Hamlin's Wizard Oil Liniment, Glass, Hand Colored, 4 x 3 1/4 In. 55.00
Thermometer, Abbott's Bitters, Flavors Cocktails, Beverages, Fruits, Jelly, Sherbet, 8 In. 35.00
Thermometer, Abbott's Bitters, Glass Front, 1899 .... 100.00
Thermometer, Ask For A Crush Carbonated Beverage, Orange, 1930s-1940s, 4 x 10 In. 290.00
Thermometer, Coca-Cola, Be Really Refreshed, Fishtail, Glass Front, Box, 1959, 12 In. 690.00
Thermometer, Coca-Cola, Bottle Shape, 1958, 17 In. 35.00
Thermometer, Coca-Cola, Bottle Shape, Die Cut, Embossed, 1930s, 17 In. .....120.00 to 345.00
Thermometer, Coca-Cola, Bottle Shape, Flat Version, 1950s, 17 In. 105.00
Thermometer, Coca-Cola, Bottle Shape, Gold Colored, 1956, 7 1/2 In. 75.00
Thermometer, Coca-Cola, Bottle Shape, Tin, Die Cut, Embossed, 17 x 5 In. 120.00
Thermometer, Coca-Cola, Double Bottle, Gold Colored, 1942, 7 x 16 In. 520.00

Thermometer, Coca-Cola, Embossed Gold-Colored Bottle, 1936, 7 x 16 In. 230.00
Thermometer, Coca-Cola, Square, Round Face, Plastic, Box, 1960s, 5 In. 70.00
Thermometer, Coca-Cola, Thirst Knows No Season, Bottle, Masonite, 7 x 17 In. 980.00
Thermometer, Coca-Cola, Thirst Knows No Season, Silhouette, 1939, 5 1/2 x 18 In. 2530.00
Thermometer, Dairy, Glass, Pat. 1893, Germany, 7 5/8 In. 15.00
Thermometer, Drink Coca-Cola In Bottles, Quality Refreshment, 1950s, 9 In. 460.00
Thermometer, Drink Frostie Root Beer, A Real Taste Treat, c.1940s, 8 x 36 In. 345.00
Thermometer, Enjoy Squirt, Embossed Tin, Self-Framed, 13 1/2 x 5 3/4 In. 160.00
Thermometer, Hills Bros. Coffee, Man In Yellow Nightshirt, 1920, 9 x 21 In. 325.00
Thermometer, McKesson's Aspirin, Best For Pain, Bottle, Porcelain, 26 x 8 In. 275.00
Thermometer, Mission Orange, Bottle, 1940s-1950s, 5 x 17 In. 110.00
Thermometer, Moxie, Man Pointing, Red, White, Blue, Yellow, Black, 1950, 25 x 10 In. 315.00
Thermometer, Pepsi-Cola, Bigger, Better, Bottle, c.1930s, 6 x 16 In. 575.00
Thermometer, Pepsi-Cola, Round, Glass Front, Box, 1960s-1970s, 18 In. 160.00
Thermometer, Regent Beverages, Metal, Plastic, Round, 10 1/2 In. 100.00
Thermometer, Sauer's Flavoring Extracts, 17 Highest Awards, Wooden, 7 x 24 In. 345.00
Thermometer, Switch To The Best, Drink Sun Crest, Bottle, 1940s-1950s, 6 x 16 In. . . . 80.00
Tin, Borden's Malted Milk, Navy Blue, Red, White, Canada, c.1925, 5 Lb., 7 3/4 In. . . . 15.00
Tin, Borden's Starlac Powdered Skimmed Milk, Elsie, Canada, c.1930, 7 3/4 In. 25.00
Tin, Store, Hire's Root Beer, Multicolored, 1950s, 16 In. 175.00
Tip Tray, Bailey's Pure Rye, Philadelphia Distiller, Tin, 1845, 4 In. 55.00
Tip Tray, Broadway Brewing, Buffalo, 4 In. 75.00
Tip Tray, Coca-Cola, Betty, 1914, Passaic Metalware Co., N.J., 4 1/4 x 6 In. 240.00
Tip Tray, Coca-Cola, Delicious, Refreshing, Woman Wearing Pendant, 1906, 4 In. 575.00
Tip Tray, Coca-Cola, Hilda Clark, 1903, 6 In. 2000.00
Tip Tray, Coca-Cola, Refreshing, Delicious, Woman At Table, 1900, 6 In. 2990.00
Tip Tray, De Laval Cream Separators, Woman With Separator, Tin, Round, 4 1/4 In. 165.00
Tip Tray, Pepsi-Cola, Woman In Green Dress, 1909, 4 In. 1265.00
Toaster, Sandwich, Coca-Cola, Original Cord, 1930s 1725.00
Token, Clinton Dairy, Clinton, Tel. HU 2-9363, Good For 1 Quart Milk, House Shape . . . 8.00
Token, Eganville Creamery, Good For 1 Pint Milk, Flower Shape, Metal 9.00
Token, Fairholme Dairy, Ltd., Clinton, Ont., Tel. HU 2-9342, Good For 2 Quarts Milk . . . 15.00
Token, Fairholme Dairy, Ltd., HU 2-9342, Good For 1 Quart Non-Fat, Arrowhead Shape 9.00
Token, Hewitts Dairy, Hagersville, Good For 2 Quart Milk, Rectangular, Tabs At Top . . . 9.00
Token, It's Lucky To Drink Green River Whiskey, Horseshoe, 4-Leaf Clover 25.00
Token, Model Dairy, Phone 10, R.M. Hagey, Good For 1 Pint, Square 15.00
Token, Mountain View Dairy, Dundas, Ont., Ph. 645, Good For 1 Qt. Milk, Heart Shape . 9.00
Token, Spring Valley Diary, Paris, Phone 442-2511, Good For 1 Pint Milk, Metal 9.00
Toy, Truck, Delivery, Canada Dry, Friction, 1950s, 8 In. 250.00
Toy, Truck, Delivery, Coca-Cola, Smitty Toys, Metal, 14 Wood Block Cases, 13 1/2 In. . . 715.00
Toy, Truck, Delivery, Coca-Cola, Sprite Boy On Sides, Yellow, 1940s, 20 In. 250.00
Toy, Truck, Pepsi-Cola, Tin, Friction, 1960s, 4 In. 65.00
Toy, Truck, Tanker, Pepsi-Cola, Metal, Ny-Lint, Box, 1990s, 26 In. 150.00
Tray, Clysmic King Of Table Waters, Woman At Spring, Bottle, Elk, 13 1/4 x 10 3/4 In. . . 210.00
Tray, Coca-Cola, Betty, 1914, Oval 460.00
Tray, Coca-Cola, Bird House, Rectangular, Canada, 1957 . . . . 45.00
Tray, Coca-Cola, Building, 25 Anos, Decorated Both Sides, Mexico, 1964 . . . . 345.00
Tray, Coca-Cola, Coke Refreshes, Hand Pouring Coke Into Glass, Pansies, 1961 . . . . 20.00
Tray, Coca-Cola, Conquistadores & Indians, Decorated Both Sides, Mexico, 1963 . . . . . . 195.00
Tray, Coca-Cola, Fishtail Logo, Hand Pouring Coke Into Glass, Pansies, Canada, 1961 . . 80.00
Tray, Coca-Cola, Fishtail Logo, Wicker Cart, 1958 . . . . 12.00
Tray, Coca-Cola, Girl With Wind In Hair, Screened Background, Rectangular, 1952 . . . . . 100.00
Tray, Coca-Cola, Girl With Wind In Hair, Solid Background, Rectangular, 1952 . . . . 345.00
Tray, Coca-Cola, Hilda Clark, 1903, 15 x 18 1/2 In. 1440.00
Tray, Coca-Cola, Menu Girl, Rectangular, 1953-1960 . . . . .30.00 to 35.00
Tray, Coca-Cola, Rooster, Rectangular, 1957 . . . . 125.00
Tray, Coca-Cola, Sandwiches & Bottles On Table, 1957 . . . . 215.00
Tray, Coca-Cola, Umbrella Girl, Rectangular, 1957 . . . . 375.00
Tray, Coca-Cola, Woman At Fair, 1909, Large Oval 980.00
Tray, Coca-Cola, Woman At Fair, 1909, Small Oval 405.00
Tray, Coca-Cola, Woman In Hat, Hamilton King Art, Oval, 1913 . . . . 1120.00
Tray, Coca-Cola, Woman With Glass, 1907, Large Oval 1840.00
Tray, Coca-Cola, Woman With Glass, 1907, Small Oval 430.00

Tray, Coca-Cola, Woman, Yellow Dress, With Glass, 1916, Rectangular, 8 1/2 x 19 In. . . .   720.00
Tray, D.G. Yuengling & Son, Inc., Pottsville, Pa., Beer, Ale, Porter, Horse, 11 3/4 In. 90.00
Tray, Dr. Pepper, Woman Holding 2 Bottles, 1940, 13 1/2 x 10 1/2 In. 320.00
Tray, Drink Hires, Pretty Girl, Haskell Coffin Art, Wood-Grained Frame, 13 x 10 In. 660.00
Tray, Falstaff Beer, Woman Pouring Beer For Portly Man, Tin, Concave, Round, 24 In. . .   110.00
Tray, Foxhead 400 Beer, Waukesha, Wis., Metal, Picture, Round 22.00
Tray, Hires, Josh Slinger, What The Doctor Ordered, 5 Cents, Tin, 1914, 13 In. 1650.00
Tray, Liditol O.K. Whiskey, Roth & Co., San Francisco, Round, 12 In. 220.00
Tray, Pepsi-Cola, Beach Scene, 1940s 50.00
Tray, Pepsi-Cola, Coast To Coast Drink Pepsi, Map Of World, Bottle In Center, 1930s . . .   400.00
Tray, Pepsi-Cola, Hits The Spot, 1940s 125.00
Wrench, For J & B Fruit Jar 25.00
Wristwatch, Guinness Time, Toucan Bird Rocks Back & Forth, Chrome, 1930s, 2 In. . .   290.00